Essential ActionScript 3.0

Other resources from O'Reilly

Related titles
ActionScript 3.0 Design
   Patterns
Dynamic HTML: The
   Definitive Reference
Ajax on Java

Ajax on Rails
Learning JavaScript
Programming Atlas
Head Rush Ajax
Rails Cookbook

oreilly.com
oreilly.com is more than a complete catalog of O'Reilly books. You'll also find links to news, events, articles, weblogs, sample chapters, and code examples.

oreillynet.com is the essential portal for developers interested in open and emerging technologies, including new platforms, programming languages, and operating systems.

Conferences
O'Reilly brings diverse innovators together to nurture the ideas that spark revolutionary industries. We specialize in documenting the latest tools and systems, translating the innovator's knowledge into useful skills for those in the trenches. Visit *conferences.oreilly.com* for our upcoming events.

Safari Bookshelf (*safari.oreilly.com*) is the premier online reference library for programmers and IT professionals. Conduct searches across more than 1,000 books. Subscribers can zero in on answers to time-critical questions in a matter of seconds. Read the books on your Bookshelf from cover to cover or simply flip to the page you need. Try it today with a free trial.

Essential ActionScript 3.0

Colin Moock

Beijing · Cambridge · Farnham · Köln · Paris · Sebastopol · Taipei · Tokyo

Essential ActionScript 3.0
by Colin Moock

Copyright © 2007 O'Reilly Media, Inc. All rights reserved.
Printed in the United States of America.

Published by O'Reilly Media, Inc., 1005 Gravenstein Highway North, Sebastopol, CA 95472.

O'Reilly books may be purchased for educational, business, or sales promotional use. Online editions are also available for most titles (*safari.oreilly.com*). For more information, contact our corporate/institutional sales department: (800) 998-9938 or *corporate@oreilly.com*.

Editor: Steve Weiss
Developmental Editor: Robyn G. Thomas
Production Editor: Philip Dangler
Proofreader: Mary Anne Weeks Mayo

Indexer: John Bickelhaupt
Cover Designer: Karen Montgomery
Interior Designer: David Futato
Illustrators: Robert Romano and Jessamyn Read

Printing History:

August 2007: First Edition.

 This book uses RepKover™, a durable and flexible lay-flat binding.

ISBN-10: 0-596-52694-6
ISBN-13: 978-0-596-52694-8
[M]

Table of Contents

Part II. Display and Interactivity

Part III. Applied ActionScript Topics

Foreword

We imagine a world where every digital interaction—whether in the classroom, the office, the living room, the airport, or the car—is a powerful, simple, efficient, and engaging experience. Flash Player is widely used to deliver these experiences and has evolved into a sophisticated platform across browsers, operating systems, and devices.

One of the main forces driving Adobe's innovation and the development of the Flash Player is seeing where developers are pushing the edge of what's possible to implement, and then enabling more developers to accomplish that kind of work.

Taking the way-back machine to 2001, you would see the web being widely used and the early signs of web sites containing not only pages but also interactive applications. These applications were primarily using HTML forms and relying on web servers for processing the form information. A handful of leading edge developers were working to implement a more responsive interaction by taking advantage of client-side processing with ActionScript in Flash. One of the earliest examples of successful interactive applications was the hotel reservation system for the Broadmoor Hotel, which moved from a multi-page HTML form to a one-screen, highly interactive reservation interface that increased their online reservations by 89%.

Clearly, responsiveness matters. It creates a much more effective, engaging experience. However, in 2001, there was a lot to be desired in terms of performance, power of the scripting language, ease of debugging, and design constraints within browsers (which were created to view pages rather than host applications).

We did a lot of brainstorming and talked extensively to developers and decided to embark on a mission to enable this trend, naming the category "Rich Internet Applications" (RIAs). To better support RIAs, we aimed to create:

- A tremendously faster virtual machine in Flash Player for ActionScript 3.0.
- A development framework called Flex, making it radically easier to build RIAs.
- An environment specifically to deliver rich Internet applications to their full potential, known now as the Adobe Integrated Runtime (AIR). During the dot-com bust, we held onto the vision of enabling this future world of rich Internet applications.

We continued to invest in building a range of technologies and prepared for the day that innovation on the web would ignite again. The days of innovation have now returned in full force, and I am delighted to see rich Internet applications coming into their own with Web 2.0. Developers are creating applications with a range of technologies and frameworks that tap into the distributed creativity of the Internet, take advantage of HTML, Flash, Flex, Ajax; and balance logic between the client and server.

The new virtual machine has been delivered now in Flash Player 9, enabling Action-Script 3.0 to run an order of magnitude faster and implement the most recent work on the ECMA standard for the language (JavaScript follows this same standard). This modern implementation has also now been released as open source with the Mozilla Foundation as the Tamarin project, enabling the Flash Player team to work with Mozilla engineers and others in the open source community to continue optimizing the virtual machine and keeping up with the most recent standards work. This core scripting engine will be incorporated over time in Firefox, bringing consistency across scripting in HTML and Flash.

The development framework has also been delivered today as Flex, enabling rapid development through common patterns for interaction and data management, with the whole framework built in ActionScript 3.0. The Flex framework is available for free, and the framework source code is included so you can see exactly how it works. You can use any editor to write code using Flex, and a specific IDE is also available, called Adobe Flex Builder.

As we saw innovation on the web returning and were pursuing this vision, we decided to unite efforts across Adobe and Macromedia. While Macromedia was driving RIAs with Flash, Adobe was innovating in delivery of electronic documents, among other areas. We saw over time that Macromedia would be adding electronic document capability to RIAs and that Adobe would add RIA capability around electronic documents. Rather than pursue those paths separately and duplicate efforts, we joined forces to deliver our vision for the next generation of documents and RIAs, bringing together the world's best technology for electronic documents and the world's best, most pervasive technology for RIAs. It's an incredibly powerful combination.

After we announced the merger, we created a "clean room" team to plan for our next generation of software, drawing on everything we've learned to date as well as from the potential of bringing Flash, PDF, and HTML together in the new Adobe AIR environment for RIAs.

The AIR project is actually our third attempt at creating this new environment. The first two attempts were part of an experimental project called Central which was code named Mercury and then Gemini after the United States space program, and with AIR code named Apollo. We learned a lot from those first two projects, and as I like to remind the team, Apollo is the one that actually went to the moon.

With AIR, you can leverage your existing web development skills (Flash, Flex, HTML, JavaScript, Ajax) to build and deploy RIAs to the desktop. Just like web publishing allowed anyone with basic HTML skills to create a web site, AIR will enable anyone with basic web development skills to create a desktop application.

As a developer, you can now create a closer connection to your users. With the browser, you have a fleeting, somewhat tenuous, connection to users. They browse to a page, and then they're gone. AIR enables you to create an experience that can keep you continuously connected to your customers. Just like a desktop application, AIR applications have an icon on the desktop, in the Windows start menu, or in the OS X dock. Also, when you're running a web application today, it's a separate world from your computer. You can't easily integrate local data with your web application. For example, you can't just drag and drop your Outlook contacts onto a web-based mapping application to get directions to your friend's house. Yet with AIR applications you can, as it bridges the chasm between your computer and the Internet.

I believe AIR represents the beginning of a new medium. And these applications are fun to build. If you start early, you'll be able to deliver capabilities in your applications that others won't have yet—especially in terms of increasing the presence of your application on the computer and bridging the web and the desktop.

The core of these RIAs is the ActionScript language, whether they run in the Flash Player in a browser, as a desktop application through AIR, or on mobile devices. Each generation of the ActionScript language has been comprehensively described by Colin Moock in this series of O'Reilly books, becoming the reference book you'll find on most Flash developer's desks. With ActionScript 3.0, you have unprecedented power in building engaging applications and with this reference you have tremendous insight to use that power effectively.

I look forward to seeing what you create and to the next generation of applications ahead. Keep pushing the boundaries of what's possible on the Internet to make the experience more engaging and effective for people around the world, and we will do our best to continue bringing more expressiveness and power to help you in your efforts.

—Kevin Lynch
Chief Software Architect, Adobe
San Francisco, 2007

Preface

ActionScript is the official programming language of Adobe's Flash platform. While originally conceived as a simple tool for controlling animation, ActionScript has since evolved into a sophisticated programming language for creating content and applications for the Web, mobile devices, and desktop computers. True to its roots, ActionScript can be used in many different ways by many different kinds of programmers and content producers. For example, an animator might use just a few lines of ActionScript to pause the playback of a web animation. Or, an interface designer might use a few hundred lines of ActionScript to add interactivity to a mobile phone interface. Or, an application developer might use thousands of lines of ActionScript to create an entire email-reading application for web browser and desktop deployment.

This book covers ActionScript programming fundamentals in truly exhaustive detail, with extreme clarity and precision. Its unparalleled accuracy and depth is the result of an entire decade of daily ActionScript research, real-world programming experience, and unmitigated insider-access to Adobe's engineers. Every word of this book has been carefully reviewed—in many cases several times over—by key members of Adobe's engineering staff, including those on the Flash Player, Flex Builder, and Flash authoring teams. (See the "Acknowledgments" section at the end of this preface.)

Beginners Welcome

This book explores ActionScript from a programmer's perspective but assumes no prior programming knowledge. If you have never programmed before, start with Chapter 1. It will guide you through the very basics of ActionScript, demystifying terms like *variable*, *method*, *class*, and *object*. Then continue through the book sequentially. Each chapter builds on the previous chapter's concepts, introducing new topics in a single, prolonged narrative that will guide you on your journey to ActionScript proficiency.

Note, however, that if you are a designer who simply wants to learn how to control animations in the Flash authoring tool, you probably don't need this book. Adobe's documentation will tell what you need to know. Come back to this book when you want to learn how to add logic and programmatic behavior to your content.

Expert Guidance

If you already have existing ActionScript experience, this book will help you fill in gaps in your knowledge, rethink important concepts in formal terms, and understand difficult subjects through plain, careful language. Consider this book an ActionScript expert that sits with you at your desk. You might ask it to explain the subtleties of ActionScript's event architecture, or unravel the intricacies of Flash Player's security system, or demonstrate the power of ActionScript's native XML support (E4X). Or you might turn to this book for information on under-documented topics, such as namespaces, embedded fonts, loaded-content access, class-library distribution, garbage collection, and screen updates.

This book is a true developer's handbook, packed with practical explanations, insightful warnings, and useful example code that demonstrates how to get the job done right.

What's In This Book

This book is divided into three parts.

Part I, *ActionScript from the Ground Up*, provides exhaustive coverage of the core ActionScript language, covering object-oriented programming, classes, objects, variables, methods, functions, inheritance, datatypes, arrays, events, exceptions, scope, namespaces, XML. Part I closes with a look at Flash Player's security architecture.

Part II, *Display and Interactivity*, explores techniques for displaying content on screen and responding to input events. Topics covered include the Flash runtime display API, hierarchical event handling, mouse and keyboard interactivity, animation, vector graphics, bitmap graphics, text, and content loading operations.

Part III, *Applied ActionScript Topics*, focuses on ActionScript code-production issues. Topics covered include combining ActionScript with assets created manually in the Flash authoring tool, using the Flex framework in Flex Builder 2, and creating a custom code library.

This book closes with a walkthrough of a fully functional example program—a virtual zoo.

What's Not In This Book

The ActionScript ecosystem is vast. No single book can cover it all. Noteworthy topics that are not covered extensively in this book include:

- MXML
- The Flex framework
- Flex Data Services
- The Flash authoring tool's built-in components
- Flash Media Server
- Flash Remoting
- ActionScript's regular expression support

For information on these topics, see Adobe's documentation and O'Reilly's Adobe Developer Library, at *http://www.oreilly.com/store/series/adl.csp*.

Authoring Tool Agnosticism

This book teaches core ActionScript concepts that apply to any ActionScript 3.0 authoring environment and any runtime that supports ActionScript 3.0. As much as possible, this book avoids tool-specific development topics and focuses on programming concepts rather than tool usage. That said, Chapter 29 covers ActionScript's use in the Flash authoring tool, and Chapter 30 covers the very basics of using the Flex framework in Flex Builder 2. Likewise, Chapter 7 describes how to compile a program using various authoring tools (Flash, Flex Builder 2, and *mxmlc*).

Now let's turn our attention to the ActionScript language itself. The following sections provide a technical introduction to ActionScript 3.0 for experienced programmers. If you are completely new to programming, you should skip down to "Typographical Conventions" and then proceed to Chapter 1.

ActionScript Overview

ActionScript 3.0 is an object-oriented language for creating applications and scripted multimedia content for playback in Flash client runtimes (such as Flash Player and Adobe AIR). With a syntax reminiscent of Java and C#, ActionScript's core language should be familiar to experienced programmers. For example, the following code creates a variable named width, of type *int* (meaning integer), and assigns it the value 25:

```
var width:int = 25;
```

The following code creates a *for* loop that counts up to 10:

```
for (var i:int = 1; i <= 10; i++) {
  // Code here runs 10 times
}
```

And the following code creates a class named *Product*:

```
// The class definition
public class Product {
  // An instance variable of type Number
  var price:Number;

  // The Product class constructor method
  public function Product () {
    // Code here initializes Product instances
  }

  // An instance method
  public function doSomething ():void {
    // Code here executes when doSomething() is invoked
  }
}
```

The Core Language

ActionScript 3.0's core language is based on the ECMAScript 4th edition language specification, which is still under development as of May 2007.

 The ECMAScript 4 specification can be viewed at *http://developer. mozilla.org/es4/spec/spec.html*. The ActionScript 3.0 specification can be viewed at *http://livedocs.macromedia.com/specs/actionscript/3*.

In the future, ActionScript is expected to be a fully conforming implementation of ECMAScript 4. Like ActionScript, the popular web browser language JavaScript is also based on ECMAScript. The future Firefox 3.0 web browser is expected to implement JavaScript 2.0 using the same code base as ActionScript, which was contributed to the Mozilla Foundation by Adobe in November 2006 (for information, see *http://www.mozilla.org/projects/tamarin*).

ECMAScript 4 dictates ActionScript's basic syntax and grammar—the code used to create things such as expressions, statements, variables, functions, classes, and objects. ECMAScript 4 also defines a small set of built-in datatypes for working with common values (such as *String*, *Number*, and *Boolean*).

Some of ActionScript 3.0's key core-language features include:

- First-class support for common object-oriented constructs, such as classes, objects, and interfaces
- Single-threaded execution model

- Runtime type-checking
- Optional compile-time type-checking
- Dynamic features such as runtime creation of new constructor functions and variables
- Runtime exceptions
- Direct support for XML as a built-in datatype
- Packages for organizing code libraries
- Namespaces for qualifying identifiers
- Regular expressions

All Flash client runtimes that support ActionScript 3.0 share the features of the core language in common. This book covers the core language in its entirety, save for regular expressions.

Flash Runtime Clients

ActionScript programs can be executed in three different client runtime environments: Adobe AIR, Flash Player, and Flash Lite.

Adobe AIR
> Adobe AIR runs Flash-platform applications intended for desktop deployment. Adobe AIR supports SWF-format content, as well as content produced with HTML and JavaScript. Adobe AIR must be installed directly on the end user's computer at the operating-system level.
>
> For more information, see *http://www.adobe.com/go/air*.

Flash Player
> Flash Player runs Flash-platform content and applications intended for web deployment. Flash Player is the runtime of choice for embedding SWF-format content on a web page. Flash Player is typically installed as a web browser add-on but can also run in standalone mode.

Flash Lite
> Flash Lite runs Flash-platform content and applications intended for mobile-device deployment. Due to the performance limitations of mobile devices, Flash Lite typically lags behind Flash Player and Adobe AIR in both speed and feature set. As of June 2007, Flash Lite does not yet support ActionScript 3.0.

The preceding Flash client runtimes offer a common core set of functionality, plus a custom set of features that cater to the capabilities and security requirements of the runtime environment. For example, Adobe AIR, Flash Player, and Flash Lite all use the same syntax for creating a variable, but Adobe AIR includes window-management and filesystem APIs, Flash Lite can make a phone vibrate, and Flash Player imposes special web-centric security restrictions to protect the end user's privacy.

Runtime APIs

Each Flash client runtime offers its own built-in set of functions, variables, classes, and objects—known as its *runtime API*. Each Flash client runtime's API has its own name. For example, the Flash client runtime API defined by Flash Player is known as the *Flash Player API*.

All Flash client runtime APIs share a core set of functionality in common. For example, every Flash client runtime uses the same basic set of classes for displaying content on screen and for dispatching events.

Key features shared by all Flash client runtime APIs include:

- Graphics and video display
- A hierarchical event architecture
- Text display and input
- Mouse and keyboard control
- Network operations for loading external data and communicating with server-side applications
- Audio playback
- Printing
- Communicating with external local applications
- Programming utilities

This book covers the first five of the preceding items. For information on other specific Flash client runtime APIs, consult the appropriate product documentation.

Components

In addition to the Flash client runtime APIs, Adobe also offers two different sets of *components* for accomplishing common programming tasks and building user interfaces. Flex Builder 2 and the free Flex 2 SDK include the *Flex framework*, which defines a complete set of user interface controls, such as *RadioButton*, *CheckBox*, and *List*. The Flash authoring tool provides a similar set of user interface components. The Flash authoring tool's components combine code with manually created graphical assets that can be customized by Flash developers and designers.

Both the Flex framework and the Flash authoring tool's component set are written entirely in ActionScript 3.0. The user interface components in the Flex framework generally have more features than those in the Flash authoring tool's component set and, therefore, also have a larger file size.

 User interface components from the Flex framework cannot be used in the Flash authoring tool, but user interface components from the Flash authoring tool *can* be used (both legally and technically) with Flex Builder 2 and *mxmlc*.

This book does not cover component use or creation in ActionScript. For information on components, see the appropriate product documentation.

The Flash File Format (SWF)

ActionScript code must be compiled into a *.swf* file for playback in one of Adobe's Flash client runtimes. A *.swf* file can include both ActionScript bytecode and embedded assets (graphics, sound, video, and fonts). Some *.swf* files contain assets only and no code, while others contain code only and no assets. A single Action-Script program might reside entirely within a single *.swf* file, or it might be broken into multiple *.swf* files. When a program is broken into multiple *.swf* files, one specific *.swf* file provides the program point of entry, and loads the other *.swf* files as required. Breaking a complex program into multiple *.swf* files makes it easier to maintain and, for Internet-delivered applications, can give the user faster access to different sections of the program.

ActionScript Development Tools

Adobe offers the following tools for creating ActionScript code:

Adobe Flash

> *http://www.adobe.com/go/flash/*
>
> A visual design and programming tool for creating multimedia content that integrates graphics, video, audio, animation, and interactivity. In Adobe Flash, developers create interactive content by combining ActionScript code with animation, manually created content, and embedded assets. Adobe Flash is also known as the *Flash authoring tool*. As of June 2007, the latest version of the Flash authoring tool is Flash CS3 (Version 9 of the software).

Adobe Flex Builder

> *http://www.adobe.com/products/flex/productinfo/overview/*
>
> A development tool for producing content using either pure ActionScript or MXML, an XML-based language for describing user interfaces. Flex Builder includes a development framework known as the Flex framework, which provides an extensive set of programming utilities and a library of skinnable, styleable user-interface controls. Based on Eclipse, the popular open source programming tool, Flex Builder 2 can be used in either hand-coding mode or in a visual-development mode similar to Microsoft's Visual Basic.

Adobe Flex 2 SDK

> *http://www.adobe.com/go/flex2_sdk*
>
> A free command-line toolkit for creating content using either pure ActionScript 3.0 or MXML. The Flex 2 SDK includes the Flex framework and a command line compiler, *mxmlc* (both of which are also included with Adobe Flex Builder 2). Using the Flex 2 SDK, developers can create content for free in the

programming editor of their choice. (For a wide variety of open source tools and utilities for ActionScript development, see *http://osflash.org*.)

This Book's Example Files

The official companion web site for this book is:

> *http://moock.org/eas3*

You can download the example files for this book at:

> *http://moock.org/eas3/examples*

Note that most of the examples in this book are presented in the context of an enclosing main class, which is intended to be compiled as a *.fla* file's *document class* (Flash authoring tool) or a project's *default application class* (Flex Builder).

Using Code Examples

This book is here to help you get your job done. In general, you can use the code in this book in your programs and documentation. You do not need to contact us for permission unless you're reproducing a significant portion of the code. For example, writing a program that uses several chunks of code from this book does not require permission. Selling or distributing a CD-ROM of examples from O'Reilly books does require permission. Answering a question by citing this book and quoting example code does not require permission. Incorporating a significant amount of example code from this book into your product's documentation does require permission.

We appreciate, but do not require, attribution. An attribution usually includes the title, author, publisher, and ISBN. For example: "*Essential ActionScript 3.0* by Colin Moock. Copyright 2007 O'Reilly Media, Inc., 0-596-52694-6".

If you feel your use of code examples falls outside fair use or the permission given above, feel free to contact us at *permissions@oreilly.com*.

Typographical Conventions

In order to indicate the various syntactic components of ActionScript, this book uses the following conventions:

Menu options
> Menu options are shown using the → character, such as File → Open.

`Constant width`
> Indicates code examples, code snippets, variable names, and parameter names.

Italic

Indicates function names, method names, class names, package names, URLs, filenames, datatypes, keywords, objects, and file suffixes such as *.swf*. In addition to being italicized in the body text, method and function names are also followed by parentheses, such as *duplicateMovieClip( )*.

`Constant width bold`

Indicates text that you must enter verbatim when following a step-by-step procedure. **`Constant width bold`** is also sometimes used within code examples for emphasis, such as to highlight an important line of code in a larger example.

`Constant width italic`

Indicates code that you must replace with an appropriate value (e.g., *yournamehere*).

This is a tip. It contains useful information about the topic at hand, often highlighting important concepts or best practices.

This is a warning. It helps you solve and avoid annoying problems. Ignore at your own peril.

This is a note about ActionScript 2.0. It compares and contrasts ActionScript 2.0 with ActionScript 3.0, helping you to migrate to ActionScript 3.0 and to understand important differences between the two versions of the language.

Coding and vocabulary conventions used in this book include:

- The keyword `this` is written in `constant-width font` because it is an implicit parameter passed to methods and functions.

- In general, the keyword `this` is not included when making reference to identifiers from within instance methods. However, `this` is used to disambiguate instance variables and instance methods from parameters and local variables.

- When discussing accessor methods and mutator methods, this book avoids the traditional terms *accessor*, *mutator*, *getter*, and *setter*. Instead, this book uses the unofficial terms *retriever method* and *modifier method*. See Chapter 3.

- In a class definition that contains static variables, static methods, instance variables, instance methods, and a constructor method, this book lists the static variables first, followed by the static methods, the instance variables, the class constructor method, and finally, the instance methods.

- This book uses ALL CAPITAL LETTERS for constant names.

- When referring to static variables and static methods, this book always includes the name of the class that defines the variable or method.
- Unless otherwise stated, *function closures* are referred to by the shorter term *function*. See Chapter 5 for a description of the difference between the two terms.
- This book assumes that all code is compiled in strict mode. Furthermore, after Chapter 7, this book supplies type annotations for all variables, parameters, and return values.
- Event listeners in this book are named using the format *eventName*`Listener`, where *eventName* is the string name of the event.

How to Contact Us

We have tested and verified the information in this book to the best of our ability, but you may find that features have changed (or even that we have made mistakes!). Please let us know about any errors you find, as well as your suggestions for future editions, by writing to:

O'Reilly Media, Inc.
1005 Gravenstein Highway North
Sebastopol, CA 95472
(800) 998-9938 (in the United States or Canada)
(707) 829-0515 (international/local)
(707) 829-0104 (fax)

We have a web page for the book, where we list errata, examples, or any additional information. You can access this page at:

http://www.oreilly.com/catalog/9780596526948

To comment or ask technical questions about this book, send email to:

bookquestions@oreilly.com

For more information about our books, conferences, software, Resource Centers, and the O'Reilly Network, see our web site at:

http://www.oreilly.com

Safari® Enabled

 When you see a Safari® Enabled icon on the cover of your favorite technology book, it means the book is available online through the O'Reilly Network Safari Bookshelf.

Safari offers a solution that's better than e-books. It's a virtual library that lets you easily search thousands of top technology books, cut and paste code samples, download chapters, and find quick answers when you need the most accurate, current information. Try it for free at *http://safari.oreilly.com*.

Acknowledgments

This book could not have been written without the abundant trust and very active support of both Adobe and O'Reilly. In the summer of 2005, in a meeting with Steve Weiss, Lisa Friendly, and Mike Chambers, I agreed to write a new book called *Essential ActionScript 3.0*. The book was originally billed as "a short update to *Essential ActionScript 2.0*." But as the ActionScript 3.0 language evolved, *Essential ActionScript 3.0* become a full work of its own. Patiently and faithfully, Adobe and O'Reilly watched the book increase vastly in scope, and agreed to let the publication deadline creep from nine months to two years. Throughout the entire process, I truly believed we were making the right choice, and I'm honored that Adobe and O'Reilly agreed.

Throughout this book's writing, Adobe graciously furnished me with full access to internal resources and official engineering time for technical reviews. I owe great thanks to JuLee Burdekin and Francis Cheng from Adobe's documentation team. JuLee and Francis coordinated my efforts internally at Adobe and answered a seemingly endless stream of questions.

Dozens of Adobe employees provided me with information and instruction during this book's research. I am deeply grateful to all of them, and would especially like to thank the following:

- Francis Cheng was a constant source of information on the core language and provided invaluable feedback on Essential ActionScript 3.0's manuscript. Francis sits on the ECMAScript 4 committee and is one of the authors of the ActionScript 3.0 specification.

- Jeff Dyer consistently took time out of his schedule to help clarify core-language concepts and investigate bugs. Jeff is one of the principal developers of the ActionScript 3.0 compiler, the principal author of the ActionScript 3.0 specification, and a key member of the ECMAScript 4 committee.

- Deneb Meketa patiently endured my misunderstanding of Flash Player's security system. Through phone calls and emails that spanned more than a month of intensive research, Deneb managed to bring clarity to Chapter 19. Deneb is the engineer responsible for implementing security in Flash Player.

- Jeff Mott, Flash Player engineer, consistently offered extensive, near instant responses to my questions about ActionScript's event system.

- Jim Corbett, Flash Player engineer, helped me understand many display list and event-loading subtleties.

- Rebecca Sun, Flash authoring engineer, answered many questions about the links between the ActionScript 3.0 compiler and Flash CS3. She also listened openly to suggestions, and endured my frequent spontaneous requests for information over instant messenger.

- Lee Thomason, Flash Player Architect, gave me a personal education in Flash Player's text rendering engine.

- Roger Gonzalez, Flex Compiler Architect, regularly fielded my questions on class loading and the Flex compiler.

- Werner Sharp, Flash Player engineer, explained many subtle nuances of bitmap programming in ActionScript.

- Paul Betlem, Senior Director of Flash Player Engineering, helped facilitate the technical review process and reviewed several chapters himself.

- Mike Chambers, Senior Product Manager of Developer Relations for Adobe AIR, provided regular technical information, and helped nurture the Essential ActionScript 3.0 project from its earliest stages.

- Gary Grossman, the original creator of ActionScript, taught me much of what I know about programming for the Flash platform. In August 2006, Gary teamed up with the inventors of Flash (Jon Gay and Robert Tatsumi) to co-found a new company, Software as Art. See *http://www.softwareasart.com*.

Other Adobe staff, past and present, that I'm honored to know and work with include Mike Downey, Kevin Lynch, Paul Betlem, Edwin Smith, Christine Yarrow, Jeff Kamerer, Nigel Pegg, Matt Wobensmith, Thomas Reilly, Jethro Villegas, Rob Dixon, Jeff Swartz, Waleed Anbar, Chris Thilgen, Gilles Drieu, Nivesh Rajbhandari, Tei Ota, Akio Tanaka, Sumi Lim, Troy Evans, John Dowdell, Bentley Wolfe, Tinic Uro, Michael Williams, Sharon Seldon, Jonathan Gay, Robert Tatsumi, Pete Santangeli, Mark Anders, John Nack, Matt Chotin, Alex Harui, Gordon Smith, Sho Kuwamoto, Craig Goodman, Stefan Gruenwedel, Deepa Subramaniam, Ethan Malasky, Sean Kranzberg, Michael Morris, Eric Wittman, Jeremy Clark, and Janice Pearce.

Table P-1 gives a statistical view of the depth of gratitude I owe this book's official technical reviewers.

Table P-1. Adobe reviewers

Reviewer	Title	Chapters reviewed	Number of emails fielded
Deneb Meketa	Computer Scientist, Flash Platform	17	75
Erica Norton	Senior Quality Engineer, Flash Player	14, 19, 21, 22	3
Francis Cheng	Senior Technical Writer	1-11, 13, 15, 16, 18	334
Jeff Dyer	Compiler Architect, ActionScript Language Group	17	106
Jeff Mott	Computer Scientist, Flash Player Engineering	12, 20-25	85
Jim Corbett	Senior Computer Scientist, Flash Player Engineering	20, 23, 24, 28	52
Lee Thomason	Architect, Flash Player	25, 27	33
Mike Chambers	Senior Product Manager, Developer Relations, Adobe AIR	1	89
Mike Richards	Computer Scientist, Mobile and Devices	22-26	9
Paul Robertson	ActionScript Developer/Writer	1, 2, 24, 27-31	14
Paul Betlem	Senior Director, Flash Player Engineering	20, 27, 26	19
Rebecca Sun	Computer Scientist, Flash Authoring	7, 29, 31	60
Robert Penner	Senior Engineer, Flash Authoring	18, 23-25	16
Roger Gonzalez	Flex Compiler Architect	25, 30, 31	64
Werner Sharp	Senior Computer Scientist, Flash Player Engineering	18, 22	35

Thanks to Robyn Thomas, this book's editor, who reviewed and polished the manuscript with great speed and precision. Thanks also to all of the members of O'Reilly's management, editorial, production, interior design, art, marketing, and sales teams including Tim O'Reilly, Steve Weiss, and Karen Montgomery. And thanks to the copy editor, Philip Dangler, for helping to ensure the text's consistency, readability, and accuracy.

In addition to being technically reviewed by Adobe staff, this book was also inspected for accuracy and quality by a keen group of beta readers, including Brett Walker, Chafic Kazoun, Derek McKenna, Edwin van Rijkom, Greg Burch, Jim Armstrong, Jon Williams, Mark Jonkman, Matthew Keefe, Mauro Di Blasi, Ralf Bokelberg, Ric Ewing, Robin Debreuil, and Victor Allen. The beta readers were indispensable, catching a great number of inconsistencies and subtle code errors. Mark Jonkman bears special mention for his extremely meticulous examination of the manuscript and its code examples.

Two mentors who helped shape me as a programmer and a writer are Bruce Epstein and Derek Clayton. Bruce was the editor for all of my previous books, and his rich lessons still inform every word I write. Derek is the creator of moock.org's Unity multiuser server (*http://www.moock.org/unity*), and a regular source of programming inspiration and friendship.

Of course, no book on any ECMAScript-based language is complete without acknowledging Brendan Eich's pioneering of JavaScript and ongoing development of ECMAScript. Thanks Brendan!

Finally, love and peace to the following for their love and friendship: James Porter, Graham Barton, Joe Duong, Tommy Jacobs, Wendy Schaffer, Andrew Harris, Dave Luxton, Dave Komlos, Marco Crawley, Eric Liphardt, Ken Reddick, Mike Linkovich, Matt Wearn, Mike Dobell, Mike "Nice," Hoss Gifford, Erik Natzke, Jared Tarbell, Marcos Weskamp, Dan Albritton, Francis Bourre, Thijs Triemstra, Veronique Brossier, Saima Khokhar, Amit Pitaru, James Patterson, Joshua Davis, Branden Hall, Robert Hodgin, Shin Matsumura, Yugo Nakamura, Claus Whalers, Darron Schall, Mario Klingeman, Fumio Nonaka, Robert Reinhardt, Grant Skinner, and the Moocks.

—Colin Moock
March 2007
Toronto, Canada

ActionScript from the Ground Up

Part I provides exhaustive coverage of the core ActionScript 3.0 language, covering object-oriented programming, classes, objects, variables, methods, functions, inheritance, datatypes, arrays, events, exceptions, scope, namespaces, and XML. Part I closes with a look at Flash Player's security architecture.

When you complete Part I, you will have gained a deep knowledge of core Action-Script 3.0, and applied that knowledge to the development of a virtual zoo example-application.

CHAPTER 1

Core Concepts

A *program* is a set of written instructions to be *executed* (i.e., carried out) by a computer or a software application. The written, human-readable text of a program is called *source code*, or just code. The person who creates a program is called a *programmer*, a *coder*, or a *developer*. Every program is written in a particular programming language, just as every book is written in a particular language (English, Russian, Japanese, etc.). Programming languages dictate the syntax and grammar that programmers must use to form the instructions in a given program. This book provides from-the-ground-up coverage of the syntax, grammar, and usage of one specific programming language, *ActionScript 3.0*. Get ready for a good time.

Tools for Writing ActionScript Code

ActionScript code is written in plain text, so an ActionScript program can be created with nothing more than a simple text editor, such as Notepad on Windows or TextEdit on Macintosh. However, most ActionScript programmers write ActionScript code using one (or both) of two commercial tools produced by Adobe Systems Incorporated: *Flex Builder* and the *Flash authoring tool*.

Flex Builder is an *integrated development environment*, or *IDE*. An IDE is an application for writing and managing code, much as a word processor is an application for creating printed documents. Developers use Flex Builder to create software applications and multimedia content using either ActionScript or *MXML*, or both. MXML is an XML-based language for describing user interfaces.

By contrast, the Flash authoring tool is a hybrid design, animation, and programming editor. Developers use the Flash authoring tool to create software applications and multimedia content by combining ActionScript code with manually drawn graphics, animation, and multimedia assets.

ActionScript 3.0 is supported by Flex Builder 2 or higher, and Flash CS3 (Version 9 of the Flash authoring tool) or higher. To obtain a copy of Flex Builder, visit *http://www.adobe.com/products/flex/productinfo/overview/*. To obtain a copy of the Flash authoring tool, visit *http://www.adobe.com/go/flash/*.

The vast majority of this book concentrates on the creation of software applications and multimedia content using pure ActionScript (i.e., code only). Chapter 29 covers the use of ActionScript in the Flash authoring tool. This book specifically does not include coverage of MXML. For coverage of MXML, see O'Reilly's *Programming Flex 2* (Kazoun and Lott, 2007) and Adobe's Flex Builder documentation.

Flash Client Runtime Environments

ActionScript programs can be executed by three different software applications (all produced by Adobe): Flash Player, Adobe AIR, and Flash Lite.

Flash Player executes ActionScript programs in a web browser or in a standalone mode on the desktop. Flash Player has very little access to the operating system (e.g., it cannot manage files, control windows, or access most hardware).

Adobe AIR executes ActionScript programs on the desktop and has full integration with the desktop operating system (e.g., can manage files, control windows, and access hardware).

Flash Lite executes ActionScript programs on mobile devices, such as cellular phones. As of the publication of this book, Flash Lite can execute ActionScript programs written in ActionScript 2.0, but not ActionScript 3.0, while Flash Player and Adobe AIR can execute programs written in ActionScript 3.0. Therefore, the techniques taught in this book apply to Flash Player and Adobe AIR, but will not apply to Flash Lite until it adds support for ActionScript 3.0.

In generic terms, Flash Player, Adobe AIR, and Flash Lite are all known as *Flash client runtime environments* (or *Flash runtimes* for short) because they manage ActionScript programs while they execute, or "run." Flash runtimes are available for Windows, Macintosh, and Linux, as well as a variety of different mobile hardware devices. Because ActionScript programs are executed by a Flash runtime, not a specific operating system or hardware device, each ActionScript program is considered *portable* because it can run on different hardware devices (phones, game consoles) and operating systems (Windows, Macintosh, and Linux).

In casual discussion, the term *ActionScript virtual machine* is sometimes used as an equivalent for *Flash client runtime environment*. There is, however, a difference between these two terms, so they should not be used interchangeably. The ActionScript virtual machine (AVM) is technically the software module *inside* Flash Player, Adobe AIR, and Flash Lite that executes ActionScript programs. But each Flash runtime also has other responsibilities, such as displaying content on screen, playing video and audio, and communicating with the operating system. The specific version of the ActionScript virtual machine that runs ActionScript 3.0 code is known as *AVM2*. The specific version of the ActionScript virtual machine that executes ActionScript 1.0 and ActionScript 2.0 code (not covered in this book) is known as *AVM1*.

Compilation

Before an ActionScript program can be executed by a Flash runtime, it must be converted from human-readable ActionScript 3.0 code to a condensed, binary format that Flash runtimes understand, known as *ActionScript bytecode*, or *ABC*. On its own, however, ActionScript bytecode cannot be executed by Flash runtimes; instead, it must be wrapped in a binary container file known as a *.swf* file. The *.swf* file stores the bytecode and any embedded media assets required by the ActionScript program in *Flash file format*, or *SWF*. The process of converting an ActionScript program to bytecode is known as *compiling the program*. The process of generating a *.swf* file is known as *compiling* the *.swf* file, or sometimes, *exporting* or *publishing* the *.swf* file.

To compile ActionScript 3.0 programs and *.swf* files, we use a software module known as a *compiler*. A compiler that compiles ActionScript code is known as an *ActionScript compiler*. A compiler that generates *.swf* files is known as a *SWF compiler*. Any SWF compiler that claims full support for the Flash file format includes an ActionScript compiler. Naturally, both Flex Builder 2 and the Flash authoring tool include a SWF compiler (and, by extension, an ActionScript compiler). Flex Builder 2 and the Flash authoring tool share the same ActionScript compiler but have different SWF compilers—known, respectively, as the *Flex compiler* and the *Flash compiler*. Adobe also offers the Flex compiler as a standalone command-line application called *mxmlc*. The *mxmlc* compiler is included in Adobe's free developer's toolkit, the *Flex 2 SDK*, available at *http://www.adobe.com/go/flex2_sdk*.

Just-In-Time Compilation

When an ActionScript program runs, the Flash runtime reads compiled ActionScript bytecode and translates it into native machine-code instructions that are executed by the specific computer hardware on which the program is running. In many cases, the native machine-code instructions are saved so they can be used again without the need to be retranslated from ActionScript bytecode.

Just as converting ActionScript 3.0 code to bytecode is called compiling, the process of translating ActionScript bytecode into native machine code and then saving that machine code for later execution is, likewise, known as compiling. Hence, most ActionScript code undergoes two levels of compilation. First, the developer compiles the code from human-readable format to a format understood by the Flash runtime (ActionScript bytecode). Then, the Flash runtime automatically compiles the ActionScript bytecode to a format understood by the hardware running the program (native machine code). The latter form of compilation (bytecode to machine code) is known as *just-in-time compilation*, or *JIT*, because it happens immediately before the specific bytecode being compiled is needed by the program. Just-in-time compilation is sometimes also called *dynamic translation*. Experienced programmers may be interested to know that code at the top level of a class definition is not just-in-time compiled (because it is executed only once).

Quick Review

The past several pages covered a lot of ground. Let's review what we've covered so far.

An ActionScript program is a set of instructions to be executed by one of the Flash runtimes: Flash Player, Adobe AIR, or Flash Lite. ActionScript programs can be written in a text editor, Flex Builder, or the Flash authoring tool. In order to run an ActionScript program, we must first compile it into a *.swf* file using a SWF compiler such as the Flash compiler included with the Flash authoring tool, or *mxmlc*, which is included with both Flex Builder 2 and the Flex 2 SDK.

Don't worry if some of the preceding concepts or terms are new to you. We'll be applying them abundantly over the next 900-plus pages.

Now let's write some code!

Classes and Objects

Imagine you are going to build an airplane, entirely from scratch. Think about the process you would follow. You very likely wouldn't just head to a metal shop and start welding. You'd have to draw up a blueprint for the airplane first. In fact, given that you are building the airplane from scratch, you'd have to draw up not just one, but many blueprints—one for each of the airplane's many parts (the wheels, the wings, the seats, the brakes, and so on). Each blueprint would describe a specific part conceptually and correspond to an actual part in the physical incarnation of the airplane. To build the airplane, you would manufacture each of the parts individually, and then assemble them according to a master blueprint. The interoperation of the airplane's assembled parts would produce the airplane's behavior.

If that all sounds logical to you, you've got what it takes to become an ActionScript programmer. Just as an airplane flying through the sky is a group of interoperating parts based on a set of blueprints, a running ActionScript program is a group of interoperating *objects*, based on a set of *classes*. ActionScript objects represent both the tangible things and the intangible concepts in a program. For example, an object might represent a number in a calculation, a clickable button in a user interface, a point in time on a calendar, or a blur effect on an image. Objects are incarnations, or *instances*, of classes. Classes are the blueprints upon which objects are based.

The first step in writing a new program is determining its classes. Each class describes, in code, both the characteristics and behavior of a particular type of object. Some of the classes in a program must be written from scratch, while others are provided by ActionScript and the various Flash runtimes. Classes written from scratch (known as *custom classes*) are used to produce specialized types of content, such as an order form for a shopping application, a car in a racing game, or a message in a chat application. By contrast, classes provided by ActionScript and the various Flash runtimes (known as *built-in classes*) are used to perform fundamental tasks such as creating numbers and text, playing sounds, displaying images, accessing the network, and responding to user input.

From the classes in a program, we make (or *instantiate*) objects and then tell those objects what to do. What the objects do determines the behavior of the program.

> Building a program with classes and objects is known as *object-oriented programming* (OOP).

In the next section we'll start writing an actual program, but before we do, let's take a brief look at an important group of classes, known as *native classes*, that are built directly into ActionScript. The native classes, listed in Table 1-1, are used to manipulate basic types of information, such as numbers and text. You can expect to use instances of at least one or two of the native classes in every program you write— much like you might use ready-made parts from a third-party supplier when building an airplane. Read over Table 1-1 for basic familiarity. In the coming chapters, we'll study the native classes in much more detail.

Table 1-1. ActionScript's native classes

Class	Description
String	Represents textual data (i.e., a string of characters)
Boolean	Represents the logical states `true` and `false`
Number	Represents floating-point numbers (i.e., numbers with a fractional value)
int	Represents integer numbers (i.e., numbers with no fractional value)
uint	Represents positive integer numbers
Array	Represents an ordered list
Error	Represents a program error (i.e., a problem in your code)
Date	Represents a specific point in time
Math	Contains common mathematical values and operations
RegExp	Defines tools for searching and replacing text
Function	Represents a reusable set of instructions that can be executed, or *called*, repeatedly
Object	Defines the basic features of every object in ActionScript

Now let's try using classes and objects in an example program—a simple simulated zoo game with virtual pets.

 Using the technique known as *timeline scripting* in the Flash authoring tool, it is possible to create an ActionScript program without first creating a class (see Chapter 29). However, even if you never expect to create classes yourself, you should still study the techniques presented in this chapter. Knowing how classes are created will greatly deepen your understanding of ActionScript and make you a better programmer.

Creating a Program

As we just learned, ActionScript programs are made up of classes, which are the blueprints for the interoperating parts (objects) of a program. Typically, the development of a new ActionScript program starts with a design phase, during which the program's functionality is broken into a logical set of classes. Each class is given a name, a set of features, and a role in the larger program. One class in particular is designated as the *main class*. The main class provides the starting point, or *program point of entry*, for the application. To start a new program, the Flash runtime automatically creates an instance of the program's main class.

For our virtual zoo example program, we'll name the main class *VirtualZoo*. As the first step in building the program, we'll create a folder on the filesystem, named *virtualzoo*. Within that folder, we'll create a subfolder named *src* (short for *source*) in which to store all *.as* files (i.e., all files containing source code).

Each program's main class code must be placed in a text file named after the main class, and given the extension *.as*. Accordingly, we'll create an empty text file named *VirtualZoo.as*. Notice that the filename *VirtualZoo.as* exactly matches the class name *VirtualZoo* and that case sensitivity matters. We'll place *VirtualZoo.as* in the folder *virtualzoo/src*. Here's the file structure for our program's source files so far:

```
virtualzoo
   |- src
      |- VirtualZoo.as
```

With *VirtualZoo.as* created, we can start writing the *VirtualZoo* class. However, first we must deal with a potential problem—if our chosen main class name conflicts with (i.e., is the same as) one of ActionScript's built-in classes, then ActionScript won't let us create the class, and our program won't be able to start. To prevent potential naming conflicts in our program, we use *packages*.

 There is a lot of ground to cover, so we won't actually compile our zoo program's code until Chapter 7. If you decide to jump ahead and compile the examples presented in Chapters 1 through 6, you are likely to encounter various warnings and errors. After Chapter 7, you'll be able to compile all versions of the example program without errors.

Packages

Like its name suggests, a package is a conceptual container for a group of classes and, as we'll learn later, for other things in a program. Each package delimits an independent physical region of a program and gives that region a name, called the *package name*. By convention, package names typically start with a lowercase letter while class names typically start with an uppercase letter. This helps distinguish package names from class names.

When a class's source code resides within a package, that class automatically adopts the package's name as part of its own name, much like a child takes on his parents' family name. For example, a class named *Player* in a package named *game* becomes known as *game.Player*. Notice that the package name comes first and is separated from the class name using a period (.) *character* (*character* is simply programming jargon for letter, number, punctuation, and so on). The package name helps distinguish the *game.Player* class from other classes also named *Player*, thus preventing name conflicts between different parts of a program or between a program's custom classes and ActionScript's built-in classes.

To create a new package, we use a *package definition directive*. Let's dissect that term. In ActionScript, all program instructions are known generally as *directives*. *Definitions* are one type of directive; they create, or define something, such as a package or a class. In this case, the thing being defined is a package, hence the term, *package definition directive*.

 A definition that creates something in a program is said to *define* or *declare* that thing. Definitions are sometimes also referred to as *declarations*.

Here's the general form of a package definition directive:

```
package packageName {
}
```

All package definitions start with a *keyword*: *package*. A *keyword* is a command name reserved for use by the ActionScript language. In this case, the *package* keyword tells ActionScript to create a package. After the *package* keyword, we provide the desired package name, represented by *packageName* in the preceding code. (Throughout this book, italicized code, such as *packageName*, indicates text that must be replaced by the programmer.) Next, we mark the beginning and end of the package contents using curly braces: { and }. To add a class to a package, we insert its source code between the curly braces, as follows:

```
package packageName {
  Class source code goes here
}
```

In technical terms, the curly braces in a package definition are a kind of statement, known as a *block statement*. Like definitions, statements are a kind of directive, or basic program instruction. A block statement marks the beginning and end of a group of directives that should be treated as a logical whole. A package definition's block statement is known as a *package block* or sometimes *package body*.

 For a complete list of ActionScript statements, see Chapter 10.

By convention (but not necessity), package names typically have the following structure:

- The reversed domain name of the organization creating the program
- Followed by a period (.)
- Followed by the general purpose package's contents

For example, a package containing classes for a mapping application created by Acme Corp., whose domain name is *acme.com*, might be named *com.acme.map*, as shown in the following code:

```
package com.acme.map {
}
```

Notice that com precedes acme (i.e., in the package name, the domain name is reversed).

 Domain names are guaranteed to be unique by the system of authorized top-level-domain registrars; thus, starting your package names with your organization's domain name avoids name conflicts with code developed by other organizations.

Now let's try using packages in our virtual zoo program. To keep our example simple, we'll use the package name *zoo*, without any leading domain name. To define the *zoo* package, we'll add the following code to the file *VirtualZoo.as*:

```
package zoo {
}
```

Now that we've added a package to the file *VirtualZoo.as*, we must change that file's location on the filesystem to match the package it contains. Due to a requirement imposed by all Adobe's ActionScript compilers, when a source file contains a class (or other definition) in a package, it must reside in a folder structure that matches that package name. For example, a file that contains a package named *com.gamecompany.zoo* must reside in a folder named *zoo*, in a folder named *gamecompany*, contained by a folder named *com* (i.e., *com/gamecompany/zoo*). Accordingly, we'll create a new folder named *zoo* in our program's file structure and move *VirtualZoo.as* into it. The file structure for our program's source files becomes:

```
virtualzoo
   |- src
      |- zoo
         |- VirtualZoo.as
```

Now that we have a package definition, let's add the *VirtualZoo* class to it.

Defining a Class

To create a new class, we use a *class definition*, as shown in the following generalized code:

```
class Identifier {
}
```

A class definition starts with the keyword *class*, followed by a class name, represented by `Identifier` in the preceding code. The term *identifier* simply refers to a name. Identifiers must not contain spaces or dashes, and cannot start with a number. Class names conventionally use a capital letter for the first, and all subsequent words in the name, as in *Date* or *TextField*. (*TextField* is a built-in Flash-runtime class whose instances represent text that can be displayed on screen.)

The curly braces ({}) following `Identifier` in the preceding class definition are a block statement, just like the block statement in a package definition. A class definition's block statement is known as the *class block* or sometimes the *class body*. The class block contains directives that describe the characteristics and behavior of the class and its instances.

Here's the basic class definition for the main class of our simulated zoo game, *VirtualZoo*. We place the class definition in the package body, in the file *VirtualZoo.as*:

```
package zoo {
  class VirtualZoo {
  }
}
```

Because the preceding *VirtualZoo* class definition resides in a package named *zoo*, the complete name of the class (known as the *fully qualified* class name) is *zoo.VirtualZoo*. In casual discussion, however, we'll use the shorter, *unqualified* class name, *VirtualZoo*.

Now that we have our program's main class defined, let's create one of the other classes in the program—*VirtualPet*. From the *VirtualPet* class, we'll create objects representing pets in the zoo.

Like *VirtualZoo*, we'll place the source code for the *VirtualPet* class in the *zoo* package, in its own file named *VirtualPet.as* saved in the *zoo* folder. Here's the code from the *VirtualPet.as* file:

```
package zoo {
  class VirtualPet {
  }
}
```

Notice that a package definition can span multiple source files. Even though *VirtualZoo* and *VirtualPet* are stored in different *.as* files, they belong to the same package, *zoo*. Any class in any file that resides in a package named *zoo* is considered part of the *zoo* package. By contrast, a class definition cannot span multiple files; it must be written, in its entirety, within a single file.

Access Control Modifiers for Classes

By default, a class in a given package can be used by code that also resides in that package only. To make a class available for use outside the package in which it is defined, we must define it with the *public attribute*. In general terms, a class's *attributes* dictate how the class and its instances can be used in a program. Attributes are listed before the keyword *class* in a class definition, as shown in the following generalized code:

```
attribute class ClassIdentifier {
}
```

For example, to add the *public* attribute to the *VirtualPet* class, we'd use:

```
package zoo {
  public class VirtualPet {
  }
}
```

However, in the case of *VirtualPet*, the *public* attribute is unnecessary because *VirtualPet* is used by the *VirtualZoo* class only, and *VirtualZoo* can use the *VirtualPet* class because both classes reside in the *zoo* package (classes in the same package can always access each other). Hence, we can return to our original *VirtualPet* definition, which implicitly allows *VirtualPet* to be used within the *zoo* package only:

```
package zoo {
  class VirtualPet {
  }
}
```

If we wish to *explicitly* indicate that we intend *VirtualPet* to be used within the *zoo* package only, we can use the *internal* attribute, as shown in the following code:

```
package zoo {
 internal class VirtualPet {
  }
}
```

A class defined with the *internal* attribute can be used within its containing package only. That is, defining a class with the *internal* attribute is identical to defining the class with no access-control modifier at all. The internal attribute simply serves to make the programmer's intention unambiguous.

The *internal* and *public* attributes are known as *access-control modifiers* because they control the region within which a class can be used (accessed) within a program.

Unlike the *VirtualPet* class, the *VirtualZoo* class must be defined with the *public* attribute because it is the application's main class.

 Adobe's compilers require an application's main class to be defined with the *public* attribute.

The following code updates *VirtualZoo* to include the necessary *public* attribute:

```
package zoo {
  public class VirtualZoo {
  }
}
```

Virtual Zoo Review

Our game now has two classes: *VirtualZoo* (the main class) and *VirtualPet* (which represents the pets in the game). The classes reside in the package *zoo*, and are stored in plain-text files named *VirtualZoo.as* and *VirtualPet.as*, respectively. By requirement of Adobe's ActionScript compilers, *VirtualZoo* is defined with the *public* attribute because it is the application's main class. By contrast, *VirtualPet* is defined with the *internal* attribute, so it can be used inside the *zoo* package only.

Example 1-1 shows the code for our game so far. The example also introduces something new—*code comments*. A code comment is a note meant to be read by programmers only and is completely ignored by the compiler. ActionScript code comments come in two varieties: single line, which start with two slashes (//), and multiline, which start with the character sequence /*, and end with the character sequence */.

This is a single-line comment:

```
// No one here but us programmers
```

This is a multiline comment:

```
/*
No one here
but us programmers
*/
```

The current code for our zoo game follows.

Example 1-1. Zoo game

```
// Contents of the file VirtualZoo.as
package zoo {
  public class VirtualZoo {
  }
}

// Contents of the file VirtualPet.as
package zoo {
  internal class VirtualPet {
  }
}
```

Now let's carry on with the development of our program, starting with the constructor method of our main class, *VirtualZoo*.

Constructor Methods

A *constructor method* (or, *constructor*, for short) is a discrete set of instructions used to initialize the instances of a class. To create a constructor method, we use a *function definition* within a class block, as shown in the following generalized code:

```
class SomeClass {
  function SomeClass () {
  }
}
```

In the preceding code, the keyword *function* begins the constructor method. Next comes the constructor method name, which must exactly match the class name (case sensitivity matters!). The constructor method name is followed by a pair of parentheses that contain a list of *constructor parameters*, which we'll study later. The curly braces ({}) following the parameter list are a block statement, just like the block statements in package and class definitions. A constructor method's block statement is known as the *constructor body*. The constructor body contains the directives that initialize instances. Whenever a new instance of `SomeClass` is created, the directives in the constructor body are executed (sequentially, from top to bottom). Executing the directives in the constructor body is known as *executing the constructor* or, more casually, *running the constructor*.

 Constructor methods are created using the *function* keyword because they are, technically speaking, a type of function. We'll study functions in Chapter 5.

When a class does not define a constructor function explicitly, ActionScript automatically provides a default constructor that performs no initialization on new instances of the class. Despite this convenience, as a best practice, always include a constructor, even if it is just an empty one. The empty constructor serves as a formal

---

indication that the class design does not require a constructor and should be accompanied by a comment to that effect. For example:

```
class SomeClass {
  // Empty constructor. This class does not require initialization.
  function SomeClass () {
  }
}
```

Unlike classes, the accessibility of constructor methods cannot be controlled with access-control modifiers. In ActionScript 3.0, all constructor methods are implicitly considered *public*. (Future versions of ActionScript might, however, allow for non-*public* constructor methods.) As a matter of style, this book always includes the *public* access-control modifier when defining constructor methods, stressing the fact that all constructor methods must be *public*. The following code demonstrates:

```
class SomeClass {
  public function SomeClass () {
  }
}
```

> The rule that constructor methods must be *public* in ActionScript 3.0 was instituted due to engineering time constraints and volatility of the ECMAScript 4 Language Specification. For details, see Sho Kuwamoto's article at: *http://kuwamoto.org/2006/04/05/as3-on-the-lack-of-private-and-protected-constructors*. (Sho is Adobe's Flex Builder 2's development team lead.)

The constructor method of an application's *main class* plays a special role in a program. It provides an opportunity to execute code immediately after the application has started. As such, the constructor method of an application's main class is considered the *program point of entry*.

The following code adds a constructor method to our *VirtualZoo* class (shown in bold):

```
package zoo {
  public class VirtualZoo {
    public function VirtualZoo () {
    }
  }
}
```

Our application now has an official point of entry. When our application starts, the Flash runtime will automatically create a *VirtualZoo* instance, executing the *VirtualZoo* constructor method in the process. Given that our application is a virtual zoo, the first thing we'll do in the *VirtualZoo* constructor method is create a *VirtualPet* object (i.e., add a pet to the zoo). We'll learn how to create objects next.

Creating Objects

To create an object from a class (known technically as *instantiating* the object), we use the keyword *new* in combination with the name of the class. The following generalized code shows the approach:

```
new ClassName
```

For example, to make an object from our *VirtualPet* class, we use the following code:

```
new VirtualPet
```

Multiple independent objects can be made from the same class. For example, the following code creates two *VirtualPet* objects:

```
new VirtualPet
new VirtualPet
```

Literal Syntax

We've just learned that the generalized syntax for creating a new object is:

```
new ClassName
```

That syntax applies to both built-in and custom classes. For example, the following code creates a new instance of the built-in *Date* class, which represents a particular point in time:

```
new Date
```

However, for some native classes, ActionScript also offers an alternative, more convenient means of creating instances, known as *literal* syntax. For example, to create a new *Number* instance representing the floating-point number 25.4, we can use the convenient literal form:

```
25.4
```

Likewise, to create a new *String* instance representing the text "hello," we can use the convenient literal form:

```
"hello"
```

Finally, to create a new *Boolean* instance representing the logical state of true, we can use the convenient literal form:

```
true
```

And to create a new *Boolean* instance representing the logical state of false, we can use the convenient literal form:

```
false
```

Literal syntax is also available for the *Object*, *Function*, *RegExp*, and *XML* classes. We'll study *Object* literal syntax in Chapter 15, *Function* literal syntax in Chapter 5, and *XML* literal syntax in Chapter 18. For information on *RegExp* literal syntax, see Adobe's documentation.

Object Creation Example: Adding a Pet to the Zoo

Now that we know how to create objects, we can add a *VirtualPet* object to our zoo program. The following code does just that:

```
package zoo {
  public class VirtualZoo {
    public function VirtualZoo () {
      new VirtualPet
    }
  }
}
```

Notice that the preceding code refers to the *VirtualPet* class by its unqualified name, *VirtualPet*—not by its qualified name, *zoo.VirtualPet*. Code in a given package can refer to the classes in that package by their unqualified names.

By contrast, code in a given package cannot refer to classes in other packages at all. To gain access to a public class in another package, we use the *import* directive, which has the following general form:

```
import packageName.className;
```

In the preceding code, *packageName* is the name of the class's package, and *className* is the name of the *public* class we wish to use. If the specified class is not *public*, the import attempt fails because a non-*public* class cannot be used outside its package. Once a class has been imported, it can then be referred to by its unqualified name. For example, to create an instance of the built-in *flash.media.Sound* class (which is used to load and play sounds), we would use the following code:

```
import flash.media.Sound
new Sound
```

Importing a class at the package-level makes that class available to code throughout the entire package body. For example, the following code imports *flash.media.Sound* at the package-level, and then later creates an instance of the *Sound* class within the *VirtualZoo* constructor method:

```
package zoo {
  import flash.media.Sound

  public class VirtualZoo {
    public function VirtualZoo () {
      new Sound
    }
  }
}
```

If a class's unqualified name conflicts with the unqualified name of another class, then qualified names must be used to differentiate the two classes. For example, if we were to define a class in the *zoo* package named *Sound*, then, within the *zoo* package, we would use the following code to create an instance of the built-in *flash.media.Sound* class (notice the use of the qualified name):

```
new flash.media.Sound
```

And we would use the following code to create an instance of the zoo package's *Sound* class:

```
new zoo.Sound
```

Use of the unqualified class name (e.g., *Sound*) on its own causes an error that prevents the offending program from compiling. Errors that prevent a program from compiling are known as *compile-time errors*.

To gain access to all the public classes in another package, we use the following code:

```
import packageName.*
```

For example, to gain access to all the public classes in the *flash.media* package, we use the following code:

```
import flash.media.*
```

Note that classes contained by a package that has no name are placed in an automatically created package known as the *unnamed package*. Classes in the unnamed package can be used directly anywhere in a program, without the need for the *import* directive. In other words:

```
package {
  // Classes defined here are in the unnamed package, and can be
  // used directly anywhere in a program
}
```

However, as a best practice, you should avoid defining classes in the unnamed package because their names might conflict with classes (and other kinds of definitions) defined by ActionScript, other programs, or even other parts of the same program.

 On a technical level, the *import* directive opens the public namespace of the specified package for the current scope and all nested scopes. But if you are new to ActionScript, you needn't worry about the technical details of the *import* directive. We'll examine everything you need to know in the chapters to come.

Now let's return to the task of creating objects in the virtual zoo program. Recall the following code, which creates a new *VirtualPet* object (shown in bold):

```
package zoo {
  public class VirtualZoo {
    public function VirtualZoo () {
      new VirtualPet
    }
  }
}
```

The preceding code successfully creates a new *VirtualPet* object, but it also suffers from a problem: after the object has been created, the program has no way to refer to it. As a result, our program cannot subsequently use or control the new pet. To give our program a way to refer to the *VirtualPet* object, we use variables.

Variables and Values

In ActionScript, every object is considered a single, self-contained piece of data (i.e., information) known as a *value*. Apart from objects, the only other legal values in ActionScript are the special values null and undefined, which represent the concept of "no value." A *variable* is an identifier (i.e., a name) associated with a value. For example, a variable might be the identifier submitBtn associated with an object representing a button in an online form. Or a variable might be the identifier productDescription associated with a *String* object that describes some product.

Variables are used to keep track of information in a program. They give us a means of referring to an object after it is created.

Variables come in four varieties: *local variables*, *instance variables*, *dynamic instance variables*, and *static variables*. We'll study the first two varieties now, and the remaining two varieties later in this book.

Local Variables

Local variables are used to track information temporarily within the physical confines of a constructor method, an instance method, a static method, or a function. We haven't studied instance methods, static methods, or functions yet so for now we'll focus on local variables in constructor methods.

To create a local variable within a constructor method, we use a *variable definition*, as shown in the following generalized code. Notice that the definition starts with the keyword *var* and, by convention, ends in a semicolon, as do all directives that do not include a block statement. The semicolon indicates the end of the directive, much like the period at the end of a sentence in a natural language.

```
class SomeClass {
  public function SomeClass () {
    var identifier = value;
  }
}
```

In the preceding code, *identifier* is the local variable's name, and *value* is the value associated with that variable. Together, the equals sign and the *value* are known as the *variable initializer* because they determine the initial value of the variable.

Associating a variable with a value is known as *assigning*, *setting*, or *writing* the variable's value.

When the variable initializer is omitted, ActionScript automatically assigns the variable a default value. Default values for variables are discussed in Chapter 8.

A local variable can be used within the method or function that contains its definition only. When the method or function finishes executing, the local variable expires and can no longer be used by the program.

Let's create a local variable to refer to the *VirtualPet* object we created earlier in the *VirtualZoo* constructor. We'll name the local variable pet, and we'll use an initializer to associate it with the *VirtualPet* object. Here's the code:

```
package zoo {
  public class VirtualZoo {
    public function VirtualZoo () {
      var pet = new VirtualPet;
    }
  }
}
```

Having associated the local variable pet with a *VirtualPet* object, we can now use that variable to refer to, and therefore control, that object. However, currently our *VirtualPet* object can't actually do anything because we haven't programmed its functionality. We'll start to rectify that shortcoming in the next section by giving pets the ability to have nicknames.

Instance Variables

Earlier we learned that a class describes the characteristics and behavior of a particular type of object. In object-oriented programming terms, a "characteristic" is a specific piece of information (i.e., *value*) that describes some aspect of an object—such as its width, speed, or color. To keep track of an object's characteristics, we use instance variables.

An *instance variable* is a variable attached to a particular object. Typically, each instance variable describes a characteristic of the object to which it is attached. For example, an instance variable might be the identifier width associated with the value 150, describing the size of the button object in an interface. Or, an instance variable might be the identifier shippingAddress associated with the value "34 Somewhere St," describing the destination of a product-order object.

Instance variables are created using variable definitions directly within class definitions, as shown in the following generalized code:

```
class SomeClass {
  var identifier = value;
}
```

Adding an instance variable definition to a class definition causes that variable to be automatically attached to each instance of the class. As with local variables, the initializer of an instance variable definition specifies the initial value of the instance variable. However, because instance variables are set independently for each individual instance of a class, the initial value of an instance variable is very often omitted and assigned later in the program.

As an example, let's add an instance variable to the *VirtualPet* class that tracks the nickname of each *VirtualPet* object. We'll call our instance variable petName. Here's the code:

```
package zoo {
  internal class VirtualPet {
    var petName = "Unnamed Pet";
  }
}
```

As a result of the preceding code, the instance variable petName is automatically attached to each new instance of the *VirtualPet* class. The initial value of petName for all *VirtualPet* instances is "Unnamed Pet." However, once each *VirtualPet* instance is created, a new, custom value can be assigned to its petName variable.

To assign an instance variable a new value, we use the following generalized code:

```
object.instanceVariable = value
```

In the preceding code, *object* is the object whose instance variable will be assigned a value, *instanceVariable* is one of *object*'s instance variables (as defined by object's class), and *value* is the value to assign.

Let's use the preceding technique to assign a nickname to the *VirtualPet* object we created earlier in the *VirtualZoo* constructor. Here's the code as we last saw it:

```
package zoo {
  public class VirtualZoo {
    public function VirtualZoo () {
      var pet = new VirtualPet;
    }
  }
}
```

According to the generalized code for assigning an instance variable a new value, we need to start by referring to an object. In this case, we use the local variable pet to refer to the desired *VirtualPet* instance:

```
pet
```

Next, we write a dot:

```
pet.
```

Then, we write the name of the instance variable whose value we wish to assign—in this case, petName:

```
pet.petName
```

Finally, we write an equals sign, then the value we wish to assign to the instance variable. Let's use "Stan":

```
pet.petName = "Stan"
```

Isn't that cute? Our pet has a name. We're making progress.

Here's the code as it appears in our program:

```
package zoo {
  public class VirtualZoo {
    public function VirtualZoo () {
      var pet = new VirtualPet;
      pet.petName = "Stan";
    }
  }
}
```

In the preceding code, notice that the petName instance variable, which is defined in the *VirtualPet* class, is set through a *VirtualPet* instance from within the *VirtualZoo* class. The petName instance variable is, therefore, said to be *accessible* to code in the *VirtualZoo* class. When a class makes its instance variables accessible to code in other classes, it is conceptually allowing those classes to modify the characteristics of its instances. The nickname of a pet is a characteristic that naturally lends itself to external modification. However, some instance variables represent characteristics that should not be modified outside the class in which they are defined. For example, later in this chapter we'll create an instance variable, caloriesPerSecond, that represents the speed with which a pet digests its food. If an inappropriately small or large value is assigned to caloriesPerSecond, a pet might starve instantly or never grow hungry. Hence, to prevent external code from assigning an inappropriate value to caloriesPerSecond, we must limit access to that variable. To limit access to a variable, we use access-control modifiers.

Access-control modifiers for instance variables

An instance variable's access-control modifier controls that variable's accessibility in a program. The access-control modifiers available for instance variable definitions are *public*, *internal*, *protected*, and *private*. The *public* and *internal* modifiers have the same effect with instance variables that they have with classes: an instance variable declared *public* can be accessed both inside and outside of the package in which it is defined; an instance variable declared *internal* can be accessed inside the package in which it is defined only. The *protected* and *private* modifiers are even more restrictive than *internal*. An instance variable declared *protected* can be accessed by code in the class that contains the variable's definition, or by code in descendants of that class only (we haven't studied inheritance yet, so if you are new to object-oriented programming, you can simply ignore *protected* for now). An instance variable declared *private* can be accessed by code in the class that contains the variable's definition only. When no modifier is specified, *internal* (package-wide access) is used.

Table 1-2 summarizes the access-control modifiers for instance variables.

Table 1-2. Instance variable access-control modifiers

Code placement	Attribute			
	Public	Internal	Protected	Private
Code in class containing variable's definition	Access allowed	Access allowed	Access allowed	Access allowed
Code in descendant of class containing variable's definition	Access allowed	Access allowed	Access allowed	Access denied
Code in different class in same package as variable's definition	Access allowed	Access allowed	Access denied	Access denied
Code not in same package as variable's definition	Access allowed	Access denied	Access denied	Access denied

By defining a class's instance variables as *private*, we can keep each instance's information safely encapsulated, preventing other code from relying too heavily on the internal structure of the class or accidentally assigning invalid values to instance variables. In general, it's good form to specify an access-control modifier explicitly for every instance variable. No instance variable should be defined as *public* unless specifically required by its class's architecture. If you are unsure which access-control modifier to use, use *private*. Down the road, you can easily make the instance variable more accessible if required. By contrast, if you start with a *public* instance variable, you'll have a tough time changing it to *private* later if external code already relies on it.

In the current version of our virtual zoo application, the petName instance variable is used within both the *VirtualPet* class and the *VirtualZoo* class, so we should define petName with the access-control modifier *internal*, as follows:

```
package zoo {
  internal class VirtualPet {
    internal var petName = "Unnamed Pet";
  }
}
```

Note that defining an instance variable with the *internal* attribute is identical to defining the variable with no access-control modifier at all (because *internal* is the default).

There are plenty more examples of instance variables throughout the remainder of this book. Now let's continue with the development of our virtual zoo program.

So far, the structure of our *VirtualPet* class requires each *VirtualPet* object's petName variable to be set voluntarily. If, however, we want to guarantee that a name is supplied for every pet, we can use constructor parameters, as described in the next section.

Constructor Parameters and Arguments

A *constructor parameter* is special type of local variable that is created as part of a constructor-method definition. Unlike regular local variables, a constructor parameter's initial value can be (or in some cases, must be) supplied externally when a new object is instantiated.

Constructor parameters are not created with the keyword *var*. Instead, to create a constructor parameter, we simply provide the desired name and variable initializer within the parentheses of a constructor function definition, as shown in the following generalized code:

```
class SomeClass {
  function SomeClass (identifier = value) {
  }
}
```

In the preceding code, `identifier` is the name of a constructor parameter, and *value* is the parameter's initial value.

To create more than one parameter for a constructor method, we list multiple parameter names, separated by commas, as shown in the following generalized code (notice the line breaks, which are both legal and common):

```
class SomeClass {
  function SomeClass (identifier1 = value1,
                      identifier2 = value2,
                      identifier3 = value3) {
  }
}
```

By default, the initial value of a constructor parameter is set to the value supplied in that parameter's definition. However, a constructor parameter's value can alternatively be supplied when an object is instantiated, using the following generalized object-creation code:

```
new SomeClass(value1, value2, value3)
```

In the preceding code, *value1*, *value2*, and *value3* are values that are assigned, in order, to the constructor parameters of *SomeClass*'s constructor method. A value supplied to a constructor parameter when an object is instantiated (as shown in the preceding code) is known as a *constructor argument*. Using a constructor argument to supply the value of a constructor parameter is known as *passing* that value to the constructor.

When a constructor parameter definition does not include a variable initializer, that parameter's initial value must be supplied via a *constructor argument*. Such a parameter is known as a *required constructor parameter*. The following generalized code shows how to create a class with a single required constructor parameter (notice that the parameter definition does not include a variable initializer):

```
class SomeClass {
  function SomeClass (requiredParameter) {
  }
}
```

Any code that creates an instance of the preceding class must supply *requiredParameter*'s value using a constructor argument, as shown in the following generalized code:

```
new SomeClass(value)
```

Failure to supply a constructor argument for a required parameter causes an error either when the program is compiled (if the program is compiled in strict mode) or when the program runs (if the program is compiled in standard mode). We'll learn the difference between strict mode and standard mode compilation in Chapter 7.

 When creating a new object *without* constructor arguments, some programmers choose to retain the constructor-argument parentheses. For example, some programmers prefer to write:

```
new VirtualPet( )
```

rather than:

```
new VirtualPet
```

The choice is entirely stylistic; ActionScript allows both formats. However, the ActionScript programming community favors the former style (with parentheses) over the latter (without parentheses). Hence, from now on, this book will always include parentheses when creating new objects, even when no constructor arguments are used.

Using the preceding generalized parameter code is a guide, let's add a new constructor method to our *VirtualPet* class, and define a single, required constructor parameter, name. We'll use the value of the name parameter to set each *VirtualPet* object's petName instance variable. Here's the basic code for the constructor method, shown, for the moment, without any code in the constructor body:

```
package zoo {
  internal class VirtualPet {
    internal var petName = "Unnamed Pet";

    public function VirtualPet (name) {
    }
  }
}
```

Because name is a required parameter, its initial value must be supplied externally at object-creation time. Accordingly, we must update the code that creates our *VirtualPet* object in the *VirtualZoo* constructor. Previously, the code looked like this:

```
package zoo {
  public class VirtualZoo {
    public function VirtualZoo () {
      var pet = new VirtualPet;
      pet.petName = "Stan";
    }
  }
}
```

Here's the updated version, which passes the value "Stan" to the *VirtualPet* constructor instead of assigning it to the new instance's petName variable:

```
package zoo {
  public class VirtualZoo {
    public function VirtualZoo () {
      var pet = new VirtualPet("Stan");
    }
  }
}
```

When the preceding code creates the *VirtualPet* instance, *VirtualPet*'s constructor runs, and the constructor argument "Stan" is assigned to the name parameter. Hence, within the *VirtualPet* constructor, we can use the name parameter to assign the value "Stan" to the new *VirtualPet* object's petName instance variable. To do that, we need to specify petName's value using an *identifier expression*. The next section describes expressions and identifier expressions.

Expressions

The written form of a value in an ActionScript program is known as an *expression*. For example, the following code shows a *new expression*—an expression representing a new object (in this case, a *Date* object):

```
new Date( )
```

Likewise, the following code shows a literal expression representing a *Number* object with the value 2.5:

```
2.5
```

Individual expressions can be combined together with *operators* to create a *compound expression*, whose value is calculated when the program runs. An *operator* is a built-in command that combines, manipulates, or transforms values (which are known as the operator's *operands*). Each operator is written using either a symbol, such as +, or a keyword, such as *instanceof*.

For example, the multiplication operator, which multiplies two numbers, is written using the asterisk symbol (*). The following code shows a compound expression that multiplies 4 and 2.5:

```
4 * 2.5
```

When the preceding code is executed, ActionScript calculates the result of multiplying 4 by 2.5, and the entire compound expression (4 * 2.5) is replaced by that single calculated result (10). Calculating the value of an expression is known as *evaluating* the expression.

 For a complete list of ActionScript operators, see Chapter 10.

To represent values that are not known when a program is compiled (at compiletime), but are supplied or calculated when the program runs (i.e., at runtime), we use variable names. When ActionScript evaluates an expression containing a variable name, it replaces that variable name with the corresponding variable's value. The process of replacing the variable name with the variable's value is known as *retrieving*, *getting*, or *reading* the variable value.

For example, consider the following compound expression, in which two values represented by variable names are multiplied together:

```
quantity * price
```

The variables quantity and price are placeholders for values that will be determined at runtime. The value of quantity might be, say, a number supplied by the user, while the value of price might be a number retrieved from a database. For the sake of this example, let's assume that the variable quantity has the value 2, and the variable price has the value 4.99.

When ActionScript evaluates the expression quantity * price, it replaces quantity with 2 and price with 4.99. Hence, during evaluation, the expression reads:

```
2 * 4.99
```

And the final value of the expression is:

```
9.98
```

 In formal terms, an expression that contains a variable name only, such as quantity, is known as an *identifier expression*.

Now let's try using an identifier expression in our virtual pet program.

Assigning One Variable's Value to Another

When we last saw our virtual zoo program, we had just finished creating a constructor method for the *VirtualPet* class. The constructor method defined a single parameter, name, whose value was supplied externally by object-creation code in the *VirtualZoo* class. Here's the code for the *VirtualPet* and *VirtualZoo* classes, as we left them:

```
// VirtualPet class
package zoo {
  internal class VirtualPet {
    internal var petName = "Unnamed Pet";

    public function VirtualPet (name) {
    }
  }
}

// VirtualZoo class
package zoo {
  public class VirtualZoo {
    public function VirtualZoo () {
      var pet = new VirtualPet("Stan");
    }
  }
}
```

Now that we know how to use variables in expressions, we can use the name parameter to assign the value "Stan" to the new *VirtualPet* object's petName instance variable.

Recall that to assign an instance variable a new value, we use the following generalized code:

```
object.instanceVariable = value
```

According to that generalized code, we need to start our variable assignment by referring to an object. In this case, that object is the new *VirtualPet* instance being created. To refer to it, we use the keyword this, which is an automatically created parameter whose value is the object being created:

```
this
```

> Within the body of a constructor method, the object being created is known as the *current object*. To refer to the current object, we use the keyword this.

After the keyword this, we write a dot, followed by the name of the instance variable whose value we wish to assign—in this case petName.

```
this.petName
```

Finally, we write an equals sign, then the value we wish to assign to the instance variable:

```
this.petName = value
```

The value we wish to assign is the value associated with the name parameter. Hence, for *value*, we write simply: name.

```
this.petName = name
```

At runtime, ActionScript replaces name, in the preceding code, with the value passed to the *VirtualPet* constructor. That value is then assigned to the instance variable petName.

Here's the assignment code as it appears in our *VirtualPet* constructor:

```
package zoo {
  internal class VirtualPet {
    internal var petName = "Unnamed Pet";

    public function VirtualPet (name) {
      this.petName = name;
    }
  }
}
```

Now that petName's value is assigned in the *VirtualPet* constructor, we can remove the redundant initial value "Unnamed Pet" in the petName variable definition. The petName variable definition used to look like this:

```
internal var petName = "Unnamed Pet";
```

From now on, it will look like this (notice the removal of the variable initializer):

```
package zoo {
  internal class VirtualPet {
    internal var petName;

    public function VirtualPet (name) {
      this.petName = name;
    }
  }
}
```

 An expression that assigns a variable a value, such as this.petName = name is known as an *assignment expression*. The equals sign in assignment expressions is an operator called the *assignment operator*.

Copies and References

In the preceding section, we learned how to assign one variable's value to another. Specifically, we assigned the value of the parameter name to the instance variable petName. Here's the code:

```
this.petName = name;
```

The result of assigning the one variable's value to another variable depends on the type of value being assigned.

In an assignment where the source variable's value is an instance of *String*, *Boolean*, *Number*, *int*, or *uint*, ActionScript makes a copy of that value and assigns the copy to the destination variable. After the assignment, two separate copies of the original value exist in system memory—the original value itself, and the copy of that value. The source variable points, or *refers*, to the *original* value in memory. The destination variable refers to the *new* value in memory.

By contrast, in an assignment where the source variable's value is an instance of a custom class or an instance of a built-in class other than *String*, *Boolean*, *Number*, *int*, or *uint*, ActionScript associates the second variable directly with the first variable's value. After the assignment, only one copy of the value exists in memory, and both variables refer to it. The variables are said to share a *reference* to the single object in memory. As a natural consequence, changes to the object made through the first variable are reflected by the second variable. For example, consider the following code, which creates two local variables, a and b, and then assigns a's value to b:

```
var a = new VirtualPet("Stan");
var b = a;
```

When the first line of the preceding code runs, ActionScript creates a new *VirtualPet* object, stores that object in memory, and then associates the local variable a with that object. When the second line of the preceding code runs, ActionScript associates the local variable b with the *VirtualPet* object already referred to by a. Changes made to the *VirtualPet* object through a are, hence, naturally reflected by b, and vice versa. For example, if we assign petName using the code b.petName = "Tom", then subsequently retrieving a.petName also yields "Tom." Or, if we assign petName using the code a.petName = "Ken", then subsequently retrieving b.petName also yields "Ken."

 A variable associated with an object does *not* store or contain that object—it simply *refers* to that object. The object, itself, is stored internally by ActionScript, in system memory.

An Instance Variable for Our Pet

Earlier, we learned that a local variable expires when the method or function in which it is defined finishes executing. To make sure that the *VirtualPet* instance in our *VirtualZoo* class will be accessible after the *VirtualZoo* constructor finishes, let's update the *VirtualZoo* class. Instead of assigning our *VirtualPet* object to a local variable, we'll assign it to an instance variable, pet. We'll make pet private so that it can be accessed by code in the *VirtualZoo* class only. Here's the code (the new instance variable is shown in bold):

```
package zoo {
  public class VirtualZoo {
    private var pet;
```

```
    public function VirtualZoo () {
      this.pet = new VirtualPet("Stan");
    }
  }
}
```

Over the preceding several sections, we've learned how to use instance variables to give characteristics to the objects of a class. Now let's explore how to use *instance methods* to give behaviors to the objects of a class.

Instance Methods

An instance method is a discrete set of instructions that carry out some task related to a given object. Conceptually, instance methods define the things an object can do. For example, the built-in *Sound* class (whose instances represent sounds in a program) defines an instance method named *play* that can start a sound playing. Likewise, the built-in *TextField* class (whose instances represent onscreen text) defines a method named *setSelection* that can change the amount of text selected in the text field.

To create an instance method, we use a function definition within a class block, as shown in the following generalized code:

```
class SomeClass {
  function identifier () {
  }
}
```

In the preceding code, the keyword *function* begins the instance method. Next comes the instance method name, which can be any legal identifier. (Recall that identifiers must not contain spaces or dashes, and cannot start with a number.) The method name is followed by a pair of parentheses that contain a list of *method parameters*, which we'll study later. The curly braces ({}) following the parameter list are a block statement. A instance method's block statement is known as the *method body*. The method body contains directives that perform some task.

 Instance methods are created using the *function* keyword because they are, technically speaking, a type of function. We'll study functions in Chapter 5.

To execute the code in a given method body, we use a *call expression*, as shown in the following generalized code. Notice the important and mandatory use of the parentheses operator, ( ), following the method name.

```
object.methodName( )
```

In the preceding code, *methodName* is the name of the method whose code should be executed, and *object* is a reference to the specific instance that will conceptually perform the task represented by the specified method. Using a call expression to execute the code in an instance method's body is known as *calling a method of an object* (or, synonymously *calling a method through an object*, or *calling an object's method*). The term *invoke* is also used to mean *call*.

 When discussing a particular method by name, most documentation includes the parentheses operator, ( ). For example, typical documentation would write *setSelection()* rather than *setSelection*. The convention of including the parentheses operator helps distinguish method names from variable names in prose. To further emphasize the distinction between variable names and method names, this book *italicizes* method names and uses constant-width font for variable names.

Let's put the preceding concepts into practice in our virtual zoo program.

To give our pets the ability to eat, we'll add a new instance variable and a new instance method to the *VirtualPet* class. The new instance variable, currentCalories, will track the amount of food each pet has eaten, as a numeric value. The new instance method, *eat()*, will implement the concept of eating by adding 100 calories to currentCalories. Eventually, the *eat()* method will be called in response to a user action—feeding a pet.

The following code shows the currentCalories variable definition. To prevent external code from tampering with the amount of calories each *VirtualPet* instance has, we define currentCalories as *private*. Notice that each new *VirtualPet* instance is given 1,000 calories to start:

```
package zoo {
  internal class VirtualPet {
    internal var petName;
    private var currentCalories = 1000;

    public function VirtualPet (name) {
      this.petName = name;
    }
  }
}
```

The following code shows the basic *eat()* method definition. Notice that, by convention, instance methods are listed after the class's constructor method, while instance variables are listed before the class's constructor method.

```
package zoo {
  internal class VirtualPet {
    internal var petName;
    private var currentCalories = 1000;

    public function VirtualPet (name) {
      this.petName = name;
    }
```

```
    function eat () {
    }
  }
}
```

Even though the *eat()* method body does not yet contain any code, with the preceding definition in place, we can already invoke the *eat()* method on a *VirtualPet* object, as shown in the following updated version of the *VirtualZoo* class:

```
package zoo {
  public class VirtualZoo {
    private var pet;

    public function VirtualZoo () {
      this.pet = new VirtualPet("Stan");
      // Invoke eat( ) on the VirtualPet object referenced by the
      // variable pet
      this.pet.eat( );
    }
  }
}
```

Within the *eat()* method body, we want to add 100 to the currentCalories variable of the object through which the *eat()* method was called. To refer to that object, we use the keyword this.

 Within the body of an instance method, the object through which the method is called is known as the *current object*. To refer to the current object, we use the keyword this. Notice that the term "current object" can refer to either the object being created in a constructor method or the object through which an instance method was called.

Adding a numeric value (such as 100) to an existing variable (such as currentCalories) is a two-step process. First, we calculate the sum of the variable and the numeric value; then we assign that sum to the variable. Here's the generalized code:

```
someVariable = someVariable + numericValue
```

In the case of the *eat()* method, we want to add 100 to the currentCalories variable of the current object (this). Hence, the code is:

```
this.currentCalories = this.currentCalories + 100;
```

As a convenient alternative to the preceding code, ActionScript offers the *addition assignment* operator, +=, which, when used with numbers, adds the value on the right to the variable on the left, as shown in the following code:

```
this.currentCalories += 100;
```

Here's the code as it appears in the *VirtualPet* class:

```
package zoo {
  internal class VirtualPet {
```

```
      internal var petName;
      private var currentCalories = 1000;

      public function VirtualPet (name) {
        this.petName = name;
      }

      function eat () {
        this.currentCalories += 100;
      }
    }
  }
```

From now on, every time a *VirtualPet* instance's *eat()* method is called, that instance's currentCalories variable will increase by 100. For example, the following code, repeated from the *VirtualZoo* constructor, increases pet's currentCalories to 1,100 (because all *VirtualPet* instances start with 1,000 calories).

```
  this.pet = new VirtualPet("Stan");
  this.pet.eat( );
```

Notice that even though the *VirtualPet* characteristic currentCalories is kept private, it can still be modified as result of a *VirtualPet* instance performing a behavior (eating) that is instigated by an external code. In some cases, however, even instance methods must be kept private. As with instance variables, we use access-control modifiers to control the accessibility of instance methods in a program.

Access Control Modifiers for Instance Methods

The access-control modifiers available for instance method definitions are identical to those available for instance variables—*public*, *internal*, *protected*, and *private*. An instance method declared *public* can be accessed both inside and outside of the package in which it is defined; an instance method declared *internal* can be accessed only inside the package in which it is defined. An instance method declared *protected* can be accessed by code in the class that contains the method's definition, or by code in descendants of that class only (we haven't studied inheritance yet, so if you are new to object-oriented programming, you can simply ignore *protected* for now). An instance method declared *private* can be accessed by code in the class that contains the method's definition only. When no modifier is specified, *internal* (package-wide access) is used.

By adding access-control modifiers to the methods of the class, we can put the "black box" principle into strict practice. In object-oriented programming, each object can be thought of as a black box that is controlled by an external assortment of metaphoric knobs. The object's internal operations are unknown (and unimportant) to the person using those knobs; all that matters is that the object performs the desired action. An object's *public* instance methods are the knobs by which any programmer can tell that object to perform some operation. An object's non-*public* methods perform other internal operations. Hence, the only methods a class should make publicly accessible are those that external code needs when instructing instances of that class to do something. Methods needed to carry out internal operations should be defined as *private*, *protected*, or *internal*. As an analogy, think of an object as a car, whose driver is the programmer using the object, and whose manufacturer is the programmer that created the object's class. To drive the car, the driver doesn't need to know how a car's engine works. The driver simply uses the gas pedal to accelerate and the steering wheel to turn. Accelerating the car in response to the driver stepping on the gas pedal is the manufacturer's concern, not the driver's.

As you manufacture your own classes, focus as much energy designing the way the class is used as you do implementing how it works internally. Remember to put yourself in the "driver's seat" regularly. Ideally, the way the class's *public* methods are used externally should change very little or not at all each time you make an internal change to the class. If you put a new engine in the car, the driver should still be able to use the gas pedal. As much as possible, keep the volatility of your classes behind the scenes, in *private* methods.

In object-oriented terms, a class's *public* instance methods and *public* instance variables are, together, sometimes called the class's *interface* to the outside world—or, synonymously, the class's API (Application Programming Interface).

The term API also refers to the collective services provided by an entire group of classes. For example, the built-in Flash-runtime classes for displaying content on screen are known as the *display API*. Likewise, a custom set of classes used to render 3D content might be known as a "3D API". In addition to classes, APIs can also include other program definitions (such as variables and functions).

In ActionScript, the term *interface* has an additional technical meaning, covered in Chapter 9. To avoid confusion, this book does not use the term "interface" to describe an object's *public* instance methods and *public* instance variables.

Returning to our virtual zoo program, let's now add an access-control modifier to the *VirtualPet* class's *eat( )* method. We'll make *eat( )* a *public* method because it is one of the official means by which external code is intended to control *VirtualPet* objects. Here's the revised code:

```
package zoo {
  internal class VirtualPet {
    internal var petName;
    private var currentCalories = 1000;

    public function VirtualPet (name) {
      this.petName = name;
    }

    public function eat () {
      this.currentCalories += 100;
```

```
        }
      }
    }
```

As it stands, the *VirtualPet* class's *eat()* method is inflexible because it adds the same amount of calories to currentCalories every time it is called. Eventually, we'll want to dynamically adjust the amount of calories added when a pet eats based on the type of food fed to it by the user. To allow the amount of calories added at feeding time to be specified externally when *eat()* is called, we need method parameters.

Method Parameters and Arguments

Like constructor parameters, a *method parameter* is special type of local variable that is created as part of a method definition, but whose initial value can be (or, in some cases, must be) supplied externally when the method is called.

To define a method parameter, we use the following generalized code. Notice that a method-parameter definition has the same general structure as a constructor-parameter definition.

```
function methodName (identifier1 = value1,
                     identifier2 = value2,
                     ...
                     identifiern = valuen) {
}
```

In the preceding code, *identifier1=value1,identifier2=value2,...identifiern=valuen* is a list of method parameter names and their corresponding initial values. By default, a method parameter's initial value is the value supplied in that parameter's definition. However, a method parameter's value can alternatively be supplied via a call expression, as shown in the following generalized code:

```
theMethod(value1, value2,...valuen)
```

In the preceding code, *theMethod* is a reference to the method being invoked, and *value1, value2,...valuen* is a list of values that are assigned, in order, to *theMethod*'s parameters. A value supplied to a method parameter through a call expression (as shown in the preceding code) is known as a *method argument*. Using a method argument to supply the value of a method parameter is known as *passing* that value to the method.

As with constructor parameters, when a method parameter definition does not include a variable initializer, that parameter's initial value must be supplied via a method argument. Such a parameter is known as a *required method parameter*. The following generalized code shows how to create a method with a single required method parameter (notice that the parameter definition does not include a variable initializer):

```
function methodName (requiredParameter) {
}
```

Any code that calls the preceding method must supply *requiredParameter*'s value using a method argument, as shown in the following generalized code:

```
theMethod(value)
```

Failure to supply a constructor argument for a required parameter causes an error either when the program is compiled (if the program is compiled in strict mode) or when the program runs (if the program is compiled in standard mode).

Now let's update the *VirtualPet* class's *eat()* method to include a required parameter, numberOfCalories. Each time *eat()* is called, we'll increase the value of the current object's currentCalories variable by the value of numberOfCalories. Here's the updated code for the *eat()* method:

```
package zoo {
  internal class VirtualPet {
    internal var petName;
    private var currentCalories = 1000;

    public function VirtualPet (name) {
      this.petName = name;
    }

    public function eat (numberOfCalories) {
      this.currentCalories += numberOfCalories;
    }
  }
}
```

Because numberOfCalories is a required parameter, its initial value must be supplied externally when *eat()* is called. Let's try it out with the *VirtualPet* object created in the *VirtualZoo* constructor. Previously, the code for the *VirtualZoo* constructor looked like this:

```
package zoo {
  public class VirtualZoo {
    private var pet;

    public function VirtualZoo () {
      this.pet = new VirtualPet("Stan");
      this.pet.eat();
    }
  }
}
```

Here's the updated version, which passes the value 50 to *eat()*:

```
package zoo {
  public class VirtualZoo {
    private var pet;
```

```
    public function VirtualZoo () {
      this.pet = new VirtualPet("Stan");
      this.pet.eat(50);
    }
  }
}
```

The preceding call expression causes *eat()* to run with the value 50 assigned to the numberOfCalories parameter. As a result, 50 is added to the currentCalories instance variable of the *VirtualPet* instance referenced by pet. After the code completes, the value of pet's currentCalories variable is 1050.

Method Return Values

Just as methods can accept values in the form of arguments, methods can also produce or *return* values. To return a value from a method, we use a *return statement*, as shown in the following general code:

```
function methodName () {
  return value;
}
```

 The value returned by a method is known as the method's *return value* or *result*.

When a method executes, its return value becomes the value of the call expression that called it.

To demonstrate the use of method return values, let's add a new method to the *VirtualPet* class that calculates and then returns the age of a pet. In order to be able to calculate a pet's age, we need a little knowledge of the *Date* class, whose instances represent specific points in time. To create a new *Date* instance, we use the following code:

```
new Date( )
```

Times represented by *Date* instances are expressed as the "number of milliseconds before or after midnight of January 1, 1970." For example, the time "one second after midnight January 1, 1970" is expressed by the number 1000. Likewise, the time "midnight January 2, 1970" is expressed by the number 86400000 (one day is 1000 milliseconds × 60 seconds × 60 minutes × 24 hours). By default, a new *Date* object represents the current time on the local system.

To access a given *Date* instance's numeric "milliseconds-from-1970" value, we use the instance variable time. For example, the following code creates a new *Date* instance and then retrieves the value of its time variable:

```
new Date( ).time;
```

On January 24, 2007, at 5:20 p.m., the preceding code yielded the value: 1169677183875, which is the precise number of milliseconds between midnight January 1, 1970 and 5:20 p.m. on January 24, 2007.

Now let's return to the *VirtualPet* class. To be able to calculate the age of *VirtualPet* objects, we must record the current time when each *VirtualPet* object is created. To record each *VirtualPet* object's creation time, we create an instance of the built-in *Date* class within the *VirtualPet* constructor, and then assign that instance to a *VirtualPet* instance variable, creationTime. Here's the code:

```
package zoo {
  internal class VirtualPet {
    internal var petName;
    private var currentCalories = 1000;
    private var creationTime;

    public function VirtualPet (name) {
      this.creationTime = new Date( );
      this.petName = name;
    }

    public function eat (numberOfCalories) {
      this.currentCalories += numberOfCalories;
    }
  }
}
```

Using creationTime, we can calculate any *VirtualPet* object's age by subtracting the object's creation time from the current time. We'll perform that calculation in a new method named *getAge()*. Here's the code:

```
public function getAge ( ) {
  var currentTime = new Date( );
  var age = currentTime.time - this.creationTime.time;
}
```

To return the calculated age, we use the following return statement:

```
public function getAge ( ) {
  var currentTime = new Date( );
  var age = currentTime.time - this.creationTime.time;

  return age;
}
```

The following code shows the *getAge()* method in the context of the *VirtualPet* class:

```
package zoo {
  internal class VirtualPet {
    internal var petName;
    private var currentCalories = 1000;
    private var creationTime;
```

```
public function VirtualPet (name) {
  this.creationTime = new Date();
  this.petName = name;
}

public function eat (numberOfCalories) {
  this.currentCalories += numberOfCalories;
}

public function getAge () {
  var currentTime = new Date();
  var age = currentTime.time - this.creationTime.time;
  return age;
}
    }
  }
```

Now let's use *getAge()*'s return value in the *VirtualZoo* class. Consider the *getAge()* call expression in the following updated version of *VirtualZoo*:

```
package zoo {
  public class VirtualZoo {
    private var pet;

    public function VirtualZoo () {
      this.pet = new VirtualPet("Stan");
      this.pet.getAge();
    }
  }
}
```

In the preceding code, the expression pet.getAge( ) has a numeric value representing the number of milliseconds since the creation of the *VirtualPet* object referenced by pet. In order to be able to access that value later in the program, we could assign it to a variable, as follows:

```
package zoo {
  public class VirtualZoo {
    private var pet;

    public function VirtualZoo () {
      this.pet = new VirtualPet("Stan");
      var age = this.pet.getAge();
    }
  }
}
```

Alternatively, in a more complete version of the virtual zoo program, we might display the returned age on screen for the user to see.

Method return values are a highly common part of object-oriented programming. We'll use them extensively throughout this book, as you will in your own code.

Note that like any other expression, a call expression can be combined with other expressions using operators. For example, the following code uses the division operator to calculate half the age of a pet:

```
pet.getAge( ) / 2
```

Likewise, the following code creates two *VirtualPet* objects, adds their ages together, and assigns the sum to a local variable, totalAge:

```
package zoo {
  public class VirtualZoo {
    private var pet1;
    private var pet2;

    public function VirtualZoo ( ) {
      this.pet1 = new VirtualPet("Sarah");
      this.pet2 = new VirtualPet("Lois");
      var totalAge = this.pet1.getAge() + this.pet2.getAge( );
    }
  }
}
```

Note that when a return statement does not include any value to return, it simply terminates the currently executing method. For example:

```
public function someMethod ( ) {
  // Code here (before the return statement) will be executed

  return;

  // Code here (after the return statement) will not be executed
}
```

The value of a call expression that calls a method with no return value (or with no return statement at all) is the special value undefined. Return statements with no return value are typically used to terminate methods based on some condition.

Method Signatures

In documentation and discussions of object-oriented programming, a method's name and parameter list are sometimes referred to as the method's *signature*. In ActionScript, a method signature also includes each parameter's datatype and the method's return type. Parameter datatypes and method return types are discussed in Chapter 8.

For example, the *signature* of the *eat( )* method is:

```
eat(numberOfCalories)
```

The *signature* of the *getAge( )* method is simply:

```
getAge( )
```

We've now covered the basics of instance methods. Before we conclude this chapter, we'll study one last issue related to ActionScript vocabulary.

Members and Properties

In the ActionScript 3.0 specification, an object's variables and methods are referred to collectively as its *properties*, where *property* means "a name associated with a value or method." Confusingly, in other ActionScript documentation (most notably Adobe's ActionScript Language Reference), the term *property* is also used to mean "instance variable." To avoid the confusion caused by this contradiction, this book avoids the use of the term "property" entirely.

Where necessary, this book uses the traditional object-oriented programming term *instance members* (or simply *members*) to refer to a class's instance methods and instance variables collectively. For example, we might say "radius is not a *member* of *Box*," meaning that the *Box* class does not define any methods or variables named radius.

Virtual Zoo Review

This chapter has introduced a large number of concepts and terms. Let's practice using them by reviewing our virtual zoo program for the last time in this chapter.

Our virtual zoo game has two *classes*: *VirtualZoo* (the main class) and *VirtualPet* (which represents the pets in the zoo).

When our program starts, the Flash runtime automatically creates an instance of *VirtualZoo* (because *VirtualZoo* is the application's main class). The act of creating the *VirtualZoo* instance causes the *VirtualZoo* constructor method to execute. The *VirtualZoo* constructor method creates an instance of the *VirtualPet* class, with a single constructor argument, "Stan."

The *VirtualPet* class defines three instance variables, petName, currentCalories, and creationTime. Those three instance variables represent the following pet characteristics: the pet's nickname, the amount of food in the pet's stomach, and the pet's birth date. For a new *VirtualPet* object, the initial value of currentCalories is a number created using the literal expression 1000. The initial value of creationTime is a *Date* object representing the time at which each *VirtualPet* object is created. When a *VirtualPet* object is created, petName is assigned the value of the required constructor parameter, name. The constructor parameter name receives its value through a constructor argument, supplied by the new expression that creates the *VirtualPet* object.

The *VirtualPet* class defines two instance methods, *eat()* and *getAge()*. The *eat()* method increases currentCalories by the specified numeric value. The *getAge()* method calculates and returns the pet's current age, in milliseconds.

Example 1-2 displays the current code for our zoo program.

Example 1-2. Zoo program

```
// VirtualPet class
package zoo {
  internal class VirtualPet {
    internal var petName;
    private var currentCalories = 1000;
    private var creationTime;

    public function VirtualPet (name) {
      this.creationTime = new Date( );
      this.petName = name;
    }

    public function eat (numberOfCalories) {
      this.currentCalories += numberOfCalories;
    }

    public function getAge ( ) {
      var currentTime = new Date( );
      var age = currentTime.time - this.creationTime.time;
      return age;
    }
  }
}

// VirtualZoo class
package zoo {
  public class VirtualZoo {
    private var pet;

    public function VirtualZoo ( ) {
      this.pet = new VirtualPet("Stan");
    }
  }
}
```

Break Time!

We've made great progress in this chapter. There's lots more to learn, but it's time for a well-deserved break. When you're ready for more ActionScript 3.0 essentials, head on to the next chapter.

CHAPTER 2

Conditionals and Loops

In this chapter, we'll depart from the general topics of classes and objects. Instead, we'll focus, on two essential types of statements: *conditionals* and *loops*. Conditionals are used to add logic to a program, while loops are used to perform repetitive tasks. Both conditionals and loops are extremely common, and can be found in nearly every ActionScript program. Once we've finished with conditionals and loops, we'll return to classes and objects, and continue developing our virtual zoo program.

This chapter presents all code examples outside the context of a functioning class or program. However, in a real program, conditionals and loops can be used within instance methods, constructor methods, static methods, functions, directly within class bodies or package bodies, and even outside package bodies.

Conditionals

A *conditional* is a type of statement that executes only when a specified condition is met. Conditionals let a program choose between multiple possible courses of action based on the current circumstances.

ActionScript provides two different conditionals: the *if* statement and the *switch* statement. ActionScript also provides a single conditional operator, ?:, which is covered briefly in Chapter 10. For details on the ?: operator, see Adobe's ActionScript language reference.

The if Statement

The *if* statement is like a two-pronged fork in the road. It contains two blocks of code and an expression (known as the *test expression*) that governs which block should execute. To create an *if* statement, we use the following generalized code:

```
if (testExpression) {
  codeBlock1
} else {
```

```
    codeBlock2
  }
```

When ActionScript encounters an *if* statement, it executes either *codeBlock1* or *codeBlock2*, depending on the value of *testExpression*. If the value of *testExpression* is the *Boolean* value true, then the first block is executed. If the value of *testExpression* is the *Boolean* value false, then the second block is executed. If the value of *testExpression* is not a *Boolean* value, ActionScript automatically converts *testExpression* to a *Boolean* object and uses the result of that conversion to decide which block to execute. (The rules for converting a value to the *Boolean* class are described in Table 8-5 in Chapter 8.)

For example, in the following *if* statement, the supplied test expression is the *Boolean* value true, so the value of the variable greeting is set to "Hello", not "Bonjour".

```
var greeting;

// Test expression is true, so...
if (true) {
  // ...this code runs
  greeting = "Hello";
} else {
  // This code doesn't run
  greeting = "Bonjour";
}
```

Of course, the preceding test expression would rarely, if ever, be used in a real program because it always produces the same result. In the vast majority of cases, the test expression's value is dynamically determined at runtime based on information calculated by the program or provided by the user.

For example, suppose we're building a social activity web site that includes gambling activities. To participate in a gambling activity, the user must be at least 18 years old. At login time, each user's status is loaded from a database. The loaded status is assigned to a variable, gamblingAuthorized. A gamblingAuthorized of true indicates that the user is 18 or older; a gamblingAuthorized of false, indicates that the user is under 18.

When the user attempts to start gambling, the application uses the following conditional statement to determine whether the attempt should be permitted or denied:

```
if (gamblingAuthorized) {
  // Code here would display the gambling activity's interface
} else {
  // Code here would display an "entry denied" message
}
```

Very often, the test expression in an *if* statement is either an *equality expression* or a *relational expression*. Equality expressions and relational expressions use *equality operators* and *relational operators* to compare two values, and express the result of that comparison as a *Boolean* value (i.e., either true or false). For example, the following equality expression uses the *equality operator* (==) to compare expression "Mike" to the expression "Margaret":

```
"Mike" == "Margaret"
```

The preceding expression evaluates to the *Boolean* value false because "Mike" is considered not equal to "Margaret".

Likewise, the following relational expression uses the *less than operator* (<) to compare the expression 6 to the expression 7:

```
6 < 7
```

This expression evaluates to the *Boolean* value true because 6 is less than 7.

As the preceding examples show, instances of the *String* class are compared based on the individual characters they represent, and instances of the *Number*, *int*, and *uint* classes are compared based on the mathematical quantities they represent. Note that string comparisons are case-sensitive; for example, "a" is considered not equal to "A". For the rules governing whether one value is equal to, greater than, or less than another value, see the entries for the ==, ===, <, and > operators in Adobe's ActionScript Language Reference.

Now let's take a look at an example of an *if* statement that uses an equality expression as its test expression. Suppose we're building an online shopping program with a virtual shopping basket. The program maintains an instance variable, numItems, whose value indicates the number of items currently in the user's shopping basket. When the basket is empty, the program displays the message "Your basket is empty". When the basket is not empty, the program instead displays the message "Total items in your basket: *n*" (where *n* represents the number of items in the basket).

The following code shows how our program might create the shopping cart status message. It assigns the value of the variable basketStatus based on the value of numItems.

```
var basketStatus;

if (numItems == 0) {
  basketStatus = "Your basket is empty";
} else {
  basketStatus = "Total items in your basket: " + numItems;
}
```

In the preceding code, if numItems is equal to zero, the program sets basketStatus to the expression:

```
"Your basket is empty"
```

Otherwise, if numItems is greater than zero, the program sets basketStatus to the expression:

```
"Total items in your basket: " + numItems
```

Notice the use of the *concatenation operator* (+) in the preceding expression. The concatenation operator converts the numeric value referenced by numItems to a string and then combines that string with the string "Total items in your basket:". The resulting value is a combination of the two expressions. For example, if numItems is 2, then the result of the concatenation expression is the following string:

```
"Total items in your basket: 2"
```

An if statement with no else

When the *else* clause of an *if* statement is not needed, it can simply be omitted. For example, suppose that, in our shopping application, if the user orders more than 10 items, the total order is discounted by 10%. At checkout time, we might use code such as the following when calculating the cost of the entire order:

```
if (numItems > 10) {
  totalPrice = totalPrice * .9;
}
```

If numItems is less than 11, totalPrice is simply not altered.

Chaining if statements

To make a decision between more than two possible courses of action, we chain multiple *if* statements together, as shown in the following generalized code for a condition with three possible outcomes:

```
if (testExpression1) {
  codeBlock1
} else if (testExpression2) {
  codeBlock2
} else {
  codeBlock3
}
```

For example, suppose we're writing a multilingual application that displays a greeting message to its users in one of four languages: English, Japanese, French, or German. When the program starts, we ask the user to choose a language, and we set a corresponding variable, language, to one of the following strings: "english", "japanese", "french", or "german" (notice that the language names are not capitalized; it's typical to use all lowercase or all UPPERCASE when comparing strings). To create the appropriate greeting message, we use the following code:

```
var greeting;

if (language == "english") {
  greeting = "Hello";
} else if (language == "japanese") {
  greeting = "Konnichiwa";
} else if (language == "french") {
```

```
    greeting = "Bonjour";
  } else if (language == "german") {
    greeting = "Guten tag";
  } else {
    // Code here (not shown) would display an error message indicating
    // that the language was not set properly
  }
```

When the preceding code runs, if language's value is "english", then greeting is set to "Hello". If language's value is "japanese", "french", or "german", then greeting is set to "Konnichiwa", "Bonjour", or "Guten tag", respectively. If language's value is not "english", "japanese", "french", or "german" (probably due to some program error), then the code in the final *else* clause is executed.

Now that we're familiar with the *if* statement, let's consider the *switch* statement, which is offered by ActionScript as a convenient way to create a condition with multiple possible outcomes.

 The behavior of a *switch* statement can also be implemented with *if* statements, but *switch* is considered more legible than *if* when working with conditions that have multiple possible outcomes.

The switch Statement

The *switch* statement lets us execute one of several possible code blocks based on the value of a single test expression. The general form of the *switch* statement is:

```
switch (testExpression) {
  case expression1:
    codeBlock1
    break;
  case expression2:
    codeBlock2
    break;
  default:
    codeBlock3
}
```

In the preceding code, *testExpression* is an expression that ActionScript will attempt to match with each of the supplied *case* expressions, from top to bottom. The *case* expressions are supplied with the statement label *case*, followed by a colon. If *testExpression* matches a *case* expression, all statements immediately following that *case* label are executed—including those in any subsequent *case* blocks! To prevent subsequent *case* blocks from executing, we must use the *break* statement at the end of each block. Alternatively, when we want more than one condition to trigger the execution of the same block of code, we can omit the *break* statement. For example, in the following code, *codeBlock1* executes when *testExpression* matches either *expression1* or *expression2*:

```
switch (testExpression) {
```

```
      case expression1:
      case expression2:
        codeBlock1
        break;
      case expression3:
        codeBlock2
        break;
      default:
        codeBlock3
    }
```

If no *case* expression matches `testExpression`, all statements following the *default* label are executed.

Though the *default* label is normally listed last, it can legally come anywhere within the *switch* statement. Furthermore, the *default* label is not mandatory in a *switch* statement. If no *default* is provided and `testExpression` does not match a *case* expression, execution flow simply continues after the end of the *switch* statement block (that is, the code within the *switch* statement is skipped).

The following code shows how to implement the preceding section's multilingual greeting condition using a *switch* statement instead of a chain of *if* statements. Both approaches implement the same behavior, but the *switch* code is arguably easier to read and scan quickly.

```
    var greeting;

    switch (language) {
      case "english":
        greeting = "Hello";
        break;

      case "japanese":
        greeting = "Konnichiwa";
        break;

      case "french":
        greeting = "Bonjour";
        break;

      case "german":
        greeting = "Guten tag";
        break;

      default:
        // Code here (not shown) would display an error message indicating
        // that the language was not set properly
    }
```

The *switch* statement implicitly uses the strict equality operator (===)—*not* the equality operator (==)—when comparing the *testExpression* with *case* expressions. For a description of the difference, see Adobe's ActionScript Language Reference.

Loops

In the preceding section, we saw that a conditional causes a statement block to execute once if the value of its test expression is true. A *loop*, on the other hand, causes a statement block to be executed repeatedly, for as long as its test expression remains true.

ActionScript provides five different types of loops: *while*, *do-while*, *for*, *for-in*, and *for-each-in*. The first three types have very similar effects but with varying syntax. The remaining two types are used to access the dynamic instance variables of an object. We haven't studied dynamic instance variables yet, so for now we'll consider the first three types of loops. For information on *for-in* and *for-each-in*, see Chapter 15.

The while Statement

Structurally, a *while* statement is constructed much like an *if* statement: a main statement encloses a code block that is executed only when a given test expression is true:

```
while (testExpression) {
  codeBlock
}
```

If *testExpression* is true, the code in *codeBlock* (called the *loop body*) is executed. But, unlike the *if* statement, when the *codeBlock* is finished, execution begins again at the beginning of the *while* statement (that is, ActionScript "loops" back to the beginning of the *while* statement). The second pass through the *while* statement works just like the first: the *testExpression* is evaluated, and if it is still true, *codeBlock* is executed again. This process continues until *testExpression* becomes false, at which point execution continues with any statements that follow the *while* statement in the program. If *testExpression* never yields false, the loop executes infinitely, eventually causing the Flash runtime to generate an error, which stops the loop (and all currently executing code). To avoid infinite execution, a *while* loop's *codeBlock* typically includes a statement that modifies the *testExpression*, causing it to yield false when some condition is met.

For example, consider the following loop, which calculates 2 to the power of 3 (i.e., 2 times 2 times 2) by executing the loop body two times:

```
var total = 2;
var counter = 0;
```

```
while (counter < 2) {
  total = total * 2;
  counter = counter + 1;
}
```

To execute the preceding *while* loop, ActionScript first evaluates the test expression:

```
counter < 2
```

Because counter is 0, and 0 is less than 2, the value of the test expression is true; so, ActionScript executes the loop body:

```
total = total * 2;
counter = counter + 1;
```

The loop body sets total to its own value multiplied by two and adds one to counter. Hence, total becomes 4, counter becomes 1. When the loop body completes, it's time to repeat the loop.

The second time the loop executes, ActionScript once again checks the value of the test expression. This time, counter's value is 1, and 1 is still less than 2, so the value of the test expression is, once again, true. Consequently, ActionScript executes the loop body for a second time. As before, the loop body sets total to its own value multiplied by two and adds one to counter. Hence, total becomes 8, counter becomes 2. When the loop body completes, it's again time to repeat the loop.

The third time the loop executes, ActionScript once again checks the value of the test expression. This time, counter's value is 2, which is *not* less than 2, so the value of the test expression is false, and the loop ends. When the entire process is complete, total, which started with the value 2, has been multiplied by itself two times, so it ends up with the value 8.

> In real code, you should use *Math.pow()*—not a loop statement—to perform exponential calculations. For example, to calculate 2 to the power of 3, use Math.pow(2, 3).

While not particularly thrilling, the preceding loop provides great flexibility. For example, if we wanted to calculate, say, 2 to the power 16, we would simply update the number in the test expression to make the loop body run 15 times, as follows:

```
var total = 2;
var counter = 0;
while (counter < 15) {
  total = total * 2;
  counter = counter + 1;
}
// Here, total has the value 65536
```

One execution of a loop body is known as an *iteration*. Accordingly, a variable, such as counter, that controls the number of times a given loop iterates is known as the

loop *iterator*, or, sometimes, the loop *index*. By convention, loop iterators are typically named i, as shown in the following code:

```
var total = 2;
var i = 0;
while (i < 15) {
  total = total * 2;
  i = i + 1;
}
```

The last line of the preceding loop body is known as the *loop update* because it
updates the value of the iterator in a way that will eventually cause the loop to end.
In this case, the loop update adds one to the value of the loop iterator. Adding one to
the value of the loop iterator is such a common task that it has its own operator: the
increment operator, written as ++. The increment operator adds one to the value of
its operand. For example, the following code adds one to the variable n:

```
var n = 0;
n++;          // n's value is now 1
```

The following code revises our loop to use the increment operator:

```
var total = 2;
var i = 0;
while (i < 15) {
  total = total * 2;
  i++;
}
```

The opposite of the increment operator is the decrement operator, written as --. The
decrement operator subtracts one from the value of its operand. For example, the
following code subtracts one from the variable n:

```
var n = 4;
n--;          // n's value is now 3
```

The decrement operator is often used with loops that count down from a given
value, rather than counting up (as our preceding examples did). We'll see both the
increment and decrement operators used throughout this book. However, in general,
the increment operator is used much more frequently than the decrement operator.

Processing Lists with Loops

Loops are typically used to process lists of things.

For example, suppose we're creating a registration form that requires the user to submit an email address. Before the form is submitted to the server, we want to check
whether the supplied email address contains an @ sign. If it doesn't, we'll warn the
user that the email address is invalid.

Note that in this example, our concept of a "valid" address is extremely rudimentary. For example, in our code, addresses that start or end with an @ character, or that contain multiple @ characters, are considered valid. Nevertheless, our example shows a decent first step towards creating an email validation algorithm.

To check for the @ sign in the email address, we'll use a loop that treats the email address as a list of individual characters. Before we start the loop, we'll create a variable, isValidAddress, and set it to false. The loop body will execute once for each character in the email address. The first time the loop body executes, it checks whether the first character in the email address is an @ sign. If it is, the loop body sets isValidAddress to true, indicating that the email address is valid. The second time the loop body executes, it checks whether the *second* character in the email address is an @ sign. Once again, if the @ sign is found, the loop body sets isValidAddress to true, indicating that the email address is valid. The loop body continues checking each character in the email address until there are no more characters to check. At the end of the loop, if isValidAddress is still false, then the @ sign was never found, so the email address is invalid. If, on the other hand, isValidAddress is true, then the @ sign *was* found, so the email address is valid.

Now let's take a look at the actual validation code. In a real application, we'd start by retrieving the user's supplied email address, However, for the sake of simplicity in this example will supply the address manually, as follows:

```
var address = "me@moock.org";
```

Next, we create the isValidAddress variable and set it to false:

```
var isValidAddress = false;
```

Then, we create our loop iterator:

```
var i = 0;
```

Next comes the *while* statement for our loop. We want it to run once for every character in address. To retrieve the number of letters in a string, we use the *String* class's instance variable length. For example, the value of the expression "abc".length is 3, indicating that there are three letters in the string "abc". Accordingly, the basic structure of our loop is as follows:

```
while (i < address.length) {
    i++;
}
```

Each time the loop body runs, we must retrieve one of the characters in address and compare it to the string "@". If the retrieved character is equal to "@", then we'll set isValidAddress to true. To retrieve a specific character from a string, we use the built-in *String* class's instance method *charAt()*. The name "charAt" is short for "character at". The *charAt()* method expects one argument—a number specifying the position, or *index*, of the character to retrieve. Character indices start at zero. For example, the following call expression has the value "m" because the character at index 0 is "m":

```
address.charAt(0);
```

Likewise, the following call expression has the value "@" because the character at index 2 is "@":

```
address.charAt(2);
```

In our loop body, the index of the character to retrieve is specified dynamically by the loop iterator, i, as shown in the following code:

```
while (i < address.length) {
  if (address.charAt(i) == "@") {
    isValidAddress = true;
  }
  i++;
}
```

Here's the validation code in its entirety:

```
var address = "me@moock.org";
var isValidAddress = false;
var i = 0;

while (i < address.length) {
  if (address.charAt(i) == "@") {
    isValidAddress = true;
  }
  i++;
}
```

For practice, let's examine how ActionScript would execute the preceding *while* statement.

First, ActionScript evaluates the test expression:

```
i < address.length
```

In this case, i is 0, and address.length is 12. The number 0 is less than 12, so the value of the test expression is true, and ActionScript executes the loop body:

```
if (address.charAt(i) == "@") {
  isValidAddress = true;
}
i++;
```

In the loop body, ActionScript must first determine whether to execute the code in the conditional:

```
if (address.charAt(i) == "@") {
  isValidAddress = true;
}
```

To decide whether to execute the code in the preceding conditional, ActionScript checks whether address.charAt(i) is equal to "@". The first time the loop body executes, i is 0, so address.charAt(i) evaluates to address.charAt(0), which, as we saw earlier, yields the character "m" (the first character in the email address). The character "m" is *not* equal to the character "@", so ActionScript does not execute the code in the conditional.

Next, ActionScript executes the loop update, incrementing i's value to 1:

```
i++;
```

With the loop body complete, it's time to repeat the loop.

The second time the loop executes, ActionScript once again checks the value of the test expression. This time, i is 1, and address.length is still 12. The number 1 is less than 12, so the value of the test expression is true, and ActionScript executes the loop body for the second time. As before, in the loop body, ActionScript must determine whether to execute the code in the conditional:

```
if (address.charAt(i) == "@") {
  isValidAddress = true;
}
```

This time, i is 1, so address.charAt(i) evaluates to address.charAt(1), which yields the character "e" (the second character in the email address). The character "e" is again not equal to the character "@", so ActionScript does not execute the code in the conditional.

Next, ActionScript executes the loop update, incrementing i's value to 2. Again, it's time to repeat the loop.

The third time the loop executes, ActionScript checks the value of the test expression. This time, i is 2, and address.length is still 12. The number 2 is less than 12, so the value of the test expression is true, and ActionScript executes the loop body for the third time. As before, in the loop body, ActionScript must determine whether to execute the code in the conditional:

```
if (address.charAt(i) == "@") {
  isValidAddress = true;
}
```

This time, i is 2, so address.charAt(i) evaluates to address.charAt(2), which yields the character "@". The character "@" *is* equal to the character "@", so ActionScript executes the code in the conditional, setting isValidAddress to true. Then, Action-Script executes the loop update, incrementing i's value to 3.

The loop repeats in the same way nine more times. When the entire process is complete, isValidAddress has been set to true, so the program knows that the email address can safely be submitted to the server for processing.

Ending a Loop with the break Statement

The loop presented in the preceding section was effective but inefficient. According to the hypothetical address-checker's simple logic, an email address is considered valid if it contains the @ character. To check for the @ character, the loop in the preceding section examined every single character in the supplied email address. In the case of the example email address "me@moock.org", the loop body executed a full 12 times, even though the address was known to be valid after the third character was examined. Hence, the loop body executed needlessly nine times.

To make the loop from the preceding section more efficient, we can use the *break* statement, which immediately terminates a loop. Here's the updated code:

```
var address = "me@moock.org";
var isValidAddress = false;
var i = 0;

while (i < address.length) {
  if (address.charAt(i) == "@") {
    isValidAddress = true;
    break;
  }
  i++;
}
```

In the preceding loop, as soon as an @ character is found in address, isValidAddress is set to true, and then the *break* statement causes the loop to terminate.

 If you create a loop whose job is to find something in a list, always use *break* to terminate that loop when it finds what it's looking for.

Reader exercise: See if you can update the preceding loop to reject addresses that start or end with an @ character, or contain multiple @ characters. You might also try to update the loop to reject addresses that contain no . character.

The do-while Statement

As we saw earlier, a *while* statement tells ActionScript to execute a block of code repeatedly while a specified condition remains true. Due to a *while* loop's structure, its body will be skipped entirely if the loop's test expression is not true the first time it is tested. A *do-while* statement lets us guarantee that a loop body will be executed at least once with minimal fuss. The body of a *do-while* loop always executes the first time through the loop. The *do-while* statement's syntax is somewhat like an inverted *while* statement:

```
do {
  codeBlock
} while (testExpression);
```

The keyword *do* begins the loop, followed by the *codeBlock* of the body. On the first pass through the *do-while* loop, the *codeBlock* is executed before the *testExpression* is ever checked. At the end of the *codeBlock* block, if *testExpression* is true, the loop is begun anew, and the *codeBlock* is executed again. The loop executes repeatedly until *testExpression* is false, at which point the *do-while* statement ends.

The for Statement

A *for* loop is essentially synonymous with a *while* loop, but it is written with more compact syntax. The *for* loop places the loop initialization and update statements together with test expression, at the top of the loop. Here's the syntax of the *for* loop:

```
for (initialization; testExpression; update) {
  codeBlock
}
```

Before the first iteration of a *for* loop, the `initialization` statement is performed (once and only once). It is typically used to set the initial value of one or more iterator variables. As with other loops, if `testExpression` is true, then the `codeBlock` is executed. Otherwise, the loop ends. Even though it appears in the loop header, the *update* statement is executed at the *end* of each loop iteration, before `testExpression` is tested again to see if the loop should continue.

Here's a *for* loop that calculates 2 to the power 3:

```
var total = 2;

for (var i = 0; i < 2; i++) {
  total = total * 2;
}
```

For comparison, here's the equivalent *while* loop:

```
var total = 2;
var i = 0;

while (i < 2) {
  total = total * 2;
  i++;
}
```

Here's a *for* loop that checks to see whether a string contains the @ character. It is functionally identical to our earlier *while* loop that performs the same task:

```
var address = "me@moock.org";
var isValidAddress = false;

for (var i = 0; i < address.length; i++) {
  if (address.charAt(i) == "@") {
    isValidAddress = true;
    break;
```

```
        }
    }
```

Once you're used to the *for* syntax, you'll find it saves space and allows for easy interpretation of the loop's body and controls.

Boolean Logic

Early in this chapter, we saw how to make logical decisions using test expressions that yield Boolean values. The decisions were based on a single factor, such as "if language is "english", then display "Hello"". But not all programming logic is so simple. Programs often need to consider multiple factors in *branching logic* (i.e., decision making). To manage multiple factors in a test expression, we use the Boolean operators: || (logical *OR*) and && (logical *AND*).

Logical OR

The *logical OR* operator is most commonly used to initiate some action when at least one of two conditions is met. For example, "If I am hungry *or* I am thirsty, I'll go to the kitchen." The symbol for logical *OR* is made using two "pipe" characters: ||. Typically, the pipe character (|) is accessible using the Shift key and the Backslash (\) key in the upper right of most Western keyboards, where it may be depicted as a dashed vertical line. Logical *OR* has the following general form:

```
    expression1 || expression2
```

When both *expression1* and *expression2* are Boolean values or evaluate to Boolean values, logical *OR* returns true if either expression is true and returns false only if *both* expression are false. In summary:

```
    true  || false    // true because first operand is true
    false || true     // true because second operand is true
    true  || true     // true (however, either operand being true is sufficient)
    false || false    // false because both operands are false
```

When *expression1* is not a Boolean value, ActionScript first converts it to a Boolean; if the result of such a conversion is true, logical *OR* returns *expression1*'s resolved value. Otherwise, logical *OR* returns *expression2*'s resolved value. Here's some code to demonstrate:

```
    0 || "hi there!"    // expression1 does not convert to true, so the
                        // operation returns expression2's value: "hi there!"

    "hey" || "dude"     // expression1 is a nonempty string, so it converts to
                        // true and the operation returns
                        // expression1's value: "hey"

    false || 5 + 5      // expression1 does not convert to true, so the
                        // value of expression2 (namely 10) is returned.
```

The results of converting various kinds of data to a Boolean value are listed in the section "Conversion to Primitive Types" in Chapter 8.

In practice, we rarely use non-Boolean values returned by a logical *OR* expression. Instead, we normally use the result in a conditional statement where it is used to make a Boolean decision. Consider the following code:

```
var x = 10;
var y = 15;
if (x || y) {
  // This code executes if one of either x or y is not zero
}
```

On line 3, we see a logical *OR* operation (x || y) being used where a Boolean is expected as the test expression of an *if* statement. The first step in determining the value of x || y is to convert 10 (the value of the first operand, x) to a Boolean. Any nonzero finite number converts to the Boolean true. Hence, the logical *OR* returns the value of x, which is 10. So, to ActionScript, the *if* statement looks like this:

```
if (10) {
  // This code executes if one of either x or y is not zero
}
```

But 10 is a number, not a Boolean. So what happens next? The *if* statement converts the return value of the logical *OR* operation to a Boolean. In this case, 10 is converted to the Boolean value true, and ActionScript sees our code as:

```
if (true) {
  // This code executes if one of either x or y is not zero
}
```

And there you have it. The test expression is true, so the code between the curly braces is executed.

Note that if the first expression in a logical *OR* operation resolves to true, it is unnecessary, and therefore inefficient, to evaluate the second expression. Hence, ActionScript evaluates the second expression only if the first expression resolves to false. This fact is useful in cases in which you don't want to resolve the second expression unless the first expression resolves to false. In the following example, we check if a number is out of range. If the number is too small, there is no need to perform the second test, in which we check whether it is too large.

```
if (xPosition < 0 || xPosition > 100) {
  // This code executes if one of either xPosition is between
  // 0 and 100, inclusive
}
```

Note that the variable xPosition must be included in each comparison. The following code shows a common mistaken attempt to check xPosition's value twice:

```
// Oops! Forgot xPosition in the comparison with 100
if (xPosition < 0 || > 100) {
  // This code executes if one of either xPosition is between
```

```
    // 0 and 100, inclusive
}
```

Logical AND

Like the logical *OR* operator, logical *AND* is used primarily to execute a block of code conditionally—in this case, only when both of two conditions are met. The logical *AND* operator has the following general form:

```
expression1 && expression2
```

Both *expression1* and *expression2* can be any valid expression. In the simplest case, in which both expressions are Boolean values, logical *AND* returns false if either operand is false and returns true only if *both* operands are true. In summary:

```
true  && false    // false because second expression is false
false && true     // false because first expression is false
true  && true     // true because both expressions are true
false && false    // false because both expressions are false
                  // (either is sufficient)
```

Let's see how the logical *AND* operator is used in two examples. First, we execute some code only when two variables are both greater than 50:

```
x = 100;
y = 51;
if (x>50 && y>50) {
   // Code here executes only if x and y are greater than 50
}
```

Next, imagine a New Year's Day-contest web site in which users are granted access only when they provide the correct password, *and* the current date is January 1. The following code shows how to use the *AND* operator to determine whether both conditions have been met (the correct password is "fun"):

```
var now = new Date();      // Create a new Date object
var day = now.getDate();   // Returns an integer between 1 and 31
var month = now.getMonth(); // Returns an integer between 0 and 11

if ( password=="fun"  &&  (month + day)>1 ) {
   // Let the user in...
}
```

The technical behavior of the logical *AND* operator is quite similar to that of the logical *OR* operator. First, *expression1* is converted to a Boolean. If the result of that conversion is false, the value of *expression1* is returned. If the result of that conversion is true, the value of *expression2* is returned.

As with *OR*, if the first expression in a logical *AND* operation resolves to false, it is unnecessary, and therefore inefficient, to evaluate the second expression. Therefore, ActionScript evaluates the second expression only if the first expression resolves to true. This fact is useful in cases in which you don't want to resolve the second expression unless the first operand resolves to true. In this example, we perform a division operation only if the divisor is nonzero:

```
if ( numItems!=0  &&  totalCost/numItems>3 ) {
  // Execute this code only when the number of items is not equal
  // to 0, and the total cost of each item is greater than 3
}
```

Logical NOT

The *logical NOT* operator (!) returns the Boolean opposite of its single operand. It takes the general form:

```
!expression
```

If *expression* is true, logical *NOT* returns false. If *expression* is false, logical *NOT* returns true. If *expression* is not a Boolean, its value is converted to a Boolean for the sake of the operation, and its opposite is returned.

Like the does-not-equal operator (!=), the logical *NOT* operator is convenient for testing what something *isn't* rather than what it *is*. For example, the body of the following conditional statement executes only when the current date is *not* January 1. Notice the extra parentheses, which force a custom order of operations (precedence), as discussed in Chapter 10.

```
var now = new Date();      // Create a new Date object
var day = now.getDate();   // Returns an integer between 1 and 31
var month = now.getMonth(); // Returns an integer between 0 and 11

if (  !( (month + day)==1)  ) {
  // Execute "not-January 1st" code
}
```

The *NOT* operator is also sometimes used to *toggle* a variable from true to false and vice versa. For example, suppose we have a single button that is used to turn an application's sound on and off. When the button is pressed, the program might use the following code to enable or disable audio playback:

```
soundEnabled = !soundEnabled // Toggle the current sound state

if (soundEnabled) {
  // Make sure sounds are audible
} else {
  // Mute all sounds
}
```

Notice that ! is also used in the inequality operator (!=). As a programming symbol, the ! character usually means *not*, or *opposite*. It is unrelated to the ! symbol used to indicate "factorial" in common mathematical notation.

Back to Classes and Objects

We're now done with our introduction to conditionals and loops, but we definitely haven't seen the last of them. Over the course of this book, we'll encounter plenty of examples of conditionals and loops used in real-world situations.

In the next chapter, we'll return to the general topics of classes and objects. If you've been yearning for our virtual pets, read on.

CHAPTER 3

Instance Methods Revisited

In Chapter 1, we learned how to create instance methods. In this chapter, we'll expand that basic knowledge by studying the following additional instance-method topics:

- Omitting the this keyword
- Bound methods
- State-retrieval and state-modification methods
- Get and set methods
- Extra arguments

Along the way, we'll continue developing the virtual zoo program that we started in Chapter 1. But before we begin, take a minute to reacquaint yourself with the virtual zoo program. Example 3-1 shows the code as we last saw it.

Example 3-1. Zoo program

```
// VirtualPet class
package zoo {
  internal class VirtualPet {
    internal var petName;
    private var currentCalories = 1000;
    private var creationTime;

    public function VirtualPet (name) {
      this.creationTime = new Date();
      this.petName = name;
    }

    public function eat (numberOfCalories) {
      this.currentCalories += numberOfCalories;
    }

    public function getAge () {
      var currentTime = new Date();
      var age = currentTime.time - this.creationTime.time;
```

Example 3-1. Zoo program (continued)

```
      return age;
    }
  }
}

// VirtualZoo class
package zoo {
  public class VirtualZoo {
    private var pet;

    public function VirtualZoo () {
      this.pet = new VirtualPet("Stan");
    }
  }
}
```

Omitting the this Keyword

In Chapter 1, we learned that the this keyword is used to refer to the current object within constructor methods and instance methods. For example, in the following code, the expression this.petName = name tells ActionScript to set the value of the instance variable petName on the object currently being created:

```
public function VirtualPet (name) {
  this.petName = name;
}
```

In the following code, the expression this.currentCalories += numberOfCalories tells ActionScript to set the value of the instance variable currentCalories on the object through which the *eat()* method was invoked:

```
public function eat (numberOfCalories) {
  this.currentCalories += numberOfCalories;
}
```

In code that frequently accesses the variables and methods of the current object, including this can be laborious and can lead to clutter. To reduce labor and improve readability, ActionScript generally allows the current object's instance variables and instance methods to be accessed without this.

Here's how it works: within a constructor method or an instance method, when ActionScript encounters an identifier in an expression, it searches for a local variable, parameter, or nested function whose name matches that identifier. (Nested functions are discussed in Chapter 5.) If no local variable, parameter, or nested function's name matches the identifier, then ActionScript automatically searches for an instance variable or instance method whose name matches the identifier. If a match is found, then the matching instance variable or instance method is used in the expression.

For example, consider what happens if we remove the keyword this from the *eat()* method, as follows:

```
public function eat (numberOfCalories) {
  currentCalories += numberOfCalories;
}
```

When the preceding method runs, ActionScript encounters numberOfCalories, and tries to find a local variable, parameter, or nested function by that name. There *is* a parameter by that name, so its value is used in the expression (in place of numberOfCalories).

Next, ActionScript encounters currentCalories, and tries to find a local variable, parameter, or nested function by that name. No variable, parameter, or nested function named currentCalories is found, so ActionScript then tries to find an instance variable or instance method by that name. This time, ActionScript's search is successful: the *VirtualPet* class *does* have an instance variable named currentCalories, so ActionScript uses it in the expression. As a result, the value of numberOfCalories is added to the instance variable currentCalories.

Therefore, within the *eat()* method, the expression this.currentCalories and currentCalories are identical.

For the sake of easier reading, many developers (and this book) avoid redundant uses of this. From now on, we'll omit this when referring to instance variables and instance methods. However, some programmers prefer to always use this, simply to distinguish instance variables and instance methods from local variables.

Note that use of the this keyword is legal within instance methods, constructor methods, functions, and code in the global scope only. (Global scope is discussed in Chapter 16.) Elsewhere, using this generates a compile-time error.

 The process ActionScript follows to look up identifiers is known as *identifier resolution*. As discussed in Chapter 16, identifiers are resolved based on the region (or scope) of the program in which they occur.

Managing Parameter/Variable Name Conflicts

When an instance variable and a method parameter have the same name, we can access the variable by including the this keyword (known as *disambiguating* the variable from the parameter). For example, the following revised version of *VirtualPet* shows the *eat()* method with a parameter, calories, whose name is identical to (i.e., conflicts with) an instance variable named calories:

```
package zoo {
  internal class VirtualPet {
    // Instance variable 'calories'
    private var calories = 1000;
```

```
    // Method with parameter 'calories'
    public function eat (calories) {
      this.calories += calories;
    }
  }
}
```

Within the body of *eat()*, the expression calories (with no this) refers to the method parameter and the expression this.calories (with this) refers to the instance variable. The calories parameter is said to *shadow* the calories instance variable because on its own, the identifier calories refers to the parameter, not the instance variable. The instance variable can be accessed only with the help of the keyword this. Note that like parameters, local variables can also shadow instance variables and instance methods of the same name. A local variable also shadows a method parameter of the same name, effectively redefining the parameter and leaving the program with no way to refer to the parameter.

Many programmers purposely use the same name for a parameter and an instance variable, and rely on this to disambiguate the two. To keep things more clearly separated in your own code, however, you can simply avoid using parameter names that have the same name as instance variables, instance methods, or local variables.

Now let's move on to our next instance-method topic, bound methods.

Bound Methods

In ActionScript, a method can, itself, be treated as a value. That is, a method can be assigned to a variable, passed to function or another method, or returned from a function or another method.

For example, the following code creates a new *VirtualPet* object, and then assigns that object's *eat()* method to the local variable consume. Notice that in the assignment statement, the method-call parentheses, ( ), are not included after the method name. As a result, the method itself—not the method's return value—is assigned to the variable consume.

```
package zoo {
  public class VirtualZoo {
    private var pet;

    public function VirtualZoo () {
      pet = new VirtualPet("Stan");
      // Assign the method eat() to a variable
      var consume = pet.eat;
    }
  }
}
```

A method assigned to a variable can be invoked via that variable using the standard parentheses operator, ( ). For example, in the following code, we invoke the method referenced by the variable consume:

```
package zoo {
  public class VirtualZoo {
    private var pet;

    public function VirtualZoo () {
      pet = new VirtualPet("Stan");
      // Assign a bound method to consume
      var consume = pet.eat;
      // Invoke the method referenced by consume
      consume(300);
    }
  }
}
```

When the preceding bolded code runs, the *eat()* method is invoked and passed the argument 300. The question is, which pet eats the food? Or, put more technically, on which object does the method execute?

When a method is assigned to a variable and then invoked through that variable, it executes on the object through which it was originally referenced. For example, in the preceding code, when the *eat()* method is assigned to the variable consume, it is referenced through the *VirtualPet* object with the name "Stan". Hence, when *eat()* is invoked via consume, it executes on the *VirtualPet* object with the name "Stan".

A method that is assigned to a variable, passed to a function or method, or returned from a function or method is known as a *bound method*. Bound methods are so named because each bound method is permanently linked to the object through which it was originally referenced. Bound methods are considered instances of the built-in *Function* class.

> When invoking a bound method, we need not specify the object on which the method should execute. Instead, the bound method will automatically execute on the object through which it was originally referenced.

Within the body of a bound method, the keyword this refers to the object to which the method is bound. For example, within the body of the bound method assigned to consume, this refers to the *VirtualPet* object named "Stan".

Bound methods are typically used when one section of a program wishes to instruct another section of the program to invoke a particular method on a particular object. For examples of such a scenario, see the discussion of event handling in Chapter 12. ActionScript's event-handling system makes extensive use of bound methods.

Continuing with this chapter's instance-method theme, the next section describes how instance methods can modify an object's state.

Using Methods to Examine and Modify an Object's State

Earlier we learned that it's good object-oriented practice to declare instance variables *private*, meaning that they cannot be read or modified by code outside of the class in which they are defined. Good object-oriented practice dictates that, rather than allow external code to modify instance variables directly, we should instead define instance methods for examining or changing an object's state.

For example, earlier, we gave our *VirtualPet* class an instance variable named currentCalories. The currentCalories variable conceptually describes the state of each pet's hunger. To allow external code to reduce the pet's hunger level, we *could* make currentCalories publicly accessible. External code could then set the pet's hunger state to any arbitrary value, as shown in the following code:

```
somePet.currentCalories = 5000;
```

The preceding approach, however, is flawed. If external code can modify currentCalories directly, then the *VirtualPet* class has no way to ensure that the value assigned to that variable is legal, or sensible. For example, external code might assign currentCalories 1000000, causing the pet to live for hundreds of years without getting hungry. Or external code might assign currentCalories a negative value, which might cause the program to malfunction.

To prevent these problems, we should declare currentCalories as private (as we did earlier in our *VirtualPet* class). Rather than allowing external code to modify currentCalories directly, we instead provide one or more public instance methods that can be used to change each pet's state of hunger in a legitimate way. Our existing *VirtualPet* class already provides a method, *eat()*, for reducing a pet's hunger. However, the *eat()* method allows any number of calories to be added to currentCalories. Let's now update the *VirtualPet* class's *eat()* method so that it prevents the value of currentCalories from exceeding 2,000. Here's the original code for the *eat()* method:

```
public function eat (numberOfCalories) {
  currentCalories += numberOfCalories;
}
```

To restrict currentCalories's value to a maximum of 2,000, we simply add an *if* statement to the *eat()* method, as follows:

```
public function eat (numberOfCalories) {
  // Calculate the proposed new total calories for this pet
  var newCurrentCalories = currentCalories + numberOfCalories;

  // If the proposed new total calories for this pet is greater
  // than the maximum allowed (which is 2000)...
  if (newCurrentCalories > 2000) {
    // ...set currentCalories to its maximum allowed value (2000)
    currentCalories = 2000;
  } else {
    // ...otherwise, increase currentCalories by the specified amount
```

```
      currentCalories = newCurrentCalories;
    }
  }
```

The *VirtualPet* class's *eat()* method provides a safe means for external code to modify a given *VirtualPet* object's hunger. However, thus far, the *VirtualPet* class does not provide a means for external code to determine how hungry a given *VirtualPet* object is. To give external code access to that information, let's define a method, *getHunger()*, which returns the number of calories a *VirtualPet* object has left, as a percentage. Here's the new method:

```
public function getHunger () {
  return currentCalories / 2000;
}
```

We now have methods for retrieving and modifying a *VirtualPet* object's current state of hunger (*getHunger()* and *eat()*). In traditional object-oriented terminology, a method that *retrieves* the state of an object is known as an *accessor method*, or more casually, a *getter method*. By contrast, a method that *modifies* the state of an object is known as a *mutator method*, or more casually, a *setter method*. However, in Action-Script 3.0, the term "accessor method" refers to a special variety of method that is invoked using variable read- and write-syntax, as described later in the section "Get and Set Methods." As noted earlier, to avoid confusion in this book, we'll avoid using the traditional terms accessor, mutator, getter, and setter. Instead, we'll use the unofficial terms *retriever method* and *modifier method* when discussing accessor methods and mutator methods. Furthermore, we'll use the terms "get method" and "set method" only when referring to ActionScript's special automatic methods.

For a little more practice with retriever and modifier methods, let's update the *VirtualPet* class again. Previously, to retrieve and assign a *VirtualPet* object's name, we accessed the petName variable directly, as shown in the following code:

```
somePet.petName = "Erik";
```

The preceding approach, however, could prove problematic later in our program. It allows petName to be assigned a very long value that might not fit on screen when we display the pet's name. It also allows petName to be assigned an empty string (""), which would not appear on screen at all. To prevent these problems, let's make petName private, and define a modifier method for setting a pet's name. Our modifier method, *setName()*, imposes a maximum name length of 20 characters and rejects attempts to set petName to an empty string (""). Here's the code:

```
public function setName (newName) {
  // If the proposed new name has more than 20 characters...
  if (newName.length > 20) {
    // ...truncate it using the built-in String.substr() method,
    // which returns the specified portion of the string on which
    // it is invoked
    newName = newName.substr(0, 20);
  } else if (newName == "") {
    // ...otherwise, if the proposed new name is an empty string,
```

```
    // then terminate this method without changing petName
    return;
  }

    // Assign the new, validated name to petName
    petName = newName;
  }
```

Now that we've made petName private, we need to provide a retriever method through which external code can access a *VirtualPet* object's name. We'll name our retriever method, *getName()*. For now, *getName()* will simply return the value of petName. (Returning an instance variable's value is often all a retriever method does.) Here's the code:

```
public function getName () {
  return petName;
}
```

The *getName()* method is currently very simple, but it gives our program flexibility. For example, in the future, we may decide we want to make pet names gender-specific. To do so, we simply update *getName()*, as follows (the following hypothetical version of *getName()* assumes that *VirtualPet* defines an instance variable, gender, indicating the gender of each pet):

```
public function getName () {
  if (gender == "male") {
    return "Mr. " + petName;
  } else {
    return "Mrs. " + petName;
  }
}
```

Example 3-2 shows the new code for the *VirtualPet* class, complete with the *getName()* and *setName()* methods. For the sake of simplicity, the instance method *getAge()* and the instance variable creationTime have been removed from the *VirtualPet* class.

Example 3-2. The VirtualPet class

```
package zoo {
  internal class VirtualPet {
    private var petName;
    private var currentCalories = 1000;

    public function VirtualPet (name) {
      petName = name;
    }

    public function eat (numberOfCalories) {
      var newCurrentCalories = currentCalories + numberOfCalories;
      if (newCurrentCalories > 2000) {
        currentCalories = 2000;
      } else {
        currentCalories = newCurrentCalories;
```

Example 3-2. The VirtualPet class (continued)

```
    }
  }

  public function getHunger () {
    return currentCalories / 2000;
  }

  public function setName (newName) {
    // If the proposed new name has more than 20 characters...
    if (newName.length > 20) {
      // ...truncate it
      newName = newName.substr(0, 20);
    } else if (newName == "") {
      // ...otherwise, if the proposed new name is an empty string,
      // then terminate this method without changing petName
      return;
    }

    // Assign the new, validated name to petName
    petName = newName;
  }

  public function getName () {
    return petName;
  }
 }
}
```

Here's a sample use of our new *getName()* and *setName()* methods:

```
package zoo {
  public class VirtualZoo {
    private var pet;

    public function VirtualZoo () {
      pet = new VirtualPet("Stan");
      // Assign the pet's old name to the local variable oldName
      var oldName = pet.getName();
      // Give the pet a new name
      pet.setName("Marcos");
    }
  }
}
```

By using a modifier method to mediate variable-value assignments, we can develop applications that respond gracefully to runtime problems by anticipating and handling illegal or inappropriate values. But does that mean each and every instance variable access in a program should happen through a method? For example, consider our *VirtualPet* constructor method:

```
public function VirtualPet (name) {
  petName = name;
}
```

Now that we have a method for setting `petName`, should we update the *VirtualPet* constructor method as follows?

```
public function VirtualPet (name) {
  setName(name);
}
```

The answer depends on the circumstances at hand. Generally speaking, it's quite reasonable to access private variables directly within the class that defines them. However, when a variable's name or role is likely to change in the future, or when a modifier or retriever method provides special services during variable access (such as error checking), it pays to use the method everywhere, even within the class that defines the variables. For example, in the preceding updated *VirtualPet* constructor method, it's wise to set `petName` through *setName()* because *setName()* guarantees that the supplied name is neither too long nor too short. That said, in cases where speed is a factor, direct variable access may be prudent (accessing a variable directly is always faster than accessing it through a method).

Programmers who prefer the style of direct variable access but still want the benefits of retriever and modifier methods, typically use ActionScript's automatic get and set methods, discussed next.

Get and Set Methods

In the previous section we learned about retriever and modifier methods, which are public methods that retrieve and modify an object's state. Some developers consider such methods cumbersome. They argue that:

```
pet.setName("Jeff");
```

is more awkward than:

```
pet.name = "Jeff";
```

In our earlier study, we saw that direct variable assignments such as `pet.name = "Jeff"` aren't ideal object-oriented practice and can lead to invalid variable assignments. To bridge the gap between the convenience of variable assignment and the safety of retriever and modifier methods, ActionScript supports get and set methods. These methods are invoked using variable retrieval- and assignment-syntax.

To define a get method, we use the following general syntax:

```
function get methodName () {
  statements
}
```

where the keyword *get* identifies the method as a get method, *methodName* is the method's name, and *statements* is zero or more statements executed when the method is invoked (one of which is expected to return the value associated with *methodName*).

To define a set method, we use the following general syntax:

```
function set methodName (newValue) {
  statements
}
```

where the *set* keyword identifies the method as a set method, *methodName* is the method's name, *newValue* receives the value assigned to an internal instance variable, and *statements* is zero or more statements executed when the method is invoked. The statements are expected to determine and internally store the value associated with *methodName*. Note that in a set method body, the *return* statement must not be used to return a value (but can be used on its own to terminate the method). Set methods have an automatic return value, discussed later.

Get and set methods have a unique style of being invoked that does not require use of the function call operator, ( ). A get method, *x()*, on an object, obj, is invoked as follows:

```
obj.x;
```

rather than:

```
obj.x( );
```

A set method, *y()*, on an object, obj, is invoked as follows:

```
obj.y = value;
```

rather than:

```
obj.y(value);
```

where *value* is the first (and only) argument passed to *y()*.

Get and set methods, therefore, appear to magically translate variable access into method calls. As an example, let's (temporarily) add a get method named *name()* to our *VirtualPet* class. Here's the code for the method:

```
public function get name ( ) {
  return petName;
}
```

With the get method *name()* in place, all attempts to retrieve the value of the instance variable name actually invoke the get method. The get method's return value appears as though it were the value of the name variable. For example, the following code invokes the get method *name()* and assigns its return value to the variable oldName:

```
var oldName = pet.name;
```

Now let's (temporarily) add a set method named *name()* to our *VirtualPet* class. Here's the code for the method:

```
public function set name (newName) {
  // If the proposed new name has more than 20 characters...
  if (newName.length > 20) {
```

```
    // ...truncate it
    newName = newName.substr(0, 20);
  } else if (newName == "") {
    // ...otherwise, if the proposed new name is an empty string,
    // then terminate this method without changing petName
    return;
  }

  // Assign the new, validated name to petName
  petName = newName;
}
```

With the set method *name()* in place, attempts to assign the value of the instance variable name invoke the set method. The value used in the name assignment statement is passed to the set method, which stores it internally in the private variable petName. For example, the following code invokes the set method *name()*, which stores "Andreas" internally in petName:

```
pet.name = "Andreas";
```

With a get and a set method named *name()* defined, the name variable becomes an external façade only; it does not exist as a variable in the class but can be used as though it did. You can, therefore, think of instance variables that are backed by get and set methods (such as name) as *pseudo-variables*.

 It is illegal to create an actual variable with the same name as a get or set method. Attempts to do so result in a compile-time error.

When a set method is called, it always invokes its corresponding get method and returns the get method's return value. This allows a program to use the new value immediately after setting it. For example, the following code shows a fragment of a fictitious music player application. It uses a set method call to tell the music player which song to play first. It then immediately plays that song by calling *start()* on the return value of the firstSong assignment.

```
// Invoke start() on new Song("dancehit.mp3")--the return value
// of the set method firstSong()
(musicPlayer.firstSong = new Song("dancehit.mp3")).start();
```

While convenient in some cases, the return-value feature of set methods imposes limits on get methods: specifically, get methods should never perform tasks beyond those required to retrieve their internal variable value. For example, a get method should not implement a global counter that tracks how many times a variable has been accessed. The automatic invocation of the get method by the set method would tarnish the counter's record keeping.

 A get/set pseudo-variable can be made read-only by declaring a get method without declaring a set method.

Choosing between retriever/modifier methods and get/set methods is a matter of personal taste. This book, for example, does not use get/set methods, but you should expect to see them used by other programmers and in some documentation.

Moving on, to complete our study of instance methods, we'll learn how to handle an unknown number of parameters. The following discussion requires a prior knowledge of arrays (ordered lists of values), which we haven't covered yet. If you are new to arrays, you should skip this section for now and return to it after you have read Chapter 11.

 The techniques described in the next section apply not only to instance methods, but also static methods and functions, which we'll study in the coming chapters.

Handling an Unknown Number of Parameters

In Chapter 1, we learned that it is illegal to call a method without supplying arguments for all required parameters. It is also illegal to call a method with *more* than the required number of arguments.

To define a method that accepts an arbitrary number of arguments, we use the ...(rest) parameter. The ...(rest) parameter defines an array to hold any arguments passed to a given method. It can be used on its own or in combination with named parameters. When used on its own, the ...(rest) parameter has the following general form:

```
function methodName (...argumentsArray) {
}
```

In the preceding code, *methodName* is the name of a method (or function), and *argumentsArray* is the name of a parameter that will be assigned an automatically created array of all arguments received by the method. The first argument (the left-most argument in the call expression) is stored at index 0 and is referred to as *argumentsArray*[0]. Subsequent arguments are stored in order, proceeding to the right—so, the second argument is *argumentsArray*[1], the third is *argumentsArray*[2], and so on.

The ...(rest) parameter allows us to create very flexible functions that operate on an arbitrary number of values. For example, the following code shows a method that finds the average value of any numbers it received as arguments:

```
public function getAverage (...numbers) {
  var total = 0;

  for (var i = 0; i < numbers.length; i++) {
    total += numbers [i];
  }

  return total / numbers.length;
}
```

Note that the preceding *getAverage()* method works with numeric arguments only. To protect *getAverage()* from being called with nonnumeric arguments, we could use the *is* operator, discussed in the section "Upcasting and Downcasting" in Chapter 8.

The ...(rest) parameter can also be used in combination with named parameters. When used with other parameters, the ...(rest) parameter must be the last parameter in the parameter list. For example, consider the following method, *initializeUser()*, used to initialize a user in a hypothetical social-networking application. The method defines a single required parameter, name, followed by a ...(rest) parameter named hobbies:

```
public function initializeUser (name, ...hobbies) {
}
```

When invoking *initializeUser()*, we must supply an argument for the name parameter, and we can optionally also supply an additional comma-separated list of hobbies. Within the method body, name is assigned the value of the first argument passed to the method, and hobbies is assigned an array of all remaining arguments passed to *initializeUser()*. For example, if we issue the following method invocation:

```
initializeUser("Hoss", "video games", "snowboarding");
```

then name is assigned the value "Hoss", and hobbies is assigned the value ["video games", "snowboarding"].

Up Next: Class-Level Information and Behavior

We're now finished our coverage of instance methods and instance variables. As we learned in Chapter 1, instance methods and instance variables define the behavior and characteristics of the objects of a class. In the next chapter, we'll learn how to create behavior and manage information that pertains not to individual objects, but to an entire class.

CHAPTER 4

Static Variables and Static Methods

In Chapter 1, we learned how to define the characteristics and behavior of an object using instance variables and instance methods. In this chapter, we'll learn how to manage information and create functionality that pertains to a class, itself, rather than its instances.

Static Variables

Over the past several chapters, we've had a fair bit of practice working with instance variables, which are variables associated with a particular instance of a class. *Static variables*, by contrast, are variables associated with a class itself, rather than a particular instance of that class. Static variables are used to keep track of information that relates logically to an entire class, as opposed to information that varies from instance to instance. For example, a class representing a dialog box might use a static variable to specify the default size for new dialog box instances, or a class representing a car in a racing game might use a static variable to specify the maximum speed of all car instances.

Like instance variables, static variables are created using variable definitions within class definitions, but static variable definitions must also include the *static* attribute, as shown in the following generalized code:

```
class SomeClass {
  static var identifier = value;
}
```

As with instance variables, access-control modifiers can be used to control the accessibility of static variables in a program. The access-control modifiers available for static-variable definitions are identical to those available for instance-variable definitions—*public*, *internal*, *protected*, and *private*. When no modifier is specified, *internal* (package-wide access) is used. When a modifier is specified, it is typically placed before the *static* attribute, as shown in the following code:

```
class SomeClass {
  private static var identifier = value;
}
```

To access a static variable, we provide the name of the class that defines the variable, followed by a dot (.), followed by the name of the variable, as shown in the following generalized code:

```
SomeClass.identifier = value;
```

Within the class that defines the variable, *identifier* can also be used on its own (without the leading class name and dot). For example, in a class, *A*, that defines a static variable v, the expression A.v is identical to the expression v. Nevertheless, to distinguish static variables from instance variables, many developers (and this book) include the leading class name even when it is not strictly required.

Static variables and instance variables of the same name can coexist within a class. If a class, *A*, defines an instance variable named v, and a static variable, also named v, then the identifier v on its own refers to the instance variable, not the static variable. The static variable can be accessed only by including the leading class name, as in A.v. The instance variable is, therefore, said to *shadow* the static variable.

Now let's add some static variables to our *VirtualPet* class. As we just learned, static variables are used to keep track of information that relates logically to an entire class and does not vary from instance to instance. There are already two such pieces of information in our *VirtualPet* class: the maximum length of a pet's name and the maximum number of calories a pet can consume. To track that information, we'll add two new static variables: maxNameLength and maxCalories. Our variables are not required outside the *VirtualPet* class, so we'll define them as *private*. The following code shows the maxNameLength and maxCalories definitions, with the rest of the *VirtualPet* class code omitted in the interest of brevity:

```
package zoo {
  internal class VirtualPet {
    private static var maxNameLength - 20;
    private static var maxCalories = 2000;

    // Remainder of class not shown...
  }
}
```

With our maxNameLength and maxCalories variables in place, we can now update the *getHunger()*, *eat()*, and *setName()* methods to use those variables. Example 4-1 shows the latest version of the *VirtualPet* class, complete with static variables. Changes since the previous version are shown in bold. Notice that, by convention, the class's static variables are listed before the class's instance variables.

Example 4-1. The VirtualPet class

```
package zoo {
  internal class VirtualPet {
    private static var maxNameLength = 20;
    private static var maxCalories = 2000;
```

Example 4-1. The VirtualPet class (continued)

```
    private var petName;
    // Give each pet 50% of the maximum possible calories to start with.
    private var currentCalories = VirtualPet.maxCalories/2;

    public function VirtualPet (name) {
      setName(name);
    }

    public function eat (numberOfCalories) {
      var newCurrentCalories = currentCalories + numberOfCalories;
      if (newCurrentCalories > VirtualPet.maxCalories) {
        currentCalories = VirtualPet.maxCalories;
      } else {
        currentCalories = newCurrentCalories;
      }
    }

    public function getHunger () {
      return currentCalories / VirtualPet.maxCalories;
    }

    public function setName (newName) {
      // If the proposed new name has more than maxNameLength characters...
      if (newName.length > VirtualPet.maxNameLength) {
        // ...truncate it
        newName = newName.substr(0, VirtualPet.maxNameLength);
      } else if (newName == "") {
        // ...otherwise, if the proposed new name is an empty string,
        // then terminate this method without changing petName
        return;
      }

      // Assign the new, validated name to petName
      petName = newName;
    }

    public function getName () {
      return petName;
    }
  }
}
```

In Example 4-1, notice that the maxNameLength and maxCalories variables help central-ize our code. For example, previously, to update the maximum allowed number of characters in a name, we would have had to change the number 20 in two places within the setName method—a process that is both time-consuming and prone to error. Now, to update the maximum allowed number of characters, we simply change the value of maxNameLength, and the entire class updates automatically.

Unexplained literal values such as the number 20 in the previous version of *setName()* are known as "magic values" because they do something important, but their purpose is not self-evident. Avoid using magic values in your code. In many cases, static variables can be used to keep track of values that would otherwise be "magic."

Static variables are often used to maintain settings whose values should not change once a program has started. To prevent a variable's value from changing, we define that variable as a constant, as discussed in the next section.

Constants

A constant is a static variable, instance variable, or local variable with a value that, once initialized, remains fixed for the remainder of the program. To create a constant, we use standard variable-definition syntax, but with the keyword *const* instead of *var*. By convention, constants are named with all capital letters. To create a constant static variable, we use the following generalized code directly within a class body:

```
static const IDENTIFIER = value
```

To create a constant instance variable, we use the following generalized code directly within a class body:

```
const IDENTIFIER = value
```

To create a constant local variable, we use the following generalized code within a method or function:

```
const IDENTIFIER = value
```

In the preceding three code examples, `IDENTIFIER` is the name of the constant, and *value* is the variable's initial value. For constant static variables and constant local variables, once *value* has been assigned by the variable initializer, it can never be reassigned.

For constant instance variables, if the program is compiled in strict mode, once *value* has been assigned by the variable initializer, it can never be reassigned. If the program is compiled in standard mode, after *value* has been assigned by the variable initializer, the variable's value can also be assigned within the constructor function of the class containing the variable definition, but not thereafter. (We'll learn the difference between strict mode and standard mode compilation in Chapter 7.)

Constants are typically used to create static variables whose fixed values define the options for a particular setting in a program. For example, suppose we're building an alarm clock program that triggers a daily alarm. The alarm has three modes: visual (a blinking icon), audio (a buzzer), or both audio and visual. The alarm clock is represented by a class named *AlarmClock*. To represent the three alarm modes, the

---

AlarmClock class defines three constant static variables: `MODE_VISUAL`, `MODE_AUDIO`, and `MODE_BOTH`. Each constant is assigned a numeric value corresponding to its mode. Mode 1 is considered "visual mode," mode 2 is considered "audio mode," and mode 3 is considered "both visual and audio mode." The following code shows the definitions for the mode constants:

```
public class AlarmClock {
  public static const MODE_VISUAL = 1;
  public static const MODE_AUDIO  = 2;
  public static const MODE_BOTH   = 3;
}
```

To keep track of the current mode for each *AlarmClock* instance, the alarm clock class defines an instance variable, `mode`. To set the mode of an *AlarmClock* object, we assign one of the mode constants' values (1, 2, or 3) to the instance variable `mode`. The following code sets the default mode for new *AlarmClock* objects to audio-only (mode 2):

```
public class AlarmClock {
  public static const MODE_VISUAL = 1;
  public static const MODE_AUDIO  = 2;
  public static const MODE_BOTH   = 3;

  private var mode = AlarmClock.MODE_AUDIO;
}
```

When it comes time to signal an alarm, the *AlarmClock* object takes the appropriate action based on its current mode. The following code shows how an *AlarmClock* object would use the mode constants to determine which action to take:

```
public class AlarmClock {
  public static const MODE_VISUAL = 1;
  public static const MODE_AUDIO  = 2;
  public static const MODE_BOTH   = 3;

  private var mode = AlarmClock.MODE_AUDIO;

  private function signalAlarm () {
    if (mode == MODE_VISUAL) {
      // Display icon
    } else if (mode == MODE_AUDIO) {
      // Play sound
    } else if (mode == MODE_BOTH) {
      // Display icon and play sound
    }
  }
}
```

Note that in the preceding code, the mode constants are not technically necessary. Strictly speaking, we could accomplish the same thing with literal numeric values (magic values). However, the constants make the purpose of the numeric values much easier to understand. For comparison, the following code shows the

AlarmClock class implemented without constants. Notice that, without reading the code comments, the meaning of the three mode values cannot easily be determined.

```
public class AlarmClock {
  private var mode = 2;

  private function signalAlarm () {
    if (mode == 1) {
      // Display icon
    } else if (mode == 2) {
      // Play sound
    } else if (mode == 3) {
      // Display icon and play sound
    }
  }
}
```

Now let's move on to the counterpart of static variables: static methods.

Static Methods

In the preceding section we learned that static variables are used to track information that relates to an entire class. Similarly *static methods* define functionality that relate to an entire class, not just an instance of that class. For example, the Flash runtime API includes a class named *Point* that represents a Cartesian point with an x-coordinate and a y-coordinate. The *Point* class defines a static method, *polar()*, which generates a *Point* object based on a given polar point (i.e., a distance and an angle). Conceptually, converting a polar point to a Cartesian point is a general service that relates to Cartesian points in general, not to a specific *Point* object. Therefore, it is defined as a static method.

Like instance methods, static methods are created using function definitions within class definitions, but static method definitions must also include the *static* attribute, as shown in the following generalized code:

```
class SomeClass {
  static function methodName (identifier1 = value1,
                              identifier2 = value2,
                              ...
                              identifiern = valuen) {

  }
}
```

As with instance methods, access-control modifiers can control the accessibility of static methods in a program. The access-control modifiers available for static-methods definitions are identical to those available for instance-method definitions—namely: *public*, *internal*, *protected*, and *private*. When no modifier is specified, *internal* (package-wide access) is used. When a modifier is specified, it is typically placed before the *static* attribute, as shown in the following code:

```
class SomeClass {
  public static function methodName (identifier1 = value1,
                                     identifier2 = value2,
                                     ...
                                     identifiern = valuen) {

  }
}
```

To invoke a static method, we use the following general code:

```
SomeClass.methodName(value1, value2,...valuen)
```

In the preceding code, *SomeClass* is the class within which the static method is defined, *methodName* is the name of the method, and *value1, value2,...valuen* is a list of zero or more method arguments. Within the class that defines the method, *methodName* can be used on its own (without the leading class name and dot). For example, in a class, *A*, that defines a static method m, the expression A.m( ) is identical to the expression m( ). Nevertheless, to distinguish static methods from instance methods, many developers (and this book) include the leading class name even when it is not strictly required.

Some classes exist solely to define static methods. Such classes group related functionality together, but objects of the class are never instantiated. For example, the built-in *Mouse* class exists solely to define the static methods *show()* and *hide()* (used to make the system pointer visible or invisible). Those static methods are accessed through *Mouse* directly (as in, Mouse.hide( )), not through an instance of the *Mouse* class. Objects of the mouse class are never created.

Static methods have two limitations that instance methods do not. First, a class method cannot use the this keyword. Second, a static method cannot access the instance variables and instance methods of the class in which it is defined (unlike instance methods, which can access static variables and static methods in addition to instance variables and other instance methods).

In general, static methods are used less frequently than static variables. Our virtual zoo program does not use static methods at all. To demonstrate the use of static methods, let's return to the email validation scenario presented earlier in Chapter 2. In that scenario, we created a loop to detect whether or not an email address contains the @ character. Now let's imagine that our application has grown large enough to warrant the creation of a utility class for working with strings. We'll call the utility class *StringUtils*. The *StringUtils* class is not meant to be used to create objects; instead, it is merely a collection of static methods. As an example, we'll define one static method, *contains()*, which returns a *Boolean* value indicating whether a specified string contains a specified character. Here's the code:

```
public class StringUtils {
  public function contains (string, character) {
    for (var i:int = 0; i <= string.length; i++) {
      if (string.charAt(i) == character) {
        return true;
```

```
      }
    }
    return false;
  }
}
```

The following code shows how our application would use the *contains()* method to check whether an email address contains the @ character:

```
StringUtils.contains("me@moock.org", "@");
```

Of course, in a real application, the email address would be supplied by the user and then *contains()* would determine whether or not to submit a form. The following code demonstrates a more realistic situation:

```
if (StringUtils.contains(userEmail, "@")) {
  // Code here would submit the form
} else {
  // Code here would display an "Invalid data" message to the user
}
```

In addition to the static methods we create ourselves, ActionScript automatically creates one static method, known as the class initializer, for every class. Let's take a look.

The Class Initializer

When ActionScript defines a class at runtime, it automatically creates a method named the *class initializer* and executes that method. In this class initializer, Action-Script places all of the class's static variable initializers and all class-level code that is not a variable definition or a method definition.

The class initializer offers an opportunity to perform one-time setup tasks when a class is defined, perhaps by invoking methods or accessing variables that are external to the current class. For example, suppose we're creating an email reader application, and we want its visual appearance to match the operating system's graphical style. To determine which graphical theme the mail reader should use, the application's main class, *MailReader*, checks the current operating system in its class initializer and sets a corresponding static variable, theme. The theme variable dictates the graphical theme used throughout the application. The following code shows the class initializer for *MailReader*. To check the operating system, *MailReader* uses the static variable, os, defined by the built-in *flash.system.Capabilities* class.

```
package {
  import flash.system.*;

  public class MailReader {
    static var theme;
    if (Capabilities.os == "MacOS") {
      theme = "MAC";
    } else if (Capabilities.os == "Linux") {
```

```
      theme = "LINUX";
    } else {
      theme = "WINDOWS";
    }
  }
}
```

Code in the class initializer runs in interpreted mode, and is not compiled by the JIT compiler. Because JIT-compiled code generally executes much more quickly than interpreted code, you should consider moving processor-intensive code out of the class initializer when performance is a priority.

Class Objects

Earlier we learned that each static method and static variable is accessed through the class that defines it. For example, to access the static variable maxCalories, which is defined by the *VirtualPet* class, we use the following code:

```
VirtualPet.maxCalories
```

In the preceding code, the use of the class name *VirtualPet* is not merely a matter of syntax; *VirtualPet* actually refers to an object that defines the variable maxCalories. The object referenced by *VirtualPet* is an automatically created instance of the built-in *Class* class.

Every class in ActionScript is represented at runtime by an instance of the *Class* class. From a programmer's perspective, *Class* objects are used primarily to access the static variables and static methods of a class. However, like other objects, *Class* objects are values that can be assigned to variables, and passed to or returned from methods and functions. For example, the following revised version of our *VirtualZoo* class assigns the *Class* object representing the *VirtualPet* class to a variable, vp, and then uses that variable to create a *VirtualPet* object:

```
package zoo {
  public class VirtualZoo {
    private var pet;

    public function VirtualZoo () {
      var vp = VirtualPet;
      pet = new vp("Stan");
    }
  }
}
```

The preceding technique is used when one *.swf* file wishes to access another *.swf* file's classes, and when embedding external assets (such as images or fonts) in a *.swf* file. We'll study both of those scenarios in Part II of this book.

We've now finished our study of static variables and static methods. Before we move on to the next chapter, let's compare some of the terms we've learned with those used in C++ and Java.

C++ and Java Terminology Comparison

The concepts of instance variables, instance methods, static variables, and static methods are found in most object-oriented languages. For comparison, Table 4-1 lists the equivalent terms used by Java and C++.

Table 4-1. Terminology comparison

ActionScript	Java	C++
instance variable	field or instance variable	data member
instance method	method	member function
static variable	class variable	static data member
static method	class method	static member function

On to Functions

We've learned that an instance method defines a behavior related to a given object and a static method defines a behavior related to a given class. In the next chapter, we'll study *functions*, which define standalone behaviors that are not related to any object or class.

CHAPTER 5

Functions

A function, or more specifically a *function closure*, is a discrete set of instructions that carry out some task, independent of any class or object. Function closures have the same basic syntax and usage as instance methods and static methods; they are defined with the *function* keyword, can define local variables, are invoked with the parentheses operator, and can optionally return a value. However, unlike instance methods (which are always associated with an object) and static methods (which are always associated with a class), function closures are created and used in standalone form, either as a subtask in a method, or a general utility available throughout a package or an entire program.

> In the strict technical jargon of the ActionScript 3.0 specification, *function closures* and *methods* are both considered types of functions, where the term *function* refers generally to a callable object representing a set of instructions. Thus, a function closure is a function that is not associated with an object or a class, while a method is a function that is associated with an object (in the case of instance methods) or a class (in the case of static methods). However, in common discussion and most documentation, the term *function closure* is shortened to *function*. Unless you are reading the ActionScript 3.0 specification or a text that specifically states otherwise, you can safely assume that function means function closure. In the remainder of this book, the term function means function closure, except where stated otherwise.

To create a function, we use the following generalized code in one of the following locations: inside a method, directly inside a package definition, directly outside a package definition, or within another function. Notice that the code used to define a function is identical to the code used to define a basic instance method. In fact, when the following code appears directly within a class body, it creates an instance method, not a function.

```
function identifier (param1, param2, ...paramn) {
}
```

In the preceding code, *identifier* is the name of the function and *param1, param2, ...paramn* is an optional list of the function's parameters, which are used exactly like the method parameters described in Chapter 1. The curly braces ({}) following the parameter list define the beginning and end of the function body, which contains the statements executed when the function is called.

To invoke a function we use the following generalized code:

```
theFunction(value1, value2, ... valuen)
```

In the preceding code, *theFunction* is a reference to the function being invoked and *value1, value2,...valuen* is a list of arguments that are assigned, in order, to *theFunction*'s parameters.

Package-Level Functions

To create a function that is available throughout a package or an entire program, we place a function definition directly within a package body. To make the function accessible within the package that contains its definition only, we precede the definition with the access-control modifier *internal*, as shown in the following code:

```
package packageName {
  internal function identifier () {
  }
}
```

To make the function accessible throughout the entire program, we precede the definition with the access control modifier *public*, as shown in the following code:

```
package packageName {
  public function identifier () {
  }
}
```

If no access-control modifier is specified, ActionScript automatically uses *internal*.

Adobe's compilers place two requirements on ActionScript source files (*.as* files) that affect package-level functions:

- Every ActionScript source file (*.as* file) must have exactly one externally visible definition, which is a class, variable, function, interface, or namespace that is defined as either *internal* or *public* within a package statement.

- An ActionScript source file's name must match the name of its sole externally visible definition.

Hence, while in theory, ActionScript does not place any limitations on package-level functions, in practice, Adobe's compilers require each package-level function to be defined as either *internal* or *public* in a separate *.as* file with a matching file name. For more information on compiler limitations, see the section "Compiler Restrictions" in Chapter 7.

The following code creates a package-level function, *isMac()*, that returns a *Boolean* value indicating whether or not the current operating system is Macintosh OS. Because the *isMac()* function is defined with the access-control modifier *internal*, it is accessible within the *utilities* package only. As discussed in the preceding note, when compiled with an Adobe compiler, the following code would be placed in a separate *.as* file named *isMac.as*.

```
package utilities {
  import flash.system.*;

  internal function isMac () {
    return Capabilities.os == "MacOS";
  }
}
```

To make *isMac()* accessible outside the *utilities* package, we would change *internal* to *public*, as follows:

```
package utilities {
  import flash.system.*;

  public function isMac () {
    return Capabilities.os == "MacOS";
  }
}
```

However, to use *isMac()* outside the *utilities* package, we must first import it. For example, suppose *isMac()* is part of a larger program with a class named *Welcome* in a package named *setup*. To use *isMac()* in *Welcome*, *Welcome*'s source file would import *utilities.isMac()*, as follows:

```
package setup {
  // Import isMac() so it can be used within this package body
  import utilities.isMac;

  public class Welcome {
    public function Welcome () {
      // Use isMac()
      if (isMac()) {
        // Do something Macintosh-specific
      }
    }
  }
}
```

Global Functions

Functions defined at the package-level within the unnamed package are known as *global functions* because they can be referenced globally, throughout a program, without the need for the *import* statement. For example, the following code defines a global function, *isLinux()*. Because the *isLinux()* function is defined within the unnamed package, it is accessible by any code in the same program.

```
package {
  import flash.system.*;

  public function isLinux () {
    return Capabilities.os == "Linux";
  }
}
```

The following code revises the preceding section's *Welcome* class to use *isLinux()* instead of *isMac()*. Notice that *isLinux()* need not be imported before being used.

```
package setup {
  public class Welcome {
    public function Welcome () {
      // Use isLinux()
      if (isLinux()) {
        // Do something Linux-specific
      }
    }
  }
}
```

Many package-level functions and global functions come built-in to each Flash runtime. For a list of available functions, see Adobe's documentation for the appropriate Flash runtime.

Perhaps the most useful built-in global function is the *trace()* function, which has the following generalized format:

```
trace(argument1, argument2, argumentn)
```

The *trace()* function is a simple tool for finding errors in a program (i.e., for debugging). It outputs the specified arguments to either a window in the ActionScript development environment or to a log file. For example, when running a program in test mode via the Flash authoring tool's Control → Test Movie command, the output of all *trace()* calls appears in the Output panel. Similarly, when running a program in test mode via Flex Builder 2's Run → Debug command, the output of all *trace()* calls appears in the Console. For information on configuring the debugger version of Flash Player to send *trace()* output to a text file, see *http://livedocs.macromedia.com/flex/2/docs/00001531.html*.

Nested Functions

When a function definition occurs within a method or another function, it creates a *nested function* that is available for use within the containing method or function only. Conceptually, a function nested in a method or function defines a reusable subtask for the exclusive use of the containing method or function. The following code shows a generic example of a nested function, *b()*, within an instance method, *a()*. The nested function *b()* can be used within the method *a()* only; outside of *a()*, *b()* is inaccessible.

```
// Define method a( )
public function a () {
  // Invoke nested function b( )
  b( );

  // Define nested function b( )
  function b () {
    // Function body would be inserted here
  }
}
```

In the preceding code, notice that the nested function can be invoked anywhere within the containing method, even *before* the nested function definition. Referring to a variable or function before it is defined is known as *forward referencing*. Further, note that access-control modifiers (*public, internal,* etc.) cannot be applied to nested functions.

The following code shows a more realistic example of a method containing a nested function. The method, *getRandomPoint()* returns a *Point* object representing a random point in a supplied rectangle. To produce the random point, the method uses a nested function, *getRandomInteger()*, to calculate the random x- and y-coordinate. In *getRandomInteger()*, notice the use of the built-in static methods *Math.random()* and *Math.floor()*. The *Math.random()* method returns a random floating-point number equal to or greater than 0 but less than 1. The *Math.floor()* method removes the fractional portion of a floating-point number. For more information on the static methods of the *Math* class, see Adobe's ActionScript Language Reference.

```
public function getRandomPoint (rectangle) {
  var randomX = getRandomInteger(rectangle.left, rectangle.right);
  var randomY = getRandomInteger(rectangle.top, rectangle.bottom);

  return new Point(randomX, randomY);

  function getRandomInteger (min, max) {
    return min + Math.floor(Math.random( )*(max+1 - min));
  }
}
```

Source-File-Level Functions

When a function definition occurs at the top-level of a source file, outside any package body, it creates a function that is available within that specific source file only. The following generalized code demonstrates. It shows the contents of a source file, *A.as*, which contains a package definition, a class definition, and a source-file-level function definition. Because the function is defined outside the package statement, it can be used anywhere within *A.as*, but is inaccessible to code outside of *A.as*.

```
package {
  // Ok to use f( ) here
  class A {
    // Ok to use f( ) here
    public function A () {
      // Ok to use f( ) here
    }
  }
}

// Ok to use f( ) here

function f () {
}
```

In the preceding code, notice that *f()*'s definition does not, and must not, include any access-control modifier (*public*, *internal*, etc.).

 Access-control modifiers cannot be included in source-file-level function definitions.

Source-file-level functions are sometimes used to define supporting tasks for a single class (such as class *A* in the preceding code). However, because private static methods can also define supporting tasks for a class, source-file-level functions are rarely seen in real-world ActionScript programs.

Accessing Definitions from Within a Function

A function's location in a program governs its ability to access the program's definitions (e.g., classes, variables, methods, namespaces, interfaces, and other functions). For a complete description of what can and cannot be accessed from code within functions, see the section "Function Scope" in Chapter 16.

Note, however, that within a function closure, the this keyword always refers to the global object, no matter where the function is defined. To access the current object within a nested function in an instance method, assign this to a variable, as shown in the following code:

```
public function m () {
  var currentObject = this;

  function f () {
    // Access to currentObject is granted here
    trace(currentObject);  // Displays the object through
                           // which m( ) was invoked
  }
}
```

Functions as Values

In ActionScript, every function is represented by an instance of the *Function* class. As such, a function can be assigned to a variable, passed to a function, or returned from a function, just like any other value. For example, the following code defines a function, *a()* and then assigns it to the variable b. Notice that the parentheses operator, ( ), is omitted; if it were included, the code would simply assign *a()*'s return value to b.

```
function a () {
}
var b = a;
```

Once a function has been assigned to a variable, it can be invoked through that variable using the standard parentheses operator, ( ). For example, the following code invokes the function *a()* through the variable b:

```
b();
```

Function values are typically used when creating dynamic classes and objects, as discussed in the sections "Dynamically Adding New Behavior to an Instance" and "Using Prototype Objects to Augment Classes" in Chapter 15.

Function Literal Syntax

As with many of ActionScript's native classes, instances of the *Function* class can be created with literal syntax. Function literals have the same syntax as standard function declarations, except that the function name is omitted. The general form is:

```
function (param1, param2, ...paramn) {
}
```

where *param1, param2, ...paramn* is an optional list of parameters.

To use the function defined by a function literal outside the expression in which the literal occurs, we can assign it to a variable, as shown in the following code:

```
var someVariable = function (param1, param2, ...paramn) {
}
```

Once assigned, the function can then be invoked through that variable, as in:

```
someVariable(arg1, arg2, ...argn)
```

For example, the following code uses a function literal to create a function that squares a number and assigns that function to the variable square:

```
var square = function (n) {
  return n * n;
}
```

To invoke the preceding function, we use the following code:

```
// Squares the number 5    and returns the result
square(5)
```

Function literals are sometimes used with the built-in function *flash.utils.setInterval()*, which takes the following form:

```
setInterval(functionOrMethod, delay)
```

The *setInterval()* function starts an *interval*, which automatically executes a specified function or method (*functionOrMethod*) every *delay* milliseconds. When an interval is created, it is assigned a number, known as an *interval ID*, that is returned by *setInterval()*. The interval ID can be assigned to a variable so that the interval can later be stopped with *clearInterval()*, as shown in the following example code:

```
// Start the interval, which invokes doSomething() every 50 milliseconds.
// Assign the returned interval ID to the variable intervalID.
var intervalID = setInterval(doSomething, 50);

// ...Some time later in the program, stop invoking doSomething()
clearInterval(intervalID);
```

 For much more sophisticated control over periodic function or method execution, see the *Timer* class, covered in the sections "Custom Events" in Chapter 12 and "Animating with the TimerEvent. TIMER Event" in Chapter 24.

The following code shows a simple class, *Clock*, which outputs the debug message "Tick!" once per second. Notice the use of the function literal and the built-in functions *setInterval()* and *trace()*.

```
package {
  import flash.utils.setInterval;

  public class Clock {
    public function Clock () {
      // Execute the function literal once per second
      setInterval(function () {
        trace("Tick!");
      }, 1000);
    }
  }
}
```

Note that function literals are used for the sake of convenience only. The preceding code could easily be rewritten with a nested function, as shown here:

```
package {
  import flash.utils.setInterval;

  public class Clock {
    public function Clock () {
      // Execute tick() once per second
      setInterval(tick, 1000);

      function tick ():void {
```

```
            trace("Tick!");
          }
        }
      }
    }
```

The nested-function version of the *Clock* class is arguably easier to read. Function literals are commonly used when assigning functions to dynamic instance variables, as described in the section "Dynamically Adding New Behavior to an Instance" in Chapter 15.

Recursive Functions

A *recursive* function is a function that calls itself. The following code shows a simple example of recursion. Every time *trouble()* runs, it calls itself again: ·

```
function trouble () {
  trouble();
}
```

A recursive function that calls itself unconditionally, as *trouble()* does, causes *infinite recursion* (i.e., a state in which a function never stops calling itself). If left unchecked, infinite recursion would theoretically trap a program in an endless cycle of function execution. To prevent this from happening, practical recursive functions call themselves only while a given condition is met. One classic use of recursion is to calculate the mathematical *factorial* of a number, which is the product of all positive integers less than or equal to the number. For example, the factorial of 3 (written as 3! in mathematical nomenclature) is 3 * 2 * 1, which is 6. The factorial of 5 is 5 * 4 * 3 * 2 * 1, which is 120. Example 5-1 shows a factorial function that uses recursion.

Example 5-1. Calculating factorials using recursion

```
function factorial (n) {
  if (n < 0) {
    return;  // Invalid input, so quit
  } else if (n <= 1) {
    return 1;
  } else {
    return n * factorial(n-1);
  }
}

// Usage:
factorial(3);  // Returns: 6
factorial(5);  // Returns: 120
```

As usual, there is more than one way to skin a proverbial cat. Using a loop, we can also calculate a factorial without recursion, as shown in Example 5-2.

Example 5-2. Calculating factorials without recursion

```
function factorial (n) {
  if (n < 0) {
    return;  // Invalid input, so quit
  } else {
    var result = 1;
    for (var i = 1; i <= n; i++) {
      result = result * i;
    }
    return result;
  }
}
```

Examples 5-1 and 5-2 present two different ways to solve the same problem. The recursive approach says, "The factorial of 6 is 6 multiplied by the factorial of 5. The factorial of 5 is 5 multiplied by the factorial of 4..." and so on. The nonrecursive approach loops over the numbers from 1 to n and multiplies them all together into one big number.

Function recursion is considered elegant because it provides a simple solution—calling the same function repeatedly—to a complex problem. However, repeated function calls are less efficient than loop iterations. The nonrecursive approach to calculating factorials is many times more efficient than the recursive approach. The nonrecursive approach also avoids the Flash runtime's maximum recursion limit, which defaults to 1000 but can be set via the compiler argument default-script-limits.

As we'll see in Chapter 18, recursion is sometimes used to process the hierarchically structured content of XML documents.

Using Functions in the Virtual Zoo Program

Let's apply our new knowledge of functions to our virtual zoo program. (For a refresher on our program's existing code, see the *VirtualPet* class in Example 4-1 in Chapter 4.)

Recall that when we last saw our virtual zoo program, pets had the ability to eat (i.e., gain calories), but not to digest (i.e., lose calories). To give our pets the ability to digest, we'll add a new method to the *VirtualPet* class, named *digest()*. The *digest()* method will subtract calories from the *VirtualPet* object on which it is invoked. To simulate digestion over time, we'll create an interval that invokes *digest()* once per second. The amount of calories consumed at each *digest()* invocation will be determined by a new static variable, caloriesPerSecond. By default, we'll set caloriesPerSecond to 100, allowing a pet to survive a maximum of 20 seconds on a "full stomach."

The following code shows the caloriesPerSecond variable definition:

```
private static var caloriesPerSecond = 100;
```

The following code shows the *digest()* method. Notice that because digestion is an internal task, *digest()* is declared *private*.

```
private function digest () {
  currentCalories -= VirtualPet.caloriesPerSecond;
}
```

To create the interval that invokes *digest()* once per second, we use the built-in *setInterval()* function. Each pet should start digesting as soon as it is created, so we'll put our *setInterval()* call in the *VirtualPet* constructor method. We'll also store *setInterval()*'s returned interval ID in a new instance variable, digestIntervalID, so that we can stop the interval later if necessary.

The following code shows the digestIntervalID variable definition:

```
private var digestIntervalID;
```

This code shows the updated *VirtualPet* constructor:

```
public function VirtualPet (name) {
  setName(name);

  // Call digest() once per second
  digestIntervalID = setInterval(digest, 1000);
}
```

Now that a *VirtualPet* object can digest food, let's use the global function *trace()* to report each pet's current status during debugging. We'll issue a status report every time *digest()* or *eat()* runs. Here's the updated *digest()* method:

```
private function digest () {
  currentCalories -= VirtualPet.caloriesPerSecond;

  trace(getName() + " digested some food. It now has " + currentCalories
      + " calories remaining.");
}
```

Here's the updated *eat()* method:

```
public function eat (numberOfCalories) {
  var newCurrentCalories = currentCalories + numberOfCalories;
  if (newCurrentCalories > VirtualPet.maxCalories) {
    currentCalories = VirtualPet.maxCalories;
  } else {
    currentCalories = newCurrentCalories;
  }

  trace(getName() + " ate some food. It now has " + currentCalories
      + " calories remaining.");
}
```

If we were to run our virtual zoo program now, we would see the following in the Output window (Flash authoring tool) or the Console (Flex Builder):

```
Stan digested some food. It now has 900 calories remaining.
Stan digested some food. It now has 800 calories remaining.
```

```
Stan digested some food. It now has 700 calories remaining.
Stan digested some food. It now has 600 calories remaining.
Stan digested some food. It now has 500 calories remaining.
Stan digested some food. It now has 400 calories remaining.
Stan digested some food. It now has 300 calories remaining.
Stan digested some food. It now has 200 calories remaining.
Stan digested some food. It now has 100 calories remaining.
Stan digested some food. It now has 0 calories remaining.
Stan digested some food. It now has -100 calories remaining.
Stan digested some food. It now has -200 calories remaining.
Stan digested some food. It now has -300 calories remaining.
```

Oops. Pets shouldn't be allowed to have negative calorie values. Instead, pets should die when currentCalories reaches 0. In our program, we'll simulate the state of death in the following ways:

- If currentCalories is 0, the program ignores attempts to increase currentCalories when *eat()* is called.

- When currentCalories reaches 0, the program stops the interval that calls *digest()* and displays a "pet death" message.

First, let's take care of the update to the *eat()* method. A simple conditional should do the trick; here's the code:

```
public function eat (numberOfCalories) {
  // If this pet is dead...
  if (currentCalories == 0) {
    // ...quit this method without modifying currentCalories
    trace(getName() + " is dead. You can't feed it.");
    return;
  }

  var newCurrentCalories = currentCalories + numberOfCalories;
  if (newCurrentCalories > VirtualPet.maxCalories) {
    currentCalories = VirtualPet.maxCalories;
  } else {
    currentCalories = newCurrentCalories;
  }
  trace(getName() + " ate some food. It now has " + currentCalories
        + " calories remaining.");
}
```

Next, we need to stop calling *digest()* if currentCalories reaches 0. To do so, we'll use *flash.utils.clearInterval()*. Here's the code:

```
private function digest () {
  // If digesting more calories would leave the pet's currentCalories at
  // 0 or less...
  if (currentCalories - VirtualPet.caloriesPerSecond <= 0) {
    // ...stop the interval from calling digest()
    clearInterval(digestIntervalID);
    // Then give the pet an empty stomach
    currentCalories = 0;
    // And report the pet's death
```

```
      trace(getName( ) + " has died.");
    } else {
      // ...otherwise, digest the stipulated number of calories
      currentCalories -= VirtualPet.caloriesPerSecond;

      // And report the pet's new status
      trace(getName( ) + " digested some food. It now has "
          + currentCalories + " calories remaining.");
    }
  }
```

Example 5-3 shows the complete code for the *VirtualPet* class, including all the changes we just made.

Example 5-3. The VirtualPet class

```
package zoo {
  import flash.utils.setInterval;
  import flash.utils.clearInterval;

  internal class VirtualPet {
    private static var maxNameLength = 20;
    private static var maxCalories = 2000;
    private static var caloriesPerSecond = 100;

    private var petName;
    private var currentCalories = VirtualPet.maxCalories/2;
    private var digestIntervalID;

    public function VirtualPet (name) {
      setName(name);
      digestIntervalID = setInterval(digest, 1000);
    }

    public function eat (numberOfCalories) {
      if (currentCalories == 0) {
        trace(getName( ) + " is dead. You can't feed it.");
        return;
      }

      var newCurrentCalories = currentCalories + numberOfCalories;
      if (newCurrentCalories > VirtualPet.maxCalories) {
        currentCalories = VirtualPet.maxCalories;
      } else {
        currentCalories = newCurrentCalories;
      }
      trace(getName( ) + " ate some food. It now has " + currentCalories
          + " calories remaining.");
    }

    public function getHunger () {
      return currentCalories / VirtualPet.maxCalories;
    }
```

Example 5-3. The VirtualPet class (continued)

```
  public function setName (newName) {
    // If the proposed new name has more than maxNameLength characters...
    if (newName.length > VirtualPet.maxNameLength) {
      // ...truncate it
      newName = newName.substr(0, VirtualPet.maxNameLength);
    } else if (newName == "") {
      // ...otherwise, if the proposed new name is an empty string,
      // then terminate this method without changing petName
      return;
    }

    // Assign the new, validated name to petName
    petName = newName;
  }

  public function getName () {
    return petName;
  }

  private function digest () {
    // If digesting more calories would leave the pet's currentCalories at
    // 0 or less...
    if (currentCalories - VirtualPet.caloriesPerSecond <= 0) {
      // ...stop the interval from calling digest()
      clearInterval(digestIntervalID);
      // Then give the pet an empty stomach
      currentCalories = 0;
      // And report the pet's death
      trace(getName() + " has died.");
    } else {
      // ...otherwise, digest the stipulated number of calories
      currentCalories -= VirtualPet.caloriesPerSecond;

      // And report the pet's new status
      trace(getName() + " digested some food. It now has "
            + currentCalories + " calories remaining.");
    }
  }
 }
 }
}
```

Back to Classes

We've finished our study of functions in ActionScript. In the next chapter, we'll return to the topic of classes, with a specific focus on using inheritance to create relationships between two or more classes. Once you understand inheritance, we'll be able to make our virtual zoo program ready to compile and run.

CHAPTER 6

Inheritance

In object-oriented programming, *inheritance* is a formal relationship between two or more classes, wherein one class borrows (or *inherits*) the variable and method definitions of another class. In the practical, technical sense, inheritance simply lets one class use the code in another class.

But the term *inheritance* implies much more than code reuse. Inheritance is as much an intellectual tool as it is a technical tool. It lets programmers conceptualize a group of classes in hierarchical terms. In biology, inheritance is a genetic process through which one living creature passes on traits to another. You are said to have inherited your mother's eyes or your father's nose, even though you don't look exactly like either of your parents. In object-oriented programming, inheritance has a similar connotation. It lets a class look and feel in many ways like another class, while adding its own unique features.

This chapter begins by examining the syntax and general use of inheritance. Once we understand inheritance on a practical level, we'll consider its benefits and alternatives. Finally, we'll apply inheritance to our virtual zoo program.

A Primer on Inheritance

Let's consider a very simple, abstract example to get a feel for how inheritance works (we'll get into practical applications once we cover the basic syntax). Here's a class named *A*, with a single instance method, *m( )*, and a single instance variable, *v*:

```
public class A {
  public var v = 10;

  public function m () {
    trace("Method m() was called");
  }
}
```

As usual, we can create an instance of class *A*, invoke method *m()*, and access variable v like this:

```
var aInstance = new A( );
aInstance.m( );         // Displays: Method m( ) was called
trace(aInstance.v);  // Displays: 10
```

Nothing new so far. Now let's add a second class, *B*, that inherits method *m()* and variable v from class *A*. To set up the inheritance relationship between *A* and *B*, we use the *extends* keyword:

```
public class B extends A {
  // No methods or variables defined
}
```

Because class *B* extends (inherits from) class *A*, instances of *B* can automatically use the method *m()* and the variable v (even though class *B* does not define that method or variable directly):

```
var bInstance:B = new B( );
bInstance.m( );         // Displays: Method m( ) was called
trace(bInstance.v);  // Displays: 10
```

When bInstance.m( ) is invoked, ActionScript checks to see if class *B* defines a method named *m()*. ActionScript does not find method *m()* defined in class *B*, so it checks *B*'s *superclass* (i.e., the class that *B* extends), for the method. There, in class *A*, ActionScript finds *m()* and invokes it on bInstance.

Notice that class *B* does not define any methods or variables of its own. In practice, there isn't much point in defining a class that doesn't add anything to the class it extends; therefore, doing so is usually discouraged. Normally, class *B* would define its own methods and/or variables in addition to inheriting *A*'s methods and variables. That is, a subclass is really a superset of the features available in its superclass; the subclass has everything available in the superclass and more. Here is a new version of class *B*, which inherits method *m()* and variable v from class *A*, and also defines its own method, *n()*:

```
public class B extends A {
  public function n () {
    trace("Method n( ) was called");
  }
}
```

Now instances of *B* can use all the methods and variables of both *B* and its superclass, *A*:

```
var bInstance = new B( );
// Invoke inherited method, defined by class A
bInstance.m( );         // Displays: Method m( ) was called
// Invoke method defined by class B
bInstance.n( );         // Displays: Method n( ) was called
// Access inherited variable
trace(bInstance.v);  // Displays: 10
```

Class B is said to *specialize* class A. It uses the features of class A as a base on which to build, adding its own features or even—as we'll see later—overriding A's features with versions modified for its own needs. Accordingly, in an inheritance relationship between two classes, the extended class (in our case, class A) is called the *base class*, and the class that does the extending (in our case, class B) is called the *derived class*. The terms *ancestor* and *descendant* are also sometimes used to refer to the base class and the derived class, respectively.

Inheritance can (and often does) involve many more than two classes. For example, even though class B inherits from class A, class B can act as a base class for another class. The following code shows a third class, C, that extends class B and also defines a new method, *o()*. Class C can use all the methods and variables defined by itself or by any of its ancestors—that is, its superclass (B), or its superclass's superclass (A).

```
public class C extends B {
  public function o () {
    trace("Method o() was called");
  }
}

// Usage:
var cInstance = new C();
// Invoke method inherited from A
cInstance.m();  // Displays: Method m() was called
// Invoke method inherited from B
cInstance.n();  // Displays: Method n() was called
// Invoke method defined by C
cInstance.o();  // Displays: Method o() was called
// Access variable inherited from A.
trace(cInstance.v);  // Displays: 10
```

Furthermore, a single superclass can have any number of subclasses (however, a superclass has no way of knowing which subclasses extend it). The following code adds a fourth class, D, to our example. Like class B, class D inherits directly from class A. Class D can use the methods and variables defined by itself and by its super-class, A.

```
public class D extends A {
  public function p () {
    trace("Method p() was called");
  }
}
```

With four classes now in our example, we've built up what's known as an *inheritance tree* or *class hierarchy*. Figure 6-1 shows that hierarchy visually. Note that a single subclass can't have more than one direct superclass.

All OOP applications can be depicted with a class diagram such as the one shown in Figure 6-1. In fact, many developers start their work by creating a class diagram before writing any code. Class diagrams can be informal—drawn according to a developer's personal iconography—or formal, drawn according to a diagramming specification such as Unified Modeling Language (UML) (see *http://www.uml.org*).

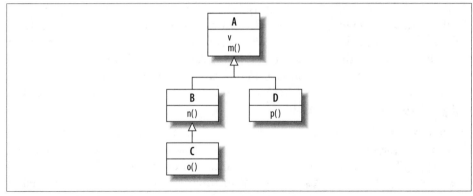

Figure 6-1. A class hierarchy

Just as we design our own class hierarchies for our OOP applications, ActionScript also organizes its built-in classes according to a hierarchy. In fact, every class in ActionScript (both built-in and custom) inherits directly or indirectly from the root of the built-in hierarchy: *Object*. The *Object* class defines some very basic methods and variables that all classes can use, through inheritance. For example, any class can use the *Object.toString( )* method, which returns a string representation of an object.

Static Methods and Static Variables Not Inherited

Unlike instance methods and instance variables, a subclass does not inherit its superclass's static methods and static variables.

For example, in the following code, we define a static method, *s( )*, in the class *A*. The method *s( )* is not inherited by *A*'s subclass, *B*, and, therefore, cannot be accessed as B.s( ).

```
public class A {
  public static function s () {
    trace("A.s() was called");
  }
}

public class B extends A {
  public function B () {
    B.s();  // Error! Illegal attempt to access A.s() through B
  }
}
```

However, within the body of either *A* or *B*, static methods and static variables defined by *A* can be referred to directly without the class name, as in *s( )* rather than *A.s( )*. Nevertheless, it's generally wise to include the class name when referring to static methods or static variables. When the class name is included, the origin of the method or variable is clear.

Overriding Instance Methods

In our study of inheritance so far, we've covered *reuse*, in which a subclass uses its superclass's methods and variables, and we've covered *extension*, in which a subclass adds its own methods and variables. We'll now turn to *redefinition*, in which a subclass provides an alternative version of a method defined by its superclass. (Bear in mind that reuse, extension, and redefinition are not mutually exclusive. A subclass might employ all three techniques.)

Redefinition lets us customize an existing class for a specific purpose by augmenting, constraining, or even nullifying one or more of its original behaviors. Redefining a method is known technically as *overriding* that method.

 ActionScript 3.0 allows instance methods to be redefined but not instance variables, static variables, or static methods.

To override a superclass's instance method, we supply an instance method definition of the same name in the subclass, and precede that definition with the keyword *override*. For example, consider the following code, which creates a class, *A*, with an instance method, *m()*:

```
public class A {
  // Declare an instance method in the superclass
  public function m () {
    trace("A's m() was called");
  }
}
```

Also consider the following code, which creates a class, *B*, that inherits from *A*:

```
// Class B is a subclass of class A
public class B extends A {
}
```

To override *m()* in *B*, we use the following code:

```
public class B extends A {
  // Override the superclass's method m()
  override public function m () {
    trace("B's m() was called");
  }
}
```

Notice that *B*'s version of *m()* has not only the same name, but also the same access-control modifier (i.e., *public*) as *A*'s version.

 An override attempt succeeds only if the overriding version of the method has the same name, access-control modifier, parameter list, and return type as the method being overridden. (We'll learn about return types in Chapter 8.) Otherwise, an error occurs.

When *m()* is invoked on an instance of class *A*, ActionScript uses *A*'s definition of the method. But when *m()* is invoked on an instance of class *B*, ActionScript uses *B*'s definition of the method instead of class *A*'s definition:

```
var aInstance = new A();
aInstance.m();  // Displays: A's m() was called

var bInstance = new B();
bInstance.m();  // Displays: B's m() was called
```

Let's consider a more realistic example. Suppose we're building a geometry program that depicts rectangles and squares. To handle the rectangles, we create a *Rectangle* class, as follows:

```
public class Rectangle {
  protected var w = 0;
  protected var h = 0;

  public function setSize (newW, newH) {
    w = newW;
    h = newH;
  }

  public function getArea () {
    return w * h;
  }
}
```

To handle squares, we *could* create a completely unrelated *Square* class. But a square is really just a rectangle with sides of equal width and height. To exploit that similarity, we'll create a *Square* class that extends *Rectangle* but alters the *setSize()* method to prevent w and h from being set unless newW equals newH. The constraint applies only to squares, not to rectangles in general, so it doesn't belong in the *Rectangle* class.

Here's the *Square* class, showing the overridden *setSize()* method:

```
public class Square extends Rectangle {
  override public function setSize (newW, newH) {
    // Here's the constraint introduced by the Square class
    if (newW == newH) {
      w = newW;
      h = newH;
    }
  }
}
```

When *setSize()* is invoked on a *Square* or *Rectangle* instance, ActionScript uses the version of the method that matches the actual class of the instance. For example, in the following code, we invoke *setSize()* on a *Rectangle* instance. ActionScript knows that the instance's class is *Rectangle*, so it invokes *Rectangle*'s version of *setSize()*:

```
var r = new Rectangle();
r.setSize(4,5);
trace(r.getArea());  // Displays: 20
```

By contrast, in the following code, we invoke *setSize()* on a *Square* instance. This time ActionScript knows that the instance's class is *Square*, so it invokes *Square*'s version of *setSize()*, not *Rectangle*'s version of *setSize()*:

```
var s = new Square( );
s.setSize(4,5);
trace (s.getArea());  // Displays: 0 (The setSize( ) method prevented the
                      //            illegal variable assignment.)
```

In the preceding code, the output of *s.getArea()*—0—indicates that values of w and h were not set by the call to *s.setSize()*; *Square*'s version of *setSize()* sets w and h only when newW and newH are equal.

Invoking an Overridden Instance Method

When a subclass overrides an instance method, the superclass's version of the method is not lost. It remains accessible to instances of the subclass via the *super* operator, which can invoke an overridden method as follows:

```
super.methodName(arg1, arg2, ...argn);
```

In the preceding code, *methodName* is the name of the overridden method to invoke, and *arg1*, *arg2*, ... *argn* are the arguments to pass to that method. (We'll discuss other uses of *super* later in this chapter.)

As an example of invoking an overridden method, let's return to the *Square* and *Rectangle* scenario. In the previous section, our *Square.setSize()* method needlessly duplicated the code in the *Rectangle.setSize()* method. The *Rectangle* version was:

```
public function setSize (newW, newH) {
  w = newW;
  h = newH;
}
```

The *Square* version of *setSize()* merely added an *if* statement:

```
override public function setSize (newW, newH) {
  if (newW == newH) {
    w = newW;
    h = newH;
  }
}
```

To avoid the duplication of setting w and h in both methods, we can use *super*, as shown in this revised version of *Square.setSize()*:

```
override public function setSize (newW, newH) {
  if (newW == newH) {
    // Invoke the superclass's setSize( ) method, on the current instance
    super.setSize(newW, newH);
  }
}
```

The *Square* class's revised *setSize()* method checks if newW and newH are equal; if they are, it invokes *Rectangle*'s *setSize()* on the current instance. The *Rectangle* class's *setSize()* method takes care of setting w and h.

The *setSize()* method example shows how a subclass can override a method to constrain its behavior. A subclass can also override a method to augment its behavior. For example, the following code creates *ScreenRectangle*, a subclass of *Rectangle* that draws a rectangle to the screen. The *ScreenRectangle* subclass overrides the *setSize()* method, retaining the behavior of the overridden method, but adding a call to *draw()*, so the rectangle changes size on screen whenever *setSize()* is invoked. Here's the code:

```
public class ScreenRectangle extends Rectangle {
  override public function setSize (newW, newH) {
    // Call Rectangle's version of setSize()
    super.setSize(newW, newH);

    // Now render the rectangle on screen
    draw();
  }

  public function draw () {
    // Screen-rendering code goes here
  }
}
```

Overriding can also be used to nullify the behavior of a method. The technique is straightforward: the subclass's version of the overridden method simply does nothing. For example, the following code shows a subclass named *ReadOnlyRectangle* that disables the *Rectangle* class's *setSize()* method, preventing an instance from changing size:

```
public class ReadOnlyRectangle extends Rectangle {
  // This effectively disables the setSize() method
  // for instances of the ReadOnlyRectangle class.
  override public function setSize (newW, newH) {
    // Do nothing
  }
}
```

Constructor Methods in Subclasses

Now that we've studied the behavior of instance methods and instance variables in relation to inheritance, let's turn our attention to constructor methods.

Recall that a constructor method initializes the instances of a class by:

- Calling methods that perform setup tasks
- Setting variables on the object being created

When a class is extended, the subclass can define a constructor method of its own. A subclass constructor is expected to:

- Perform setup tasks related to the subclass
- Set variables defined by the subclass
- Invoke the superclass constructor method (sometimes called the *superconstructor*)

A subclass constructor method, if provided, is required to invoke its superclass constructor, via the keyword *super*. Furthermore, the superclass constructor invocation must occur before any instance variable or instance method is accessed. If no such invocation is provided, the compiler adds a no-argument superclass constructor call automatically. Finally, *super* must not be used twice in a constructor method.

Forbidding the use of *super* after any instance variable or instance method is accessed has the following benefits:

- Prevents methods from being called on an object that has not yet been initialized
- Prevents variable access on an object that has not yet been initialized
- Prevents variable assignments in the superclass constructor from overwriting variable assignments in the subclass constructor

Don't confuse the two forms of the *super* operator. The first form, *super()*, invokes a superclass's constructor method. The second form, *super.methodName()*, invokes a superclass's method. The first form is allowed in a constructor method only. The second form is allowed anywhere in a constructor method or instance method, and can be used multiple times.

Let's try using *super* to invoke a superclass's constructor method in a simplified situation. The following code defines a class, *A*, with an empty constructor method:

```
public class A {
  public function A () {
  }
}
```

The following code defines a class, *B*, which extends *A*. Within *B*'s constructor method, we use *super* to invoke *A*'s constructor method:

```
public class B extends A {
  // Subclass constructor
  public function B () {
    // Invoke superclass's constructor method
    super();
  }
}
```

The following two constructor method definitions are functionally synonymous. In the first case, we call the superclass's constructor method explicitly; in the second case, ActionScript calls the superclass's constructor method implicitly:

```
public function B () {
  // Invoke superclass's constructor method explicitly
  super();
}

public function B () {
  // No constructor call. ActionScript provides one implicitly
}
```

If a subclass does not define a constructor method at all, ActionScript automatically creates one and adds a *super* call as its only statement. The following two definitions of the class *B* are functionally identical; the first is an explicit version of what the compiler creates automatically in the second:

```
// Explicitly provide constructor
public class B extends A {
  // Declare a constructor explicitly
  public function B () {
    // Invoke superclass's constructor method explicitly
    super();
  }
}

// Let compiler create default constructor automatically
public class B extends A {
}
```

A subclass constructor method can (and often does) define different parameters than its superclass counterpart. For example, our *Rectangle* class might define a constructor with width and height parameters. And our *Square* subclass might provide its own constructor that defines a single side parameter (squares have the same width and height, so specifying both is redundant). Example 6-1 shows the code.

Example 6-1. The Rectangle and Square constructors

```
public class Rectangle {
  protected var w = 0;
  protected var h = 0;

  // Rectangle constructor
  public function Rectangle (width, height) {
    setSize(width, height);
  }

  public function setSize (newW, newH) {
    w = newW;
    h = newH;
  }
```

Example 6-1. The Rectangle and Square constructors (continued)

```
  public function getArea ( ) {
    return w * h;
  }
}

public class Square extends Rectangle {
  // Square constructor
  public function Square (side) {
    // Pass the side parameter onto the Rectangle constructor
    super(side, side);
  }

  override public function setSize (newW, newH) {
    if (newW == newH) {
      // Invoke the superclass's setSize( ) method, on the current instance
      super.setSize(newW, newH);
    }
  }
}
```

Incidentally, you might wonder whether the *Square* class's *setSize()* method is better off defining a single side parameter rather than separate width and height parameters. The following version of *setSize()* demonstrates (notice that the method no longer needs to check whether newW equals newH):

```
    override public function setSize (side) {
      // Invoke the superclass's setSize( ) method, on the current instance
      super.setSize(side, side);
    }
```

While the preceding version of *setSize()* is definitely more appropriate for a *Square* class, it would cause an error because it defines fewer parameters than the *Rectangle* class's version of *setSize()* (remember that the number of parameters defined by an overriding method must match that of the overridden method). Later, under "Inheritance Versus Composition," we'll consider an alternate, legal approach for implementing the single-parameter version of *setSize()* in the *Square* class.

When defining a subclass's constructor method, be sure to supply all required arguments to the superclass's constructor. In the following example, the *ColoredBall* class erroneously defines a constructor method that doesn't supply necessary information to its superclass's constructor method:

```
    public class Ball {
      private var r;
      public function Ball (radius) {
        r = radius;
      }
    }

    public class ColoredBall extends Ball {
      private var c;
```

```
    // Here's the problematic constructor...
    public function ColoredBall (color) {
      // OOPs! No call to super( ). An error will occur here because
      // Ball's constructor requires an argument for the radius parameter
      c = color;
    }
  }
```

Here's the corrected version of *ColoredBall*, which supplies the necessary argument to the *Ball* constructor's behavior:

```
  public class ColoredBall extends Ball {
    private var c;

    // All fixed up...
    public function ColoredBall (radius, color) {
      super(radius);
      c = color;
    }
  }
```

Notice that, as a matter of good form, the subclass constructor lists the superclass's constructor parameters first (in this case, radius), then the additional subclass constructor arguments (in this case, color).

Preventing Classes from Being Extended and Methods from Being Overridden

To prevent a class from being extended or a method from being overridden, we precede that class or method definition with the *final* attribute. For example, the following code defines a class, *A*, that cannot be extended:

```
  final public class A {
  }
```

Because class *A* is defined with the *final* attribute, the following attempt to extend *A*:

```
  public class B extends A {
  }
```

yields this compile-time error:

```
  Base class is final.
```

Likewise, the following code defines a method, *m( )*, that cannot be overridden:

```
  public class A {
    final public function m ( ) {
    }
  }
```

Because class *m( )* is defined with the *final* attribute, the following attempt to override *m( )*:

```
public class B extends A {
  override public function m ( ) {
  }
}
```

yields this compile-time error:

```
Cannot redefine a final method.
```

The *final* attribute is used for two reasons in ActionScript:

- In some situations, *final* methods execute faster than non-*final* methods. If you are looking to improve your application's performance in every possible way, try making its methods *final*. Note, however, that in future Flash runtimes, Adobe expects non-*final* methods to execute as quickly as *final* methods.

- Methods that are *final* help hide a class's internal details. Making a class or a method *final* prevents other programmers from extending the class or overriding the method for the purpose of examining the class's internal structure. Such prevention is considered one of the ways to safeguard an application from being maliciously exploited.

Efficiency and safeguarding aside, the programming community is divided on whether making methods and classes *final* is good object-oriented programming practice. On one hand, some argue that *final* methods and classes are useful because they allow a programmer to guarantee that an object has an intended behavior, rather than an unexpected (and potentially problematic) overridden behavior. On the other hand, others argue that *final* methods and classes contradict the general object-oriented principle of polymorphism, wherein an instance of a subclass can be used anywhere an instance of its superclass is expected. We'll learn more about polymorphism later in this chapter.

Subclassing Built-in Classes

Just as we can create subclasses of our own custom classes, we can also create subclasses of any non-*final* built-in class, allowing us to implement specialized functionality based on an existing ActionScript class. For an example of extending the built-in *Array* class, see Programming ActionScript 3.0 → Core ActionScript 3.0 Data Types and Classes → Working with Arrays → Advanced Topics, in Adobe's Programming ActionScript 3.0. For an example of extending the built-in Flash runtime class, *Shape,* see the section "Custom Graphical Classes" in Chapter 20.

Some built-in ActionScript classes are simply collections of class methods and class variables—for example, the *Math, Keyboard,* and *Mouse* classes exist merely to store related methods and variables (e.g., *Math.random( )* and Keyboard.ENTER). Such classes are known as *static method libraries,* and are typically declared *final.* Rather than extending these classes, you must distribute your own static method libraries separately. For example, rather than adding a *factorial( )* method to a subclass of the *Math* class, you would create a custom class, say *AdvancedMath*, to hold your *factorial( )* method. The *AdvancedMath* class cannot be related to the *Math* class via inheritance.

The Theory of Inheritance

So far this chapter has focused mainly on the practical details of using inheritance in ActionScript. But the theory of why and when to use inheritance runs much deeper than the technical implementation. Before we conclude, let's consider some basic theoretical principles, bearing in mind that a few pages is hardly enough room to do the topic justice. For a much more thorough consideration of inheritance theory, see "Using Inheritance Well" (*http://archive.eiffel.com/doc/manuals/technology/oosc/ inheritance-design/page.html*), an online excerpt from Bertrand Meyer's illuminating work *Object-Oriented Software Construction* (Prentice Hall).

Why Inheritance?

Superficially, the obvious benefit of inheritance is code reuse. Inheritance lets us separate a core feature set from customized versions of that feature set. Code for the core is stored in a superclass while code for the customizations is kept neatly in a subclass. Furthermore, more than one subclass can extend the superclass, allowing multiple customized versions of a particular feature set to exist simultaneously. If the implementation of a feature in the superclass changes, all subclasses automatically inherit the change.

But inheritance also lets us express the architecture of an application in hierarchical terms that mirror the real world and the human psyche. For example, in the real world, we consider plants different from animals, but we categorize both as living things. We consider cars different from planes, but we see both as vehicles. Correspondingly, in a human resources application, we might have an *Employee* superclass with *Manager*, *CEO*, and *Worker* subclasses. Or, in a banking application, we might create a *BankAccount* superclass with *CheckingAccount* and *SavingsAccount* subclasses. These are canonical examples of one variety of inheritance sometimes called *subtype inheritance*, in which the application's class hierarchy is designed to model a real-world situation (a.k.a. the *domain* or *problem domain*).

However, while the *Employee* and *BankAccount* examples make attractive demonstrations of inheritance, not all inheritance reflects the real world. In fact, overemphasizing real-world modeling can lead to miscomprehension of inheritance and its subsequent misuse. For example, given a *Person* class, we might be tempted to create *Female* and *Male* subclasses. These are logical categories in the real world, but if the application using those classes were, say, a school's reporting system, we'd be forced to create *MaleStudent* and *FemaleStudent* classes just to preserve the real-world hierarchy. In our program, male students do not define any operations differently from female students and, therefore, should be used identically. The real-world hierarchy in this case conflicts with our application's hierarchy. If we need gender information, we're better off creating a single *Student* class and adding a gender variable to the *Person* class. As tempting as it may be, we should avoid creating inheritance structures based solely on the real world rather than the needs of our program.

Finally, in addition to code reuse and logical hierarchy, inheritance allows types of objects to be used where a single type is expected. Known as polymorphism, this important benefit warrants a discussion all its own.

Polymorphism and Dynamic Binding

Polymorphism is a feature of all truly object-oriented languages, wherein an instance of a subclass can be used anywhere an instance of its superclass is expected. The word *polymorphism* itself means literally "many forms"—each single object can be treated as an instance of its own class or as an instance of any of its superclasses.

Polymorphism's partner is *dynamic binding*, which guarantees that a method invoked on an object will trigger the behavior defined by that object's actual class.

The canonical example of polymorphism and dynamic binding is a graphics application that displays shapes. The application defines a *Shape* class with an unimplemented *draw()* method:

```
public class Shape {
  public function draw () {
    // No implementation. In some other languages, draw() would be
    // declared with the abstract attribute, which syntactically
    // forces subclasses of Shape to provide an implementation.
  }
}
```

The *Shape* class has several subclasses—a *Circle* class, a *Rectangle* class, and a *Triangle* class, each of which provides its own definition for the *draw()* method:

```
public class Circle extends Shape {
  override public function draw () {
    // Code to draw a Circle on screen, not shown...
  }
}

public class Rectangle extends Shape {
  override public function draw () {
    // Code to draw a Rectangle on screen, not shown...
  }
}

public class Triangle extends Shape {
  override public function draw () {
    // Code to draw a Triangle on screen, not shown...
  }
}
```

To add a new shape to the screen, we pass a *Circle*, *Rectangle*, or *Triangle* instance to the *addShape()* method of the application's main class, *DrawingApp*. Here's *DrawingApp*'s *addShape()* method:

```
public function addShape (newShape) {
  newShape.draw();

  // Remainder of method (code not shown) would add the new shape
  // to an internal list of shapes on screen
}
```

Here's how we add a *Circle* shape to the screen:

```
drawingApp.addShape(new Circle());
```

The *addShape()* method invokes the new shape's *draw()* method and adds the new shape to an internal list of shapes on screen. And here's the key point—*addShape()* invokes *draw()* without knowing (or caring) whether the new shape is a *Circle*, *Rectangle*, or *Triangle* instance. Through the runtime process of *dynamic binding*, ActionScript uses the appropriate implementation of that method. That is, if the instance is a *Circle*, ActionScript invokes *Circle.draw()*; if it's a *Rectangle*, Action-Script invokes *Rectangle.draw()*; and if it's a *Triangle*, ActionScript invokes *Triangle.draw()*. Importantly, the specific class of the new shape is not known at compile time. Hence, dynamic binding is often called *late binding*: the method call is *bound* to a particular implementation "late" (i.e., at runtime).

The key benefit of dynamic binding and polymorphism is containment of changes to code. Polymorphism lets one part of an application remain fixed even when another changes. For example, let's consider how we'd handle the drawing of shapes if polymorphism didn't exist. First, we'd have to use unique names for each version of *draw()*:

```
public class Circle extends Shape {
  public function drawCircle () {
    // Code to draw a Circle on screen, not shown...
  }
}

public class Rectangle extends Shape {
  public function drawRectangle () {
    // Code to draw a Rectangle on screen, not shown...
  }
}

public class Triangle extends Shape {
  public function drawTriangle () {
    // Code to draw a Triangle on screen, not shown...
  }
}
```

Then, within *DrawingApp*'s *addShape()* method we'd have to use the *is* operator to check the class of each new shape manually and invoke the appropriate draw method, as shown in the following code. An *is* operation returns the value true if the specified expression belongs to the specified datatype; otherwise, it returns false. We'll study datatypes and the *is* operator in Chapter 8.

```
public function addShape (newShape) {
  if (newShape is Circle) {
    newShape.drawCircle( );
  } else if (newShape is Rectangle) {
    newShape.drawRectangle( );
  } else if (newShape is Triangle) {
    newShape.drawTriangle( );
  }

  // Remainder of method (code not shown) would add the new shape
  // to an internal list of shapes on screen
}
```

That's already more work. But imagine what would happen if we added 20 new kinds of shapes. For each one, we'd have to update the *addShape()* method. In a polymorphic world, we don't have to touch the code that invokes *draw()* on each *Shape* instance. As long as each *Shape* subclass supplies its own valid definition for *draw()*, our application will "just work" without other changes.

Polymorphism not only lets programmers collaborate more easily, but it allows them to use and expand on a code library without requiring access to the library's source code. Some argue that polymorphism is object-oriented programming's greatest contribution to computer science.

Inheritance Versus Composition

In this chapter, we've focused most of our attention on one type of inter-object relationship: inheritance. But inheritance isn't the only game in town. *Composition*, an alternative form of inter-object relationship, often rivals inheritance as an object-oriented design technique. In composition, one class (the *front-end class*) stores an instance of another class (the *back-end class*) in an instance variable. The front-end class delegates work to the back-end class by invoking methods on that instance. Here's the basic approach, shown in generalized code:

```
// The back end class is analogous to the superclass in inheritance
public class BackEnd {
  public function doSomething () {
  }
}

// The front end class is analogous to the subclass in inheritance
public class FrontEnd {
  // An instance of the back end class is stored in
  // a private instance variable, in this case called bc
  private var be;
```

```
    // The constructor creates the instance of the back end class
    public function FrontEnd () {
      be = new BackEnd();
    }

    // This method delegates work to BackEnd's doSomething() method
    public function doSomething () {
      be.doSomething();
    }
  }
```

Notice that the *FrontEnd* class does not extend the *BackEnd* class. Composition does not require or use its own special syntax, as inheritance does. Furthermore, the front-end class might use a subset of the methods of the back end class, or it might use all of them, or it might add its own unrelated methods. The method names in the front-end class might match those exactly in the back-end class, or they might be completely different. The front-end class can constrain, extend, or redefine the back-end class's features, just like a subclass in inheritance.

Earlier we learned how, using inheritance, a *Square* class could constrain the behavior of a *Rectangle* class. Example 6-2 shows how that same class relationship can be implemented with composition instead of inheritance. In Example 6-2, the *Rectangle* class is unchanged. But this time, the *Square* class does not extend *Rectangle*. Instead, it defines a variable, r, that contains a *Rectangle* instance. All operations on r are filtered through *Square*'s *public* methods. The *Square* class forwards, or *delegates*, method calls to r. Notice that because the *Square* class's *setSize()* method does not override the *Rectangle* class's *setSize()* method, its signature need not be compatible with the *Rectangle* class's *setSize()* method. The *Square* class's *setSize()* method is free to define a single parameter, contrasting with the *Rectangle* class's *setSize()* method, which defines two parameters.

Example 6-2. An example composition relationship

```
// The Rectangle class
public class Rectangle {
  protected var w = 0;
  protected var h = 0;

  public function Rectangle (width, height) {
    setSize(width, height);
  }

  public function setSize (newW, newH) {
    w = newW;
    h = newH;
  }

  public function getArea () {
    return w * h;
  }
}
```

Example 6-2. An example composition relationship (continued)

```
}

// Here's the new Square class
public class Square {
  private var r;

  public function Square (side) {
    r = new Rectangle(side, side);
  }

  public function setSize (side) {
    r.setSize(side, side);
  }

  public function getArea () {
    return r.getArea();
  }
}
```

Is-A, Has-A, and Uses-A

In object-oriented language, an inheritance relationship is known colloquially as an Is-A relationship because an instance of the subclass can be seen literally as being an instance of the superclass (i.e., the subclass instance can be used wherever a superclass instance is expected). In our earlier polymorphic example, a *Circle* instance Is-A *Shape* because the *Circle* class inherits from the *Shape* class and can, therefore, be used anywhere a *Shape* is used.

A composition relationship is known as a "Has-A relationship because the front-end class maintains an instance of the back-end class. The Has-A relationship should not be confused with the Uses-A relationship, in which a class instantiates an object of another class but does not assign it to an instance variable. In a "Uses-A relationship, the class uses the object and throws it away. For example, a *Circle* might store its numeric color in a variable, color (Has-A *uint* object), but then use a *Color* object temporarily to actually set that color on screen (Uses-A *Color* object).

In Example 6-2, our *Square* class Has-A *Rectangle* instance and adds restrictions to it that effectively turn it into a *Square*. In the case of *Square* and *Rectangle*, the Is-A relationship seems natural, but the Has-A relationship can also be used. Which begs the question: which relationship is best?

When to use composition over inheritance

Example 6-2 raises a serious design question. How do you choose between composition and inheritance? In general, it's fairly easy to spot a situation in which inheritance is inappropriate. An *AlertDialog* instance in an application "has an" OK button, but an *AlertDialog* instance, itself, "isn't an" OK button. However, spotting a situation in which composition is inappropriate is trickier because any time you can use inheritance to establish the relationship between two classes, you could use composition instead. If both techniques work in the same situation, how can you tell which is the best option?

If you're new to object-oriented programming, you may be surprised to hear that composition is often favored over inheritance as an application design strategy. In fact, some of the best-known object-oriented design theoreticians explicitly advocate composition over inheritance (see *Design Patterns: Elements of Reusable Object-Oriented Software*, Gamma et al., 1995, Addison-Wesley). Hence, conventional wisdom tells us to at least consider composition as an option even when inheritance seems obvious. That said, here are some general guidelines to consider when deciding whether to use inheritance or composition:

- If you want to take advantage of polymorphism, consider using inheritance.
- If a class just needs the services of another class, consider a composition relationship.
- If a class you're designing behaves very much like an existing class, consider an inheritance relationship.

For more advice on choosing between composition and inheritance, read Bill Venner's excellent JavaWorld article, archived at his site: *http://www.artima.com/designtechniques/compoinh.html*. Mr. Venner offers compelling evidence that, generally speaking:

- Changing code that uses composition has fewer consequences than changing code that uses inheritance.
- Code based on inheritance often executes faster than code based on composition.

Abstract Not Supported

Many object-oriented designs require the use of a so-called *abstract class*. An abstract class is any class that defines zero or more *abstract methods*—methods that have a name, parameters, and a return type but no implementation (i.e., no method body). A class that wishes to extend an abstract class must either implement all of the superclass's abstract methods, or be abstract itself; otherwise, a compile-time error occurs. Subclasses of an abstract class effectively promise to provide some real code to do a job the abstract class only describes in theory.

Abstract classes are a common, important part of polymorphic designs. For example, in our earlier discussion of polymorphism, we studied a *Shape* class with *Circle*, *Rectangle*, and *Triangle* subclasses. Traditionally, the *Shape* class's *draw()* method would be defined as an abstract method, guaranteeing that:

- Each *Shape* subclass provides a means of drawing itself to the screen.
- External code can safely call *draw()* on any *Shape* subclass (because the compiler will not let a class extend *Shape* without implementing *draw()*).

Unfortunately, ActionScript does not support abstract classes or abstract methods. Instead of defining an abstract method in ActionScript, you should simply define a method with no code in its body, and document the method as "abstract." It's left up to the programmer (not the compiler) to ensure that the subclasses of a would-be abstract class implement the appropriate method(s).

In many cases, ActionScript interfaces can be used in place of abstract classes to enforce a particular object-oriented architecture. See Chapter 9.

We've finished our study of inheritance. Let's close this chapter by applying our new knowledge to the virtual zoo program.

Using Inheritance in the Virtual Zoo Program

In our virtual zoo program, we'll use inheritance in two different ways. First, we'll use it to define types of food for our pets to eat—replacing our earlier approach of adding raw calories to pets through the *eat()* method. Second, we'll use inheritance to make our application's main class, *VirtualZoo*, displayable on screen.

Creating Types of Pet Food

Until now, our implementation of eating in the virtual zoo program has been overly simplistic. To make a pet eat, we simply invoke *eat()* on the desired *VirtualPet* object and specify an arbitrary number of calories for the pet to eat. To improve the realism of our simulation, let's add *types of food* to the zoo program.

To keep things simple, we'll allow our pet to eat only two types of food: sushi and apples. We'll represent sushi with a new class, *Sushi*, and apples with a new class, *Apple*. Because the *Sushi* and *Apple* classes both conceptually represent food, they have nearly identical functionality. Hence, in our application, we'll implement the functionality needed by both *Sushi* and *Apple* in a single superclass, *Food*. The *Sushi* and *Apple* classes will extend *Food* and, through inheritance, adopt its features.

The *Food* class defines four simple methods for retrieving and modifying the name and calorie value of a given piece of food. Here's the code:

```
package zoo {
  public class Food {
    private var calories;
    private var name;

    public function Food (initialCalories) {
      setCalories(initialCalories);
    }

    public function getCalories () {
      return calories;
    }
```

```
      public function setCalories (newCalories) {
        calories = newCalories;
      }

      public function getName () {
        return name;
      }

      public function setName (newName) {
        name = newName;
      }
    }
  }
```

The *Apple* class sets the default number of calories for a given *Apple* object, and defines the food name for all *Apple* objects. Here's the code:

```
package zoo {
  public class Apple extends Food {
    // Set the default number of calories for an Apple object to 100
    private static var DEFAULT_CALORIES = 100;

    public function Apple (initialCalories = 0) {
      // If no calorie value or a negative calorie value was specified
      // for this particular object...
      if (initialCalories <= 0) {
        // ...use the default value
        initialCalories = Apple.DEFAULT_CALORIES;
      }
      super(initialCalories);

      // Set the food name for all Apple objects
      setName("Apple");
    }
  }
}
```

The *Sushi* class sets the default number of calories for a given *Sushi* object, and defines the food name for all *Sushi* objects. Here's the code:

```
package zoo {
  public class Sushi extends Food {
    private static var DEFAULT_CALORIES = 500;

    public function Sushi (initialCalories = 0) {
      if (initialCalories <= 0) {
        initialCalories = Sushi.DEFAULT_CALORIES;
      }
      super(initialCalories);

      setName("Sushi");
    }
  }
}
```

To enable *VirtualPet* objects to eat apples and sushi, we need to update the *VirtualPet* class's *eat()* method. Here's what the *eat()* method used to look like:

```
public function eat (numberOfCalories) {
  if (currentCalories == 0) {
    trace(getName() + " is dead. You can't feed it.");
    return;
  }

  var newCurrentCalories = currentCalories + numberOfCalories;
  if (newCurrentCalories > VirtualPet.maxCalories) {
    currentCalories = VirtualPet.maxCalories;
  } else {
    currentCalories = newCurrentCalories;
  }
  trace(getName() + " ate some food. It now has " + currentCalories
        + " calories remaining.");
}
```

In the new version of the *eat()* method, we'll change the numberOfCalories parameter to foodItem, introducing the logical convention that *eat()*'s argument must be an instance of any class that inherits from *Food*. (Note that Chapter 8 teaches how to enforce that convention with a *datatype declaration*.) Within the *eat()* method, we'll calculate newCurrentCalories by adding the calorie value of the food item (i.e., foodItem.getCalories()) to the pet's existing calories (i.e., currentCalories). Finally, when reporting that the pet ate some food, we'll use the *Food* class's *getName()* method to list the name of the food that was eaten. Here's the updated *eat()* method:

```
public function eat (foodItem) {
  if (currentCalories == 0) {
    trace(getName() + " is dead. You can't feed it.");
    return;
  }

  var newCurrentCalories = currentCalories + foodItem.getCalories();
  if (newCurrentCalories > VirtualPet.maxCalories) {
    currentCalories = VirtualPet.maxCalories;
  } else {
    currentCalories = newCurrentCalories;
  }
  trace(getName() + " ate some " + foodItem.getName() + "."
        + " It now has " + currentCalories  + " calories remaining.");
}
```

Now let's try feeding some sushi and an apple to the pet in the *VirtualZoo* constructor. Here's the code:

```
package zoo {
  public class VirtualZoo {
    private var pet;

    public function VirtualZoo () {
      pet = new VirtualPet("Stan");
```

```
      pet.eat(new Apple());  // Feed Stan an apple
      pet.eat(new Sushi());  // Feed Stan some sushi
    }
  }
}
```

The *Sushi* and *Apple* classes are currently very simple, but they provide the foundation for more sophisticated behavior. For example, now that our zoo program includes types of food, we could quite easily make pets that like only apples or eat sushi after 6 p.m. We can also easily customize the behavior of each type of food. As an example, let's randomly give 50% of all apples a worm, and make pets reject apples with worms.

To track whether a given *Apple* object has a worm, we'll add a new instance variable to the *Apple* class, wormInApple:

```
private var wormInApple;
```

Next, within the *Apple* constructor, we'll use *Math.random()* to pick a random number between 0 and 0.9999.... If the number is equal to or greater than 0.5, we'll assign wormInApple the value true, indicating that the *Apple* object has a worm; otherwise we'll assign wormInApple the value false, indicating that the *Apple* object does not have a worm. Here's the code:

```
wormInApple = Math.random() >= .5;
```

To give other classes a way to check whether an *Apple* object has a worm, we'll define a new public method, *hasWorm()*, which simply returns the value of wormInApple. Here's the code:

```
public function hasWorm () {
  return wormInApple;
}
```

Finally, we'll update the *VirtualPet* class's *eat()* method to make pets reject apples with worms. Here's the code, excerpted from the *eat()* method:

```
if (foodItem is Apple) {
  if (foodItem.hasWorm()) {
    trace("The " + foodItem.getName() + " had a worm. " + getName()
        + " didn't eat it.");
    return;
  }
}
```

In the preceding code, notice the use of the *is* operator, which checks whether an object is an instance of a specified class or any class that inherits from that class. The expression foodItem is Apple yields the value true if foodItem refers to an instance of *Apple* (or any class that inherits from *Apple*); otherwise, it yields false. If the foodItem is an *Apple* object, and its *hasWorm()* method returns true, then the *eat()* method is terminated without increasing the value of currentCalories.

Beyond types of food, there's one other use of inheritance in the virtual zoo program. Let's take a look.

Preparing VirtualZoo for Onscreen Display

Because ActionScript is used to create graphical content and user interfaces, the main class of every ActionScript program must extend either the *flash.display.Sprite* class or the *flash.display.MovieClip* class. Both *Sprite* and *MovieClip* represent containers for onscreen graphical content. The *MovieClip* class is sometimes used when the program's main class is associated with a *.fla* file (Flash authoring tool document), as described in Chapter 29. Otherwise, the *Sprite* class is used.

When a Flash runtime opens a new *.swf* file, it creates an instance of that *.swf* file's main class and adds that instance to a hierarchical list of objects that are currently displayed on screen, known as the *display list*. Once the instance is on the display list, it can then use the inherited methods of the *DisplayObject* class (from which *Sprite* or *MovieClip* both descend) to add other graphical content to the screen.

Our virtual zoo program will eventually add graphical content to the screen. But before it does, we have much to learn about the display list and graphics programming. Part II of this book, explores those topics in great detail. For now, however, in order to run our program in its current state, we must meet the requirement that the main class of every ActionScript program must extend either the *Sprite* class or the *MovieClip* class.

Our program contains no Flash authoring tool content, so its main class, *VirtualZoo*, extends the *Sprite* class. Here's the code:

```
package zoo {
  import flash.display.Sprite;

  public class VirtualZoo extends Sprite {
    private var pet;

    public function VirtualZoo () {
      pet = new VirtualPet("Stan");
      pet.eat(new Apple());
      pet.eat(new Sushi());
    }
  }
}
```

We've made quite a few changes to our virtual zoo program in this chapter. Let's review the code in its entirety.

Virtual Zoo Program Code

Example 6-3 shows the code for the *VirtualZoo* class, the program's main class.

Example 6-3. The VirtualZoo class

```
package zoo {
  import flash.display.Sprite;

  public class VirtualZoo extends Sprite {
    private var pet;

    public function VirtualZoo () {
      pet = new VirtualPet("Stan");
      pet.eat(new Apple());
      pet.eat(new Sushi());
    }
  }
}
```

Example 6-4 shows the code for the *VirtualPet* class, whose instances represent pets in the zoo.

Example 6-4. The VirtualPet class

```
package zoo {
  import flash.utils.setInterval;
  import flash.utils.clearInterval;

  internal class VirtualPet {
    private static var maxNameLength = 20;
    private static var maxCalories = 2000;
    private static var caloriesPerSecond = 100;

    private var petName;
    private var currentCalories = VirtualPet.maxCalories/2;
    private var digestIntervalID;

    public function VirtualPet (name) {
      setName(name);
      digestIntervalID = setInterval(digest, 1000);
    }

    public function eat (foodItem) {
      if (currentCalories == 0) {
        trace(getName() + " is dead. You can't feed it.");
        return;
      }

      if (foodItem is Apple) {
        if (foodItem.hasWorm()) {
          trace("The " + foodItem.getName() + " had a worm. " + getName()
                + " didn't eat it.");
```

Example 6-4. The VirtualPet class (continued)

```
      return;
    }
  }

  var newCurrentCalories = currentCalories + foodItem.getCalories();
  if (newCurrentCalories > VirtualPet.maxCalories) {
    currentCalories = VirtualPet.maxCalories;
  } else {
    currentCalories = newCurrentCalories;
  }
  trace(getName() + " ate some " + foodItem.getName() + "."
        + " It now has " + currentCalories  + " calories remaining.");
}

public function getHunger () {
  return currentCalories / VirtualPet.maxCalories;
}

public function setName (newName) {
  // If the proposed new name has more than maxNameLength characters...
  if (newName.length > VirtualPet.maxNameLength) {
    // ...truncate it
    newName = newName.substr(0, VirtualPet.maxNameLength);
  } else if (newName == "") {
    // ...otherwise, if the proposed new name is an empty string,
    // then terminate this method without changing petName
    return;
  }

  // Assign the new, validated name to petName
  petName = newName;
}

public function getName () {
  return petName;
}

private function digest () {
  // If digesting more calories would leave the pet's currentCalories at
  // 0 or less...
  if (currentCalories - VirtualPet.caloriesPerSecond <= 0) {
    // ...stop the interval from calling digest()
    clearInterval(digestIntervalID);
    // Then give the pet an empty stomach
    currentCalories = 0;
    // And report the pet's death
    trace(getName() + " has died.");
  } else {
    // ...otherwise, digest the stipulated number of calories
    currentCalories -= VirtualPet.caloriesPerSecond;

    // And report the pet's new status
```

Example 6-4. The VirtualPet class (continued)

```
        trace(getName( ) + " digested some food. It now has "
            + currentCalories + " calories remaining.");
      }
    }
  }
}
```

Example 6-5 shows the code for the *Food* class, the superclass of the various types of food that pets eat.

Example 6-5. The Food class

```
package zoo {
  public class Food {
    private var calories;
    private var name;

    public function Food (initialCalories) {
      setCalories(initialCalories);
    }

    public function getCalories ( ) {
      return calories;
    }

    public function setCalories (newCalories) {
      calories = newCalories;
    }

    public function getName ( ) {
      return name;
    }

    public function setName (newName) {
      name = newName;
    }
  }
}
```

Example 6-6 shows the code for the *Apple* class, which represents a specific type of food that pets eat.

Example 6-6. The Apple class

```
package zoo {
  public class Apple extends Food {
    private static var DEFAULT_CALORIES = 100;
    private var wormInApple;

    public function Apple (initialCalories = 0) {
      if (initialCalories <= 0) {
        initialCalories = Apple.DEFAULT_CALORIES;
```

Example 6-6. The Apple class (continued)

```
      }
      super(initialCalories);

      wormInApple = Math.random( ) >= .5;

      setName("Apple");
    }

    public function hasWorm ( ) {
      return wormInApple;
    }
  }
}
```

Finally, Example 6-7 shows the code for the *Sushi* class, which represents a specific type of food that pets eat.

Example 6-7. The Sushi class

```
package zoo {
  public class Sushi extends Food {
    private static var DEFAULT_CALORIES = 500;

    public function Sushi (initialCalories = 0) {
      if (initialCalories <= 0) {
        initialCalories = Sushi.DEFAULT_CALORIES;
      }
      super(initialCalories);

      setName("Sushi");
    }
  }
}
```

It's Runtime!

With the changes we made to the virtual zoo program in this chapter, our application is now ready to compile and run. I hope it is with more than a little excitement that you precede to the next chapter, where we'll learn how to run our program after compiling it with the Flash authoring tool, Flex Builder, or *mxmlc*.

CHAPTER 7

Compiling and Running a Program

After all our hard work on the virtual zoo program, we are now ready to compile and run our code. In this chapter, we'll learn how to compile a program with the Flash authoring tool, Flex Builder 2, and *mxmlc*. In each case, we'll assume that the program being compiled resides in the folder */virtualzoo/*, and that the source code for the program (i.e., the *.as* files) resides in the folder */virtualzoo/src/*.

Now let's do some compiling!

Compiling with the Flash Authoring Tool

To compile the virtual zoo program using the Flash authoring tool, we must first associate the program's main class with a *.fla* file, as described in the following steps:

1. In the Flash authoring tool, select File → New.
2. On the New Document dialog, select Flash File (ActionScript 3.0), then click OK.
3. Select File → Save As.
4. On the Save As dialog, for Save in, browse to the */virtualzoo/src* folder.
5. On the Save As dialog, for File name, enter **VirtualZoo.fla**, then click OK.
6. On the Properties panel, under Document class, enter **zoo.VirtualZoo**.

Once the program's main class has been associated with a *.fla* file (as described in the preceding steps), we then select Control → Test Movie to compile the program and run the resulting *.swf* file in a test version of Flash Player directly within the Flash authoring tool. When the program runs in "Test Movie" mode, *trace()* messages appear in the Flash authoring tool's Output panel. (You should see Stan getting hungry!)

When a program is compiled using Test Movie, the Flash authoring tool generates a *.swf* file with a name matching the corresponding *.fla* file. For example, when we compile the virtual zoo program using Test Movie, a new file, *VirtualZoo.swf*, appears in the */src/* folder. For information on changing the folder in which the generated *.swf* file is placed, see the Flash authoring tool's documentation for the File → Publish Settings command.

To distribute *VirtualZoo.swf* over the Web, we would typically embed it in an HTML page. For details, see the Flash authoring tool's documentation for the File → Publish command. To distribute *VirtualZoo.swf* as a desktop application, we would bundle it into an installable *.air* file. For details see the product documentation for Adobe AIR.

Compiling with Flex Builder 2

Before we can compile the virtual zoo program using Flex Builder 2, we must first make some changes to our code in order to meet the requirements of Flex Builder 2's compiler. Flex Builder 2's compiler stipulates that a program's main class must reside in the unnamed package. Currently, our *VirtualZoo* class resides in the package *zoo*, not the unnamed package.

Moving the Main Class to the Unnamed Package

To move *VirtualZoo* from *zoo* to the unnamed package, we must follow these steps:

1. Move the file *VirtualZoo.as* from */virtualzoo/src/zoo* to */virtualzoo/src/*.
2. In the *VirtualZoo.as* file, add the following code immediately before the *VirtualZoo* class definition statement (this code imports the classes from the *zoo* package):

   ```
   import zoo.*;
   ```
3. In the *VirtualZoo.as* file, remove the package name "zoo" from the package declaration statement. That is, change this code:

   ```
   package zoo {
   ```
   to this:

   ```
   package {
   ```
4. In the *VirtualPet.as* file, change the access-control modifier for the *VirtualPet* class from *internal* to *public*, as follows (this gives the *VirtualZoo* class access to the *VirtualPet* class):

   ```
   public class VirtualPet {
   ```

Once the preceding changes have been made, we can then compile the program.

Compiling the Program

To compile the virtual zoo program, we first create an ActionScript Project, as described in the following steps:

1. Select File → New → ActionScript Project.
2. On the New ActionScript Project dialog, for Project name, enter **virtualzoo**.

3. Under Project Contents, uncheck "Use default location".

4. Under Project Contents, for Folder, enter (or browse to) the location of the *virtualzoo* folder on your hard drive.

5. Click Next.

6. For Main source folder, enter **src**.

7. For Main application file, enter **VirtualZoo.as**.

8. Click Finish.

Running the Program

Once the ActionScript Project has been created, we can then follow these steps to run the virtual zoo program in debugging mode so that *trace()* messages appear in the Console panel:

1. In the navigator panel, select any class in the virtual zoo project.

2. Select Run → Debug VirtualZoo. By default, the program will launch in the system default web browser.

In the process of compiling the program, Flex Builder 2 generates the following assets, which it places in an automatically created folder, */virtualzoo/bin/*:

- A *.swf* file named *VirtualZoo.swf*

- A *.swf* file named *VirtualZoo-debug.swf*, used for debugging

- An HTML file named *VirtualZoo.html*, which embeds *VirtualZoo.swf* for web distribution

- An HTML file named *VirtualZoo-debug .html*, which embeds *VirtualZoo-debug. swf* for testing in a web browser

- A series of supporting files for web browser-based detection of Flash Player and automatic Flash Player installation

To distribute *VirtualZoo.swf* over the Web, simply place all the files from the */bin/* folder—except for *VirtualZoo-debug.html* and *VirtualZoo-debug.swf*—in a folder on a public web server. To distribute the program as a desktop application, see the product documentation for Adobe AIR.

 Compiling the virtual zoo program as described in this section will cause a series of compiler warnings such as "var 'pet' has no type declaration." For now, you can simply ignore these warnings. In the next chapter, we'll learn why they occur.

Compiling with mxmlc

Like Flex Builder 2's compiler, *mxmlc* stipulates that a program's main class must reside in the unnamed package. Therefore, before compiling the virtual zoo program with *mxmlc*, we must first move *VirtualZoo* from *zoo* to the unnamed package by following the steps listed in the earlier section "Moving the Main Class to the Unnamed Package."

Next, we must locate the compiler itself, which is named *mxmlc.exe*. The location of the compiler varies by version and operating system. Typically, it resides in a folder called *Flex SDK [version]\bin*, but you should confirm the location for your computer according to the documentation provided with Flex SDK. For the purposes of this example, we'll assume that we're compiling on Windows XP, and that the compiler resides in the following location:

```
C:\Flex SDK 2\bin\mxmlc.exe
```

We'll also assume that our */virtualzoo/* program folder resides in the following location:

```
C:\data\virtualzoo\
```

To compile the virtual zoo program using *mxmlc*, we follow these steps:

1. From the Windows start menu, open a command prompt by choosing Start → All Programs → Accessories → Command Prompt.

2. At the command prompt, change to the *C:\Flex SDK 2\bin* directory by entering the following command:

   ```
   cd C:\Flex SDK 2\bin
   ```

3. At the command prompt, enter the following command, then press Enter:

   ```
   mxmlc C:\data\virtualzoo\src\VirtualZoo.as
   ```

In response to the preceding steps, *mxmlc* compiles the program, and generates a *.swf* file named *VirtualZoo.swf*, which it places in the *virtualzoo\src* folder. Note that *mxmlc* has a wide variety of compilation options; for details, see the documentation provided with Flex SDK.

To run the *VirtualZoo.swf* file generated by *mxmlc*, simply open it in the standalone version of Flash Player or in a web browser with Flash Player installed. To view the *trace()* messages generated by the program, use the debugger version of Flash Player (included with Flex SDK) and configure it to output *trace()* messages to a logfile. For details, see *http://livedocs.adobe.com/flex/201/html/logging_125_07.html*.

 Compiling the virtual zoo program as described in this section will cause a series of compiler warnings such as "var 'pet' has no type declaration." For now, you can simply ignore these warnings. In the next chapter, we'll learn why they occur.

Compiler Restrictions

When compiling ActionScript programs with the Flash authoring tool, Flex Builder, or *mxmlc*, bear in mind the following compiler restrictions:

- The program's main class must be public.
- In Flex Builder 2 and *mxmlc*, the program's main class must reside in the unnamed package.
- The program's main class must extend either *Sprite* or *MovieClip*, as discussed in Chapter 6.
- Every ActionScript source file (*.as* file) in the program must have exactly one externally visible definition. An "externally visible definition" is a class, variable, function, interface, or namespace that is defined as either *internal* or *public* within a package statement.
- An ActionScript source file's name must match the name of its sole externally visible definition.

For example, the following source file would be considered illegal because it contains two externally visible classes:

```
package {
  public class A {
  }

  public class B {
  }
}
```

Likewise, the following source file would be considered illegal because it does not contain any externally visible definition.

```
class  C {
}
```

The Compilation Process and the Classpath

When a *.swf* file is exported, the ActionScript compiler makes a list of all the classes that the *.swf* requires. Specifically, the list of required classes includes:

- All classes referenced directly or indirectly by the program's main class
- In the case of the Flash authoring tool, all the classes referenced directly or indirectly by the *.swf*'s source *.fla* file (i.e., in frame scripts)

The compiler searches the filesystem for source *.as* files that correspond to all referenced classes, and compiles each source file into the *.swf*, in bytecode format. The set of folders in which the compiler searches for *.as* files is known as the *classpath*.

Class files that exist on the filesystem but are not required by the *.swf* are not compiled into the *.swf*, classes that are required but not found cause a compile-time error.

Each ActionScript authoring tool includes some folders in the classpath automatically and also allows you to specify directories that should be included in the classpath. For example, the Flash authoring tool automatically includes the folder containing the *.swf*'s source *.fla* file in a classpath. Likewise, Flex Builder 2 and *mxmlc* both automatically include the folder containing the program's main class in the classpath. For instructions on including other folders in the classpath, see the appropriate product's documentation.

The classpath is sometimes also referred to as the *build path* or the *source path*.

Strict-Mode Versus Standard-Mode Compilation

ActionScript offers two different modes for compiling a program: *strict mode* and *standard mode*. In strict mode, the compiler reports more errors than in standard mode. The extra strict-mode errors are intended to help programmers locate potential sources of problems in a program before the program actually runs. Strict mode is, therefore, enabled by default in all of Adobe's compilers. Programmers who wish to use ActionScript's dynamic features (as described in Chapter 15,), or who simply prefer to solve problems (i.e., debug) at runtime rather than at compile time can choose to compile using standard mode.

The following questionable acts of programming will cause a compiler error in strict mode, but not in standard mode:

- Supplying the wrong number or types of parameters to a function (see Chapter 8)
- Defining two variables or methods with the same name
- Accessing methods and variables that are not defined at compile time (but might be defined at runtime using the techniques described in Chapter 15)
- Assigning a value to a nonexistent instance variable of an object whose class is not dynamic
- Assigning a value to a constant variable anywhere other than the variable's initializer or, for instance variables, the constructor method of the class containing the variable's definition
- Attempting to delete (via the *delete* operator) an instance method, instance variable, static method, or static variable
- Comparing two incompatibly typed expressions (see the section "Compatible Types" in Chapter 8)

- Assigning a value to a type-annotated variable where the value is not a member of the declared type (for exceptions to this rule, see the section "Strict Mode's Three Special Cases" in Chapter 8)
- Referring to nonexistent packages

Enabling Standard-Mode Compilation in Flex Builder 2

To enable standard-mode compilation for a project in Flex Builder 2, follow these steps:

1. In the Navigator, select the project folder.
2. Select Project → Properties.
3. Under ActionScript Compiler, uncheck "Enable strict type checking."

Enabling Standard-Mode Compilation in the Flash Authoring Tool

To enable standard-mode compilation for a document in the Flash authoring tool, follow these steps:

1. Select File → Publish Settings.
2. On the Publish Settings dialog, on the Flash tab, click the Settings button.
3. On the ActionScript 3.0 Settings dialog, under Errors, uncheck Strict Mode.

To enable standard-mode compilation when compiling with *mxmlc*, set the compiler option strict to false.

The Fun's Not Over

We've now compiled and run our virtual zoo program, but our program isn't done yet. To make the zoo fully interactive, complete with graphics and buttons for feeding pets, we need to continue our study of ActionScript essentials. In the next chapter, we'll learn how ActionScript's type-checking system helps detect common errors in a program.

CHAPTER 8

Datatypes and Type Checking

So far, we've developed our virtual zoo program without making a single coding error. Error-free development happens in training courses and books—and *nowhere else*. In real-world development, programmers make errors all the time. For example, when invoking *eat()* on a *VirtualPet* object, a programmer might make a typographical error, such as the following (notice the extra "t"):

```
pet.eatt(new Sushi())
```

Or, a programmer might make a mistaken assumption about the capabilities of an object. For example, a programmer might mistakenly attempt to invoke a method named *jump()* on a *VirtualPet* object, even though *VirtualPet* defines no such method:

```
pet.jump()
```

In both the preceding cases, when the program runs in the debugger version of a Flash runtime, ActionScript will generate a *reference error*, indicating that the program attempted to reference a variable or method that doesn't exist.

 Errors that occur at runtime are known as *exceptions*. We'll study exceptions and the techniques for handling them in Chapter 13.

When an error occurs in a program you're writing, you should be happy. Errors indicate the precise location and cause of something in your program that would likely cause a malfunction without your attention. For example, in response to the earlier "*eatt()*" typo, the debugger version of a Flash runtime would display an alert dialog containing the following message:

```
ReferenceError: Error #1069: Property eatt not found on
      zoo.VirtualPet and there is no default value.
    at VirtualZoo$iinit()[C:\data\virtualzoo\src\VirtualZoo.as:8]
```

The error message tells us not only the name of the file in which the error occurred, but also the specific line of code containing the error. Now that's service. (Notice that the error message uses the term *property* to mean "variable or method," as discussed in Chapter 1 under "Members and Properties.")

As useful as runtime errors are, they have a potential drawback. They occur only when the erroneous line of code actually runs. Therefore, in a very large program, a runtime error might take a long time to surface. For example, in an adventure game that takes 10 hours to complete, an error in the final stage would take 10 hours of game-play to surface!

Luckily, rather than waiting for reference errors to occur at runtime, we can tell the compiler to report them at compiletime, before a program ever runs. To do so, we use *type annotations* in combination with strict mode compilation.

Datatypes and Type Annotations

In ActionScript, the term *datatype* means, simply, "a set of values." ActionScript defines three fundamental datatypes: *Null*, *void*, and *Object*. The *Null* and *void* datatypes each include a single value only—null and undefined, respectively (null and undefined are discussed in the later section "null and undefined"). The *Object* datatype includes all instances of all classes.

In addition to the three fundamental datatypes (*Null*, *void*, and *Object*), each and every built-in or custom class constitutes a unique datatype whose set of values includes its direct instances and instances of its descendant classes. For example, the *Food* class from our virtual zoo program constitutes a datatype whose set of values includes all instances of *Food* and all instances of *Apple* and *Sushi* (because *Apple* and *Sushi* both inherit from *Food*). Thus, an *Apple* instance and a *Sushi* instance are both said to belong to the *Food* datatype.

But the *Apple* class and the *Sushi* class each also constitute their own datatype. For example, the set of values in the *Apple* datatype includes all *Apple* instances and all instances of any class that inherits from *Apple*. Likewise, the set of values in the *Sushi* datatype includes all *Sushi* instances and all instances of any class that inherits from *Sushi*. Thus, in addition to belonging to the *Food* datatype, an *Apple* instance *also* belongs to the *Apple* datatype. But an *Apple* instance does *not* belong to the *Sushi* datatype because *Sushi* does not inherit from *Apple*. In the same way, a *Sushi* instance belongs to the *Food* and *Sushi* datatypes, but does not belong to the *Apple* datatype because *Sushi* does not inherit from *Apple*. Finally, while an *Apple* instance and a *Sushi* instance both belong to the *Food* datatype, a *Food* instance does not belong to either the *Apple* or *Sushi* datatypes because the *Food* class does not inherit from the *Apple* or *Sushi* classes.

Notice the important distinction between a given *class* and the *datatype* that it represents. The set of values that belong to the *class* includes the class's instances only. But the set of values that belong to the class's *datatype* includes the class's instances and instances of its descendant classes.

Just as each class constitutes a datatype, each *interface* also constitutes a datatype. The set of values in an interface's datatype includes every instance of every class that implements the interface, and every instance of every class that inherits from a class that implements the interface. We haven't studied interfaces yet, so we'll defer our examination of interfaces as datatypes until Chapter 9.

Given two datatypes *A* and *B*, where the class (or interface) represented by *B* inherits from the class (or interface) represented by *A*, *A* is referred to as a *supertype* of *B*. Conversely, *B* is referred to as a *subtype* of *A*. For example, *Food* is considered a supertype of *Apple*, while *Apple* is considered a subtype of *Food*.

Compatible Types

Because a given class can, through inheritance, use all the nonprivate instance members of its superclass (or superinterface), a given subtype is considered *compatible* with any of its supertypes. For example, the *Apple* datatype is considered compatible with the *Food* datatype because it is a subtype of *Food*.

The opposite, however, is not true. A class cannot use any of the instance members defined by its descendant classes. Hence, a given supertype is considered *incompatible* with any of its subtypes. For example, the *Food* datatype is considered incompatible with the *Apple* datatype because *Food* is not a subtype of *Apple*.

Conceptually, the subtype is considered compatible with the supertype because a program can treat an instance of the subtype as though it were an instance of the supertype. For example, a program can treat any *Apple* instance as though it were a *Food* instance—perhaps by invoking the *Food* class's *getCalories()* method on it.

```
// Create a new Apple instance
var apple = new Apple();

// Legally invoke getCalories() on the Apple instance
apple.getCalories();
```

By comparison, the supertype is considered *incompatible* with the subtype because a program *cannot* treat an instance of the supertype as though it were an instance of the subtype. For example, a program cannot invoke the *Apple* class's *hasWorm()* method on a *Food* instance:

```
// Create a new Food instance
var food = new Food(200);
```

```
// The following line causes a reference error because the Food class
// has no access to the hasWorm( ) method
food.hasWorm( );  // Error!
```

Detecting Type Mismatch Errors with Type Annotations

A *type annotation* (or, synonymously, a *type declaration*) is a suffix that constrains the datatype of a variable, parameter, or function return value. The general syntax for a type annotation is a colon (:) followed by a datatype, as in:

```
:type
```

For example, a variable definition with a type annotation has the following generalized form:

```
var identifier:type = value;
```

In the preceding code, the *type* must be the name of a class or interface (representing the datatype), or the special symbol * (indicating "untyped").

A function or method definition with a parameter type annotation and a return type annotation has the following generalized form:

```
function identifier (param:paramType):returnType {
}
```

In the preceding code, the parameter type annotation is the specified *paramType* and the colon (:) that precedes it; the return type annotation is the specified *returnType* and the colon (:) that precedes it. The *paramType* must be one of the following:

- The name of a class or interface (representing the datatype)
- The special symbol, * (indicating "untyped")

The *returnType* must be one of the following:

- The name of a class or interface (representing the datatype)
- The special symbol, * (indicating "untyped")
- The special "no-return" type annotation, void (indicating that the function does not return a value)

 ActionScript 2.0 programmers should note that Void is no longer capitalized in ActionScript 3.0.

A type annotation for a variable, parameter, or function result constrains the value of that variable, parameter, or result to the specified type. The means by which the value is constrained depends on the compilation mode used to compile the code (recall that strict mode is the default compilation mode for Adobe compilers).

In both standard mode and strict mode, if the value belongs to the specified datatype, then the assignment or return attempt succeeds.

If the value does *not* belong to the specified datatype, then in strict mode, the compiler generates an error (known as a *type mismatch error*), and refuses to compile the code. In standard mode, the code compiles, and at runtime ActionScript attempts to convert the value to the specified datatype. If the specified datatype is one of the built-in classes *String*, *Boolean*, *Number*, *int*, or *uint* (known as the *primitive types*) then the conversion proceeds according to the rules described in the section "Conversion to Primitive Types," later in this chapter. Otherwise, the conversion fails, and ActionScript generates a runtime type mismatch error. In formal terms, automatic runtime-conversion is known as *coercion*.

For example, the following code defines a variable, meal, of type *Food*, and assigns that variable an instance of the *Apple* class:

```
var meal:Food = new Apple( );
```

In both strict mode and standard mode, the preceding code compiles successfully because *Apple* extends *Food*, so instances of *Apple* belong to the *Food* datatype.

By contrast, the following code assigns meal an instance of the *VirtualPet* class:

```
var meal:Food = new VirtualPet("Lucky");
```

In strict mode, the preceding code causes a type mismatch error because *VirtualPet* instances do not belong to the *Food* datatype. Therefore, the code fails to compile.

In standard mode, the preceding code compiles happily. However, because the value (the *VirtualPet* instance) does not belong to the variable's datatype (*Food*), ActionScript attempts to coerce (i.e., convert) the value to the variable's datatype at runtime. In this case, the variable's datatype is not one of the primitive types, so the conversion fails, and ActionScript generates a runtime type mismatch error.

Let's look at another example. The following code defines a variable, petHunger, of type *int*, and assigns that variable an instance of the *VirtualPet* class:

```
var pet:VirtualPet = new VirtualPet("Lucky");
var petHunger:int = pet;
```

In strict mode, the preceding code causes a type mismatch error because *VirtualPet* instances do not belong to the *int* datatype. Hence, the code fails to compile.

In standard mode, the preceding code compiles happily. However, because the value (the *VirtualPet* instance) does not belong to the variable's datatype (*int*), ActionScript attempts to convert the value to the variable's datatype at runtime. In this case, the variable's datatype *is* one of the primitive types, so the conversion proceeds according to the rules described in the section "Conversion to Primitive Types," later in this chapter. Hence, after the code runs, petHunger has the value 0.

Of course, assigning the value 0 to petHunger was likely *not* the intention of the preceding code. More likely, the programmer simply forgot to invoke *getHunger()* on the *VirtualPet* instance, as in:

```
var pet:VirtualPet = new VirtualPet("Lucky");
var petHunger:int = pet.getHunger( );
```

Strict mode faithfully warned us of the problem, but standard mode did not. Instead, standard mode assumed that because petHunger's datatype was *int*, we wanted to convert the *VirtualPet* object to the *int* type. For our purposes, that assumption was incorrect, and resulted in an unexpected value in our program.

Some programmers consider standard mode's lenience convenient, particularly in simple programs. In more complex programs, however, standard mode's flexibility often leaves would-be errors unreported, leading to difficult-to-diagnose bugs.

> The remainder of this book assumes that all code is compiled in strict mode and supplies type annotations for all variables, parameters, and return values.

Untyped Variables, Parameters, Return Values, and Expressions

A variable or parameter whose definition includes a type annotation is said to be a *typed variable* or *typed parameter*. Likewise, a function definition that includes a return-type annotation is said to have a *typed return value*. Furthermore, an expression that refers to a typed variable or a typed parameter, or calls a function with typed return value is known as a *typed expression*.

Conversely, a variable or parameter whose definition does not include a type annotation is said to be an *untyped variable* or *untyped parameter*. Likewise, a function definition that does not include a return-type annotation is said to have an *untyped return value*. An expression that refers to untyped variable or an untyped parameter, or calls a function with an untyped return value is known as a *untyped expression*.

Untyped variables, parameters, and return values are not constrained to a specific datatype (as typed variables, parameters, and return values are). For example, an untyped variable can be assigned a *Boolean* value on one line, and a *VirtualPet* object on another without error:

```
var stuff = true;
stuff = new VirtualPet("Edwin");  // No error
```

> ActionScript does not generate type-mismatch errors for untyped variables, parameters, and return values.

Programmers wishing to explicitly indicate that a variable, parameter, or return value is intentionally untyped can use the special type annotation, `:*`. For example, the following code defines an *explicitly* untyped variable, `totalCost`:

```
var totalCost:* = 9.99;
```

The following code defines the same variable, but this time it is *implicitly* untyped:

```
var totalCost = 9.99;
```

Implicitly untyped variables, parameters, and return values, are typically used when an entire program does not use type annotations, preferring to handle any type errors at runtime. Explicitly untyped variables, parameters, and return values are typically used when a strict-mode program wishes to specify individual cases where multiple data types are allowed. The `:*` type annotation prevents an untyped variable from generating a "missing type annotation" warning. For details, see the upcoming section "Warnings for Missing Type Annotations."

Strict Mode's Three Special Cases

There are three situations in which the compiler ignores type mismatch errors in strict mode, deferring possible type errors until runtime:

- When an untyped expression is assigned to a typed variable or parameter, or returned from a function with a declared return type
- When any expression is assigned to a typed variable or parameter whose declared type is *Boolean*, or returned from a function whose declared return type is *Boolean*
- When any numeric value is used where an instance of a different numeric type is expected

Let's look at each of the preceding cases with an example. First, we'll create an untyped variable, pet, and assign the value of that variable to a typed variable, d:

```
var pet:* = new VirtualPet("Francis");
pet = new Date( );
var d:Date = pet;
```

Because pet can contain any type of value, on line 3, the compiler cannot determine whether pet's value belongs to the datatype *Date*. To determine whether the value in pet belongs to the datatype *Date*, the code must be executed, not just compiled. Once the code is actually executing, ActionScript can then determine the result of the assignment attempt. In the case of the preceding code, the value in pet (assigned on line 2) does indeed belong to the datatype *Date* (even though pet's value on line 1 was originally incompatible with *Date*). Hence, the assignment proceeds without causing an error.

Next, consider the following code which defines a variable, b, of type *Boolean*, and assigns b an integer value, 5:

```
var b:Boolean = 5;
```

Even though the value 5 does not belong to the *Boolean* datatype, the compiler does not generate a type mismatch error. Instead, it assumes that the programmer wishes to convert the value 5 to the *Boolean* datatype (according to the rules described in the later section "Conversion to Primitive Types") and issues a warning to that effect. This lenience can cut down on the amount of code in a program. For example, suppose the *VirtualPet* class's *getHunger()* method's return type were declared as *Number*. A program could then create a variable indicating whether a pet is alive or dead using the following code:

```
var isAlive:Boolean = somePet.getHunger();
```

According to the rules described in the section "Conversion to Primitive Types," the number 0 converts to the value false, while all other numbers convert to the value true. Hence, if *getHunger()* returns anything other than 0, isAlive is set to true; otherwise, *isAlive* is set to false (the pet is dead when it has no calories left).

For comparison, here's the alternative, slightly longer code that would be necessary if the compiler enforced type checking for variables of type *Boolean* (rather than allowing a runtime conversion):

```
var isAlive:Boolean = somePet.getHunger() > 0;
```

Finally, consider the following code that defines a variable, xCoordinate, of type *int*, and assigns xCoordinate a *Number* value, 4.6459:

```
var xCoordinate:int = 4.6459;
```

Even though the value 4.6459 does not belong to the *int* datatype, the compiler does not generate a type mismatch error. Instead, the compiler assumes that you wish to convert the value 4.6459 to the *int* datatype (according to the rules described in the section "Conversion to Primitive Types"). This lenience allows easy interoperation between ActionScript's numeric data types with minimal fuss.

Warnings for Missing Type Annotations

As we've seen over the past several sections, ActionScript's strict compilation mode provides a valuable way to detect program errors as early as possible. Not surprisingly, in an effort to write problem-free code, many developers rely heavily on strict mode's compile-time type checking. However, as we learned in the earlier section "Untyped Variables, Parameters, Return Values, and Expressions," strict-mode's type-mismatch errors are reported for typed variables, parameters, and return values only. Any time a type annotation is accidentally omitted, the programmer loses the benefit of strict mode's compile-time type checking.

Luckily, Adobe's ActionScript compilers offer a warning mode in which missing type annotations are reported at compiletime. Developers can use those warnings to help locate accidentally omitted type annotations. In Flex Builder 2 and *mxmlc*, warnings for missing type annotations are enabled by default. In the Flash authoring tool, type annotation warnings must be enabled manually, using the following steps:

1. Using a text editor, in the Flash CS3 installation folder, under */en/Configuration/ActionScript 3.0/*, open *EnabledWarnings.xml*.

2. Locate the following line:

   ```
   <warning id="1008" enabled="false" label="kWarning_NoTypeDecl">
       Missing type declaration.</warning>
   ```

3. Change enabled="false" to enabled="true".

4. Save *EnabledWarnings.xml*.

Note that missing type-annotation warnings are issued for implicitly untyped variables, parameters, and return values only. Missing type-annotation warnings are not issued for explicitly untyped variables, parameters, and return values (i.e., those that use the special type annotation, :*).

Detecting Reference Errors at Compile Time

At the beginning of this chapter, we learned that an attempt to access a nonexistent variable or method results in a reference error. When a program is compiled in standard mode, reference errors are not reported by the compiler. Instead, when the program runs in the debugger version of a Flash runtime, reference errors manifest as runtime exceptions. By contrast, when a program is compiled in strict mode, references to nonexistent variables or methods made through typed expressions *are* reported by the compiler, and cause compilation to fail.

For example, the following code creates a variable, pet, of type *VirtualPet*, and assigns that variable an instance of the *VirtualPet* class:

```
var pet:VirtualPet = new VirtualPet("Stan");
```

Next, the following code attempts to access a nonexistent method, *eatt()*, through the typed variable pet:

```
pet.eatt(new Sushi());
```

In standard mode, the preceding code compiles, but generates a runtime reference error. In strict mode, the preceding code generates the following compile-time reference error and fails to compile.

```
1061: Call to a possibly undefined method eatt through a
   reference with static type zoo:VirtualPet.
```

Service with a smile.

Note, however, that the compiler does not report reference errors made through untyped expressions. Furthermore, references to nonexistent variables and methods made through instances of dynamic classes (such as *Object*) do not generate reference errors of any kind; instead, such references yield the value undefined. For more information on dynamic classes, see Chapter 15.

 Here's a type-annotation bonus: in Flex Builder and the Flash authoring tool, type annotations for variables, parameters, and return values activate *code hints*. A code hint is a handy pop-up menu that lists the properties and methods of objects as you write them in your code.

Casting

In the preceding section, we learned that in strict mode, the compiler reports reference errors at compiletime. To detect reference errors, the compiler relies on type annotations. For example, suppose the compiler encounters a method reference made through a typed variable. To determine whether the reference is valid, the compiler checks for the method's definition in the class or interface specified by the variable's type annotation. If the class or interface does not define the referenced method, the compiler generates a reference error.

 Notice that it is the class or interface specified by the type annotation—*not* the actual class of the value—that determines whether the reference error occurs.

Consider the following code, in which the *hasWorm()* method is invoked on an *Apple* object through a variable of type *Food*:

```
var meal:Food = new Apple( );
meal.hasWorm( );  // Attempt to call hasWorm( ) on meal
```

When compiling the preceding code in strict mode, the compiler must decide whether the *hasWorm()* method can be invoked on meal's value. To do so, the compiler checks to see whether the *Food* class (i.e., the class specified by meal's type annotation) defines *hasWorm()*. The *Food* class defines no such method, so the compiler generates a reference error. Of course, by looking at the code, *we* know that meal's value (an *Apple* object) supports the *hasWorm()* method. *But compiler doesn't.* ActionScript must wait until runtime to learn that the variable's value is actually an *Apple* object.

Solution? Use a *cast operation* to force the compiler to allow the preceding *hasWorm()* invocation. A cast operation tells the compiler to treat a given expression as though it belongs to a specified datatype. A cast operation has the following generalized form:

type(expression)

In the preceding code, *type* is any datatype, and *expression* is any expression. The operation is said to "cast the *expression* to the specified *type*." For example, the following code casts the expression meal to the *Apple* datatype before invoking *hasWorm()* on meal's value:

```
Apple(meal).hasWorm( )
```

No matter what the actual value of meal, the compiler believes that the datatype of the expression meal is *Apple*. Therefore, when deciding whether the *hasWorm()* method can be invoked on meal's value, the compiler checks to see whether the *Apple* class—*not* the *Food* class—defines *hasWorm()*. The *Apple* class does define *hasWorm()*, so the compiler generates no errors.

However, a cast operation is not merely a compile-time mechanism; it also has a runtime behavior. At runtime, if the *expression* resolves to an object that belongs to the specified *type*, then ActionScript simply returns that object. But if the *expression* resolves to an object that *does not* belong to the specified *type*, then the cast operation has one of two results. If the specified *type* is not a primitive type, the cast operation causes a runtime error; otherwise, the object is converted to the specified type (according to the rules listed in the section "Conversion to Primitive Types") and the converted value is returned.

For example, in the following code, the runtime value of meal belongs to the *Apple* datatype, so the cast operation on line 2 simply returns the *Apple* object referenced by meal:

```
var meal:Food = new Apple( );
Apple(meal);  // At runtime, returns the Apple object
```

By comparison, in the following code, the runtime value of meal does not belong to the *VirtualPet* datatype, and *VirtualPet* is not a primitive type, so the cast operation on line 2 causes a type error:

```
var meal:Food = new Apple( );
VirtualPet(meal);  // At runtime, causes a type error
```

Finally, in the following code, the runtime value of meal does not belong to the *Boolean* datatype, but *Boolean* is a primitive type, so the cast operation on line 2 converts meal's value to the specified type, and returns the result of that conversion (true):

```
var meal:Food = new Apple( );
Boolean(meal);  // At runtime, returns the value true
```

Avoiding Unwanted Type Mismatch Errors

So far, we've learned that cast operations can be used to avoid unwanted compile-time reference errors. Similarly, cast operations can be used to avoid unwanted type-mismatch errors.

As an example, imagine a program that converts a supplied Fahrenheit temperature to Celsius. The value of the Fahrenheit temperature is entered into a text field, which is represented by an instance of the built-in *TextField* class. To retrieve the input value, we access the text variable of the *TextField* instance, as shown in the following code:

```
var fahrenheit:Number = inputField.text;
```

As it stands, the preceding code causes a type mismatch error because the text variable's datatype is *String*. To avoid that error, we use a cast operation, as follows:

```
var fahrenheit:Number = Number(inputField.text);
```

At runtime, the preceding cast converts the string value in inputField.text to a *Number* that is then assigned to fahrenheit.

Upcasting and Downcasting

Casting an object to one of its supertypes (superclass or superinterface) is known as an *upcast*. For example, the following operation is considered an upcast because *Food* is a supertype of *Apple*:

```
Food(new Apple( ))
```

Conversely, casting an object to one of its subtypes (subclass or subinterface) is known as a *downcast* because it casts the object's type to a type further down the type hierarchy. The following operation is considered a downcast because *Apple* is a subtype of *Food*:

```
Apple(new Food( ))
```

An upcast is said to "widen" the object's type because a supertype is more generalized than its subtype. A downcast is said to "narrow" the object's type because a subtype is more specialized than its supertype.

An upcast is also described as a *safe cast* because it never generates a runtime error. As we learned earlier, an instance of a subtype can always be safely treated as an instance of any of its supertypes because it is guaranteed (through inheritance) to have all of its supertypes' non-*private* instance methods and variables.

Conversely, a downcast is described as an *unsafe cast* because it has the potential to cause a runtime error. To guarantee that a downcast operation will not generate a runtime error, we must first check whether the object in question is actually an instance of the target datatype before performing the cast. To check the datatype of an object, we use the *is* operator, which has the following form:

```
expression is type
```

In the preceding code, *expression* is any expression, and *type* is any class or interface (and must not be undefined or null). An *is* operation returns the value true if the specified expression belongs to the specified *type*; otherwise, it returns false.

The following code uses the *is* operator to guarantee that a downcast operation will not generate a runtime error:

```
var apple:Food = new Apple();
if (apple is Apple) {
  Apple(apple).hasWorm();
}
```

In the preceding code, the statement block of the conditional statement will execute only if the variable apple refers to an object belonging to the *Apple* type. Hence, the cast operation Apple(apple) can never generate an error because it executes only when apple's value belongs to the *Apple* type.

Using the as Operator to Cast to Date and Array

For legacy reasons, the cast syntax described in the preceding sections cannot be used to cast a value to the built-in *Date* or *Array* classes. The result of the expression Date(*someValue*) is identical to new Date().toString() (which returns a string representing the current time). The result of the expression Array(*someValue*) is identical to new Array(*someValue*) (which creates a new *Array* object with *someValue* as its first element).

To cast an expression to either the *Date* class or the *Array* classes, we use the *as* operator, which has the same behavior as a cast operation, except that it returns the value null in all cases where a cast operation would generate a runtime error. An *as* operation has the following form:

expression as *type*

In the preceding code, *expression* is any expression, and *type* is any class or interface (and must not be undefined or null). An *as* operation returns the value of *expression* if the specified *expression* belongs to the specified *type*; otherwise, it returns null.

For example, in the following code, the expression (meal as Apple) has the same result as the cast operation Apple(meal):

```
var meal:Food = new Apple();
(meal as Apple).hasWorm();
```

The following code uses the *as* operator to "cast" an *Array* object to the *Array* datatype so it can be assigned to a variable of type *Array*.

```
public function output (msg:Object):void {
  if (msg is String) {
    trace(msg);
  }

  if (msg is Array) {
    var arr:Array = msg as Array;  // "Cast" to Array here
    trace(arr.join("\n"));
  }
}
```

The following code shows the result of passing an example *Array* object to *output( )*:

```
var numbers:Array = [1,2,3]
output(numbers);

// Output:
1
2
3
```

Conversion to Primitive Types

In the preceding section we learned that when an expression is cast to a primitive type to which it does not belong, then that expression is converted to the specified type. For example, consider the following code, which casts a *Date* object to the primitive datatype *Boolean*:

```
Boolean(new Date( ))
```

Because *Boolean* is a primitive type, and the *Date* object does not belong to the *Boolean* type, ActionScript converts the *Date* object to the *Boolean* type. The result is the *Boolean* value true (see Table 8-5).

Cast operations are sometimes used not to tell the compiler the type of a given expression but to convert that expression to a primitive datatype.

 A cast operation can convert any value to a particular primitive type.

For example, the following code converts a floating-point number (a number with a fractional value) to an integer (a number with no fractional value):

```
int(4.93)
```

The result of the preceding cast operation is the integer 4. Likewise, the following code converts the *Boolean* value true to the integer 1, and the *Boolean* value false to the integer 0:

```
int(true);  // Yields 1
int(false);  // Yields 0
```

The preceding technique might be used to reduce the size of data transmitted to a server when submitting a series of *Boolean* options.

Table 8-1 shows the results of converting various datatypes to the *Number* type.

Table 8-1. Conversion to Number

Original data	Result after conversion
undefined	NaN (the special numeric value "Not a Number," which represents invalid numeric data).
null	0
int	The same number
uint	The same number
Boolean	1 if the original value is true; 0 if the original value is false
Numeric string	Equivalent numeric value if string is composed only of base-10 or base-16 numbers, whitespace, exponent, decimal point, plus sign, or minus sign (e.g., "-1.485e2" becomes -148.5)
Empty string	0
"Infinity"	Infinity
"-Infinity"	-Infinity
Other strings	NaN
Object	NaN

Table 8-2 shows the results of converting various datatypes to the *int* type.

Table 8-2. Conversion to int

Original data	Result after conversion
undefined	0
null	0
Number or uint	An integer in the range -2^{31} through $2^{31}-1$, out of range values are brought into range using the algorithm listed in section 9.5 of the Standard ECMA-262, Third Edition
Boolean	1 if the original value is true; 0 if the original value is false
Numeric string	Equivalent numeric value, converted to signed-integer format
Empty string	0
"Infinity"	0
"-Infinity"	0
Other strings	0
Object	0

Table 8-3 shows the results of converting various datatypes to the *uint* type.

Table 8-3. Conversion to uint

Original data	Result after conversion
undefined	0
null	0
Number or Int	An integer in the range 0 through 2^{31} 1, out of range values are brought into range using the algorithm listed in section 9.6 of the Standard ECMA-262, Third Edition
Boolean	1 if the original value is true; 0 if the original value is false

Table 8-3. Conversion to uint (continued)

Original data	Result after conversion
Numeric string	Equivalent numeric value, converted to unsigned-integer format
Empty string	0
"Infinity"	0
"-Infinity"	0
Other strings	0
Object	0

Table 8-4 shows the results of converting various datatypes to the *String* type.

Table 8-4. Conversion to String

Original data	Result after conversion
undefined	"undefined"
null	"null"
Boolean	"true" if the original value was true; "false" if the original value was false.
NaN	"NaN"
0	"0"
Infinity	"Infinity"
-Infinity	"-Infinity"
Other numeric value	String equivalent of the number. For example, 944.345 becomes "944.345".
Object	The value that results from calling *toString( )* on the object. By default, the *toString( )* method of an object returns "[object *className*]", where *className* is the object's class. The *toString( )* method can be overridden to return a more useful result. For example, *toString( )* of a *Date* object returns the time in human-readable format, such as: "Sun May 14 11:38:10 EDT 2000"), while *toString( )* of an *Array* object returns comma-separated list of element values.

Table 8-5 shows the results of converting various datatypes to the *Boolean* type.

Table 8-5. Conversion to Boolean

Original data	Result after conversion
undefined	false
null	false
NaN	false
0	false
Infinity	true
-Infinity	true
Other numeric value	true
Nonempty string	true
Empty string ("")	false
Object	true

Default Variable Values

When a variable is declared *without* a type annotation and without an initial value, then its initial value is automatically set to the value undefined (the sole value of the datatype *void*). When a variable is declared *with* a type annotation but no initial value, then its initial value is automatically set to a default value for its specified datatype.

Table 8-6 lists the default values, by datatype, for variables in ActionScript.

Table 8-6. Default variable values

Datatype	Default value
String	null
Boolean	false
int	0
uint	0
Number	NaN
All other types	null

null and undefined

Earlier we learned that, the *Null* and *void* datatypes each include a single value only—null and undefined, respectively. Now that we have studied datatypes and type annotations, let's consider the difference between those two values.

Both null and undefined conceptually represent the absence of data. The null value represents the absence of data for variables, parameters, and return values with a specified type annotation set to anything but *Boolean*, *int*, *uint*, and *Number*. For example, the following code creates a typed instance variable, pet, of type *VirtualPet*. Before the variable is explicitly assigned a value in the program, its value is null.

```
package {
  import flash.display.Sprite;
  import zoo.*;

  public class VirtualZoo extends Sprite {
    private var pet:VirtualPet;

    public function VirtualZoo () {
      trace(pet);  // Displays: null
    }
  }
}
```

By contrast, the undefined value represents the absence of data for variables, parameters, and return values *without* a specified type annotation. For example, the following code creates an object with two dynamic instance variables, city and country. When assigning the country variable an initial value, the code uses undefined to indicate that country does not yet have a meaningful value.

```
var info = new Object( );
info.city = "Toronto";
info.country = undefined;
```

The undefined value also represents the complete absence of a variable or method on an object whose class is defined as *dynamic*. For example, the following attempt to access a nonexistent variable through the object referenced by info yields undefined:

```
trace(info.language);  // Displays: undefined
```

We'll learn more about ActionScript's dynamic features and the undefined value in Chapter 15.

Datatypes in the Virtual Zoo

Now that we've learned all about datatypes, let's add type annotations to our virtual zoo program. Example 8-1 shows the updated code for the *VirtualZoo* class, the program's main class.

Example 8-1. The VirtualZoo class

```
package {
  import flash.display.Sprite;
  import zoo.*;

  public class VirtualZoo extends Sprite {
    private var pet:VirtualPet;

    public function VirtualZoo ( ) {
      pet = new VirtualPet("Stan");
      pet.eat(new Apple( ));
      pet.eat(new Sushi( ));
    }
  }
}
```

Example 8-2 shows the code for the *VirtualPet* class, whose instances represent pets in the zoo. Notice the cast operation in the *eat( )* method, discussed in the earlier section "Upcasting and Downcasting."

Example 8-2. The VirtualPet class

```
package zoo {
  import flash.utils.setInterval;
  import flash.utils.clearInterval;

  public class VirtualPet {
    private static var maxNameLength:int = 20;
```

Example 8-2. The VirtualPet class (continued)

```
private static var maxCalories:int = 2000;
private static var caloriesPerSecond:int = 100;

private var petName:String;
private var currentCalories:int = VirtualPet.maxCalories/2;
private var digestIntervalID:int;

public function VirtualPet (name:String):void {
  setName(name);
  digestIntervalID = setInterval(digest, 1000);
}

public function eat (foodItem:Food):void {
  if (currentCalories == 0) {
    trace(getName() + " is dead. You can't feed it.");
    return;
  }

  if (foodItem is Apple) {
    // Note the cast to Apple
    if (Apple(foodItem).hasWorm()) {
      trace("The " + foodItem.getName() + " had a worm. " + getName()
            + " didn't eat it.");
      return;
    }
  }

  var newCurrentCalories:int = currentCalories + foodItem.getCalories();
  if (newCurrentCalories > VirtualPet.maxCalories) {
    currentCalories = VirtualPet.maxCalories;
  } else {
    currentCalories = newCurrentCalories;
  }
  trace(getName() + " ate some " + foodItem.getName() + "."
        + " It now has " + currentCalories  + " calories remaining.");
}

public function getHunger ():Number {
  return currentCalories / VirtualPet.maxCalories;
}

public function setName (newName:String):void {
  // If the proposed new name has more than maxNameLength characters...
  if (newName.length > VirtualPet.maxNameLength) {
    // ...truncate it
    newName = newName.substr(0, VirtualPet.maxNameLength);
  } else if (newName == "") {
    // ...otherwise, if the proposed new name is an empty string,
    // then terminate this method without changing petName
    return;
  }
```

Example 8-2. The VirtualPet class (continued)

```
      // Assign the new, validated name to petName
      petName = newName;
    }

    public function getName ():String {
      return petName;
    }

    private function digest ():void {
      // If digesting more calories would leave the pet's currentCalories at
      // 0 or less...
      if (currentCalories - VirtualPet.caloriesPerSecond <= 0) {
        // ...stop the interval from calling digest()
        clearInterval(digestIntervalID);
        // Then give the pet an empty stomach
        currentCalories = 0;
        // And report the pet's death
        trace(getName() + " has died.");
      } else {
        // ...otherwise, digest the stipulated number of calories
        currentCalories -= VirtualPet.caloriesPerSecond;

        // And report the pet's new status
        trace(getName() + " digested some food. It now has "
              + currentCalories + " calories remaining.");
      }
    }
  }
}
```

Example 8-3 shows the code for the *Food* class, the superclass of the various types of food that pets eat.

Example 8-3. The Food class

```
package zoo {
  public class Food {
    private var calories:int;
    private var name:String;

    public function Food (initialCalories:int) {
      setCalories(initialCalories);
    }

    public function getCalories ():int {
      return calories;
    }

    public function setCalories (newCalories:int):void {
      calories = newCalories;
    }
```

Example 8-3. The Food class (continued)

```
    public function getName ():String {
      return name;
    }

    public function setName (newName:String):void {
      name = newName;
    }
  }
}
```

Example 8-4 shows the code for the *Apple* class, which represents a specific type of food that pets eat.

Example 8-4. The Apple class

```
package zoo {
  public class Apple extends Food {
    private static var DEFAULT_CALORIES:int = 100;
    private var wormInApple:Boolean;

    public function Apple (initialCalories:int = 0) {
      if (initialCalories <= 0) {
        initialCalories = Apple.DEFAULT_CALORIES;
      }
      super(initialCalories);

      wormInApple = Math.random() >= .5;

      setName("Apple");
    }

    public function hasWorm ():Boolean {
      return wormInApple;
    }
  }
}
```

Finally, Example 8-5 shows the code for the *Sushi* class, which represents a specific type of food that pets eat.

Example 8-5. The Sushi class

```
package zoo {
  public class Sushi extends Food {
    private static var DEFAULT_CALORIES:int = 500;

    public function Sushi (initialCalories:int = 0) {
      if (initialCalories <= 0) {
        initialCalories = Sushi.DEFAULT_CALORIES;
      }
      super(initialCalories);
```

Example 8-5. The Sushi class (continued)

```
      setName("Sushi");
    }
  }
}
```

More Datatype Study Coming Up

In this chapter, we learned how to use datatypes to help identify and resolve potential problems in a program. In the next chapter, we'll conclude our general exploration of datatypes by studying *interfaces*. Like classes, interfaces are used to create custom datatypes.

CHAPTER 9

Interfaces

An *interface* is an ActionScript language construct that defines a new datatype, much as a class defines a datatype. However, whereas a class both defines a datatype and provides the implementation for it, an interface defines a datatype in abstract terms only, and provides no implementation for that datatype. That is, a class doesn't just declare a bunch of methods and variables, it also supplies concrete behavior; the method bodies and variable values that make the class actually do something. An interface, instead of providing its own implementation, is adopted by one or more classes that agree to provide the implementation. Instances of a class that provides an implementation for an interface belong both to the class's datatype and to the datatype defined by the interface. As a member of multiple datatypes, the instances can then play multiple roles in an application.

Don't confuse the term *interface*, as discussed in this chapter, with other uses of the word. In this chapter, "interface" refers to an Action-Script language construct, not a graphical user interface (GUI) or the public API of a class, sometimes also called an interface in general object-oriented programming theory.

Unless you're familiar with interfaces already, theoretical descriptions of them can be hard to follow, so let's dive right into an example.

The Case for Interfaces

Suppose we're creating a logging class, *Logger*, that reports status messages ("log entries") for a program as it runs. Many classes receive the *Logger*'s status messages and respond to them in different ways. For example, one class, *LogUI*, displays log messages on screen; another class, *LiveLog*, alerts a live support technician via a networked administration tool; yet another class, *LogTracker*, adds log messages to a database for statistics tracking. To receive log messages, each class defines an *update()* method. To send a message to objects of each interested class, the *Logger* class invokes the *update()* method.

That all seems logical enough so far, but what happens if we forget to define the *update()* method in the *LogUI* class? The status message will be sent, but *LogUI* objects won't receive it. We need a way to guarantee that each log recipient defines the *update()* method.

To make that guarantee, suppose we add a new requirement to our program: any object that wants to receive log messages from *Logger* must be an instance of a generic *LogRecipient* class (which we'll provide) or an instance of one of *LogRecipient*'s subclasses. In the *LogRecipient* class, we implement the *update()* method in a generic way—by simply displaying the log message using *trace()*:

```
public class LogRecipient {
  public function update (msg:String):void {
    trace(msg);
  }
}
```

Now any class that wishes to receive log messages from *Logger* simply extends *LogRecipient* and if specialized behavior is wanted, overrides *LogRecipient*'s *update()* method, providing the desired behavior. For example, the following class, *LogTracker*, extends *LogRecipient* and overrides *update()*, providing database-specific behavior:

```
public class LogTracker extends LogRecipient {
  // Override LogRecipient's update()
  override public function update (msg:String):void {
    // Send problem report to database. Code not shown...
  }
}
```

Back in the *Logger* class, we define a method, *addRecipient()*, that registers an object to receive log messages. The basic code for *addRecipient()* follows. Notice that only instances of the *LogRecipient* class and its subclasses can be passed to *addRecipient()*:

```
public class Logger {
  public function addRecipient (lr:LogRecipient):Boolean {
    // Code here should register lr to receive status messages,
    // and return a Boolean value indicating whether registration
    // succeeded (code not shown).
  }
}
```

If an object passed to *addRecipient()* is not of type *LogRecipient*, then the compiler generates a type mismatch error. If the object is an instance of a *LogRecipient* subclass that doesn't implement *update()*, at least the generic *update()* (defined by *LogRecipient*) will execute.

Sounds reasonable, right? Almost. But there's a problem. What if a class wishing to receive events from *LogRecipient* already extends another class? For example, suppose the *LogUI* class extends *flash.display.Sprite*:

```
public class LogUI extends Sprite {
```

```
    public function update (msg:String):void {
      // Display status message on screen, code not shown...
    }
  }
```

In ActionScript, a single class cannot extend more than one class. The *LogUI* class already extends *Sprite,* so it can't also extend *LogRecipient*. Therefore, instances of *LogUI* can't register to receive status messages from *Logger*. What we really need in this situation is a way to indicate that *LogUI* instances actually belong to two datatypes: *LogUI* and *LogRecipient*.

Enter…interfaces!

Interfaces and Multidatatype Classes

In the preceding section, we created the *LogRecipient* datatype by creating a *LogRecipient* class. That approach forces every *Logger* message-recipient to be an instance of either *LogRecipient* or a *LogRecipient* subclass. To loosen that restriction, we can define the *LogRecipient* datatype by creating a *LogRecipient* interface rather than a *LogRecipient* class. That way, instances of any class that formally agrees to provide an implementation for *update()* can register for log messages. Let's see how this works.

Syntactically, an interface is simply a list of methods. For example, the following code creates an interface named *LogRecipient* that contains a single method, *update()*. (Notice that, like classes, interfaces can be defined as either *public* or *internal*.)

```
  public interface LogRecipient {
    function update(msg:String):void;
  }
```

Once an interface has been defined, any number of classes can use the keyword *implements* to enter into an agreement with it, promising to define the methods it contains. Once such a promise has been made, the class's instances are considered members of both the class's datatype and the interface's datatype.

For example, to indicate that the *LogUI* class agrees to define the method *update()* (defined by the *LogRecipient* interface), we use the following code:

```
  class LogUI extends Sprite implements LogRecipient {
    public function update (msg:String):void {
      // Display status message on screen, code not shown...
    }
  }
```

Instead of extending the *LogRecipient* class, the *LogUI* class extends *Sprite* and implements the *LogRecipient* interface. Because *LogUI* implements *LogRecipient*, it must define an *update()* method. Otherwise, the compiler generates the following error:

```
  Interface method update in namespace LogRecipient not implemented by class LogUI.
```

Because *LogUI* promises to implement *LogRecipient*'s methods, *LogUI* instances can be used anywhere the *LogRecipient* datatype is required. Instances of *LogUI* effectively belong to two datatypes: *LogUI* and *LogRecipient*. Thus, despite the fact that *LogUI* extends *Sprite*, *LogUI* instances still belong to the *LogRecipient* type and can be passed safely to *Logger*'s *addRecipient()* method. (Wow, Ron, that's amazing! It's a pasta maker *and* a juicer!)

Compiler errors are the key to the entire interface system. They guarantee that a class lives up to its implementation promises, which allows external code to use it with the confidence that it will behave as required. That confidence is particularly important when designing an application that will be extended by another developer or used by third parties.

Now that we have a general idea of what interfaces are and how they're used, let's get down to some syntax details.

Interface Syntax and Use

Recall that an interface defines a new datatype without implementing any of the methods of that datatype. Thus, to create an interface, we use the following syntax:

```
interface SomeName {
    function method1 (param1:datatype,...paramn:datatype):returnType;
    function method2 (param1:datatype,...paramn:datatype):returnType;
    ...
    function methodn (param1:datatype,...paramn:datatype):returnType;
}
```

where *SomeName* is the name of the interface, *method1*, ...*methodn* are the methods in the interface, *param1:datatype*, ...*paramn:datatype* are the parameters of the methods, and *returnType* is the datatype of each method's return value.

In interfaces, method declarations do not (and must not) include curly braces. The following method declaration causes a compile-time error in an interface because it includes curly braces:

```
function method1 (param:datatype):returnType {
}
```

The error generated is:

```
Methods defined in an interface must not have a body.
```

All methods declared in an interface must not include an access-control modifier. Variable definitions are not allowed in ActionScript interfaces; neither can interface definitions be nested. However, interfaces can include get and set methods, which can be used to simulate variables (from the perspective of the code using the methods). Like class definitions, interface definitions can be placed directly within a *package* statement or outside of any *package* statement, but nowhere else.

As we saw in the preceding section, a class that wishes to adopt an interface's datatype must agree to implement that interface's methods. To form such an agreement, the class uses the *implements* keyword, which has the following syntax:

```
class SomeName implements SomeInterface {
}
```

In the preceding code, *SomeName* is the name of the class that promises to implement *SomeInterface*'s methods, and *SomeInterface* is the name of the interface. The *SomeName* class is said to "implement the *SomeInterface* interface." Note that *implements* must always come after any *extends* clause that might also be present. Furthermore, if you specify a class instead of an interface after the *implements* keyword, the compiler generates this error:

```
An interface can only extend other interfaces, but ClassName is a class.
```

The class *SomeName* must implement all methods defined by *SomeInterface*, otherwise a compile-time error such as the following occurs:

```
Interface method methodName in namespace InterfaceName not
    implemented by class ClassName.
```

The implementing class's method definitions must be public and must match the interface's method definitions exactly, including number of parameters, parameter types, and return type. If any of those aspects differs between the interface and the implementing class, the compiler generates the following error:

```
Interface method methodName in namespace InterfaceName is
    implemented with an incompatible signature in class ClassName.
```

A class can legally implement more than one interface by separating interface names with commas, as follows:

```
class SomeName implements SomeInterface, SomeOtherInterface {
}
```

in which case, instances of the class *SomeName* belongs to all three of the following datatypes: *SomeName*, *SomeInterface*, and *SomeOtherInterface*. If a class implements two interfaces that define a method by the same name, but with different signatures (i.e., method's name, parameter list, and return type), the compiler generates an error indicating that one of the methods was not implemented properly.

If, on the other hand, a class implements two interfaces that define a method by the same name and with the exact same signature, no error occurs. The real question is whether the class can provide the services required by both interfaces within a single method definition. In most cases, the answer is no.

 Once an interface has been implemented by one or more classes, adding new methods to it will cause compile-time errors in those implementing classes (because the classes won't define the new methods)! Hence, you should think carefully about the methods you want in an interface and be sure you're confident in your application's design before you commit it to code.

If a class declares that it implements an interface, but that interface cannot be found by the compiler, the following error occurs:

```
Interface InterfaceName was not found.
```

Interface Naming Conventions

Like classes, interfaces should be named with an initial capital letter so they're easy to identify as datatypes. Most interfaces are named after the additional ability they describe. For example, suppose an application contains a series of classes that represent visual objects. Some of the objects can be repositioned; others cannot. In our design, objects that can be repositioned must implement an interface named *Moveable*. Here is a theoretical *ProductIcon* class that implements *Moveable*:

```
public class ProductIcon implements Moveable {
  public function getPosition ():Point {
  }
  public function setPosition (pos:Point):void {
  }
}
```

The interface name, *Moveable*, indicates the specific capability that the interface adds to a class. An object might be a piece of clip art or a block of text, but if it implements *Moveable*, it can be repositioned. Other similar names might be *Storable*, *Killable*, or *Serializable*. Some developers also preface interface names with an "I," as in *IMoveable*, *IKillable*, and *ISerializable*.

Interface Inheritance

As with classes, an interface can use the *extends* keyword to inherit from another interface. For example, the following code shows an interface, *IntA*, that extends another interface, *IntB*. In this setup, interface *IntB* is known as the *subinterface,* and interface *IntA* is known as the *superinterface*.

```
public interface IntA {
  function methodA ():void;
}
public interface IntB extends IntA {
  function methodB ():void;
}
```

Classes that implement interface *IntB* must provide definitions for both *methodA()* and *methodB()*. Interface inheritance lets us define a type hierarchy much as we would with class inheritance, but without accompanying method implementations.

ActionScript interfaces also support multiple interface inheritance; that is, an interface can extend more than one interface. For example, consider the following three interface definitions:

```
public interface IntC {
  function methodC ():void;
}
```

```
public interface IntD {
  function methodD ():void;
}

public interface IntE extends IntC, IntD {
  function methodE ():void;
}
```

Because *IntE* extends both *IntC* and *IntD*, classes that implement interface *IntE* must provide definitions for *methodC()*, *methodD()*, and *methodE()*.

Marker Interfaces

Interfaces need not contain any methods at all to be useful. Occasionally, empty interfaces, called *marker interfaces*, are used to "mark" (designate) a class as having some feature. Requirements for the *marked classes* (classes implementing the marker interface) are provided by the documentation for the marker interface. For example, the Flash runtime API includes a marker interface, *IBitmapDrawable,* which designates a class as eligible for drawing into a *BitmapData* object. The *BitmapData* class will draw only those classes that implement *IBitmapDrawable* (even though *IBitmapDrawable* does not actually define any methods). The *IBitmapDrawable* interface is simply used to "approve" a given class for drawing into a bitmap. Here's the source code for the *IBitmapDrawable* interface:

```
package flash.display {
  interface IBitmapDrawable {
  }
}
```

Another Multiple-Type Example

In our earlier logging example, we learned that a class can inherit from another class while also implementing an interface. Instances of the subclass belong to both the superclass's datatype and the interface's datatype. For example, instances of the earlier *LogUI* class belonged to both the *Sprite* and *LogRecipient* datatypes because *LogUI* inherited from *Sprite* and implemented *LogRecipient*. Let's take a closer look at this important architectural structure with a new example.

 The following discussion requires a prior knowledge of arrays (ordered lists of values), which we haven't covered yet. If you are new to arrays, you should skip this section for now and return to it after you have read Chapter 11.

Suppose we're creating an application that stores objects on a server via a server-side script. Each stored object's class is responsible for providing a method, *serialize()*, that can return a string-representation of its instances. The string representation is used to reconstitute a given object from scratch.

One of the classes in the application is a simple *Rectangle* class with width, height, fillColor, and lineColor instance variables. To represent *Rectangle* objects as strings, the *Rectangle* class implements a *serialize()* method that returns a string of the following format:

```
"width=value|height=value|fillColor=value|lineColor=value"
```

To store a given *Rectangle* object on the server, we invoke *serialize()* on the object and send the resulting string to our server-side script. Later, we can retrieve that string and use it to create a new *Rectangle* instance matching the original's size and colors.

To keep things simple for this example, we'll presume that every stored object in the application must store only variable names and values. We'll also presume that no variable values are, themselves, objects that would need serialization.

When the time comes to save the state of our application, an instance of a custom *StorageManager* class performs the following tasks:

- Gathers objects for storage
- Converts each object to a string (via *serialize()*)
- Transfers the objects to disk

In order to guarantee that every stored object can be serialized (i.e., converted to a string), the *StorageManager* class rejects any instances of classes that do not belong to the *Serializable* datatype. Here's an excerpt from the *StorageManager* class that shows the method an object uses to register for storage—*addObject()* (notice that only instances belonging to the *Serializable* type can be passed to *addObject()*):

```
package {
  public class StorageManager {
    public function addObject (o:Serializable):void {
    }
  }
}
```

The *Serializable* datatype is defined by the interface *Serializable*, which contains a single method, *serialize()*, as follows:

```
package {
  public interface Serializable {
    function serialize():String;
  }
}
```

To handle the serialization process, we create a class, *Serializer*, which implements *Serializable*. The *Serializer* class provides the following general methods for serializing any object:

setSerializationObj()
  Specifies which object to serialize

setSerializationVars()
  Specifies which of the object's variables should be serialized

setRecordSeparator()

 Specifies the string to use as a separator between variables

serialize()

 Returns a string representing the object

Here's the class listing for *Serializer*:

```
package {
  public class Serializer implements Serializable {
    private var serializationVars:Array;
    private var serializationObj:Serializable;
    private var recordSeparator:String;

    public function Serializer () {
      setSerializationObj(this);
    }

    public function setSerializationVars (vars:Array):void {
      serializationVars = vars;
    }

    public function setSerializationObj (obj:Serializable):void {
      serializationObj = obj;
    }

    public function setRecordSeparator (rs:String):void {
      recordSeparator = rs;
    }

    public function serialize ():String {
      var s:String = "";
      // Notice that the loop counts down to 0, and performs the
      // iterator update (decrementing i) within the loop's test expression
      for (var i:int = serializationVars.length; --i >= 0; ) {
        s += serializationVars[i]
          + "=" + String(serializationObj[serializationVars[i]]);
        if (i > 0) {
          s += recordSeparator;
        }
      }
      return s;
    }
  }
}
```

To use the *Serializer* class's serialization services, a class can simply extend *Serializer*. By extending *Serializer* directly, the extending class inherits both the *Serializable* interface and the *Serializer* class's implementation of that interface.

Notice the general structure of our serialization system: *Serializer* implements *Serializable*, providing a generalized implementation for other classes to use via inheritance. But classes can still choose to implement *Serializable* directly, supplying their own custom behavior for the *serialize()* method.

For example, the following code shows a *Point* class that defines x and y variables, which need to be serialized. The *Point* class extends *Serializer* and uses *Serializer*'s services directly.

```
package {
  public class Point extends Serializer {
    public var x:Number;
    public var y:Number;

    public function Point (x:Number, y:Number) {
      super();

      setRecordSeparator(",");
      setSerializationVars(["x", "y"]);

      this.x = x;
      this.y = y;
    }
  }
}
```

Code that wishes to save a *Point* instance to disk simply calls *serialize()* on that instance, as follows:

```
var p:Point = new Point(5, 6);
trace(p.serialize());  // Displays: y=6,x=5
```

Notice that the *Point* class does not implement *Serializable* directly. It extends *Serializer*, which in turn implements *Serializable*.

The *Point* class does not extend any other class, so it's free to extend *Serializer*. However, if a class wants to use *Serializer* but already extends another class, it must use composition instead of inheritance. That is, rather than extending *Serializer*, the class implements *Serializable* directly, stores a *Serializer* object in an instance variable, and forwards *serialize()* method calls to that object. For example, here's the *Rectangle* class mentioned earlier. It extends a *Shape* class but uses *Serializer* via composition (refer specifically to the sections in bold):

```
// The Shape superclass
package {
 public class Shape {
    public var fillColor:uint = 0xFFFFFF;
    public var lineColor:uint = 0;

    public function Shape (fillColor:uint, lineColor:uint) {
      this.fillColor = fillColor;
      this.lineColor = lineColor;
    }
  }
}

// The Rectangle class
package {
  // The Rectangle subclass implements Serializable directly
```

```
public class Rectangle extends Shape implements Serializable {
  public var width:Number = 0;
  public var height:Number = 0;
  private var serializer:Serializer;

  public function Rectangle (fillColor:uint, lineColor:uint) {
    super(fillColor, lineColor)

    // Here is where the composition takes place
    serializer = new Serializer();
    serializer.setRecordSeparator("|");
    serializer.setSerializationVars(["height", "width",
                                     "fillColor", "lineColor"]);
    serializer.setSerializationObj(this);
  }

  public function setSize (w:Number, h:Number):void {
    width = w;
    height = h;
  }

  public function getArea ():Number {
    return width * height;
  }

  public function serialize ():String {
    // Here is where the Rectangle class forwards the serialize()
    // invocation to the Serializer instance stored in serializer
    return serializer.serialize();
  }
 }
}
```

As with the *Point* class, code that wishes to store a *Rectangle* instance simply invokes *serialize()* on that instance. Through composition, the invocation is forwarded to the *Serializer* instance stored by the *Rectangle* class. Here is an example of its use:

```
var r:Rectangle = new Rectangle(0xFF0000, 0x0000FF);
r.setSize(10, 15);
// Displays: lineColor=255|fillColor=16711680|width=10|height=15
trace(r.serialize());
```

If a class would rather implement its own custom *serialize()* method instead of using the generic one provided by *Serializer*, then the class simply implements the *Serializable* interface directly, providing the *serialize()* method definition and body itself.

Separating the *Serializable* datatype's interface from its implementation allows any class to flexibly choose from among the following options when providing an implementation for the *serialize()* method:

- Extend *Serializer*
- Use *Serializer* via composition
- Provide its own *serialize()* method directly

If the class does not already extend another class, it can extend *Serializer* (this option involves the least work). If the class already extends another class, it can still use *Serializer* via composition (this option is the most flexible). Finally, if the class needs its own special serialization routine, it can implement *Serializable* directly (this option involves the most work but may be required by the situation at hand).

The flexibility of the preceding structure led Sun Microsystems to formally recommend that, in a Java application, any class that is expected to be subclassed should be an implementation of an interface. As such, it can be subclassed directly, or it can be used via composition by a class that inherits from another class. Sun's recommendation is also sensible for large-scale ActionScript applications.

Figure 9-1 shows the generic structure of a datatype whose implementation can be used via either inheritance or composition.

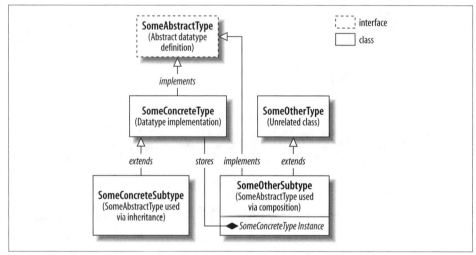

Figure 9-1. Multiple datatype inheritance via interfaces

Figure 9-2 shows the structure of the specific *Serializable*, *Point*, and *Rectangle* example.

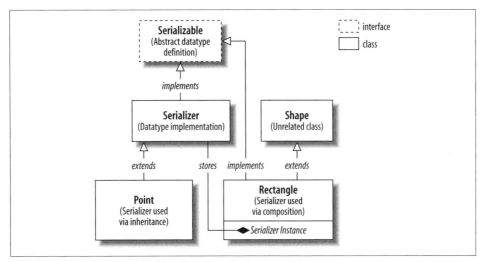

Figure 9-2. Multiple datatype inheritance Serializable example

More Essentials Coming

Having covered classes, objects, inheritance, datatypes, and interfaces, we've now finished our study of the basic concepts of object-oriented programming. In the remainder of Part I, we'll explore a variety of other fundamental topics in Action-Script. But the object-oriented concepts we've studied will never be far behind. Object-oriented programming is the true foundation of ActionScript. The concepts presented in remainder of this book will all build and rely upon that foundation.

Up next, an overview of ActionScript's statements and operators.

CHAPTER 10

Statements and Operators

This chapter provides a reference-style overview of ActionScript's statements and operators—many of which we've already seen in this book. Rather than discussing each statement and operator in isolation, this book teaches the use of statements and operators in the context of other programming topics. Accordingly, this chapter lists many crossreferences to discussion and usage examples found elsewhere in this book. For information on operators not covered in this book, see Adobe's Action-Script Language Reference.

Statements

Statements are one kind of directive, or basic program instruction, consisting of a keyword (command name reserved for use by the ActionScript language) and, typically, a supporting expression.

Table 10-1 lists ActionScript's statements, their syntax, and purpose.

Table 10-1. ActionScript statements

Statement	Usage	Description
break	break	Aborts a loop or *switch* statement. See Chapter 2.
case	case *expression*: *substatements*	Identifies a statement to be executed conditionally in a *switch* statement. See Chapter 2.
continue	continue;	Skips the remaining statements in the current loop and begins the next iteration at the top of the loop. See Adobe documentation.
default	default: *substatements*	Identifies the statement(s) to execute in a *switch* statement when the test expression does not match any *case* clauses. See Chapter 2.
do-while	do { *substatements* } while (*expression*);	A variation of a *while* loop that ensures at least one iteration of the loop is performed. See Chapter 2.

Table 10-1. ActionScript statements (continued)

Statement	Usage	Description

for	```for (init; test; update) {```
	``` statements```
	```}```
		Executes a statement block repetitively (a *for* loop). It is synonymous with a *while* loop but places the loop initialization and update statements together with the test expression at the top of the loop. See Chapter 2.

for-in	```for (variable in object) {```
	``` statements```
	```}```
		Enumerates the names of the dynamic instance variables of an object or an array's elements. See Chapter 15.

for-each-in	```for each```
	```(variableOrElementValue in```
	```object) {```
	``` statements```
	```}```
		Enumerates the values of an object's dynamic instance variables or an array's elements. See Chapter 15.

if-else if-else	```if (expression) {```
	``` substatements```
	```} else if (expression) {```
	``` substatements```
	```} else {```
	``` substatements```
	```}```
		Executes one or more statements, based on a condition or a series of conditions. See Chapter 2.

label	```label: statement``` ```label: statements```	Associates a statement with an identifier. Used with *break* or *continue*. See Adobe documentation.
return	```return;``` ```return expression;```	Exits and optionally returns a value from a function. See Chapter 5.

super	```super(arg1, arg2, ...argn)```
	```super.method(arg1, arg2, ..```
	```.argn)```
		Invokes a superclass's constructor method or overridden instance method. See Chapter 6.

switch	```switch (expression) {```
	``` substatements```
	```}```
		Executes specified code, based on a condition or a series of conditions (alternative to *if-else if-else*). See Chapter 2.

throw	```throw expression```	Issues a runtime exception (error). See Chapter 13.

try/catch/finally	```try {```
	``` // Code that might```
	``` // generate an exception```
	```} catch (error:ErrorType1) {```
	``` // Error-handling code```
	``` // for ErrorType1.```
	```} catch (error:ErrorTypeN) {```
	``` // Error-handling code```
	``` // for ErrorTypeN.```
	```} finally {```
	``` // Code that always```
	```executes```
	```}```
		Wraps a block of code to respond to potential runtime exceptions. See Chapter 13.

while	```while (expression) {```
	``` substatements```
	```}```
		Executes a statement block repetitively (a *while* loop). See Chapter 2.

with	```with (object) {```
	``` substatements```
	```}```
		Executes a statement block in the scope of a given object. See Chapter 16.

Operators

An *operator* is a symbol or keyword that manipulates, combines, or transforms data. For example, the following code uses the multiplication operator (*) to multiply 5 times 6:

```
5 * 6;
```

Though each operator has its own specialized task, all operators share a number of general characteristics. Before we consider the operators individually, let's see how they behave generally.

Operators perform actions using the data values (*operands*) supplied. For example, in the operation 5 * 6, the numbers 5 and 6 are the *operands* of the multiplication operator (*).

Operations can be combined to form complex expressions. For example:

```
((width * height) - (Math.PI * radius * radius)) / 2
```

When expressions become very large, consider using variables to hold interim results for both convenience and clarity. Remember to name your variables descriptively. For example, the following code has the same result as the preceding expression but is much easier to read:

```
var radius:int = 10;
var height:int = 25;
var circleArea:Number = (Math.PI * radius * radius);
var cylinderVolume:Number = circleArea * height;
```

Number of Operands

Operators are sometimes categorized according to how many operands they take (i.e., require or *operate on*). Some ActionScript operators take one operand, some take two, and one even takes three:

```
-x                                      // One operand
x * y                                   // Two operands
(x == y) ? "true result" : "false result"  // Three operands
```

Single-operand operators are called *unary* operators; operators that take two operands are called *binary* operators; operators that take three operands are called *ternary* operators. For our purposes, we'll look at operators according to what they do, not the number of operands they take.

Operator Precedence

Operators' *precedence* determines which operation is performed first in an expression with multiple operators. For example, when multiplication and addition occur in the same expression, multiplication is performed first:

```
4 + 5 * 6 // Yields 34, because 4 + 30 = 34
```

The expression 4 + 5 * 6 is evaluated as "4 plus the product of 5 * 6" because the * operator has higher precedence than the + operator.

Similarly, when the less-than (<) and concatenation (+) operators occur in the same expression, concatenation is performed first. For example, suppose we want to compare two strings and then display the result of that comparison during debugging. Without knowing the precedence of the < and + operators, we might mistakenly use the following code:

```
trace("result: " + "a" < "b");
```

Due precedence of the < and + operators, the preceding code yields the value:

```
false
```

whereas we were expecting it to yield:

```
result: true
```

To determine the result of the expression "result: " + "a" < "b", ActionScript performs the concatenation operation first (because + has a higher precedence than <). The result of concatenating "result: " with "a" is a new string, "result: a". ActionScript then compares that new string with "b", which yields false because the first character in "result: a" is alphabetically greater than "b".

When in doubt, or to ensure a different order of operation, use parentheses, which have the highest precedence:

```
"result: " + ("a" < "b")  // Yields: "result: true"
(4 + 5) * 6               // Yields 54, because 9 * 6 = 54
```

Even if not strictly necessary, parentheses can make a complicated expression more readable. The expression:

```
x > y || y == z  // x is greater than y, or y equals z
```

may be difficult to comprehend without consulting a precedence table. It's a lot easier to read with parentheses added:

```
(x > y) || (y == z)  // Much better!
```

The precedence of each operator is listed later in Table 10-2.

Operator Associativity

As we've just seen, operator precedence indicates the pecking order of operators: those with a higher precedence are executed before those with a lower precedence. But what happens when multiple operators occur together and have the same level of precedence? In such a case, we apply the rules of *operator associativity*, which indicate the direction of an operation. Operators are either left-associative (performed left to right) or right-associative (performed right to left). For example, consider this expression:

```
b * c / d
```

The * and / operators are left-associative, so the * operation on the left (b * c) is performed first. The preceding example is equivalent to:

```
(b * c) / d
```

In contrast, the = (assignment) operator is right-associative, so the expression:

```
a = b = c = d
```

says, "assign d to c, then assign c to b, then assign b to a," as in:

```
a = (b = (c = d))
```

Unary operators are right-associative; binary operators are left-associative, except for the assignment operators, which are right-associative. The conditional operator (?:) is also right-associative. Operator associativity is fairly intuitive, but if you're getting an unexpected value from a complex expression, add extra parentheses to force the desired order of operations. For further information on operator associativity in ActionScript, see Adobe's documentation.

Datatypes and Operators

The operands of most operators are typed. In strict mode, if a value used for an operand does not match that operand's datatype, the compiler generates a compile-time error and refuses to compile the code. In standard mode, the code compiles, and at runtime, if the operand's type is a primitive type, ActionScript converts the value to the operand's datatype (according to the rules described in Chapter 8, in the section "Conversion to Primitive Types"). If the operand's type is not a primitive type, ActionScript generates a runtime error.

For example, in strict mode, the following code causes a type mismatch error because the datatype of the division (/) operator's operands is *Number*, and the value "50" does not belong to the *Number* datatype:

```
"50" / 10
```

In standard mode, the preceding code does not cause a compile-time error. Instead, at runtime, ActionScript converts the *String* value "50" to the *Number* datatype, yielding 50, and the entire expression has the value 5.

To compile the preceding code without causing an error in strict mode, we must cast the *String* value to the required datatype, as follows:

```
Number("50") / 10
```

Some operators' operands are untyped, which allows the result of the operation to be determined at runtime based on the datatypes of the supplied values. The + operator, for example, performs addition when used with two numeric operands, but it performs concatenation when either operand is a string.

The datatypes of each operator's operands are listed in Adobe's ActionScript Language Reference.

Operator Overview

Table 10-2 lists ActionScript's operators, their precedence value, a brief description, and a typical example of their use. Operators with the highest precedence (at the top of the table) are executed first. Operators with the same precedence are performed in the order they appear in the expression, usually from left to right, unless the associativity is right to left.

Note that with the exception of the E4X operators, this book does not provide exhaustive reference information for ActionScript's operators. For details on a specific operator, consult Adobe's ActionScript Language Reference. For information on the bitwise operators, see the article "Using Bitwise Operators in ActionScript" at *http://www.moock.org/asdg/technotes/bitwise*.

Table 10-2. ActionScript operators

Operator	Precedence	Description	Example

.	15	Multiple uses:	`// Access a variable`
			`product.price`
			`// Reference a class`
			`flash.display.Sprite`
			`// Access an XML child element`
			`novel.TITLE`

		• Accesses a variable or method	
		• Separates package names from class names and other package names	
		• Accesses children of an *XML* or *XMLList* object (E4X)	

[]	15	Multiple uses:	`// Initialize an array`
			`["apple", "orange", "pear"]`
			`// Access fourth element of an array`
			`list[3]`
			`// Access a variable`
			`product["price"]`
			`// Access an XML child element`
			`novel["TITLE"]`

		• Initializes an array	
		• Accesses an array element	
		• Accesses a variable or method using any expression that yields a string	
		• Accesses children or attributes of an *XML* or *XMLList* object (E4X)	

()	15	Multiple uses:	`// Force addition before multiplication`
			`(5 + 4) * 2`
			`// Invoke a function`
			`trace()`
			`// Filter an XMLList`
			`staff.*.(SALARY <= 35000)`

		• Specifies a custom order of operations (precedence)	
		• Invokes a function or method	
		• Contains an E4X filtering predicate	
@	15	Accesses XML attributes	`// Retrieve all attributes of novel` `novel.@*`
::	15	Separates a qualifier namespace from a name	`// Qualify orange with namespace fruit` `fruit::orange`

..	15	Accesses XML descendants	`// Retrieve all descendant elements`
			`// of loan named DIRECTOR`
			`loan..DIRECTOR`

{x:y}	15	Creates a new object and initializes its dynamic variables	`// Create an object with dynamic variables,`
			`// width and height`
			`{width:30, height:5}`

new	15	Creates an instance of a class	`// Create TextField instance` `new TextField()`

Table 10-2. ActionScript operators (continued)

Operator	Precedence	Description	Example
`<tag></tag>`	15	Defines an XML element	`// Create an XML element named BOOK` `<BOOK>Essential ActionScript 3.0</BOOK>`
`x++`	14	Adds one to *x* and returns *x*'s former value (postfix increment)	`// Increase i by 1, and return i` `i++`
`x--`	14	Subtracts one from *x* and returns *x*'s former value (postfix decrement)	`// Decrease i by 1, and return i` `i--`
`++x`	14	Adds one to *x* and returns *x*'s new value (prefix increment)	`// Increase i by 1, and return the result` `++i`
`--x`	14	Subtracts one from *x* and returns *x*'s new value (prefix decrement)	`// Decrease i by 1, and return the result` `--i`

`-`	14	Switches the operand's sign (positive becomes negative, and negative becomes positive)	`var a:int = 10;`
			`// Assign -10 to b`
			`var b:int = -b;`

`~`	14	Performs a bitwise NOT	`// Clear bit 2 of options` `options &= ~4;`

`!`	14	Returns the Boolean opposite of its single operand	`// If under18's value is not true,`
			`// execute conditional body`
			`if (!under18) {`
			`  trace("You can apply for a credit card")`
			`}`

`delete`	14	Multiple uses:
		
		• Removes the value of an array element
		• Removes an object's dynamic instance variable
		• Removes an XML element or attribute
			`// Create an array`
			`var genders:Array = ["male","female"]`
			`// Remove the first element's value`
			`delete genders[0];`
			`// Create an object`
			`var o:Object = new Object();`
			`o.a = 10;`
			`// Remove dynamic instance variable a`
			`delete o.a;`
			`// Remove the <TITLE> element from the XML`
			`// object referenced by novel`
			`delete novel.TITLE;`

179

Table 10-2. ActionScript operators (continued)

Operator	Precedence	Description	Example
typeof	14	Returns a simple string description of various types of objects. Used for backwards compatibility with ActionScript 1.0 and ActionScript 2.0 only.	`// Retrieve string description of 35's type` `typeof 35`

void	14	Returns the value undefined	`var o:Object = new Object();`
			`o.a = 10;`
			`// Compare undefined to the value of o.a`
			`if (o.a == void) {`
			`  trace("o.a does not exist, or has no value");`
			`}`

*	13	Multiplies two numbers	`// Calculate four times six` `4 * 6`
/	13	Divides left operand by right operand	`// Calculate 30 divided by 5` `30 / 5`
%	13	Returns the remainder (i.e., *modulus*) that results when the left operand is divided by the right operand	`// Calculate remainder of 14 divided by 4` `14 % 4`

+	12	Multiple uses:
		• Adds two numbers
		• Combines(concatenate) two strings
		• Combines (concatenate) two XML or XMLList objects
			`// Calculate 25 plus 10`
			`25 + 10`
			`// Combine "He" and "llo" to form "Hello"`
			`"He" + "llo"`
			`// Combine two XML objects`
			`<JOB>Programmer</JOB> + <AGE>52</AGE>`

-	12	Subtracts right operand from left operand	`// Subtract 2 from 12` `12 - 2`
<<	11	Performs a bitwise left shift	`// Shift 9 four bits to the left` `9 << 4`
>>	11	Performs a bitwise signed right shift	`// Shift 8 one bit to the right` `8 >> 1`

>>>	11	Performs a bitwise unsigned right shift	`// Shift 8 one bit to the right, filling`
			`// vacated bits with zeros`
			`8 >>> 1`

Table 10-2. ActionScript operators (continued)

Operator	Precedence	Description	Example
`<`	10	Checks if the left operand is less than the right operand. Depending upon the evaluation of the operands, returns true or false.	```// Check if 5 is less than 6
5 < 6
// Check if "a" has a lower character code point
// than "z"
"a" < "z"```
`<=`	10	Checks if the left operand is less than or equal to the right operand. Depending on the evaluation of the operands, returns true or false.	```// Check if 10 is less than or equal to 5
10 <= 5
// Check if "C" has a lower character code point
// than "D", or the same code point as "D"
"C" <= "D"```
`>`	10	Checks if the left operand is greater than the right operand. Depending upon the evaluation of the operands, returns true or false.	```// Check if 5 is greater than 6
5 > 6
// Check if "a" has a higher character code point
// than "z"
"a" > "z"```
`>=`	10	Checks if the left operand is greater than or equal to the right operand. Depending on the evaluation of the operands, returns true or false.	```// Check if 10 is greater than or equal to 5
10 >= 5
// Check if "C" has a higher character code point
// than "D", or the same code point as "D"
"C" >= "D"```
`as`		Checks if the left operand belongs to the datatype specified by the right operand. If yes, returns the object; otherwise returns null	```var d:Date = new Date()
// Check if d's value belongs to
// the Date datatype
d as Date```
`is`		Checks if the left operand belongs to the datatype specified by the right operand. If yes, returns the true; otherwise returns false.	```var a:Array = new Array()
// Check if a's value belongs to
// the Array datatype
a is Array```
`in`		Checks if an object has a specified public instance variable or public instance method. Depending on the evaluation of the operands, returns true or false.	```var d:Date = new Date()
// Check if d's value has a public variable or
// public method named getMonth
"getMonth" in d```

Table 10-2. ActionScript operators (continued)

Operator	Precedence	Description	Example

instanceof	10	Checks if the left operand's prototype chain includes the right operand. Depending on the evaluation of the operands, returns true or false.	`var s:Sprite = new Sprite()`
			`// Check if s's value's prototype chain`
			`// includes DisplayObject`
			`s instanceof DisplayObject`

==	9	Checks whether two expressions are considered equal (equality). Depending on the evaluation of the operands, returns true or false.	`// Check whether the expression "hi" is equal to`
			`// the expression "hello"`
			`"hi" == "hello"`

!=	9	Checks whether two expressions are considered not equal (in equality). Depending upon the evaluation of the operands, returns true or false.	`// Check whether the expression 3 is not equal to`
			`// the expression 3`
			`3 != 3`

===	9	Checks whether two expressions are considered equal without datatype conversion for primitive types (strict equality). Depending on the evaluation of the operands, returns true or false.	`// Check whether the expression "3" is equal to`
			`// the expression 3. This code compiles in`
			`// standard mode only.`
			`"3" === 3`

!==	9	Checks whether two expressions are considered not equal without datatype conversion for primitive types (strict equality). Depending on the evaluation of the expression, returns true or false.	`// Check whether the expression "3" is not equal to`
			`// the expression 3. This code compiles in`
			`// standard mode only.`
			`"3" === 3`

&	8	Performs a bitwise AND	`// Combine bits of 15 and 4 using bitwise AND` `15 & 4`
^	7	Performs a bitwise XOR	`// Combine bits of 15 and 4 using bitwise XOR` `15 ^ 4`
|	6	Performs a bitwise OR	`// Combine bits of 15 and 4 using bitwise OR` `15 | 4`

&&	5	Compares two expressions using a logical *AND* operation. If the left operand is false or converts to false, && returns the left operand; otherwise && returns the right operand.	`var validUser:Boolean = true;`
			`var validPassword:Boolean = false;`
			`// Check if both validUser and validPassword`
			`// are true`
			`if (validUser || validPassword) {`
			`    // Do login...`
			`}`

Table 10-2. ActionScript operators (continued)

Operator	Precedence	Description	Example

`||`	4	Compares two expressions using a logical *OR* operation. If the left operand is `true` or converts to `true`, `||` returns the left operand; otherwise `||` returns the right operand.	```var promotionalDay:Boolean = false;```
			 ```var registeredUser:Boolean = false;```
			 ```// Check if either promotionalDay or registeredUser```
			 ```// is true```
			 ```if (promotionalDay || registeredUser) {```
			 ``` // Show premium content...```
			 ```}```

`?:`	3	Performs a simple conditional. If the first operand is `true` or converts to `true`, the value of the second operand is evaluated and returned. Otherwise, the value of the third operand is evaluated and returned.	```// Invoke one of two methods based on```
			 ```// whether soundMuted is true```
			 ```soundMuted ? displayVisualAlarm() : playAudioAlarm()```

`=`	2	Assigns a value to a variable or array element	```// Assign 36 to variable age```
			 ```var age:int = 36;```
			 ```// Assign a new array to variable seasons```
			 ```var seasons:Array = new Array();```
			 ```// Assign "winter" to first element of seasons```
			 ```seasons[0] = "winter";```

`+=`	2	Adds (or concatenates) and reassigns	```// Add 10 to n's value```
			 ```n += 10; // same as n = n + 10;```
			 ```// Add an exclamation mark to the end of msg```
			 ```msg += "!"```
			 ```// Add an <AUTHOR> tag after the first <AUTHOR>```
			 ```// tag child of novel```
			 ```novel.AUTHOR[0] += <AUTHOR>Dave Luxton</AUTHOR>;```

`-=`	2	Subtracts and reassigns	```// Subtract 10 from n's value``` ```n -= 10; // same as n = n - 10;```
`*=`	2	Multiplies and reassigns	```// Multiply n's value by 10``` ```n *= 10; // same as n = n * 10;```
`/=`	2	Divides and reassigns	```// Divide n's value by 10``` ```n /= 10; // same as n = n / 10;```
`%=`	2	Performs modulo division and reassigns	```// Assign n%4 to n``` ```n %= 4; // same as n = n % 4;```

Table 10-2. ActionScript operators (continued)

Operator	Precedence	Description	Example
<<=	2	Shifts bits left and reassigns	`// Shift n's bits two places to the left` `n <<= 2; // same as n = n << 2;`
>>=	2	Shifts bits right and reassigns	`// Shift n's bits two places to the right` `n >>= 2; // same as n = n >> 2;`

>>>=	2	Shifts bits right (unsigned) and reassigns	`// Shift n's bits two places to the right, filling`
			`// vacated bits with zeros`
			`n >>>= 2; // same as n = n >>> 2;`

&=	2	Performs bitwise AND and reassigns	`// Combine n's bits with 4 using bitwise AND` `n &= 4 // same as n = n & 4;`
^=	2	Performs bitwise XOR and reassigns	`// Combine n's bits with 4 using bitwise XOR` `n ^= 4 // same as n = n ^ 4;`
|=	2	Performs bitwise OR and reassigns	`// Combine n's bits with 4 using bitwise OR` `n |= 4 // same as n = n | 4;`

,	1	Evaluates left operand, then right operand	`// Initialize and increment two loop counters`
			`for (var i:int = 0, j:int = 10; i < 5; i++, j++) {`
			`  // i counts from 0 through 4`
			`  // j counts from 10 through 14`
			`}`

Up Next: Managing Lists of Information

This chapter covered some of ActionScript's basic built-in programming tools. In the next chapter, we'll study another essential ActionScript tool: arrays. Arrays are used to manage lists of information.

CHAPTER 11

Arrays

Arrays store and manipulate ordered lists of information and are, therefore, a fundamental tool in sequential, repetitive programming. We use arrays to do everything from storing user input, to generating pull-down menus, to keeping track of enemy spacecraft in a game. Practically speaking, an array is just a list of items, like your grocery list or the entries in your checkbook ledger. The items just happen to be ActionScript values.

What Is an Array?

An array is a data structure that can encompass multiple individual data values in an ordered list. Here is a simple example showing two separate strings, followed by an array that contains two strings:

```
"cherries"              // A single string
"peaches"               // Another string
["oranges", "apples"]   // A single array containing two strings
```

An array can contain any number of items, including items of different types. An array can even contain other arrays. Here is a simple example showing an array that contains both strings and numbers. It might represent your shopping list, showing how many of each item you intend to buy:

```
["oranges", 6, "apples", 4, "bananas", 3];
```

Though an array can keep track of many values, it's important to recognize that the array itself is a single data value. Arrays are represented as instances of the *Array* class. As such, an array can be assigned to a variable or used as part of a complex expression:

```
// Assign an array to a variable
var product:Array = ["ladies downhill skis", 475];

// Pass that array to a function
display(product);
```

The Anatomy of an Array

Each item in an array is called an array *element*, and each element has a unique numeric position (*index*) by which we can refer to it.

Array Elements

Like a variable, each array element can be assigned any value. An entire array, then, is akin to a collection of sequentially named variables, but instead of each item having a different name, each item has an element number (the first element is number 0, not number 1). To manipulate the values in an array's elements, we ask for them by number.

Array Element Indexing

An element's position in the array is known as its index. We use an element's index to set or retrieve the element's value or to work with the element in various ways. Some of the array-handling methods, for example, use element indexes to specify ranges of elements for processing.

We can also insert and delete elements from the beginning, end, or even middle of an array. An array can have gaps (that is, some elements can be empty). We can have elements at positions 0 and 4, without requiring anything in positions 1, 2, and 3. Arrays with gaps are called *sparse arrays*.

Array Size

At any point during its life span, a given array has a specific number of elements (both empty and occupied). The number of elements in an array is called the array's *length*, which we'll discuss later in this chapter.

Creating Arrays

To create a new array, we use an array literal or the *new* operator (i.e., new Array( )).

Creating Arrays with Array Literals

In an array literal, square brackets demarcate the beginning and end of the array. Inside the square brackets, the values of the array's elements are specified as a comma-separated list. Here's the general syntax:

```
[expression1, expression2, expression3]
```

Arrays in Other Programming Languages

Almost every high-level computer language supports arrays or array-like entities. That said, there are differences in the ways arrays are implemented across different languages. For example, many languages do not allow arrays to contain differing types of data. In many languages, an array can contain numbers or strings, but not both in the same array. Interestingly, in C, there is no primitive *string* datatype. Instead, C has a single-character datatype named *char*; strings are considered a complex datatype and are implemented as an array of *chars*.

In ActionScript, the size of an array changes automatically as items are added or removed. In many languages, the size of an array must be specified when the array is first *declared* or *dimensioned* (i.e., when memory is *allocated* to hold the array's data).

Languages differ as to what happens when a program attempts to access an element whose index is outside the bounds (limits) of the array. ActionScript adds elements if a program attempts to set a value for an element beyond the existing bounds of the array. If a program attempts to access an element by an index outside the array bounds, ActionScript returns undefined, whereas C, for example, pays no attention to whether the element number is valid. It lets the program retrieve and set elements outside the bounds of the array, which usually results in the access of meaningless data that is not part of the array, or causes other data in memory to be overwritten (C gives you plenty of rope with which to hang yourself).

The expressions are resolved and then assigned to the elements of the array being defined. Any valid expression can be used, including function calls, variables, literals, and even other arrays (an array within an array is called a *nested* array or a *two-dimensional array*).

Here are a few examples:

```
// Simple numeric elements
[4, 5, 63];

// Simple string elements
 ["apple", "orange", "pear"]

// Numeric expressions with an operation
[1, 4, 6 + 10]

// Variable values and strings as elements
[firstName, lastName, "tall", "skinny"]

// A nested array literal
["month end days", [31, 30, 28]]
```

Creating Arrays with the new Operator

To create an array with the *new* operator, we use the following generalized code:

```
new Array(arguments)
```

The result of the preceding code depends on the number and type of arguments supplied to the *Array* constructor. When more than one argument is supplied, or when a single nonnumeric argument is supplied, each argument becomes one of the element values in the new array. For example, the following code creates an array with three elements:

```
new Array("sun", "moon", "earth")
```

When exactly one numeric argument is supplied to the *Array()* constructor, it creates an array with the specified number of empty placeholder elements (creating such an array with an array literal is cumbersome). For example, the following code creates an array with 14 empty elements:

```
new Array(14)
```

Arguments passed to the *Array()* constructor can be any legal expression, including compound expressions. For example, the following code creates an array whose first element is an 11 and second element is 50:

```
var x:int = 10;
var y:int = 5;
var numbers:Array = new Array(x + 1, x * y);
```

For direct comparison, the following code creates the arrays from the previous section, but using the *new* operator instead of array literals:

```
new Array(4, 5, 63)
new Array("apple", "orange", "pear")
new Array(1, 4, 6 + 10)
new Array(firstName, lastName, "tall", "skinny")
new Array("month end days", new Array(31, 30, 28))
```

Referencing Array Elements

Once we've created an array, we'll inevitably want to retrieve or change the value of its elements. To do so, we use the *array access operator*, [].

Retrieving an Element's Value

To access an individual element, we provide a reference to the array followed by the element's index within square brackets, as follows:

```
theArray[elementNumber]
```

In the preceding code, *theArray* is a reference to the array (usually a variable with an array as a value), and *elementNumber* is an integer specifying the element's index. The first element is number 0, and the last element number is 1 less than the array's length. Specifying an element number greater than the last valid element number causes ActionScript to return undefined (because the specified index is outside the bounds of the array).

Let's try retrieving some element values. The following code creates an array using an array literal, and assigns it to the variable trees:

```
var trees:Array = ["birch", "maple", "oak", "cedar"];
```

The following code assigns the value of the first element of trees ("birch") to a variable, firstTree:

```
var firstTree:String = trees[0];
```

The following code assigns the third element's value ("oak") to the variable favoriteTree (remember that indexes start at 0, so index 2 is the third element!)

```
var favoriteTree:String = trees[2];
```

Now here's the fun part. Because we can specify the index of an element as any number-yielding expression, we can use variables or complex expressions just as easily as we use numbers to specify an element index. For example, the following code assigns the fourth element's value ("cedar") to the variable lastTree:

```
var i = 3;
var lastTree:String = trees[i];
```

We can even use call expressions that have numeric return values as array indexes. For example, the following code sets randomTree to a randomly chosen element of trees by calculating a random number between 0 and 3:

```
var randomTree:String = trees[Math.floor(Math.random( ) * 4)];
```

Nice. You might use a similar approach to pick a random question from an array of trivia questions or to pick a random card from an array that represents a deck of cards.

Note that accessing an array element is very similar to accessing a variable value. Array elements can be used as part of any complex expression, as follows:

```
var ages:Array = [12, 4, 90];
var totalAge:Number = ages[0] + ages[1] + ages[2];   // Sum the array
```

Summing the values of an array's elements manually isn't exactly the paragon of optimized code. Later, we'll see a much more convenient way to access an array's elements sequentially.

Setting an Element's Value

To set an element's value, we use *arrayName[elementNumber]* as the left-side operand of an assignment expression. The following code demonstrates:

```
// Make an array
var cities:Array = ["Toronto", "Montreal", "Vancouver", "Waterloo"];
// cities is now: ["Toronto", "Montreal", "Vancouver", "Waterloo"]
```

```
// Set the value of the array's first element
cities[0] = "London";
// cities becomes ["London", "Montreal", "Vancouver", "Waterloo"]

// Set the value of the array's fourth element
cities[3] = "Hamburg";
// cities becomes ["London", "Montreal", "Vancouver", "Hamburg"]

// Set the value of the array's third element
cities[2] = 293.3;  // Notice that the datatype change is not a problem
// cities becomes ["London", "Montreal", 293.3, "Hamburg"]
```

Note that we can use any nonnegative numeric expression as the index when setting an array element:

```
var i:int = 1;
// Set the value of element i
cities[i] = "Tokyo";
// cities becomes ["London", "Tokyo", 293.3, "Hamburg"]
```

Determining the Size of an Array

All arrays come with an instance variable named length, which indicates the current number of elements in the array (including undefined elements). To access an array's length variable, we use the dot operator, like so:

> *theArray*.length

Here are a few examples:

```
var list:Array = [34, 45, 57];
trace(list.length);             // Displays: 3

var words:Array = ["this", "that", "the other"];
trace(words.length);            // Displays: 3

var cards:Array = new Array(24);  // Note the single numeric argument
                                  // used with the Array( ) constructor
trace(cards.length);            // Displays: 24
```

The length of an array is always 1 greater than the index of its last element. For example, an array with elements at indexes 0, 1, and 2 has a length of 3. And an array with elements at indexes 0, 1, 2, and 50 has a length of 51. 51? Yes, 51. Even though indexes 3 through 49 are empty, they still contribute to the length of the array. The index of the last element of an array is always *theArray*.length - 1 (because index numbers begin at 0, not 1). Therefore, to access the last element of *theArray*, we use the following code:

> *theArray*[*theArray*.length - 1]

If we add and remove elements, the array's length variable is updated to reflect our changes. In fact, we can even set the length variable to add or remove elements at the end of an array. This is in contrast to the *String* class's length variable, which is read-only. Shortening the length of an array removes elements beyond the new length.

Using an array's length variable, we can create a loop that accesses all the elements of an array. Looping through an array's elements is a fundamental task in programming. To get a sense of what's possible when we combine loops and arrays, study Example 11-1, which hunts through a soundtracks array to find the location of the element with the value "hip hop."

Example 11-1. Searching an array

```
// Create an array
var soundtracks:Array = ["electronic", "hip hop",
                          "pop", "alternative", "classical"];

// Check each element to see if it contains "hip hop"
for (var i:int = 0; i < soundtracks.length; i++) {
  trace("Now examining element: " + i);
  if (soundtracks[i] == "hip hop") {
    trace("The location of 'hip hop' is index: " + i);
    break;
  }
}
```

Let's extend Example 11-1 into a generalized search method that can check any array for any matching element. The method will return the position within the array where the element was found or -1 if it was not found. Example 11-2 shows the code.

Example 11-2. A generalized array-searching function

```
public function searchArray (theArray:Array, searchElement:Object):int {
  // Check each element to see if it contains searchElement
  for (var i:int = 0; i < theArray.length; i++) {
    if (theArray[i] == searchElement) {
      return i;
    }
  }
  return -1;
}
```

Here's how to use our new search method to check whether or not "Dan" is one of the names in our userNames array, which is a hypothetical array of authorized usernames:

```
if (searchArray(userNames, "Dan") == -1) {
  trace("Sorry, that username wasn't found");
} else {
  trace("Welcome to the game, Dan.");
}
```

 The *searchArray()* method demonstrates the code required to loop through an array's elements but is not intended for use in a real program. To search for a given element's index in a real program, you should use the *Array* class's *indexOf()* and *lastIndexOf()* methods.

The remainder of this chapter explains more about the mechanics of manipulating arrays, including the use of *Array* methods.

Adding Elements to an Array

To add elements to an array, we use one of the following techniques:

- Specify a value for a new element at an index equal to or greater than the array's length
- Increase the array's length variable
- Invoke *push()*, *unshift()*, *splice()* or *concat()* on the array

The following sections discuss these techniques in detail.

Adding New Elements Directly

To add a new element to an existing array at a specific index, we simply assign a value to that element. The following code demonstrates:

```
// Create an array, and assign it three values
var fruits:Array = ["apples", "oranges", "pears"];

// Add a fourth value
fruits[3] = "tangerines";
```

The new element does not need to be placed immediately after the last element of the array. If we place the new element more than one element beyond the end of the array, ActionScript automatically creates undefined elements for the intervening indexes:

```
// Leave indexes 4 to 38 empty
fruits[39] = "grapes";

trace(fruits[12]); // Displays: undefined
```

If the element already exists, it will be replaced by the new value. If the element doesn't exist, it will be added.

Adding New Elements with the length Variable

To extend an array without assigning values to new elements, we can simply increase the length variable, and ActionScript will add enough elements to reach that length:

```
// Create an array with three elements
var colors = ["green", "red", "blue"];
// Add 47 empty elements, numbered 3 through 49, to the array
colors.length = 50;
```

You can use this approach to create a number of empty elements to hold some data you expect to accumulate, such as student test scores. Even though the elements are empty, they can still be used to indicate that an expected value has not yet been assigned. For example, a loop that displays test scores on screen could generate default output, "No Score Available," for empty elements.

Adding New Elements with Array Methods

We can use *Array* methods to handle more complex element-addition operations.

The push( ) method

The *push()* method appends one or more elements to the end of an array. It automatically appends the data after the last numbered element of the array, so there's no need to worry about how many elements already exist. The *push()* method can also append multiple elements to an array at once. The *push()* method has the following general form:

```
theArray.push(item1, item2,...itemn);
```

In the preceding code, *theArray* is a reference to an *Array* object, and *item1, item2, ...itemn* is a comma-separated list of items to be appended to the end of the array as new elements. Here are some examples:

```
// Create an array with two elements
var menuItems:Array = ["home", "quit"];

// Add an element
menuItems.push("products");
// menuItems becomes ["home", "quit", "products"]

// Add two more elements
menuItems.push("services", "contact");
// menuItems becomes ["home", "quit", "products", "services", "contact"]
```

The *push()* method returns the new length of the updated array (i.e., the value of the length variable):

```
var list:Array = [12, 23, 98];
trace(myList.push(28, 36));
// Appends 28 and 36 to list and displays: 5
```

Note that the items added to the list can be any expression. The expression is resolved before being added to the list:

```
var temperature:int = 22;
var sky:String = "sunny";
var weatherListing:Array = new Array();

// Add 22 and "sunny" to the array
weatherListing.push(temperature, sky);
```

The unshift( ) method

The *unshift()*method is much like *push()*, but it adds one or more elements to the beginning of the array, bumping all existing elements up to make room (i.e., the

Pushing, Popping, and Stacks

The *push()* method takes its name from a programming concept called a *stack*. A stack can be thought of as a vertical array, like a stack of dishes. If you frequent cafeterias or restaurants with buffets, you should be familiar with the spring-loaded racks that hold plates for the customers. When clean dishes are added, they are literally *pushed* onto the top of the stack, and the older dishes sink lower into the rack. When a customer *pops* a dish from the top of the stack, she is removing the dish that was most recently pushed onto the stack. This is known as a last-in-first-out (LIFO) stack and is typically used for things like history lists. For example, if you hit the Back button in your browser, it will take you to the previous web page you visited. If you hit the Back button again, you'll be brought to the page before that, and so on. This is achieved by *pushing* the URL of each page you visit onto the stack and *popping* it off when the Back button is clicked.

LIFO stacks can also be found in real life. The last person to check her luggage on an airplane usually receives her luggage first when the plane lands, because the luggage is unloaded in the reverse order from which it was loaded. The early bird who checked his luggage first must wait the longest at the luggage conveyor belt after the plane lands. A first-in-first-out (FIFO) stack is more egalitarian; it works on a first-come-first-served basis. A FIFO stack is like the line at your local bank. Instead of taking the last element in an array, a FIFO stack deals with the first element in an array next. It then deletes the first element in the array, and all the other elements "move up," just as you move up in line when the person in front of you is "deleted" (i.e., either she is served and then leaves, or she chooses to leave in disgust because she is tired of waiting). Therefore, the word *push* generally implies that you are using a LIFO stack, whereas the word *append* implies that you are using a FIFO stack. In either case, elements are added to the "end" of the stack; the difference lies in which end of the array holds the element that is taken for the next operation.

indexes of existing elements increase to accommodate the new elements at the beginning of the array). The *unshift()* method has the following general form:

```
theArray.unshift(item1, item2,...itemn);
```

In the preceding code, *theArray* is a reference to an *Array* object, and *item1, item2, ...itemn* is a comma-separated list of items to be added to the beginning of the array as new elements. Note that multiple items are added in the order that they are supplied. Here are some examples:

```
var versions:Array = new Array();
versions[0] = 6;
versions.unshift(5);       // versions is now [5, 6]
versions.unshift(2,3,4);   // versions is now [2, 3, 4, 5, 6]
```

The *unshift()* method, like *push()*, returns the length of the newly enlarged array.

The splice( ) method

The *splice()* method can add elements to, or remove elements from, an array. It is typically used to insert elements into the middle of an array (later elements are renumbered to make room) or to delete elements from the middle of an array (later elements are renumbered to close the gap). When *splice()* performs both tasks in a single invocation, it effectively replaces some elements with new elements (though not necessarily with the same number of elements). The *splice()* method has the following general form:

```
theArray.splice(startIndex, deleteCount, item1, item2,...itemn)
```

In the preceding code, *theArray* is a reference to an *Array* object; *startIndex* is a number that specifies the index at which element removal and optional insertion should commence (remember that the first element's index is 0); *deleteCount* is an optional argument that dictates how many elements should be removed (including the element at *startIndex*). When *deleteCount* is omitted, every element after and including *startIndex* is removed. The optional *item1, item2, ...itemn* parameters are items to be added to the array as elements starting at *startIndex*.

Example 11-3 shows the versatility of the *splice()* method.

Example 11-3. Using the splice() array method

```
// Make an array...
var months:Array = new Array("January", "Friday",
                        "April", "May", "Sunday", "Monday", "July");
// Hmmm. Something's wrong with our array. Let's fix it up.
// First, let's get rid of "Friday".
months.splice(1,1);
  // months is now:
  // ["January", "April", "May", "Sunday", "Monday", "July"]

// Now, let's add the two months before "April".
// Note that we won't delete anything here (deleteCount is 0).
months.splice(1, 0, "February", "March");
  // months is now:
  // ["January", "February", "March", "April",
  //  "May", "Sunday", "Monday", "July"]

// Finally, let's remove "Sunday" and "Monday" while inserting "June".
months.splice(5, 2, "June");
  // months is now:
  // ["January", "February", "March", "April", "May", "June", "July"]

// Now that our months array is fixed, let's trim it
// so that it contains only the first quarter of the year,
// by deleting all elements starting with index 3 (i.e., "April").
months.splice(3); // months is now: ["January", "February", "March"]
```

The *splice()* method returns an array of the elements it removes. Thus it can be used to extract a series of elements from an array:

```
var letters:Array = ["a", "b", "c", "d"];
trace(letters.splice(1, 2));  // Displays: "b,c"
                              // letters is now ["a", "d"]
```

If no elements are removed, *splice()* returns an empty array (that is, an array with no elements).

The concat( ) method

The *concat()* method combines two or more arrays into a single, new array, which it returns. The *concat()* method has the following general form:

```
origArray.concat(elementList)
```

The *concat()* method appends the elements contained in `elementList`, one by one, to the end of *origArray* and returns the result as a *new* array, leaving *origArray* untouched. Normally, we store the returned array in a variable. Here, simple numbers are used as the items to be added to the array:

```
var list1:Array = new Array(11, 12, 13);
var list2:Array = list1.concat(14, 15);  // list2 becomes
                                         // [11, 12, 13, 14, 15]
```

In the following example, we use *concat()* to combine two arrays:

```
var guests:Array = ["Panda", "Dave"];
var registeredPlayers:Array = ["Gray", "Doomtrooper", "TRK9"];
var allUsers:Array = registeredPlayers.concat(guests);
// allUsers is now: ["Gray", "Doomtrooper", "TRK9", "Panda", "Dave"]
```

Notice that *concat()* broke apart, or "flattened" the guests array when adding it to allUsers; that is, each element of the guests array was added to allUsers individually. However, *concat()* does not flatten nested arrays (elements that are themselves arrays within the main array), as you can see from the following code:

```
var x:Array = [1, 2, 3];
var y:Array = [[5, 6], [7, 8]];
var z:Array = x.concat(y);  // Result is [1, 2, 3, [5, 6], [7, 8]].
                            // Elements 0 and 1 of y were not "flattened"
```

Removing Elements from an Array

To remove elements from an array, we use one of the following techniques:

- Delete the specific element with the *delete* operator
- Decrease the array's length variable
- Invoke *push()*, *unshift()*, or *splice()* on the array

The following sections discuss these techniques in detail.

Removing Elements with the delete Operator

The *delete* operator sets an array element to undefined, using the following syntax:

```
delete theArray[index]
```

In the preceding code, *theArray* is a reference to an array, and *index* is the number or name of the element whose value should be set to undefined. The name *delete* is, frankly, misleading. It does *not* remove the numbered element from the array; it merely sets the target element's value to undefined. A *delete* operation, therefore, is identical to assigning the undefined value to an element. We can verify this by checking the length variable of an array after deleting one of its elements:

```
var list = ["a", "b", "c"];
trace(list.length);  // Displays: 3
delete list[2];
trace(list.length);  // Still displays 3...the element at index 2 is
                      // undefined instead of "c", but it still exists
```

To truly delete elements, use *splice()* (to delete them from the middle of an array), or use *shift()* and *pop()* (to delete them from the beginning or end of an array).

Removing Elements with the length Variable

To delete elements from the end of the array (i.e., truncate the array), we can set the array's length variable to a number smaller than the current length:

```
var toppings:Array = ["pepperoni", "tomatoes",
                       "cheese", "green pepper", "broccoli"];
toppings.length = 3;
trace(toppings);  // Displays: "pepperoni,tomatoes,cheese"
                  // We trimmed elements 3 and 4 (the last two)
```

Removing Elements with Array Methods

Arrays come equipped with several built-in methods for removing elements. We've already seen how *splice()* can delete a series of elements from the middle of an array. The *pop()* and *shift()* methods are used to prune elements from the end or beginning of an array.

The pop( ) method

The *pop()* method is the antithesis of *push()*: it removes the last element of an array. The syntax of *pop()* is simple:

```
theArray.pop( )
```

I don't know why, but I always think that "popping" an array is kinda funny. Anyway, *pop()* decrements the array's length by 1 and returns the value of the element it removed. For example:

```
var numbers:Array = [56, 57, 58];
trace(numbers.pop());  // Displays: 58 (the value of the popped element)
                       // numbers is now [56, 57]
```

As we saw earlier, *pop()* is often used in combination with *push()* to perform LIFO stack operations.

The shift( ) method

Remember *unshift()*, the method we used to add an element to the beginning of an array? Meet its alter ego, *shift()*, which removes an element from the beginning of an array:

```
theArray.shift()
```

Not as funny as *pop()*. Oh well.

Like *pop()*, *shift()* returns the value of the element it removes. The remaining elements all move up in the pecking order toward the beginning of the array. For example:

```
var sports:Array = ["quake", "snowboarding", "inline skating"];
trace(sports.shift());  // Displays: quake
                        // sports is now ["snowboarding", "inline skating"]
trace(sports.shift());  // Displays: snowboarding
                        // sports is now ["inline skating"]
```

Because *shift()* truly deletes an element, it is more useful than *delete* for removing the first element of an array.

The splice( ) method

Earlier we saw that *splice()* can both remove elements from and add elements to an array. Because we've already looked at *splice()* in detail, we won't reexamine it here. However, for reference, the following code specifically demonstrates *splice()*'s element-removal capabilities:

```
var letters:Array = ["a", "b", "c", "d", "e", "f"];
// Remove elements 1, 2, and 3, leaving ["a", "e", "f"]
letters.splice(1, 3);
// Remove elements 1 through the end leaving just ["a"]
letters.splice(1);
```

Checking the Contents of an Array with the toString( ) Method

The *toString()* method, common to all objects, returns a string representation of the object upon which it is invoked. In the case of an *Array* object, the *toString()* method returns a list of the array's elements, converted to strings and separated by commas. The *toString()* method can be called explicitly, as follows:

```
theArray.toString()
```

Typically, however, *toString()* isn't used explicitly; rather, it is invoked automatically whenever *theArray* is used in a string context. For example, the expression trace(*theArray*) outputs a list of comma-separated element values during debugging; trace(*theArray*) is equivalent to trace(*theArray*.toString()). The *toString()* method is often helpful during debugging when we need a quick, unformatted look at the elements of an array. For example:

```
var sites = ["www.moock.org", "www.adobe.com", "www.oreilly.com"];
trace("The sites array is " + sites);
```

Note that the *join()* method offers greater formatting flexibility than *toString()*. For details, see Adobe's ActionScript Language Reference.

Multidimensional Arrays

So far, we've limited our discussion to *one-dimensional* arrays, which are akin to a single row or a single column in a spreadsheet. But what if we want to create the equivalent of a spreadsheet with both rows and columns? We need a second dimension. ActionScript natively supports only one-dimensional arrays, but we can simulate a multidimensional array by creating arrays within arrays. That is, we can create an array that contains elements that are themselves arrays (sometimes called *nested* arrays).

The simplest type of multidimensional array is a two-dimensional array, in which elements are organized conceptually into a grid of rows and columns; the rows are the first dimension of the array, and the columns are the second.

Using a practical example, let's consider how a two-dimensional array works. Suppose we're processing an order that contains three products, each with a quantity and a price. We want to simulate a spreadsheet with three rows (one for each product) and two columns (one for the quantity and one for the price). We create a separate array for each row, with each row's elements representing the values in each column:

```
var row1:Array = [6, 2.99];    // Quantity 6, Price 2.99
var row2:Array = [4, 9.99];    // Quantity 4, Price 9.99
var row3:Array = [1, 59.99];   // Quantity 1, Price 59.99
```

Next, we place the rows into a container array named spreadsheet:

```
var spreadsheet:Array = [row1, row2, row3];
```

Now we can find the total cost of the order by multiplying the quantity and price of each row and adding them all together. We access a two-dimensional array's elements using two indexes (one for the row and one for the column). The expression spreadsheet[0], for example, represents the first row's two-column array. Hence, to access the second column in the first row of spreadsheet, we use spreadsheet[0][1] (which yields 2.99). Here's how to calculate the total price of the items in spreadsheet:

```
// Create a variable to store the total cost of the order.
var total:Number;

// Now find the cost of the order. For each row, multiply the columns
// together, and add that to the total.
for (var i:int = 0; i < spreadsheet.length; i++) {
  total += spreadsheet[i][0] * spreadsheet[i][1];
}

trace(total);  // Displays: 117.89
```

On to Events

This chapter offered an introduction to arrays but is by no means exhaustive. The *Array* class offers many useful methods for reordering and sorting array elements, filtering elements, converting elements to strings, and extracting arrays from other arrays. For details, see the *Array* class in Adobe's ActionScript Language Reference.

Our next topic of study is event handling—a built-in system for managing communication between objects.

CHAPTER 12

Events and Event Handling

In general terms, an *event* is a noteworthy runtime occurrence that has the potential to trigger a response in a program. In ActionScript, events can be broken into two categories: *built-in events*, which describe changes to the state of the runtime environment, and *custom events*, which describe changes to the state of a program. For example, a built-in event might be the clicking of the mouse or the completion of a file-load operation. By contrast, a custom event might be the ending of a game or the submission of an answer in a quiz.

Events are ubiquitous in ActionScript. In fact, in a pure ActionScript program, once the main-class constructor method has finished executing, all subsequent code is triggered by events. Accordingly, ActionScript supports a rich event architecture that provides the foundation for both built-in and custom events.

 ActionScript's event architecture is based on the W3C Document Object Model (DOM) Level 3 Events Specification, available at *http:// www.w3.org/TR/DOM-Level-3-Events*.

This chapter teaches the fundamentals of ActionScript's event architecture, covering both how to respond to built-in events and how to implement custom events in an ActionScript program. Note, however, that this chapter covers event fundamentals only. Later, in Chapter 21, we'll study how ActionScript's event architecture caters to display objects (objects that represent onscreen content). Then, in Chapter 22, we'll examine a variety of specific built-in user-input events.

ActionScript Event Basics

In order to *handle* (respond to) events in an ActionScript program, we use *event listeners*. An event listener is a function or method that registers to be executed when a given event occurs. Event listeners are so named because they conceptually wait (listen) for events to happen. To notify a program that a given event has occurred,

ActionScript executes any and all event listeners that have registered for that event. The notification process is known as an *event dispatch*.

When a given event dispatch is about to begin, ActionScript creates an object—known as the *event object*—that represents the event. The event object is always an instance of the *Event* class or one of its descendants. All event listeners executed during the event dispatch are passed a reference to the event object as an argument. Each listener can use the event object's variables to access information relating to the event. For example, a listener for an event representing mouse activity might use the variables of the event object to determine the location of the mouse pointer at the time of the event.

Every type of event in ActionScript—whether built-in or custom—is given a string name. For example, the name of the "mouse click" event type is "click." During an event dispatch, the name of the event being dispatched can be retrieved via the type variable of the event object passed to every listener.

Each event dispatch in ActionScript has an *event target*, which is the object to which the event conceptually pertains. For example, for input events, the event target is typically the object that was manipulated (clicked on, typed into, moved over, etc.). Likewise, for network events, the event target is typically the object that instigated the network operation.

To respond to a given event, listeners typically register with the event target. Accordingly, all event target objects are instances of a class that inherits from the *EventDispatcher* class or that implements the *IEventDispatcher* interface. The *EventDispatcher* class provides methods for registering and unregistering event listeners (*addEventListener()* and *removeEventListener()*, respectively).

In Chapter 21, we'll learn that when the event target is a *display object* (an object that can be displayed on screen), event listeners can also register with the event target's *display ancestors* (i.e., objects that visually contain the event target). For now, however, we'll concentrate solely on nondisplayable event-target objects.

Registering an Event Listener for an Event

The general process for responding to an event in ActionScript is as follows:

1. Determine the name of the event's event type.
2. Determine the datatype of the event object representing the event.
3. Create an event listener to respond to the event. The event listener must define a single parameter matching the datatype of the event object from Step 2.
4. Use *EventDispatcher* class's instance method *addEventListener()* to register the event listener with the event target (or, any display ancestor of the event target).
5. Sit back and wait for the event to occur.

Let's apply the preceding steps to an example: registering for the built-in "complete" event.

Step 1: Determine the event type's name

Flash client runtimes offer a wide range of built-in event types, representing everything from user input to network and sound activity. Each event type's name is accessible via a constant of the *Event* class or one of its descendants. For example, the constant for the "operation complete" event type is `Event.COMPLETE`, whose value is the string name "complete." Likewise, the constant for the "mouse pressed" event type is `MouseEvent.MOUSE_DOWN`, whose value is the string name "mouseDown."

In order to respond to a given built-in event type, we must first find the constant that represents it. In Adobe's ActionScript Language Reference, event constants are listed under the Events heading for any class that supports events (i.e., inherits from *EventDispatcher*). Hence, to find the constant for a given built-in event, we check the Events heading in the documentation for the class to which the event pertains.

For example, suppose we're loading an external text file using the *URLLoader* class, and we want to execute some code when the file finishes loading. We check the Events heading of the *URLLoader* class to see if the appropriate "done loading" event is available. Under the Events heading we find an entry for the "complete" event that seems to suit our purpose. Here's what the "complete" event entry looks like:

> **complete** event
>
> **Event object type:** `flash.events.Event`
>
> **Event.type property** = `flash.events.Event.COMPLETE`
>
> Dispatched after all the received data is decoded and placed in the data property of the URLLoader object. The received data may be accessed once this event has been dispatched.

The "Event.type property" tells us the constant for the "complete" event—`flash.events.Event.COMPLETE`. We'll use that constant when registering for the "complete" event, as shown in bold in the following generic code:

```
theURLLoader.addEventListener(Event.COMPLETE, someListener);
```

 From now on, when referring to any built-in event, we'll use the event constant (e.g., `Event.COMPLETE`) rather than the string-literal name (e.g., "complete"). While slightly verbose, this style promotes developer familiarity with the event constants actually used in ActionScript programs.

Step 2: Determine the event object's datatype

Now that we've determined our event type's name (`Event.COMPLETE`), we must determine the datatype of its event object. Once again, we use the "complete" event entry under the *URLLoader* class in Adobe's ActionScript Language Reference. The "Event object type" subheading of the "complete" entry (shown in the previous section) tells us the datatype of Event.COMPLETE's *Event* object—*flash.events.Event*.

Step 3: Create the event listener

Now that we know the constant and event object datatype for our event (Event.COMPLETE and *Event*, respectively), we can create our event listener. Here's the code:

```
private function completeListener (e:Event):void {
  trace("Load complete");
}
```

Notice that our listener defines a parameter (e) that will receive the event object at event-dispatch time. The parameter's datatype matches the datatype for the Event.COMPLETE event, as determined in Step 2.

By convention, all event listeners have a return type of void. Furthermore, event listeners that are methods are typically declared *private* so that they cannot be invoked by code outside of the class in which they are defined.

While there is no standard for naming event listener functions or methods, event listeners in this book are named using the format *eventName*Listener, where *eventName* is the string name of the event (in our example, "complete").

Step 4: Register for the event

With our event listener now defined, we're ready to register for the event. Recall that we're loading an external text file using an instance of the *URLLoader* class. That instance will be our event target (because it initiates the load operation that eventually results in the Event.COMPLETE event). The following code creates the *URLLoader* instance:

```
var urlLoader:URLLoader = new URLLoader( );
```

And the following code registers our listener, *completeListener()*, with our event target, urlLoader, for Event.COMPLETE events:

```
urlLoader.addEventListener(Event.COMPLETE, completeListener);
```

The first argument to *addEventListener()* specifies the name of the event type for which we are registering. The second argument to *addEventListener()* provides a reference to the listener being registered.

Here's the complete method signature for *addEventListener()*:

```
addEventListener(type, listener, useCapture, priority, useWeakReference)
```

The first two parameters (*type* and *listener*) are required; the remaining parameters are optional. We'll study *priority* and *useWeakReference* later in this chapter, and we'll study *useCapture* in Chapter 21.

Step 5: Wait for the event to occur

We've now created an event listener for the Event.COMPLETE event, and registered it with the event target. To make the Event.COMPLETE event occur, in turn causing the execution of *completeListener()*, we initiate a file-load operation, as follows:

```
urlLoader.load(new URLRequest("someFile.txt"));
```

When *someFile.txt* finishes loading, ActionScript dispatches an Event.COMPLETE event targeted at urlLoader, and *completeListener()* executes.

Example 12-1 shows the code for the preceding five steps in the context of a functional class, *FileLoader*.

Example 12-1. Registering for Event.COMPLETE events

```
package {
  import flash.display.*;
  import flash.net.*;
  import flash.events.*;

  public class FileLoader extends Sprite {
    public function FileLoader () {
      // Create the event target
      var urlLoader:URLLoader = new URLLoader( );
      // Register the event listener
      urlLoader.addEventListener(Event.COMPLETE, completeListener);
      // Start the operation that will trigger the event
      urlLoader.load(new URLRequest("someFile.txt"));
    }

    // Define the event listener
    private function completeListener (e:Event):void {
      trace("Load complete");
    }
  }
}
```

For practice, let's now register two more events.

Two More Event Listener Registration Examples

When the code in Example 12-1 runs, if the Flash client runtime cannot find *someFile.txt*, it dispatches an IOErrorEvent.IO_ERROR event targeted at urlLoader. Let's register for that event so that our application can handle load failures gracefully. We'll start by creating a new event listener, *ioErrorListener()*, as follows:

```
private function ioErrorListener (e:Event):void {
  trace("Error loading file.");
}
```

Next, we register *ioErrorListener()* with urlLoader for IOErrorEvent.IO_ERROR events:

```
urlLoader.addEventListener(IOErrorEvent.IO_ERROR, ioErrorListener);
```

Nice and simple.

Example 12-2 shows our new IOErrorEvent.IO_ERROR code in the context of the *FileLoader* class.

Example 12-2. Registering for IOErrorEvent.IO_ERROR events

```
package {
  import flash.display.*;
  import flash.net.*;
  import flash.events.*;

  public class FileLoader extends Sprite {
    public function FileLoader () {
      var urlLoader:URLLoader = new URLLoader( );
      urlLoader.addEventListener(Event.COMPLETE, completeListener);
      urlLoader.addEventListener(IOErrorEvent.IO_ERROR, ioErrorListener);
      urlLoader.load(new URLRequest("someFile.txt"));
    }

    private function completeListener (e:Event):void {
      trace("Load complete");
    }

    private function ioErrorListener (e:Event):void {
      trace("Error loading file.");
    }
  }
}
```

Now let's try responding to a completely different built-in Flash client runtime event, Event.RESIZE. The Event.RESIZE event is dispatched whenever a Flash runtime is in "no-scale" mode, and the application window changes width or height. The event target for Event.RESIZE events is the Flash client runtime's *Stage* instance. We'll access that instance through the stage variable of our application's main class, *ResizeMonitor*. (If you're not familiar with the *Stage* instance, for now simply think of it as representing the Flash client runtime's display area. We'll study the *Stage* class in more detail in Chapter 20.)

Here's the code:

```
package {
  import flash.display.*;
  import flash.net.*;
  import flash.events.*;

  public class ResizeMonitor extends Sprite {
    public function ResizeMonitor () {
      // Use "no-scale" mode. (Otherwise, the content
      // scales automatically when the application window is resized, and
      // no Event.RESIZE events are dispatched.)
      stage.scaleMode = StageScaleMode.NO_SCALE;
```

```
      // Register resizeListener( ) with the Stage instance for
      // Event.RESIZE events.
      stage.addEventListener(Event.RESIZE, resizeListener);
    }

    // Define the event listener, executed whenever the Flash runtime
    // dispatches the Event.RESIZE event
    private function resizeListener (e:Event):void {
      trace("The application window changed size!");
      // Output the new Stage dimensions to the debugging console
      trace("New width:  " + stage.stageWidth);
      trace("New height: " + stage.stageHeight);
    }
  }
}
```

Notice that within the *resizeListener()* function, stage is directly accessible, just as it is within the *ResizeMonitor* constructor method.

 When an event listener is an instance method, it retains full access to the methods and variables of its instance. See "Bound Methods" in Chapter 3.

Unregistering an Event Listener for an Event

To stop an event listener from receiving event notifications, we unregister it using the *EventDispatcher* class's instance method *removeEventListener()*, which has the following general form:

```
eventTargetOrTargetAncestor.removeEventListener(type, listener, useCapture)
```

In most cases, only the first two parameters (*type* and *listener*) are required; we'll study *useCapture* in Chapter 21.

 To reduce memory and processor usage, event listeners should always be unregistered when they are no longer needed in a program.

The following code demonstrates the use of *removeEventListener()*; it stops *mouseMoveListener()* from receiving notification of MouseEvent.MOUSE_MOVE events targeted at the *Stage* instance:

```
stage.removeEventListener(MouseEvent.MOUSE_MOVE, mouseMoveListener);
```

For more information on important event-related memory issues, see the section "Event Listeners and Memory Management" later in this chapter.

Event Vocabulary Review

The following list of terms reviews the key event vocabulary we've encountered so far:

Event

Conceptually, something that has happened (some "asynchronous occurrence"), such as a mouse click or the completion of a load operation. Each event is identified by an *event name*, which is typically accessible via a constant. Constants for the built-in events are defined either by the *Event* class or by the *Event* subclass most closely related to the event.

Event object

An object representing a specific single occurrence of an event. The event object's class determines what information about the event is available to event listeners. All event objects are instances either of the *Event* class or of one of its subclasses.

Event target

The object to which the event conceptually pertains. Acts as the destination object of a dispatched event, as determined uniquely by each type of event. Every event target (and target ancestor in the case of targets on the display list) can register event listeners to be notified when an event occurs.

Event listener

A function or method registered to receive event notification from an event target (or from an event target's ancestor in the case of targets on the display list).

Event dispatching

Sending notification of the event to the event target, which triggers registered listeners. (If the target is on the display list, the event dispatch proceeds through the event flow, from the root of the display list to the target, and, for bubbling events, back to the root. (See Chapter 21 for information on the display list and the event flow.) Event dispatching is also known as *event propagation*.

Looking ahead, here's a little more event vocabulary that we'll encounter in future event-handling discussions: listeners executed in response to an event are said to have been *triggered* by that event. Once a triggered listener has finished executing, it is said to have *processed the event*. Once all of an object's listeners have processed a given event, the object itself is said to have finished processing the event.

Now that we're familiar with the basics of events and event handling, let's take a deeper look at a variety of specific event-handling topics.

Accessing the Target Object

During every event dispatch, the *Event* object passed to every event listener defines a target variable that provides a reference to the target object. Hence, to access the target of an event dispatch, we use the following general event-listener code, which simply outputs the event target's *String* value during debugging:

```
public function someListener (e:SomeEvent):void {
  // Access the target of the event dispatch
  trace(e.target);
}
```

Programs typically use the *Event* class's instance variable `target` to control the target object in some way. For example, recall the code we used to respond to the completion of a file-load operation (shown in Example 12-1):

```
package {
  import flash.display.*;
  import flash.net.*;
  import flash.events.*;

  public class FileLoader extends Sprite {
    public function FileLoader () {
      var urlLoader:URLLoader = new URLLoader( );
      urlLoader.addEventListener(Event.COMPLETE, completeListener);
      urlLoader.load(new URLRequest("someFile.txt"));
    }

    private function completeListener (e:Event):void {
      trace("Load complete");
    }
  }
}
```

In the preceding code, within the *completeListener()* function, we might want to access the `urlLoader` object in order to retrieve the content of the loaded file. Here's the code we'd use (notice that, for added type safety, we cast `target` to *URLLoader*—the actual datatype of the target object):

```
private function completeListener (e:Event):void {
  var loadedText:String = URLLoader(e.target).data;
}
```

After the preceding code runs, `loadedText`'s value is the contents of the loaded text file (*someFile.txt*).

Example 12-3 provides another example of accessing an event's target object, this time for a target object that is on the display list. In the example, we set a text field's background color to red when it has focus. To access the *TextField*, the *focusInListener()* method uses the *Event* class's instance variable `target` variable.

> Example 12-3 uses several techniques that we haven't yet covered—creating text, focusing an object, working with the display list, and the event flow. We'll study each of those topics in Part II of this book. If you are new to display programming, consider skipping this example and returning to it after you have read Part II.

Example 12-3. Accessing the target object
```
package {
  import flash.display.*;
  import flash.events.*;
  import flash.text.*;

  // Changes a text field's background color to red when focused
  public class HighlightText extends Sprite {

    // Constructor
    public function HighlightText () {
      // Create a Sprite object
      var s:Sprite = new Sprite( );
      s.x = 100;
      s.y = 100;

      // Create a TextField object
      var t:TextField = new TextField( );
      t.text = "Click here";
      t.background = true;
      t.border = true;
      t.autoSize = TextFieldAutoSize.LEFT;

      // Put the TextField in the Sprite
      s.addChild(t);

      // Add the Sprite to this object's display hierarchy
      addChild(s);

      // Register to be notified when the user focuses any of the Sprite
      // object's descendants (in this case, there's only one descendant:
      // the TextField, t)
      s.addEventListener(FocusEvent.FOCUS_IN, focusInListener);
    }

    // Listener executed when one of the Sprite object's descendants
    // is focused
    public function focusInListener (e:FocusEvent):void {
      // Displays: Target of this event dispatch: [object TextField]
      trace("Target of this event dispatch: " + e.target);

      // Set the text field's background to red. Notice that, for added type
      // safety, we cast Event.target to TextField--the actual datatype of
      // the target object.
      TextField(e.target).backgroundColor = 0xFF0000;
    }
  }
}
```

Reader exercise: try adding a FocusEvent.FOCUS_OUT listener to Example 12-3 that changes the text field's background color to white.

Accessing the Object That Registered the Listener

During every event dispatch, the *Event* object passed to every event listener defines a currentTarget variable that provides a reference to the object with which the event listener registered. The following general event-listener code demonstrates; it outputs the *String* value of the object with which *someListener()* registered:

```
public function someListener (e:SomeEvent):void {
  // Access the object with which this event listener registered
  trace(e.currentTarget);
}
```

For events targeted at nondisplay objects, the value of the *Event* class's instance variable currentTarget is always equal to target (because listeners always register with the event target). For example, returning once again to the *FileLoader* class from Example 12-1, if we check the value of both e.currentTarget and e.target within *completeListener()*, we find that those two variables refer to the same object:

```
package {
  import flash.display.*;
  import flash.net.*;
  import flash.events.*;

  public class FileLoader extends Sprite {
    public function FileLoader () {
      var urlLoader:URLLoader = new URLLoader();
      urlLoader.addEventListener(Event.COMPLETE, completeListener);
      urlLoader.load(new URLRequest("someFile.txt"));
    }

    private function completeListener (e:Event):void {
      trace(e.currentTarget == e.target);  // Displays: true
    }
  }
}
```

However, as we'll learn in Chapter 21, for events targeted at display objects in a display hierarchy, listeners can register both with the event target and with the event target's display ancestors. For event listeners registered with an event target's display ancestor, currentTarget refers to that display ancestor, while target refers to the event target object.

For example, suppose a *Sprite* object that contains a *TextField* object registers a MouseEvent.CLICK event listener, *clickListener()*. When the user clicks the text field, a MouseEvent.CLICK event is dispatched, and *clickListener()* is triggered. Within *clickListener()*, currentTarget refers to the *Sprite* object, while target refers to the *TextField* object.

Programs typically use currentTarget to control the object that registered a listener in some way. As an applied example, let's revise the *focusInListener()* function from Example 12-3. This time, when the *TextField* object is focused, our new *focusInListener()* function will display a blue oval behind the text field. The blue oval is drawn in the *Sprite* object, which is accessed via currentTarget.

```
public function focusInListener (e:FocusEvent):void {
  // Set the text field's background to red
  TextField(e.target).backgroundColor = 0xFF0000;

  // Obtain a reference to the Sprite object
  var theSprite:Sprite = Sprite(e.currentTarget);

  // Draw the ellipse in the Sprite object
  theSprite.graphics.beginFill(0x0000FF);
  theSprite.graphics.drawEllipse(-10, -10, 75, 40);
}
```

Preventing Default Event Behavior

Some events in ActionScript are associated with a side effect known as a *default behavior*. For example, the default behavior of a TextEvent.TEXT_INPUT event is text being added to the target text field. Likewise, the default behavior for a MouseEvent.MOUSE_DOWN event targeted at a *SimpleButton* object displays the button's "down state" graphic.

In some cases, events with a default behavior offer the option to prevent that behavior programmatically. Events with a default behavior that can be prevented are said to be *cancelable*. For example, the TextEvent.TEXT_INPUT event is cancelable, as are FocusEvent.KEY_FOCUS_CHANGE and FocusEvent.MOUSE_FOCUS_CHANGE.

To prevent the default behavior for a cancelable event, we invoke the *Event* class's instance method *preventDefault()* on the *Event* object passed to any listener registered for that event. For example, in the following code, we prevent the default behavior for all TextEvent.TEXT_INPUT events targeted at the text field t. Instead of allowing the user-entered text to appear in the text field, we simply add the letter "x" to the text field.

```
package {
  import flash.display.*;
  import flash.text.*;
  import flash.events.*;

  // Changes all user-entered text to the character "x"
  public class InputConverter extends Sprite {
    private var t:TextField;

    public function InputConverter () {
      // Create the text field
      t = new TextField();
      t.border     = true;
      t.background = true;
      t.type = TextFieldType.INPUT;
      addChild(t);
```

```
    // Register for the TextEvent.TEXT_INPUT event
    t.addEventListener(TextEvent.TEXT_INPUT, textInputListener);
}

// Listener executed when the TextEvent.TEXT_INPUT event occurs
private function textInputListener (e:TextEvent):void {
    // Show what the user tried to enter
    trace("Attempted text input: " + e.text);

    // Stop the user-entered text from appearing in the text field
    e.preventDefault( );

    // Add the letter "x" to the text field instead of
    // the user-entered text
    t.appendText("x");
    }
  }
}
```

To determine whether a given event has default behavior that can be canceled, check the value of *Event* class's instance variable cancelable within a listener registered for that event. For built-in events, see also the event's entry in Adobe ActionScript Language Reference.

To determine whether an event currently being dispatched has had its default behavior prevented, check the return value of the *Event* class's instance method *isDefaultPrevented( )* within a listener registered for that event.

Note that just like built-in events, custom events can define default behavior that can be canceled via *preventDefault( )*. For more information and example code, see the section "Preventing Default Behavior for Custom Events" later in this chapter.

 For another example showing how to use *preventDefault( )* with the TextEvent.TEXT_INPUT event, see Example 22-8 in Chapter 22.

Event Listener Priority

By default, when multiple event listeners are registered for a single event type with a given object, those listeners are triggered in the order in which they registered. For example, in the following code two event listeners—*completeListenerA( )* and *completeListenerB( )*—register with urlLoader for the Event.COMPLETE event. When the Event.COMPLETE event occurs, *completeListenerA( )* executes before *completeListenerB( )* because *completeListenerA( )* registered before *completeListenerB( )*.

```
package {
  import flash.display.*;
  import flash.net.*;
  import flash.events.*;

  public class FileLoader extends Sprite {
    public function FileLoader ( ) {
```

```
      var urlLoader:URLLoader = new URLLoader( );
      // Registration order determines execution order
      urlLoader.addEventListener(Event.COMPLETE, completeListenerA);
      urlLoader.addEventListener(Event.COMPLETE, completeListenerB);
      urlLoader.load(new URLRequest("someFile.txt"));
    }

    private function completeListenerA (e:Event):void {
      trace("Listener A: Load complete");
    }

    private function completeListenerB (e:Event):void {
      trace("Listener B: Load complete");
    }
  }
}
```

To alter the default order in which event listeners are triggered, we can use the *addEventListener( )* method's priority parameter, shown in the following generic code:

```
addEventListener(type, listener, useCapture, priority, useWeakReference)
```

The priority parameter is an integer indicating the order in which the event listener being registered should be triggered, relative to other listeners registered for the same event with the same object. Listeners registered with a higher priority are triggered before listeners registered with a lower priority. For example, a listener registered with priority 3 will be triggered before a listener registered with priority 2. When two listeners are registered with the same priority, they are executed in the order in which they were registered. When priority is not specified, it defaults to 0.

The following code demonstrates the general use of the priority parameter; it forces *completeListenerB( )* to execute before *completeListenerA( )* even though *completeListenerA( )* registers before *completeListenerB( )*.

```
package {
  import flash.display.*;
  import flash.net.*;
  import flash.events.*;

  public class FileLoader extends Sprite {
    public function FileLoader ( ) {
      var urlLoader:URLLoader = new URLLoader( );
      // Priority parameter determines execution order
      urlLoader.addEventListener(Event.COMPLETE,
                                 completeListenerA,
                                 false,
                                 0);
      urlLoader.addEventListener(Event.COMPLETE,
                                 completeListenerB,
                                 false,
                                 1);
      urlLoader.load(new URLRequest("someFile.txt"));
    }
```

```
      private function completeListenerA (e:Event):void {
        trace("Listener A: Load complete");
      }

      private function completeListenerB (e:Event):void {
        trace("Listener B: Load complete");
      }
    }
  }
```

The priority parameter is rarely needed, but can prove useful in specific situations. For example, an application framework might use a high priority listener to perform initialization on a loaded application before other listeners have a chance to execute. Or a testing suite might use a high priority listener to disable other listeners that would otherwise interfere with a given test (see the section "Stopping an Event Dispatch" in Chapter 21).

 Use caution when altering event listener execution order. Programs that depend on an execution order are prone to error because event listener priorities are volatile, difficult to maintain, and make source code more difficult to follow.

Event Listeners and Memory Management

As we've seen throughout this chapter, ActionScript's event architecture is based on two key participants: the listener (either a function or a method) and the object with which that listener registers. Each object that registers a listener for a given event keeps track of that listener by assigning a reference to it in an internal array known as a *listener list*. For example, in the following code (repeated from Example 12-1) the *completeListener()* method registers with urlLoader for Event.COMPLETE events. As a result, urlLoader's internal *listener list* gains a reference to *completeListener()*.

```
    package {
      import flash.display.*;
      import flash.net.*;
      import flash.events.*;

      public class FileLoader extends Sprite {
        public function FileLoader () {
          var urlLoader:URLLoader = new URLLoader();
          // Register completeListener()
          urlLoader.addEventListener(Event.COMPLETE, completeListener);
          urlLoader.load(new URLRequest("someFile.txt"));
        }

        private function completeListener (e:Event):void {
          trace("Load complete");
        }
      }
    }
```

By default, any object that has a reference to a listener maintains that reference until the listener is explicitly unregistered via the *removeEventListener()* method. Furthermore, the object maintains its reference to the listener even when no other references to the listener remain in the program. The following simple class, *AnonymousListener*, demonstrates. It creates an anonymous function and registers that function for MouseEvent.MOUSE_MOVE events with the Flash client runtime's *Stage* instance. Even though the *AnonymousListener* class has no references to the anonymous function, the function is permanently retained by the *Stage* instance, and continues to be triggered every time the MouseEvent.MOUSE_MOVE occurs, long after the *AnonymousListener* constructor method exits.

```
package {
  import flash.display.*;
  import flash.events.*;

  public class AnonymousListener extends Sprite {
    public function AnonymousListener () {
      // Adds an anonymous function to the Stage instance's
      // listener list
      stage.addEventListener(MouseEvent.MOUSE_MOVE,
                             function (e:MouseEvent):void {
                               trace("mouse move");
                             });

    }
  }
}
```

In the preceding code, the anonymous function is permanently stranded in the *Stage* instance's listener list. The program cannot unregister the anonymous function because it has no reference to that function.

 Stranded listeners are a potential source of serious memory waste and can cause other problematic side effects in ActionScript programs.

Let's consider an applied example demonstrating the potential risks of stranding listeners, and ways to avoid those risks.

Suppose we're building a butterfly-catching game in which the player catches butterflies by touching them with the mouse. Butterflies try to avoid being caught by flying away from the mouse pointer. The application's main class is *ButterflyGame*. Each butterfly is represented by an instance of the *Butterfly* class. To manage butterfly movement, the game uses a central *Timer* object that triggers a TimerEvent.TIMER event every 25 milliseconds. Each *Butterfly* object registers a listener with the central *Timer* object, and calculates a new position for itself every time a TimerEvent.TIMER event occurs.

Here's the code for the *Butterfly* class:

```
package {
  import flash.display.*;
  import flash.events.*;
  import flash.utils.*;

  public class Butterfly extends Sprite {
    // Each Butterfly object receives a reference to the central
    // timer through the gameTimer constructor parameter
    public function Butterfly (gameTimer:Timer) {
      gameTimer.addEventListener(TimerEvent.TIMER, timerListener);
    }

    private function timerListener (e:TimerEvent):void {
      trace("Calculating new butterfly position...");
      // Calculate new butterfly position (code not shown)
    }
  }
}
```

And here's the code for the *ButterflyGame* class, highly simplified to isolate the butterfly creation and removal code. In this version of the code, the game contains one butterfly only.

```
package {
  import flash.display.*;
  import flash.utils.*;

  public class ButterflyGame extends Sprite {
    private var timer:Timer;
    private var butterfly:Butterfly;

    public function ButterflyGame () {
      // The game timer
      timer = new Timer(25, 0);
      timer.start();
      addButterfly();
    }

    // Adds the butterfly to the game
    public function addButterfly ():void {
      butterfly = new Butterfly(timer);
    }

    // Removes the butterfly from the game
    public function removeButterfly ():void {
      butterfly = null;
    }
  }
}
```

To add the butterfly to the game, *ButterflyGame* uses the following code:

```
butterfly = new Butterfly(timer);
```

When that code runs, the *Butterfly* constructor runs, and the *Butterfly* object's *timerListener()* method registers with gameTimer for TimerEvent.TIMER events.

When the player catches the butterfly, *ButterflyGame* removes the *Butterfly* object from the program using the following code:

```
butterfly = null;
```

However, even though the preceding code removes *ButterflyGame*'s reference to the *Butterfly* object, gameTimer's listener list retains its reference to the *Butterfly* object's *timerListener()* method—and, by extension, to the *Butterfly* object itself. Furthermore, *timerListener()* continues to execute every time a TimerEvent.TIMER occurs. The *Butterfly* object, hence, continues to consume memory and processor time, and has the potential to trigger unexpected or unwanted side effects in the program. To avoid these problems, when we remove a *Butterfly* object from our game, we must first unregister its *timerListener()* method for TimerEvent.TIMER events.

In order to facilitate TimerEvent.TIMER event unregistration, let's add a new variable, gameTimer, and a new method, *destroy()*, to the *Butterfly* class. The central game timer is assigned to the gameTimer variable. The *destroy()* method unregisters *timerListener()* for TimerEvent.TIMER events. Here's the updated *Butterfly* class, with additions shown in bold:

```
package {
  import flash.display.*;
  import flash.events.*;
  import flash.utils.*;

  public class Butterfly extends Sprite {
    private var gameTimer:Timer;

    public function Butterfly (gameTimer:Timer) {
      this.gameTimer = gameTimer;
      this.gameTimer.addEventListener(TimerEvent.TIMER, timerListener);
    }

    private function timerListener (e:TimerEvent):void {
      trace("Calculating new butterfly position...");
      // Calculate new butterfly position (code not shown)
    }

    public function destroy ():void {
      gameTimer.removeEventListener(TimerEvent.TIMER, timerListener);
    }
  }
}
```

In the *ButterflyGame* class's instance method *removeButterfly()*, we invoke *destroy()* before removing the reference to the *Butterfly* object, as follows:

```
public function removeButterfly ():void {
  butterfly.destroy();
```

```
      butterfly = null;
  }
```

By invoking *destroy()* before removing the *Butterfly* object from the game, we prevent *timerListener()* from being stranded in the *Timer* object's listener list.

 When you register an event listener with an object, be sure your program also eventually unregisters that listener.

Weak Listener References

In the preceding section we learned that, by default, an object that registers a listener for a given event maintains a reference to that listener until it is explicitly unregistered for that event—even when no other references to the listener remain in the program. This default behavior can, however, be altered with *addEventListener()*'s useWeakReference parameter.

 This topic requires a prior understanding of garbage collection in ActionScript, which is covered in Chapter 14.

Registering a listener with useWeakReference set to true prevents that listener from becoming stranded in the listener list of the object with which it registered. For example, suppose an object, 0, registers a listener, L, for an event, E, with useWeakReference set to true. Further suppose that the only reference the program has to L is the one held by 0. Normally, L would be held by 0 until L is unregistered for the event E. However, because L originally registered with useWeakReference set to true, and because 0 holds the only remaining reference to L in the program, L immediately becomes eligible for garbage collection. Subsequently, the garbage collector, at its discretion, can choose to automatically remove L from 0's listener list, and delete it from memory.

To demonstrate useWeakReference, let's return to the *AnonymousListener* class. Recall that *AnonymousListener* creates an anonymous function and registers that function for MouseEvent.MOUSE_MOVE events with the Flash client runtime's *Stage* instance. This time, however, when we register the function for MouseEvent.MOUSE_MOVE events, we set useWeakReference set to true.

```
package {
  import flash.display.*;
  import flash.events.*;

  public class AnonymousListener extends Sprite {
    public function AnonymousListener () {
      // Add an anonymous function to the Stage instance's
      // listener list
```

```
stage.addEventListener(MouseEvent.MOUSE_MOVE,
                       function (e:MouseEvent):void {
                         trace("mouse move");
                       },
                       false,
                       0,
                       true);

      }
    }
  }
```

When the preceding code runs, the program's only reference to the anonymous function is the one held by the *Stage* instance. Because the anonymous function was registered with useWeakReference set to true, it immediately becomes eligible for garbage collection. Hence, the garbage collector, at its discretion, can subsequently choose to automatically remove the anonymous function from the *Stage* instance's listener list, and delete it from memory.

Of course, just because the anonymous function is *eligible* for garbage collection does not mean it *will be* garbage collected. In fact, in the case of the preceding simple example, the function will likely *not* be garbage collected because the application does not use enough memory to trigger a garbage collection. As a result, the function will continue to be executed anytime a MouseEvent.MOUSE_MOVE event dispatch targets the *Stage* instance, even though theoretically it could be garbage collected at any time. Hence, in general, useWeakReference should not be relied on as a way to automatically remove event listeners. As a best practice, simply *avoid stranding event listeners*.

A previous note can't be emphasized enough, so it bears repeating:

> When you register an event listener with an object, be sure your program also eventually unregisters that listener.

So far in this chapter we've worked exclusively with ActionScript's built-in events. Now let's consider how to implement our own custom events in a program.

Custom Events

Dispatching a new custom event in ActionScript is as simple as extending the *EventDispatcher* class, giving the new event a name, and invoking the *EventDispatcher* class's instance method *dispatchEvent()*. To learn how to create custom events in a program, we'll study two examples: first, an event in a game, and then an event for a user interface widget.

To target an event dispatch at an instance of a class that already extends a class another, use the composition approach discussed in Chapter 9: implement the *IEventDispatcher* interface directly, and use *EventDispatcher*'s services via composition rather than inheritance.

A Custom "gameOver" Event

Suppose we're creating a general framework for video game development. The framework includes the following two classes: *Game*, which handles the basic needs of any video game; and *Console*, which represents a launchpad from which to start new games. The *Console* class instantiates a *Game* object whenever a new game is started. Each *Game* class instance created by the *Console* class is the target of a custom "gameOver" event, which is dispatched when a game ends.

In order to allow *Game* objects to act as event targets, the *Game* class extends *EventDispatcher*, as follows:

```
package {
  import flash.events.*;

  public class Game extends EventDispatcher {
  }
}
```

The *Game* class also defines a constant, Game.GAME_OVER, whose value is the name of the custom event: gameOver. By convention, event constants are written with all capital letters, and words separated by an underscore, as in GAME_OVER. Custom event constants are typically defined either by the event target class (in this case, *Game*) or, if an *Event* subclass is used, by that *Event* subclass (as shown in our upcoming widget example). Our present game example does not include an *Event* subclass, so we define the event constant for gameOver in the *Game* class, as follows:

```
package {
  import flash.events.*;

  public class Game extends EventDispatcher {
    public static const GAME_OVER:String = "gameOver";
  }
}
```

When a game is over, the *Game* object calls the *endGame()* method, which resets the game environment and prepares for the possibility of a new game. Here's the *endGame()* method:

```
package {
  import flash.events.*;

  public class Game extends EventDispatcher {
    public static const GAME_OVER:String = "gameOver";
```

```
    private function endGame ():void {
      // Perform game-ending duties (code not shown)
    }
  }
}
```

When all game-ending duties are complete, *endGame()* uses *dispatchEvent()* to dispatch a Game.GAME_OVER event signaling the end of the game:

```
package {
  import flash.events.*;

  public class Game extends EventDispatcher {
    public static const GAME_OVER:String = "gameOver";

    private function endGame ():void {
      // Perform game-ending duties (code not shown)...

      //      ...then ask ActionScript to dispatch an event indicating that
      // the game is over
      dispatchEvent(new Event(Game.GAME_OVER));
    }
  }
}
```

Note that because *dispatchEvent()* is invoked on the *Game* object, that object is the target of the event.

> The object on which *dispatchEvent()* is invoked is the event target.

The *dispatchEvent()* method shown in the preceding code takes a single parameter—an *Event* object representing the event being dispatched. The *Event* constructor, itself, it takes three parameters—*type*, *bubbles*, and *cancelable* as shown in the following generalized code:

```
Event(type, bubbles, cancelable)
```

In most cases, however, only the first argument, *type*, is needed; it specifies the string name of the event (in our case, Game.GAME_OVER). The bubbles parameter is used when the event target is a display object only; it indicates whether the event flow should include a bubbling phase (true) or not (false). (See the section "Custom Events and the Event Flow" in Chapter 21.) The cancelable parameter is used to create custom events with preventable default behavior, as discussed later, in the section "Preventing Default Behavior for Custom Events."

To register an event listener for our custom Game.GAME_OVER event, we use *addEventListener()*, just as we would when registering for a built-in event. For example, suppose that, when a game ends, we want the *Console* class to display a dialog box that gives the player the option to return to the launchpad or to play the current

game again. In the *Console* class, we detect the ending of a game by registering for
Game.GAME_OVER events, as follows:

```
package {
  import flash.display.*;
  import flash.events.*;

  public class Console extends Sprite {

    // Constructor
    public function Console () {
      var game:Game = new Game();
      game.addEventListener(Game.GAME_OVER, gameOverListener);
    }

    private function gameOverListener (e:Event):void {
      trace("The game has ended!");
      // Display "back to console" UI (code not shown)
    }
  }
}
```

Notice that the datatype of the event object passed to *gameOverListener()* matches
the datatype of the event object originally passed to *dispatchEvent()* in the *Game*
class's instance method *endGame()* (shown in the previous code).

When creating a listener for a custom event, set the datatype of the listener's parameter to match the datatype of the event object originally
passed to *dispatchEvent()*.

Example 12-4 shows the code for our custom Game.GAME_OVER event in its entirety,
and adds a timer that forces a call to *endGame()*, simulating the ending of an actual
game. (For details on the *Timer* class, see Adobe's ActionScript Language Reference.)

Example 12-4. A custom "gameOver" event

```
// The Game class (the event target)
package {
  import flash.events.*;
  import flash.utils.*;  // Required for the Timer class

  public class Game extends EventDispatcher {
    public static const GAME_OVER:String = "gameOver";

    public function Game () {
      // Force the game to end after one second
      var timer:Timer = new Timer(1000, 1);
      timer.addEventListener(TimerEvent.TIMER, timerListener);
      timer.start();
      // A nested function that is executed one second after this object
      // is created
      function timerListener (e:TimerEvent):void {
```

Example 12-4. A custom "gameOver" event (continued)

```
      endGame( );
    }
  }

  private function endGame ( ):void {
    // Perform game-ending duties (code not shown)...

    //     ...then ask ActionScript to dispatch an event indicating that
    // the game is over
    dispatchEvent(new Event(Game.GAME_OVER));
  }
 }
}

// The Console class (registers a listener for the event)
package {
  import flash.display.*;
  import flash.events.*;

  public class Console extends Sprite {

    // Constructor
    public function Console ( ) {
      var game:Game = new Game( );
      game.addEventListener(Game.GAME_OVER, gameOverListener);
    }

    private function gameOverListener (e:Event):void {
      trace("The game has ended!");
      // Display "back to console" UI (code not shown)
    }
  }
}
```

Now let's take a look at another example, an event for a user interface widget.

A Custom "toggle" Event

Suppose we're creating a toggle-switch widget with an on and off state. Our toggle switch is represented by the *ToggleSwitch* class. Whenever the switch is toggled on or off, we dispatch a custom event named "toggle."

In the preceding section, the event object for our custom Game.GAME_OVER event was an instance of the built-in *Event* class. This time, our custom event will be represented by its own class, *ToggleEvent*. The *ToggleEvent* class has the following two purposes:

- Define the constant for the toggle event (ToggleEvent.TOGGLE)
- Define a variable, isOn, which listeners use to determine the state of the target *ToggleSwitch* object

The code for the *ToggleEvent* class follows. Note that every custom *Event* subclass must override both *clone()* and *toString()*, providing versions of those methods that account for any custom variables in the subclass (e.g., isOn).

The toggle switch code in this section focuses solely on the implementation of the toggle event; the code required to create interactivity and graphics is omitted.

```
package {
  import flash.events.*;

  // A class representing the custom "toggle" event
  public class ToggleEvent extends Event {
    // A constant for the "toggle" event type
    public static const TOGGLE:String = "toggle";

    // Indicates whether the switch is now on or off
    public var isOn:Boolean;

    // Constructor
    public function ToggleEvent (type:String,
                                 bubbles:Boolean = false,
                                 cancelable:Boolean = false,
                                 isOn:Boolean = false) {
      // Pass constructor parameters to the superclass constructor
      super(type, bubbles, cancelable);

      // Remember the toggle switch's state so it can be accessed within
      // ToggleEvent.TOGGLE listeners
      this.isOn = isOn;
    }

    // Every custom event class must override clone()
    public override function clone( ):Event {
      return new ToggleEvent(type, bubbles, cancelable, isOn);
    }

    // Every custom event class must override toString(). Note that
    // "eventPhase" is an instance variable relating to the event flow.
    // See Chapter 21.
    public override function toString( ):String {
      return formatToString("ToggleEvent", "type", "bubbles",
                            "cancelable", "eventPhase", "isOn");
    }
  }
}
```

Next, let's turn to the *ToggleSwitch* class, which represents the toggle switch. The *ToggleSwitch* class's sole method, *toggle()*, changes the state of the toggle switch, and then dispatches a ToggleEvent.TOGGLE event indicating that the switch's state has changed. The following code shows the *ToggleSwitch* class. Notice that the *ToggleSwitch* class extends *Sprite*, which provides support for onscreen display. As a descendant of *EventDispatcher*, the *Sprite* class also provides the required event-dispatching capabilities:

```
package {
  import flash.display.*;
  import flash.events.*;

  // Represents a simple toggle-switch widget
  public class ToggleSwitch extends Sprite {
    // Remembers the state of the switch
    private var isOn:Boolean;

    // Constructor
    public function ToggleSwitch () {
      // The switch is off by default
      isOn = false;
    }

    // Turns the switch on if it is currently off, or off if it is
    // currently on
    public function toggle ():void {
      // Toggle the switch state
      isOn = !isOn;

      // Ask ActionScript to dispatch a ToggleEvent.TOGGLE event, targeted
      // at this ToggleSwitch object
      dispatchEvent(new ToggleEvent(ToggleEvent.TOGGLE,
                                    true,
                                    false,
                                    isOn));
    }
  }
}
```

To demonstrate the use of the ToggleEvent.TOGGLE event, let's create a simple example class, *SomeApp*. The *SomeApp* class defines a method, *toggleListener()*, and registers it with a *ToggleSwitch* object for ToggleEvent.TOGGLE events. For demonstration purposes, the *SomeApp* class also programmatically toggles the switch on, triggering a ToggleEvent.TOGGLE event.

```
package {
  import flash.display.*;

  // A generic application that demonstrates the use of the custom
  // ToggleEvent.TOGGLE event
  public class SomeApp extends Sprite {
    // Constructor
    public function SomeApp () {
      // Create a ToggleSwitch
      var toggleSwitch:ToggleSwitch = new ToggleSwitch();
      // Register for ToggleEvent.TOGGLE events
      toggleSwitch.addEventListener(ToggleEvent.TOGGLE,
                                    toggleListener);
```

```
    // Toggle the switch (normally the switch would be toggled by the
    // user, but for demonstration purposes, we toggle
    // it programmatically)
    toggleSwitch.toggle();
  }

  // Listener executed whenever a ToggleEvent.TOGGLE event occurs
  private function toggleListener (e:ToggleEvent):void {
    if (e.isOn) {
      trace("The ToggleSwitch is now on.");
    } else {
      trace("The ToggleSwitch is now off.");
    }
  }
 }
}
```

Now that we have some experience implementing custom events, let's consider an advanced scenario: a custom event type with a default behavior.

Preventing Default Behavior for Custom Events

In the earlier section, "Preventing Default Event Behavior," we saw that some built-in events are associated with a default behavior. For example, the TextEvent.TEXT_INPUT event is associated with the default behavior of adding text to a text field. We also saw that, for built-in events that are classified as cancelable, the default behavior can be prevented using the *Event* class's instance method *preventDefault()* method.

Custom events can also be associated with custom default behavior that can likewise be prevented via *preventDefault()*. A custom event's default behavior is entirely program determined and implemented. The general approach for implementing events associated with preventable default behavior is as follows:

1. At event-dispatch time, create an event object representing the event, making sure to set the *Event* constructor's cancelable parameter to true.

2. Use *dispatchEvent()* to dispatch the event.

3. After *dispatchEvent()* completes, use the *Event* class's instance method *isDefaultPrevented()* to check whether any listeners requested the prevention of the default behavior.

4. If the event object's *isDefaultPrevented()* method returns false, then proceed with the default behavior; otherwise, do not carry out the default behavior.

Here's the generic code for implementing an event with a preventable default behavior:

```
// Create the event object, with the desired values for type and
// bubbles. Set cancelable (the third parameter) to true.
var e:Event = new Event(type, bubbles, true);
```

```
// Dispatch the event
dispatchEvent(e);

// Check whether any listeners requested the prevention of the
// default behavior. If no listener called preventDefault()...
if (!e.isDefaultPrevented()) {
  // ...then carry out the default behavior
}
```

Let's apply these steps to an example that builds on the toggle switch example. Suppose we're using our toggle switch widget in a control-panel application that assigns different privileges to its users depending on their status. Guest users are prevented from using some of the switches in the panel, while administrative users are allowed to use all switches in the panel.

To accommodate the different user levels in the application, we define a new toggle switch event type: ToggleEvent.TOGGLE_ATTEMPT. The ToggleEvent.TOGGLE_ATTEMPT occurs anytime the user attempts to turn a toggle switch on or off. The default behavior associated with the ToggleEvent.TOGGLE_ATTEMPT event is the toggling of the switch.

For the sake of simplicity, we'll assume that our toggle switch can only be turned on or off via a mouse click (not via the keyboard). Whenever the user clicks the toggle switch, we dispatch a ToggleEvent.TOGGLE_ATTEMPT. Then, if no listener prevents the default behavior, we carry out the toggle request. Here's the relevant code:

```
private function clickListener (e:MouseEvent):void {
  // The user has attempted to turn the switch on or off, so ask
  // ActionScript to dispatch a ToggleEvent.TOGGLE_ATTEMPT event,
  // targeted at this ToggleSwitch object. First create the event object...
  var toggleEvent:ToggleEvent =
                      new ToggleEvent(ToggleEvent.TOGGLE_ATTEMPT,
                                      true,
                                      true);
  // ... then request the event dispatch
  dispatchEvent(toggleEvent);

  // The ToggleEvent.TOGGLE_ATTEMPT event dispatch is now complete.
  // If no listener prevented the default event behavior...
  if (!toggleEvent.isDefaultPrevented()) {
    // ...then toggle the switch
    toggle();
  }
}
```

In our control-panel application, we register a ToggleEvent.TOGGLE_ATTEMPT listener for every *ToggleSwitch* object. Within that listener, we evaluate the user's status. For restricted switches, if the user is a guest, we prevent the default behavior. Here's the code:

```
// Listener executed whenever a ToggleEvent.TOGGLE_ATTEMPT event occurs
private function toggleAttemptListener (e:ToggleEvent):void {
```

```
  // If the user is a guest...
  if (userType == UserType.GUEST) {
    // ...deny the attempted use of the toggle switch
    e.preventDefault( );
  }
}
```

Example 12-5 shows the control-panel application in its entirety, complete with a fully functioning, albeit simple, graphical version of the toggle switch widget. The comments will guide you through the code.

Example 12-5. The control panel application classes

```
// The ToggleEvent class
package {
  import flash.events.*;

  // A class representing the custom "toggle" event
  public class ToggleEvent extends Event {
    // A constant for the "toggle" event type
    public static const TOGGLE:String = "toggle";

    // A constant for the "toggleAttempt" event type
    public static const TOGGLE_ATTEMPT:String = "toggleAttempt";

    // Indicates whether the switch is now on or off
    public var isOn:Boolean;

    // Constructor
    public function ToggleEvent (type:String,
                                 bubbles:Boolean = false,
                                 cancelable:Boolean = false,
                                 isOn:Boolean = false) {
      // Pass constructor parameters to the superclass constructor
      super(type, bubbles, cancelable);

      // Remember the toggle switch's state so it can be accessed within
      // ToggleEvent.TOGGLE listeners
      this.isOn = isOn;
    }

    // Every custom event class must override clone( )
    public override function clone( ):Event {
      return new ToggleEvent(type, bubbles, cancelable, isOn);
    }

    // Every custom event class must override toString( ).
    public override function toString( ):String {
      return formatToString("ToggleEvent", "type", "bubbles",
                            "cancelable", "eventPhase", "isOn");
    }
  }
}
```

Example 12-5. The control panel application classes (continued)

```
// The ToggleSwitch class
package {
  import flash.display.*;
  import flash.events.*;

  // Represents a simple toggle-switch widget with preventable default
  // behavior
  public class ToggleSwitch extends Sprite {
    // Remembers the state of the switch
    private var isOn:Boolean;
    // Contains the toggle switch graphics
    private var icon:Sprite;

    // Constructor
    public function ToggleSwitch () {
      // Create the Sprite to contain the toggle switch graphics
      icon = new Sprite();
      addChild(icon);

      // Set the switch to off by default
      isOn = false;
      drawOffState();

      // Register to be notified when the user clicks the switch graphic
      icon.addEventListener(MouseEvent.CLICK, clickListener);
    }

    // Listener executed when the user clicks the toggle switch
    private function clickListener (e:MouseEvent):void {
      // The user has attempted to turn the switch on or off, so ask
      // ActionScript to dispatch a ToggleEvent.TOGGLE_ATTEMPT event,
      // targeted at this ToggleSwitch object. First create the event
      // object...
      var toggleEvent:ToggleEvent =
                            new ToggleEvent(ToggleEvent.TOGGLE_ATTEMPT,
                                            true, true);
      // ...then request the event dispatch
      dispatchEvent(toggleEvent);

      // The ToggleEvent.TOGGLE_ATTEMPT event dispatch is now complete.
      // If no listener prevented the default event behavior...
      if (!toggleEvent.isDefaultPrevented()) {
        // ...then toggle the switch
        toggle();
      }
    }

    // Turns the switch on if it is currently off, or off if it is
    // currently on. Note that the switch can be toggled programmatically,
    // even if the user does not have privileges to toggle it manually.
    public function toggle ():void {
      // Toggle the switch state
      isOn = !isOn;
```

Example 12-5. The control panel application classes (continued)

```
      // Draw the matching graphic for the new switch state
      if (isOn) {
        drawOnState( );
      } else {
        drawOffState( );
      }

      // Ask ActionScript to dispatch a ToggleEvent.TOGGLE event, targeted
      // at this ToggleSwitch object
      var toggleEvent:ToggleEvent = new ToggleEvent(ToggleEvent.TOGGLE,
                                                    true, false, isOn);
      dispatchEvent(toggleEvent);
    }

    // Draws the graphics for the off state
    private function drawOffState ( ):void {
      icon.graphics.clear( );
      icon.graphics.lineStyle(1);
      icon.graphics.beginFill(0xFFFFFF);
      icon.graphics.drawRect(0, 0, 20, 20);
    }

    // Draws the graphics for the on state
    private function drawOnState ( ):void {
      icon.graphics.clear( );
      icon.graphics.lineStyle(1);
      icon.graphics.beginFill(0xFFFFFF);
      icon.graphics.drawRect(0, 0, 20, 20);
      icon.graphics.beginFill(0x000000);
      icon.graphics.drawRect(5, 5, 10, 10);
    }
  }
}

// The ControlPanel class (the application's main class)
package {
  import flash.display.*;

  // A generic application that demonstrates the prevention of
  // default behavior for custom events
  public class ControlPanel extends Sprite {
    // Set this application user's privilege level. In this example, only
    // users with UserType.ADMIN privileges can use the toggle switch.
    private var userType:int = UserType.GUEST;

    // Constructor
    public function ControlPanel ( ) {
      // Create a ToggleSwitch
      var toggleSwitch:ToggleSwitch = new ToggleSwitch( );
      // Register for ToggleEvent.TOGGLE_ATTEMPT events
      toggleSwitch.addEventListener(ToggleEvent.TOGGLE_ATTEMPT,
                                    toggleAttemptListener);
```

Example 12-5. The control panel application classes (continued)

```
      // Register for ToggleEvent.TOGGLE events
      toggleSwitch.addEventListener(ToggleEvent.TOGGLE,
                                    toggleListener);
      // Add the toggle switch to this object's display hierarchy
      addChild(toggleSwitch);
    }

    // Listener executed whenever a ToggleEvent.TOGGLE_ATTEMPT event occurs
    private function toggleAttemptListener (e:ToggleEvent):void {
      // If the user is a guest...
      if (userType == UserType.GUEST) {
        // ...deny the attempted use of the toggle switch
        e.preventDefault( );
      }
    }

    // Listener executed whenever a ToggleEvent.TOGGLE event occurs
    private function toggleListener (e:ToggleEvent):void {
      if (e.isOn) {
        trace("The ToggleSwitch is now on.");
      } else {
        trace("The ToggleSwitch is now off.");
      }
    }
  }
}

// The UserType class
package {
  // Defines constants representing levels of user privilege for the
  // control panel application
  public class UserType {
    public static const GUEST:int = 0;
    public static const ADMIN:int = 1;
  }
}
```

Now that we've covered custom events in ActionScript, let's turn our attention to two final advanced event topics.

Type Weakness in ActionScript's Event Architecture

ActionScript's listener-based event architecture involves many different participants—the event listener, the object that registers the listener, the event target, the event object, and the event name. A given event dispatch (and response) succeeds only when those participants interoperate properly. In order for the participants to interoperate properly, the following basic assumptions must be met:

- The event type for which the listener registered must exist
- The listener, itself, must exist

- The listener must know how to handle the event object dispatched when the event occurs
- The object that registered the listener must support the specified event type

When a listener registers with an object for an event, it enters into a datatype-based contract that guarantees the first three of the preceding four assumptions. If that contract is not upheld, ActionScript generates a datatype error. For example, consider the following event-listener registration and definition code, which includes three intentional event-listener-contract violations (shown in bold):

```
urlLoader.addEventListener(Event.COMPLTE, completeListenr);

private function completeListener (e:MouseEvent):void {
  trace("Load complete");
}
```

The event-listener contract violations in the preceding code are as follows:

- The constant Event.COMPLTE has a typo: it is missing an "E." ActionScript generates an error warning the programmer that the event type for which the listener is attempting to register does not exist.
- The event listener name, completeListenr, has a typo: another missing "e." ActionScript generates an error warning the programmer that the listener being registered does not exist.
- The datatype specified for *completeListener()*'s first parameter is *MouseEvent*, which does not match the datatype of the event object for a Event.COMPLETE event. At event dispatch time, ActionScript generates an error warning the programmer that the listener cannot handle the dispatched event object.

If we were to change the preceding code to address its three datatype errors, the event dispatch and response would proceed successfully.

 The datatype-based contract between an event listener and the object that registers that listener helps us ensure that our event-response code runs properly.

However, the contract between a listener and the object that registers that listener has a weakness: it does not guarantee that the object supports the specified event type. For example, consider the following code, which registers a listener with urlLoader for TextEvent.TEXT_INPUT events:

```
urlLoader.addEventListener(TextEvent.TEXT_INPUT, textInputListener);
```

Even though, in practical terms, we can safely assume that a *URLLoader* object will never be the target of a TextEvent.TEXT_INPUT event, the preceding code does not generate an error. In ActionScript, listeners can register for events by any name. For example, the following nonsensical code is also legal:

```
urlLoader.addEventListener("dlrognw", dlrognwListener);
```

While it may seem self-evident that urlLoader will never be the target of an event named "dlrognw," it *is* actually possible for a program to cause such an event to be dispatched. The following code demonstrates:

```
urlLoader.dispatchEvent(new Event("dlrognw"));
```

To account for the possibility that a program might target an event dispatch of any event type at any object, ActionScript intentionally does not enforce the concept of "supported events." This flexibility is the subject of some debate because it leads to potentially difficult-to-diagnose bugs in code. For example, suppose we use the *Loader* class to load an external image, as follows:

```
var loader:Loader = new Loader();
loader.load(new URLRequest("image.jpg"));
```

Also suppose we assume that loader will be the target of load-progress events for the loading asset (much as a *URLLoader* object is the target of load-progress events for a loading asset). We, therefore, attempt to handle the Event.COMPLETE event for our loading asset by registering directly with the *Loader* object, as follows:

```
loader.addEventListener(Event.COMPLETE, completeListener);
```

When we run our code, we're surprised to find that even though no errors occur, *completeListener()* is never triggered. Because no errors are generated, we have no immediate way to diagnose the problem in our code. The ensuing research and debugging costs us time and, in all likelihood, no small amount of frustration. Only by consulting Adobe's documentation do we find the problem: *Loader* objects, in fact, are *not* the target of load-progress events; instead, load-progress events must be handled through each *Loader* object's *LoaderInfo* instance, as follows:

```
loader.contentLoaderInfo.addEventListener(Event.COMPLETE, completeListener);
```

In the future, ActionScript might allow classes to declare the events they support, and corresponding compiler warnings for attempts to register for unsupported events. In the meantime, by overriding the *addEventListener()* method, classes that implement custom events can optionally throw a custom error when listeners register for unsupported events, as shown in the following code:

```
public override function addEventListener(eventType:String,
                                          handler:Function,
                                          capture:Boolean = false,
                                          priority:int = 0,
                                          weakRef:Boolean = false):void {
  // The canDispatchEvent() method (not shown) checks the specified
  // eventType against the class's list of supported events, and
  // returns a Boolean indicating whether the specified and eventType is
  // a supported event
  if(canDispatchEvent(eventType)) {
    // The event is supported, so proceed with registration
    super.addEventListener(eventType, handler, capture, priority, weakRef);
```

```
  } else {
    // The event is not supported, so throw an error
    throw new Error(this + " does not support events of type '"
                    + eventType + "'" );
  }
}
```

The moral of the story is: be extra cautious when registering a listener for an event. Always ensure that the object with which the listener is registered actually supports the required event.

Now let's consider one last event-architecture issue: event handling in applications comprised of *.swf* files from different Internet domains. The following section requires a basic understanding of *.swf*-file-loading techniques, covered in Chapter 28.

Handling Events Across Security Boundaries

In the upcoming Chapter 19, we'll study a variety of scenarios in which security restrictions prevent one *.swf* file from *cross-scripting* (programmatically controlling) another. When two *.swf* files are prevented from cross-scripting each other due to Flash Player security restrictions, they are subject to the following important event-handling limitations:

- Event listeners in one *.swf* file are forbidden from registering for events with objects in the other *.swf* file.
- When an event-dispatch targets an object in a display hierarchy, any objects inaccessible to the target's *.swf* file are not included in the event flow.

Fortunately, the preceding limitations can be completely circumvented using the *flash.system.Security* class's static method, *allowDomain()*. Let's consider two examples showing how *allowDomain()* can be used to circumvent each of the preceding limitations.

 For information on loading *.swf* files see Chapter 28.

Module.swf Listener Registers with Main.swf Object

Suppose a *.swf* file from one site (*site-a.com/Main.swf*) loads a *.swf* file from another site (*site-b.com/Module.swf*). Further suppose that *Module.swf* defines a listener that wishes to register with an object created by *Main.swf*. To permit the registration, *Main.swf* must execute the following line of code before *Module.swf* registers the listener:

```
Security.allowDomain("site-b.com");
```

The preceding line of code allows all *.swf* files from *site-b.com* (including *Module.swf*) to register listeners with any object created by *Main.swf*.

Main.Swf Listener Receives Notification for an Event Targeted at a Module.swf Display Object

Continuing with the *"Main.swf* loads *Module.swf"* scenario from the preceding section, suppose *Main.swf*'s main class instance adds the *Loader* object containing *Module.swf* to its display hierarchy, as follows:

```
package {
  import flash.display.*;
  import flash.net.*;
  import flash.events.*;

  public class Main extends Sprite {
    private var loader:Loader;

    public function Main( ) {
      loader = new Loader( );
      loader.load(new URLRequest("http://site-b.com/Module.swf"));
      // Add the Loader object containing Module.swf to this object's
      // display hierarchy
      addChild(loader);
    }
  }
}
```

Also suppose that *Main.swf*'s main class instance wishes to be notified any time an object in *Module.swf* is clicked. Accordingly, *Main.swf*'s main class instance registers a listener with loader for MouseEvent.CLICK events, as follows:

```
package {
  import flash.display.*;
  import flash.net.*;
  import flash.events.*;

  public class Main extends Sprite {
    private var loader:Loader;

    public function Main( ) {
      loader = new Loader( );
      loader.load(new URLRequest("http://site-b.com/Module.swf"));
      addChild(loader);
      loader.addEventListener(MouseEvent.CLICK, clickListener);
    }

    private function clickListener (e:MouseEvent):void {
      trace("Module.swf was clicked");
    }
  }
}
```

However, because *Main.swf* and *Module.swf* are from different Internet domains, security limitations prevent *clickListener()* from being triggered by MouseEvent.CLICK events targeted at loader's display descendants (i.e., display objects in *Module.swf*).

To circumvent this limitation, *Module.swf*'s main-class constructor includes the following code:

```
Security.allowDomain("site-a.com");
```

After the preceding line of code runs, *Main.swf* (and all *.swf* files from *site-a.com*) are trusted by *Module.swf*, so *Main.swf*'s main class instance is included in the event flow when the Flash client runtime dispatches MouseEvent.CLICK events targeted at objects in *Module.swf*. As a result, *clickListener()* is triggered anytime an object in *Module.swf* is clicked.

 For complete information on *allowDomain()* and Flash Player security, see the section "Creator Permissions (allowDomain())" in Chapter 19.

Note that calling *allowDomain()* does more than just permit event handling across security boundaries: it gives all *.swf* files from the permitted domain full license to cross-script the *.swf* file in which the *allowDomain()* invocation occurs. But there's an alternative to *allowDomain()*'s broad-based permissions.

An Alternative to allowDomain( ): Shared Events

In some cases, *.swf* files from different domains may wish to share events without allowing full cross-scripting privileges. To account for such situations, Flash Player provides the *LoaderInfo* class's instance variable sharedEvents. The sharedEvents variable is a simple, neutral object through which two *.swf* files can pass events to each other, regardless of security restrictions. The technique allows event-based inter-*.swf* communication without security concessions but involves more code than the *allowDomain()* alternative.

Let's explore sharedEvents through an example scenario. Suppose Tommy runs a fireworks company with a Flash-based promotional web site, *www.blast.ca*. Tommy hires a contractor, Derek, to produce a self-contained mouse effect that randomly generates animated firework explosions behind the mouse pointer. Derek creates a *.swf* file, *MouseEffect.swf*, containing the effect, and posts it at *www.dereksflasheffects.com/MouseEffect.swf*. Derek tells Tommy to load *MouseEffect.swf* into his application, *www.blast.ca/BlastSite.swf*. Derek and Tommy agree that *MouseEffect.swf* should be hosted at *www.dereksflasheffects.com* so that Derek can easily update the file without requiring any changes to Tommy's web site.

Tommy asks Derek to make *MouseEffect.swf* stop generating explosions when the mouse pointer leaves Flash Player's display area. Derek thinks that's a sensible idea and starts writing the appropriate code. Normally, in order to detect the mouse's departure from Flash Player's display area, code in *MouseEffect.swf* would register for Event.MOUSE_LEAVE events with the *Stage* instance. However, because *MouseEffect.swf* and *BlastSite.swf* come from different domains, *MouseEffect.swf* does not have access

to the *Stage* instance. Tommy decides that, rather than give *MouseEffect.swf* full
access to *BlastSite.swf*, he'll simply forward all Event.MOUSE_LEAVE events to
MouseEffect.swf via sharedEvents.

Example 12-6 shows the relevant event-forwarding code from *BlastSite.swf*.

Example 12-6. Forwarding an event through sharedEvents

```
package {
  import flash.display.*;
  import flash.net.*;
  import flash.events.*;
  import flash.system.*;

  public class BlastSite extends Sprite {
    private var loader:Loader;

    public function BlastSite ( ) {
      // Load MouseEffect.swf
      loader = new Loader( );
      loader.load(
        new URLRequest("http://www.dereksflasheffects.com/MouseEffect.swf"));
      addChild(loader);

      // Register for Event.MOUSE_LEAVE events
      stage.addEventListener(Event.MOUSE_LEAVE, mouseLeaveListener);
    }

    // When Event.MOUSE_LEAVE occurs...
    private function mouseLeaveListener (e:Event):void {
      // ...forward it to MouseEffect.swf
      loader.contentLoaderInfo.sharedEvents.dispatchEvent(e);
    }
  }
}
```

Example 12-7 shows the relevant event-handling code from *MouseEffect.swf*:

Example 12-7. Handling an Event Targeted at sharedEvents

```
package {
  import flash.display.Sprite;
  import flash.events.*;

  public class MouseEffect extends Sprite {
    public function MouseEffect ( ) {
      // Register for Event.MOUSE_LEAVE with sharedEvents
      loaderInfo.sharedEvents.addEventListener(Event.MOUSE_LEAVE,
                                               mouseLeaveListener);
    }

    // Handles Event.MOUSE_LEAVE events targeted at sharedEvents
    private function mouseLeaveListener (e:Event):void {
      trace("MouseEffect.mouseLeaveListener( ) was invoked...");
      // Stop the explosions effect here...
    }
```

Example 12-7. Handling an Event Targeted at sharedEvents (continued)

```
  }
}
```

Derek gets paid and puts the money towards a trip to Japan. Tommy is happy with the explosion effect, although he's not sure it has increased his sales.

What's Next?

We're making good progress in our study of ActionScript fundamentals. If you've read and understood the concept in the past 12 chapters, you now have enough knowledge of ActionScript to start learning about most Flash client runtime APIs. So it's time to choose your own adventure. If you want to continue exploring Action-Script's core features, head on to Chapter 13, where we'll learn to write code that recovers from runtime error conditions. If, on the other hand, you'd prefer to learn how to use ActionScript to display content on screen, then skip ahead to Part II.

Exceptions and Error Handling

In this chapter, we'll explore ActionScript's system for generating and responding to runtime errors—or *exceptions*. In ActionScript, errors can be generated both by the Flash runtime and by the program that is executing. Errors generated by the Flash runtime are known as *built-in errors*; errors generated by a program are known as *custom errors*. In a program, we can respond to, or *handle*, any error (whether built-in or custom) using the *try/catch/finally* statement; we can generate an error via the *throw* statement.

To learn how to generate and respond to errors in a program, we'll revisit our virtual zoo program.

 This chapter's updates to the virtual zoo program are the last we'll make until the end of this book. To complete the virtual zoo program we must discuss display programming and mouse input, both of which are covered in Part II. After you read Part II, consult the "The Final Virtual Zoo," (Appendix) to see how to add graphics and interactivity to the virtual zoo program.

The Exception-Handling Cycle

Recall that the *VirtualPet* class defines a *setName()* method that sets the petName variable of *VirtualPet* instances. As a refresher, here's the relevant *VirtualPet* class code (portions of the class that do not pertain to setting the petName variable are omitted):

```
public class VirtualPet {
  private var petName:String;

  public function setName (newName:String):void {
    // If the proposed new name has more than maxNameLength characters...
    if (newName.length > VirtualPet.maxNameLength) {
      // ...truncate it
      newName = newName.substr(0, VirtualPet.maxNameLength);
    } else if (newName == "") {
      // ...otherwise, if the proposed new name is an empty string,
```

```
      // then terminate this method without changing petName
      return;
    }

    // Assign the new, validated name to petName
    petName = newName;
  }
}
```

The *setName()* method checks whether a new pet name has a legal number of characters before changing the petName variable. If the new pet name is not valid, the change is not made; otherwise, the change is allowed.

Let's revise the *setName()* method so that it generates an exception (signals an error) when the newName parameter is passed an illegal number of characters. Later we'll write some error-recovery code to handle *setName()*'s new exception.

To generate an exception in our code, we use the *throw* statement, which takes the following form:

```
throw expression
```

In the preceding code, *expression* is a data value that describes some unusual or problematic situation. Using *throw* to signal an error is sometimes referred to as "throwing an exception." ActionScript allows any value to act as the *expression* of a *throw* statement. For example, the *expression* value could be the string literal "Something went wrong!" or it could be a numeric error code. However, as a best practice, Adobe recommends using an instance of the built-in *Error* class (or one of its subclasses) as the value of *expression*. The *Error* class is a standard class for representing error conditions in a program. Its instance variable message is used to describe an error.

The *throw* statement halts all currently executing code and passes *expression* to a special section of code known as a *catch* block that will respond to, or *handle*, the problem. Before we consider how *catch* blocks works, let's rewrite *setName()* so that it generates an exception with a *throw* statement when an invalid petName is received. Here's the code:

```
public function setName (newName:String):void {
  // If the proposed new name has an illegal number of characters...
  if (newName.length > VirtualPet.maxNameLength || newName == "") {
    // ...generate an error
    throw new Error("Invalid pet name specified.");
  }

  // Assign the new valid name to petName
  petName = newName;
}
```

In our revised *setName()* method, when the value of newName is illegal, we use *throw* to halt the method's execution rather than simply truncating the name as we did previously. We also supply a description of the problem—"Invalid pet name specified"—as an argument to the *Error* constructor, indicating what went wrong. The *Error* constructor assigns that description to the new *Error* object's message variable.

If *setName()* encounters no problems with newName, then the method completes normally, and the code that called it can rest assured that it performed its job successfully. Otherwise, a *catch* block must handle the problem. A *catch* block is part of a larger statement known as the *try/catch/finally* statement. The *try/catch/finally* statement provides a backup plan for code that might throw an exception. Here's the general structure of a typical *try/catch/finally* statement:

```
try {
  // Code here might generate an exception
} catch (e:type) {
  // Code here deals with the problem
} finally {
  // Code here executes whether or not code in the try block
  // throws an exception
}
```

In the preceding code, the keyword *try* tells ActionScript that we're about to execute some code that might generate an exception. The *catch* block handles exceptions generated by the *try* block. Code in the *catch* block executes if, and only if, code in the *try* block generates an exception. Code in the *finally* block always executes after either the *try* block or the *catch* block has finished. The *finally* block of a *try/catch/finally* statement typically contains cleanup code that must execute whether or not an exception occurs in the corresponding *try* block.

Notice the typical structure:

- The *try* block executes code that might throw an exception.
- Code in the *try* block uses the *throw* statement to indicate any errors.
- If no error is thrown in the *try* block, then the *try* block executes in full, and the program skips the *catch* block.
- If an error is thrown in the *try* block, the *try* block is aborted, and the *catch* block executes. The *catch* block deals with any errors that occur in the *try* block.
- The *finally* block executes

In many cases, the *finally* block is not required, and is, therefore, omitted. In the coming examples, we'll omit the *finally* block. Later in the section "The finally Block," we'll study a *finally* block example.

When the *catch* block is executed, it receives the *expression* of the *throw* statement as a parameter. In the *catch* block, we can use that expression to help diagnose the error thrown by the *try* block. Metaphorically, the code that encounters a problem *throws* an exception (passes an *Error* object) to the *catch* block, which receives it as a parameter (*catches* it).

We'll find out what happens if an error is never caught later in the section "Uncaught Exceptions," later in this chapter.

Here's an example *try/catch/finally* statement.

```
try {
  somePet.setName("James");
  // If we get this far, no exception occurred; proceed as planned.
  trace("Pet name set successfully.");
} catch (e:Error) {
  // ERROR! Invalid data. Display a warning.
  trace("An error occurred: " + e.message);
}
```

When we invoke pet.setName( ) within the preceding *try* block, if *setName()*'s *throw* statement doesn't execute (if no error occurs), then the subsequent statements in the *try* block execute normally, and the program skips the *catch* block entirely. But if *setName()* throws an exception, the program immediately skips to and executes the *catch* block. Within the *catch* block, the value of the parameter e is the *Error* object from the *throw* statement in *setName()*. In the preceding example, the code in the *catch* block simply displays that *Error* object's message variable during debugging. But in a more sophisticated application, the *catch* block might attempt to recover from the error, perhaps by displaying a dialog box requesting that the user supply a valid name.

Handling Multiple Types of Exceptions

The exception example from the preceding section was simplistic. What happens if our method generates more than one kind of error? Are they all sent to the same *catch* block? Well, that's up to the developer; they certainly could be, but it's more typical and better practice for different kinds of errors to be handled by separate *catch* blocks. Let's examine why.

Suppose we want a finer-grained set of error messages in our *setName()* method: one for general invalid data, one for a name that's too short, and one for a name that's too long. The body of our revised *setName()* method might look like this:

```
if (newName.indexOf(" ") == 0) {
  // Names can't start with a space...
  throw new Error("Invalid pet name specified.");
} else if (newName == "") {
  throw new Error("Pet name too short.");
} else if (newName.length > VirtualPet.maxNameLength) {
  throw new Error("Pet name too long.");
}
```

To handle the three possible error messages in our new *setName()* message, we might be tempted to code our *try/catch/finally* statement as follows:

```
try {
  somePet.setName("somePetName");
  // If we get this far, no exception occurred; proceed as planned.
  trace("Pet name set successfully.");
} catch (e:Error) {
  switch (e.message) {
    case "Invalid pet name specified.":
    trace("An error occurred: " + e.message);
    trace("Please specify a valid name.");
    break;

    case "Pet name too short.":
    trace("An error occurred: " + e.message);
    trace("Please specify a longer name.");
    break;

    case "Pet name too long.":
    trace("An error occurred: " + e.message);
    trace("Please specify a shorter name.");
    break;
  }
}
```

Admittedly, that code does work, but it's fraught with problems. First, and most serious, the errors are distinguished from one another only by the text in a string that is hidden within the *VirtualPet* class. Each time we want to check what kind of errors might occur in *setName()*, we have to look inside the *VirtualPet* class and find the error message strings. Using message strings for error identification across multiple methods and classes is highly prone to human error and makes our code difficult to maintain. Second, the *switch* statement itself is hard to read. We're not much farther ahead than we would be if we had used, say, numeric error codes instead of formal exceptions.

Fortunately, there's a formal (and elegant) way to handle multiple exception types. Each *try* block can have any number of supporting *catch* blocks. When an exception is thrown in a *try* block that has multiple *catch* blocks, ActionScript executes the *catch* block whose parameter's datatype matches the datatype of the value originally thrown.

Here's the general syntax of a *try* statement with multiple *catch* blocks:

```
try {
  // Code that might generate an exception.
} catch (e:ErrorType1) {
  // Error-handling code for ErrorType1.
} catch (e:ErrorType2) {
  // Error-handling code for ErrorType2.
} catch (e:ErrorTypen) {
  // Error-handling code for ErrorTypen.
}
```

If a *throw* statement in the preceding *try* block were to throw an expression of type *ErrorType1*, then the first *catch* block would be executed. For example, the following code causes the first *catch* block to execute:

```
throw new ErrorType1();
```

If a *throw* statement were to pass an expression of type *ErrorType2*, then the second *catch* clause would be executed, and so on. As we learned earlier, in ActionScript the *throw* statement expression can belong to any datatype. However, remember that, as a best practice, most programs throw instances of the *Error* class or one of its subclasses only.

If we want to throw multiple kinds of exceptions in an application, we define an *Error* subclass for each kind of exception. It is up to you as the developer to decide what level of granularity you require (i.e., to what degree you need to differentiate among different error conditions).

Determining Exception Type Granularity

Should you define an *Error* subclass for each and every error condition? Typically, no, you won't need that level of granularity because in many cases multiple error conditions can be treated in the same way. If you don't need to differentiate among multiple error conditions, you can group them together under a single custom *Error* subclass. For example, you might define a single *Error* subclass named *InvalidInputException* to handle a wide range of input problems.

That said, you should define a separate *Error* subclass for each error condition that you want to distinguish from other possible conditions. To help you understand when you should create a new subclass for a given error condition and to demonstrate how to group multiple conditions into a single subclass, let's return to the *setName()* method.

Earlier we generated three exceptions from the *setName()* method. All three exceptions used the generic *Error* class. Here's the code again:

```
if (newName.indexOf(" ") == 0) {
  // Names can't start with a space...
  throw new Error("Invalid pet name specified.");
} else if (newName == "") {
  throw new Error("Pet name too short.");
} else if (newName.length > VirtualPet.maxNameLength) {
  throw new Error("Pet name too long.");
}
```

In the preceding code, to differentiate *VirtualPet* exceptions from all other exceptions in our application, we used the *Error* class's message variable, which, as we just learned, made our exceptions awkward to use and prone to human error. A better way to set *VirtualPet*-related data errors apart from other errors in our application is to define a custom *Error* subclass, *VirtualPetNameException*, as follows:

```
// Code in VirtualPetNameException.as:
package zoo {
  public class VirtualPetNameException extends Error {
    public function VirtualPetNameException () {
      // Pass an error message to the Error constructor, to be
      // assigned to this object's message variable
      super("Invalid pet name specified.");
    }
  }
}
```

With our *VirtualPetNameException* class in place, our *setName()* method can throw its very own type of error, as follows:

```
public function setName (newName:String):void {
  if (newName.indexOf(" ") == 0) {
    throw new VirtualPetNameException();
  } else if (newName == "") {
    throw new VirtualPetNameException();
  } else if (newName.length > VirtualPet.maxNameLength) {
    throw new VirtualPetNameException();
  }

  petName = newName;
}
```

Notice that the preceding method definition throws the same error type (*VirtualPetNameException*) for all three *VirtualPet*-related error conditions. As developers of the *VirtualPet* class, we now face the crux of the error-granularity issue. We must decide not only how distinguishable we want *VirtualPet* error messages to be from other application errors, but also how distinguishable we want those errors to be from one another. We have the following options:

Option 1: Use a single VirtualPet error class.
> In this option, we leave the preceding *setName()* method definition as it is. As we'll see shortly, this option lets us distinguish *VirtualPet* errors from other generic errors in the program, but it does not help us distinguish internally among the three varieties of *VirtualPet*-related errors (invalid data, too short a pet name, and too long a pet name).

Option 2: Simplify code, but still use a single VirtualPet error class.
> In this option, we modify the *setName()* method so it checks for all three error conditions using a single *if* statement. This option is the same as the previous option, but uses cleaner code.

Option 3: Use debugging messages to distinguish among errors.
> In this option, we add configurable debugging messages to the *VirtualPetNameException* class. This option adds slightly more granularity than the previous two options but only for the sake of the developer and only during debugging.

Option 4: Create a custom exception class for each error condition.

In this option, we create two custom *VirtualPetNameException* subclasses, *VirtualPetInsufficientDataException* and *VirtualPetExcessDataException*. This option provides the most granularity; it lets a program respond independently to the three varieties of *VirtualPet*-related errors using formal branching logic.

Let's consider the preceding options in turn.

Options 1 and 2: Using a single custom-exception type

Our first option is to accept the preceding *setName()* definition, which throws the same error type (*VirtualPetNameException*) for all three *VirtualPet*-related error conditions. Because the method uses *VirtualPetNameException* and not *Error* to throw exceptions, *VirtualPet* exceptions are already distinguishable from other generic exceptions. Users of the *setName()* method can use code such as the following to discriminate between *VirtualPet*-related errors and other generic errors:

```
try {
  // This call to setName() will generate a VirtualPetNameException.
  somePet.setName("");
  // Other statements in this try block might generate other generic errors.
  // For demonstration purposes, we'll throw a generic error directly.
  throw new Error("A generic error.");
} catch (e:VirtualPetNameException) {
  // Handle VirtualPet name errors here.
  trace("An error occurred: " + e.message);
  trace("Please specify a valid name.");
} catch (e:Error) {
  // Handle all other errors here.
  trace("An error occurred: " + e.message);
}
```

For many applications, the level of error granularity provided by *VirtualPetNameException* is enough. In such a case, we should at least rewrite the *setName()* method so that it doesn't contain redundant code (throwing the *VirtualPetNameException* three times). Here's the rewritten code (which was Option 2 in our earlier list):

```
public function setName (newName:String):void {
  if (newName.indexOf(" ") == 0
      || newName == ""
      || newName.length > VirtualPet.maxNameLength) {
    throw new VirtualPetNameException();
  }

  petName = newName;
}
```

Rewriting code to improve its structure without changing its behavior is known as *refactoring*.

Option 3: Using configurable debugging messages

Option 3 adds configurable debugging messages to the *VirtualPetNameException* class. Options 1 and 2 let us distinguish a *VirtualPet* exception from other exceptions in the application but didn't help us distinguish a "too long" exception from a "too short" exception. If you feel that it's difficult to debug a *VirtualPet* name problem without knowing whether a *VirtualPet* object's name is too big or too small, you can adjust the *VirtualPetNameException* class so that it accepts an optional description (the equivalent of a proverbial "note to self"). Here's the adjusted *VirtualPetNameException* class:

```
package zoo {
  public class VirtualPetNameException extends Error {
    // Provide a constructor that allows a custom message to be supplied,
    // but uses the default error message when no custom message is supplied
    public function VirtualPetNameException (
                      message:String = "Invalid pet name specified.") {
      super(message);
    }
  }
}
```

To make use of our adjusted *VirtualPetNameException* class in *setName()*, we revert to our *setName()* code used in Option 1 and add debugging error messages, as follows:

```
public function setName (newName:String):void {
  if (newName.indexOf(" ") == 0) {
    // The default error message is fine in this case,
    // so don't bother specifying a custom error message.
    throw new VirtualPetNameException();
  } else if (newName == "") {
    // Here's the custom "too short" error message.
    throw new VirtualPetNameException("Pet name too short.");
  } else if (newName.length > VirtualPet.maxNameLength) {
    // Here's the custom "too long" error message.
    throw new VirtualPetNameException("Pet name too long.");
  }

  petName = newName;
}
```

Now that *setName()* supplies custom error messages, we'll have an easier time debugging a *VirtualPet* problem because we'll know more information when an error occurs. Our use of the *setName()* method has not changed, but we're better informed when something goes wrong, as shown next:

```
try {
  // This call to setName() will generate a VirtualPetNameException.
  somePet.setName("");
} catch (e:VirtualPetNameException) {
  // Handle VirtualPet name errors here.
  // In this case, the helpful debugging output is:
  // An error occurred: Pet name too short.
  trace("An error occurred: " + e.message);
} catch (e:Error) {
  // Handle all other errors here.
  trace("An error occurred: " + e.message);
}
```

Option 4: Multiple custom VirtualPetNameException subclasses

Option 3 added configurable debugging messages to the *VirtualPetNameException* class. It helped us investigate a problem in our code during development, but it doesn't help the program take independent action to recover from individual *VirtualPet* errors. To allow the program to execute independent code branches based on the type of *VirtualPet* error thrown, we need custom *VirtualPetNameException* subclasses, which is Option 4.

 If you want a program to differentiate among error conditions, implement a separate *Error* subclass for each one. Don't rely on the *message* variable alone to implement program branching logic. If your custom *Error* subclass defines a constructor that accepts an error message, you should use that message for debugging only, not for branching logic.

To independently differentiate among the *VirtualPet* class's three error conditions, we'll create three *Error* subclasses: *VirtualPetNameException*, *VirtualPetInsufficientDataException*, and *VirtualPetExcessDataException*. The *VirtualPetNameException* class extends *Error* directly. The *VirtualPetInsufficientDataException* and *VirtualPetExcessDataException* classes both extend *VirtualPetNameException* because we want to differentiate these specific error types from a more general invalid data exception.

Here's the source code for our three *VirtualPetError* subclasses:

```
// Code in VirtualPetNameException.as:
package zoo {
  public class VirtualPetNameException extends Error {
    public function VirtualPetNameException (
                        message:String = "Invalid pet name specified.") {
      super(message);
    }
  }
}

// Code in VirtualPetInsufficientDataException.as:
package zoo {
  public class VirtualPetInsufficientDataException
                                extends VirtualPetNameException {
```

```
    public function VirtualPetInsufficientDataException () {
      super("Pet name too short.");
    }
  }
}

// Code in VirtualPetExcessDataException.as:
package zoo {
  public class VirtualPetExcessDataException
                              extends VirtualPetNameException {
    public function VirtualPetExcessDataException () {
      super("Pet name too long.");
    }
  }
}
```

Each class specifies the value of its *message* variable directly and does not allow it to be customized on a per-use basis. When catching any of the preceding *VirtualPet* exceptions, our program will use the exception's datatype (not the *message* variable) to distinguish between the three kinds of exceptions.

Now that we have three exception types, let's update our *setName()* method to throw those types. Here's the code:

```
public function setName (newName:String):void {
  if (newName.indexOf(" ") == 0) {
    throw new VirtualPetNameException();
  } else if (newName == "") {
    throw new VirtualPetInsufficientDataException();
  } else if (newName.length > VirtualPet.maxNameLength) {
    throw new VirtualPetExcessDataException();
  }

  petName = newName;
}
```

Notice that we do not pass any error description to the various *VirtualPet* exception constructors. Once again, the description of each exception is set by each custom *Error* subclass using its message variable.

With each *VirtualPet* exception represented by its own class, the errors that can be generated by the *setName()* method are well-known to programmers working with *VirtualPet* instances. The exception types are visible outside the *VirtualPet* class, exposed appropriately to programmers working on the application. Just by glancing at the application class hierarchy, the programmer can determine the exceptions that relate to the *VirtualPet* class. Furthermore, if the programmer mistakenly uses the wrong name for an exception, the compiler generates a datatype error.

Now let's see how to add branching logic to our code based on the types of exceptions that can be generated by *setName()*. Pay close attention to the datatype of each *catch* block parameter and the placement of each *catch* block.

```
try {
  b.setName("somePetName");
} catch (e:VirtualPetExcessDataException) {
  // Handle "too long" case.
  trace("An error occurred: " + e.message);
  trace("Please specify a shorter name.");
} catch (e:VirtualPetInsufficientDataException) {
  // Handle "too short" case.
  trace("An error occurred: " + e.message);
  trace("Please specify a longer name.");
} catch (e:VirtualPetNameException) {
  // Handle general name errors.
  trace("An error occurred: " + e.message);
  trace("Please specify a valid name.");
}
```

In the preceding code, if the *setName()* method generates a *VirtualPetExcessDataException*, the first *catch* block executes. If *setName()* generates a *VirtualPetInsufficientDataException*, the second *catch* block executes. And if *setName()* generates a *VirtualPetNameException*, the third *catch* block executes. Notice that the error datatypes in the *catch* blocks progress from specific to general. When an exception is thrown, the *catch* block executed is the first one that matches the datatype of the exception.

Hence, if we changed the datatype of the first *catch* block parameter to *VirtualPetNameException*, the first catch block would execute for all three kinds of exceptions! (Remember, *VirtualPetNameException* is the superclass of both *VirtualPetInsufficientDataException* and *VirtualPetExcessDataException*, so they are considered matches for the *VirtualPetNameException* datatype.) In fact, we could prevent all of the *catch* blocks from executing simply by adding a new first *catch* block with a parameter datatype of *Error*:

```
try {
  b.setName("somePetName");
} catch (e:Error) {
  // Handle all errors. No other catch blocks will ever execute.
  trace("An error occurred:" + e.message);
  trace("The first catch block handled the error.");
} catch (e:VirtualPetExcessDataException) {
  // Handle "too long" case.
  trace("An error occurred: " + e.message);
  trace("Please specify a shorter name.");
} catch (e:VirtualPetInsufficientDataException) {
  // Handle "too short" case.
  trace("An error occurred: " + e.message);
  trace("Please specify a longer name.");
} catch (e:VirtualPetNameException) {
  // Handle general name errors.
  trace("An error occurred: " + e.message);
  trace("Please specify a valid name.");
}
```

Obviously, the addition of the first *catch* clause in the preceding code is self-defeating, but it does illustrate the hierarchical nature of exception handling. By placing a very generic *catch* block at the beginning of the catch list, we can handle all errors in a single location. Conversely, by placing a very generic *catch* block at the *end* of the catch list, we can provide a safety net that handles any errors not caught by earlier *catch* blocks. For example, in the following code, the final *catch* block executes only if the *try* block generates an exception that doesn't belong to the *VirtualPetExcessDataException*, *VirtualPetInsufficientDataException*, or *VirtualPetNameException* datatypes:

```
try {
  b.setName("somePetName");
} catch (e:VirtualPetExcessDataException) {
  // Handle overflow.
  trace("An error occurred: " + e.message);
  trace("Please specify a smaller value.");
} catch (e:VirtualPetInsufficientDataException) {
  // Handle under zero.
  trace("An error occurred: " + e.message);
  trace("Please specify a larger value.");
} catch (e:VirtualPetNameException) {
  // Handle general dimension errors.
  trace("An error occurred: " + e.message);
  trace("Please specify a valid dimension.");
} catch (e:Error) {
  // Handle any errors that don't qualify as VirtualPetNameException errors.
}
```

Remember, error granularity is a choice. In Option 4 we created a custom *Error* subclass for each variety of exception generated by the *VirtualPet* class. This approach gives our program the greatest ability to respond independently to different types of errors. But such flexibility is not necessarily required in many situations. Let the needs of your program's logic dictate how granular you make your errors.

Exception Bubbling

In ActionScript, an exception can be thrown anywhere in a program, even on a frame in a timeline script! Given that an exception can be thrown anywhere, how does ActionScript find the corresponding *catch* block to handle it? And what if no *catch* block exists? These mysteries are resolved through the magic of *exception bubbling*. Let's follow along a bubbly ride with ActionScript as it encounters a *throw* statement in a program. During the following dramatization, ActionScript's musings are shown in code comments.

When a *throw* statement executes, ActionScript immediately stops normal program flow and looks for an enclosing *try* block. For example, here's a *throw* statement:

```
// ActionScript: Hmm. A throw statement.
// Is there an enclosing try block for it?
throw new Error("Something went wrong");
```

If the *throw* statement is enclosed in a *try* block, ActionScript next tries to find a *catch* block whose parameter's datatype matches the datatype of the value thrown (in this case, *Error*):

```
// ActionScript: Great, I found a try block.
// Is there a matching catch block?
try {
  throw new Error("Something went wrong");
}
```

If a matching *catch* block is found, ActionScript transfers program control to that block:

```
try {
  throw new Error("Something went wrong");
// ActionScript: Found a catch block whose parameter datatype is Error!
//               The hunt's over. I'll execute this catch block now...
} catch (e:Error) {
  // Handle problems...
}
```

But if a matching *catch* block cannot be found or if the *throw* statement did not appear within a *try* block in the first place, then ActionScript checks whether the *throw* statement occurred within a method or function. If the *throw* statement occurred in a method or function, ActionScript searches for a *try* block around the code that invoked the method or function. The following code demonstrates how ActionScript reacts when, within a method, it encounters a *throw* statement that has no enclosing *try* block:

```
public function doSomething ():void {
  // ActionScript: Hmm. No try block here.
  // I'll check who called this method.
  throw new Error("Something went wrong");
}
```

If the code that invoked the method or function is enclosed in a *try* block, ActionScript looks for a matching *catch* block there and, if it finds a match, executes it. The following code demonstrates an exception thrown out of a method and caught where the method is invoked (i.e., one level up the *call stack*):

```
public class ProblemClass {
  public function doSomething ():void {
    // ActionScript: Hmm. No try block here.
    // I'll check who called this method.
    throw new Error("Something went wrong");
  }
}

public class ErrorDemo extends Sprite {
  public function ErrorDemo () {
    // ActionScript: Aha, here's who called doSomething(). And here's
    //               an enclosing try block with a catch block whose
    //               parameter datatype is Error! My work's done. catch
```

```
    //              block, please execute now...
    try {
      var problemObject:ProblemClass = new ProblemClass( );
      problemObject.doSomething( );
    } catch (e:Error) {
      // Handle problems...
      trace("Exception caught in ErrorDemo, thrown by doSomething( ).");
    }
  }
}
```

 The *call stack* is the list of functions and methods currently being executed by ActionScript at any given point in a program. The list includes the functions and methods in the reverse order from which they were called, from top to bottom. When a function is immediately below another function in the call stack, then the lower function was invoked by the higher. The lowest function in the call stack is the function currently executing.

In Flex Builder and the Flash authoring tool, you can use the debugger to view the call stack for the current program, as described in Adobe's documentation.

In the preceding code, an exception thrown by a method was caught by a *try/catch* block enclosing the method call statement. However, if no *try* block is found around the function or method caller, ActionScript searches up the entire call stack for a *try* block with a matching *catch* block. The following code shows a method throwing an error that is caught two levels up the call stack:

```
public class ProblemClass {
  public function doSomething ( ):void {
    // ActionScript: Hmm. No try block here.
    // I'll check who called this method.
    throw new Error("Something went wrong");
  }
}

public class NormalClass {
  public function NormalClass ( ) {
    // ActionScript: Aha, here's who called doSomething( ). But still
    //              no try block here. I'll check who called this method.
    var problemObject:ProblemClass = new ProblemClass( );
    problemObject.doSomething( );
  }
}

public class ErrorDemo extends Sprite {
  public function ErrorDemo ( ) {
    // ActionScript: Aha! Found a try block that has a catch block whose
    //              parameter's datatype is Error! My work's done.
    //              catch block, please execute now...
    try {
```

```
      var normalObject:NormalClass = new NormalClass();
    } catch (e:Error) {
      // Handle problems...
      trace("Exception caught in ErrorDemo.");
    }
  }
}
```

Notice that ActionScript finds the *try/catch* block despite the fact that it surrounds not the error-throwing code, nor the caller of the error-throwing method, but the caller of the method that called the error-throwing method!

The following code shows the preceding bubbling example in the context of our virtual pet program. In the following code listing, for brevity, only the pet-naming code is shown. Comments in the code describe how the exception bubbles.

```
package {
  import flash.display.Sprite;
  import zoo.*;

  public class VirtualZoo extends Sprite {
    private var pet:VirtualPet;

    public function VirtualZoo () {
      try {
        // This code attempts to give a pet a name that is too long.
        // As a result, the setName() method throws an error.
        // However, the exception is not caught in the VirtualPet
        // constructor (where setName() is called). Instead, the exception
        // is caught here, where the VirtualPet constructor was
        // called (i.e., two levels up the call stack).
        pet = new VirtualPet("Bartholomew McGillicuddy");
      } catch (e:Error) {
        trace("An error occurred: " + e.message);
        // If attempting to create a VirtualPet object causes an exception,
        // then the object won't be created. Hence, we create a new
        // VirtualPet object here with a known-to-be-valid name.
        pet = new VirtualPet("Unnamed Pet");
      }
    }
  }
}

package zoo {
  public class VirtualPet {
    public function VirtualPet (name:String):void {
      // Even though the setName() method is called here, exceptions thrown
      // by setName() are not handled here. They are handled up the call
      // stack, by the code that created this VirtualPet object.
      setName(name);
    }

    public function setName (newName:String):void {
      // Exceptions thrown in this method are not handled here. They are
```

```
// handled two-levels up the call stack, by the code that created
// this VirtualPet object.
if (newName.indexOf(" ") == 0) {
  throw new VirtualPetNameException();
} else if (newName == "") {
  throw new VirtualPetInsufficientDataException();
} else if (newName.length > VirtualPet.maxNameLength) {
  throw new VirtualPetExcessDataException();
}

petName = newName;
      }
    }
  }
```

Uncaught Exceptions

We've seen a number of scenarios in which we've caught various errors. But what happens if ActionScript never finds a *catch* block that can handle a thrown exception? If no eligible *catch* block is found anywhere in the call stack, then ActionScript aborts execution of all code currently remaining in the call stack. In addition, if the program is running in the debugger version of the Flash runtime, the error is reported via either a dialog box, the Output panel (Flash authoring tool), or the Console panel (Flex Builder). Execution of the program then resumes normally.

The following code demonstrates a method that throws an error that is never caught:

```
public class ProblemClass {
  public function doSomething ():void {
    // ActionScript: Hmm. No try block here.
    // I'll check who called this method.
    throw new Error("Something went wrong");
  }
}

public class ErrorDemo extends Sprite {
  public function ErrorDemo () {
    // ActionScript: Aha, here's who called doSomething(). But still
    // no try block here. Hmm. I searched all the way to the top, and found
    // no try block. If this Flash runtime is a debugger version, I'll
    // report the problem. Maybe the programmer will know what to do.
    var problemObject:ProblemClass = new ProblemClass();
    problemObject.doSomething();
  }
}
```

As we've just seen, because exceptions bubble up the call stack, it's not necessary for a method to catch its own exceptions. And it's not even necessary for the caller of a method to catch its exceptions. The exception can legally be caught at any level in the call stack. Any method can delegate exception handling to the code that calls it. That said, it's bad form and harmful to a program to throw an exception and then never catch it. You should always catch exceptions or, having encountered an uncaught exception, revise your code so that the exception isn't thrown in the first place.

The finally Block

So far, we've discussed only the *try* and *catch* blocks in the *try/catch/finally* statement. As we've seen, a *try* block contains code that might throw an exception, and a *catch* block contains code that executes in response to a thrown exception. The *finally* block, by comparison, contains code that always executes, whether or not code in the *try* block throws an exception.

The *finally* block is placed once (and only once) as the last block in a *try/catch/finally* statement. For example:

```
try {
  // substatements
} catch (e:ErrorType1) {
  // Handle ErrorType1 exceptions.
} catch (e:ErrorTypen) {
  // Handle ErrorTypen exceptions.
} finally {
  // This code always executes, no matter how the try block exits.
}
```

Misplacing the *finally* block causes a compile-time error.

In the preceding code, the *finally* block executes in one of these four circumstances:

- Immediately after the *try* block completes without errors
- Immediately after a *catch* block handles an exception generated in the *try* block
- Immediately before an uncaught exception bubbles up
- Immediately before a *return*, *continue*, or *break* statement transfers control out of the *try* or *catch* blocks

The *finally* block of a *try/catch/finally* statement typically contains cleanup code that must execute whether or not an exception occurs in the corresponding *try* block. For example, suppose we're creating a space shooter game, and we define a class, *SpaceShip*, to represent spaceships in the game. The *SpaceShip* class has a method, *attackEnemy( )*, which performs the following tasks:

- Sets the spaceship's current target
- Fires on that target
- Clears the current target (by setting the *SpaceShip* object's currentTarget variable to null)

In our hypothetical application, we'll assume that the first two of the preceding tasks might generate an exception. Further, we'll assume that the *attackEnemy( )* method doesn't handle those exceptions itself; instead, it passes them up to the calling method. Regardless of whether an exception is generated, the *attackEnemy()* method must set the currentTarget variable to null.

Here's what the *attackEnemy()* method would look like if we coded it with a *catch* statement (i.e., without using *finally*):

```
public function attackEnemy (enemy:SpaceShip):void {
  try {
    setCurrentTarget(enemy);
    fireOnCurrentTarget( );
  } catch (e:Error) {
    // Clear the current target if an exception occurs.
    setCurrentTarget(null);
    // Pass the exception up to the calling method.
    throw e;
  }
  // Clear the current target if no exception occurs.
  setCurrentTarget(null);
}
```

Notice that we must duplicate the statement, setCurrentTarget(null). We place it both in the *catch* block and after the *try/catch* statement, guaranteeing that it will run whether or not there's an exception in the *try* block. However, duplicating the statement is error prone. In the preceding method, a programmer could have easily forgotten to clear the current target after the *try/catch* block.

If we change our strategy by clearing the current target in a *finally* block, we remove the redundancy in the preceding code:

```
public function attackEnemy (enemy:SpaceShip):void {
  try {
    setCurrentTarget(enemy);
    fireOnCurrentTarget( );
  } finally {
    setCurrentTarget(null);
  }
}
```

In the revised version, the *finally* block clears the current target whether there's an exception or not. Because both situations are handled, we no longer have any need for a *catch* block; we can simply let the exception bubble up to the calling method automatically.

You might be wondering why we need the *finally* block at all. That is, why not just use the following code?

```
// This code might look decent, but there's a problem. Can you spot it?
public function attackEnemy (enemy:SpaceShip):void {
  setCurrentTarget(enemy);
  fireOnCurrentTarget( );
  setCurrentTarget(null);
}
```

Remember that when an exception is thrown, program control is transferred to the nearest suitable *catch* block in the call stack. Hence, if *fireOnCurrentTarget()* throws an exception, control transfers out of *attackEnemy()*, never to return, and setCurrentTarget(null) would never execute. By using a *finally* block, we guarantee that setCurrentTarget(null) executes before the exception bubbles up.

The *attackEnemy()* method example reflects the most common use of *finally* in multithreaded languages like Java, where a program can have multiple sections of code executing simultaneously. In Java, the following general structure is commonplace; it guards against the possibility that an object busy with a task might be inappropriately altered by another object during the execution of that task:

```
// Set a state indicating this object's current task.
// External objects should check this object's state
// before accessing or manipulating this object.
doingSomething = true;
try {
  // Perform the task.
  doSomething();
} finally {
  // Unset the "in-task" state (whether or not
  // the task generated an exception).
  doingSomething = false;
}
```

In ActionScript, the preceding state-management code is effectively unnecessary because the language is single-threaded, so no external object will ever attempt to alter the state of an object while it is busy executing a method. Therefore, *finally* is used much more rarely in ActionScript than it is in multithreaded languages. However, it can still be used for organizational purposes, to contain code that performs cleanup duties after other code has executed.

Nested Exceptions

So far we've used only single-level *try/catch/finally* statements, but exception-handling logic can also be nested. A *try/catch/finally* statement can appear inside the *try*, *catch*, or *finally* block of another *try/catch/finally* statement. This hierarchical nesting allows any block in a *try/catch/finally* statement to execute code that might, itself, throw an error.

For example, suppose we were writing a multiuser, web-based message board system. We define the following classes: *BulletinBoard*, the application's main class; *GUIManager*, which manages the user interface; and *User*, which represents a user on the board. We give *BulletinBoard* a method, *populateUserList()*, which displays the list of current active users. The *populateUserList()* method splits its work into two stages: first it retrieves an instance of a *List* class from the application's *GUIManager* instance. The *List* class represents an onscreen user list. Then *populateUserList()* populates that *List* instance with users from a supplied array of *User* instances. These two stages can both potentially generate an exception, so a nested *try/catch/finally* structure is used in the *populateUserList()* method. Let's take a closer look at this nested structure.

During the first stage of *populateUserList()*, if the *List* instance isn't available, a *UserListNotFound* exception is thrown by the *GUIManager*. The *UserListNotFound* exception is caught by the outer *try/catch/finally* statement.

If, on the other hand, the *List* instance is available, the *populateUserList()* method proceeds with stage two, during which a loop populates the *List* instance with users from the supplied array. For each iteration through the loop, if the current user's ID cannot be found, the *User.getID()* method throws a *UserIdNotSet* exception. The *UserIdNotSet* exception is caught by the nested *try/catch/finally* statement.

Here's the code:

```
public function populateUserList (users:Array):void {
  try {
    // Start stage 1...get the List instance.
    // If getUserList() throws an exception, the outer catch executes.
    var ulist:List = getGUIManager().getUserList();
    // Start stage 2...populate the List.
    for (var i:Number = 0; i < users.length; i++) {
      try {
        var thisUser:User = User(users[i]);
        // If getID() throws an exception, the nested catch executes.
        // If not, the user is added to the List instance via addItem().
        ulist.addItem(thisUser.getName(), thisUser.getID());
      } catch (e:UserIdNotSet) {
        trace(e.message);
        continue;  // Skip this user.
      }
    }
  } catch (e:UserListNotFound) {
    trace(e.message);
  }
}
```

Now that we've had a look at a specific nested exception example, let's consider how nested exceptions are handled in general.

If an exception occurs in a *try* block that is nested within another *try* block, and the inner *try* block has a *catch* block that can handle the exception, then the inner *catch* block is executed, and the program resumes at the end of the inner *try/catch/finally* statement.

```
try {
  try {
    // Exception occurs here.
    throw new Error("Test error");
  } catch (e:Error) {
```

```
      // Exception is handled here.
      trace(e.message);  // Displays: Test error
    }
    // The program resumes here.
  } catch (e:Error) {
    // Handle exceptions generated by the outer try block.
  }
```

If, on the other hand, an exception occurs in a *try* block that is nested within another *try* block, but the inner *try* block does not have a *catch* block that can handle the exception, then the exception bubbles up to the outer *try/catch/finally* statement (and, if necessary, up the call stack) until a suitable *catch* block is found, or the exception is not caught. If the exception is caught somewhere in the call stack, the program resumes at the end of the *try/catch/finally* statement that handled the exception. Note that in the following code example (and subsequent examples), the hypothetical error datatype *SomeSpecificError* is a placeholder used to force the thrown exception to not be caught. In order to test the code example in your own code, you'd have to create a subclass of *Error* called *SomeSpecificError*.

```
try {
  try {
    // Exception occurs here.
    throw new Error("Test error");
  } catch (e:SomeSpecificError) {
    // Exception is not handled here.
    trace(e.message);  // Never executes because the types don't match.
  }
} catch (e:Error) {
  // Exception is handled here.
  trace(e.message);  // Displays: Test error
}
// The program resumes here, immediately after the outer catch block
// has handled the exception.
```

If an exception occurs in a *try* block that is nested within a *catch* block, and the inner *try* block does not have a *catch* block that can handle the exception, then the search for a matching *catch* block begins outside the outer *try/catch/finally* statement:

```
try {
  // Outer exception occurs here.
  throw new Error("Test error 1");
} catch (e:Error) {
  // Outer exception handled here.
  trace(e.message);  // Displays: Test error 1
  try {
    // Inner exception occurs here.
    throw new Error("Test error 2");
  } catch (e:SomeSpecificError) {
    // Inner exception is not handled here.
    trace(e.message);  // Never executes because the types don't match.
  }
}
```

```
// The search for a matching catch block for the
// inner exception starts here.
```

Last, if an exception occurs in a *try* block that is nested within a *finally* block, but a prior exception is already in the process of bubbling up the call stack, then the new exception is handled before the prior exception continues to bubble up.

```
// This method throws an exception in a finally block.
public function throwTwoExceptions ( ):void {
  try {
    // Outer exception occurs here. Because there is no catch block for this
    // try block, the outer exception starts to bubble up,
    // out of this method.
    throw new Error("Test error 1");
  } finally {
    try {
      // Inner exception occurs here. The inner exception is
      // handled before the outer exception actually bubbles up.
      throw new Error("Test error 2");
    } catch (e:Error) {
    // Inner exception is handled here.
    trace("Internal catch: " + e.message);
    }
  }
}

// Elsewhere, within another method that calls the preceding method.
try {
  throwTwoExceptions( );
} catch (e:Error) {
  // The outer exception, which has bubbled up from throwTwoExceptions( ),
  // is handled here.
  trace("External catch: " + e.message);
}

// Output (notice that the inner exception is caught first):
Internal catch: Test error 2
External catch: Test error 1
```

If, in the preceding example, the exception thrown in the *finally* block had never been caught, then ActionScript would have reported the error during debugging, and aborted all other code in the call stack. As a result, the original, outer exception would have been discarded along with all code in the call stack. The following code demonstrates the preceding principle. It throws an uncaught exception from a *finally* statement. As a result, the exception thrown by the outer *try* block is discarded.

```
try {
  // Outer exception occurs here.
  throw new Error("Test error 1");
} finally {
  try {
    // Inner exception occurs here.
    throw new Error("Test error 2");
```

```
    } catch (e:SomeSpecificError) {
      // Inner exception is not handled here.
      trace("internal catch: " + e.message); // Never executes because
                                              // the types don't match.
    }
  }
  // The search for a matching catch block for the inner exception starts
  // here. If no match is ever found, then the inner exception is reported
  // during debugging, and the bubbling of the outer exception is aborted.
```

The preceding code demonstrates the effect of an uncaught exception in one scenario, but once again, it's not appropriate to allow an exception to go uncaught. In the preceding case, we should either catch the exception or revise our code so that the exception isn't thrown in the first place.

Control-Flow Changes in try/catch/finally

As we've seen throughout this chapter, the *throw* statement changes the flow of a program. When ActionScript encounters a *throw* statement, it immediately stops what it's doing and transfers program control to eligible *catch* and *finally* blocks. However, it is also quite legal for those *catch* and *finally* blocks to change program flow again via *return* (in the case of a method or function) or *break* or *continue* (in the case of a loop). Furthermore, a *return*, *break*, or *continue* statement can also appear in a *try* block.

To learn the rules of flow changes in the *try/catch/finally* statement, let's look at how the *return* statement affects program flow in a *try*, *catch*, and *finally* block. The following code examples contain a function, *changeFlow()*, which demonstrates a control flow in various hypothetical situations.

Example 13-1 shows a *return* statement in a *try* block, placed before an error is thrown. In this case, the method returns normally, and no error is ever thrown or handled. However, before the method returns, the *finally* block is executed. Note that you're unlikely to see code exactly like Example 13-1 in the real world. In most applied cases, the *return* statement would occur in a conditional statement and execute in response to some specific condition in the program.

Example 13-1. Using return in try, before throw

```
public function changeFlow ():void {
  try {
    return;
    throw new Error("Test error.");
  } catch (e:Error) {
    trace("Caught: " + e.message);
  } finally {
    trace("Finally executed.");
  }
  trace("Last line of method.");
```

Example 13-1. Using return in try, before throw (continued)

```
}

// Output when changeFlow( ) is invoked:
Finally executed.
```

Example 13-2 shows a *return* statement in a *try* block, placed after an error is thrown. In this case, the *return* statement is never executed because an error is thrown before it is reached. Once the error is caught and the *try/catch/finally* completes, execution resumes after the *try/catch/finally* statement, and the method exits at the end of the method body. Again, Example 13-2 demonstrates a principle but is atypical of real-world code, which would normally throw the error based on some condition.

Example 13-2. Using return in try, after throw

```
public function changeFlow ( ):void {
  try {
    throw new Error("Test error.");
    return;
  } catch (e:Error) {
    trace("Caught: " + e.message);
  } finally {
    trace("Finally executed.");
  }
  trace("Last line of method.");
}

// Output when changeFlow( ) is invoked:
Caught: Test error.
Finally executed.
Last line of method.
```

Example 13-3 shows a *return* statement in a *catch* block. In this case, the *return* statement executes when the work of error handling is done, and the code after the *try/catch/finally* statement never executes. However, as usual, before the method returns, the *finally* block is executed. Unlike Examples 13-1 and 13-2, this code *is* typical of a real-world scenario in which a method is aborted due to the occurrence of an error.

Example 13-3. Using return in catch

```
public function changeFlow ( ):void {
  try {
    throw new Error("Test error.");
  } catch (e:Error) {
    trace("Caught: " + e.message);
    return;
  } finally {
    trace("Finally executed.");
  }
  trace("Last line of function.");
```

Example 13-3. Using return in catch (continued)

```
}
```

```
// Output when changeFlow( ) is invoked:
Caught: Test error.
Finally executed.
```

 Due to a known bug, the code in Examples 13-2 and 13-3 causes a stack underflow in Flash Player 9. Adobe expects to fix the problem in a future version of Flash Player.

Example 13-4 shows a *return* statement in a *finally* block. In this case, the *return* statement executes when the *finally* block executes (as we learned earlier, a *finally* block executes when its corresponding *try* block completes in one of the following ways: without errors; with an error that was caught; with an error that was not caught; or due to a *return*, *break*, or *continue* statement). Notice that the *return* statement in Example 13-4 prevents any code in the method beyond the *try/catch/finally* statement from executing. You might use a similar technique to quit out of a method after invoking a block of code, whether or not that code throws an exception. In such a case, you'd typically surround the entire *try/catch/finally* block in a conditional statement (otherwise the remainder of the method would never execute!).

Example 13-4. Using return in finally

```
public function changeFlow ( ):void {
  try {
    throw new Error("Test error.");
  } catch (e:Error) {
    trace("Caught: " + e.message);
  } finally {
    trace("Finally executed.");
    return;
  }
  trace("Last line of method.");  // Not executed.
}
```

```
// Output when changeFlow( ) is invoked:
Caught: Test error.
Finally executed.
```

 If a *return* statement occurs in a *finally* block after a *return* has already been issued in the corresponding *try* block, then the *return* in the *finally* block replaces the *return* already in progress.

Handling a Built-in Exception

At the very beginning of this chapter, we learned that we can respond to both built-in and custom errors using the *try/catch/finally* statement. So far, the errors we've handled have all been custom errors. To close this chapter, let's examine a *try/catch/finally* statement that handles a built-in error.

Suppose we're building a chat application in which the user is asked to specify a port number when connecting to the chat server. We assign the specified port number to a variable named userPort. Then, we use the *Socket* class to attempt to connect to the specified port. In some cases, the connection will fail due to security limitations. To indicate that a security limitation has been breached when a connection attempt is made, the Flash runtime throws a *SecurityError*. Therefore, when attempting to make a connection, we wrap the connection code in the *try* block. If the connection fails due to security reasons, we display an error message to the user indicating what went wrong.

```
var socket:Socket = new Socket();
try {
  // Attempt to connect to the specified port
  socket.connect("example.com", userPort);
} catch (e:SecurityError) {
  // Code here displays message to the user
}
```

 For a list of circumstances that can cause socket connection failures, see the *Socket* class's *connect()* method in Adobe's ActionScript Language Reference.

Error Events for Problem Conditions

In the preceding section, we saw how to handle an exception caused by an illegal socket-connection attempt. But not all error conditions in ActionScript result in exceptions. Problems that occur asynchronously (i.e., after some time passes) are reported via error events, not exceptions. For example, if we attempt to load a file, ActionScript must first asynchronously check to see if that file exists. If the file does not exist, ActionScript dispatches an IOErrorEvent.IO_ERROR event. To handle the problem, the code that instigated the load operation must register a listener for the IOErrorEvent.IO_ERROR event. If no listener is registered for that event, then a run-time error occurs. For an error event-handling example, see the examples in the section "Two More Event Listener Registration Examples" in Chapter 12.

More Gritty Work Ahead

Exceptions are not the most glamorous aspect of programming. It's usually more fun to build something than to diagnose what went wrong with it. Nevertheless, exception handling is an important part of any program's development. In the coming chapter, we'll study another similarly gritty topic, *garbage collection*. Garbage collection helps prevent a program from running out of system memory.

CHAPTER 14

Garbage Collection

Every time a program creates an object, ActionScript stores it in system memory (for example, in RAM). As a program creates hundreds, thousands, or even millions of objects, it slowly occupies more and more memory. To prevent system memory from being fully depleted, ActionScript automatically removes objects from memory when they are no longer needed by the program. The automatic removal of objects from memory is known as *garbage collection*.

Eligibility for Garbage Collection

In an ActionScript program, an object becomes eligible for garbage collection as soon as it becomes *unreachable*. An object is unreachable when it cannot be accessed directly or indirectly through at least one *garbage collection root*. The most significant garbage collection roots in ActionScript are as follows:

- Package-level variables
- Local variables of a currently executing method or function
- Static variables
- Instance variables of the program's main class instance
- Instance variables of an object on the Flash runtime display list
- Variables in the scope chain of a currently executing function or method

For example, consider the following version of the *VirtualZoo* class from our zoo program. Notice that in this version, the *VirtualPet* object created in the *VirtualZoo* constructor is not assigned to a variable.

```
package {
  import flash.display.Sprite;
  import zoo.*;

  public class VirtualZoo extends Sprite {
    public function VirtualZoo () {
      new VirtualPet("Stan");
```

```
      }
    }
  }
```

In the preceding code, when the *VirtualZoo* constructor runs, the expression new
VirtualPet("Stan") creates a new *VirtualPet* object. After that object is created, however, it cannot be accessed via any variable. As a result, it is considered unreachable
and immediately becomes eligible for garbage collection.

Next, consider the following version of the *VirtualZoo* class. Focus on the constructor method body, shown in bold:

```
package {
  import flash.display.Sprite;
  import zoo.*;

  public class VirtualZoo extends Sprite {
    public function VirtualZoo () {
      var pet:VirtualPet = new VirtualPet("Stan");
    }
  }
}
```

As before, when the preceding *VirtualZoo* constructor runs, the expression new
VirtualPet("Stan") creates a new *VirtualPet* object. However, this time the
VirtualPet object is assigned to a local variable, pet. Throughout the *VirtualZoo* constructor, the *VirtualPet* object can be accessed via that local variable, so it is not eligible for garbage collection. However, as soon as the *VirtualZoo* constructor finishes
running, the variable pet expires, and the *VirtualPet* object can no longer be accessed
via any variable. As a result, it becomes unreachable and eligible for garbage collection.

Next, consider the following version of the *VirtualZoo* class:

```
package {
  import flash.display.Sprite;
  import zoo.*;

  public class VirtualZoo extends Sprite {
    private var pet:VirtualPet;

    public function VirtualZoo () {
      pet = new VirtualPet("Stan");
    }
  }
}
```

In the preceding code, when the *VirtualZoo* constructor runs, the expression new
VirtualPet("Stan") again creates a new *VirtualPet* object. This time, however, the
VirtualPet object is assigned to an instance variable of the program's main class. As
such, it is considered reachable, and therefore not eligible for garbage collection.

Now consider the following version of the *VirtualZoo* class (again, focus on the bold sections):

```
package {
  import flash.display.Sprite;
  import zoo.*;

  public class VirtualZoo extends Sprite {
    private var pet:VirtualPet;

    public function VirtualZoo () {
      pet = new VirtualPet("Stan");
      pet = new VirtualPet("Tim");
    }
  }
}
```

As before, line 1 of the preceding constructor creates a *VirtualPet* object and assigns it to the instance variable, pet. However, line 2 of the preceding constructor method then creates *another VirtualPet* object and also assigns it to the instance variable, pet. The second assignment replaces pet's first value (i.e., the pet "Stan") with a new value (i.e., the pet "Tim"). As a result, the *VirtualPet* object named "Stan" becomes unreachable, and eligible for garbage collection. Note that we could have also made the *VirtualPet* object named "Stan" unreachable by assigning null (or any other legal value) to pet, as in:

```
pet = null;
```

Finally, consider the following version of the *VirtualZoo* class, which defines two instance variables, pet1 and pet2:

```
package {
  import flash.display.Sprite;
  import zoo.*;

  public class VirtualZoo extends Sprite {
    private var pet1:VirtualPet;
    private var pet2:VirtualPet;

    public function VirtualZoo () {
      pet1 = new VirtualPet("Stan");
      pet2 = pet1;
      pet1 = null;
      pet2 = null;
    }
  }
}
```

As before, line 1 of the preceding constructor creates a *VirtualPet* object; for convenience, let's call it "Stan." Line 1 also assigns Stan to the instance variable, pet1. Line 2 then assigns that same object to the instance variable, pet2. After line 2 is finished executing, and before line 3 executes, the program can access Stan through both pet1 and pet2, so Stan is not eligible for garbage collection. When line 3 executes, pet1's value is replaced with the value null, so Stan can no longer be accessed through pet1. However, Stan *can* still be accessed through pet2, so it is still not eligible for garbage collection. Finally, line 4 executes, and pet2's value is replaced with the value null. As a result, Stan can no longer be accessed through any variable. Poor Stan is unreachable, and officially becomes eligible for garbage collection.

 There are two special cases in ActionScript where an object that *is* reachable becomes eligible for garbage collection. For details, see the section "Weak Listener References" in Chapter 12, and "Events and Event Handling" and the Dictionary class in Adobe's ActionScript Language Reference.

Incremental Mark and Sweep

In the preceding section, we learned that an object becomes eligible for garbage collection (automatic removal from memory) when it is unreachable. But we didn't learn exactly when unreachable objects are removed from memory. In an ideal world, objects would be removed from memory immediately upon becoming unreachable. However, in practice, removing unreachable objects immediately would be very time consuming and would cause most nontrivial programs to run slowly or become unresponsive. Accordingly, ActionScript does not remove unreachable objects from memory immediately. Instead, it checks for and removes unreachable objects only periodically, during *garbage collection cycles*.

ActionScript's unreachable-object removal strategy is known as *incremental mark and sweep* garbage collection. Here's how it works: when the Flash runtime starts, it asks the operating system to set aside, or *allocate,* an arbitrary amount of memory in which to store the objects of the currently running program. As the program runs, it accumulates objects in memory. At any given time, some of the program's objects will be reachable, and others might not be reachable. If the program creates enough objects, ActionScript will eventually decide to perform a garbage collection cycle. During the cycle, all objects in memory are audited for "reachability." All reachable objects are said to be *marked* for keeping, and all unreachable objects are said to be *swept* (removed) from memory. However, for a large program, the process of auditing objects for reachability can be time-consuming. Accordingly, ActionScript breaks garbage collection cycles into small chunks, or *increments*, which are interwoven with the program's execution. ActionScript also uses deferred reference counting to help improve garbage collection performance. For information on deferred reference counting, see "The Memory Management Reference: Beginner's Guide: Recycling," at *http://www.memorymanagement.org/articles/recycle.html#reference.deferred.*

ActionScript's garbage collection cycles are typically triggered when the amount of memory required to store a program's objects approaches the amount of memory currently allocated to the Flash runtime. However, ActionScript makes *no guarantee* as to when its garbage collection cycles will occur. Furthermore, the programmer cannot force ActionScript to perform a garbage collection cycle.

Disposing of Objects Intentionally

In ActionScript, there is no direct way to remove an object from system memory. All object-removal happens indirectly, through the automatic garbage collection system.

However, while a program cannot remove an object from system memory, it can at least make an object eligible for removal by eliminating all program references to it. To eliminate all references to an object, we must manually remove it from any arrays that contain it and assign null (or some other value) to any variable that references it.

Making an object eligible for garbage collection does not immediately remove that object from memory. It simply gives ActionScript authorization to remove the object when and if a garbage collection cycle occurs.

Note, however, that creating and then removing objects from memory is often less efficient than reusing objects.

> Wherever possible, you should strive to reuse objects rather than dispose them.

Returning, once again, to the virtual zoo program, consider the following code. It feeds a pet five apples.

```
package {
  import flash.display.Sprite;
  import zoo.*;

  public class VirtualZoo extends Sprite {
    private var pet:VirtualPet;

    public function VirtualZoo () {
      pet = new VirtualPet("Stan");
      pet.eat(new Apple());
      pet.eat(new Apple());
      pet.eat(new Apple());
      pet.eat(new Apple());
      pet.eat(new Apple());
    }
  }
}
```

Notice that each time the preceding code feeds the pet, it creates a new *Apple* instance and passes that instance to the *eat()* method. Each time the *eat()* method completes, all references to the *Apple* instance it was passed are lost, so the *Apple* instance becomes eligible for garbage collection. Now consider what would happen if we were to feed the pet 1,000 *Apple* objects. Our program would incur the processing cost not only of creating the *Apple* objects but also of garbage collecting them. To avoid that cost, we're better off creating a single, reusable *Apple* object, and using that single object any time the pet eats an apple. The following code demonstrates by feeding the pet the same *Apple* object five times:

```
package {
  import flash.display.Sprite;
  import zoo.*;

  public class VirtualZoo extends Sprite {
    private var pet:VirtualPet;
    private var apple:Apple;

    public function VirtualZoo () {
      pet = new VirtualPet("Stan");
      apple = new Apple();

      pet.eat(apple);
      pet.eat(apple);
      pet.eat(apple);
      pet.eat(apple);
      pet.eat(apple);
    }
  }
}
```

The preceding pet-feeding code incurs the cost of a single object-creation and incurs *no* garbage collection cost whatsoever. That's much more efficient than our earlier approach of creating and garbage collecting a new *Apple* object for each *eat()* method invocation!

Deactivating Objects

We've learned that removing all references to an object makes that object eligible for garbage collection. However, even after an object becomes eligible for garbage collection, it continues to exist in memory until ActionScript decides to "sweep" it away during a garbage collection cycle. After the object becomes eligible for garbage collection, but before it is actually removed from system memory, the object continues to receive events and, in the case of *Function* objects, can still be triggered by *setInterval()*.

For example, imagine a slideshow application that uses a class, *ImageLoader*, to load images from a server at regular intervals. The code for the *ImageLoader* class is as follows:

```
package {
  import flash.events.*;
  import flash.utils.*;
```

```
public class ImageLoader {
  private var loadInterval:int;

  public function ImageLoader (delay:int = 1000) {
    loadInterval = setInterval(loadImage, delay);
  }

  public function loadImage ():void {
    trace("Now loading image...");
    // Image-loading code not shown
  }
 }
}
```

Further imagine that the application's main class, *SlideShow*, implements code to start and stop the slideshow. To start the slideshow, *SlideShow* creates an *ImageLoader* instance that manages image loading. The *ImageLoader* instance is stored in the instance variable imgLoader, as follows:

```
imgLoader = new ImageLoader();
```

To stop or pause a slideshow, *SlideShow* discards the *ImageLoader* instance, as follows:

```
imgLoader = null;
```

When imgLoader is set to null, the *ImageLoader* instance becomes eligible for garbage collection. However, until the instance is actually removed from system memory, the *setInterval()*-based load operation in the *ImageLoader* instance continues executing on a regular basis. The following very simple class demonstrates. It creates and then immediately discards an *ImageLoader* instance. But even after imgLoader is set to null, the message "Now loading image..." continues to appear in the debugging console, once per second.

```
package {
  import flash.display.*;

  public class SlideShow extends Sprite {
    private var imgLoader:ImageLoader;
    public function SlideShow () {
      // Create and immediately discard an ImageLoader instance
      imgLoader = new ImageLoader();
      imgLoader = null;
    }
  }
}
```

If the memory required by the slideshow application never becomes significant enough to trigger a garbage collection cycle, then the *setInterval()*-based load operation in the *ImageLoader* instance will execute indefinitely. The unnecessary execution of code in the discarded *ImageLoader* instance wastes system and network resources, and could cause undesired side effects in the slideshow program.

To avoid unnecessary code execution in discarded objects, a program should always deactivate objects before discarding them. *Deactivating* an object means putting the object in an idle state where nothing in the program can cause it to execute code. For example, to deactivate an object, we might perform any or all of the following tasks:

- Unregister the object's methods for events
- Stop all timers and intervals
- Stop the playhead of timelines (for instances of movie clips created in the Flash authoring tool)
- Deactivate any objects that would become unreachable if the object, itself, became unreachable

To allow objects to be deactivated, any class whose instances register for events or uses timers should provide a public method for deactivating instances.

For example, our preceding *ImageLoader* class should have provided a method to stop its interval. Let's add such a method now and call it *dispose()*. The name *dispose()* is arbitrary; it could also be called *kill()*, *destroy()*, *die()*, *clean()*, *disable()*, *deactivate()*, or anything else. Here's the code:

```
package {
  import flash.events.*;
  import flash.utils.*;

  public class ImageLoader {
    private var loadInterval:int;

    public function ImageLoader (delay:int = 1000) {
      loadInterval = setInterval(loadImage, delay);
    }

    public function loadImage ():void {
      trace("Now loading image...");
      // Image-loading code not shown
    }

    public function dispose ():void {
      clearInterval(loadInterval);
    }
  }
}
```

Any code that creates an *ImageLoader* instance would then be required to invoke *ImageLoader.dispose()* before discarding it, as follows:

```
package {
  import flash.display.*;

  public class SlideShow extends Sprite {
    private var imgLoader:ImageLoader;
    public function SlideShow () {
```

```
      // Create and immediately discard an ImageLoader instance
      imgLoader = new ImageLoader( );
      imgLoader.dispose( );
      imgLoader = null;
    }
  }
}
```

Garbage Collection Demonstration

Example 14-1 shows a very simple program that demonstrates garbage collection at
work. The program creates a *Sprite* object that displays a message repeatedly in the
debugging output console. Because the *Sprite* object is reachable only via a local variable, it becomes eligible for garbage collection immediately after the program's main
class constructor completes. Meanwhile, the program also runs a timer that repeatedly creates objects, occupying system memory. When enough system memory is
consumed, the garbage collector runs. During garbage collection, the original *Sprite*
object is removed from memory, and its messages stop appearing in the debugging
output console.

Example 14-1. Garbage collection demonstration

```
package {
  import flash.display.*;
  import flash.text.*;
  import flash.utils.*;
  import flash.events.*;
  import flash.system.*;

  public class GarbageCollectionDemo extends Sprite {
    public function GarbageCollectionDemo () {
      // This Sprite object is garbage collected after enough memory
      // is consumed
      var s:Sprite = new Sprite( );
      s.addEventListener(Event.ENTER_FRAME, enterFrameListener);

      // Repeatedly create new objects, occupying system memory
      var timer:Timer = new Timer(1, 0);
      timer.addEventListener(TimerEvent.TIMER, timerListener);
      timer.start( );
    }

    private function timerListener (e:TimerEvent):void {
      // Create an object to take up some system memory. Could be
      // any object, but TextField objects are nice and meaty.
      new TextField( );
    }

    // This function is executed until the Sprite object is
    // garbage collected
    private function enterFrameListener (e:Event):void {
```

Example 14-1. Garbage collection demonstration (continued)

```
    // Display the amount of memory occupied by this program
    trace("System memory used by this program: " + System.totalMemory);
  }
 }
}
```

On to ActionScript Backcountry

Garbage collection is an immensely important part of ActionScript programming. You should consider memory management in every ActionScript program you write. If you create an object, you should decide whether that object is needed for the entire lifespan of the program. If not, you should add code that deactivates and then disposes of the object.

For more general information on garbage collection in programming languages, see "Garbage collection (computer science)" in Wikipedia, The Free Encyclopedia at *http://en.wikipedia.org/wiki/Garbage_collection_(computer_science)*, and The Memory Management Reference, at *http://www.memorymanagement.org*.

For a series of self-published articles on garbage collection in ActionScript 3.0 by Grant Skinner, see *http://www.gskinner.com/blog/archives/2006/06/as3_resource_ma. html* and *http://gskinner.com/talks/resource-management/*.

In the next chapter, we'll explore some of ActionScript's less commonly used tools for altering the structure of classes and objects at runtime.

CHAPTER 15

Dynamic ActionScript

ActionScript was originally conceived of as a language for adding basic programmatic behavior to content created manually in the Flash authoring tool. In early versions of ActionScript, most code was intended to be written in short scripts that implemented limited functionality compared with the code required to create a complex desktop application. As such, ActionScript's original feature set stressed flexibility and simplicity over formality and sophistication.

ActionScript originally allowed the structure of all classes and even all individual objects to be modified dynamically at runtime. For example, at runtime, a program could:

- Add new instance methods or instance variables to any class
- Add new instance methods or instance variables to any single, specific object
- Create a new class entirely from scratch
- Change a given class's superclass

With the advent of ActionScript 3.0, Flash Player 9, Adobe AIR, and Flex, the Flash platform has evolved to a stage where the complexity of an ActionScript-based program may well rival the complexity of a full-featured desktop application. Accordingly, as a language, ActionScript has taken on many of the formal structures required for large-scale application development—structures such as a formal *class* keyword an inheritance syntax, formal datatypes, a built-in event framework, exception handling, and built-in XML support. Nevertheless, ActionScript's dynamic features remain available in the language and still constitute an important part of ActionScript's internal makeup.

This chapter explores ActionScript's dynamic programming techniques. Note, however, that the flexibility inherent in dynamic ActionScript programming limits or removes most of the benefits of type checking we studied in Chapter 8. As a result, most complex programs use the features described in this chapter only sparingly, if at all. For example, in the over 700 classes defined by the Flex framework, there are approximately only 10 uses of dynamic programming techniques. That said, even if you never intend to use dynamic programming in your code, the information presented in this chapter will improve your understanding ActionScript's internal workings.

For our first dynamic programming technique, we'll study dynamic instance variables—instance variables added to an individual object at runtime.

Dynamic Instance Variables

The very beginning of this book compared writing an ActionScript program to designing and building an airplane. The comparison likened the airplane's blueprints to ActionScript's classes, and the actual parts in a specific physical airplane to ActionScript's objects. In that analogy, a single individual airplane is guaranteed to have the same structure as all other airplanes because all airplanes are based on the same blueprint. By comparison, all instances of a given class are guaranteed to have the same structure because they are based on the same class.

But what if the owner of a specific airplane mounts a custom light on the top of his airplane? That airplane now has a specific characteristic not shared by all other airplanes. In ActionScript, "adding a new light to an individual airplane" is analogous to adding a new instance variable to a single, specific object without adding that light to any other instance of that object's class. Such an instance variable is known as a *dynamic instance variable*. When contrasted with dynamic instance variables, "regular" instance variables are referred to as *fixed variables*.

Dynamic instance variables can be added to instances of classes defined with the attribute *dynamic* only (such classes are referred to as *dynamic classes*). Dynamic instance variables cannot be added to instances of classes that are not defined with the attribute *dynamic* (such classes are referred to as *sealed classes*). A subclass of a dynamic class is not considered dynamic unless its definition also includes the *dynamic* attribute.

The following code creates a new class, *Person*, which might represent a person in a statistics program that tracks demographics. Because *Person* is declared with the attribute *dynamic*, dynamic instance variables can be added to any individual *Person* object at runtime.

```
dynamic public class Person {
}
```

Once a class has been defined as dynamic, we can add a new dynamic instance variable to any instance of that class via a standard variable assignment statement. For example, the following code adds a dynamic instance variable, eyeColor, to a *Person* object:

```
var person:Person = new Person( );
person.eyeColor = "brown";
```

As we learned in Chapter 8, if the *Person* class were not declared *dynamic*, the preceding code would cause a reference error because the *Person* class does not define an instance variable named eyeColor. However, in this case, the *Person* class *is* declared *dynamic*. As a result, when ActionScript encounters the attempt to assign a value to the nonexistent instance variable eyeColor, rather than reporting an error, it simply creates a dynamic instance variable named eyeColor, and assigns it the specified value ("brown"). In the preceding code, notice that the dynamic instance variable definition does not, and must not, include a datatype definition or an access-control modifier.

 All dynamic instance variables are untyped and public.

The following code, which attempts to include a datatype definition when creating eyeColor, causes a compile-time error:

```
person.eyeColor:String = "brown";  // Error! :String is not allowed here
```

To retrieve the value of a dynamic instance variable, we use a standard variable access expression as shown in the following code:

```
trace(person.eyeColor);  // Displays: brown
```

If the specified instance variable (dynamic or not dynamic) does not exist, ActionScript returns the value undefined, as shown in the following code:

```
trace(person.age);  // Displays undefined because the person object
                    // has no instance variable named age
```

ActionScript's most significant use of dynamic instance variables occurs in the Flash authoring tool, where each animated timeline is represented by a subclass of the built-in *MovieClip* class. In the Flash authoring tool, automatically generated subclasses of *MovieClip* are dynamic so that programmers can define new variables on manually created movie clip instances. For details on this technique, and other timeline-scripting techniques, see Chapter 29.

Dynamic instance variables are sometimes used to create a simple "lookup table," as discussed later in the section "Using Dynamic Instance Variables to Create Lookup Tables."

Remember that allowing a program to be modified dynamically can lead to hard-to-diagnose problems. For example, when a class is defined as dynamic in order to support dynamic instance variables, then legitimate reference errors made through that class's instances can easily go unnoticed (because referencing an instance variable that does not exist generates neither a compile-time error nor a runtime error). The only way to know for sure whether the dynamically modified program works is to run it and observe its behavior. Such observation is time-consuming and prone to human error, so most programmers avoid using dynamic variables in complex programs.

 ActionScript takes longer to access a dynamic instance variable than it does to access a fixed variable. Where performance is a concern, avoid using dynamic instance variables.

Processing Dynamic Instance Variables with for-each-in and for-in Loops

The *for-each-in* loop provides easy access to the values of an object's dynamic instance variables (or an array's elements). It takes the general form:

```
for each (variableOrElementValue in someObject) {
  statements
}
```

The *statements* of a *for-each-in* loop run once for each dynamic instance variable or array element of *someObject*. During each iteration of the loop, the value of the variable or element being iterated over (*enumerated*) is assigned to the variable *variableOrElementValue*. Code within the body of the loop then has the opportunity to operate on that value in some way.

For example, consider the object definition and subsequent *for-each-in* loop shown in the following code. Note that the built-in *Object* class is declared *dynamic*, and, hence, supports dynamic instance variables.

```
var info:Object = new Object( );
info.city = "Toronto";
info.country = "Canada";

for each (var detail:* in info) {
  trace(detail);
}
```

The preceding loop runs twice, once for each of the two dynamic instance variables of the object referenced by info. The first time the loop runs, the variable detail is assigned the value "Toronto" (i.e., the value of the city variable). The second time the loop runs, detail has the value "Canada" (i.e., the value of the country variable). So the output of the loop is:

```
Toronto
Canada
```

In most cases, the order in which *for-each-in* and *for-in* loops enumerate an object's variables is not guaranteed. There are two exceptions: variables of *XML* and *XMLList* instances are enumerated in ascending sequential order according to their numeric variable names (i.e., document order for XML objects; see Chapter 18). For all other types of objects, the enumeration order used by *for-each-in* and *for-in* loops might vary across different versions of ActionScript or different Flash runtimes. Therefore, you should not write code that depends on a *for-each-in* or *for-in* loop's enumeration order unless you are processing XML data.

The following code shows a *for-each-in* loop used to access the values of an array's elements:

```
var games:Array = ["Project Gotham Racing",
                   "Shadow of the Colossus",
                   "Legend of Zelda"];

for each (var game:* in games) {
  trace(game);
}
```

The preceding loop runs three times, once for each of the three elements in the games array. The first time the loop runs, the variable game is assigned the value "Project Gotham Racing" (i.e., the first element's value). The second time the loop runs, game has the value "Shadow of the Colossus." And the third time it has the value "Legend of Zelda." So the output of the loop is:

```
Project Gotham Racing
Shadow of the Colossus
Legend of Zelda
```

The *for-each-in* loop is a companion for the ActionScript *for-in* loop. Whereas the *for-each-in* loop iterates over variable *values*, the *for-in* loop iterates over variable *names*. For example, the following *for-in* loop lists the names of dynamic instance variables of the object referenced by info:

```
for (var detailName:* in info) {
  trace(detailName);
}
// Output:
city
country
```

Notice that the preceding code outputs the *names* of the variables city and country, *not the values*. To access the values of those properties, we could use the [ ] operator, as discussed in the later section "Dynamic References to Variables and Methods." The following code demonstrates:

```
for (var detailName:* in info) {
  trace(info[detailName]);
}
```

```
// Output:
Toronto
Canada
```

To prevent a dynamic instance variable from being included in *for-in* and *for-each-in* loops, use the *Object* class's *setPropertyIsEnumerable( )* method, as shown in the following code:

```
info.setPropertyIsEnumerable("city", false);

for (var detailName:* in info) {
  trace(info[detailName]);
}
// Outputs: Canada
// (the "city" variable was not processed by the for-in loop)
```

We'll see the *for-each-in* loop used in a practical situation in the later section, under "Using Dynamic Instance Variables to Create Lookup Tables."

Dynamically Adding New Behavior to an Instance

Having just learned how to create dynamic instance variables, you might wonder whether ActionScript also supports dynamic instance methods—adding a new instance method to a single, specific object without adding it to any other instances of that object's class. In fact, there is no formal means of adding a true instance method to an object dynamically. However, by assigning a function closure to a dynamic instance variable, we can emulate the effect of giving an individual object a new method (for a refresher on the term *function closure*, see Chapter 5). The following code demonstrates the general approach:

```
someObject.someDynamicVariable = someFunction;
```

In the preceding code, *someObject* is an instance of a dynamic class, *someDynamicVariable* is the name of a dynamic instance variable (which can be a new variable or an existing variable), and *someFunction* is a reference to a function closure. Typically, *someFunction* is supplied using a function literal, as shown in the following code:

```
someObject.someDynamicVariable = function (param1, param2, ...paramn) {
  // Function body
}
```

Once *someFunction* has been assigned to the dynamic instance variable, it can be invoked through the object, exactly like a regular instance method, as shown in the following code:

```
someObject.someDynamicVariable(value1, value2, ...valuen);
```

To demonstrate the preceding generic syntax, let's return to the info example from the preceding section:

```
var info:Object = new Object( );
info.city = "Toronto";
info.country = "Canada";
```

Suppose we want to give the object referenced by info a new behavior—the ability to format and return its details as a string. We create a new instance variable, getAddress, to which we assign the desired formatting function, as follows:

```
info.getAddress = function ( ):String {
  return this.city + ", " + this.country;
}
```

To invoke the function, we use the following code:

```
trace(info.getAddress( ));
```

Notice that within the body of the function assigned to getAddress, we can use the keyword *this* to access the variables and methods of the object through which the function was invoked. In fact, in the case of function closures, the variables and methods of the object through which the function was invoked cannot be accessed without the keyword this. For example, suppose we omit this from the *getAddress()* function definition, as follows:

```
info.getAddress = function ( ):String {
  return city + ", " + country;
}
```

When searching for the variables city and country, ActionScript does not automatically consider instance variables of the object referenced by info. Therefore, the preceding code causes an error (unless other variables by the name city and country actually exist higher up in the *getAddress()* function's scope chain).

If the assignment of a function to an object's instance variable occurs within that object's class, then the function can access the object's *private*, *protected*, *internal*, and *public* variables and methods. If the assignment occurs within a subclass of the object's class, then the function can access the object's *protected*, *internal*, and *public* variables and methods only. If the assignment occurs within the same package as the object's class, then the function can access the object's *internal* and *public* variables and methods only. If the assignment occurs in a different package than the object's class, then the function can access the object's *public* variables and methods only.

For example, consider the following code, which creates a dynamic class, *Employe*:

```
dynamic public class Employee {
  public var startDate:Date;
  private var age:int;
}
```

The following code assigns a function to a dynamic instance variable, doReport, of an *Employee* instance. The assignment occurs outside the *Employee* class, but within a class in the same package as the *Employee* class. As a result, the function can access the *Employee* object's *internal* and *public* variables, but not its *protected* or *private* variables.

```
public class Report {
  public function Report (employee:Employee) {
    // Assign a function to doReport
    employee.doReport = function ():void {
      trace(this.startDate);  // Access to public variable allowed
      trace(this.age);        // Access to private variable denied
    }
  }
}
```

Dynamic References to Variables and Methods

Because dynamic instance variable names are often not known until runtime, Action-Script provides a way to specify a variable's name using an arbitrary string expression. The following code shows the general approach:

```
someObject[someExpression]
```

In the preceding code, `someObject` is a reference to the object whose variable is being accessed, and `someExpression` is any expression that yields a string (indicating that variable's name). The preceding code can be used both to assign a value to a variable and to retrieve a variable's value.

For example, the following code assigns the value "Toronto" to a variable whose name is specified by the literal string expression "city":

```
var info:Object = new Object();
info["city"] = "Toronto";
```

The following code assigns the value "Canada" to a variable whose name is specified by the literal string expression "country":

```
info["country"] = "Canada";
```

The following code retrieves the value of the variable whose name is specified by the identifier expression, `detail`:

```
var detail:String = "city";
trace(info[detail]);  // Displays: Toronto
```

When ActionScript encounters the code, info[detail], it first determines the value of detail, which is "city," and then looks up the variable named "city" of the object referenced by *info*.

The syntactic rules for identifiers don't apply to variables created using the [ ] operator. For example, the following code creates a dynamic instance variable whose name starts with a number:

```
var info:Object = new Object();
info["411"] = "Information Line";
```

Using the dot (.) operator to create the same variable causes an error because it violates the syntactic rules for identifiers:

```
var info:Object = new Object();
info.411 = "Information Line";  // ERROR! Identifiers must not start
                               // with a number
```

Note that the preceding technique can be used to access any kind of variable or method, not just dynamic instance variables; but it's most commonly used with dynamic instance variables. The next section shows dynamic references used in an applied situation: creating a lookup table.

Using Dynamic Instance Variables to Create Lookup Tables

A *lookup table* is a data structure that maps a set of names to a corresponding set of values. For example, the following pseudocode shows a lookup table representing the courses of a meal:

```
appetizer:  tortilla chips
maincourse: bean burrito
dessert:    cake
```

To represent the lookup table using dynamic instance variables, we would use the following code:

```
var meal:Object = new Object();
meal.appetizer  = "tortilla chips";
meal.maincourse = "bean burrito";
meal.dessert    = "cake";
```

Now let's consider a more involved scenario. Imagine an inventory application for a bookstore in which the user can browse books by ISBN number. Information for each book is loaded from an external server. To minimize communication with the server, the application loads the information for 500 books at a time. For the sake of simplicity, we'll assume that each book's information takes the form of a single string, in the following format:

```
"Price: $19.99. Title: Path of the Paddle"
```

To store the loaded book information in ActionScript, we create an instance of the *Object* class, which will act as a lookup table for the books:

```
var bookList:Object =  new Object();
```

As each book's information is loaded, we assign it to a new dynamic instance variable of the preceding *bookList* object. Each variable's name corresponds to a book's ISBN number, preceded by the string "isbn". For example, the variable for a book with the ISBN number 155209328X would be named isbn155209328X. The following code demonstrates how we would create a given book's dynamic instance variable if we knew its ISBN number in advance:

```
bookList.isbn155209328X = "Price: $19.95. Title: Path of the Paddle";
```

In the real application, however, we won't know a book's ISBN number until it is loaded from the server. Hence, we must define each book's dynamic-instance variable name dynamically, based on data loaded at runtime. For the sake of demonstration, let's create a variable, bookData, whose value represents the data as it would be loaded from the server. In this simplified example, each book's ISBN number and details are separated with a single tilde character (~). Meanwhile, entire books are separated from each other by two tilde characters (~~).

```
var bookData:String = "155209328X~Price: $19.95. Title: Path of the Paddle"
                    + "~~"
                    + "0072231726~Price: $24.95. Title: High Score!";
```

To convert the loaded book data from a string to an array of books for processing, we use the *String* class's *split()* method, as follows:

```
var bookDataArray:Array = bookData.split("~~");
```

To convert the array of books to a lookup table, we use the following code:

```
// Create a variable to track each book's information as it is processed
var book:Array;

// Loop once for every item in the array of books
for (var i:int = 0; i < bookDataArray.length; i++) {
  // Convert the current item in the array from a string to its
  // own array. For example, the string:
  // "155209328X~Price: $19.95. Title: Path of the Paddle"
  // becomes the array:
  // ["155209328X", "Price: $19.95. Title: Path of the Paddle"]
  book = bookDataArray[i].split("~");

  // Create a dynamic instance variable whose name matches the ISBN number
  // of the current item in the array of books, and assign that variable
  // the description of the current item in the array. Note that the ISBN
  // number is book[0], while the description is book[1].
  bookList["isbn" + book[0]] = book[1];
}
```

Once we've added all 500 books to the *bookList* object, each with its own dynamic instance variable, the user can then select a book to view by entering its ISBN number in a text-input field, isbnInput. Here's how we would display the user's selected book during debugging:

```
trace(bookList["isbn" + isbnInput.text]);
```

Here's how we would display the user's selected book on screen in a text field referenced by bookDescription:

```
bookDescription.text = bookList["isbn" + isbnInput.text];
```

To list all of the books in the *bookList* object, we would use a *for-each-in* loop, as follows:

```
for each (var bookInfo:* in bookList) {
  // Display the value of the dynamic instance variable currently
  // being processed
  trace(bookInfo);
}
```

The preceding loop produces the following debugging output:

```
Price: $19.95. Title: Path of the Paddle
Price: $24.95. Title: High Score!
```

Making Lookup Tables with Object Literals

For the sake of convenience, to create a lookup table whose content is limited and known in advance, we can use an object literal. An object literal creates a new instance of the *Object* class from a series of comma-separated dynamic-variable name/value pairs, enclosed in curly braces. Here's the general syntax:

```
{varName1:varValue1, varName2:varValue2,...varNameN:varValueN}
```

For example, the following code creates an *Object* instance with a dynamic instance variable named city (whose value is "Toronto"), and a dynamic instance variable named country (whose value is "Canada"):

```
var info:Object = {city:"Toronto", country:"Canada"};
```

The preceding code is identical to the following code:

```
var info:Object = new Object();
info.city = "Toronto";
info.country = "Canada";
```

If there were only two books in the preceding section's book-inventory application, we might have used the following object literal to create the bookList lookup table:

```
var bookList:Object = {
                isbn155209328X:"Price: $19.95. Title: Path of the Paddle",
                isbn0072231726:"Price: $24.95. Title: High Score!"
                };
```

Using Functions to Create Objects

As we've seen throughout this book, most objects in ActionScript are created using classes. However, it is also possible to create objects using standalone function closures. The following code shows the basic approach. It uses an example function, *Employee()*, to create an object:

```
// Create the function
function Employee () {
}
```

```
// Use the function to create an object, and assign that
// object to the variable, worker
var worker = new Employee( );
```

Notice that the variable worker is untyped. From a datatype perspective, the object referenced by worker is an instance of the *Object* class. There is no *Employee* class, so there is no *Employee* datatype. The following code, therefore, causes an error (because the *Employee* datatype does not exist):

```
// ERROR!
var worker:Employee = new Employee( );
```

A function closure used to create an object is referred to as a *constructor function* (not to be confused with a constructor *method*, which is part of a class definition). In ActionScript 3.0, standalone functions declared at the package-level cannot be used as constructor functions. Hence, the preceding code would have to appear within a method, in code outside of a package statement or in a frame script on a timeline in the Flash authoring tool. For the sake of brevity, however, this section shows all constructor functions outside the required containing method or frame script.

All objects created from constructor functions are implicitly dynamic. Hence, a constructor function can use the this keyword to add new dynamic instance variables to an object at creation time. Dynamic instance variables created in a constructor function are typically assigned values passed to the function as arguments. The following code demonstrates:

```
function Employee (age, salary) {
  // Define dynamic instance variables
  this.age = age;
  this.salary = salary;
}

// Pass arguments to use as the values of
// this object's dynamic instance variables
var worker = new Employee(25, 27000);
trace(worker.age);  // Displays: 25
```

To allow objects created via a particular constructor function to share information and behavior, ActionScript defines a special static variable named prototype on every function. A function's prototype variable references an object (known as the function's *prototype object*) whose dynamic instance variables can be accessed through any object created by that function. Initially, ActionScript assigns every function's prototype variable an instance of the generic *Object* class. By adding dynamic instance variables to that object, we can create information and behavior that is shared by all objects created from a particular function.

For example, the following code adds a dynamic instance variable, company, to the *Employee()* function's prototype object:

```
Employee.prototype.company = "AnyCorp";
```

As a result, any object created from the *Employee()* function can access company as though it were its own dynamic instance variable:

```
var worker = new Employee(25, 27000);
trace(worker.company);  // Displays: AnyCorp
```

In the preceding code, when ActionScript realizes that the object created from the *Employee()* function (*worker*) does not have an instance variable or instance method named "company," it then checks whether *Employee.prototype* defines a dynamic instance variable by that name. The *Employee.prototype* object does define such a variable, so ActionScript uses it as though it were the *worker* object's own variable.

If, on the other hand, the *worker* object defined its own variable named company, then that variable would be used instead of the *Employee.prototype* object's variable. The following code demonstrates:

```
var worker = new Employee(25, 27000);
worker.company = "CarCompany";
trace(worker.company);  // Displays: CarCompany (not AnyCorp)
```

Using the technique we learned in the section "Dynamically Adding New Behavior to an Instance," we can assign a function to a dynamic instance variable of any constructor function's *prototype* object. The function can then be used by any object created from that constructor function.

For example, the following code defines a dynamic instance variable, getBonus, on the *Employee()* function's *prototype* object and assigns that variable a function that calculates and returns an annual bonus:

```
Employee.prototype.getBonus = function (percentage:int):Number {
  // Return a bonus based on a specified percentage of the
  // employee's salaray
  return this.salary * (percentage/100);
}
```

As a result, all objects created from the *Employee()* function can use the *getBonus()* function as though it were assigned to their own dynamic instance variable:

```
var worker = new Employee(25, 27000);
trace(worker.getBonus(10));  // Displays: 2700
```

Using Prototype Objects to Augment Classes

We've learned that ActionScript defines a special static variable named prototype on every function. Using the prototype variable of a given function, we can share information and behavior among all objects created from that function.

Just as ActionScript defines a prototype variable on every function, it also defines a static prototype variable on every class. Using the static prototype variable, we can add shared information and behavior to all instances of a given class at runtime.

For example, the following code defines a new dynamic instance variable, isEmpty, on the built-in *String* class's *prototype* object and assigns that variable a function. The function returns true when a string has no characters in it; otherwise the function returns false:

```
String.prototype.isEmpty = function () {
  return (this == "") ? true : false;
};
```

To invoke the function *isEmpty()* on a *String* object, we use the following code:

```
var s1:String = "Hello World";
var s2:String = "";

trace(s1.isEmpty()); // Displays: false
trace(s2.isEmpty()); // Displays: true
```

However, the previous code example—and this entire technique—has a problem: the dynamic instance variable isn't added until runtime; therefore, the compiler has no idea that it exists and will generate an error if it is used in strict mode. For example, in strict mode, the code in the preceding example yields this error:

```
Call to a possibly undefined method isEmpty through a reference with static type
String.
```

In order to refer to *isEmpty()* in strict mode without causing a compile-time error, we must use a dynamic reference, as shown in the following code:

```
s1["isEmpty"]()
```

On the other hand, if the *String* class were declared *dynamic*, then the original approach (i.e., s1.isEmpty()) would not generate an error.

Note that fixed variables and methods are always preferred over prototype variables. In the preceding example, if the *String* class already defined an instance method or instance variable named isEmpty, then all references to isEmpty would refer to that instance variable or instance method—not to dynamic instance variable on the *String* class's prototype object.

The Prototype Chain

In the preceding sections, we learned that a prototype object can be used to share information and behavior with the objects created from a particular constructor function or class. In fact, the reach of a given prototype object goes beyond the objects created from the function or class to which it is attached.

In the case of a class, the dynamic instance variables defined on the class's prototype object can be accessed not just through the class's instances but also through the instances of the class's descendants. The following generic code demonstrates:

```
// Create a simple class, A
dynamic public class A {
```

```
  }

  // Create another simple class, B, that extends A
  dynamic public class B extends A {
  }

  // Create an application's main class
  public class Main extends Sprite {
    public function Main () {
      // Add a dynamic instance variable to class A's prototype object
      A.prototype.day = "Monday";

      // Access A.prototype.day through an instance of B
      var b:B = new B();
      trace(b.day);  // Displays: "Monday"
    }
  }
```

In the case of a function, the dynamic instance variables defined on the function's prototype object can be accessed not just through any object created from that function but also through any object whose *prototype chain* includes that function's prototype object.

Let's explore how prototype chains work through an example. Suppose we create a function, *Employee()*, just as we did earlier, whose prototype object has a dynamic instance variable named company:

```
function Employee () {
}
Employee.prototype.company = "AnyCorp";
```

Any object created from *Employee()* can access company through *Employee()*'s prototype object. Nothing new so far. Now suppose we create another function, *Manager()*:

```
function Manager () {
}
```

Suppose also that we wish to give objects created from *Manager()* access to company through *Employee()*'s prototype object. To do so, we assign an object created from *Employee()* to *Manager()*'s prototype variable.

```
Manager.prototype = new Employee();
```

Now, let's consider what happens when we access the name "company" through an object created from the *Manager()* function, as follows:

```
var worker = new Manager();
trace(worker.company);
```

When the preceding code runs, ActionScript checks whether the *worker* object has an instance variable or instance method named "company." The *worker* object does not have an instance variable or instance method by that name, so ActionScript then checks whether the *Manager()* function's prototype object defines a dynamic instance variable named "company." The *Manager()* function's prototype object is, itself, an object created from the *Employee()* function. However, objects created from the *Employee()* function do not define a dynamic instance variable named "company." Hence, ActionScript next checks whether the *Employee()* function's prototype object defines a dynamic instance variable named "company." The *Employee()* function's prototype object does define such a variable, so ActionScript uses it as though it were the *worker* object's own variable.

Here's the trail ActionScript follows to find "company":

1. Search worker for company. Not found.
2. Search Manager.prototype for company. Not found.
3. Manager.prototype was created from *Employee()*, so search Employee.prototype for company. Found!

The list of prototype objects ActionScript searches when attempting to resolve a variable's value is known as the *prototype chain*. Prior to ActionScript 3.0, the prototype chain was the primary mechanism for sharing reusable behavior among various kinds of objects. As of ActionScript 3.0, class inheritance plays that role.

Note the following limitations imposed on the prototype chain in ActionScript 3.0:

- An object assigned to a function's prototype variable must, itself, be an object created from a function or an instance of the *Object* class (instances of other classes are not allowed).
- The value of a class's prototype variable is set automatically by ActionScript and cannot be reassigned.

Onward!

In most mid- to large-scale projects, the dynamic techniques we learned in this chapter play only a minor role. Nevertheless, an understanding of ActionScript's dynamic programming features should increase your overall comfort with the language. In a similar way, knowledge of *scope*, the topic of the next chapter, will increase your confidence as an ActionScript programmer (but might not get you asked out on any dates). Scope governs the availability and life span of a program's definitions.

CHAPTER 16

Scope

A *scope* is a physical region of a program in which code executes. In ActionScript there are five possible scopes:

- A function body
- An instance method body
- A static method body
- A class body
- Everywhere else (i.e., *global scope*)

At any specific point in the execution of a program, the availability of variables, functions, classes, interfaces, and namespaces is governed by the scope of the code currently being executed. For example, code in a function can access that function's local variables because it executes inside the function's scope. By contrast, code outside the function cannot access the function's local variables because it executes outside the function's scope.

In ActionScript, scopes can be nested. For example, a function might be nested in an instance method, which, itself, is nested in a class body:

```
public class SomeClass {
  public function someMethod ():void {
    function someNestedFunction ():void {
      // This function's scope is nested inside someMethod()'s scope,
      // which is nested inside SomeClass's scope
    }
  }
}
```

When one scope is nested within another, the definitions (i.e., variables, functions, classes, interfaces, and namespaces) available to the enclosing scope become available to the nested scope. For example, a function nested inside an instance method can access that method's local variables. The entire list of nested scopes surrounding the code currently being executed is known as the *scope chain*.

This chapter describes the availability of variables, functions, classes, interfaces, and namespaces within ActionScript's various scopes.

Note that in addition to the definitions listed as "accessible" in each of the following sections, the public definitions of an external package can also be made visible in a given scope via the *import* directive. For details, see the section "Object Creation Example: Adding a Pet to the Zoo" in Chapter 1.

In combination, a definition's location and access-control modifier governs its accessibility throughout a program. For reference, Table 16-1 lists the accessibility of definitions according to their location and access-control modifier.

Table 16-1. Definition accessibility by location and access-control modifier

Definition	Accessibility
Definition outside of any package	Accessible within containing source file only
Definition in the unnamed package	Accessible to entire program
Public definition in a named package	Accessible within the package containing the definition and anywhere the definition is imported
Internal definition in a named package	Accessible within the package containing the definition only
Public method or variable	Accessible anywhere the containing class can be accessed
Internal method or variable	Accessible within the containing class's package
Protected method or variable	Accessible within the containing class and its descendant classes
Private method or variable	Accessible within the containing class only
Definition in instance method, static method, or function	Accessible within the containing method or function, and all of its nested functions

Global Scope

Code placed directly outside a package body or at the top-level of a package body resides in the global scope. In other words:

```
package {
  // Code here is in the global scope
}
// Code here is also in the global scope
```

Code in the global scope can access the following definitions:

- Functions, variables, classes, interfaces, and namespaces defined at the top level of the unnamed package

- Functions, variables, classes, interfaces, and namespaces defined outside of any package, but in the same source (*.as*) file

In other words:

```
package {
  // Definitions here are accessible to all code in the global scope
```

```
  }
  // Definitions here are accessible to all code in the same source file
```

Note that code placed at the top-level of a named package body can also access the definitions placed at the top-level of that package. Those definitions are accessible because within a named package, ActionScript automatically opens the namespace corresponding to that package (see Chapter 17). In other words:

```
package somePackage {
  // Definitions here are automatically accessible to
  // all code in somePackage
}
```

Class Scope

Code placed at the top-level of a class body resides in that class's scope. Here's the code:

```
package {
  public class SomeClass {
    // Code here is in the someClass scope
  }
}
```

 Remember that code placed at the top-level of a class body is wrapped in an automatically created static method (the *class initializer*), which executes when ActionScript defines the class at runtime. See the section "The Class Initializer" in Chapter 4.

Via the scope chain, code in a classs scope can access the following definitions:

- All definitions available to code in the global scope

Additionally, code in a class's scope can access the following definitions:

- Static methods and static variables defined by the class
- Static methods and static variables defined by the class's ancestors, if any (i.e., superclass, superclass's superclass, etc.)

In other words:

```
package {
  public class SomeClass extends SomeParentClass {
    // Static variables and static methods defined here are
    // accessible througout SomeClass
  }
}

package {
  public class SomeParentClass {
    // Static variables and static methods defined here are
```

```
    // accessible througuot SomeClass
  }
}
```

Remember that even though a class can access its ancestors' static variables and methods, static variables and methods are not inherited. See the section "Static Methods and Static Variables Not Inherited" in Chapter 6.

Static Method Scope

Code placed in a static method body resides in that method's scope. To demonstrate:

```
package {
  public class SomeClass {
    public static function staticMeth () {
      // Code here is in the staticMeth scope
    }
  }
}
```

Via the scope chain, code in a static method's scope can access these definitions:

- All definitions available to code in the global scope
- All definitions available to code in the scope of the class containing the static method definition

Additionally, code in a static method's scope can access the following definition:

- All local variables, nested functions, and namespaces defined within the static method

In other words:

```
package {
  public class SomeClass extends SomeParentClass {
    public static function staticMeth () {
      // Local variables, nested functions, and namespaces defined here
      // are accessible throughout staticMeth
    }
  }
}
```

Instance Method Scope

Code placed in an instance method body resides in that method's scope. Here's the code:

```
package {
  public class SomeClass {
    public function instanceMeth () {
      // Code here is in the instanceMeth scope
```

```
      }
    }
  }
```

Via the scope chain, code in an instance method's scope can access these definitions:

- All definitions available to code in the global scope
- All definitions available to code in the scope of the class containing the instance method definition

Additionally, code in an instance method's scope can access these definitions:

- All instance methods and instance variables of the object through which the instance method was invoked (subject to the limitations imposed by access-control modifiers)
- All local variables, nested functions, and namespaces defined within the instance method

The following code demonstrates:

```
package {
  public class SomeClass extends SomeParentClass {
    public function instanceMeth () {
      // 1) All instance methods and instance variables of the current
      //    object (i.e., this) are accessible throughout instanceMeth()
      //    (subject to the limitations imposed by access-control modifiers)

      // 2) Local variables, nested functions, and namespaces defined here
      //    are accessible throughout instanceMeth()
    }
  }
}
```

Function Scope

Code placed in a function body resides in that function's scope. The specific list of definitions available to code in a function's scope depends on the location of that function in the program.

Code in a function defined at the package-level or outside any package can access the following definitions:

- All definitions available to code in the global scope
- All local variables, nested functions, and namespaces defined within the function

Code in a function defined within a static method can access these definitions:

- All definitions available to code in the global scope
- All definitions available to code in the scope of the static method
- All local variables, nested functions, and namespaces defined within the function

Code in a function defined within an instance method can access the following definitions:

- All definitions available to code in the global scope
- All definitions available to code in the scope of the instance method
- All local variables, nested functions, and namespaces defined within the function

Code in a function defined within another function can access these definitions:

- All definitions available to code in the global scope
- All definitions available to code in the enclosing function
- All local variables, nested functions, and namespaces defined within the function

Scope Summary

The following code summarizes ActionScript available scopes:

```
package {
  // Code here is in the global scope

  public class SomeClass {
    // Code here is in the SomeClass scope

    public static function staticMeth ():void {
      // Code here is in the staticMeth scope
    }

    public function instanceMeth ():void {
      // Code here is in the instanceMeth scope

      function nestedFunc ():void {
        // Code here is in the nestedFunc scope
      }
    }
  }
}
// Code here is in the global scope
```

The Internal Details

Internally, ActionScript uses a list of objects to keep track of the definitions in the scope chain. The objects used to track the definitions of each scope are as follows:

Global scope
> The global object (an object created automatically by ActionScript to hold global definitions)

Class scope
> The class's *Class* object (and the *Class* objects of the class's ancestors)

Static method scope
> The class's *Class* object (and the *Class* objects of the class's ancestors)

Instance method scope
> The current object (*this*) and an activation object (an *activation object* is an object created and stored internally by ActionScript and maintains the local variables and parameters of function or method)

Function scope
> An activation object

When ActionScript encounters an identifier expression in an program, it searches for that identifier among the objects in the scope chain. For example, consider the following code:

```
package {
  public class SomeClass {
    public function instanceMeth ():void {
      function nestedFunc ():void {
        trace(a);
      }
    }
  }
}
var a:int = 15;
```

In the preceding code, when ActionScript encounters the identifier a, it begins a search for the value of that identifier with *nestedFunc()*'s activation object. But *nestedFunc()* does not define any local variables or parameters named a, so ActionScript next searches for a on the current object (i.e., the object through which *instanceMeth()* was invoked). But *SomeClass* does not define or inherit an instance method or instance variable named a, so ActionScript next searches for a on *SomeClass*'s class object. But *SomeClass* does not define a static method or static variable named a, so ActionScript next searches for a on the class object of *SomeClass*'s superclass—which is *Object*. But *Object* does not define a static method or static variable named a, so ActionScript next searches for a on the global object. There, ActionScript finds a, and determines its value to be 15. With a's value in hand, ActionScript then outputs 15 during debugging. Quite a lot of work for li'l 'ol a!

Here are the objects ActionScript searched for a, in the order they were searched:

- *nestedFunc()*'s activation object
- The object through which *instanceMeth()* was invoked
- *SomeClass*'s class object
- *Object*'s class object
- The global object

If a is not found on the global object, ActionScript reports a reference error.

Note that in the preceding example, a is defined on the global object but is accessible in the source file that contains a's definition only.

 Variables defined outside a package definition are accessible within the containing source file only.

Now that we know all about the scope chain, let's close this chapter with a quick look at ActionScript's only tool for manipulating the scope chain directly—the *with* statement.

Expanding the Scope Chain via the with Statement

The *with* statement provides a shorthand way to refer to the variables and methods of an object without having to specify the object's name repeatedly. A *with* statement takes the general form:

```
with (object) {
  substatements
}
```

When an identifier is referenced within a *with* statement block, `object` is checked for the specified name—before the remainder of the scope chain is consulted. In other words, *with* temporarily adds `object` to the end of ActionScript's internal list of objects in the scope chain.

For example, to refer to the built-in *Math* class's PI variable, we normally use the following code:

```
Math.PI;
```

But using the *with* statement, we can to refer to the built-in *Math* class's PI variable without the preceding reference to the *Math* class:

```
with (Math) {    // Execute statements in the context of Math
  trace(PI);     // Displays: 3.1459... (because PI is defined on Math)
}
```

Some developers find the *with* statement convenient when writing code that makes repeated references to a particular object's variables and methods.

On to Namespaces

In this chapter we learned how ActionScript manages the availability of definitions in different scopes. In the next chapter, we'll learn to use namespaces to manage the visibility of definitions. Note that namespaces are an important part of Action-Script's internal makeup but are typically used in custom code in advanced situations only. Newer programmers may wish to skip the next chapter and proceed directly to Chapter 18.

CHAPTER 17

Namespaces

In very general terms, a *namespace* is a set of names that contains no duplicates. That is, within the set, each name is unique. For example, in English, the names of fruits could be considered a namespace because each fruit has its own unique name—apple, pear, orange, and so on. Likewise, the names of colors could be considered a namespace because each color has its own unique name—blue, green, orange, and so on.

Notice that the name "orange" appears in both groups of names. The name "orange" itself is not unique, it is unique only within each group. Depending on whether you're talking about a fruit or a color, the same name, "orange," refers to two different things. That's the purpose of namespaces. They let the same name (identifier) have different meanings depending on the context in which it is used.

When applied to programming, this "same name, different meaning" feature of namespaces offers two general benefits:

- It helps programmers avoid name conflicts
- It lets a program's behavior adapt to the current context

Over the course of this chapter, we'll explore the many nooks and crannies of namespaces in ActionScript. Try not to let the various details distract you from the relative simplicity of namespaces. Fundamentally, namespaces are nothing more than a two-part naming system. They are used to distinguish one group of names from another, much like an area code distinguishes one phone number from other phone numbers around the world.

Namespace Vocabulary

In this chapter, we'll encounter quite a few new namespace-related terms. Below you'll find some of the most important ones listed for quick reference. Skim the list quickly now for familiarity and return to it whenever you need a refresher during the upcoming discussions. The remainder of this chapter covers each of these terms in much greater depth.

local name

> The local part of a qualified identifier; that is, the name being qualified by the namespace. For example, "orange" in `fruit::orange`.

namespace name

> The uniquely identifying name of a namespace, in the form of a uniform resource identifier (URI). In ActionScript, the namespace name is accessible via the `Namespace` class's instance variable `uri`. In XML, the namespace name is accessible via the `xmlns` attribute.

namespace prefix

> An alias to the namespace name. Namespace prefixes are used in XML only, but can be accessed in ActionScript via the *Namespace* class's `prefix` variable for the sake of E4X operations.

namespace identifier

> The identifier used for a namespace in an ActionScript namespace definition. For example, `fruit` in the following namespace definition:
>
> ```
> namespace fruit = "http://www.example.com/games/kidsgame/fruit";
> ```

open namespace

> A namespace that has been added to the set of open namespaces via the *use namespace* directive.

open namespaces

> The set of namespaces ActionScript consults when attempting to resolve unqualified references.

qualifier namespace

> The namespace that qualifies a variable or method definition or the namespace identifier in a qualified identifier.

qualified identifier

> A two-part ActionScript identifier that includes a namespace identifier and a local name, separated by two colons. For example, `fruit::orange`.

ActionScript Namespaces

In ActionScript, a namespace is a qualifier for the name of a variable, method, XML tag, or XML attribute. A *qualifier* limits, or "qualifies" the meaning of an identifier, giving us the ability to say in code "this orange variable is a fruit, not a color" or "this *search()* method applies to Japanese language searching, not English" or "this `<TABLE>` tag describes HTML page layout, not a piece of furniture."

Using ActionScript namespaces to qualify variable and method names we can:

- Prevent naming conflicts (see the section "Namespaces for Access-Control Modifiers")
- Implement custom levels of method and variable visibility across an entire program, independent of the program's package structure (see the mx_internal namespace example, in the section "Example: Framework-Internal Visibility")
- Implement permission-based access control wherein classes must request access to variables and methods (see Example 17-5 in the section "Example: Permission-Based Access Control")
- Implement multiple "modes" in a program (see Example 17-7 in the section "Example: Program Modes")

ActionScript namespaces also provide direct access to XML namespaces in XML documents. For coverage of XML namespaces in ActionScript see the section "Working with XML Namespaces" in Chapter 18.

C++ Namespaces Versus ActionScript Namespaces

Even though some of ActionScript's namespace syntax is similar to C++'s namespace syntax, namespaces are used differently in ActionScript than they are in C++.

In C++, a namespace is a syntactic container, just as packages are in ActionScript and Java. In C++, an identifier is considered "in" a given namespace only if it physically resides in that namespace's statement block. For example, in the following code, the variable a is in the namespace n because of the physical placement of the variable's declaration within the namespace statement:

```
namespace n {
  int a;
}
```

C++ namespaces are, therefore, used primarily to prevent naming conflicts between physical sections of code and to restrict one section of code from accessing another.

By contrast, in ActionScript, a namespace can include any variable or method, regardless of physical code structure. ActionScript namespaces define visibility rules for methods and variables that transcend the structural limits (classes and packages) of a program.

C++ programmers looking for the equivalent of C++ namespaces in ActionScript should investigate ActionScript packages, covered in Chapter 1. There is no direct analog for ActionScript namespaces in C++.

Before we get to applied namespace examples, let's look at the basic concepts and syntax involved in using ActionScript namespaces. Over the next few introductory sections we'll create two namespaces: fruit and color, then use the fruit and color namespaces to qualify the definitions of two variables, and finally refer to those variables using so-called "qualified identifiers." Along the way, we'll progress towards a simple example application: a child's learn-to-read game. Let's get started.

Creating Namespaces

To create a namespace, we must give it a name. The name of each namespace—known formally as the *namespace name*—is a string that, by convention, specifies a uniform resource identifier, or *URI*. The URI uniquely identifies the namespace among all other namespaces in a program and potentially even among any program in the world.

The term URI refers to the generalized resource-identification standard of which the familiar Internet address standard, URL, is a subtype. See *http://www.ietf.org/rfc/rfc2396.txt*.

ActionScript's use of URIs as namespace names is based on the standard set by the World Wide Web Consortium (W3C) in their "Namespaces in XML" recommendation. See *http://www.w3.org/TR/xml-names11*.

The first step in creating a namespace, then, is to decide on a URI to use as its name.

Choosing the Namespace URI

Typically, the URI used as a namespace name is a URL within the control of the organization producing the code. For example, my web site is *www.moock.org*, so for a new namespace name, I might use a URI generally structured like this:

```
http://www.moock.org/app/namespace
```

For the child's game that we're going to build, we'll use the following URIs for the namespaces fruit and color:

```
http://www.example.com/games/kidsgame/fruit
http://www.example.com/games/kidsgame/color
```

Note that the URI need not—and generally does not—exist online. The URI is used only to identify the namespace; it is not a web page address, or an XML document address, or any other online resource. Any URI is allowed, but using a URL from your own web site as the namespace name minimizes the likelihood that other organizations will use the same name.

Defining the Namespace

Once we've settled on a URI to use as the namespace name, we create the namespace using the *namespace* keyword, followed by the namespace's identifier, then an equal sign, and finally the namespace name (the URI):

```
namespace identifier = URI;
```

The namespace *identifier* is the name of the ActionScript constant to which the namespace value is assigned (where the namespace value is an instance of the *Namespace* class automatically generated by the preceding statement). The URI is the namespace name.

For example, to create a namespace with the identifier `fruit` and the URI `"http://www.example.com/games/kidsgame/fruit"`, we use:

```
namespace fruit = "http://www.example.com/games/kidsgame/fruit";
```

To create a namespace with the identifier `color` and the URI `"http://www.example.com/games/kidsgame/color"`, we use:

```
namespace color = "http://www.example.com/games/kidsgame/color";
```

Notice that no datatype declaration is required or allowed. The implicit datatype of the namespace identifier is always *Namespace*. Namespaces can be defined anywhere variables can be defined, namely:

- In the top level of a package definition
- In the top level of a class definition
- In a function or method
- On a movie clip timeline in a *.fla* file

In practice, namespaces are nearly always defined at the top level of a package or class definition (unless they're used for XML, as discussed in Chapter 18). For now, we'll define all our namespaces at the package level.

To create a package-level namespace for use throughout a program, place the namespace definition in a separate file, with the extension *.as*, and a name that exactly matches the namespace identifier's name, as in the following for the `fruit` namespace:

```
// File fruit.as
package kidsgame {
  namespace fruit = "http://www.example.com/games/kidsgame/fruit";
}
```

and for the color namespace:

```
// File color.as
package kidsgame {
  namespace color = "http://www.example.com/games/kidsgame/color";
}
```

In the later section "Namespace Accessibility," we'll study examples of namespaces defined at the class or function level. Namespaces defined in a movie clip timeline are treated as though they were defined at the class level in the class representing the containing movie clip (for more information on timeline-level definitions, see the section "Variable and Function Definitions in Frame Scripts" in Chapter 29.)

Explicit Versus Implicit URIs

So far, all our namespace definitions have included an explicit URI, such as the one shown in bold in the following namespace definition:

```
namespace fruit = "http://www.example.com/games/kidsgame/fruit";
```

But when a namespace declaration does not explicitly provide a namespace name (URI), ActionScript automatically generates one. For example, the following namespace definition provides no URI, so ActionScript automatically creates one:

```
package {
  namespace ns1;
}
```

To prove it, we can display the automatically generated URI for the namespace ns1 like this:

```
namespace ns1;
trace(ns1.uri);  // Displays: ns1
```

The *Namespace* class's instance method *toString()* also returns the value of the instance variable uri, so the *trace()* call can be shortened to:

```
trace(ns1);  // Also displays: ns1
```

However, it's generally wise to specify a URI when defining namespaces because explicit URIs are universally identifiable in any context, even across multiple *.swf* files, whereas automatically generated URIs are not. In this chapter, we'll provide an explicit URI for all namespaces.

 As a best practice, always provide a URI for each namespace definition.

Namespace Terminology Review

In just a few short pages we've encountered quite a lot of new terminology. Let's review.

- A *namespace name* is a URI that identifies a namespace.
- The *Namespace class* represents a namespace in an object-oriented way.
- A *namespace value* is an instance of the *Namespace* class.
- A *namespace identifier* is the name of an ActionScript constant that refers to a namespace value.

Generally speaking, the complexity of these terms can be captured by the simple term "namespace." For example, in this book, we often use the simple phrase, "the namespace fruit," in place of the more technically precise phrase, "the namespace "http://www.example.com/games/kidsgame/fruit" that is represented by a *Namespace* object referenced by the identifier `fruit`."

For the sake of easier reading, we'll normally use the simpler, if less precise, phrase "the namespace `fruit`." Nevertheless, the distinction between a namespace name and a namespace identifier is important to some of the ensuing discussion, so you should familiarize yourself with the preceding terminology.

Using a Namespace to Qualify Variable and Method Definitions

Now that we've defined the `fruit` and `color` namespaces, we can use them to specify the so-called *qualifier namespace* for new methods and variables. The qualifier namespace is the namespace within which the variable or method name is unique.

To specify the qualifier namespace for a new variable or method, we use that namespace's identifier as an attribute of the variable or method definition, as follows:

```
// Specify the qualifier namespace for a variable
namespaceIdentifier var propName:datatype = optionalInitialValue;

// Specify the qualifier namespace for a method
namespaceIdentifier function methodName (params):ReturnType {
  statements
}
```

The following rules apply to the *namespaceIdentifier*:

- It must be accessible to the scope where the variable or method is defined, as discussed later in the section "Namespace Accessibility."
- It cannot be a literal value; specifically it cannot be a string literal containing a namespace name (URI).
- It must be a compile-time constant.

These three rules effectively mean that the *namespaceIdentifier* can only be a namespace identifier created with the *namespace* keyword, and specifically cannot be a variable that refers to a namespace value. (We'll learn about variables that refer to namespace values later in the section "Assigning and Passing Namespace Values.")

Here's how to specify the qualifier namespace `fruit` for an instance variable named `orange`:

```
fruit var orange:String = "Round citrus fruit";
```

And here's how to specify the qualifier namespace `color` for an instance variable also named `orange`:

```
color var orange:String = "Color obtained by mixing red and yellow";
```

It's legal and common to use one qualifier namespace to qualify many different variables, providing that each variable's name is unique in that namespace (that's the whole idea!). For example, here's another variable, purple, also qualified by the namespace color:

```
color var purple:String = "Color obtained by mixing red and blue";
```

When multiple variables and methods are qualified by the same namespace, *n*, those variables and methods can be thought of as forming a logical group. From a theoretical point of view, then, it is natural to say that a variable or method "belongs to" or "is in" its declared namespace. However, on a technical level, an ActionScript "namespace" is not a data structure that physically contains variables or methods. Namespaces are *not* data containers, nor arrays. Namespaces serve only to qualify names. To avoid confusion, from now on, we'll use the phrase "the namespace n qualifies the variable name p" rather than "the variable name p belongs to the namespace n" or "the variable name p is in the namespace n."

Namespaces do not contain names; they simply qualify them.

Note that multiple namespaces cannot be specified for a single variable or method definition. Each definition can include a single qualifier namespace only. For example, this code is not legal:

```
// Attempt to specify two namespaces for a single definition.
fruit color var orange:String;  // Yields the following error:
                                // Only one namespace attribute
                                // may be used per definition
```

User-Defined Namespace Attributes in the Top-Level of a Class Only

In the previous section we learned how to use our own namespaces as attributes for method and variable definitions. In fact, that's the only place a user-defined namespace can legally be used as an attribute of a definition.

User-defined namespaces can be used as attributes within the top level of a class definition only.

If you attempt to use a user-defined namespace as an attribute of a definition anywhere else, you'll receive the following error:

```
A user-defined namespace attribute can only be used at the top level of a class
definition.
```

Specifically, this means you cannot specify a user-defined namespace for the definition of a class, package-level variable, package-level function, local variable, or nested function. The following definitions are illegal:

```
// Illegal class definition.  Namespace color not allowed here!
color class Picker {
}

public function doSomething ():void {
  // Illegal local variable definition.  Namespace color not allowed here!
  color var tempSwatch;
}

package p {
  // Illegal package-level variable definition.
  // Namespace color not allowed here!
  color var favorites:Array;
}
```

By contrast, namespaces built-in to ActionScript can be used as attributes of a definition wherever ActionScript specifically allows it. For example, as we'll learn in the later section "Namespaces for Access-Control Modifiers," the access-control modifiers (*public*, *internal*, *protected*, and *private*) are built-in namespaces, and two of them (*public* and *internal*) can be used at the package level.

Right, back to our code. We've now seen how to create two namespaces and three variables qualified by those namespaces, as follows:

```
// Create two namespaces
package kidsgame {
  namespace fruit = "http://www.example.com/games/kidsgame/fruit";
}

package kidsgame {
  namespace color = "http://www.example.com/games/kidsgame/color";
}

// Elsewhere, within a class, create three variables
fruit var orange:String = "Round citrus fruit";
color var orange:String = "Color obtained by mixing red and yellow";
color var purple:String = "Color obtained by mixing red and blue";
```

Next we'll learn how to refer to those variables using *qualified identifiers*.

Qualified Identifiers

So far all the identifiers we've encountered in this book have been so-called *simple identifiers*—identifiers with "simple" one-part names such as box, height, and border. But in order to work with namespaces we must use *qualified identifiers*. A qualified identifier is a special type of identifier that includes both a name and a namespace that qualifies that name. Accordingly, qualified identifiers have two parts instead of just one:

- The *local name* (the name that is unique within the specified namespace)
- The *qualifier namespace* (the namespace within which the local name is unique)

In ActionScript code, qualified identifiers are written as follows,

```
qualifierNamespace::localName
```

where the local name and qualifier namespace are joined together with the *name-qualifier operator*, written as two colons (::). The *qualifierNamespace* must be either a namespace identifier or a variable with a namespace as a value. We'll learn about assigning namespaces to variables in the later section "Assigning and Passing Namespace Values." The *qualifierNamespace* cannot, however, be a literal string that is the namespace name (URI).

Let's take a look at a real-life example of a qualified identifier. First, recall our earlier definition of the variable orange qualified by the namespace fruit:

```
fruit var orange:String = "Round citrus fruit";
```

Here's how we refer to that variable with a qualified identifier:

```
fruit::orange
```

Likewise, here's the qualified identifier for the variable with the local name orange qualified by the namespace color:

```
color::orange
```

In the preceding examples, notice that the local names are the same (orange), but the qualifier namespace is different. ActionScript uses the qualifier namespace to distinguish between the two local names. Qualified identifiers are used exactly like simple identifiers in ActionScript; they just happen to include a qualifier namespace. The format *qualifierNamespace::localName* applies to method and variable names alike:

```
someNamespace::p     // Access variable p
someNamespace::m()   // Invoke method m( )
```

A reference to a qualified identifier through an object uses the familiar dot operator, as follows:

```
someObject.qualifierNamespace::localName
```

For example, this code accesses someObj's variable p, which is qualified by someNamespace:

```
someObj.someNamespace::p
```

And this code invokes someObj's method m( ), which is qualified by someNamespace:

```
someObj.someNamespace::m( )
```

Expanded Names

We've just learned that a qualified identifier is a two-part name that includes a qualifier namespace and a local name:

```
qualifierNamespace::localName
```

The *qualifierNamespace* in a qualified identifier is a reference to a *Namespace* object whose uri variable identifies the namespace name.

An expanded name, by comparison, is a two-part name that includes a literal namespace name (URI) and a local name. Expanded names are used for documentation purposes only, never in code, and are typically written in the following format:

```
{namespaceName}localName
```

For example, once again consider the definition of the namespace fruit:

```
namespace fruit = "http://www.example.com/games/kidsgame/fruit";
```

And consider the definition of the variable orange, which is qualified by the namespace fruit:

```
fruit var orange:String = "Round citrus fruit";
```

In code, we refer to that variable using the qualified identifier fruit::orange. However, in documentation, we may wish to discuss that variable in reference to its actual namespace name, rather than its namespace identifier. We can do so using the following *expanded name*:

```
{http://www.example.com/games/kidsgame/fruit}orange
```

Expanded names are rarely used in this book, but are relatively common in the documentation of XML namespaces. If you do not use XML namespaces, simply be aware that the syntax {namespaceName}localName is a documentation convention only, not a supported form of code.

A Functional Namespace Example

Let's put our new knowledge of namespaces to work in a simplified program. Example 17-1 contains the beginnings of an application we'll develop over the coming sections—a child's word-recognition game. In the game, the player is shown a picture of either a color or a fruit, and asked to choose its name from a list of options. Figure 17-1 depicts two different screens in the game.

For now, each item in the game will be represented by a variable whose value is a string description. We'll define the catalog of all item variables in a class called *Items. Using namespaces,* we'll separate the "fruit" variables from the "color" variables; fruit variable names will be qualified by the fruit namespace, and color variable names will be qualified by the color namespace.

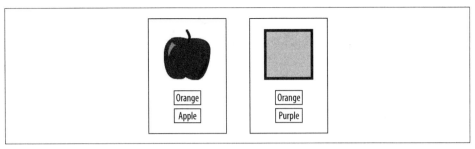

Figure 17-1. A child's learn-to-read game

Take a look at the code in Example 17-1, then we'll review it.

Example 17-1. Kids Game: a functional namespace example

```
// File fruit.as
package {
  namespace fruit = "http://www.example.com/games/kidsgame/fruit";
}

// File color.as
package {
  namespace color = "http://www.example.com/games/kidsgame/color";
}

// File Items.as
package {
  public class Items {
    fruit var orange:String = "Round citrus fruit";
    color var orange:String = "Color obtained by mixing red and yellow";

    public function Items () {
      trace(fruit::orange);
      trace(color::orange);
    }
  }
}
```

In the preceding code, we start by defining the game's namespaces. We define the namespace fruit in the file *fruit.as*, as follows:

```
package {
  namespace fruit = "http://www.example.com/games/kidsgame/fruit";
}
```

Then we define the namespace color in the file *color.as*, as follows:

```
package {
  namespace color = "http://www.example.com/games/kidsgame/color";
}
```

We create each namespace at the package level so that it can be accessed by any class in the application.

Next we define the class *Items* in the file *Items.as*. In *Items*, we define two variables, both of which have the local name orange. For the first variable, we specify the qualifier namespace fruit; for the second we specify the qualifier namespace color.

```
package {
  public class Items {
    fruit var orange:String = "Round citrus fruit";
    color var orange:String = "Color obtained by mixing red and yellow";
  }
}
```

Finally, to test that our code is working so far, in the *Items* constructor method we use the *trace()* function to display the value of both orange variables. To distinguish one orange variable from the other, we use the qualified identifiers fruit::orange and color::orange.

```
package {
  public class Items {
    fruit var orange:String = "Round citrus fruit";
    color var orange:String = "Color obtained by mixing red and yellow";

    public function Items () {
      trace(fruit::orange); // Displays: Round citrus fruit
      trace(color::orange); // Displays: Color obtained by
                            //           mixing red and yellow
    }
  }
}
```

Can you guess what would happen if we modified the preceding *Items* constructor to access the simple identifier orange, without including any qualifier namespace, as follows:

```
public function Items () {
  trace(orange); // What happens here?
}
```

The answer is that the following compile-time error occurs:

```
Access of undefined property orange.
```

The compiler cannot find a variable or method (i.e., a "property") by the name orange because no variable or method with the simple identifier orange exists in the scope of the *Items* constructor method. The variables fruit::orange and color::orange are qualified by namespaces, so they are invisible to our attempt to reference them with an unqualified identifier. That said, in the later section "Open Namespaces and the use namespace Directive," we'll learn a shortcut for referring to qualified identifiers without including the qualifier namespace.

Example 17-1 obviously doesn't show a fully functional game, but it should give you a sense of basic namespace syntax and usage. We'll finish making our game later in this chapter.

At this early state of our game's development, you might wonder if, rather than using namespaces, we should simply define variables with longer names, such as `orangeFruit` and `orangeColor`. Or you might wonder if we should separate the two kinds of "oranges" by assigning them to individual arrays, as in:

```
var fruitList:Array = ["orange", "apple", "banana"];
var colorList:Array = ["orange", "red", "blue"];
```

Those are valid considerations. In fact, at our current level of simplicity, we would indeed be better served with arrays or longer variable names. But don't lose faith in namespaces yet; we're building towards more compelling usage scenarios.

Namespace Accessibility

Like variable and method definitions, namespace definitions can be modified by the access-control modifiers *public*, *internal*, *protected*, and *private*. Taken in combination, the location of a namespace definition and the access-control modifier of that definition determine where the resulting namespace identifier can be used.

Here are some general rules to help you decide where to define your namespaces:

- When you need a namespace throughout a program or across a group of classes, define it at the package level.

- When you need a namespace to define the visibility of variables and methods within a single class only, define it at the class level.

- When you need a namespace only temporarily within a function, and you know the URI of the namespace, but you cannot access that namespace directly, define it at the function level.

Let's look at some examples, starting with namespaces defined at the package level.

Accessibility of Package-Level Namespace Definitions

In the following code, we define a namespace identifier, `fruit`, in the package `kidsgame`:

```
package kidsgame {
  public namespace fruit = "http://www.example.com/games/kidsgame/fruit";
}
```

Because `fruit` is declared at the package level with the access-control modifier *public*, it can be used to qualify any variable or method in the program. Of course, code outside the `kidsgame` package would have to import the namespace `fruit` before using it, as in:

```
package anyPackage {
  // Import the fruit namespace
  import kidsgame.fruit;
```

```
    public class AnyClass {
      // Ok to use fruit here now that it has been imported
      fruit var banana:String = "Long yellow fruit";
    }
  }
```

Now let's set the accessibility of the namespace color to package-only using the access-control modifier *internal*:

```
  package kidsgame {
    internal namespace color = "http://www.example.com/games/kidsgame/color";
  }
```

When a namespace identifier is defined as *internal* at the package level, it can be used within the containing package only. The following code demonstrates.

```
  package kidsgame {
    public class Items {
      // Ok to use color here. This use of the color namespace is valid
      // it occurs within the kidsgame package
      color var green:String = "Color obtained by mixing blue and yellow";
    }
  }

  package cardgame {
    import kidsgame.color;
    public class CardGame {
      // Illegal.
      // The color namespace can be used in the kidsgame package only.
      color var purple:String = "Color obtained by mixing blue and red";
    }
  }
```

Package-level namespaces can be defined as *public* or *internal*, but not *private* nor *protected*. Further, if the access modifier for a package-level namespace definition is omitted, then *internal* is assumed. For example, this code:

```
  package kidsgame {
    // Explicitly internal
    internal namespace fruit;
  }
```

is the same as this code:

```
  package kidsgame {
    // Implicitly internal
    namespace fruit;
  }
```

Next, let's consider the class-level case.

Accessibility of Class-Level Namespace Definitions

A namespace identifier defined as *private* in a class is accessible throughout that class only, not in subclasses or any other external code:

```
public class A {
  private namespace n = "http://www.example.com/n";

  // Fine. Namespace identifier n is accessible here.
  n var someVariable:int;
}

public class B extends A {
  // Error. Namespace identifier n is not accessible here.
  n var someOtherVariable:int;
}
```

We can use a *private* namespace in a class to implement a permission-based access control system, as discussed in the later section "Example: Permission-Based Access Control."

A namespace identifier defined as *protected*, *internal*, or *public* in a class is directly accessible throughout that class and its subclasses but not directly accessible in any other external code. Contrast this with a package-level *public* namespace definition, which creates a namespace identifier that can be accessed directly throughout a program. The following code demonstrates:

```
public class A {
  public namespace n = "http://www.example.com/n";

  // Fine. Namespace identifier n is directly accessible here.
  n var someVariable:int;
}

public class B extends A {
  // Fine. Namespace identifier n is directly accessible here.
  n var someOtherVariable:int;
}

public class C {
  // Error. Namespace identifier n is not directly accessible here.
  // (But n would be accessible if defined at the package level.)
  n var yetAnotherVariable:int;
}
```

Note that while a namespace identifier defined as *internal* or *public* in a class is directly accessible throughout that class and its subclasses only, the *Namespace* object referenced by the namespace identifier can still be accessed using static-variable syntax.

For example, to access the *Namespace* object referenced by the namespace identifier n in the preceding code, we would use the expression: A.n. Static-variable style access to *Namespace* objects is subject to the normal restrictions imposed on *protected*, *internal*, and *public* static variables. For example, in the preceding code, because n is declared as *public*, the expression A.n is valid in any code that has access to the class A. If n were declared as *internal*, then the reference A.n would be valid within the containing package only. If n were declared as *protected*, then the reference A.n would be valid within the class *A* and its subclasses only.

However, references to namespaces made through a class (such as A.n) cannot be used as an attribute of a variable or method definition. The following syntax is illegal because an attribute of a variable or method definition must be a compile-time constant value:

```
A.n var p:int;  // Illegal. A.n is not a compile-time constant.
```

So, if we can't use A.n to qualify definitions, what *can* we use A.n for? Stay tuned, we'll learn the answer to that question soon in the section "Assigning and Passing Namespace Values."

Now let's consider one final namespace accessibility topic: namespace definitions in methods and functions.

Accessibility of Function-Level Namespace Definitions

Like other function-level definitions, a namespace identifier defined at the function level cannot take any access-control modifiers (i.e., cannot be defined as *public*, *private*, etc.) and is accessible in the scope of that function only:

```
public function doSomething ():void {
  // This is illegal
  private namespace n = "http://www.example.com/n";
}
```

Furthermore, local variables and nested function definitions cannot take namespaces as attributes:

```
public function doSomething ():void {
  // This is also illegal
  namespace n = "http://www.example.com/n";
  n var someLocalVariable:int = 10;
}
```

Hence, namespace identifiers defined in a function can be used to form qualified identifiers only. (The following code assumes that the namespace n has already been declared elsewhere and has been used to qualify the instance variable someVariable.)

```
public function doSomething ():void {
  // This is legal
  namespace n = "http://www.example.com/n";
  trace(n::someVariable);
}
```

Function-level namespace definitions are used only in the rare circumstance in which a namespace that is required temporarily by a function cannot be accessed directly but the namespace URI is known. For example, a function that processes an XML fragment containing qualified element names might use code such as the following:

```
public function getPrice ():void {
```

```
   namespace htmlNS = "http://www.w3.org/1999/xhtml";
   output.text = htmlNS::table.htmlNS::tr[1].htmlNS::td[1].price;
}
```

For coverage of XML namespaces, see Chapter 18.

Qualified-Identifier Visibility

Perhaps you noticed that none of the qualified-identifier definitions in this book include any access-control modifiers (*public*, *internal*, *protected*, or *private*). We've seen plenty of this:

```
fruit var orange:String = "Round citrus fruit";
```

But none of this (note the addition of the access-control modifier *private*):

```
private fruit var orange:String = "Round citrus fruit";
```

And for good reason: it is *illegal* to use access-control modifiers with definitions that include a qualifier namespace. For example, the following code:

```
private fruit var orange:String;
```

yields the error:

```
Access specifiers not allowed with namespace attributes
```

But if access-control modifiers are illegal, then what governs the accessibility of a qualified identifier? Answer: the accessibility of the identifier's qualifier namespace.

> The accessibility of the qualifier namespace in a qualified identifier determines that identifier's accessibility. If the qualifier namespace is visible in a given scope, then the qualified identifier is also visible.

For example, in the expression gameitems.fruit::orange, the variable fruit::orange is accessible if and only if the namespace fruit is accessible in the scope where the expression occurs. The accessibility of the variable fruit::orange is entirely determined by the accessibility of the namespace fruit.

Example 17-2 demonstrates qualified identifier visibility with generic code.

Example 17-2. Qualified identifier visibility demonstration

```
// Create namespace n, set to package-only visibility, in package one
package one {
  internal namespace n = "http://www.example.com/n";
}

// Create variable n::p in class A, package one
package one {
  public class A {
    n var p:int = 1;
  }
```

Example 17-2. Qualified identifier visibility demonstration (continued)

```
}

// Because namespace n's visibility is internal, the
// variable n::p is accessible anywhere within the package one
package one {
  public class B {
    public function B () {
      var a:A = new A();
      trace(a.n::p);  // OK
    }
  }
}

// But the variable n::p is not accessible to code outside of
// package one
package two {
  import one.*;

  public class C {
    public function C () {
      var a:A = new A();
      trace(a.n::p);  // Illegal because n is internal to package one, and
                      // is, therefore, not accessible within package two
    }
  }
}
```

Comparing Qualified Identifiers

Two namespaces are considered equal if, and only if, they have the same namespace name (URI). For example, to determine whether the namespaces in the qualified identifiers fruit::orange and color::orange are equal, ActionScript does not check whether the characters "fruit" in the first identifier match the characters "color" in second. Instead, ActionScript checks whether the *Namespace* instance referred to by fruit and the *Namespace* instance referred to by color have a matching uri variable value. If fruit.uri equals color.uri, then the namespaces are considered equal.

Therefore, when we write the following comparison:

```
trace(fruit::orange == color::orange);
```

ActionScript performs this comparison (notice the use of expanded names, discussed in the earlier section "Expanded Names"):

```
{http://www.example.com/games/kidsgame/fruit}orange
    == {http://www.example.com/games/kidsgame/color}orange
```

Hence, even though two qualified identifiers may look different on the surface, they might be the same, leading to perhaps surprising name conflicts. For example, in the following code, the attempted definition of the variable ns2::p is considered a compile-time error because a variable with the expanded name {http://www.example.com/general}p already exists:

```
namespace ns1 = "http://www.example.com/general"
namespace ns2 = "http://www.example.com/general"
ns1 var p:int = 1;
ns2 var p:int = 2;  // Error! Duplicate variable definition!
```

Even though the identifiers ns1 and ns2 are different, the variables ns1::p and ns2::p are considered identical because they have the same expanded name ({http://www.example.com/general}p).

Note that namespace names (URIs) are compared as strings, and case sensitivity matters. So, whereas two URIs that differ in case only would be considered the same by a web browser, ActionScript considers them different. The following two URIs are considered different by ActionScript because "example" is not capitalized in the first but is capitalized in the second:

```
namespace ns1 = "http://www.example.com"
namespace ns2 = "http://www.Example.com"
trace(ns1 == ns2);  // Displays: false
```

Assigning and Passing Namespace Values

Because every namespace is represented by an instance of the *Namespace* class, namespaces can be assigned to variables or array elements, passed to methods, returned from methods, and generally used like any other object. This flexibility lets us:

- Pass a namespace from one scope to another
- Choose between multiple namespaces dynamically at runtime

These activities are critical to namespace usage in ActionScript. Let's see how.

Assigning a Namespace Value to a Variable

To assign a namespace value to a variable, we use the same assignment syntax we'd use with any other value. For example, the following code assigns the namespace value in fruit to the variable currentItemType (recall that a *namespace value* is a *Namespace* object):

```
// File fruit.as
package {
  namespace fruit = "http://www.example.com/games/kidsgame/fruit";
}

// File Items.as
package {
  public class Items {
    // Assign the value in fruit to currentItemType
```

```
    private var currentItemType:Namespace = fruit;
  }
}
```

A variable referencing a *Namespace* object can be used to form a qualified identifier. For example, consider the following variable definition:

```
fruit var orange:String = "Round citrus fruit";
```

To refer to that variable, we can use either the expression `fruit::orange` or the expression `currentItemType::orange`. By changing the value of `currentItemType` to some other namespace, we can dynamically adjust the meaning of the identifier `currentItemType::orange`, and of all other methods and variables qualified by `currentItemType` across an entire program. If we organize groups of methods and variables with namespaces, we can use dynamic namespace selection to switch between operational modes in the program.

For example, suppose we're writing an instant messaging application with two modes represented by corresponding namespaces, `offline` and `online`. The application defines two versions of a method named *sendMessage()*—one to use in online mode and one to use in offline mode.

```
online sendMessage (msg:String):void {
  // Send message now...
}

offline sendMessage (msg:String):void {
  // Queue message and send later...
}
```

The application keeps track of the currently active mode using a variable, `currentMode`. Whenever the server connection is established or lost, `currentMode` is updated.

```
private function connectListener (e:Event):void {
  currentMode = online;
}

private function closeListener (e:Event):void {
  currentMode = offline;
}
```

All calls to *sendMessage()* use `currentMode` as a qualifier namespace, as shown in the following code:

```
currentMode::sendMessage("yo dude");
```

By updating the `currentMode` variable, the application dynamically switches between the two versions of *sendMessage()*, depending on the connection status.

In the later section "Example: Program Modes," we'll revisit the concept of namespaces as modes in a Japanese/English dictionary example that switches between different search modes.

Just remember that while a variable can be used to specify the namespace of a qualified identifier, variables *cannot* be used to specify the namespace for a variable or method definition. The third line of the following code:

```
namespace fruit;
var currentItemType:Namespace = fruit;
currentItemType var orange:String = "Round citrus fruit";
```

yields this error:

```
Namespace was not found or is not a compile-time constant.
```

Similarly, variables cannot be used to specify the namespace in a *use namespace* directive. We'll cover the *use namespace* directive in the later section "Open Namespaces and the use namespace Directive."

Namespaces as Method Arguments and Return Values

In addition to being assigned to variables and array elements, namespace values can be passed to and returned from methods. For example, the following code defines a method, *doSomething()*, that accepts a namespace value as an argument:

```
public function doSomething (n:Namespace):void {
  trace(n);
}
```

This code passes the namespace fruit to the method *doSomething()*:

```
doSomething(fruit);
```

A namespace might be passed to a method in order to send one part of a program's context to another. For example, a shopping cart application might pass the namespace currentLocale to a *Checkout* class that would then dynamically select the appropriate currency and time-sensitive greeting based on the user's location.

This code defines a method, *getNamespace()* that returns the namespace fruit:

```
public function getNamespace ():Namespace {
  return fruit;
}
```

A namespace might be returned from a method in order to grant the caller privileged access to restricted variables and methods. For a full example of returning a namespace from a method as part of permission-based access control, see the section "Example: Permission-Based Access Control," later in this chapter.

A Namespace Value Example

Now that we've studied how namespace values work in theory, let's revisit our earlier child's game example to see how namespace values can be used in an actual application. Recall that the game is a reading exercise in which the player tries to identify a randomly chosen color or fruit. The first version of the game code (Example 17-1) showed a single, extremely simplified section of the game. In this updated version, we'll make the game fully functional, providing a deeper look at how namespaces help manage multiple sets of data.

Skim the code in Example 17-3 for familiarity. In the example, namespaces are used within the *Items* and *KidsGame* classes only, so you should focus most of your attention on those classes. For information on the techniques used to generate the user interface in the example, see Part II. A detailed analysis follows the example listing.

Example 17-3. Kids Game: a namespace value example

```
// File fruit.as
package {
  public namespace fruit = "http://www.example.com/games/kidsgame/fruit";
}

// File color.as
package {
  public namespace color = "http://www.example.com/games/kidsgame/color";
}

// File Items.as
package {
  // A simple data-storage class containing the Item objects for the game.
  public class Items {
    // The fruits
    fruit var orange:Item = new Item("Orange", "fruit-orange.jpg", 1);
    fruit var apple:Item  = new Item("Apple", "fruit-apple.jpg", 2);

    // The colors
    color var orange:Item = new Item("Orange", "color-orange.jpg", 3);
    color var purple:Item = new Item("Purple", "color-purple.jpg", 4);

    // Arrays that track complete sets of items (i.e., all the fruits, or
    // all the colors)
    fruit var itemSet:Array = [fruit::orange, fruit::apple];
    color var itemSet:Array = [color::orange, color::purple];

    // An array of namespaces representing the types of the item
    // sets in the game
    private var itemTypes:Array = [color, fruit];

    // Returns all the fruit items in the game
    fruit function getItems ():Array {
      return fruit::itemSet.slice(0);
    }

    // Returns all the color items in the game
    color function getItems ():Array {
      return color::itemSet.slice(0);
    }

    // Returns the list of available item types in the game
    public function getItemTypes ():Array {
```

Example 17-3. Kids Game: a namespace value example (continued)

```
      return itemTypes.slice(0);
    }
  }
}

// File KidsGame.as
package {
  import flash.display.*;
  import flash.events.*;
  import flash.utils.*;

  // The main application class for a child's learn-to-read game
  // demonstrating the basic usage of namespaces in ActionScript.
  // The player is shown a picture of a color or a fruit, and asked to
  // choose its name from a list of options.
  public class KidsGame extends Sprite {
    private var gameItems:Items;  // The list of all items in the game
    private var thisQuestionItem:Item; // The item for each question
    private var questionScreen:QuestionScreen;  // The user interface

    // Constructor
    public function KidsGame( ) {
      // Retrieve the game items (the fruits and colors which the user must
      // name)
      gameItems = new Items( );
      // Display the first question
      newQuestion( );
    }

    // Creates and displays a new random game question
    public function newQuestion ( ):void {
      // Get the full list of item types (an array of namespaces)
      var itemTypes:Array = gameItems.getItemTypes( );
      // Pick a random item type (one of the namespaces in itemTypes)
      var randomItemType:Namespace = itemTypes[Math.floor(
                              Math.random( )*itemTypes.length)];

      // Retrieve the randomly chosen item set
      var items:Array = gameItems.randomItemType::getItems( );

      // Randomly pick the item for this question from the item set
      thisQuestionItem = items[Math.floor(Math.random( )*items.length)];

      // Remove the previous question, if there was one
      if (questionScreen != null) {
        removeChild(questionScreen);
      }

      // Display the new question
      questionScreen = new QuestionScreen(this, items, thisQuestionItem);
      addChild(questionScreen);
    }
```

Example 17-3. Kids Game: a namespace value example (continued)

```
    // Handles a player's guess
    public function submitGuess (guess:int):void {
      trace("Guess: " + guess + ", Correct: " + thisQuestionItem.id);
      if (guess == thisQuestionItem.id) {
        questionScreen.displayResult("Correct!");
        // Disable the answer buttons while the
        // player waits for the next question.
        questionScreen.disable();
        // Wait 3 seconds then show another question.
        var timer:Timer = new Timer(3000, 1);
        timer.addEventListener(TimerEvent.TIMER, doneResultDelay);
        timer.start();
      } else {
        questionScreen.displayResult("Incorrect. Please try again.");
      }
    }

    // Makes a new question after the previous question is finished.
    private function doneResultDelay (e:TimerEvent):void {
      newQuestion();
    }
  }
}

// File Item.as
package {
  // A simple data container that tracks an item's information.
  public class Item {
    // The item's name (for example, "apple")
    public var name:String;
    // The URL from which to load an image representing the item
    public var src:String;
    // A unique identifier for the item, used to evaluate player guesses
    public var id:int;

    // Constructor
    public function Item (name:String, src:String, id:int) {
      this.name = name;
      this.src = src;
      this.id = id;
    }
  }
}

// File QuestionScreen.as
package {
  import flash.events.*;
  import flash.display.*;
  import flash.text.*;
  import flash.net.*;
```

Example 17-3. Kids Game: a namespace value example (continued)

```
// Creates the user interface for a question
public class QuestionScreen extends Sprite {
  private var status:TextField;
  private var game:KidsGame;
  private var items:Array;
  private var thisQuestionItem:Item;

  // Constructor
  public function QuestionScreen (game:KidsGame,
                                  items:Array,
                                  thisQuestionItem:Item) {
    // Keep a reference to the main game engine
    this.game = game;

    // Assemble question data
    this.items = items;
    this.thisQuestionItem = thisQuestionItem;

    // Put the question on screen
    makeQuestion( );
  }

  // Creates and displays a question's interface
  public function makeQuestion ( ):void {
    // Display the graphic for the item
    var imgLoader:Loader = new Loader( );
    addChild(imgLoader);
    imgLoader.load(new URLRequest(thisQuestionItem.src));

    // Add a selection of clickable words for the player to choose
    // from. For the sake of simplicity, we'll display the name of every
    // item in the item set.
    var wordButton:WordButton;
    for (var i:int = 0; i < items.length; i++) {
      wordButton = new WordButton( );
      wordButton.setButtonText(items[i].name);
      wordButton.setID(items[i].id);
      wordButton.y = 110 + i*(wordButton.height + 5);
      wordButton.addEventListener(MouseEvent.CLICK, clickListener);
      addChild(wordButton);
    }

    // Create a text field in which to display question status
    status = new TextField( );
    status.autoSize = TextFieldAutoSize.LEFT;
    status.y = wordButton.y + wordButton.height + 10;
    status.selectable = false;
    addChild(status);
  }

  // Displays a message in the status field
  public function displayResult (msg:String):void {
```

Example 17-3. Kids Game: a namespace value example (continued)

```
      status.text = msg;
    }

    // Displays user input for this question
    public function disable ():void {
      // Disables mouse events for all children of this Sprite.
      mouseChildren = false;
    }

    // Responds to the clicking of a word button
    private function clickListener (e:MouseEvent):void {
      // The player's guess is the item id associated with
      // the WordButton object, as set in makeQuestion().
      game.submitGuess(e.target.getID());
    }
  }
}

// File WordButton.as
package {
  import flash.text.*;
  import flash.display.*;

  // Represents a clickable word on screen (i.e., an available choice for
  // a question). The ID indicates the item id of the player's
  // guess (see Item.id).
  public class WordButton extends Sprite {
    private var id:int;  // The ID of the item this button represents
    private var t:TextField;

    // Constructor
    public function WordButton () {
      t = new TextField();
      t.autoSize   = TextFieldAutoSize.LEFT;
      t.border     = true;
      t.background = true;
      t.selectable = false;
      addChild(t);

      buttonMode     = true;
      mouseChildren = false;
    }

    // Assigns the text to display on the button
    public function setButtonText (text:String):void {
      t.text = text;
    }

    // Assigns the ID of the item this button represents
    public function setID (newID:int):void {
      id = newID;
    }
```

Example 17-3. Kids Game: a namespace value example (continued)

```
  // Returns the ID of the item this button represents
  public function getID ():int {
    return id;
  }
 }
}
```

Done skimming the code? Great, let's examine it in more detail. You probably noticed that the namespace definitions in the game haven't changed at all since Example 17-1. However, the *Items* class has changed substantially and there are several new classes, including:

- *KidsGame*—the main application class
- *Item*—provides information about a particular game item
- *QuestionScreen*—builds the each question's user interface
- *WordButton*—represents a clickable word on screen

Because our present focus is namespaces, we'll examine the *Items* and *KidsGame* classes only; study of the remaining classes is left as an exercise for the reader.

Let's start by looking at how *Items* has been updated since Example 17-1. First, we've added two new item variables, fruit::apple and color::purple. These new variables give the fruit and color item categories a total of two items each—orange and apple for the fruits, and orange and purple for the colors. We've also replaced Example 17-1's simple item descriptions (such as "Round citrus fruit") with instances of the *Item* class. The *Item* instances track the item's name, image URL, and ID. The following code shows the updated item variables. As in Example 17-1, each variable is qualified by a namespace corresponding to the variety of item.

```
fruit var orange:Item = new Item("Orange", "fruit-orange.jpg", 1);
fruit var apple:Item  = new Item("Apple", "fruit-apple.jpg", 2);

color var orange:Item = new Item("Orange", "color-orange.jpg", 3);
color var purple:Item = new Item("Purple", "color-purple.jpg", 4);
```

Next, the *Items* class also adds two arrays to manage the items as groups. Each array maintains a complete list of its group's items (either the fruits or the colors). The arrays are assigned to variables with the same local name (itemSet) but qualified by different namespaces (fruit and color).

```
fruit var itemSet:Array = [fruit::orange, fruit::apple];
color var itemSet:Array = [color::orange, color::purple];
```

To give other classes access to the different item sets in the game, *Items* defines two methods with the same local name, *getItems()*, but qualified by different namespaces, fruit and color. Each *getItems()* method returns a copy of the item set that corresponds to its namespace. Hence, the appropriate item-set can be accessed dynamically based on the current question type (either color or fruit).

```
fruit function getItems ():Array {
  // Return the fruits.
  return fruit::itemSet.slice(0);
}

color function getItems ():Array {
  // Return the colors.
  return color::itemSet.slice(0);
}
```

Finally, *Items* defines the variable itemTypes and a corresponding accessor method *getItemTypes()*. The itemTypes variable maintains a list of all the different varieties of items in the game. Our game has only two varieties—fruit and color—but more could easily be added. Each item variety corresponds to a namespace, so itemTypes is an array of namespaces. The *getItemTypes()* method returns a copy of that array, giving external code a central location from which to obtain the official list of item types in the game.

```
// The itemTypes variable
private var itemTypes:Array = [color, fruit];

// The getItemTypes() method
public function getItemTypes ():Array {
  return itemTypes.slice(0);
}
```

That's it for the changes to *Items*. Now let's turn to the new main application class, *KidsGame*. In contrast with the *Items* class, *KidsGame* never uses the namespace identifiers fruit and color directly. Instead, it refers to those namespaces via the *Items* class's instance method *getItemTypes()*.

The *KidsGame* class's gameItems variable provides *KidsGame* with access to the game data, in the form of an *Items* object. Meanwhile, the *KidsGame* class's *newQuestion()* method generates a new question based on the data in gameItems. The *newQuestion()* method contains the majority of the namespace code we're interested in, so let's look at it line-by-line.

Recall that each question displays an item from one of the predetermined item sets maintained by the *Items* class (fruit::itemSet or color::itemSet). Accordingly, the first task in *newQuestion()* is to randomly choose the item set for the question being generated. We start by retrieving the entire array of possible item sets (i.e., namespaces) from the *Items* class, using *gameItems.getItemTypes()*:

```
var itemTypes:Array = gameItems.getItemTypes();
```

Then we randomly choose a namespace from the resulting array. For convenience, we assign the chosen namespace to a local variable, randomItemType.

```
var randomItemType:Namespace = itemTypes[Math.floor(
                  Math.random()*itemTypes.length)];
```

Notice that randomItemType's datatype is *Namespace* because it refers to a namespace value. Once an item set (namespace) for the question has been chosen, we must retrieve the array of actual items in that set. To retrieve the appropriate array of items (either fruits or colors), we invoke the method that corresponds to our chosen namespace—either *Items*'s *fruit::getItems()* or *Items*'s *color::getItems()*. But instead of referring to the method we want directly, we dynamically generate the method's qualified identifier using the randomItemType variable to specify the namespace, like this:

```
gameItems.randomItemType::getItems()
```

The returned array is assigned to a local variable, items:

```
var items:Array = gameItems.randomItemType::getItems();
```

 In the preceding method call, notice that the *behavior* of the program is determined by the *context* of the program. This can be thought of as a kind of polymorphism, one based not on class inheritance but on the arbitrary groups of methods and variables delineated by namespaces.

With our array of items cheerfully in hand, we can get on with the everyday work of putting a question on screen. First we randomly pick the item to display from among the array of items:

```
thisQuestionItem = items[Math.floor(Math.random( )*items.length)];
```

Then we put the item image and text choices for the chosen item on screen using the *QuestionScreen* class:

```
// Remove the previous question, if there was one
if (questionScreen != null) {
  removeChild(questionScreen);
}

// Display the new question
questionScreen = new QuestionScreen(this, items, thisQuestionItem);
addChild(questionScreen);
```

Here's another look at the *newQuestion()* method. Pay special attention to its use of namespace values as you review it one last time.

```
public function newQuestion ():void {
  // Get the full list of item types (an array of namespaces)
  var itemTypes:Array = gameItems.getItemTypes();
  // Pick a random item type (one of the namespaces in itemTypes)
  var randomItemType:Namespace = itemTypes[Math.floor(
                                      Math.random( )*itemTypes.length)];

  // Retrieve the randomly chosen item set
  var items:Array = gameItems.randomItemType::getItems();

  // Randomly pick the item for this question from the item set
  thisQuestionItem = items[Math.floor(Math.random( )*items.length)];

  // Remove the previous question, if there was one
```

```
    if (questionScreen != null) {
      removeChild(questionScreen);
    }

    // Display the new question
    questionScreen = new QuestionScreen(this, items, thisQuestionItem);
    addChild(questionScreen);
  }
```

The remainder of the code in Example 17-3 relates to game logic and user interface creation, which are not our present focus. As mentioned earlier, you should study the rest of the code on your own. For information on user interface coding techniques, see Part II of this book.

Well that was a nice, practical example. And there are more examples coming, but first we have to cover two more fundamental namespace concepts: open namespaces and namespaces for access-control modifiers.

Open Namespaces and the use namespace Directive

Remember the simple *Items* class from Example 17-1?

```
package {
  public class Items {
    fruit var orange:String = "Round citrus fruit";
    color var orange:String = "Color obtained by mixing red and yellow";

    public function Items () {
      trace(fruit::orange);
      trace(color::orange);
    }
  }
}
```

As we learned earlier, one way to access the orange variables in the preceding code is to use qualified identifiers, as in:

```
trace(fruit::orange); // Displays: Round citrus fruit
trace(color::orange); // Displays: Color obtained by
               //          mixing red and yellow
```

But, for the sake of convenience, ActionScript also provides another tool for accessing variables qualified by a namespace: the *use namespace* directive. The *use namespace* directive adds a given namespace to the so-called *open namespaces* for a particular scope of a program. The *open namespaces* is the set of namespaces Action-Script consults when attempting to resolve unqualified references. For example, if namespace n is in the open namespaces, and ActionScript encounters an unqualified reference to a variable p, then ActionScript will automatically check for the existence of n::p.

Here's the general form of the *use namespace* directive:

```
use namespace namespaceIdentifier
```

where *namespaceIdentifier* is the namespace identifier that should be added to the set of open namespaces. Note that *namespaceIdentifier* must be a compile-time constant, so it cannot be a variable that references a namespace value.

Let's see how *use namespace* works by referring directly to the local name orange after adding the namespace fruit to the set of open namespaces in the preceding *Items* constructor (this is also described as "opening the namespace fruit").

```
public function Items () {
  use namespace fruit;
  trace(orange);
}
```

Because we added fruit to the open namespaces, when ActionScript encounters the code:

```
trace(orange);
```

it automatically checks to see if the qualified identifier fruit::orange exists. In our example, that identifier does exist, so it is used in place of orange. In other words, in the *Items* constructor, this code:

```
trace(fruit::orange); // Displays: Round citrus fruit
```

has the same result as this code:

```
use namespace fruit;
trace(orange);         // Displays: Round citrus fruit
```

Open Namespaces and Scope

Each scope of an ActionScript program maintains a separate list of open namespaces. A namespace opened in a given scope will be open for that entire scope, including nested scopes but will not be open in other scopes. The opened namespace is available even prior to the occurrence of the *use namespace* statement (however, the best practice is to place the *use namespace* directive at the top of the enclosing code block).

 Recall that "scope" means "region of a program." In ActionScript, a unique scope is defined for each package, class, and method. Conditionals and loops do not have their own scope.

Example 17-4 uses generic code to demonstrate two separate scopes and their separate list of open namespaces. Comments will guide you through the code.

Example 17-4. Open namespace demo

```
public class ScopeDemo {
  // Create a namespace.
  private namespace n1 = "http://www.example.com/n1";
```

Example 17-4. Open namespace demo (continued)

```
// Create two variables qualfied by the namespace n1.
n1 var a:String = "a";
n1 var b:String = "b";

// Constructor
public function ScopeDemo () {
  // Call a method that accesses the variable n1::a.
  showA();
}

public function showA ():void {
  // This unqualified reference a matches the fully qualified
  // identifier n1::a because the following line opens the namespace n1.
  trace(a);  // OK!

  // Open namespace n1.
  use namespace n1;

  // Unqualified reference a again matches n1::a.
  trace(a);  // OK!

  // Create a nested function.
  function f ():void {
    // The namespace n1 is still open in nested scopes...
    trace(a);  // OK! Matches n1::a.
  }

  // Call the nested function.
  f();
}

public function showB ():void {
  // The following code makes a misguided attempt to access n1::b.
  // The namespace n1 is open in the scope of showA() only, not showB(),
  // so the attempt fails. Furthermore, no variable with the simple
  // identifier b exists in the scope of showB(), so the compiler
  // generates the following error:
  //    Attempted access of inaccessible property b through a reference
  //    with static type ScopeDemo.
  trace(b);  // ERROR!
  }
}
```

Because an open namespace remains open in nested scopes, we can open a namespace at the class or package level in order to use it throughout the entire *class* or *package* statement. Note, however, that once a namespace is opened, it cannot be "closed." There is no "unuse namespace" directive, and no way to remove a namespace from the open namespaces in a particular scope.

Opening Multiple Namespaces

It's perfectly legal to open multiple namespaces in the same scope. For example, here are four variables divided into two namespaces (the variables are excerpted from the *Items* class in Example 17-3):

```
fruit var orange:Item = new Item("Orange", "fruit-orange.jpg", 1);
fruit var apple:Item  = new Item("Apple", "fruit-apple.jpg", 2);
color var orange:Item = new Item("Orange", "color-orange.jpg", 3);
color var purple:Item = new Item("Purple", "color-purple.jpg", 4);
```

Suppose we add a method to the *Items* class, *showItems()*, to display all game items. In *showItems()*, we can open both the fruit and color namespaces, and then refer to fruit::apple and color::purple without specifying a qualifier namespace:

```
public function showItems ():void {
  use namespace fruit;
  use namespace color;
  // Look mom! No namespaces!
  trace(apple.name);   // Displays: Apple
  trace(purple.name);  // Displays: Purple
}
```

Let's consider how this works. Earlier we learned that *open namespaces* means "the set of namespaces ActionScript consults when attempting to resolve unqualified references." If multiple namespaces are open in a given scope, then ActionScript examines them all for each and every unqualified reference in that scope. For example, in *showItems()*, the fruit and color namespaces are both open. Therefore, when Action-Script encounters the unqualified reference apple it looks for both fruit::apple and color::apple. In apple's case, the unqualified reference matches fruit::apple but does not match color::apple. Because apple matches only one qualified identifier (namely, fruit::apple), that qualified identifier is used in place of the unqualified reference, apple.

But what happens if we use an unqualified reference, such as orange, that matches *two* qualified identifiers:

```
public function showItems ():void {
  use namespace fruit;
  use namespace color;
  // Matches fruit::orange and color::orange--what happens here?
  trace(orange);
}
```

When an unqualified reference matches a name in more than one open namespace, a runtime error occurs. The preceding code yields the following error:

```
Ambiguous reference to orange.
```

Due to a bug in some Adobe ActionScript compilers, the preceding error might go unreported.

If we open both the fruit and color namespaces, then we must use the qualified identifiers fruit::orange or color::orange to refer to our orange variables unambiguously, as follows:

```
public function showItems ():void {
  use namespace fruit;
  use namespace color;

  trace(apple);    // Displays: Apple
  trace(purple);   // Displays: Purple

  // Both fruit and color are open so references to orange
  // must be fully qualified.
  trace(fruit::orange);
  trace(color::orange);
}
```

Namespaces for Access-Control Modifiers

Just as we use namespaces to control variable and method visibility in our own programs, so ActionScript uses namespaces to control the visibility of every variable and method in every program! Remember the four access-control modifiers in ActionScript—*public, internal, protected, private*? ActionScript, itself, enforces those visibility rules using namespaces. For example, from ActionScript's perspective, the variable definition:

```
class A {
  private var p:int;
}
```

means "create a new variable p qualified by the class *A*'s private namespace."

In each scope, ActionScript implicitly opens the appropriate namespaces for the various access-control modifiers. For example, in every scope ActionScript always adds the global public namespace to the set of open namespaces. At the top level of a package, ActionScript also adds that package's internal and public namespaces. In code within a class that resides in a package, ActionScript also adds the class's private and protected namespaces. The set of open namespaces, then, includes not just user-opened namespaces, but also the access-control namespaces that are implicitly opened by ActionScript in each scope.

 You cannot use the *use namespace* directive to open one of the access-control namespaces explicitly. ActionScript opens the access-control namespaces automatically according to the current scope.

The access-control modifier namespaces determine the accessibility of identifiers and prevent naming conflicts. For example, in the following code, a superclass, *Parent*, and a subclass, *Child*, each define a *private* variable with the same name: description. The Parent class's description variable is not accessible to code within the *Child* class because description is qualified by the *Parent* class's private namespace, which is not open in the scope of the *Child* class. As a result, the variable names do not conflict.

```
package p {
  public class Parent {
    private var description:String = "A Parent object";
    public function Parent () {
      trace(description);
    }
  }
}

package p {
  public class Child extends Parent {
    private var description:String = "A Child object";
    public function Child () {
      trace(description); // No conflict
    }
  }
}
```

But if we change the access modifier for the *Parent* class's description variable to protected, a conflict arises. Let's consider exactly why. First let's change the access modifier for description to protected:

```
public class Parent {
  protected var description:String = "A Parent object";
}
```

Now let's pretend we're ActionScript attempting to run the code in the *Child* class constructor. We enter the constructor and encounter a reference to the identifier description. In order to resolve that identifier, we must check for it in the open namespaces. And what are the open namespaces in the *Child* class constructor? As we just learned, in code within a class that resides in a package, ActionScript opens the class's *private* and *protected* namespaces, the package's *internal* and *public* namespaces, and the global *public* namespace. So the open namespaces are:

- The *Child* class's private namespace
- The *Child* class's protected namespace (which qualifies all members inherited from the direct superclass)
- The package p's internal namespace
- The package p's public namespace
- The global public namespace
- All explicitly opened custom namespaces

When ActionScript checks for description in the open namespaces, it finds two matches: Child's private::description and Child's protected::description. As we learned in the previous section, when an unqualified reference matches a name in more than one open namespace, an ambiguous-reference error occurs. Furthermore, when multiple names are qualified by different implicitly opened namespaces, a definition-conflict error occurs. In the case of description, the specific conflict error is:

```
A conflict exists with inherited definition Parent.description
in namespace protected.
```

If you create conflicting method and variable names in your code, ActionScript will describe the conflict in relation to the namespace where the conflict occurred. For example, the following code:

```
package {
  import flash.display.*;
  public class SomeClass extends Sprite {
    private var prop:int;
    private var prop:int;  // Illegal duplicate property definition
  }
}
```

yields the following error:

```
A conflict exists with definition prop in namespace private.
```

(Actually, due to a compiler bug in Flex Builder 2 and Flash CS3, the preceding message erroneously reads "namespace internal" whereas it should read "namespace private.")

Likewise, the following code:

```
package {
  import flash.display.*;
  public class SomeClass extends Sprite {
    private var x;
  }
}
```

yields the following error (because—as we can learn by reading Adobe's Action-Script Language Reference—*DisplayObject* already defines the public variable x):

```
A conflict exists with inherited definition flash.display:DisplayObject.x in
namespace public.
```

Import Opens Public Namespaces

Note that technically, importing a package, as in:

```
import somePackage.*;
```

opens the public namespace of the imported package. However, it does not open the internal namespace of the imported package. Even when a package is imported, its internal identifiers remain inaccessible to outside code.

Applied Namespace Examples

This chapter's introduction cited four practical scenarios for namespace use:

- Prevent naming conflicts
- Framework-level member visibility
- Permission-based access control
- Program modes

In the preceding section we learned how namespaces prevent naming conflicts. In this section we'll explore each of the remaining three scenarios with a real-world example.

Example: Framework-Internal Visibility

Our first applied namespace example comes from Adobe's Flex framework, a library of user interface components and utilities for rich Internet application development.

The Flex framework contains a lot of code—hundreds of classes in dozens of packages. Some methods and variables in those classes must be accessible across different packages but are still considered internal to the overall framework. This presents a dilemma: if the methods and variables are declared *public*, then code outside the framework will have unwanted access to them, but if they are declared *internal*, they cannot be shared across packages.

To address this issue, the Flex framework defines the namespace mx_internal, and uses it to qualify methods and variables that should not be used outside the framework but must be accessible across different packages within the framework.

Here's the declaration of the mx_internal namespace:

```
package mx.core {
  public namespace mx_internal =
      "http://www.adobe.com/2006/flex/mx/internal";
}
```

Let's look at a specific mx_internal example from the Flex framework.

To work with grids of data, such as would be required in a spreadsheet application, the Flex framework provides the *DataGrid* component. The *DataGrid* class resides in the mx.controls package. Helper classes for *DataGrid* live in a separate package: mx.controls.gridclasses. To make communication as efficient as possible between the *DataGrid* and its helper classes, *DataGrid* accesses some of its helper classes' internal variables directly rather than via publicly accessible getter methods. These internal variables, however, should not be used by classes outside the Flex framework, so they are qualified by the mx_internal namespace. For example, the helper class *mx.controls.gridclasses.DataGridColumn* tracks the index of a column in the variable mx_internal::colNum.

```
// File DataGridColumn.as
mx_internal var colNum:Number;
```

To retrieve the column index, the *DataGrid* class first opens the mx_internal namespace:

```
use namespace mx_internal;
```

and then accesses mx_internal::colNum directly, as shown in this setter method excerpt:

```
// File DataGrid.as
public function set columns(value:Array):void {
  // Initialise "colNum" on all columns
  var n:int = value.length;
  for (var i:int = 0; i < n; i++) {
    var column:DataGridColumn = _columns[i];
    column.owner = this;

    // Access  mx_internal::colNum directly. (Remember that the
    // mx_internal namespace is open, so column.colNum is equivalent
    // to column.mx_internal::colNum.)
    column.colNum = i;
  }
  // Remainder of method not shown
}
```

Classes outside the framework use the public method *getColumnIndex()* to retrieve the column index instead of accessing mx_internal::colNum directly.

Intent is 9/10 of the law. Placing variables or methods in the mx_internal namespace certainly reduces their immediate visibility, but it does not technically restrict code outside the Flex framework from accessing them. Any developer who knows the URI of the mx_internal namespace can use it to access any of the variables or methods qualified by mx_internal.

The goal of mx_internal, however, is not to technically secure variables and methods against developer use. Rather, it is to erect a bold warning sign indicating that the variables and methods are not for external use and might change without warning or cause erratic behavior if accessed by code outside the Flex framework.

Example: Permission-Based Access Control

Our second namespace example demonstrates a custom form of access control where a class defines a group of methods and variables that only designated classes can access. Here are the participants in this example:

The sheltered class
> The class that grants access to its restricted methods and variables

The restricted methods and variables
> The group of methods and variables to which access is limited

The authorized classes
    Classes that are granted access to the restricted methods and variables

Here's the basic code for the sheltered class:

```
package {
  // This is the sheltered class.
  public class ShelteredClass {
    // The namespace restricted qualifies variables and
    // methods to which access is restricted.
    private namespace restricted;

    // This is the array of authorized classes. In this
    // example there is only one authorized class: Caller.
    private var authorizedClasses:Array = [ Caller ];

    // This is a restricted variable.
    // It can be accessed by authorized classes only.
    restricted var secretData:String = "No peeking";

    // This is a restricted method.
    // It can be accessed by authorized classes only.
    restricted function secretMethod ( ):void {
      trace("Restricted method secretMethod( ) called");
    }
  }
}
```

The sheltered class keeps an array of the authorized classes. It also defines a *private* namespace to qualify its restricted methods and variables. The namespace is *private* so that other classes cannot access it directly. Additionally, the URI for the namespace is automatically generated so that it cannot be discovered and used outside the class. Finally, the sheltered class defines the restricted variables and methods themselves.

To access a restricted method or variable (e.g., secretData or *secretMethod()*), a prospective class must obtain the proverbial keys to the front door. That is, it must retrieve a reference to the namespace that qualifies the restricted methods and variables. But the sheltered class will grant that reference only if the prospective class— lets call it the "caller class"—is in the authorizedClasses array.

In our example, the caller class will ask *ShelteredClass* for a reference to the restricted namespace using *ShelteredClass*'s instance method *getRestrictedNamespace()*. The *getRestrictedNamespace()* method accepts an instance of the caller class as an argument. If the caller instance is authorized, *getRestrictedNamespace()* returns a reference to the restricted namespace. Otherwise, *getRestrictedNamespace()* returns null, indicating to the caller that access to the restricted methods and variables is denied. Here's the code for the *getRestrictedNamespace()* method:

```
    public function getRestrictedNamespace
                         (callerObject:Object):Namespace {
      // Check to see if the callerObject is in the authorizedClasses array.
      for each (var authorizedClass:Class in authorizedClasses) {
        // If the caller object is an instance of an authorized class...
        if (callerObject is authorizedClass) {
          // ...pass back a reference to the restricted namespace (the
          // keys to the front door)
          return restricted;
        }
      }
      // The caller object is not an instance of
      // an authorized class, so abort
      return null;
    }
```

Example 17-5 shows the code for *ShelteredClass* in its entirety, complete with the *getRestrictedNamespace()* method.

Example 17-5. The ShelteredClass class

```
package {
  // This is the sheltered class
  public class ShelteredClass {
    // The namespace restricted qualifies variables and
    // methods to which access is restricted
    private namespace restricted;

    // This is the array of authorized classes. In this
    // example there is only one authorized class: Caller.
    private var authorizedClasses:Array = [ Caller ];

    // This is a restricted variable.
    // It can be accessed by authorized classes only
    restricted var secretData:String = "No peeking";

    // This is a restricted method.
    // It can be accessed by authorized classes only
    restricted function secretMethod ():void {
      trace("Restricted method secretMethod() called");
    }

    public function getRestrictedNamespace
                         (callerObject:Object):Namespace {
      // Check to see if the callerObject is in the authorizedClasses array.
      for each (var authorizedClass:Class in authorizedClasses) {
        // If the caller object is an instance of an authorized class...
        if (callerObject is authorizedClass) {
          // ...pass back a reference to the restricted namespace (the
          // keys to the front door)
          return restricted;
        }
      }
      // The caller object is not an instance of
      // an authorized class, so abort
```

Example 17-5. The ShelteredClass class (continued)

```
      return null;
    }
  }
}
```

Now let's look at *Caller*, a class that wishes to access *ShelteredClass*'s restricted methods and variables. Having already seen the authorizedClasses array in *ShelteredClass*, we know that *Caller* is a legal class. In our example, *Caller* is also the main application class, so it extends *Sprite*. The *Caller* class creates an instance of *ShelteredClass* in its constructor method and assigns that instance to the variable shelteredObject.

```
package {
  import flash.display.*;

  public class Caller extends Sprite {
    private var shelteredObject:ShelteredClass;

    public function Caller () {
      shelteredObject = new ShelteredClass();
    }
  }
}
```

To invoke *secretMethod()* on *ShelteredClass*, a *Caller* object must first retrieve a reference to the restricted namespace. To do so, the *Caller* object passes itself to *getRestrictedNamespace()* and assigns the result (either restricted or null) to a variable, key, for later use.

```
var key:Namespace = shelteredObject.getRestrictedNamespace(this);
```

Then, before calling *secretMethod()*, *Caller* first checks whether key refers to a valid namespace. If it does, then *Caller* uses key as the namespace when invoking *secureMethod()*:

```
if (key != null) {
  shelteredObject.key::secureMethod();
}
```

For convenience, our *Caller* class wraps the code that calls *secretMethod()* in a method named *callSecretMethod()*:

```
public function callSecretMethod ():void {
  var key:Namespace = shelteredObject.getRestrictedNamespace(this);
  if (key != null) {
    shelteredObject.key:: secretMethod();
  }
}
```

Example 17-6 shows the entire code for the *Caller* class, including *callSecretMethod()* and another convenience method, *displaySecret()*, which accesses the restricted variable secretData using the same basic technique.

Example 17-6. The Caller class

```
package {
  import flash.display.*;

  public class Caller extends Sprite {

    private var shelteredObject:ShelteredClass;

    public function Caller () {
      shelteredObject = new ShelteredClass();
      callSecretMethod();
      displaySecret();
    }

    public function callSecretMethod ():void {
      var key:Namespace = shelteredObject.getRestrictedNamespace(this);
      if (key != null) {
        shelteredObject.key::secretMethod();
      }
    }

    public function displaySecret ():void {
      var key:Namespace = shelteredObject.getRestrictedNamespace(this);
      if (key != null) {
        trace(shelteredObject.key::secretData);
      }
    }
  }
}
```

Example: Program Modes

Our last example is an electronic dictionary that translates from Japanese to English and vice versa. The dictionary demonstrates program modes—perhaps the area of namespace programming in ActionScript with the greatest potential. When in "Japanese mode," the dictionary returns English translations for Japanese queries; when in "English mode," the dictionary returns Japanese translations for English queries. Each mode is represented by a namespace—japanese for Japanese-to-English mode and english for English-to-Japanese mode.

Here are the participants in this example:

japanese
: A namespace for Japanese-specific variables and methods

english
: A namespace for English-specific variables and methods

QueryManager class
: Performs searches for words

SearchOptions class
: Contains the basic options for a search operation

JapaneseSearchOptions class
  Contains options specific to a Japanese search operation

EnglishSearchOptions class
  Contains options specific to an English search operation

JEDictionary class
  The main application class

Let's look at these participants one at a time, bearing in mind that this example is not fully functional, and uses placeholder code where actual database searches would occur.

We'll start with the japanese and english namespace definitions, whose code should be familiar by now:

```
package {
  public namespace english = "http://www.example.com/jedict/english";
}

package {
  public namespace japanese = "http://www.example.com/jedict/japanese";
}
```

Next comes the *QueryManager* class, which defines two methods to look up a word, *japanese::search()* and *english::search()*. The appropriate search method is invoked depending on the current mode of the program. Each search method accepts an options argument that specifies search options in the form of either a *JapaneseSearchOptions* or an *EnglishSearchOptions* object, respectively. Later, in the *JEDictionary* class, we'll see that the search options are selected according to the current program mode. Here's the code for *QueryManager*:

```
package {
  public class QueryManager {

    japanese function search (word:String,
                              options:JapaneseSearchOptions):Array {
      trace("Now searching for '" + word + "'.\n"
            + " Match type: " + options.getMatchType() + "\n"
            + " English language variant: " + options.getEnglishVariant());

      // Code here (not shown) would search the Japanese-to-English
      // dictionary and return the results, but we'll just return a
      // hard-coded list of results as a proof-of-concept:
      return ["English Word 1", "English Word 2", "etc"];
    }

    english function search (word:String,
                             options:EnglishSearchOptions):Array {
      trace("Now searching for '" + word + "'.\n"
            + " Match type: " + options.getMatchType() + "\n"
            + " Use kanji in results: " + options.getKanjiInResults());

      // Code here (not shown) would search the English-to-Japanese
```

```
      // dictionary and return the results, but we'll just return a
      // hard-coded list of results as a proof-of-concept:
      return ["Japanese Word 1", "Japanese Word 2", "etc"];
    }
  }
}
```

Now let's examine the three search-options classes: *SearchOptions* and its two sub-classes, *JapaneseSearchOptions* and *EnglishSearchOptions*. The *SearchOptions* class specifies how the program should look for the requested search string, either using an "exact match" (the matching word must be identical to the search string), a "starts-with match" (all matching words must start with the search string), or a "contains match" (all matching words must contain the search string).

The different types of matches are represented by the constants MATCH_EXACT, MATCH_STARTSWITH, and MATCH_CONTAINS. The match type for a given search can be set and retrieved via the methods *setMatchType()* and *getMatchType()*. Here's the *SearchOptions* class:

```
package {
  public class SearchOptions {
    public static const MATCH_EXACT:String      = "Exact";
    public static const MATCH_STARTSWITH:String = "StartsWith";
    public static const MATCH_CONTAINS:String   = "Contains";

    private var matchType:String;

    public function SearchOptions () {
      // Default to exact matching.
      setMatchType(SearchOptions.MATCH_EXACT);
    }

    public function getMatchType ():String {
      return matchType;
    }

    public function setMatchType (newMatchType:String):void {
      matchType = newMatchType;
    }
  }
}
```

The *JapaneseSearchOptions* class extends *SearchOptions*, adding options relevant to Japanese-to-English searches only—namely, whether results should be returned in U.S. English or U.K. English. These two English variants are represented by the constants ENGLISH_UK and ENGLISH_US. The English variant for a given search can be set and retrieved via the methods *setEnglishVariant()* and *getEnglishVariant()*.

```
package {
  public class JapaneseSearchOptions extends SearchOptions {
    public static const ENGLISH_UK:String = "EnglishUK";
    public static const ENGLISH_US:String = "EnglishUS";
```

```
    private var englishVariant:String;

    public function JapaneseSearchOptions () {
      setEnglishVariant(JapaneseSearchOptions.ENGLISH_UK);
    }

    public function getEnglishVariant ():String {
      return englishVariant;
    }

    public function setEnglishVariant (newEnglishVariant:String):void {
      englishVariant = newEnglishVariant;
    }
  }
}
```

Like *JapaneseSearchOptions*, the *EnglishSearchOptions* class extends *SearchOptions*, adding options relevant to English-to-Japanese searches only—namely, whether results should be returned in kanji (a ideographic character set) or hiragana (a phonetic character set). The character set for a given search can be set and retrieved via the methods *setKanjiInResults()* and *getKanjiInResults()*:

```
package {
  public class EnglishSearchOptions extends SearchOptions {
    private var kanjiInResults:Boolean = false;

    public function getKanjiInResults ():Boolean {
      return kanjiInResults;
    }

    public function setKanjiInResults (newKanjiInResults:Boolean):void {
      kanjiInResults = newKanjiInResults;
    }
  }
}
```

Finally let's turn to *JEDictionary*, the application's main class, where most of the namespace magic happens. Skim the class code in Example 17-7, then we'll study it line by line.

Example 17-7. The JEDictionary class

```
package {
  import flash.display.Sprite;

  public class JEDictionary extends Sprite {
    private var queryMan:QueryManager;

    japanese var options:JapaneseSearchOptions;
    english var options:EnglishSearchOptions;

    private var lang:Namespace;
```

Example 17-7. The JEDictionary class (continued)

```
    public function JEDictionary( ) {
      queryMan = new QueryManager( );

      japanese::options = new JapaneseSearchOptions( );
      japanese::options.setMatchType(SearchOptions.MATCH_STARTSWITH);
      japanese::options.setEnglishVariant(JapaneseSearchOptions.ENGLISH_US);

      english::options = new EnglishSearchOptions( );
      english::options.setMatchType(SearchOptions.MATCH_CONTAINS);
      english::options.setKanjiInResults(true);

      // Do a Japanese search...
      setModeJapaneseToEnglish( );
      findWord("sakana");

      // Do an English search...
      setModeEnglishToJapanese( );
      findWord("fish");
    }

    public function findWord (word:String):void {
      var words:Array = queryMan.lang::search(word, lang::options);
      trace(" Words found: " + words);
        }

    public function setModeEnglishToJapanese ( ):void {
      lang = english;
    }

    public function setModeJapaneseToEnglish ( ):void {
      lang = japanese;
    }
  }
}
```

To begin, the application's main class, *JEDictionary* extends *Sprite*:

```
    public class JEDictionary extends Sprite {
```

To perform searches, *JEDictionary* creates a *QueryManager* instance, which it assigns to the variable queryMan:

```
    private var queryMan:QueryManager;
```

Next, *JEDictionary* creates two variables, both with the local name options, but qualified by the japanese and english namespaces. These hold the search options that will be passed to the *QueryManager* class's instance method *search()*. Notice that their datatypes correspond to the type of search being performed:

```
    japanese var options:JapaneseSearchOptions;
    english  var options:EnglishSearchOptions;
```

Then comes the definition of the important lang variable, which refers to the namespace corresponding to the current dictionary mode (either Japanese or English):

```
private var lang:Namespace;
```

That's it for *JEDictionary*'s variables; now let's examine its methods: *setModeEnglishtoJapanese()*, *setModeJapaneseToEnglish()*, and *findWord()*. The *setModeEnglishtoJapanese()* and *setModeJapaneseToEnglish()* methods activate the different modes of the dictionary by setting the variable lang to the english namespace or japanese namespace, respectively:

```
public function setModeEnglishToJapanese ():void {
  lang = english;
}

public function setModeJapaneseToEnglish ():void {
  lang = japanese;
}
```

The *findWord()* method uses *QueryManager* to perform a dictionary lookup using the appropriate *search()* method. The call to *search()* is the most important line of code in our dictionary example:

```
queryMan.lang::search(word, lang::options)
```

Notice that the namespace (the program mode) determines both the type of search to perform (the behavior) and the type of options to be used for that search (the data). When lang is set to japanese, then *japanese::search()* is invoked and passed a *JapaneseSearchOptions* object. When lang is set to english, then *english::search()* is invoked and passed an *EnglishSearchOptions* object.

The result of the *search()* invocation is assigned to the local variable words and then displayed in a debugging message:

```
public function findWord (word:String):void {
  var words:Array = queryMan.lang::search(word, lang::options);
  trace(" Words found: " + words);
}
```

For demonstration purposes, the *JEDictionary* constructor method performs two example dictionary searches (though, in a full-featured application, dictionary searches would normally be performed in response to user input). Searches are carried out by the application's *QueryManager* instance, which is created in the constructor, as follows:

```
queryMan = new QueryManager();
```

Default options for all Japanese-to-English searches and English-to-Japanese searches are also set in the constructor:

```
japanese::options = new JapaneseSearchOptions();
japanese::options.setMatchType(SearchOptions.MATCH_STARTSWITH);
```

```
japanese::options.setEnglishVariant(JapaneseSearchOptions.ENGLISH_US);

english::options = new EnglishSearchOptions();
english::options.setMatchType(SearchOptions.MATCH_CONTAINS);
english::options.setKanjiInResults(true);
```

To perform a search, the constructor sets the dictionary mode, then passes the search string to the *JEDictionary* class's instance method *findWord()*:

```
// Do a Japanese search...
setModeJapaneseToEnglish();
findWord("sakana");

// Do an English search...
setModeEnglishToJapanese();
findWord("fish");
```

According to the current dictionary mode, the appropriate *search()* method is called, and the appropriate search options are used.

And that completes our dictionary! And it also completes our study of namespaces. Remember you can download the source code for the dictionary application and other examples from this chapter at *http://www.moock.org/eas3/examples*.

Final Core Topics

We're almost finished with our exploration of the core ActionScript language. The coming two chapters cover two final subjects: creating and manipulating XML-based data and Flash Player security restrictions.

CHAPTER 18

XML and E4X

Since Flash Player 5, ActionScript has included tools for working with XML-structured data. In ActionScript 1.0 and ActionScript 2.0, XML data was created and manipulated with the variables and methods of the built-in *XML* class (e.g., firstChild, nextSibling, *appendChild()*, etc.). The *XML* class was based on the W3C Document Object Model, or DOM, a standard for interacting with XML documents programmatically (see *http://www.w3.org/DOM*).

As of ActionScript 3.0, the toolset for creating and manipulating XML has been completely overhauled. ActionScript 3.0 implements *ECMAScript for XML* ("E4X"), an official ECMA-262 language extension for working with XML as a native datatype. E4X seeks to improve the usability and flexibility of working with XML in ECMA-262-based languages (including ActionScript and JavaScript).

Understanding XML Data as a Hierarchy

Before we can learn to manipulate XML data with E4X, we must first understand the general principle of XML as hierarchical data. Both the legacy *XML* class and E4X treat XML data as a hierarchical tree in which each element and text block is considered a tree node (i.e., a branch or a leaf). For example, consider the XML fragment in Example 18-1. (An XML *fragment* is a section of XML excerpted from an XML document.)

Example 18-1. An example XML fragment

```
<BOOK ISBN="0141182806">
  <TITLE>Ulysses</TITLE>
  <AUTHOR>Joyce, James</AUTHOR>
  <PUBLISHER>Penguin Books Ltd</PUBLISHER>
</BOOK>
```

The elements <BOOK>, <TITLE>, <AUTHOR>, and <PUBLISHER>, and the text "Ulysses", "Joyce, James", and "Penguin Books Ltd" are all considered nodes on the tree, as depicted in Figure 18-1.

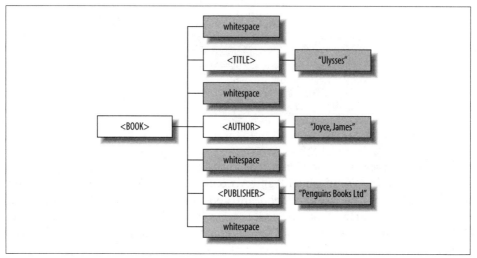

Figure 18-1. An example XML hierarchy

The element <BOOK> is the root of the tree—known as the *root node* of the XML data structure. Every well-formed XML document must have an all-encompassing root element, such as <BOOK>, that contains every other element.

When a node is contained by another node, the contained node is said to be a *child* of the containing node; conversely, the containing node is known as the child node's *parent*. In our example, the <TITLE> element is a child of <BOOK>, and <BOOK> is <TITLE>'s parent.

Perhaps surprisingly, <TITLE> is not the first child of <BOOK>; it is the second. The first child is actually the so-called *insignificant whitespace* (the new line and two spaces) in the XML source code between the <BOOK> and <TITLE> tags. In E4X, *insignificant whitespace* means any of the following four formatting characters: space (\u0020), carriage return (\u000D), line feed (\u000A), and tab (\u0009). In an XML tree, text blocks—even ones that contain whitespace only—are considered nodes on the tree. Accordingly, the <BOOK> element has not three children but seven, four of which are so-called whitespace nodes (text nodes that contain insignificant whitespace only).

The <BOOK> node's seven children are known as *siblings* of one another because they reside on the same level in the hierarchy. For example, we say that <TITLE>'s *next sibling* is a whitespace node, and <AUTHOR>'s *previous sibling* is another whitespace node. You can see how the text nodes get in the way when moving from sibling to sibling in a hierarchy. Fortunately, by default, whitespace nodes are ignored by the E4X parser. E4X lets us treat <AUTHOR> as <TITLE>'s next sibling, which is what we want in most cases. You won't have to process whitespace nodes yourself in E4X unless you specifically want to (see the *XML* class's instance variable `ignoreWhitespace`, discussed in the later section "Converting an XML Element to a String").

On the last tier in the hierarchy, we find that the `<TITLE>`, `<AUTHOR>`, and `<PUBLISHER>` nodes each have a single text-node child: `"Ulysses"`, `"Joyce, James"`, and `"Penguin Books Ltd"`, respectively. The text nodes are the last nodes in the tree.

> The text contained by an element in XML source code is considered a child node of that element in the corresponding XML tree hierarchy.

We've now finished examining the XML tree for Example 18-1, but we still haven't learned where the attributes fit into the hierarchy. You might expect `<BOOK>`'s `ISBN` attribute to be depicted as a child node called `ISBN`. But in practice, an attribute is not considered a *child* of the element that defines it, but rather a *characteristic* of that element. We'll learn how attributes are accessed in E4X in the later section "Accessing Attributes."

Now that we've learned how XML data can be thought of as a conceptual hierarchy, we can explore how XML is represented, created, and manipulated using E4X techniques.

Representing XML Data in E4X

In E4X, XML data is represented by one of two native ActionScript datatypes, *XML* and *XMLList* and their corresponding classes, also named *XML* and *XMLList*.

> Due to the introduction of the E4X *XML* datatype, the legacy *XML* class from ActionScript 1.0 and ActionScript 2.0 has been renamed to *XMLDocument* in ActionScript 3.0 and moved to the `flash.xml` package.

Each *XML* instance represents one of the following five possible kinds of XML content, known as *node kinds*:

- An element
- An attribute
- A text node
- A comment
- A processing instruction

If an XML element has any child elements (e.g., `<BOOK>`'s child `<AUTHOR>`) or child text nodes (e.g., `<TITLE>`'s child "Ulysses"), those children are wrapped in an *XMLList* by their parent *XML* instance. Each *XMLList* instance is an arbitrary collection of one or more *XML* instances. For example, an *XMLList* might be any of the following:

- A series of attributes or elements returned by a search
- A group of XML fragments, each with its own root element
- A collection of the text nodes in a document
- A collection of the comments in a document
- A collection of the processing instructions in a document

The child nodes of an *XML* element are always wrapped in an *XMLList*. Even if an element has only one child (say, just a text node), that child is still wrapped in an *XMLList*. If an XML element has any attributes, comments, or processing instructions, those are likewise wrapped in an *XMLList* by the parent *XML* instance. However, comments and processing instructions are, by default, ignored by the E4X parser. (To prevent them from being ignored, set the static variables `XML.ignoreComments` and `XML.ignoreProcessingInstructions` to false.)

Let's look at an example showing how an XML fragment would be represented by instances of *XML* and *XMLList* classes in E4X. Recall the XML source code from Example 18-1:

```
<BOOK ISBN="0141182806">
  <TITLE>Ulysses</TITLE>
  <AUTHOR>Joyce, James</AUTHOR>
  <PUBLISHER>Penguin Books Ltd</PUBLISHER>
</BOOK>
```

From the E4X perspective, the element `<BOOK>` in the preceding code is represented by an *XML* instance. That *XML* instance contains two *XMLList* instances—one for `<BOOK>`'s attributes and the other for its child elements. The `<BOOK>` element has only one attribute, so the *XMLList* for `<BOOK>`'s attributes contains one *XML* instance only (representing the attribute `ISBN`). The *XMLList* for `<BOOK>`'s child elements contains three *XML* instances, representing the three elements `<TITLE>`, `<AUTHOR>`, and `<PUBLISHER>`. Each of those *XML* instances, itself, has an *XMLList* containing exactly one *XML* instance representing, respectively, the child text nodes "Ulysses", "Joyce, James", and "Penguin Books Ltd". Figure 18-2 summarizes. In the figure, each item in the `<BOOK>` hierarchy is labeled with a letter (A through M) so it can be referenced easily in the coming sections.

Now let's put some of the preceding theory into practice by creating the `<BOOK>` fragment from Example 18-1 using E4X techniques.

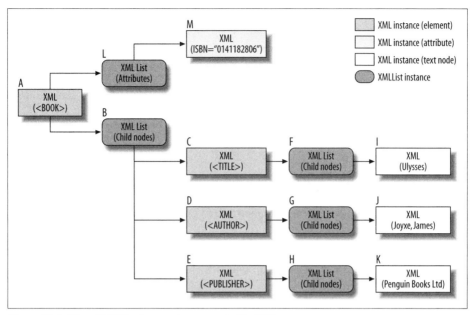

Figure 18-2. The <BOOK> fragment, represented in E4X

Creating XML Data with E4X

To create the <BOOK> XML fragment from Example 18-1 via E4X, we have three general options:

- Use the *XML* constructor to create a new *XML* instance, and then create the remainder of the fragment programmatically using the techniques covered in later section "Changing or Creating New XML Content."

- Use the *XML* constructor to create a new *XML* instance, and then import the fragment from an externally loaded file, as discussed in the later section "Loading XML Data."

- Write our *XML* data in literal form, just like a string or a number, anywhere literals are allowed by ActionScript.

For now, we'll use the third approach—creating the XML fragment with an XML literal. Example 18-2 demonstrates; it assigns a literal XML value (the XML fragment from Example 18-1) to the variable novel.

Example 18-2. Assigning an XML literal to a variable

```
var novel:XML = <BOOK ISBN="0141182806">
    <TITLE>Ulysses</TITLE>
    <AUTHOR>Joyce, James</AUTIIOR>
    <PUBLISHER>Penguin Books Ltd</PUBLISHER>
</BOOK>;
```

When the preceding code runs, ActionScript generates a new E4X *XML* instance representing the literal XML fragment and assigns it to the variable novel.

> To view the XML source code for an *XML* instance (such as the one referenced by novel), use the *XML* class's instance method *toXMLString()*, as in:
>
> ```
> trace(novel.toXMLString());
> ```
>
> The *toXMLString()* method is covered later in the section "Converting XML and XMLList to a String."

Notice that the line breaks and quotation marks in the preceding XML literal are perfectly normal. ActionScript knows they are part of the XML data, and interprets them as such. Where possible, ActionScript even converts certain reserved characters to XML entities. For details see the section "Using XML Entities for Special Characters."

ActionScript also allows dynamic expressions to be used within an XML literal so that element names, attribute names, attribute values, and element content can be generated programmatically. To specify a dynamic expression within an XML literal, surround it in curly braces ({ }). For example, the following code specifies the name of the <BOOK> tag dynamically:

```
var elementName:String = "BOOK";
var novel:XML = <{elementName}/>;
```

The following code presents a slightly exaggerated example that creates the same XML hierarchy as that shown in Example 18-2, but dynamically specifies all element names, attribute names, attribute values, and element contents.

```
var rootElementName:String = "BOOK";
var rootAttributeName:String = "ISBN";
var childElementNames:Array = ["TITLE", "AUTHOR", "PUBLISHER"];
var bookISBN:String = "0141182806";
var bookTitle:String = "Ulysses";
var bookAuthor:String = "Joyce, James";
var bookPublisher:String = "Penguin Books Ltd";
var novel:XML = <{rootElementName} {rootAttributeName}={bookISBN}>
    <{childElementNames[0]}>{bookTitle}</{childElementNames[0]}>
    <{childElementNames[1]}>{bookAuthor}</{childElementNames[1]}>
    <{childElementNames[2]}>{bookPublisher}</{childElementNames[2]}>
  </{rootElementName}>;
```

Note that because the characters { } are used to delimit a dynamic expression, they are not allowed in some parts of an XML literal. Specifically, within an element name, an attribute name, or element content, the entities { and } must be used to represent { and }, respectively. However, { and } can be used in literal form within an attribute value, a CDATA section, a processing instruction, or a comment.

Now that we have a variable, novel, defined in Example 18-2 that references the XML fragment from Example 18-1, let's see how its various parts can be accessed using E4X coding techniques.

Accessing XML Data

E4X offers two general sets of tools for accessing data in an XML hierarchy:

- The *XML* and *XMLList* content-access methods (*attribute()*, *attributes()*, *child()*, *children()*, *comments()*, *descendants()*, *elements()*, *parent()*, *processingInstructions()*, and *text()*)
- Variable-style access with the dot (.), descendant (..), and attribute (@) operators

Variable-style access is offered as a convenience to the programmer and always equates to one of the methods of either the *XML* or *XMLList* classes. However, the two approaches do not overlap completely; the following types of content must be accessed using the appropriate method of the *XML* or *XMLList* class:

- An *XML* instance's parent (accessed via *parent()*)
- Comments (accessed via *comments()*)
- Processing instructions (accessed via *processingInstructions()*)
- Elements or attributes whose names include characters considered illegal in an ActionScript identifier (accessed via *attribute()*, *child()*, *descendants()*, or *elements()*)

Continuing with our <BOOK> example, let's take a look at some of the most common ways to access XML data.

Accessing the Root XML Node

In Example 18-2 we assigned the XML fragment from Example 18-1 to the variable novel. To access the root <BOOK> element of that fragment (item A in Figure 18-2) we refer to it as, simply, novel. For example, the following code passes the <BOOK> element (and, by extension, all its children) to the hypothetical *addToOrder()* method:

```
addToOrder(novel);
```

Notice that the <BOOK> element is not named. That is, we write addToOrder(novel), not either of the following:

```
addToOrder(novel.BOOK);            // Wrong.
addToOrder(novel.child("BOOK"));   // Also wrong.
```

The preceding two examples mistakenly treat the <BOOK> element as though it were a child of novel, which is not. We'll learn how to access child elements in the next section.

Note that there is no direct way to access the root node relative to any given child. However, we can use the *XML* class's instance method *parent()* (covered later) to ascend a tree recursively to its root, as shown in Example 18-3.

Example 18-3. A custom root-access method

```
// Returns the root of an XML hierarchy, relative to a given child
public function getRoot (childNode:XML):XML {
  var parentNode:XML = childNode.parent( );
  if (parentNode != null) {
    return getRoot(parentNode);
  } else {
    return childNode;
  }
}

// Usage:
getRoot(someChild);
```

Accessing Child Nodes

To access the *XMLList* representing <BOOK>'s child nodes (item B in Figure 18-2), we use the *XML* class's instance method *children()*, which takes no arguments. For example:

```
novel.children( )  // Returns an XMLList representing <BOOK>'s child nodes
```

Alternatively, we can access <BOOK>'s child nodes using E4X's more convenient *properties wildcard* (*). For example:

```
novel.*  // Also returns an XMLList, representing <BOOK>'s child nodes
```

To access a specific child in an *XMLList* we use the familiar array-element access operator, []. For example, to access the <BOOK> element's second child, <AUTHOR> (item D in Figure 18-2), we use:

```
novel.children( )[1]  // A reference to <BOOK>'s second child node
```

or:

```
novel.*[1]  // Also a reference to <BOOK>'s second child node
```

Although there is no firstChild or lastChild variable in E4X (as there is in the legacy *XMLDocument* class), the first child in a list of child nodes can be accessed as follows:

```
theNode.children( )[0]
```

And the last child in a list of child nodes can be accessed as follows:

```
theNode.children( )[theNode.children().length( )-1]
```

However, accessing a child node according to its position in a list can be cumbersome, and has, therefore, been deemphasized by E4X. In E4X, child nodes are typically accessed by their element names rather than their position. To access child nodes by name, we use the *XML* class's instance method *child()*, which returns an *XMLList* of all child elements matching a specified name. For example, to retrieve an *XMLList* of all children of <BOOK> named "AUTHOR", we use:

```
novel.child("AUTHOR") // Returns all child elements of <BOOK> named "AUTHOR"
```

Alternatively, we can access child nodes by name using E4X's more convenient variable-access syntax. The following code has the identical result as the preceding code but uses E4X's more convenient variable-access syntax:

```
novel.AUTHOR  // Also returns all child elements of <BOOK> named "AUTHOR"
```

If <BOOK> contained two <AUTHOR> elements, then novel.AUTHOR would return an *XMLList* with two *XML* instances, representing those elements. To access the first element, we would use novel.AUTHOR[0]. To access the second element, we would use novel.AUTHOR[1], as shown in the following code:

```
var novel:XML = <BOOK>
    <AUTHOR>Jacobs, Tom</AUTHOR>
    <AUTHOR>Schumacher, Jonathan</AUTHOR>
  </BOOK>;

novel.AUTHOR[0];  // Access <AUTHOR>Jacobs, Tom</AUTHOR>
novel.AUTHOR[1];  // Access <AUTHOR>Schumacher, Jonathan</AUTHOR>
```

Of course, the <BOOK> element from Example 18-1 contains only one child named "AUTHOR", so the *XMLList* returned by the expression novel.AUTHOR has just one *XML* instance (representing the lone <AUTHOR> element). To access that <AUTHOR> element, we *could* use this code:

```
novel.AUTHOR[0]  // A reference to the <AUTHOR> instance
```

However (and this is the exciting part!), in most cases we don't have to include the [0]. In order to make node access more convenient, E4X implements special behavior for *XMLList* objects that have only one *XML* instance (as our example novel. AUTHOR does). When an *XML* method is invoked on an *XMLList* with only one *XML* instance, the method invocation is automatically forwarded to that *XML* instance. By forwarding the method invocation, E4X lets the programmer treat an *XMLList* with only one *XML* instance as though it were that instance. As the E4X specification puts it, E4X "intentionally blurs the distinction between an individual *XML* object and an *XMLList* containing only that object."

For example, suppose we want to change the <AUTHOR> element's name from "AUTHOR" to "WRITER". We *could* use this code, which explicitly refers to the <AUTHOR> instance:

```
novel.AUTHOR[0].setName("WRITER");
```

But we would typically use this more convenient code, which implicitly refers to the <AUTHOR> instance by omitting the array-element access (the [0] following novel.AUTHOR):

```
novel.AUTHOR.setName("WRITER");
```

When we invoke *setName()* directly on the *XMLList* returned by novel.AUTHOR, ActionScript recognizes that the list has only one *XML* instance (<AUTHOR>) and automatically forwards the *setName()* invocation to that instance. As a result, the name of the sole element contained by novel.AUTHOR is changed from "AUTHOR" to "WRITER".

In most cases, this sleight-of-hand performed by ActionScript makes XML code easier to write and more intuitive to read. However, some caution is required when using this technique. For example, the following code invokes *setName()* on an *XMLList* with more than one *XML* instance:

```
var novel:XML = <BOOK>
    <AUTHOR>Jacobs, Tom</AUTHOR>
    <AUTHOR>Schumacher, Jonathan</AUTHOR>
  </BOOK>;
novel.AUTHOR.setName('WRITER');
```

When the preceding code runs, ActionScript generates the following runtime error:

```
The setName method works only on lists containing one item.
```

The act of treating an *XMLList* with only one *XML* instance as though it were that instance is an important and often misunderstood aspect of E4X programming, so we'll return to this topic several times over the course of this chapter.

Accessing Text Nodes

As we learned in the earlier section "Understanding XML Data as a Hierarchy," the text contained by an element is represented as a node in an XML hierarchy. For example, in the following XML fragment (repeated from Example 18-2) the text "Ulysses" is a text node. It is represented by an *XML* instance whose node kind is "text," as are the text nodes "Joyce, James", and "Penguin Books Ltd".

```
var novel:XML = <BOOK ISBN="0141182806">
    <TITLE>Ulysses</TITLE>
    <AUTHOR>Joyce, James</AUTHOR>
    <PUBLISHER>Penguin Books Ltd</PUBLISHER>
  </BOOK>;
```

We access text nodes in different ways depending on our needs. When we need to reference a text node as an *XML* instance, we must use the child-node access syntax discussed in the previous section. For example, to access the text "Ulysses", which is <TITLE>'s first child, we can use this code:

```
novel.TITLE.children()[0]  // A reference to the text node Ulysses
```

Or, alternatively, we can use the properties wildcard to do the same thing:

```
novel.TITLE.*[0]  // Also a reference to the text node Ulysses
```

Both of the preceding examples return an *XML* object (not a string) that represents the element text "Ulysses". We can invoke *XML* methods on that object, just as we can with any *XML* object. For example:

```
novel.TITLE.*[0].parent( )    // Reference to the <TITLE> element
novel.TITLE.*[0].nodeKind( )  // Returns the string "text"
novel.TITLE.*[0].toString( )  // Returns the string "Ulysses"
```

However, if we simply want to access the content of a text node as a *String*, not an *XML* instance, we can use the *XML* class's instance method *toString()* on its parent element. For elements such as <TITLE> that contain one child text node only (with no other interspersed elements), *toString()* returns the text of that child node, omitting the parent element's start and end tags. Hence, the expression novel.TITLE.toString( ) yields the string "Ulysses":

```
trace(novel.TITLE.toString( ));  // Displays: Ulysses
```

As you're mulling over the preceding line of code, remember that it is actually a shorthand version of:

```
trace(novel.TITLE[0].toString( ));  // Displays: Ulysses
```

The shorthand expression novel.TITLE.toString( ) returns "Ulysses" because ActionScript recognizes that the *XMLList* referred to by novel.TITLE has only one *XML* instance (<TITLE>) and automatically forwards the *toString()* invocation to that instance.

When accessing the content of a text node as a *String*, we can typically omit the explicit call to *toString()* because ActionScript invokes *toString()* automatically whenever a nonstring value is used where a string is expected. For example, the *trace()* function expects a string as an argument, so instead of explicitly invoking *toString()*, as in:

```
trace(novel.TITLE.toString( ));  // Displays: Ulysses
```

we can let ActionScript invoke it implicitly:

```
trace(novel.TITLE);  // Also displays: Ulysses
```

Likewise, when assigning the content of the text node Ulysses to a variable of type *String*, instead of this fully explicit code:

```
var titleName:String = novel.TITLE[0].toString( );
```

we can use, simply:

```
var titleName:String = novel.TITLE;
```

Now that's snazzy. And it's also the typical way to retrieve the text contained by an element in E4X.

For text nodes that are interspersed with other elements, we can use the *XML* class's instance method *text()* to retrieve the text nodes not contained by elements. To illustrate how this works, let's temporarily add a <DESCRIPTION> element to <BOOK>, as follows:

```
var novel:XML = <BOOK ISBN="0141182806">
    <TITLE>Ulysses</TITLE>
    <AUTHOR>Joyce, James</AUTHOR>
    <PUBLISHER>Penguin Books Ltd</PUBLISHER>
    <DESCRIPTION>A <B>very</B> thick book.</DESCRIPTION>
  </BOOK>;
```

The <DESCRIPTION> element contains both element and text child nodes:

- A (text node)
- <B>very</B> (element node with a child text node)
- thick book. (text node)

To retrieve an *XMLList* with the two text nodes A and thick book., we use:

```
novel.DESCRIPTION.text( )
```

To access those text nodes, we use the array-element access operator:

```
trace(novel.DESCRIPTION.text( )[0]);  // Displays: A
trace(novel.DESCRIPTION.text( )[1]);  // Displays: thick book.
```

The *text()* method can also be used to retrieve the text nodes from an entire *XMLList*, not just a single *XML* element. For example, suppose we have an *XMLList* representing the children of the <BOOK> element from Example 18-2 (as it existed before we added the <DESCRIPTION> element):

```
novel.*
```

To place the text nodes from each of those children into an *XMLList* for easy processing, such as for the creation of a user interface, we use:

```
novel.*.text( )
```

Once again, to access the text nodes, we use the array-element access operator:

```
trace(novel.*.text( )[0]);  // Displays: Ulysses
trace(novel.*.text( )[1]);  // Displays: Joyce, James
trace(novel.*.text( )[2]);  // Displays: Penguin Books Ltd
```

However, the *XMLList* class's instance method *text()* is less useful when applied to a list of elements that contain both text and element child nodes. For any node that contains both text and element child nodes (such as the <DESCRIPTION> node), only the first child text node is returned; other children are ignored. For example:

```
var novel:XML = <BOOK ISBN="0141182806">
    <TITLE>Ulysses</TITLE>
    <AUTHOR>Joyce, James</AUTHOR>
    <PUBLISHER>Penguin Books Ltd</PUBLISHER>
    <DESCRIPTION>A <B>very</B> thick book.</DESCRIPTION>
  </BOOK>;

trace(novel.*.text( )[3]);  // Displays: A
```

```
// The other child nodes, <B>very</B> and
// thick book., are ignored.
```

Accessing Parent Nodes

To access a node's parent node, we use the *XML* class's instance method *parent()*, which takes no arguments. For example, suppose a variable, pub, has a reference to the <PUBLISHER> element from Example 18-2.

```
var pub:XML = novel.PUBLISHER[0];
```

To access <PUBLISHER>'s parent (which is <BOOK>), we use:

```
pub.parent()
```

The *parent()* method can also be used successively to access any ancestor node, as shown in the following code:

```
// Create a 3-tier XML hierarchy.
var doc:XML = <grandparent><parent><child></child></parent></grandparent>;

// Assign a reference to <child>
var kid:XML = doc.parent.child[0];

// Use parent() successively to access <grandparent> from <child>
var grandparent:XML = kid.parent().parent();
```

 Unlike *children()* and *child()*, the *XML* class's instance method *parent()* method has no alternative variable-access syntax.

When used on an *XMLList* instance, the *parent()* method returns null unless all items in the list have the same parent, in which case that parent is returned. For example, in the following code, we retrieve an *XMLList* representing the <BOOK> element's three children, and then invoke *parent()* on that list. Because the three children have the same parent, that parent is returned.

```
var bookDetails:XMLList = novel.*;
var book:XML = bookDetails.parent();  // Returns the <BOOK> element
```

Invoking *parent()* on an *XMLList* with a single *XML* instance is identical to invoking *parent()* on that instance itself. For example, the following two lines of code are identical:

```
novel.PUBLISHER[0].parent()  // Accesses <BOOK>
novel.PUBLISHER.parent()     // Also accesses <BOOK>
```

When *parent()* is invoked on an *XML* instance that represents an attribute, it returns the element on which the attribute is defined. The following code demonstrates, using an attribute-access technique that we haven't yet covered (but will very shortly):

```
novel.@ISBN.parent()  // Returns the <BOOK> element
```

Accessing Sibling Nodes

As we learned in the section "Understanding XML Data as a Hierarchy," a sibling node is a node that resides directly beside another node on a given level of an XML hierarchy. For example, in our familiar <BOOK> hierarchy, <TITLE> is the previous sibling of <AUTHOR> and <PUBLISHER> is the next sibling of <AUTHOR>.

```
var novel:XML = <BOOK ISBN="0141182806">
    <TITLE>Ulysses</TITLE>                       <!--Previous sibling-->
    <AUTHOR>Joyce, James</AUTHOR>
    <PUBLISHER>Penguin Books Ltd</PUBLISHER>  <!--Next sibling-->
  </BOOK>;
```

In E4X there is no built-in support for moving between sibling nodes in an XML hierarchy. The DOM-based nextSibling, previousSibling variables are not part of the E4X API. However, the next sibling of any given node can be deduced using the following code, provided that the node has a valid parent node:

```
someNode.parent( ).*[someNode.childIndex( )+1];
```

And the previous sibling can be found using the following code:

```
someNode.parent( ).*[someNode.childIndex( )-1];
```

For example, the following code accesses <AUTHOR>'s previous and next siblings:

```
var author:XML = novel.AUTHOR[0];
// Previous sibling
trace(author.parent().*[author.childIndex( )-1]);  // Displays: Ulysses
// Next sibling
trace(author.parent().*[author.childIndex( )+1]);  // Displays:
                                                   //    Penguin Books Ltd
```

Example 18-4 wraps the code for accessing a node's previous sibling in a custom method. Notice that the method adds code to check that the specified node actually has a previous sibling before returning it.

Example 18-4. A custom previousSibling() method

```
public function previousSibling (theNode:XML):XML {
  // Make sure the node actually has a previous sibling before
  // attempting to return it
  if (theNode.parent() != null && theNode.childIndex( ) > 0) {
    return theNode.parent().*[theNode.childIndex( )-1];
  } else {
    return null;
  }
}

// Usage:
previousSibling(someNode);
```

Example 18-5 defines *nextSibling()*, the companion custom method to the *previousSibling()* method defined in Example 18-4. Notice that the method adds code to check that the specified node actually has a next sibling before returning it.

Example 18-5. A custom nextSibling() method

```
public function nextSibling (theNode:XML):XML {
  if (theNode.parent( ) != null
      && theNode.childIndex() < theNode.parent().children().length( )-1) {
    return theNode.parent().*[theNode.childIndex( )+1];
  } else {
    return null;
  }
}

// Usage:
nextSibling(someNode);
```

> E4X reduces the emphasis on accessing siblings due to its increased focus on accessing elements by name. For example, to access the `<TITLE>` element in E4X, we would typically use, simply, novel.TITLE, not author.parent().*[author.childIndex( )-1]).

Accessing Attributes

To access an *XMLList* representing all of an element's attributes, we use the *XML* class's instance method *attributes()*, which takes no arguments, and has the general form:

```
someElement.attributes( )
```

For example, the following code returns an *XMLList* representing `<BOOK>`'s attributes (item L in Figure 18-2):

```
novel.attributes( )
```

Alternatively, we can access an *XMLList* representing an element's attributes using the more convenient E4X *attributes wildcard* (@*), which is written as:

```
someElement.@*   // Returns an XMLList representing
                 // all of someElement's attributes
```

For example, the following code, which is equivalent to novel.attributes( ), returns an *XMLList* representing `<BOOK>`'s attributes (again, item L in Figure 18-2):

```
novel.@*
```

As with elements, attributes in an *XMLList* can be accessed using the array-access operator ([ ]). For example, the following code accesses the first, and only, attribute of the `<BOOK>` element, ISBN (item M in Figure 18-2):

```
novel.attributes( )[0]
```

The following code also accesses `<BOOK>`'s first attribute (again, ISBN), but uses E4X's attributes wildcard syntax:

```
novel.@*[0]
```

However, neither `novel.@*[0]` nor `novel.attributes()[0]` represents typical E4X code. In E4X, it's rare to access attributes according to their order in an XML document. Normally, attributes are accessed by name, using either the *attribute()* method or E4X's more convenient variable-access syntax. The general form for accessing an attribute by name using the *attribute()* method is:

```
someElement.attribute("attributeName")
```

The preceding code returns an *XMLList* containing the attribute named *attributeName* of the element *someElement*. For example, the following code returns an *XMLList* that contains one *XML* instance, representing `<BOOK>`'s ISBN attribute (item M in Figure 18-2):

```
novel.attribute("ISBN")
```

Here's the equivalent form for accessing an attribute by name using variable-access syntax is:

```
someElement.@attributeName
```

For example, the following also returns an *XMLList* that contains one *XML* instance, representing `<BOOK>`'s ISBN attribute, but uses variable-access syntax:

```
novel.@ISBN
```

Like *child()*, *attribute()* returns an *XMLList* of *XML* instances matching a given name. However, because it is an error for two or more attributes of the same element to have the same name, the *XMLList* returned by *attribute()* always contains one *XML* instance only (representing the attribute by the specified name).

To access the *XML* instance contained by the *XMLList* returned by `novel.@ISBN`, we *could* use:

```
novel.@ISBN[0]
```

But, when invoking an *XML* method on that instance, we normally omit the array-access operation ([0]), as in:

```
novel.@ISBN.someXMLMethod()
```

We can omit [0] because, as we learned earlier, when an *XML* method is invoked on an *XMLList* with only one *XML* instance, the method invocation is automatically forwarded to that *XML* instance. For example, the following explicit code:

```
novel.@ISBN[0].parent()  // Returns the <BOOK> node
```

is equivalent to the following implicit code:

```
novel.@ISBN.parent()  // Also returns the <BOOK> node
```

That said, *XML* instances representing attributes never have children, and, hence, have no need for the majority of the *XML* class's methods. Instead, an *XML* instance representing an attribute is used nearly exclusively for the simple attribute value it represents. To access the value of an attribute, we use the *XML* class's instance method *toString()*. For example, the following code assigns the value of <BOOK>'s ISBN attribute to the variable bookISBN using fully explicit code:

```
var bookISBN:String = novel.@ISBN[0].toString();
```

But remember, we can invoke *toString()* directly on novel.@ISBN (rather than on novel.@ISBN[0]) because it is an *XMLList* with only one *XML* instance. Here is the shorter, more typical code:

```
var bookISBN:String = novel.@ISBN.toString();  // Removed [0]
```

But we can make the preceding line of code shorter still. The *XML* class is dynamic. Hence, we can use ActionScript's automatic datatype conversion to convert the value of any *XML* instance's variables to a string. (ActionScript's datatype conversion rules are described in Chapter 8.) Here's the technique:

```
var bookISBN:String = novel.@ISBN;
```

In the preceding code, novel is an instance of a dynamic class (*XML*). Hence, when we assign its ISBN variable to the typed variable bookISBN, ActionScript defers type checking until runtime. At runtime, because bookISBN's datatype is a primitive type (*String*), ISBN's value is automatically converted to that primitive type.

Pretty handy. And it works for converting to other primitive datatypes, too. For example, the following code converts the ISBN attribute value to a number simply by assigning it to a variable whose datatype is *Number*:

```
var bookISBN:Number = novel.@ISBN;
```

When working with attributes, remember that an attribute's value is always type *String*, even if it contains what appears to be another type of data. To be used as a datatype other than *String*, that value must be converted either explicitly or implicitly. To avoid unwelcome surprises, stay mindful of the rules for datatype conversion, covered in Chapter 8. In particular, remember that the string value "false" converts to the Boolean value true! When working with attributes that contain Boolean information, it's, therefore, easier to use string comparisons than it is to convert to the *Boolean* datatype. For example, the following code adds a new attribute, INSTOCK, to the <BOOK> element, indicating whether or not the book is currently in stock. To print a message indicating the availability of the book, we compare novel.@INSTOCK to the string "false" rather than convert novel.@INSTOCK to a *Boolean* value. As a precaution, we also convert the attribute value to all lowercase before making the comparison.

When comparing attributes, remember that attributes are always strings and that comparisons are case-sensitive.

```
var novel:XML = <BOOK ISBN="0141182806" INSTOCK="false">
    <TITLE>Ulysses</TITLE>
    <AUTHOR>Joyce, James</AUTHOR>
    <PUBLISHER>Penguin Books Ltd</PUBLISHER>
  </BOOK>;

// Compare to the string "false" instead of converting to Boolean
if (novel.@INSTOCK.toLowerCase() == "false") {
  trace("Not Available!");
} else {
  trace("Available!");
}
```

Accessing Comments and Processing Instructions

The final two kinds of nodes we can access in E4X are comments and processing instructions. XML comments take the for:

```
<!--Comment text goes here-->
```

and XML processing instructions take the form:

```
<?someTargetApp someData?>
```

These two ancillary forms of data can be accessed using the *XML* class's instance methods *comments()* and *processingInstructions()*. Both methods return an *XMLList* representing all direct children of an element that are either comments or processing instructions, respectively. However, by default, the E4X parser ignores both comments and processing instructions. In order to make the comments of an XML document or fragment accessible, we must set XML.ignoreComments to false before parsing the data, as in:

```
XML.ignoreComments = false;
```

Similarly, in order to make the processing instructions of an XML document or fragment accessible, we must set XML.ignoreProcessingInstructions to false before parsing the data, as in:

```
XML.ignoreProcessingInstructions = false;
```

Note that both XML.ignoreComments and XML.ignoreProcessingInstructions are static variables, set through the *XML* class, not an individual *XML* instance. Once set, XML.ignoreComments and XML.ignoreProcessingInstructions affect all future XML parsing operations.

Example 18-6 adds two comments and two processing instructions to the <BOOK> example, and demonstrates how to access them. Notice that XML.ignoreProcessingInstructions and `XML.ignoreComments` are set to `false` *before* the XML literal is assigned to the variable novel. Notice also that even though the comments and processing instructions are interspersed within `<BOOK>`'s children, *comments()* and *processingInstructions()* ignore the other children, and return a clean list of the comments and processing instructions.

Example 18-6. Accessing comments and processing instructions

```
XML.ignoreComments = false;
XML.ignoreProcessingInstructions = false;

// Create an XML fragment that contains both
// comments and processing instructions
var novel:XML = <BOOK ISBN="0141182806">
    <!--Hello world-->
    <?app1 someData?>
    <TITLE>Ulysses</TITLE>
    <AUTHOR>Joyce, James</AUTHOR>
    <?app2 someData?>
    <PUBLISHER>Penguin Books Ltd</PUBLISHER>
    <!--Goodbye world-->
  </BOOK>

trace(novel.comments()[0]);                // <!--Hello world-->
trace(novel.comments()[1]);                // <!--Goodbye world-->
trace(novel.processingInstructions()[0]);  // <?app1 someData?>
trace(novel.processingInstructions()[1]);  // <?app2 someData?>
```

To obtain an *XMLList* representing all comments and processing instructions within an entire XML tree (not just within the direct children of a node), use the descendants operator in combination with the properties wildcard, as follows:

```
var tempRoot:XML = <tempRoot/>;
tempRoot.appendChild(novel);
trace(tempRoot..*.comments()[0]);  // First comment in the document
```

We'll study the preceding technique more closely in the later section "Traversing XML Trees."

Accessing Attributes and Elements Whose Names Contain Reserved Characters

When an attribute or element name contains a character that is considered illegal in an ActionScript identifier (e.g., a hyphen), that attribute or element cannot be accessed using the dot operator. Instead, we must use the *attribute()* method, the *child()* method, or the [ ] operator. For example:

```
var saleEndsDate:XML = <DATE TIME-ZONE="PST">February 1, 2006</DATE>
trace(saleEndsDate.@TIME-ZONE);              // ILLEGAL! Don't do this.
trace(saleEndsDate.attribute("TIME-ZONE"));  // Legal. Do do this.
trace(saleEndsDate.@["TIME ZONE"]);          // Also Legal.
```

In the specific case of the illegal code `saleEndsDate.@TIME-ZONE`, ActionScript treats the hyphen as a subtraction operation, and interprets the expression to mean `saleEndsDate.@TIME` *minus* `ZONE`! In all likelihood, no variable (or method) named `ZONE` exists, and ActionScript will generate the following error message:

```
Access of undefined property 'ZONE'
```

However, if a variable named `ZONE` did exist, its value would be subtracted from the empty *XMLList* object represented by `saleEndsDate.@TIME`, and no error would occur! Without any error message, the failed reference to `saleEndsDate.@TIME-ZONE` would be very difficult to track down. Given that the attribute `saleEndsDate.@TIME` does not exist, we would ideally like ActionScript to generate a "nonexistent attribute" error, but unfortunately the version of the E4X specification implemented by ActionScript 3.0 stipulates that references to nonexistent attributes should return an empty *XMLList* object rather than causing an error. Future versions of Action-Script may improve this situation.

We've now covered the basics of accessing XML data. Before we continue our study of E4X, let's return one more time to the important topic of treating an *XMLList* instance as though it were an *XML* instance.

Treating XMLList as XML, Revisited

Earlier we learned that in E4X, a reference to an *XMLList* with only one *XML* instance can be treated as though it were that instance. For example, we saw that the expression:

```
novel.AUTHOR[0].setName("WRITER");
```

was equivalent to the expression:

```
novel.AUTHOR.setName("WRITER");  // Removed [0]
```

The two are equivalent because `novel.AUTHOR` refers to an *XMLList* with a single *XML* instance (the element `<AUTHOR>`).

Treating an *XMLList* instance as though it were an *XML* instance enables much of E4X's convenience and usability, but also introduces some potentially confusing subtleties, particularly when used in combination with automatic string conversion. Let's take a deeper look at this issue.

Suppose we're building a user interface for an online book store in which each book is represented by an XML fragment matching the structure of our ongoing `<BOOK>` example. When the user chooses a book from the store, the corresponding author's name appears onscreen.

In our code, we create a method, *displayAuthor()*, that handles the display of the author's name. In our first attempt to code the *displayAuthor()* method, we require that the name of the author be supplied as a string:

```
public function displayAuthor (name:String):void {
  // authorField refers to a TextField instance in which to
  // display the author name
  authorField.text = name;
}
```

When the user chooses a book, we retrieve the name of the author for that book from the <AUTHOR> element and pass it to the *displayAuthor()* method like this:

```
displayAuthor(novel.AUTHOR);
```

That statement is pleasingly simple and intuitive, but as we've learned in this chapter, there's a lot going on behind the scenes. As a review, let's dissect how it works. First, ActionScript passes novel.AUTHOR to the *displayAuthor()* method as the value of the name parameter. The name parameter's datatype is *String*, so ActionScript automatically attempts to convert novel.AUTHOR to a string using:

```
novel.AUTHOR.toString()
```

By default, calling *toString()* on an object yields a string in the format [object *ClassName*], but novel.AUTHOR is an *XMLList* instance, and *XMLList* overrides *toString()* with custom behavior. Specifically, the *XMLList* version of *toString()* recognizes that novel.AUTHOR contains only one item, and, therefore, returns the result of calling *XML*'s *toString()* on that item. So the invocation, novel.AUTHOR.toString(), is automatically redirected to novel.AUTHOR[0].toString(). And what is the return value of novel.AUTHOR[0].toString()? As we learned earlier, the answer hinges on the fact that novel.AUTHOR[0] represents a simple XML element that does not contain any child elements. For an XML element that contains no other elements, *XML*'s *toString()* returns the child text node of that element, as a string, with the containing tags removed. So novel.AUTHOR[0].toString() returns "Joyce, James" (not "<AUTHOR>Joyce, James</AUTHOR>") as the final value passed to *displayAuthor()*. In summary:

- Passing novel.AUTHOR to a parameter of type *String* forces an implicit conversion of novel.AUTHOR to a string.
- novel.AUTHOR is converted to a string via novel.AUTHOR.toString().
- novel.AUTHOR.toString() automatically returns novel.AUTHOR[0].toString() because novel.AUTHOR is an *XMLList* with only one item.
- novel.AUTHOR[0].toString() returns the text contained by the <AUTHOR> element ("Joyce, James") as per the implementation of *XML*'s *toString()* (see the later section "Converting XML and XMLList to a String").

After all is said and done, the expression:

```
displayAuthor(novel.AUTHOR);
```

results in:

```
displayAuthor("Joyce, James");
```

which is what we intuitively expected in the first place.

Most of the time, we can ignore the preceding complexity because E4X, in unscientific terms, "does what it looks like it will do." But there are times where we must understand the E4X autopilot in order to take manual control. For example, suppose we decide that our bookstore should display not just the name, but also the birth date of each author. We modify our XML structure to include the birth date as a child of the <AUTHOR> element, as shown in the following code:

```
var novel:XML = <BOOK ISBN="0141182806">
  <TITLE>Ulysses</TITLE>
  <AUTHOR>
    <NAME>Joyce, James</NAME>
    <BIRTHDATE>February 2 1882</BIRTHDATE>
  </AUTHOR>
  <PUBLISHER>Penguin Books Ltd</PUBLISHER>
</BOOK>
```

Accordingly, we modify the *displayAuthor()* method so that it accepts the entire <AUTHOR> element as a parameter, and retrieves the author name and birth date from the <NAME> and <BIRTHDATE> child elements directly:

```
public function displayAuthor (author:XML):void {
  authorField.text = "Name: " + author.NAME
                   + " Birthdate: " + author.BIRTHDATE;
}
```

In the preceding code, notice that the parameter datatype has changed from *String* to *XML*. If we now attempt to pass novel.AUTHOR to the *displayAuthor()* method, we receive a type mismatch error at runtime because ActionScript cannot implicitly convert novel.AUTHOR (which is an *XMLList*) to an instance of the *XML* class:

```
displayAuthor(novel.AUTHOR);  // TypeError: Error #1034: Type Coercion
                              // failed: cannot convert XMLList to XML
```

To fix the error, we must refer to the *XML* instance representing <AUTHOR> explicitly when passing it to *displayAuthor()*, as in:

```
displayAuthor(novel.AUTHOR[0]);  // Pass the lone XML instance
                                 // in novel.AUTHOR to displayAuthor()
```

Notice the important difference: when we want to access the text contained by the <AUTHOR> element as a *String*, we can rely on E4X's automatic behavior; but when we want to access the actual *XML* instance representing the <AUTHOR> element, we must refer to that instance explicitly.

Now suppose later, we're asked to modify our store to handle books with multiple authors. Once again we alter our XML structure, this time to accommodate multiple <AUTHOR> elements. Example 18-7 contains a sample XML fragment showing the new structure (the authors' birth dates are fabricated).

Example 18-7. A multiple-author <BOOK> fragment

```
var oopBook:XML = <BOOK ISBN="0596007124">
  <TITLE>Head First Design Patterns</TITLE>
```

Example 18-7. A multiple-author <BOOK> fragment (continued)

```
  <AUTHOR>
    <NAME>Eric Freeman</NAME>
    <BIRTHDATE>January 1 1970</BIRTHDATE>
  </AUTHOR>
  <AUTHOR>
    <NAME>Elisabeth Freeman</NAME>
    <BIRTHDATE>January 1 1971</BIRTHDATE>
  </AUTHOR>
  <AUTHOR>
    <NAME>Kathy Sierra</NAME>
    <BIRTHDATE>January 1 1972</BIRTHDATE>
  </AUTHOR>
  <AUTHOR>
    <NAME>Bert Bates</NAME>
    <BIRTHDATE>January 1 1973</BIRTHDATE>
  </AUTHOR>
  <PUBLISHER>O'Reilly Media, Inc</PUBLISHER>
</BOOK>;
```

To handle the new XML structure, we modify *displayAuthor()* so that it accepts an *XMLList* representing multiple <AUTHOR> elements (instead of the previous single <AUTHOR> element). The new version of *displayAuthor()* uses the *for-each-in* statement to iterate over the <AUTHOR> elements (we'll study *for-each-in* in the later section "Processing XML with for-each-in and for-in").

```
public function displayAuthor (authors:XMLList):void {
  for each (var author:XML in authors) {
    authorField.text += "Name: " + author.NAME
                + ", Birthdate: " + author.BIRTHDATE + "\n";
  }
}
```

To pass a list of the <AUTHOR> elements to *displayAuthor()*, we use the following code:

```
displayAuthor(oopBook.AUTHOR);
```

The preceding line of code matches our original approach, which was:

```
displayAuthor(novel.AUTHOR);
```

But this time, the *XMLList* is passed directly to the *displayAuthor()* method without any conversion because the receiving parameter's datatype is *XMLList* not *String*. Again, notice the difference: when passing an *XMLList* object to a function, if we want to convert the list to a *String*, we specify *String* as the datatype of the receiving parameter and let E4X's automatic behavior work its magic; but if we want to preserve the datatype of the list, we must specify *XMLList* as the datatype of the receiving parameter. Both the reference itself (oopBook.author) and the datatype of the receiving parameter (authors) affect the behavior of the code.

Table 18-1 reviews the results of passing the various E4X expressions we've just studied to parameters of various datatypes.

Table 18-1. Review: E4X expressions and results

Expression	Parameter datatype	Result
novel.AUTHOR	*String*	"Joyce, James"
novel.AUTHOR	*XML*	Type mismatch error (can't convert *XMLList* to *XML*)
novel.AUTHOR[0]	*String*	"Joyce, James"
novel.AUTHOR[0]	*XML*	*XML* instance representing the <AUTHOR> element
oopBook.AUTHOR	*String*	String containing XML source code for the four <AUTHOR> elements
oopBook.AUTHOR	*XMLList*	*XMLList* with four *XML* instances representing the four <AUTHOR> elements

Don't panic. E4X is well thought out. Don't let its automatic behavior distress you. Most of the time it will serve you well. However, when accessing XML nodes using variable-access syntax (the dot operator), bear the following potential points of confusion in mind:

- *parentNode.childNodeName* is equivalent to *parentNode*.child(*childNodeName*) and always refers to an *XMLList* instance, not an *XML* instance.

- When an *XMLList* instance has one *XML* instance only, *XML* methods can be invoked on it; the *XMLList* instance automatically forwards the invocations to the *XML* instance.

- To obtain an object reference to an *XML* instance contained by *parentNode. childNodeName*, you must use the form *parentNode.childNodeName*[*index*], even if the *XML* instance you want is the only item in the *XMLList* (in which case it is referred to as *parentNode.childNodeName*[0]).

- If an XML element contains text only (and *does not* contain child elements), converting it to a string yields the text it contains, stripped of enclosing tags (e.g., converting <TITLE>Ulysses</TITLE> to a string yields "Ulysses" not "<TITLE> Ulysses</TITLE>").

- If an XML element contains text *and* contains child elements, converting it to a string yields the element's source code, complete with tags. For example, converting:

```
<AUTHOR>Joyce, <FIRSTNAME>James</FIRSTNAME></AUTHOR>
```

to a string yields:

```
"<AUTHOR>Joyce, <FIRSTNAME>James</FIRSTNAME></AUTHOR>"
```

not:

```
Joyce, James
```

When in doubt, consider using the methods of the *XML* class to access the content you're interested in. The explicit names of the *XML* class's methods are sometimes easier to understand, though more verbose.

Processing XML with for-each-in and for-in

XML-structured documents often contain data sets that need to be processed systematically. For example, an XML document might contain population information for the countries of the world, or points on a map, or the costs of items in an order. Whatever the data, the basic approach is the same—each item must be examined and used in some uniform way by the application. In order to make XML-formatted information easy to process, E4X adds a new kind of loop to ActionScript called the *for-each-in* loop.

The *for-each-in* loop, which we first saw in Chapter 15, provides easy access to the values of an object's dynamic instance variables or an array's elements. Recall the generalized syntax for a *for-each-in* loop:

```
for each (variableOrElementValue in someObject) {
  statements
}
```

We can use the preceding syntax to process *XML* instances in an *XMLList* just as easily as we process an array's elements or an object's dynamic instance variables. Example 18-8 demonstrates.

Example 18-8. Using for-in-each to process XML instances

```
var novel:XML = <BOOK ISBN="0141182806">
    <TITLE>Ulysses</TITLE>
    <AUTHOR>Joyce, James</AUTHOR>
    <PUBLISHER>Penguin Books Ltd</PUBLISHER>
  </BOOK>;

for each (var child:XML in novel.*) {
  trace(child);
}
```

The *for-each-in* loop in Example 18-8 runs three times, once for each child node in the *XMLList* returned by novel.*. The first time the loop runs, the variable child is assigned a reference to <BOOK>'s first child node (i.e., the *XML* instance representing <TITLE>). The second time the loop runs, child is assigned a reference to <BOOK>'s second child node (the *XML* instance representing <AUTHOR>). The third time the loop runs, child is assigned a reference to <BOOK>'s third child node (the *XML* instance representing <PUBLISHER>). So the output of the loop is:

```
Ulysses
Joyce, James
Penguin Books Ltd
```

Example 18-9 presents a more involved scenario—calculating the total cost of a customer order. The comments will guide you through the code.

Example 18-9. Calculating an order total

```
// Create the order. Normally the order would be generated programmatically
// in response to user input, but we hard code it for this example.
var order:XML = <ORDER>
  <ITEM SKU="209">
    <NAME>Trinket</NAME>
    <PRICE>9.99</PRICE>
    <QUANTITY>3</QUANTITY>
  </ITEM>

  <ITEM SKU="513">
    <NAME>Gadget</NAME>
    <PRICE>149.99</PRICE>
    <QUANTITY>1</QUANTITY>
  </ITEM>

  <ITEM SKU="374">
    <NAME>Toy</NAME>
    <PRICE>39.99</PRICE>
    <QUANTITY>2</QUANTITY>
  </ITEM>
</ORDER>

// Create a text field in which to display the order details.
var outField:TextField = new TextField( );
outField.width = 300;
outField.height = 300;
outField.text = "Here is your order:\n";
addChild(outField);

// Set the initial total cost to 0.
var total:Number = 0;

// This loop runs once for every <ITEM> element.
for each (var item:XML in order.*) {
  // Display the details for this item in the outField text field.
  outField.text += item.QUANTITY
            + " " + item.NAME + "(s)."
            + " $" + item.PRICE + " each.\n";

  // Add the cost of this item to the total cost of the order.
  // Notice that the quantity and price values are automatically
  // converted to numbers by the multiplication operation.
  total += item.QUANTITY * item.PRICE;
}

// Display the total cost of the order.
outField.appendText("TOTAL: " + total);
```

Here is the output of the code from Example 18-9:

```
Here is your order:
3 Trinket(s). $9.99 each.
1 Gadget(s). $149.99 each.
```

```
2 Toy(s). $39.99 each.
TOTAL: 259.94
```

Here's one final example, showing how we can manipulate the order's content using a *for-each-in* loop. It assigns the same value to all <PRICE> elements from Example 18-9:

```
// Big SALE! Everything's $1!
for each (var item:XML in order.*) {
  item.PRICE = 1;
}
```

We'll learn more about changing the content of an XML element later in the section "Changing or Creating New XML Content."

Be careful not to mistakenly assume that the *XML* instances in an *XMLList* have variable names matching their *XML* element names. Instead, like array elements, the *XML* instances in an *XMLList* are arranged in order, and have their numeric position as variable names. The following code uses a *for-in* loop to demonstrate. Notice that the variable names are 0, 1, and 2, not "ITEM". The names 0, 1, and 2 represent each *XML* instance's numeric position in the *XMLList* returned by order.*.

```
for (var childName:String in order.*) {
  trace(childName);
}
Output:
0
1
2
```

 For more information on the *for-each-in* and *for-in* statements, see Chapter 15.

Accessing Descendants

We've now had plenty of practice accessing the child nodes of an XML element. Next let's consider how to access not just an element's child nodes, but also its so-called *descendant* nodes. An element's descendants are all the nodes it contains, at any level of the XML hierarchy (i.e., grandchild nodes, great-grandchild nodes and so on).

For example, consider the XML fragment in Example 18-10, representing a book and movie loan transaction from a library.

Example 18-10. A library loan record

```
var loan:XML = <LOAN>
  <BOOK ISBN="0141182806" DUE="1136091600000">
    <TITLE>Ulysses</TITLE>
    <AUTHOR>Joyce, James</AUTHOR>
```

Example 18-10. A library loan record (continued)

```
    <PUBLISHER>Penguin Books Ltd</PUBLISHER>
  </BOOK>

  <DVD ISBN="0790743086" DUE="1136610000000">
    <TITLE>2001 A Space Odyssey</TITLE>
    <DIRECTOR>Stanley Kubrick</DIRECTOR>
    <PUBLISHER>Warner Home Video</PUBLISHER>
  </DVD>

  <DVD ISBN="078884461X" DUE="1137214800000">
    <TITLE>Spirited Away</TITLE>
    <DIRECTOR>Hayao Miyazaki</DIRECTOR>
    <PUBLISHER>Walt Disney Video</PUBLISHER>
  </DVD>
</LOAN>
```

In the preceding example, the <LOAN> element's descendants include:

- The direct children: <BOOK> and the two <DVD> elements
- The grandchildren: every <TITLE>, <AUTHOR>, <PUBLISHER>, and <DIRECTOR> element
- The great-grandchildren: every text node contained by the <TITLE>, <AUTHOR>, <PUBLISHER>, and <DIRECTOR> elements

To access an element's descendants we use the E4X descendant operator (..), which is used as follows:

```
    theElement..identifier
```

A descendant-access expression returns an *XMLList* representing all descendants of *theElement* whose names match *identifier*. For example, the following expression yields an *XMLList* that has two *XML* instances, representing the two <DIRECTOR> elements from Example 18-10.

```
    loan..DIRECTOR
```

Notice that the <DIRECTOR> elements are not direct children of the <LOAN> element; they are grandchildren. The descendant operator gives us direct, easy access to nodes anywhere in an XML hierarchy. For example, to retrieve a list of all <TITLE> elements in the library loan record, we use:

```
    loan..TITLE
```

To print the titles of all items being loaned, we can use code such as the following:

```
    trace("You have borrowed the following items:");
    for each (var title:XML in loan..TITLE) {
      trace(title);
    }

    // Output:
    You have borrowed the following items:
```

```
Ulysses
2001 A Space Odyssey
Spirited Away
```

That's super handy!

 The expression a.b is a list of all *direct child* elements of a named b; the expression a..b is a list of all *descendant* elements of a named b. The syntax is intentionally similar the only difference is the depth of the nodes returned.

The descendant operator also works with attributes. To retrieve a list of descendant attributes rather than elements, use the following form:

```
theElement..@attributeName
```

For example, the following expression yields an *XMLList* that has three *XML* instances, representing the three DUE attributes from Example 18-10.

```
loan..@DUE
```

Here's another handy bit of code:

```
trace("Your items are due on the following dates:");
for each (var due:XML in loan..@DUE) {
  trace(new Date(Number(due)));
}

// In Eastern Standard Time, the output is:
Your items are due:
Sun Jan 1 00:00:00 GMT-0500 2006
Sat Jan 7 00:00:00 GMT-0500 2006
Sat Jan 14 00:00:00 GMT-0500 2006
```

To retrieve an *XMLList* that includes every single node descending from a given element, use:

```
theElement..*
```

For example, the following code returns an *XMLList* with all 21 descendants of the <LOAN> element:

```
loan..*
```

Can you identify all 21 descendants? Example 18-11 presents them all, rendered in comforting ASCII art. Each node's position in the *XMLList* returned by loan..* is indicated in parentheses. (You didn't forget the text nodes, did you? Remember, they count as descendants.)

Example 18-11. The nodes of loan..*

```
BOOK (1)
  |-TITLE (2)
  |    |-Ulysses (3)
  |
  |-AUTHOR (4)
  |    |-Joyce, James (5)
  |
  |-PUBLISHER (6)
       |-Penguin Books Ltd (7)

DVD (8)
  |-TITLE (9)
  |    |-2001 A Space Odyssey (10)
  |
  |-AUTHOR (11)
  |    |-Stanley Kubrick (12)
  |
  |-DIRECTOR (13)
       |-Warner Home Video (14)

DVD (15)
  |-TITLE (16)
  |    |-Spirited Away (17)
  |
  |-AUTHOR (18)
  |    |- Hayao Miyazaki (19)
  |
  |-DIRECTOR (20)
       |- Walt Disney Video (21)
```

To retrieve an *XMLList* that includes every single attribute defined both on an element and on all of its descendants, use:

```
theElement..@*
```

For example, the following code returns an *XMLList* with all attributes defined by descendants of <LOAN> (there are six total). Note that if <LOAN> defined any attributes (it doesn't), they would be included in the list.

```
loan..@*
```

The following code prints the attributes returned by loan..@* using a *for-each-in* loop. For each attribute, the code shows the attribute name and value, and the contents of its parent's child <TITLE> element.

```
for each (var attribute:XML in loan..@*) {
  trace(attribute.parent( ).TITLE
       + ": " + attribute.name( ) + "=" + attribute);
}

// Output:
Ulysses: ISBN=0141182806
Ulysses: DUE=1136091600000
```

```
2001 A Space Odyssey: ISBN=0790743086
2001 A Space Odyssey: DUE=1136610000000
Spirited Away: ISBN=078884461X
Spirited Away: DUE=1137214800000
```

To retrieve an *XMLList* that includes every attribute defined on an element's descendants, but *not* on the element itself, use:

```
theElement..*.@*
```

or the following more verbose, but less arcane code:

```
theElement..*.attributes( )
```

In English the preceding code reads "invoke the *XMLList* class's instance method *attributes( )* on the *XMLList* representing *theElement*'s descendants." The result is an *XMLList* representing every attribute defined on *theElement*'s descendants. For a refresher on *attributes( )* see the earlier section "Accessing Attributes."

 To access attributes or elements whose names contain characters considered illegal in an ActionScript identifier, we must use the *XML* class's instance method *descendants( )* instead of the descendants operator. The format `theElement..["someName"]` is not allowed with the descendants operator.

The descendants operator is useful on its own, but it becomes indispensable when combined with E4X's filtering capabilities. Once you understand the descendants operator and E4X filtering, you'll be able to meet nearly all your XML processing needs quickly and easily. We'll find out how in the next section.

Filtering XML Data

The E4X *filtering predicate operator* is a simple but powerful search tool. It can take any *XMLList* and return a subset of items from that list based on a specified condition. (The term predicate is borrowed from the W3C's XPath Language. See *http:// www.w3.org/TR/xpath20/#id-predicates*.)

The filtering predicate operator takes the general form:

```
theXMLList.(conditionExpression)
```

For each item in `theXMLList`, the `conditionExpression` is executed once. If the `conditionExpression` yields true for an item, that item is added to an *XMLList* that is returned after all items have been processed. Note that during each execution of the `conditionExpression`, the current item is temporarily added to the front of the scope chain, allowing the item's child elements and attributes to be referenced directly by name within the expression.

The filtering predicate operator is extremely intuitive to use. Let's take a look at a new XML fragment and do some filtering! Example 18-12, the new fragment, represents a company's staff list.

Example 18-12. An employee list

```
var staff:XML = <STAFF>
  <EMPLOYEE ID="501" HIRED="1090728000000">
    <NAME>Marco Crawley</NAME>
    <MANAGER>James Porter</MANAGER>
    <SALARY>25000</SALARY>
    <POSITION>Designer</POSITION>
  </EMPLOYEE>

  <EMPLOYEE ID="500" HIRED="1078462800000">
    <NAME>Graham Barton</NAME>
    <MANAGER>James Porter</MANAGER>
    <SALARY>35000</SALARY>
    <POSITION>Designer</POSITION>
  </EMPLOYEE>

  <EMPLOYEE ID="238" HIRED="1014699600000">
    <NAME>James Porter</NAME>
    <MANAGER>Dorian Schapiro</MANAGER>
    <SALARY>55000</SALARY>
    <POSITION>Manager</POSITION>
  </EMPLOYEE>
</STAFF>
```

Now for our first filtering operation: suppose we want a list of the employees with James Porter as a manager. We can filter the list of <EMPLOYEE> elements from Example 18-12 like this:

```
// First obtain an XMLList object representing all <EMPLOYEE> elements
var allEmployees:XMLList = staff.*;

// Now filter the list of <EMPLOYEE> elements
var employeesUnderJames:XMLList = allEmployees.(MANAGER == "James Porter");
```

The expression allEmployees.(MANAGER == "James Porter") returns an *XMLList* of all items in allEmployees whose <MANAGER> element contains the text "James Porter." You have to love the simplicity and readability of E4X. Just remember that the preceding line of code works because each item in allEmployees is added to the scope chain each time that (MANAGER == "James Porter") is evaluated. So every time the expression (MANAGER == "James Porter") runs, it has the following conceptual meaning, expressed in pseudocode:

```
if (currentEmployee.MANAGER == "James Porter")
   add currentEmployee to results
```

For comparison, here is some actual ActionScript code that does the same thing as the expression allEmployees.(MANAGER == "James Porter"):

```
var resultList:XMLList = new XMLList( );
var counter:int = 0;
for each (var employee:XML in allEmployees) {
  if (employee.MANAGER == "James Porter") {
    resultList[counter] = employee;
    counter++;
  }
}
```

Let's look at some more examples that demonstrate how to access the information in Example 18-12 based on a variety of conditions. The following expression returns a list of employees with a salary less than or equal to $35,000.

```
staff.*.(SALARY <= 35000)
```

The next expression returns a list of employees with a salary between $35,000 and $50,000:

```
staff.*.(SALARY >= 35000 && SALARY <= 50000)
```

This expression returns a list of the designers in the company:

```
staff.*.(POSITION == "Designer")
```

This one returns a list of employees whose ID number is 238 (it so happens that there's only one, but it's still wrapped in an *XMLList* instance).

```
staff.*.(@ID == "238")
```

Here we retrieve a list of employees hired in the year 2004 (to represent time, we use the standard milliseconds-from-1970 format used by the *Date* class):

```
staff.*.(@HIRED >= 1072933200000 && @HIRED <= 1104555600000)
```

Finally, we print the date on which Graham was hired:

```
// In Eastern Standard Time, displays: Fri Mar 5 00:00:00 GMT-0500 2004
trace(new Date(Number(staff.*.(NAME == "Graham Barton").@HIRED)));
```

Fun, ain't it? Predicates are great!

 To filter a list where not every item has a given attribute or child element, we must use *hasOwnProperty()* to check for the existence of that attribute or child before filtering on it. Otherwise, a reference error occurs. For example, the following code returns every element in *someDocument* that has a color attribute set to "red":

```
someDocument..*.(hasOwnProperty("@color") && @color == "red")
```

We've now seen lots of ways to access various specific nodes or groups of nodes within an XML document. Next up: using tree traversal to access not just some of the nodes in a document, but *every* node in a document.

Traversing XML Trees

In general programming terms, *to traverse* means to access every node in a data structure and process it in some way. *Tree traversal* means using a recursive algorithm to traverse the nodes of a tree structure.

In DOM-based XML implementations (such as the legacy *flash.xml.XMLDocument* class), programmers often write custom code to traverse XML trees when searching for information. For example, a human resources program might include traversal code that searches through an XML document looking for all employees classified as managers or all employees in a certain salary bracket. As we saw in the previous section, such custom tree-traversal code is largely unnecessary in E4X because most searches can be performed using E4X's descendants and filtering predicate operators. However, there are still some situations in which a tree must be traversed, even in E4X. Fortunately, the E4X code for doing so is trivial.

In E4X, we can use the descendants operator in combination with the properties wildcard to retrieve an *XMLList* containing every descendant node for a given element, as follows:

```
someElement..*  // Returns a list containing
                // all of someElement's descendants
```

And we can use the *for-each-in* statement to iterate over every item in an *XMLList*. By combining these techniques, we can easily traverse every node in an XML tree as follows:

```
for each (var child:XML in someElement..*) {
  // Process child...
}
```

Note, however, that the preceding code does not strictly conform to the classic definition of tree traversal because it never accesses the root of the hierarchy (*someElement*). In situations that require the root node to be processed along with its children, simply add the root node to another *XML* instance temporarily, as in:

```
var tempRoot:XML = <root/>;
tempRoot.appendChild(someElement);
for each (var child:XML in tempRoot..*) {
  // Process child...
}
```

Let's look at a simple real-world traversal example. Suppose we're creating a blog posting system that allows users to contribute responses that can include HTML markup. In order to make the responses XHTML-compliant, we want to convert all tag names found in user responses to lowercase. Here's an example of a response that includes problematic uppercase and mixed case tag names:

```
var message:XML = <message>
<B>HEY!</B> I just wanted to say that your site is so cool!!
You should <A Href="http://mysiteiscooltoo.com/">visit mine</A> sometime.
</message>;
```

Here's the tree traversal code that converts every element and attribute name in the preceding XML fragment to lowercase:

```
for each (var child:XML in message..*) {
  // If the node is an element...
  if (child.nodeKind( ) == "element") {
    // ...change its name to lowercase.
    child.setName(child.name().toString().toLowerCase( ));
    // If the node has any attributes, change their names to lowercase.
    for each (var attribute:XML in child.@*) {
      attribute.setName(attribute.name().toString().toLowerCase( ));
    }
  }
}
```

Here is the new XML resulting from the preceding code, with all tag and attribute names converted to lowercase:

```
<message>
<b>HEY!</b>I just wanted to say that your site is so cool!!
You should <a href="http://mysiteiscooltoo.com/">visit mine</a> sometime.
</message>
```

We've spent most of this chapter exploring how to access content in an existing XML document. Next we'll consider how to add to and change that content.

Changing or Creating New XML Content

In E4X, most common additions and modifications to an existing *XML* instance can be achieved using simple assignment statements. E4X assignments, however, have different results depending on the type of value being assigned and the target of the assignment. Let's look at the various scenarios one at a time.

Changing the Contents of an Element

To change the contents of an XML element, we assign that element any value other than an *XMLList* or *XML* object. The value is converted to a string and replaces the element's content. Recall our <BOOK> fragment:

```
var novel:XML = <BOOK ISBN="0141182806">
  <TITLE>Ulysses</TITLE>
  <AUTHOR>Joyce, James</AUTHOR>
  <PUBLISHER>Penguin Books Ltd</PUBLISHER>
</BOOK>
```

To change the contents of the <TITLE> element from "Ulysses" to "The Sun Also Rises", we use:

```
novel.TITLE[0] = "The Sun Also Rises";
```

But remember that E4X lets us treat an *XMLList* like an *XML* object wherever possible, so because the *XMLList* returned by novel.TITLE has a single XML instance only, we can use this more convenient code:

```
novel.TITLE = "The Sun Also Rises";  // Removed [0]
```

However, if the *XMLList* returned by novel.TITLE had more than one <TITLE> element, the assignment would have a different meaning, as described in the later section "Assigning Values to an XMLList." (If you need a refresher on the difference between novel.TITLE[0] and novel.TITLE, see the earlier section, "Treating XMLList as XML, Revisited.")

Now let's change the author and publisher of the book too:

```
novel.AUTHOR = "Hemingway, Ernest";
novel.PUBLISHER = "Scribner";
```

Alternatively, the content of an element can be changed using the *XML* class's instance method *setChildren()*. For example:

```
novel.TITLE.setChildren("The Sun Also Rises");
```

Changing an Attribute Value

To change an XML attribute value, simply assign the attribute any new value in an assignment statement. The new value is converted to a string and then replaces the attribute's existing value. For example, the following code changes the ISBN attribute value from "0141182806" to "0684800713":

```
novel.@ISBN = "0684800713";
```

In the preceding assignment, using a string rather than a number as the new value preserves the leading zero.

If the value assigned to the attribute is an *XMLList* containing attributes, the attribute values in the *XMLList* are concatenated into a single string separated by spaces, which is then assigned to the attribute. This slightly unusual behavior can be used to collect a group of attributes into a single attribute. For example:

```
var books:XML = <BOOKS>
    <BOOK ISBN="0141182806"/>
    <BOOK ISBN="0684800713"/>
    <BOOK ISBN="0198711905"/>
  </BOOKS>;

var order:XML = <ORDER ITEMS=""/>;
order.@ITEMS = books.*.@ISBN;

// Yields:
<ORDER ITEMS="0141182806 0684800713 0198711905"/>
```

Replacing an Entire Element

To replace an XML element with new elements, we assign either an *XMLList* or *XML* object to that element. For example, in the following code, the <DIV> element replaces the <P> element:

```
var doc:XML = <DOC>
    <P ALIGN="CENTER">E4X is fun</P>
  </DOC>;
doc.P = <DIV>E4X is convenient</DIV>;

// Yields:
<DOC>
  <DIV>E4X is convenient</DIV>
</DOC>
```

The content of an element can also be changed using the *XML* class's instance method *replace()*. For example:

```
// Same as: doc.P = <DIV>E4X is convenient</DIV>
doc.replace("P", <DIV>E4X is convenient</DIV>);
```

Note that when an XML element is replaced by content from another document, the new content is a copy of, not a reference to, the other document's content. For example, consider the following two XML fragments:

```
var user1:XML = <USERDETAILS>
    <LOGIN>joe</LOGIN>
    <PASSWORD>linuxRules</PASSWORD>
  </USERDETAILS>;

var user2:XML = <USERDETAILS>
    <LOGIN>ken</LOGIN>
    <PASSWORD>default</PASSWORD>
  </USERDETAILS>;
```

We can replace the <PASSWORD> element of user2 with the <PASSWORD> element of user1 as follows:

```
user2.PASSWORD = user1.PASSWORD;
```

After the replacement, the two <PASSWORD> elements have the same content:

```
trace(user1.PASSWORD[0] == user2.PASSWORD[0]); // Displays: true
```

But they do not refer to the same *XML* instance:

```
trace(user1.PASSWORD[0] === user2.PASSWORD[0]); // Displays: false
```

For information on the difference between the preceding two equality expressions, see the later section "Determining Equality in E4X."

Adding New Attributes and Elements

We can add new attributes and elements to a document using the same assignment syntax we use to modify and replace existing attributes and elements.

In E4X, when a value is assigned to an attribute or element that does not already exist, ActionScript automatically adds the specified attribute or element to the document. As an example, let's rebuild our <BOOK> fragment from scratch. We'll start with an empty <BOOK> element:

```
var novel:XML = <BOOK/>;
```

Next, we add the ISBN attribute:

```
novel.@ISBN = "0141182806";
```

Finally, we add the <TITLE>, <AUTHOR>, and <PUBLISHER> elements:

```
novel.TITLE = "Ulysses";
novel.AUTHOR = "Joyce, James";
novel.PUBLISHER = "Penguin Books Ltd";
```

For each assignment, the new element is appended to the <BOOK> tag as its new last child. So the result of the preceding code is the following XML fragment:

```
<BOOK ISBN="0141182806">
  <TITLE>Ulysses</TITLE>
  <AUTHOR>Joyce, James</AUTHOR>
  <PUBLISHER>Penguin Books Ltd</PUBLISHER>
</BOOK>
```

Assignment syntax can also be used to add a nested XML structure with a single assignment. For example, suppose we want to add the following nested content to the <BOOK> element, describing the novel's setting:

```
<SETTING>
  <CITY>Dublin</CITY>
  <COUNTRY>Ireland</COUNTRY>
</SETTING>
```

To do so, we would use the following code:

```
novel.SETTING.CITY = "Dublin";
novel.SETTING.COUNTRY = "Ireland";
```

At runtime, when ActionScript executes the first statement, it recognizes that neither the <SETTING> nor the <CITY> elements are already in the document, and, hence, creates them both. When ActionScript executes the second statement, it sees that the <SETTING> element already exists, and, therefore, doesn't recreate it. Instead, ActionScript simply adds the <COUNTRY> element to the existing <SETTING> element. Here's the resulting XML:

```
<BOOK ISBN="0141182806">
  <TITLE>Ulysses</TITLE>
  <AUTHOR>Joyce, James</AUTHOR>
  <PUBLISHER>Penguin Books Ltd</PUBLISHER>
```

```
  <SETTING>
    <CITY>Dublin</CITY>
    <COUNTRY>Ireland</COUNTRY>
  </SETTING>
</BOOK>
```

We can use a similar approach to represent the setting information in a single element, of the following format:

```
<SETTING CITY="Dublin" COUNTRY="Ireland"/>
```

To do so, we simply assign the desired attributes the desired values, as in:

```
novel.SETTING.@CITY = "Dublin";
novel.SETTING.@COUNTRY = "Ireland";

//Yields:
<BOOK ISBN="0141182806">
  <TITLE>Ulysses</TITLE>
  <AUTHOR>Joyce, James</AUTHOR>
  <PUBLISHER>Penguin Books Ltd</PUBLISHER>
  <SETTING CITY="Dublin" COUNTRY="Ireland"/>
</BOOK>
```

In this section we've learned that assigning a value to an element that does not already exist causes that element to be added to the document. But what if we want to add an element by the same name as an existing element? For example, how would we add multiple <AUTHOR> elements to the <BOOK> element? The answers to that question is covered next. As you read over the following sections, notice the use of the additive operator (+), which creates a new *XMLList* from a series of *XML* or *XMLList* instances. The additive operator takes the form:

```
XMLOrXMLListInstance1 + XMLOrXMLListInstance2
```

It returns a new *XMLList* instance that contains a flattened list of all *XML* instances in *XMLOrXMLListInstance1* and *XMLOrXMLListInstance2*.

Adding a new child after all existing children

To add a new last child to an existing element, use one of the following techniques:

```
parent.insertChildAfter(parent.*[parent.*.length( )-1], <newchild/>)
```

or:

```
parent.*[parent.*.length( )-1] = parent.*[parent.*.length( )-1] + <newchild/>
```

or:

```
parent.appendChild(<newchild/>)
```

For example, the following code adds a new <DESCRIPTION> element to <BOOK>, immediately following the existing <PUBLISHER> element:

```
var novel:XML = <BOOK ISBN="0141182806">
  <TITLE>Ulysses</TITLE>
  <AUTHOR>Joyce, James</AUTHOR>
```

```
<PUBLISHER>Penguin Books Ltd</PUBLISHER>
</BOOK>

novel.insertChildAfter(novel.*[novel.*.length( )-1],
                       <DESCRIPTION>A modern classic</DESCRIPTION>);
```

The preceding line is synonymous with the following code, which replaces <BOOK>'s last child (<PUBLISHER>) with an *XMLList* containing <BOOK>'s last child (<PUBLISHER>) and the <DESCRIPTION> element:

```
novel.*[novel.*.length()-1] = novel.*[novel.*.length( )-1]
                             + <DESCRIPTION>A modern classic</DESCRIPTION>;
```

For the sake of easier comprehension, here's the preceding line again, in pseudocode:

```
// PSEUDO-CODE:
<PUBLISHER> = <PUBLISHER> + <DESCRIPTION>A modern classic</DESCRIPTION>
```

We can write the same thing more succinctly (in real ActionScript code) as follows:

```
novel.*[novel.*.length( )-1] += <DESCRIPTION>A modern classic</DESCRIPTION>;
```

But here is the most convenient approach:

```
novel.appendChild(<DESCRIPTION>A modern classic</DESCRIPTION>);
```

Adding a new child after a specific existing child

To add a new child after a specific existing child, use one of the following techniques:

```
parent.insertChildAfter(parent.existingChild[n], <newchild/>)
```

or:

```
parent.existingChild[n] = parent.existingChild[n] + <newchild/>
```

or:

```
parent.*[childIndex] = parent.*[childIndex] + <newchild/>
```

For example, the following code adds a second <AUTHOR> element to <BOOK>, immediately following the existing <AUTHOR> element:

```
novel.insertChildAfter(novel.AUTHOR[0], <AUTHOR>Dave Luxton</AUTHOR>);
```

insertChildAfter() requires an *XML* instance (not an *XMLList* instance!) as its first argument, so we must make direct reference to the *XML* instance novel.AUTHOR[0].

> For a refresher on the difference between *XML* and *XMLList* instances, see the earlier section "Treating XMLList as XML, Revisited."

As an alternative to the *insertChildAfter()* approach, we can use the following code:

```
novel.AUTHOR[0] = novel.AUTHOR[0] + <AUTHOR>Dave Luxton</AUTHOR>;
```

Or, more succinctly:

```
novel.AUTHOR[0] += <AUTHOR>Dave Luxton</AUTHOR>;
```

Here is yet another synonymous approach:

```
// Add a new XML element after novel's second child
novel.*[1] = novel.*[1] + <AUTHOR>Dave Luxton</AUTHOR>;
```

Again, the preceding line can be written more succinctly as,

```
novel.*[1] += <AUTHOR>Dave Luxton</AUTHOR>;
```

Adding a new child before a specific existing child

To add a new child before a specific existing child, use one of these techniques:

```
parent.insertChildBefore(parent.existingChild[n], <newchild/>)
// or
parent.existingChild[n] = parent.existingChild[n] + <newchild/>
// or
parent.*[childIndex] = parent.*[childIndex] + <newchild/>
```

For example, the following code adds a new `<PRICE>` element to our book, immediately following the first `<AUTHOR>` element:

```
novel.insertChildBefore(novel.AUTHOR[0], <PRICE>19.99</PRICE>);
```

As with *insertChildAfter()*, note that *insertChildBefore()* requires an *XML* instance (not an *XMLList* instance!) as its first argument.

The preceding line is synonymous with:

```
novel.AUTHOR = <PRICE>19.99</PRICE> + novel.AUTHOR;
```

Here is yet another synonymous approach:

```
// Add a new XML element before novel's second child
novel.*[1] = <PRICE>19.99</PRICE> + novel.*[1];
```

Adding a new child before all existing children

To add a new element as the *first* child of an existing element, use any of the following techniques:

```
parent.insertChildBefore(parent.*[0], <newchild/>)
// or
parent.*[0] = <newchild/> + parent.*[0]
// or
parent.prependChild(<newchild/>)
```

For example, the following code adds a new `<PAGECOUNT>` element to our book, immediately preceding the existing `<TITLE>` element:

```
novel.insertChildBefore(novel.*[0], <PAGECOUNT>1040</PAGECOUNT>);
```

The preceding line is synonymous with:

```
novel.*[0] = <PAGECOUNT>1040</PAGECOUNT> + novel.*[0];
```

Here is the most convenient approach:

```
novel.prependChild(<PAGECOUNT>1040</PAGECOUNT>);
```

Deleting Elements and Attributes

To remove an element or attribute from a document, use the *delete* operator as follows:

```
delete elementOrAttribute
```

For example, the following code removes the ISBN attribute from the <BOOK> element:

```
delete novel.@ISBN;
```

The following code removes the <TITLE> element from the <BOOK> element:

```
delete novel.TITLE;
```

Here's how to delete all children contained by an element:

```
delete novel.*;   // Removes <TITLE>, <AUTHOR>, and <PUBLISHER>
                  // from the original XML fragment.
```

The same technique can be used to remove the text content of an element:

```
delete novel.TITLE.*;  // Removes "Ulysses"
                       // from the original XML fragment.
```

Here's how to delete all attributes of an element:

```
delete novel.@*;  // Removes all attributes (in this case, ISBN)
```

References to Parts of a Document Are Not Live

As you change or add new content to an *XML* object, bear in mind that any updates you make will not be reflected by variables that refer to part of that document. For example, the following code creates a variable, children, that a refers to <BOOK>'s child nodes:

```
var novel:XML = <BOOK ISBN="0141182806">
  <TITLE>Ulysses</TITLE>
  <AUTHOR>Joyce, James</AUTHOR>
  <PUBLISHER>Penguin Books Ltd</PUBLISHER>
</BOOK>

var children:XMLList = novel.*;
```

If we now remove the <PUBLISHER> element, the change is made to the original document, but is not reflected by the children variable:

```
// Remove <PUBLISHER>
delete novel.PUBLISHER;
trace(novel);  // Displays: <BOOK ISBN="0141182806">
               //             <TITLE>Ulysses</TITLE>
               //             <AUTHOR>Joyce, James</AUTHOR>
               //           </BOOK>

trace(children);  // Displays: <TITLE>Ulysses</TITLE>
                  //           <AUTHOR>Joyce, James</AUTHOR>
                  //           <PUBLISHER>Penguin Books Ltd</PUBLISHER>
                  // <PUBLISHER> is still there!
```

Future versions of E4X may support live references to parts of a document.

Using XML Entities for Special Characters

E4X implements special treatment and rules for certain punctuation characters when they appear in an XML literal or XML assignment. Table 18-2 explains how to include these characters in an XML document in ActionScript. The left column of the table lists the characters, while the remaining columns show the code required to include these characters, in four different contexts. For reference, the following code shows an example of each of the four types of contexts (the context is represented by *someText*):

```
// Text of an attribute literal
var xml:XML = <someElement someAttribute="someText"/>

// Text assigned to an attribute
xml.@someOtherAttribute = "someText"

// Text node in an element literal
var xml:XML = <someElement>someText</someElement>

// Text node assigned to an element
xml.someOtherElement = "someText";
```

Table 18-2. Assignments of special punctuation characters

Character	Text of an attribute literal	Text assigned to an attribute	Text node in an element literal	Text node assigned to an element
\	\\	\\	****	\\
&	&	&	&	&
"	&quot;	\" or "	"	\"
'	'**	'	'	'
<	&lt;	<	&lt;	<
>	>	>	>	>
Newline (\n)	Unsupported*	Unsupported*	Unsupported*,***	\n
{	{	{	&#x7B;	{
}	}	}	&#x7D;	}

* In these contexts, the newline sequence \n is automatically converted to the entity
.
** To include ' within an attribute value delimited by ', use the escape sequence '.
*** The sequence \n can be used if the element value is computed. For example: var val:String = "Newlines \n are \n okay \n here!";
var paragraph:XML = <p>{val}</p>;
**** Unlike in strings, in an XML literal, the backslash (\) character is never interpreted as the beginning of an escape sequence.

Note that although the characters > and & can be used in literal form anywhere in an XML literal, when ActionScript encounters them in a text node while parsing XML, it automatically converts them to the entities > and &, respectively. Likewise, when ActionScript encounters & in an attribute value while parsing XML, it automatically converts it to the entity &. However, when used in a string context, those entities will be converted back to their original characters. To view the text node with its entities intact, use the *XML* class's instance method *toXMLString()*. The following code illustrates:

```
var p:XML = <p>&></p>;
trace(p.toString());     // Displays: &>
trace(p.toXMLString());  // Displays: <p>&amp;&gt;</p>
```

Finally, note also that although the ' character can be used to delimit an attribute value in an XML literal, it is converted to the " character during parsing. The following code illustrates:

```
var p:XML = <p align='left'/>;
trace(p.toXMLString());  // Displays: <p align="left"/>
```

Assigning Values to an XMLList

As we learned in the section "Changing the Contents of an Element," there's no difference between assigning a value to an *XMLList* with a single *XML* instance and assigning that value to the instance directly. However, assigning a value to an *XMLList* with more than one *XML* instance can have a variety of different results. Depending on the type of value being assigned and the type of *XML* instances in the list, the list might be changed or even replaced entirely.

Assignment to an *XMLList* instance has only one typical usage scenario: replacing the children of a parent element with a new XML element or list of elements. For example, the following code replaces <DOC>'s two <P> children with a single <P> element:

```
var doc:XML = <DOC TOPIC="Code Tips" AUTHOR="Colin">
    <P>Errors are your friends</P>
    <P>Backup often</P>
  </DOC>;

doc.* = <P>Practice coding everyday</P>;

// Yields:
<DOC TOPIC="Code Tips" AUTHOR="Colin">
  <P>Practice coding everyday</P>
</DOC>
```

Assigning a value to an *XMLList* is uncommon, and therefore, not exhaustively covered in this book. Readers interested in grotesque acts of programming—such as attempting to assign a list of processing instructions to a list of attributes—are left to explore such indecency on their own.

Loading XML Data

For instructive purposes, most XML examples in this chapter have been written in literal form. However, in real applications it's much more common to load *XML* from an external source.

To load external XML data into an *XML* instance, follow these general steps:

1. Create a *URLRequest* object describing the location of the external XML (either a file or a server-side script that returns XML).

2. Create a *URLLoader* object, and use its *load()* method to load the XML.

3. Wait for the XML to load.

4. Pass the loaded XML to the constructor of a new *XML* instance.

While a full discussion of the *URLRequest* and *URLLoader* classes is beyond the scope of this chapter, Example 18-13 demonstrates the code required to load XML data into an *XML* instance. The class in the example, *XMLLoader*, extends *Sprite* so that it can be compiled as an application's main class for testing. For information on the *URLRequest* and *URLLoader* classes see Adobe's ActionScript Language Reference. For information on event handling, see Chapter 12.

Example 18-13. Loading external XML

```
package {
  import flash.display.*;
  import flash.events.*;
  import flash.net.*;

  // Demonstrates the code required to load external XML
  public class XMLLoader extends Sprite {
    // The variable to which the loaded XML will be assigned
    private var novel:XML;
    // The object used to load the XML
    private var urlLoader:URLLoader;

    // Constructor
    public function XMLLoader () {
      // Specify the location of the external XML
      var urlRequest:URLRequest = new URLRequest("novel.xml");
      // Create an object that can load external text data
      urlLoader = new URLLoader();
      // Register to be notified when the XML finishes loading
      urlLoader.addEventListener(Event.COMPLETE, completeListener);
      // Load the XML
      urlLoader.load(urlRequest);
    }

    // Method invoked automatically when the XML finishes loading
    private function completeListener(e:Event):void {
      // The string containing the loaded XML is assigned to the URLLoader
```

Example 18-13. Loading external XML (continued)

```
        // object's data variable (i.e., urlLoader.data). To create a new XML
        // instance from that loaded string, we pass it to the XML constructor
        novel = new XML(urlLoader.data);
        trace(novel.toXMLString());  // Display the loaded XML, now converted
                                     // to an XML object
    }
  }
}
```

Note that all ActionScript load operations, including that shown in Example 18-13, are subject to Flash Player's security limitations. For complete information on security considerations, see Chapter 19.

Working with XML Namespaces

XML uses namespaces to prevent name conflicts in markup, with the ultimate goal of allowing markup from different XML-based vocabularies to coexist peacefully in a single document. ActionScript supports namespaces both as part of E4X and as a general programming tool. This section describes how to work with namespaces using E4X syntax but assumes prior knowledge of the concepts expressed by the W3C definition of namespaces in XML. For an introduction to namespaces in XML, see the following online resources:

Ronald Bourret's "XML Namespaces FAQ":
  http://www.rpbourret.com/xml/NamespacesFAQ.htm

"Namespaces in XML 1.1" (W3C recommendation):
  http://www.w3.org/TR/xml-names11/

"Plan to use XML namespaces, Part 1," by David Marston:
  http://www-128.ibm.com/developerworks/library/x-nmspace.html

For information on the non-XML uses of namespaces in ActionScript programming, see Chapter 17.

Accessing Namespace-Qualified Elements and Attributes

We've already learned how to access elements and attributes not qualified by a namespace. To learn the additional techniques required to access elements and attributes qualified by a namespace, let's look at a new XML fragment example, shown in Example 18-14. The fragment depicts part of a hypothetical furniture catalog. As you read the example, pay attention to the following namespace-related items:

- The namespace URI *http://www.example.com/furniture*, and its companion prefix shop

- The default namespace, *http://www.w3.org/1999/xhtml*

- Three elements qualified by the namespace *http://www.example.com/furniture*: `<shop:table>`, `<shop:desc>`, and `<shop:price>`

- One attribute qualified by the namespace *http://www.example.com/furniture*: `shop:id`

Example 18-14. Using namespaces in a furniture catalog

```
var catalog:XML = <html xmlns:shop="http://www.example.com/furniture"
    xmlns="http://www.w3.org/1999/xhtml">
  <head>
    <title>Catalog</title>
  </head>
  <body>
    <shop:table shop:id="4875">
      <table border="1">
        <tr align="center">
          <td>Item</td>
          <td>Price</td>
        </tr>
        <tr align="left">
          <td><shop:desc>3-legged Coffee Table</shop:desc></td>
          <td><shop:price>79.99</shop:price></td>
        </tr>
      </table>
    </shop:table>
  </body>
</html>
```

Example 18-14 is primarily an XHTML document intended to be rendered by web browsers, but it also contains markup representing items in the furniture catalog. The furniture markup gives the document semantic structure, allowing it to be processed by clients other than a web browser. The catalog uses a namespace to disambiguate XHTML markup from furniture markup. As a result, the element `<table>` can represent, on one hand, a piece of furniture and, on the other, the graphical layout of a web page—all without name conflicts.

To access the elements and attributes qualified by the namespaces in Example 18-14, we must first obtain a reference to those namespaces. To obtain a reference to the namespace *http://www.example.com/furniture*, we invoke the *XML* class's instance method *namespace()* on the document's root node, passing the prefix "shop" as an argument. As a result, the *namespace()* method returns a *Namespace* object representing the namespace *http://www.example.com/furniture*. We assign that object to the variable shopNS for later use.

```
var shopNS:Namespace = catalog.namespace("shop");
```

Alternatively, if we know the namespace's URI, we can create a reference to the *Namespace* using the *Namespace* constructor:

```
var shopNS:Namespace = new Namespace("http://www.example.com/furniture");
```

To retrieve a reference to the default namespace, we invoke the *namespace()* method on the document's root node without passing any namespace prefix:

```
var htmlNS:Namespace = catalog.namespace();
```

Alternatively, if we know the namespace's URI, we can create a reference to the default *Namespace* using the *Namespace* constructor:

```
var htmlNS:Namespace = new Namespace("http://www.w3.org/1999/xhtml");
```

The *inScopeNamespaces()* and *namespaceDeclarations()* methods can also be used to access the namespaces in a document. For details see Adobe's ActionScript Language Reference.

 In E4X, XML namespace attributes are not represented as attributes (i.e., cannot be accessed via *attributes()* or *someElement.@**). Instead, the namespace declarations for an element are accessed via the *XML* class's instance method *namespaceDeclarations()*.

Once we have a *Namespace* reference, we can access namespace-qualified elements and attributes, using qualified names, which have the following general format:

```
theNamespace::elementLocalName
theNamespace::@attributeLocalName
```

For example, here's the qualified name of <shop:price> in ActionScript:

```
shopNS::price
```

Notice the use of the name-qualifier operator (::), which separates the namespace name from the local name.

Here's how to access the element <body>, which is qualified by the default namespace (*http://www.w3.org/1999/xhtml*):

```
catalog.htmlNS::body
```

To access the element <shop:table>, which is a child of <body>, we use:

```
catalog.htmlNS::body.shopNS::table
```

To access the attribute shop:id, we use:

```
catalog.htmlNS::body.shopNS::table.@shopNS::id
```

To access the element <shop:price> we could use this nightmarish code:

```
catalog.htmlNS::body.shopNS::table.htmlNS::table.htmlNS::tr[
    1].htmlNS::td[1].shopNS::price
```

But we'll sleep a little easier if we take advantage of the descendants operator (..) in two places, as in:

```
catalog..shopNS::table..shopNS::price
```

Still, the repetition of shopNS:: is a bit irritating. We can save some keystrokes by asking ActionScript to automatically qualify all unqualified element and attribute names with a namespace of our choosing. To do so, we use the default XML namespace statement, which takes the form:

```
default xml namespace = namespaceOrStringURI
```

For example, the following code causes ActionScript to automatically qualify all unqualified element and attribute names with the namespace *http://www.example.com/furniture*:

```
default xml namespace = shopNS;
```

Subsequent to issuing that statement, the namespace *http://www.example.com/furniture* is implied in all unqualified element and attribute references, so we can reduce this code:

```
catalog..shopNS::table..shopNS::price
```

to this:

```
catalog..table..price
```

It's like a massage and a hot bath!

 Due to a bug in Flash Player 9, the preceding example code (catalog..table..price) yields undefined the first time it runs.

In a more complete example, the catalog document would likely contain more than one <shop::table> element. To access a specific table we'd have to use the filtering predicate, as in:

```
catalog..table.(@id == 4875)..price
```

Example 18-15 shows the code we would use to access and display information about all of the tables in the catalog.

Example 18-15. Showing the tables in the catalog

```
var shopNS:Namespace = catalog.namespace("shop");
default xml namespace = shopNS;
for each (var table:XML in catalog..table) {
  trace(table..desc + ": " + table..price);
}
```

As with element and attribute names, we can use the properties wildcard (*) with namespaces. For example, the following code returns an *XMLList* representing all <table> elements in all namespaces:

```
catalog..*::table
```

To retrieve all descendants at every level in all namespaces or in no namespace, use:

```
theXMLObj..*::*   // elements
theXMLObj..@*::*  // attributes
```

To retrieve all children in all namespaces or in no namespace, use:

```
theXMLObj.*::*   // elements
theXMLObj.@*::*  // attributes
```

Creating Namespace-Qualified Elements and Attributes

To create elements and attributes that are qualified by namespaces, we combine the qualified-names syntax covered in the previous section with the creation techniques covered in the earlier section "Changing or Creating New XML Content."

Before we can create namespace-qualified names, we must create (or obtain) a reference to a *Namespace* object. For example, the following code creates two *Namespace* objects and assigns them to the variables htmlNS and shopNS for later use in qualified names:

```
var htmlNS:Namespace = new Namespace("html",
                           "http://www.w3.org/1999/xhtml");
var shopNS:Namespace = new Namespace("shop",
                           "http://www.example.com/furniture");
```

When creating an entire document rather than a single element or attribute, it's customary and convenient to use a default namespace, which is specified using the default XML namespace statement. For example, the following code sets the default namespace to *http://www.w3.org/1999/xhtml*:

```
default xml namespace = htmlNS;
```

Once the default namespace has been established, all subsequently created elements (but not attributes) without an explicit namespace are automatically qualified by the default namespace. For example, the following code creates an element with the local name "html"; it has no explicit namespace, so it is automatically qualified by the default namespace (*http://www.w3.org/1999/xhtml*):

```
var catalog:XML = <html/>;
```

The XML source code generated by the previous line is:

```
<html xmlns="http://www.w3.org/1999/xhtml" />
```

To add a namespace declaration to a given element, we use the *XML* class's instance method *addNamespace()*. For example, the following code adds a new namespace declaration to the preceding element:

```
catalog.addNamespace(shopNS);
```

The resulting XML source code is:

```
<html xmlns:shop="http://www.example.com/furniture"
      xmlns="http://www.w3.org/1999/xhtml" />
```

You probably recognize the preceding element as the first line of code in the catalog document from Example 18-14. Let's build the rest of that document. Here are the `<head>` and `<title>` tags. Their names are automatically qualified by the default namespace (*http://www.w3.org/1999/xhtml*).

```
        catalog.head.title = "Catalog";
```

Next up, the <shop:table> element and its shop:id attribute. Both of those items have names qualified by the namespace *http://www.example.com/furniture*. The XML source code we want to generate looks like this:

```
<shop:table shop:id="4875">
```

The ActionScript code we use to generate it is:

```
        catalog.body.shopNS::table = "";
        catalog.body.shopNS::table.@shopNS::id = "4875";
```

The preceding code should be very familiar. Except for the namespace qualifier syntax, shopNS::, it's identical to the code we used earlier to create elements and attributes. The namespace qualifier simply specifies the namespace for the local names table and id. Example 18-16 uses the same technique to generate the rest of the catalog document. In the example, notice the following line of code:

```
        catalog.body.shopNS::table.table.tr.td[1] = "Price";
```

That line creates a new element named "td" immediately following the existing element at catalog.body.shopNS::table.table.tr.td[0].

Example 18-16. Creating the furniture catalog

```
// Create the namespaces
var htmlNS:Namespace = new Namespace("html",
                                     "http://www.w3.org/1999/xhtml");
var shopNS:Namespace = new Namespace("shop",
                                     "http://www.example.com/furniture");
// Set the default namespace
default xml namespace = htmlNS;

// Create the root element
var catalog:XML = <html/>;

// Add the furniture namespace to the root element
catalog.addNamespace(shopNS);

// Create the remainder of the document
catalog.head.title = "Catalog";
catalog.body.shopNS::table = "";
catalog.body.shopNS::table.@shopNS::id = "4875";
catalog.body.shopNS::table.table = "";
catalog.body.shopNS::table.table.@border = "1";
catalog.body.shopNS::table.table.tr.td = "Item";
catalog.body.shopNS::table.table.tr.td[1] = "Price";
catalog.body.shopNS::table.table.tr.@align = "center";
catalog.body.shopNS::table.table.tr[1] = "";
catalog.body.shopNS::table.table.tr[1].@align = "left";
catalog.body.shopNS::table.table.tr[1].td.shopNS::desc =
                                        "3-legged Coffee Table";
catalog.body.shopNS::table.table.tr[1].td[1] = "";
catalog.body.shopNS::table.table.tr[1].td[1].shopNS::price = "79.99";
```

We've now finish studying all of the major topics in E4X. The remainder of this chapter covers two supplementary subjects: XML conversion and equality.

Converting XML and XMLList to a String

As we've seen throughout this chapter, E4X implements custom rules for converting *XML* and *XMLList* instances to a string. For reference and review, this section describes E4X's *XML*-to-string and *XMLList*-to-string conversion rules. Remember that an *XML* instance can represent five different kinds of content: an element, an attribute, a text node, a comment, or a processing instruction. We'll consider the conversion rules for each kind separately, but we'll start with *XMLList*-to-string conversion in preparation for the subsequent discussion.

Converting XMLList to a String

When an *XMLList* has only one *XML* instance, the result of *XMLList*'s *toString()* is exactly the same as the result of calling *toString()* on that one instance. For example, in the following code, the title variable refers to an *XMLList* whose single *XML* instance represents the <TITLE> element. Converting title to a string yields Ulysses, exactly as if *toString()* had been invoked on the single *XML* instance directly:

```
var novel:XML = <BOOK ISBN="0141182806">
    <TITLE>Ulysses</TITLE>
    <AUTHOR>Joyce, James</AUTHOR>
    <PUBLISHER>Penguin Books Ltd</PUBLISHER>
  </BOOK>

// Create an XMLList with only one XML instance
var title:XMLList = novel.TITLE;
// Convert the XMLList to a string, and display that string.
trace(title);  // Displays: Ulysses
```

When an *XMLList* has more than one *XML* instance, *XMLList*'s *toString()* returns the result of calling *toXMLstring()* on each *XML* instance and concatenating those strings together, each on its own line. For example, in the following code, the *XMLList* object assigned to details has three *XML* instances representing the three elements <TITLE>, <AUTHOR>, and <PUBLISHER>:

```
// Create an XMLList with three XML instances
var details:XMLList = novel.*;
```

Converting details to a string yields the source XML code for <TITLE>, <AUTHOR>, and <PUBLISHER>:

```
// Convert the XMLList to a string, and display that string
trace(details);  // Displays:
             //  <TITLE>Ulysses</TITLE>
             //  <AUTHOR>Joyce, James</AUTHOR>
             //  <PUBLISHER>Penguin Books Ltd</PUBLISHER>
```

Converting an XML Element to a String

For *XML* instances that represent elements, *XML*'s *toString()* has one of two results, depending on the content of that element. If an element contains child elements, then *XML*'s *toString()* returns XML source code for the element and its children, formatted according to the settings of `XML.ignoreWhitespace`, `XML.prettyPrinting`, and `XML.prettyIndent`. For example, in the following code the element `<BOOK>` has three child elements (`<TITLE>`, `<AUTHOR>`, and `<PUBLISHER>`):

```
var novel:XML = <BOOK ISBN="0141182806">
    <TITLE>Ulysses</TITLE>
    <AUTHOR>Joyce, James</AUTHOR>
    <PUBLISHER>Penguin Books Ltd</PUBLISHER>
  </BOOK>;
```

Because the element `<BOOK>` has child elements, converting it to a string yields XML source code:

```
trace(novel.toString());  // Displays:
                          // <BOOK ISBN="0141182806">
                          //    <TITLE>Ulysses</TITLE>
                          //    <AUTHOR>Joyce, James</AUTHOR>
                          //    <PUBLISHER>Penguin Books Ltd</PUBLISHER>
                          // </BOOK>;
```

For an element that contains no child elements, *XML*'s *toString()* returns the text contained by that element, omitting the element's start and end tags. For example, the following code converts the `<TITLE>` element to a string. The result is `Ulysses`, not `<TITLE>Ulysses</TITLE>`.

```
trace(novel.TITLE.toString());  // Displays: Ulysses
```

If we want to retrieve a string including the text node and its containing tags, we use *XML*'s *toXMLString()*, as in:

```
trace(novel.TITLE.toXMLString());  // Displays: <TITLE>Ulysses</TITLE>
```

Notice how E4X's string conversion rules for XML elements change the way leaf text nodes are accessed in ActionScript. In ActionScript 1.0 and ActionScript 2.0, text nodes were accessed using the variable *XML* class's instance variable `firstChild` (which, in ActionScript 3.0, is now the *XMLDocument* class's instance variable `firstChild`). For example, the legacy equivalent to the E4X statement:

```
trace(novel.TITLE.toString());
```

would be:

```
trace(novel.firstChild.firstChild.firstChild);
```

In E4X, the text of an element that contains no child elements can be accessed directly via its containing element's name when used in a string context. Here are two more E4X examples (this time, we've omitted the explicit call to *toString()*

because ActionScript automatically invokes *toString()* on any argument passed to *trace()*):

```
trace(novel.AUTHOR);      // Displays: Joyce, James
trace(novel.PUBLISHER);   // Displays: Penguin Books Ltd
```

And here is a direct comparison between legacy text node access and E4X text node access:

```
// E4X text node access
var msg:XML = <GREETING>
    <TO>World</TO>
    <FROM>J. Programmer</FROM>
    <MESSAGE>Hello</MESSAGE>
    </GREETING>
trace(msg.TO);       // Displays: World
trace(msg.FROM);     // Displays: J. Programmer
trace(msg.MESSAGE);  // Displays: Hello


// Legacy text node access
var msgDoc:XMLDocument = new XMLDocument("<GREETING>"
    + "<TO>World</TO>"
    + "<FROM>J. Programmer</FROM>"
    + "<MESSAGE>Hello</MESSAGE>"
    + "</GREETING>");
trace(msgDoc.firstChild.firstChild.firstChild);    // Displays: World
trace(msgDoc.firstChild.childNodes[1].firstChild); // Displays:
                                                   //      J. Programmer
trace(msgDoc.firstChild.childNodes[2].firstChild); // Displays: Hello
```

Converting an Attribute to a String

For XML instances that represent attributes, *XML*'s *toString()* returns the attribute value only, not the entire attribute definition. For example, the following code converts the preceding <BOOK> element's ISBN attribute to a string. The result is 0141182806 not ISBN='0141182806'.

```
trace(novel.@ISBN.toString());  // Displays: 0141182806
```

Converting Comments and Processing-Instructions to Strings

When *XML*'s *toString()* is called on an *XML* instance that represents a comment or a processing instruction, the entire comment or processing instruction is returned:

```
XML.ignoreComments = false;
XML.ignoreProcessingInstructions = false;

// Create an XML fragment that contains both a comment and a processing
// instruction (shown in bold)
var novel:XML = <BOOK ISBN="0141182806">
    <!--This is a comment-->
    <?someTargetApp someData?>
    <TITLE>Ulysses</TITLE>
```

```
    <AUTHOR>Joyce, James</AUTHOR>
    <PUBLISHER>Penguin Books Ltd</PUBLISHER>
  </BOOK>;

// Convert the comment to a string.
// Displays: <!--This is a comment-->
trace(novel.comments()[0].toString());

// Convert the processing instruction to a string.
// Displays: <?someTargetApp someData?>
trace(novel.processingInstructions()[0].toString());
```

Determining Equality in E4X

The following sections describe ActionScript's special rules for determining the equality of *XML*, *XMLList*, *QName*, and *Namespace* objects. Note, however, that the following sections apply to the equality operator (==) only, not to the strict equality (===) operator. E4X does not modify the semantics of the strict equality operator. Specifically, the strict equality operator considers two instances of *XML*, *XMLList*, *QName* (qualified name), or *Namespace* equal if, and only if, they point to the same object reference.

XML Equality

Two *XML* instances representing elements are considered equal by the equality operator (==) if the XML hierarchy they represent is identical. For example, in the following code, the variables x1 and x2 point to different object references but are considered equal because they represent the same XML hierarchy.

```
var x1:XML = <a><b></b></a>;
var x2:XML = <a><b></b></a>;
trace(x1 == x2);  // Displays: true
```

By default, E4X ignores whitespace nodes, so two *XML* instances representing elements are considered equal when they have the same markup even if they have different formatting. For example, in the following code the XML source code for the *XML* instance in x1 contains no whitespace nodes, while the XML source code for the *XML* instance in x2, contains two whitespace nodes; despite this difference, the instances are still considered equal because the whitespace is ignored, so the XML hierarchies are the same.

```
var x1:XML = <a><b></b></a>;
var x2:XML = <a>
                <b></b>
             </a>;
trace(x1 == x2);  // Still displays: true
```

However, if we force ActionScript not to ignore whitespace nodes prior to parsing, then the *XML* instances will not be considered not equal, as shown next:

```
XML.ignoreWhitespace = false;  // Don't ignore whitespace nodes
var x1:XML = <a><b></b></a>;
var x2:XML = <a>
                <b></b>
             </a>;
trace(x1 == x2);  // Now displays: false
```

An *XML* instance representing an element is considered equal to an *XML* instance representing an attribute if the element contains no child elements and the text contained by the element matches the attribute value. For example, in the following code, the QUANTITY attribute is considered equal to the <COST> element because <COST> has no child elements and contains text that matches QUANTITY's value:

```
var product:XML = <PRODUCT QUANTITY="1"><COST>1</COST></PRODUCT>;
trace(product.@QUANTITY == product.COST);  // Displays: true
```

Similarly, an *XML* instance representing an element is considered equal to an *XML* instance representing a text node if the element contains no child elements, and the text it contains matches the text node's value. For example, in the following code, the text node contained by <COST> is considered equal to the element <QUANTITY> because <QUANTITY> has no child elements and contains text that matches the <COST>'s child text node's value:

```
var product:XML = <PRODUCT>
                    <COST>1</COST>
                    <QUANTITY>1</QUANTITY>
                  </PRODUCT>;
trace(product.COST.*[0] == product.QUANTITY);  // Displays: true
```

In all other cases, if the node kind of two *XML* instances is different, the two are not considered equal. If the node kind is the same, the two are considered equal if:

- The node kind is "attribute," and the attribute values are the same.
- The node kind is "text," and the text of the node is the same.
- The node kind is "comment," and the text between the comments start and end delimiters (<!-- and -->) is the same.
- The node kind is "processing-instruction," and the text between the processing instruction start and end delimiters (<? and ?>) is the same.

XMLList Equality

To determine whether two *XMLList* instances are equal, ActionScript compares each of the instances they contain, in order, using the rules for *XML* equality discussed in the preceding section. If any item in the first *XMLList* instance is considered not equal to any corresponding item in the second *XMLList* instance, then the two *XMLList* instances are not equal. For example, in the following code the *XMLList* returned by msg1.* is considered equal to msg2.* because each *XML* instance in msg1.* is equal to an *XML* instance in the corresponding position in msg2.*:

```
var msg1:XML = <GREETING>
    <TO>World</TO>
    <FROM>J. Programmer</FROM>
    <MESSAGE>Hello</MESSAGE>
  </GREETING>;

var msg2:XML = <GREETING>
    <TO>World</TO>
    <FROM>J. Programmer</FROM>
    <MESSAGE>Hello</MESSAGE>
  </GREETING>;

trace(msg1.* == msg2.*);  // Displays: true
```

A comparison between an *XML* instance and an *XMLList* with only one *XML* instance is treated as a direct comparison between the two *XML* instances:

```
trace(msg1.FROM == msg2.*[1]);  // Displays: true
```

This means that the equality operator (==) considers an *XMLList* containing only one *XML* instance equal to that instance!

```
trace(msg1.FROM == msg1.FROM[0]);  // Displays: true
```

To distinguish an *XMLList* containing only one *XML* instance from the instance it contains, use the strict equality operator (===):

```
trace(msg1.FROM === msg1.FROM[0]);  // Displays: false
```

QName Equality

The *QName* class represents an element or attribute name qualified by a namespace. Two *QName* instances are considered equal if their namespace name and local names both match (i.e., if they have identical values for the uri and localName variables). For example, the following code creates a *QName* object using the *QName* constructor and compares it to a *QName* object retrieved from an XML document. The two *QName* objects have the same namespace name and local name, so they are considered equal.

```
var product:XML = <someCorp:PRODUCT
                   xmlns:someCorp="http://www.example.com/someCorp">
                    <someCorp:PRICE>99.99</someCorp:PRICE>
                  </someCorp:PRODUCT>;

var someCorp:Namespace = product.namespace("someCorp");
var qn1:QName = new QName("http://www.example.com/someCorp", "PRICE");
var qn2:QName = product.someCorp::PRICE.name();

trace(qn1 == qn2);  // Displays: true
```

Namespace Equality

The *Namespace* class represents the qualifier part of a qualified name. Two *Namespace* objects are considered equal if, and only if, they have the same namespace name (i.e., if their uri variables have the same value), regardless of their prefix. For example, the following code creates a *Namespace* object using the *Namespace* constructor and compares it to a *Namespace* object retrieved from an XML document. The two *Namespace* objects have the same URI, so they are considered equal, despite the fact that they have different prefixes.

```
var product:XML = <someCorp:PRODUCT
                      xmlns:someCorp="http://www.example.com/someCorp">
                      <someCorp:PRICE>99.99</someCorp:PRICE>
                  </someCorp:PRODUCT>;
var ns1:Namespace = product.namespace("someCorp");
var ns2:Namespace = new Namespace("sc", "http://www.example.com/someCorp");
trace(ns1 == ns2);  // Displays: true
```

More to Learn

This chapter has covered the majority of E4X's core functionality, but completely exhaustive coverage is beyond the scope of this book. For further study, see the methods and variables of the *XML* an *XMLList* classes in Adobe's ActionScript Language Reference. For deep technical details, consider reading the E4X specification at *http://www.ecma-international.org/publications/standards/Ecma-357.htm*.

Up next, we'll explore Flash Player security restrictions. If researching Flash Player security isn't your idea of a good time, you might want to consider skipping ahead to Part II, where we'll learn how to display things on screen. Just remember that Chapter 19 is there to help if you find yourself faced with security errors during development.

Flash Player Security Restrictions

To protect data from being transferred to unauthorized destinations without appropriate permission, Flash Player scrutinizes all requests to load or access external resources, or interact with other *.swf* files or HTML files. Each request a *.swf* file makes for an external resource (a resource not compiled into the *.swf* file making the request) is rejected or approved based on the following factors:

- The ActionScript operation used to access the resource
- The security status of the *.swf* file performing the request
- The location of the resource
- The explicit access-permissions set for the resource as determined by either the resource's creator or distributor
- The explicit access-permissions granted by the user (e.g., permission to connect to the user's camera or microphone)
- The type of Flash Player running the *.swf* file (e.g., plug-in version, standalone version, Flash authoring tool test version)

In the preceding list, and throughout this chapter, the following terms have the following meanings:

Resource distributor
> The party that delivers a given resource. Typically a server operator such as a web site administrator or socket server administrator.

Resource creator
> The party that actually authors the resource. For *.swf* files, the *resource creator* is the ActionScript developer that compiles the *.swf*.

User
> The user of the computer on which Flash Player is running.

This chapter explains Flash Player security restrictions in general terms, and then explores how security specifically affects loading content and accessing external data.

This chapter covers security restrictions in one specific Flash runtime: Flash Player (both the web browser add-on, and standalone player versions). For information on security limitations imposed by other Flash runtimes (e.g., Adobe AIR and Flash Lite), see Adobe's documentation.

What's Not in This Chapter

Before we start, let's be clear: security is a deep topic. Complete coverage of Flash Player security is beyond the scope of this book. Moreover, this chapter covers security features designed to protect users of Flash content in general but does not discuss the development of secure applications such as e-commerce web sites. For much more information on security—including secure-application development topics such as using Secure Sockets Layer (SSL), coding custom encryption algorithms, and guarding data streamed over RTMP—see the following key resources:

- Adobe's documentation, under Programming ActionScript 3.0 → Flash Player APIs → Flash Player Security
- Adobe's Security Topic Center at *http://www.adobe.com/devnet/security/*
- Adobe's security white paper at: *http://www.adobe.com/go/fp9_0_security*
- Deneb Meketa's "Security Changes in Flash Player 8," which primarily covers local security, at: *http://www.adobe.com/devnet/flash/articles/fplayer8_security.html*
- Deneb Meketa's "Security Changes in Flash Player 7," which primarily covers policy files, at: *http://www.adobe.com/devnet/flash/articles/fplayer_security.html*
- Adobe's Flash Player Help, which covers security settings available to users, at: *http://www.adobe.com/support/documentation/en/flashplayer/help/index.html*

Now let's explore how Flash Player security affects loading content and accessing external data.

The Local Realm, the Remote Realm, and Remote Regions

As we'll see throughout this chapter, ActionScript often bases security restrictions on the locations of *.swf* files and external resources. When evaluating a location from a security perspective, ActionScript makes a distinction between resources in remote locations and resources in local locations. In this chapter, we'll use the term *remote realm* when referring to the logical group of all possible remote locations, such as the Internet. Correspondingly, we'll use the term *local realm* when referring to the logical group of all possible local locations. A local location is any location that the user of the computer on which Flash Player is running can access using either the file:

protocol (typically used to access the local filesystem) or a universal naming convention (UNC) path (typically used to access computers on a local area network).

The remote realm is, itself, further divided into distinct regions delimited conceptually by resource distributor. We'll call these distributor-delimited regions *remote regions*. Specifically, a remote region is any one of the following:

- An Internet domain
- An Internet subdomain
- An IP address that points to a computer in the remote realm

Hence, according to the preceding list:

- *sitea.com* is a different remote region than *siteb.com*
- *games.example.com* is a different remote region than *finances.example.com*
- 192.150.14.120 is a different remote region than 205.166.76.26
- 192.150.14.120 is a different remote region than *adobe.com*, even though 192.150.14.120 resolves to *adobe.com* (because Flash Player considers numerically specified IP addresses distinct from their equivalent domain names)

 The terms *remote realm*, *local realm*, and *remote region* are not currently part of Adobe's official security vocabulary. They are used by this book for expository purposes only.

Security-Sandbox-Types

ActionScript assigns a security status known as a *security-sandbox-type* to every *.swf* file opened by or loaded into Flash Player. There are four possible security-sandbox-types: *remote*, *local-with-filesystem*, *local-with-networking*, and *local-trusted*. Each security-sandbox-type defines a distinct set of rules that governs a *.swf* file's ability to perform external operations. Specifically, the types of external operations a security-sandbox-type can potentially prohibit include:

- Loading content
- Accessing content as data
- Cross-scripting
- Loading data
- Connecting to a socket
- Sending data to an external URL
- Accessing the user's camera and microphone
- Accessing local shared objects
- Uploading or downloading files selected by the user

- Scripting an HTML page from a *.swf* file and vice versa
- Connecting to a *LocalConnection* channel

In this chapter, we'll see how each security-sandbox-type governs the first five of the preceding types of external operations. To learn how security-sandbox-types govern the remaining types of external operations, see Adobe's documentation, under Programming ActionScript 3.0 → Flash Player APIs → Flash Player Security. Note that when an operation fails due to Flash Player security restrictions, ActionScript either generates a *SecurityError* or dispatches a `SecurityErrorEvent.SECURITY_ERROR` event. For details on handling security error conditions, see the section "Handling Security Violations," near the end of this chapter.

How Security-Sandbox-Types Are Assigned

To determine a given *.swf* file's security-sandbox-type, ActionScript first considers the location from which the *.swf* file was loaded or opened. All *.swf* files from the remote realm are assigned the security-sandbox-type *remote*. By contrast, *.swf* files from the local realm are assigned one of the remaining three security-sandbox-types—*local-trusted*, *local-with-networking*, or *local-with-filesystem*. The specific security-sandbox-type assigned to a local *.swf* file depends on two factors:

- Whether the *.swf* file was compiled with network support (see the section "Choosing a Local Security-Sandbox-Type," later in this chapter)
- Whether the *.swf* file is explicitly trusted (a *.swf* file is said to be explicitly trusted if it is opened from a trusted local location; see the section "Granting Local Trust," later in this chapter)

All *.swf* files from the local realm that are explicitly trusted are assigned the security-sandbox-type *local-trusted*. Likewise, executable projector files (i.e., standalone files containing a *.swf* file and a particular version of Flash Player) are always trusted.

All *.swf* files from the local realm that are not explicitly trusted are assigned either the security-sandbox-type *local-with-networking* (for *.swf* files compiled with network support) or the security-sandbox-type *local-with-filesystem* (for *.swf* files compiled without network support).

For brevity in this chapter, we'll refer to *.swf* files whose security-sandbox-type is *remote* as *remote .swf files*. Likewise, we'll use the terms *local-with-filesystem .swf file*, *local-with-networking .swf file*, and *local-trusted .swf file* when referring to *.swf* files whose security-sandbox-type is *local-with-filesystem*, *local-with-networking*, and *local-trusted*, respectively.

As a rule, *local-with-networking .swf* files have more access to the remote realm than to the local realm. By contrast, *local-with-filesystem .swf* files have more access to the local realm than to the remote realm.

To check a *.swf* file's security-sandbox-type at runtime, retrieve the value of the `flash.system.Security.sandboxType` variable from within that *.swf* file.

Because Flash Player assigns all *.swf* files from the remote realm a security-sandbox-type of *remote*, developers creating *.swf* content for the Web must always work within the limitations of the *remote* security-sandbox-type. By contrast, developers creating *.swf* content intended to be loaded or opened locally can use compiler settings, configuration files, installers, and instructions to choose between the three local security-sandbox-types. By choosing a security-sandbox-type, developers creating local *.swf* content effectively select a logical set of external-access capabilities for their content. In the upcoming sections we'll explore how security-sandbox-types govern a *.swf* file's external-access capabilities, then we'll take a closer look at the mechanisms for, and rationale behind, selecting from among the three local security-sandbox-types.

Security Generalizations Considered Harmful

Over the remainder of this chapter, we'll study specific operations and specific security limitations in precise detail. When describing security rules, this book is careful not to generalize at the expense of the accuracy because security generalizations are often the source of frustrating misconceptions. During your study of Flash Player security, you should likewise be wary of forming overly general impressions. Be mindful that when documentation or third-party resources generalize about Flash Player security, they could be underemphasizing important exceptions. For example, the following statement is mostly true, and, therefore, makes a tempting generalization:

> A *.swf* file whose security-sandbox-type is *local-with-filesystem* has full access to the local realm.

However, there are many notable exceptions to that statement, including:

- *local-with-filesystem* *.swf* files cannot connect to sockets.
- *local-with-filesystem* *.swf* files cannot load *local-with-networking* *.swf* files.
- *local-with-filesystem* *.swf* files cannot access the data of *local-trusted* *.swf* files without creator permissions.
- Accessing the user's camera and microphone requires the user's permission.
- Users can disable or limit any *.swf* file's ability to store data in local shared objects.

In order to avoid confusion, when you face a security issue in your development, always focus on specifics. Determine the specific operation you wish to perform, this security-sandbox-type of your *.swf* file, and the specific limitations that security-sandbox-type imposes on the operation you are performing. Once you have this information, you can confidently decide how to work within or around any security limitations.

 This chapter does not cover every single security limitation imposed by ActionScript. To determine the limitations ActionScript places on any operation not covered in this chapter, consult that operation's entry in Adobe's ActionScript Language Reference.

Now let's explore how each of the four security-sandbox-types govern loading content, accessing content as data, cross-scripting, and loading data.

Restrictions on Loading Content, Accessing Content as Data, Cross-Scripting, and Loading Data

Most developers encounter ActionScript's security system for the first time when an operation they expect to succeed is blocked for security reasons. In this section, we'll study four of the most-often blocked external operations: loading content, accessing content as data, cross-scripting, and loading data. After defining each, we'll look at the circumstances under which these common operations are blocked.

Loading Content

Loading content means retrieving any external resource in order to subsequently display or play it. Conceptually, loading-content operations enable developers to present external content to the user, even in cases where ActionScript's security rules restrict programmatic access to that content's data.

The ActionScript methods considered to be "loading-content" operations from a security perspective are listed in the leftmost column of Table 19-1.

Table 19-1. Content-loading operations

Content-loading method	Type of content	Specific file formats supported by Flash Player 9
flash.display.Loader.load( )	Image, Adobe Flash	JPEG, GIF, PNG, SWF
flash.media.Sound.load( )	Audio	MP3
flash.net.NetStream.play( )	Progressive Video	FLV

For convenience, this chapter occasionally uses the term *content resources* when referring to resources loaded using one of the methods listed in Table 19-1. Note, however, that it is the specific method used to load the resource—not the file type of the resource—that makes an external operation a loading-content operation. For example, loading a JPEG using the *Loader* class's instance method *load( )* is considered a loading-content operation, but loading the very same *JPEG* over a binary socket or using the *URLLoader* class's instance method *load()* is not considered a content load operation. The distinction is important because different security rules apply to different categories of operations.

Accessing Content as Data

Accessing content as data means reading the internal information of a content resource—for example, reading the pixels of a bitmap or the spectrum of a sound. Table 19-2 presents the ActionScript methods considered "accessing-content-as-data" operations from a security perspective.

Table 19-2. Accessing content as data, example operations

Operation	Description
Access an image via the *Loader* class's instance variable content	Retrieve the ActionScript *Bitmap* object representing a loaded image
Invoke the *BitmapData* class's instance method *draw( )*	Copy the pixels of a display asset to a *BitmapData* object
Invoke the *SoundMixer* class's instance method *computeSpectrum( )*	Copy the current sound wave data to a *ByteArray*
Access the *Sound* class's instance variable id3	Read a sound's ID3 metadata

Cross-Scripting

Cross-scripting means accessing a loaded *.swf* file programmatically. Many Action-Script operations can be used to cross-script a *.swf* file, including, but not limited to:

- Using the *Loader* class's instance variable content to retrieve the object representing the loaded *.swf* file
- Accessing the loaded *.swf* file's variables
- Calling the loaded *.swf* file's methods
- Referencing a class defined by the loaded *.swf* file
- Using the *BitmapData* class's instance method *draw()* to copy the loaded *.swf* file's pixels to a *BitmapData* object

Other cross-scripting operations can be found in Adobe's ActionScript Language Reference, which explicitly notes any security restrictions that apply to each Action-Script operation.

Loading Data

In a general sense, the term "loading data" could be used to describe a wide variety of Flash Player load operations, including downloading files from a server via the *FileReference* class's instance method *download()*, loading objects with Flash Remoting, loading binary data over a *Socket* object, and so on. However, for the purposes of the current discussion (and the remainder of this chapter), *loading data* means either:

- Loading external text, binary data, or variables using the *URLLoader* class's instance method *load( )*
- Loading data using the *URLStream* class's instance method *load( )*

 To determine the limitations ActionScript places on data load operations not covered in this chapter, consult Adobe's ActionScript Language Reference.

For the *URLLoader* class's instance method *load( )*, the format of the loaded data (text, binary, or variables) is determined by the *URLLoader* class's instance variable dataFormat variable. Typical text file formats include XML, TXT, and HTML. Typical binary data formats include images, *.swf* files, and serialized objects encoded in ActionScript Message Format (AMF); however, binary data can be any file or content loaded into a *ByteArray* for processing in raw binary format. Variables come in one format only: URL-encoded variables loaded as name/value pairs from an external text file or script.

Note that, similar to content loading, the specific method used to load the resource—not the file type of the resource—makes an external operation a loading-data operation. For example, loading a *.swf* file using *URLLoader*'s *load( )* method is considered a *loading-data* operation; loading that same *.swf* file using *Loader*'s *load( )* method is considered a *loading-content* operation.

Restrictions on Loading Content, Accessing Content as Data, Loading Data, and Cross-Scripting

Now that we understand specifically what constitutes loading content, accessing content as data, cross-scripting, and loading data, let's look at how each of Flash Player's four security-sandbox-types limits those operations.

The upcoming four tables—Tables 19-3, 19-4, 19-5, and 19-6—catalog the circumstances under which each security-sandbox-type allows and prohibits loading content, accessing content as data, cross-scripting, and loading data. Each table presents the specific regulations enforced by a single security-sandbox-type, indicating whether the external operations listed in the leftmost column are allowed or prohibited when used to access the resources listed in the remaining columns. As indicated in the tables, some operations are allowed by creator or distributor permission only. *Creator permission* means a *.swf* file contains the appropriate call to the *Security* class's static method *allowDomain( )* (or, in rare cases, to *allowInsecureDomain( )*). *Distributor permission* means the resource distributor has made the appropriate cross-domain policy file available. For more information, see the sections "Creator Permissions (allowDomain())" and "Distributor Permissions (Policy Files)," later in this chapter.

As Table 19-3 through Table 19-6 reveal, loading content is allowed in more situations than accessing content as data, cross-scripting, or loading data. For example, an application might be permitted to load and display a bitmap image but be denied access to that image's underlying pixel data. Likewise, an application might be permitted to load and display an external *.swf* file but require permission to cross-script that *.swf* file.

Note that Tables 19-3 through 19-6 cover permissions for a single direction of communication only, a *.swf* file loads or accesses an external resource. The tables do not cover the reverse direction of communication in which a loaded *.swf* file communicates with the *.swf* file that loaded it. For information on bidirectional communication between *.swf* files, see Adobe's documentation, under Programming ActionScript 3.0 → Flash Player APIs → Flash Player Security → Cross-scripting.

Table 19-3 lists the regulations imposed by the *remote* security-sandbox-type. In the table, the phrase ".*swf*'s region of origin" means the remote region from which the *.swf* file was opened or loaded. For example, if *hiscores.swf* is loaded from the remote location *http://coolgames.com/hiscores.swf*, then *hiscores.swf*'s *region of origin* is *coolgames.com* (for details on remote regions, see the earlier section "The Local Realm, the Remote Realm, and Remote Regions").

Table 19-3 illustrates the following key *remote* security-sandbox-type rules:

- Loading-content, accessing-content-as-data, cross-scripting, and loading-data operations cannot be used with resources from the local realm.
- All resources from the entire remote realm can be loaded as content.
- Loading-content, accessing-content-as-data, cross-scripting, and loading-data operations can be used with all resources from the *.swf* file's region of origin.
- Remote realm resources outside the *.swf*'s region of origin can be accessed as data or loaded as data if the appropriate distributor permission is granted.
- Remote realm *.swf* files outside the *.swf*'s region of origin can be cross-scripted if the appropriate creator permission is granted.

Table 19-3. Remote sandbox, selected authorized, and prohibited operations

Operation	Local realm	Remote realm resources from .swf's region of origin	Remote realm resources outside .swf's region of origin
Loading content	Prohibited	Allowed	Allowed
Accessing content as data	Prohibited	Allowed	Allowed by distributor permission only
Cross-scripting	Prohibited	Allowed	Allowed by creator permission only

Table 19-3. Remote sandbox, selected authorized, and prohibited operations (continued)

Operation	Local realm	Remote realm resources from .swf's region of origin	Remote realm resources outside .swf's region of origin
Loading data	Prohibited	Allowed	Allowed by distributor permission only

Table 19-4 lists the regulations imposed by the *local-with-filesystem* security-sandbox-type. The table illustrates the following key *local-with-filesystem* security-sandbox-type rules:

- Loading-content, accessing-content-as-data, cross-scripting, and loading-data operations cannot be used with resources from the remote realm.
- Loading-content, accessing-content-as-data, and loading-data operations can be used with all non-.*swf* resources from the local realm.
- Loading *local-with-networking* .*swf* files is strictly prohibited.
- Loading and cross-scripting other *local-with-filesystem* .*swf* files is allowed.
- Cross-scripting *local-trusted* .*swf* files requires creator permission.

Table 19-4. Local-with-filesystem sandbox, selected authorized, and prohibited operations

Operation	Non-.swf resources in the local realm	local-with-filesystem .swf files	local-with-networking .swf files	local-trusted .swf files	Remote-realm resources
Loading content	Allowed	Allowed	Prohibited	Allowed	Prohibited
Accessing content as data	Allowed	n/a	n/a	n/a	Prohibited
Cross-scripting	n/a	Allowed	Prohibited	Allowed by creator permission only	Prohibited
Loading data	Allowed	n/a	n/a	n/a	Prohibited

Table 19-5 lists the regulations imposed by the *local-with-networking* security-sandbox-type. The table illustrates the following key *local-with-networking* security-sandbox-type rules:

- Loading-content operations can be used with resources from the remote realm.
- Loading-data and accessing-content-as-data operations can be used with remote-realm resources if the appropriate distributor permission is granted.
- Loading-content operations can be used with non-.*swf* resources from the local realm.
- Loading-data and accessing-content-as-data operations cannot be used with resources from the local realm.
- Loading *local-with-filesystem* .*swf* files is strictly prohibited.

- Loading and cross-scripting other *local-with-networking .swf* files is allowed.
- Cross-scripting *local-trusted .swf* files or *remote .swf* files requires creator permission.

Table 19-5. Local-with-networking sandbox, selected authorized, and prohibited operations

Operation	Non-*.swf* resources in the local realm	*local-with-filesystem .swf* files	*local-with-networking .swf* files	*local-trusted .swf* files	Remote-realm resources
Loading content	Allowed	Prohibited	Allowed	Allowed	Allowed
Accessing content as data	Prohibited	n/a	n/a	n/a	Allowed by distributor permission only
Cross-scripting	n/a	Prohibited	Allowed	Allowed by creator permission only	Allowed by creator permission only
Loading data	Prohibited	n/a	n/a	n/a	Allowed by distributor permission only

Table 19-6 lists the regulations imposed by the *local-trusted* security-sandbox-type. The table illustrates the only *local-trusted* security-sandbox-type rule:

- Loading-content, accessing content as data, cross-scripting, and loading-data operations can be used with any resource from both the local and remote realms

The local trusted *security-sandbox-type* gives a *.swf* file the greatest possible level of freedom Flash Player offers.

Table 19-6. Local-trusted sandbox, selected authorized, and prohibited operations

Operation	Non-*.swf* resources in the local realm	*local-with-filesystem .swf* files	*local-with-networking .swf* files	*local-trusted .swf* files	Remote-realm resources
Content loading	Allowed	Allowed	Allowed	Allowed	Allowed
Accessing content as data	Allowed	n/a	n/a	n/a	Allowed
Cross-scripting	n/a	Allowed	Allowed	Allowed	Allowed
Data loading	Allowed	n/a	n/a	n/a	Allowed

We've now seen how four types of operations are regulated by each of the four security-sandbox-types. Before we move to other security topics, let's look at one last type of operation: connecting to a socket.

Socket Security

In ActionScript, socket connections are made with the *XMLSocket*, *Socket*, and *NetConnection* classes. Table 19-7 and Table 19-8 list the specific locations and ports to which the *XMLSocket* and *Socket* methods can open socket connections. The tables do not cover the *NetConnection* class, which is used with Adobe Flash Media Server and Adobe Flex. For information on *NetConnection* security, see the documentation for those products.

In both Table 19-7 and Table 19-8, *distributor permission* means the socket-server operator has made the appropriate cross-domain policy file available; see the section "Distributor Permissions (Policy Files)," later in this chapter.

Table 19-7 describes whether a *remote* .swf file can make a socket connection to the four locations listed.

Table 19-7. Remote sandbox authorized and prohibited socket connections

Local realm, any port	Remote realm, within .swf's region of origin, port 1024 and higher	Remote realm, within .swf's region of origin, port 1023 and lower	Remote realm, outside .swf's region of origin, any port
Allowed by distributor permission only	Allowed	Allowed by distributor permission only	Allowed by distributor permission only

Table 19-8 describes whether a .swf file with the security-sandbox-type in the leftmost column can make a socket connection to the locations listed in the remaining columns.

Table 19-8. Local sandboxes authorized and prohibited socket connections

Security-sandbox-type	Local realm, any port	Remote realm, any port
Local-with-filesystem	Prohibited	Prohibited
Local-with-networking	Allowed by distributor permission only	Allowed by distributor permission only
Local-trusted	Allowed	Allowed

Example Security Scenarios

To give the information we've studied so far a practical context, let's look at a few examples where Flash Player's security system prevents data from being retrieved by an unauthorized party. Each scenario presents the technique a hacker would use to access data if there were no Flash Player security and then describes how Flash Player's security system prevents the hacker from accessing the target data.

Snoopy Email Attachment—Without Flash Player Security

Joe Hacker wants to perform an identity theft on Dave User. Joe knows that Dave reports his taxes using ABCTax software on Microsoft Windows. Joe does a little research, and finds that ABCTax keeps each year's tax return information in an XML file stored in the following location: *c:\ABCTax\taxreturn.xml*. If Joe can get that file, he can use the information it contains to open a bank account and apply for credit cards in Dave's name. So Joe sends Dave an email with a harmless looking animation, *cartoon.swf*, as an attachment. Dave opens the email and watches the cartoon in a web browser on his local machine. Without Dave's knowledge, *cartoon.swf* secretly uses *URLLoader.load()* to retrieve *taxreturn.xml* from the local filesystem. Then, *cartoon.swf* uses *flash.net.sendToURL()* to upload *taxreturn.xml* to Joe's web site.

Joe gets a credit card in Dave's name and buys a Nintendo Wii with lots of great games.

Snoopy Email Attachment—With Flash Player Security

As before, Joe sends Dave an email with a harmless looking animation, *cartoon.swf*, as an attachment. Dave opens the email and watches the cartoon in a web browser on his local machine. Because *cartoon.swf* is opened from the local realm, Flash Player checks whether the *cartoon.swf* file was compiled with network support. Let's first suppose that *cartoon.swf* was compiled without network support. In that case, Flash Player assigns *cartoon.swf* the *local-with-filesystem* security-sandbox-type. As before, *cartoon.swf* secretly uses *URLLoader.load()* to retrieve *taxreturn.xml* from the local filesystem. According to Table 19-4, *cartoon.swf* is allowed to load that local data. Then, *cartoon.swf* attempts to use *flash.net.sendToURL()* to upload *taxreturn.xml* to Joe's web site, but the attempt is blocked because *local-with-filesystem .swf* files are not allowed to perform *flash.net.sendToURL()* operations. (Our earlier tables didn't specifically cover the security restrictions for *flash.net.sendToURL()*, but as mentioned earlier, you can determine the security restrictions that apply to any method in the Flash Player API by consulting Adobe's ActionScript Language Reference.)

Now let's suppose that *cartoon.swf* was compiled with network support. In that case, Flash Player assigns *cartoon.swf* the *local-with-networking* security-sandbox-type. As before, *cartoon.swf* attempts to secretly use *URLLoader.load()* to retrieve *taxreturn.xml* from the local filesystem. But the attempt is blocked because, per Table 19-5, *local-with-networking .swf* files cannot use data-load operations with resources from the local realm.

Joe has to buy his own Nintendo Wii.

Internal Corporate Information—Without Flash Player Security

Joe Hacker wants some insider information for a stock deal. Joe used to work at WYZ Corporation. WYZ Corporation's public web site is *www.wyzcorp.com*. Joe left WYZ on good terms, so WYZ has hired him on contract to update the company profile, *profile.swf*, on *www.wyzcorp.com*. Joe knows that WYZ is planning to release an important product that will affect the company's stock price. Joe also knows that WYZ Corporation keeps its future product release dates on an internal web site that is behind the company firewall, at the following location: *strategy.wyzcorp.com/releasedates.html*. If Joe can secretly obtain the new product's release date, he can buy WYZ stock the day before the product ships and sell it at a profit later.

So Joe adds some code to *profile.swf* that uses *URLLoader.load( )* to attempt to load the file: *strategy.wyzcorp.com/releasedates.html*. An employee of WYZ then views the company's profile at, *www.wyzcorp.com/profile.swf*. Because the employee's computer is behind the firewall, it has access to *strategy.wyzcorp.com*, so the attempt to load *releasedates.html* succeeds! Without the employee's knowledge, *profile.swf* uses *flash.net.sendToURL( )* to upload *releasedates.html* to Joe's web site.

WYZ's stock takes off, and Joe retires to a life of painting and urban exploration.

Internal Corporate Information—With Flash Player Security

As before, Joe posts *profile.swf* to *www.wyzcorp.com*, and *profile.swf* uses *URLLoader. load( )* to attempt to load the file: *strategy.wyzcorp.com/releasedates.html*. An employee of WYZ then views the company's profile at, *www.wyzcorp.com/profile.swf*. Because *profile.swf* is opened from the remote realm, ActionScript assigns it the *remote* security-sandbox-type. When *www.wyzcorp.com/profile.swf* attempts to load *strategy.wyzcorp.com/releasedates.html,* the attempt is blocked because, per Table 19-3, a *remote .swf* file cannot use data-load operations with resources outside its remote region of origin.

Joe hopes to get a gig making banner ads for WYZ's new product so he can pay next month's rent.

Cross-Web Site Information—Without Flash Player Security

Joe Hacker wants to steal some bank account information. Joe works at Hipster Ad Agency, which produces advertising for ReallyHuge Bank. ReallyHuge Bank has an online banking application posted at *www.reallyhugebank.com/bank.swf*. The *bank.swf* application loads advertising from *www.hipsteradagency.com/ad.swf*. Joe has looked at *bank.swf* with a *.swf* decompiler, and knows the variables in which *bank.swf* stores its users' bank account numbers and passwords. Maliciously, Joe adds code to *ad.swf* that reads those variables from its parent, *bank.swf* and then uses *flash.net.sendToURL( )* to send the stolen information to Joe's web site. Whenever a *bank.swf* user logs into an account, Joe receives the account number and password.

Joe donates a mysteriously large amount of money to Greenpeace.

Cross-Web Site Information—With Flash Player Security

As before, Joe adds code to *ad.swf* that reads those variables from its parent, *bank.swf*. A user launches *www.reallyhugebank.com/bank.swf*, and *bank.swf* loads Joe's ill-intentioned *www.hipsteradagency.com/ad.swf*. Because *ad.swf* is opened from the remote realm, ActionScript assigns it the *remote* security-sandbox-type. When *ad.swf* attempts to read *bank.swf*'s variables, the attempt is blocked because, per Table 19-3, a *remote* *.swf* file cannot use data-load operations with resources outside its remote region of origin.

Joe donates a modest amount of money to Greenpeace.

Choosing a Local Security-Sandbox-Type

We now have a good understanding of the safeguards provided by each security-sandbox-type. We've also seen that *.swf* files opened or loaded from remote realm locations are always assigned the *remote* security-sandbox-type, and that *.swf* files opened or loaded from local realm locations are assigned one of three local security-sandbox-types. Now let's take a closer look at the mechanisms involved in choosing between those three local security-sandbox-types. Each of the following three sections presents a scenario in which a developer uses one of the three local security-sandbox-types. Each scenario describes both the rationale for, and mechanism for choosing, each security-sandbox-type.

Compiling a Local-with-Filesystem .swf File

Susan is developing a calendar application, *calendar.swf*, to be posted on a hotel's web site. The calendar loads holiday information from an external XML file, *holiday.xml*. The application is near complete, so Susan needs to send it to her client for review. Even though *calendar.swf* will eventually be posted on a web site, the client wants to demonstrate it to a variety of people at the hotel. The client won't always have an Internet connection available during demonstrations. Hence, Susan sends both *calendar.swf* file and *holiday.xml* to the client.

In order to allow *calendar.swf* to load *holiday.xml* from the local filesystem during the client's demonstrations, Susan compiles calendar *.swf* with the -use-network compiler flag set to `false`. Depending on the authoring tool Susan is using, she uses different mechanisms to set the -use-network compiler flag. In Flex Builder 2, Susan follows these steps to set the -use-network compiler flag to `false`:

1. In the Navigator panel, Susan selects the project folder for the calendar application.

2. On the Project Menu, she chooses Properties.

3. On the Properties dialog, she chooses ActionScript Compiler.

4. Under Additional compiler arguments, she enters: -use-network=false.

5. To confirm the setting, Susan clicks OK.

In Flash authoring tool, Susan follows these steps to set the -use-network compiler flag to false:

1. On the File menu, Susan chooses Publish Settings.

2. On the Publish Settings dialog, she chooses the Flash tab.

3. In the Local playback security pulldown-menu she chooses Access local files only.

4. To confirm the setting, Susan clicks OK.

When using the Flex SDK command-line compiler, Susan specifies the value of the -use-network flag as an argument to *mxmlc*. Here is the command Susan issues when she's working on Microsoft Windows:

```
mxmlc.exe -use-network=false -file-specs c:\projects\calendar\Calendar.as
-output c:\projects\calendar\bin\Calendar.swf
```

Compiling a Local-with-Networking .swf File

Dorian is making a video game, *race.swf*, for her company's web site. Visitors to the web site can play the game online and submit their high scores. Dorian wants to make a downloadable version of the game available for people to play when they are not connected to the Internet. When the user is not connected, the downloadable game will retain the user's high score in a local shared object and submit the score to the high-score server the next time the user connects to the Internet.

Dorian knows that the general public prefers not to run executable files from unknown sources, so she chooses to make her game available as a downloadable *.swf* file rather than an executable projector. To allow the game to connect to the high-score server when running as a local *.swf* file, Dorian compiles *race.swf* with the -use-network compiler flag set to true.

To set the -use-network flag, Dorian uses the exact same techniques that Susan used in the preceding *calendar.swf* scenario but specifies the value true instead of false when setting -use-network. When using Flash, for "Local playback security," Dorian chooses "Access network only" instead of "Access local files only."

Granting Local Trust

Colin is making an administrator tool, *admin.swf*, for a socket server application. The *admin.swf* file is intended to run either on the same domain as the socket server or on the server administrator's local filesystem. The administrator tool connects to a remote socket server and does not load any local files, so Colin compiles it as a *local-with-networking .swf* file.

The administrator tool's first screen presents a simple server name and password login form. When the user logs in, the administrator tool offers to remember the server's password. If the user accepts the offer, the administrator tool stores the password in a local shared object. Next time the user logs in, the administrator tool automatically populates the login form's password text field.

During development, Colin suddenly realizes that because *admin.swf* is a *local-with-networking .swf* file, other *local-with-networking .swf* files on the same computer as *admin.swf* will be permitted to load *admin.swf* and read the password out of the text field!

To prevent this possible breach of security, Colin wisely decides that *admin.swf* must be assigned the *local-trusted* security-sandbox-type. If *admin.swf* 's security-sandbox-type is *local-trusted*, then other *local-with-networking .swf* files will not be able to read the password text field.

To make *admin.swf* a local trusted *.swf* file, Colin writes an installer that designates *admin.swf* 's location as a trusted location by placing a configuration file in the local machine's Global Flash Player Trust directory. Following ActionScript's official format for local-trust configuration files, the configuration file contains only a single line of text: the local filesystem location of *admin.swf*. As a result, when Flash Player loads *admin.swf* from that specified location, it sets *admin.swf* 's security-sandbox-type to *local-trusted*.

 For complete coverage of creating and managing local-trust configuration files, see Adobe's documentation, under Programming ActionScript 3.0 → Flash Player APIs → Flash Player Security → Overview of permission controls → Administrative user controls.

Colin also recognizes that users of the administration tool might want to move *admin.swf* to arbitrary new locations. To allow the user to move *admin.swf* to a new location without losing its *local-trusted* status, Colin includes the instructions in the administration tool's documentation (see sidebar).

The socket-server-administration-tool scenario just presented demonstrates the two available mechanisms for classifying a local *.swf* file as trusted: configuration files on the computer running Flash Player (which Colin's installer provided) and the Flash Player Settings Manager (accessed by the user). For complete coverage of the Flash

Player Settings Manager, see Adobe's documentation, under Programming Action-Script 3.0 → Flash Player APIs → Flash Player Security → Overview of permission controls → User controls.

Note that if Flash Player is running when trust is granted (via either configuration files or the Flash Player Settings Manager), the new trust status for the affected *.swf* file(s) does not come into effect until Flash Player is restarted. For the plug-in and ActiveX control versions of Flash Player "restarting" means shutting down all instances of Flash Player—even those in other browser windows!

Developers Automatically Trusted

To simplify the testing of local content that is intended for web deployment, Adobe's Flex Builder 2 automatically grants trust to projects under development. To grant trust, it adds a path entry for each project's output folder (typically, */bin/*) to the *flexbuilder.cfg* file in the User Flash Player Trust directory. Likewise, the Flash authoring tool's Test Movie-mode Player automatically trusts all local-realm *.swf* files it opens or loads.

Consequently, when loading assets during development, you might not encounter security violations that would affect your enduser. For example, a *.swf* file in a project's */bin/* folder would be allowed to load a local file, even if it has network-only permissions.

To test your application as your end user will see it, be sure to run it in its target environment. For example, for web-based applications, be sure to test over the Web. For nontrusted local applications created in Flex Builder 2, test from a local nontrusted directory (the system desktop is typically a nontrusted directory). For nontrusted local applications created in the Flash authoring tool, use File → Publish Preview → HTML to preview in a browser (the Flash authoring tool does not automatically trust content previewed in a browser).

During testing you should always explicitly verify that your application's security-sandbox-type matches the security-sandbox-type you intend to use during deployment.

To check a *.swf* file's security-sandbox-type at runtime, retrieve the value of the `flash.system.Security.sandboxType` variable from within that *.swf* file.

To manually verify which directories are trusted on a given computer, consult the trust files in the User Flash Player Trust directory and the Global Flash Player Trust directory, and the online Flash Player Settings Manager at: *http://www.adobe.com/ support/documentation/en/flashplayer/help/index.html*.

To remove trust for a Flex Builder 2 project (thus simulating the end-user experience for nontrusted applications), delete the appropriate path entry in the *flexbuilder.cfg* file in the User Flash Player Trust directory. Note, however, that because Flex Builder 2 automatically restores the *flexbuilder.cfg* file when it creates a new project, you will have to delete the path entry every time you create or import a project. For the location of the User and Global trust directories, see Adobe's documentation, under Programming ActionScript 3.0 → Flash Player APIs → Flash Player Security → Overview of permission controls.

Default Local Security-Sandbox-Type

Both Flex Builder 2 and the command line compiler *mxmlc* set the `-use-network` compiler flag to `true` when it is not specified. Hence, by default, when a *.swf* file compiled with either Flex Builder 2 or *mxmlc* runs in the local realm in any nontrusted location, it will be assigned the *local-with-networking* security-sandbox-type.

By perhaps surprising contrast, the Flash authoring tool's default value for the "Local playback security" publishing option is "Access local files only." Therefore, by default, when a *.swf* file compiled with the Flash authoring tool runs in the local realm in any nontrusted location, it will be assigned the *local-with-filesystem* security-sandbox-type.

To avoid confusion, always explicitly specify your desired value for the `-use-network` compiler flag and the Flash authoring tool's "Local playback security" publishing option.

Distributor Permissions (Policy Files)

Throughout this chapter, we've seen plenty of ways in which Flash Player's security system restricts a *.swf* file's access to foreign resources. Now let's examine how, in some cases, a resource distributor can use *distributor permissions* to override those restrictions.

Recall that a "resource distributor" is the party that delivers a resource from a given remote region. For example, a web site administrator and a socket-server administrator are both resource distributors.

As the party responsible for a given remote region's resources, a resource distributor can grant *.swf* files from foreign origins access to those resources. To grant *.swf* files access to a given set of resources, a resource distributor uses a special permission mechanism known as a *policy file*. A policy file is a simple XML document that contains a list of trusted *.swf* file origins. In general terms, a policy file gives *.swf* files from its list of trusted origins access to resources that would otherwise be inaccessible due to Flash Player's security restrictions.

The types of operations a policy file can potentially authorize are:

- Accessing content as data
- Loading data
- Connecting to a socket
- Import loading (discussed separately in the later section "Import Loading")

A policy file cannot authorize cross-scripting operations. For information on authorizing cross-scripting, see the section "Creator Permissions (allowDomain( ))."

Typically, policy files are used to enable interoperation between different remote regions. For example, a policy file might give *http://site-a.com/map.swf* permission to read the pixels of *http://site-b.com/satellite-image.jpg* or permission to load *http://site-b.com/map-data.xml*.

Per Table 19-3, Table 19-5, Table 19-7, and Table 19-8, a policy file can give a *.swf* file access to otherwise inaccessible resources in the following situations:

- When a *remote .swf* file attempts to perform an accessing-content-as-data operation on a remote-realm resource outside its region of origin
- When a *remote .swf* file attempts to perform a loading-data operation on a remote-realm resource outside its region of origin
- When a *local-with-networking .swf* file attempts to perform an accessing-content-as-data operation on a remote-realm resource
- When a *local-with-networking .swf* file attempts to perform a loading-data operation on a remote-realm resource
- When a *remote .swf* file attempts to connect to a socket within its region of origin, but below port 1024
- When a *remote .swf* file attempts to connect to a socket outside its region of origin

- When a *local-with-networking* *.swf* file attempts to connect to a socket in the remote realm

The upcoming sections explore how a resource distributor can use a policy file to authorize access to resources in each of the preceding situations.

For additional policy-file coverage, see Adobe's documentation, under Programming ActionScript 3.0 → Flash Player APIs → Flash Player Security → Overview of permission controls → Web Site controls (cross-domain policy files).

 In Flash Player 6, policy files were used to allow cross-domain communication only, and were, therefore, called *cross-domain policy files*. Since Flash Player 7.0.19.0, policy files have also been used to allow socket connections to low-range ports. To reflect this broader purpose, this book uses the shorter term *policy file*, but you should expect to see the original term, *cross-domain policy file*, in other documentation.

Authorizing Loading-Data and Accessing-Content-as-Data Operations

To grant *.swf* files from a given set of origins authorization to perform loading-data or accessing-content-as-data operations on a given set of remote resources, follow these general steps:

1. Create a policy file.
2. Post the policy file within the same remote region (i.e., domain or IP address) as the resource to which authorization is being granted.

The next two sections cover the preceding steps in detail. Once we've studied how to create and post policy files, we'll examine the process by which a *.swf* file obtains permission from a policy file to perform loading-data and accessing-content-as-data operations.

Creating the policy file

To create a policy file, follow these steps:

1. Create a new text file.
2. Add a list of the desired authorized origins to the policy file, using Adobe's official policy-file syntax.
3. Save the text file.

Adobe's official policy-file syntax is XML-based and has the following structure:

```
<?xml version="1.0"?>
<!DOCTYPE cross-domain-policy
  SYSTEM "http://www.adobe.com/xml/dtds/cross-domain-policy.dtd">
```

```
<cross-domain-policy>
  <allow-access-from domain="domainOrIP"/>
</cross-domain-policy>
```

where *domainOrIP* specifies the domain name or IP address of an authorized origin. A *.swf* file loaded from an authorized origin is permitted to perform loading-data and accessing-content-as-data operations on a given set of resources. As we'll learn in the next section, the specific set of resources to which a policy file grants access is determined by the location from which the policy file is served.

Any number of <allow-access-from> tags can be included in a policy file. For example, the following policy file defines three authorized origins: example1.com, example2.com, and example3.com.

```
<?xml version="1.0"?>
<!DOCTYPE cross-domain-policy
  SYSTEM "http://www.adobe.com/xml/dtds/cross-domain-policy.dtd">
<cross-domain-policy>
  <allow-access-from domain="example1.com"/>
  <allow-access-from domain="example2.com"/>
  <allow-access-from domain="example3.com"/>
</cross-domain-policy>
```

Within the value of the domain attribute, the * character indicates a wildcard. For example, the following policy file authorizes example1.com and any subdomain of example1.com, no matter how deeply nested (e.g., games.example1.com, driving. games.example1.com, and so on):

```
<?xml version="1.0"?>
<!DOCTYPE cross-domain-policy
  SYSTEM "http://www.adobe.com/xml/dtds/cross-domain-policy.dtd">
<cross-domain-policy>
  <allow-access-from domain="*.example1.com"/>
</cross-domain-policy>
```

When used on its own, the * character authorizes all origins:

```
<?xml version="1.0"?>
<!DOCTYPE cross-domain-policy
  SYSTEM "http://www.adobe.com/xml/dtds/cross-domain-policy.dtd">
<cross-domain-policy>
  <allow-access-from domain="*"/>
</cross-domain-policy>
```

To include the local realm as an authorized origin, a policy file must explicitly trust *all* origins by specifying * (any origin) for the domain attribute. Hence, a web site wishing to make XML files loadable by *local-with-networking .swf* files *must* specify * for the domain attribute.

Posting the policy file

Once a policy file has been created, it must be posted within the same remote region (i.e., domain or IP address) as the resource to which access is being granted. For example, if the policy file grants access to content at *www.example.com*, then the policy file must also be posted at *www.example.com*.

The set of resources to which a policy file grants access is determined by the specific location at which it is posted. When a policy file is posted in the root directory of a web site, it grants access to the entire web site. For example, a policy file posted at *http://www.example.com* grants access to all content at *www.example.com*.

When a policy file is posted in a subdirectory of a web site, it grants access to that directory and its child subdirectories only. For example, a policy file posted at *http://www.example.com/assets* grants access to all content in the */assets/* directory and its subdirectories, but does not grant access to content in the root directory of *www.example.com*, nor to any other subdirectory on *www.example.com*.

To help automate the loading of policy files, ActionScript defines a default name and location for policy files. Any policy file that is named *crossdomain.xml* and is placed in the root directory of a web site is said to reside in the *default policy file location*, and is known as the web site's *default policy file*. As we'll learn in the next two sections, placing a policy file in the default policy file location reduces the amount of code required to obtain that policy file's permissions.

Obtaining a policy file's permission to load data

When a web site has a default policy file authorizing a given remote region, *.swf* files from that remote region can load data from that web site by simply performing the desired loading-data operation. For example, suppose *site-a.com* has the following default policy file, which authorizes *site-b.com* and *www.site-b.com*:

```
<?xml version="1.0"?>
<!DOCTYPE cross-domain-policy
  SYSTEM "http://www.adobe.com/xml/dtds/cross-domain-policy.dtd">
<cross-domain-policy>
  <allow-access-from domain="www.site-b.com"/>
  <allow-access-from domain="site-b.com"/>
</cross-domain-policy>
```

To load *http://site-a.com/assets/file.xml*, any *.swf* file from *www.site-b.com* or *site-b.com* would use the following code:

```
var urlloader:URLLoader = new URLLoader();
urlloader.load(new URLRequest("http://site-a.com/assets/file.xml"));
```

Because *site-a.com*'s policy file is in the default location, Flash Player finds it automatically and allows *file.xml* to load.

On the other hand, if a web site's policy file is posted in a nondefault location, *.swf* files from authorized remote regions must manually load that policy file before attempting to load data from that web site. To manually load a policy file, we use the *Security* class's static method *loadPolicyFile()*, which has the following general form:

```
Security.loadPolicyFile("http://domainOrIP/pathToPolicyFile");
```

In the preceding generalized code, *domainOrIP* is the domain or IP address at which the policy file is posted, and *pathToPolicyFile* is the location of the policy file on that server. Note that, as mentioned earlier, Flash Player considers numerically specified IP addresses distinct from their equivalent domain names.

For example, suppose *site-c.com* posts the following policy file at *http://site-c.com/assets/policy.xml*; the policy file authorizes *site-d.com* and *www.site-d.com*.

```
<?xml version="1.0"?>
<!DOCTYPE cross-domain-policy
  SYSTEM "http://www.adobe.com/xml/dtds/cross-domain-policy.dtd">
<cross-domain-policy>
  <allow-access-from domain="www.site-d.com"/>
  <allow-access-from domain="site-d.com"/>
</cross-domain-policy>
```

To load *http://site-c.com/assets/file.xml*, any *.swf* file from *www.site-d.com* or *site-d.com* would use the following code:

```
// Load policy file first
Security.loadPolicyFile("http://site-c.com/assets/policy.xml");
// Then perform the load operation
var urlloader:URLLoader = new URLLoader();
urlloader.load(new URLRequest("http://site-c.com/assets/file.xml"));
```

Notice that the preceding code issues the loading-data command immediately after issuing the policy-file-loading command. Flash Player automatically waits for the policy file to load before proceeding with the loading-data operation.

Once a policy file has been loaded via *Security.loadPolicyFile()*, its authorization remains in effect for all future loading-data operations issued by the *.swf* file. For example, the following code manually loads a policy file, and then performs two load operations that both rely on that policy file's authorization:

```
// Load policy file once
Security.loadPolicyFile("http://site-c.com/assets/policy.xml");
// Perform two authorized load operations
var urlloader1:URLLoader = new URLLoader();
urlloader1.load(new URLRequest("http://site-c.com/assets/file1.xml"));
var urlloader2:URLLoader = new URLLoader();
urlloader2.load(new URLRequest("http://site-c.com/assets/file2.xml"));
```

Let's consider a practical example showing how a policy file posted in a web site's subdirectory might be used in a real-world situation. Suppose Graham runs a free stock-information web site, *stock-feeds-galore.com*. Graham stores his latest stock feed in an XML file, in the following location:

```
stock-feeds-galore.com/latest/feed.xml
```

Graham wants to make the contents of the */latest/* directory publicly accessible to all Flash files from any origin but does not want to make the entire web site accessible.

Hence, Graham posts the following policy file, named *policy.xml*, in the */latest/* directory (notice the use of the domain wildcard, *):

```
<?xml version="1.0"?>
<!DOCTYPE cross-domain-policy
  SYSTEM "http://www.adobe.com/xml/dtds/cross-domain-policy.dtd">
<cross-domain-policy>
  <allow-access-from domain="*"/>
</cross-domain-policy>
```

Graham then posts a notice on *stock-feeds-galore.com* telling ActionScript developers that the location of the policy file is:

```
stock-feeds-galore.com/latest/policy.xml
```

Meanwhile, James is creating a stock-ticker application, *stockticker.swf*, which he intends to post at his web site, *www.some-news-site.com*. James' application loads Graham's stock feed. Because *www.stock-feeds-galore.com*'s policy file is not in the default location, James must load the policy file before loading the stock feed. Here's the code James uses to load Graham's policy file:

```
Security.loadPolicyFile("http://stock-feeds-galore.com/latest/policy.xml")
```

After issuing the request to load the policy file, James uses a *URLLoader* object to load the *feed.xml* file, as follows:

```
var urlLoader:URLLoader = new URLLoader( );
urlLoader.load(new URLRequest(
                    "http://stock-feeds-galore.com/latest/feed.xml"));
```

In response, Flash Player loads *http://stock-feeds-galore.com/latest/policy.xml*, finds the required authorization within that policy file, and then proceeds with the loading of *feed.xml*.

Now that we've seen how to obtain a policy file's permission to load data, let's explore how to obtain a policy file's permission to perform an accessing-content-as-data operation.

Obtaining a policy file's permission to access content as data

The code we use to obtain a policy file's permission to access content as data varies according to the type of data being accessed. To obtain a policy file's permission to access an *image* as data, follow these steps:

1. If the policy file is not in the default location, load it with *Security.loadPolicyFile()* (as discussed in the previous section).
2. Create a LoaderContext object, and set its checkPolicyFile variable to true.
3. Load the desired image with *Loader.load()*; for *Loader.load()*'s context parameter, pass the LoaderContext object from Step 2.
4. Once the image has loaded, perform the accessing-content-as-data operation.

For example, suppose *site-a.com* posts the following policy file at *http://site-a.com/assets/policy.xml*; the policy file authorizes *site-b.com* and *www.site-b.com*.

```
<?xml version="1.0"?>
<!DOCTYPE cross-domain-policy
  SYSTEM "http://www.adobe.com/xml/dtds/cross-domain-policy.dtd">
<cross-domain-policy>
  <allow-access-from domain="www.site-b.com"/>
  <allow-access-from domain="site-b.com"/>
</cross-domain-policy>
```

To access *http://site-a.com/assets/image.jpg* as data, any *.swf* file from *www.site-b.com* or *site-b.com* would use the following code:

```
// Step 1: The policy file is not in the default location,
//         so load it manually.
Security.loadPolicyFile("http://site-a.com/assets/policy.xml");

// Step 2: Create a LoaderContext object and set
//         its checkPolicyFile variable to true.
var loaderContext = new LoaderContext();
loaderContext.checkPolicyFile = true;

// Step 3: Load the image. Pass the LoaderContext object to Loader.load().
theLoader.load(new URLRequest("http://site-a.com/assets/image.jpg"),
                            loaderContext);

// Step 4: Later, once the application has verified that the image
//         has finished loading, access the image as data
trace(theLoader.content);
```

To obtain a policy file's permission to access a foreign *sound* as data, follow these steps:

1. If the policy file is not in the default location, load it with *Security.loadPolicyFile()* (as discussed in the preceding section).

2. Create a SoundLoaderContext object, and set its checkPolicyFile variable to true.

3. Load the desired sound with the *Sound* class's instance method *load()*. For *load()*'s context parameter, pass the SoundLoaderContext object from Step 2.

4. Once the sound has sufficiently loaded (as determined by using the *Sound* class's load-progress events), perform the authorized accessing-content-as-data operation.

For example, suppose *site-c.com* has the following default policy file, which authorizes *site-d.com* and *www.site-d.com*:

```
<?xml version="1.0"?>
<!DOCTYPE cross-domain-policy
  SYSTEM "http://www.adobe.com/xml/dtds/cross-domain-policy.dtd">
<cross-domain-policy>
  <allow-access-from domain="www.site-d.com"/>
  <allow-access-from domain="site-d.com"/>
</cross-domain-policy>
```

To access *http://site-c.com/sounds/song.mp3* as data, any *.swf* file from *www.site-d. com* or *site-d.com* would use the following code:

```
// Step 1: The policy file is in the default location, so no need to
//         manually load it

// Step 2: Create a SoundLoaderContext object and set
//         its checkPolicyFile variable to true.
var soundLoaderContext = new SoundLoaderContext();
soundLoaderContext.checkPolicyFile = true;

// Step 3: Load the sound. Pass the SoundLoaderContext object
//         to Loader.load().
theSound.load(new URLRequest("http://example.com/sounds/song.mp3"),


// Step 4: Later, once the application has verified that the sound's
// ID3 data loaded (as indicated by the Event.ID3 event), access the
// sound as data
trace(theSound.id3);
```

Note that setting either the *LoaderContext* or the *SoundLoaderContext* class's instance variable checkPolicyFile to true does not determine whether an asset is loaded. When either *Loader's load()* or *SoundLoader's load()* method runs, the asset is always loaded, even when no policy file authorizes the requesting *.swf* file's region of origin; however, if code in that *.swf* file later attempts to access the loaded asset as data, Flash Player will throw a *SecurityError* exception.

Let's look at a real-world example showing how a web site's default policy file might be used to authorize an accessing-content-as-data operation.

Remember Graham's *stock-feeds-galore.com* web site? It's doing so well that Graham finds himself with some time on his hands. He decides to experiment with Action-Script bitmap programming and creates a facial-recognition application that can automatically add a funny party hat to any photo of a person's face. Graham's pretty pleased with himself.

Graham's friend Andy runs a lottery corporation with a promotional web site, *www.lotterylotterylottery.com*. Andy sees Graham's party-hat application and decides it would make a good marketing campaign. In the campaign, lottery winners post their photos to *photos.lotterylotterylottery.com*. The main site, *www.lotterylotterylottery.com*, then picks a random photo for the home page, showing a lottery winner wearing a party hat. Andy hires Graham to produce the code for the campaign.

Graham puts his facial-recognition application, *partyhat.swf*, on *www.lotterylotterylottery.com*. He then writes a Perl script, *randompic.pl*, that returns a random photo (*.jpg* file) from *photos.lotterylotterylottery.com*. He places *randompic.pl* in *photos.lotterylotterylottery.com/cgi-bin*.

The *partyhat.swf* file from *www.lotterylotterylottery.com* needs access to the pixels of loaded photos from *photos.lotterylotterylottery.com*. To authorize that access,

Graham places the following policy file in the root of *photos.lotterylotterylottery.com* and names it *crossdomain.xml*:

```
<?xml version="1.0"?>
<!DOCTYPE cross-domain-policy
  SYSTEM "http://www.adobe.com/xml/dtds/cross-domain-policy.dtd">
<cross-domain-policy>
  <allow-access-from domain="www.lotterylotterylottery.com"/>
  <allow-access-from domain="lotterylotterylottery.com"/>
</cross-domain-policy>
```

Notice that Graham is careful to include both *www.lotterylotterylottery.com* and *lotterylotterylottery.com* in the policy file. That way, *partyhat.swf* will function properly when loaded from either of those URLs. Graham is also careful to exclude the domain "*" because his policy applies to specific domains only, not to the entire world.

To load a photo, Graham uses the following code. (Notice that *Security.loadPolicyFile()* is not needed because Graham posted the policy file in the default policy file location.)

```
var loaderContext = new LoaderContext();
loaderContext.checkPolicyFile = true;
loader.load(
    new URLRequest("http://photos.lotterylotterylottery.com/randompic.pl"),
    loaderContext);
```

In response, Flash Player loads *http://photos.lotterylotterylottery.com/crossdomain.xml*, finds the required authorization within that policy file, loads the photo returned by *randompic.pl*, and then allows *partyhat.swf* to access to the pixels of the loaded photo.

Once the photo is loaded, *partyhat.swf* safely accesses the loaded photo. For example, here's the code Graham uses to run the *partyhat.swf* method that adds the party hat to the loaded photo (notice that the loaded image's *Bitmap* object, `loader.content`, is referenced by permission):

```
addHat(loader.content);
```

Now that we've seen how to use a policy file to authorize loading-data and accessing-content-as-data operations, let's explore how to use a policy file to authorize socket connections.

Using a Policy File to Authorize Socket Connections

To authorize socket connections with a policy file follow these general steps:

1. Create the policy file.
2. Serve the policy file via a socket server or an HTTP server running on the same domain or IP as the desired socket connection.

The next three sections cover the preceding steps in detail.

Create the policy file

Policy files that grant permission to perform socket connections have the same basic syntax as policy files that grant permission to perform loading-data and accessing-content-as-data operations. However, in policy files that grant permission to perform socket connections, the `<allow-access-from>` tag includes an additional attribute, to-ports, as shown in the following code:

```
<?xml version="1.0"?>
<!DOCTYPE cross-domain-policy
  SYSTEM "http://www.adobe.com/xml/dtds/cross-domain-policy.dtd">
<cross-domain-policy>
  <allow-access-from domain="domainOrIP" to-ports="ports"/>
</cross-domain-policy>
```

The *to-ports* attribute specifies the ports to which a *.swf* file from *domainOrIP* is authorized to connect. The ports can be listed individually (separated by commas), or in ranges (separated by the - character). For example, the following policy file grants the following permissions:

- *.swf* files from *example1.com* can connect to ports 9100 and 9200.
- *.swf* files from *example2.com* can connect to ports 10000 through 11000.

```
<?xml version="1.0"?>
<!DOCTYPE cross-domain-policy
  SYSTEM "http://www.adobe.com/xml/dtds/cross-domain-policy.dtd">
<cross-domain-policy>
  <allow-access-from domain="example1.com" to-ports="9100,9200"/>
  <allow-access-from domain="example2.com" to-ports="10000-11000"/>
</cross-domain-policy>
```

Within the value of *to-ports*, the * character acts as a wildcard; when a policy file is retrieved over a socket on a port less than 1024, * indicates that access to any port is authorized; when a policy file is retrieved over a socket on a port greater than or equal to 1024, * indicates that access to any port greater than or equal to 1024 is authorized.

> Because ports under 1024 are considered sensitive, a policy file served over port 1024 or greater can never authorize access to ports below 1024, even if those ports are listed specifically.

For example, if the following policy file is served on port 2000, it grants *.swf* files from *example3.com* permission to connect to all ports greater than or equal to 1024.

```
<?xml version="1.0"?>
<!DOCTYPE cross-domain-policy
  SYSTEM "http://www.adobe.com/xml/dtds/cross-domain-policy.dtd">
<cross-domain-policy>
  <allow-access-from domain="example3.com" to-ports="*"/>
</cross-domain-policy>
```

But when the very same policy file is served on port 1021 (which is less than 1024), it grants *.swf* files from *example3.com* permission to connect to *any* port.

Therefore, to grant *.swf* files from *any* location permission to connect to *any* port, we would serve the following policy file on a port below 1024:

```
<?xml version="1.0"?>
<!DOCTYPE cross-domain-policy
  SYSTEM "http://www.adobe.com/xml/dtds/cross-domain-policy.dtd">
<cross-domain-policy>
  <allow-access-from domain="*" to-ports="*"/>
</cross-domain-policy>
```

When a policy file is retrieved over a socket, to-ports is mandatory; if it is not specified, access is not granted to any port.

Now that we know how to create a policy file that authorizes a socket connection, let's examine how a *.swf* file can obtain that policy file's authorization.

Socket-based policy-file retrieval

Policy files that authorize socket connections can be served either directly over a socket or via HTTP. Policy files served over a socket must be served on the same domain or IP as the desired socket connection, either on the same port as the desired socket connection, or on a different port. In either case, the server running on the port over which the policy file is served must communicate with Flash Player using a very simple policy-file-retrieval protocol. The protocol consists of a single tag, <policy-file-request/>, which Flash Player sends over the socket when it wishes to load a policy file authorizing a socket connection. In response, the socket server is expected to send Flash Player the text of the policy file in ASCII format, plus a zero byte (i.e., the ASCII null character), and then close the connection.

Hence, custom servers that wish to handle both policy file requests and normal communications over the same port must implement code to respond to policy-file requests as well as code to manage normal socket communications. When a server handles policy file requests and normal communications over the same port, *.swf* files from authorized regions can connect to that server by performing the desired socket connection operation. For example, suppose a multiuser game server running at *site-a.com* is designed to handle both game communication and policy file requests over port 3000. The game server's policy file authorizes *www.site-b.com* and *site-b.com*, as follows:

```
<?xml version="1.0"?>
<!DOCTYPE cross-domain-policy
  SYSTEM "http://www.adobe.com/xml/dtds/cross-domain-policy.dtd">
<cross-domain-policy>
  <allow-access-from domain="www.site-b.com" to-ports="3000"/>
  <allow-access-from domain="site-b.com" to-ports="3000"/>
</cross-domain-policy>
```

To connect to port 3000 at *site-a.com*, any *.swf* file loaded from *www.site-b.com* or *site-b.com* would use the following code:

```
var socket:Socket = new Socket();
try {
  socket.connect("site-a.com", 3000);
} catch (e:SecurityError) {
  trace("Connection problem!");
  trace(e.message);
}
```

When the preceding code runs, before the requested connection to port 3000 is allowed, Flash Player automatically makes a separate connection to port 3000 and sends a ⟨policy-file-request/⟩ message to the game server. The game server responds with *site-a.com*'s policy file and then closes the connection. That policy file contains the connecting *.swf* file's origin as an authorized region, so the original socket connection is then allowed to proceed. In all, two separate connections are made: one for the policy file, and, subsequently, one for the original socket-connection request.

In some situations, it might not be practical or possible for a server to respond to a Flash Player policy-file request. For example, a *.swf* file might wish to connect to an existing SMTP mail server that does not understand the meaning of the instruction ⟨policy-file-request/⟩. To authorize the connection, the mail server administrator must make a policy file available via a different port at the same domain or IP address as the mail server. The server at that different port can be an extremely simple socket server that merely listens for connections, receives ⟨policy-file-request/⟩ instructions, returns a policy file in response, and then closes the connection.

When a policy file is served on a different port than the desired socket connection (as is the case in our mail server example), *.swf* files from authorized regions must load that policy file manually before requesting the desired socket connection. To load a policy file manually from an arbitrary port, we use the following general code:

```
Security.loadPolicyFile("xmlsocket://domainOrIP:portNumber");
```

where *domainOrIP* is the domain or IP address of the server, and *portNumber* is the port number over which to retrieve the policy file. Once again, Flash Player considers numerically specified IP addresses distinct from their equivalent domain names. In the preceding code, notice the mandatory use of the special xmlsocket:// protocol. The protocol name, "xmlsocket," describes the type of connection used to retrieve the policy file, not the type of connection the policy file authorizes.

 A policy file loaded using the xmlsocket:// protocol authorizes connections made via both *Socket* and *XMLSocket*, not just *XMLSocket*.

Once a manual request to load a policy file has been issued, a follow-up request to connect to the desired port can immediately be issued. For example, suppose *site-c.com* runs a simple policy file server on port 1021, and that *site-c*'s policy file authorizes *site-d.com* and *www.site-d.com* to connect to port 25. Here's the policy file:

```
<?xml version="1.0"?>
<!DOCTYPE cross-domain-policy
  SYSTEM "http://www.adobe.com/xml/dtds/cross-domain-policy.dtd">
<cross-domain-policy>
  <allow-access-from domain="www.site-d.com" to-ports="25"/>
  <allow-access-from domain="site-d.com" to-ports="25"/>
</cross-domain-policy>
```

To connect to port 25 at *site-c.com*, any *.swf* file loaded from *site-d.com* or *www.site-d.com* would use the following code. Notice that the *.swf* file requests the socket connection to port 25 immediately after issuing the request to load the policy file over port 1021. Flash Player patiently waits for the policy file to load before proceeding with the connection to port 25.

```
// Load the policy file manually
Security.loadPolicyFile("xmlsocket://site-c.com:1021");
var socket:Socket = new Socket();
try {
  // Attempt the connection (immediately after policy file has
  // been requested)
  socket.connect("site-c.com", 25);
} catch (e:SecurityError) {
  trace("Connection problem!");
  trace(e.message);
}
```

When the preceding code runs, before allowing the requested connection to port 25, Flash Player makes a separate connection to port 1021 and sends a <policy-file-request/> message to the server listening on that port. The server on port 1021 responds with *site-c.com*'s policy file and then closes the connection. That policy file contains the connecting *.swf* file's origin as an authorized region, so the connection to port 25 is then allowed to proceed.

Now let's take a look at an alternative way to authorize a socket-connection: HTTP-based policy files.

HTTP-based policy-file retrieval

Prior to Flash Player 7.0.19.0, Flash Player required policy files authorizing socket connections to be served over HTTP. Primarily for backwards compatibility, Action-Script 3.0 continues to support the authorization of socket connections by policy files served over HTTP. However, in order to authorize a socket connection, a policy file served via HTTP must meet the following requirements:

- It must be named *crossdomain.xml*.
- It must reside in the web server's root directory.

- It must be served over port 80 at the domain or IP address of the desired socket connection.
- In ActionScript 3.0, it must be manually loaded via *Security.loadPolicyFile()*.

Furthermore, policy files served via HTTP do not use the to-ports attribute; instead, they simply grant access to all ports greater than or equal to 1024.

 A policy file served via HTTP cannot authorize socket connections to ports under 1024. (However, note that due to a bug, this rule was not enforced prior to Flash Player Version 9.0.28.0.)

To gain an HTTP-based policy file's permission to perform a given socket connection, we must manually load that policy file before attempting the connection, as shown in the following general code:

```
Security.loadPolicyFile("http://domainOrIP/crossdomain.xml");
```

In the preceding code, *domainOrIP* is the exact domain or IP address of the desired socket connection.

Once a request to load a policy file over HTTP has been issued, a follow-up request to connect to the desired port can immediately be issued. For example, suppose *site-a.com* has the following policy file posted on a web server at *http://site-a.com/crossdomain.xml*; the policy file authorizes *site-b.com* and *www.site-b.com*:

```
<?xml version="1.0"?>
<!DOCTYPE cross-domain-policy
  SYSTEM "http://www.adobe.com/xml/dtds/cross-domain-policy.dtd">
<cross-domain-policy>
  <allow-access-from domain="www.site-b.com"/>
  <allow-access-from domain="site-b.com"/>
</cross-domain-policy>
```

To connect to port 9100 at *site-a.com*, any *.swf* file loaded from *site-b.com* or *www.site-b.com* would use the following code.

```
// Request policy file via HTTP before making connection attempt
Security.loadPolicyFile("http://site-a.com/crossdomain.xml");
var socket:Socket = new Socket();
try {
  // Attempt connection (immediately after policy file has
  // been requested)
  socket.connect("site-a.com", 9100);
} catch (e:SecurityError) {
  trace("Connection problem!");
  trace(e.message);
}
```

When the preceding code runs, before allowing the requested connection to port 9100, Flash Player loads *site-c.com*'s policy file over HTTP. That policy file contains the connecting *.swf* file's origin as an authorized region, so the connection to port 9100 is then allowed to proceed.

We're now finished studying the ways in which a resource distributor can give foreign *.swf* files permission to load data, access content as data, and connect to sockets. In the next section, we'll continue our study of Flash Player's permission mechanisms, examining how a *.swf* file's creator can grant cross-scripting permissions to *.swf* files from foreign origins.

Creator Permissions (allowDomain( ))

We've just learned that distributor permissions are used to authorize accessing-content-as-data, loading-data, and socket-connection operations. Distributor permissions are so named because they must be put in place by the distributor of the resource to which they grant access.

By contrast, *creator permissions* are permissions put in place by the creator of a *.swf* file rather than its distributor. Creator permissions are more limited than distributor permissions; they affect cross-scripting and HTML-to-SWF scripting operations only.

 This book does not cover HTML-to-SWF-scripting operations. For details on security and HTML-to-SWF scripting, see the entries for the *Security* class's static methods *allowDomain()* and *allowInsecureDomain()* in Adobe's ActionScript Language Reference.

Unlike distributor permissions, which are served independently of the content to which they grant access, creator permissions are issued from within *.swf* files. By calling *Security.allowDomain()* in a *.swf* file, a developer can grant *.swf* files from foreign origins permission to cross-script that *.swf* file. For example, if *app.swf* includes the following line of code:

```
Security.allowDomain("site-b.com");
```

then any *.swf* file loaded from *site-b.com* can cross-script *app.swf*. Furthermore, because the call to *allowDomain()* occurs within a *.swf* file, the permissions granted are effective no matter where that *.swf* file is posted.

 In contrast to distributor permissions, creator permissions travel with the *.swf* file in which they occur.

The *allowDomain()* method has the following general form:

```
Security.allowDomain("domainOrIP1", "domainOrIP2",..."domainOrIPn")
```

where *"domainOrIP1"*, *"domainOrIP2"*,...*"domainOrIPn"* is a list of strings containing the domain names or IP addresses of authorized origins. A *.swf* file loaded from an authorized origin can perform cross-scripting operations on the *.swf* file that invoked *allowDomain()*.

As with policy files, the * character indicates a wildcard. For example, the following code authorizes all origins (i.e., any *.swf* file from any origin can cross-script the *.swf* file that contains the following line of code):

```
Security.allowDomain("*");
```

To include the local realm as an authorized origin, *allowDomain()* *must* specify * (any origin) as an authorized domain. For example, a *.swf* file wishing to allow cross-scripting by *local-with-networking .swf* files must specify * as an authorized domain.

However, when used with *allowDomain()*, the * character cannot be used as a sub-domain wildcard. (This contrasts, somewhat confusingly, with policy file wildcard usage.) For example, the following code does not authorize all subdomains of *example.com*:

```
// Warning: Do not use this code! Subdomain wildcards are not supported.
Security.allowDomain("*.example.com");
```

Once an *allowDomain()* invocation completes, any *.swf* file from an authorized origin can immediately perform authorized operations. For example, suppose a television network maintains a generic animation player application posted at *www.sometvnetwork.com*. The animation player loads animations in *.swf*-format from *animation.sometvnetwork.com*. To control the playback of the loaded animations, the animation player invokes basic *MovieClip* methods (*play()*, *stop()*, etc.) on them. Because the animation player and the animations it loads originate from different subdomains, the animation player must obtain permission to invoke *MovieClip* methods on the animations. Each animation's main class constructor, hence, includes the following line of code, which gives the animation player the permission it needs:

```
Security.allowDomain("www.sometvnetwork.com", "sometvnetwork.com");
```

Notice that because the animation player can be opened via *www.sometvnetwork.com* or *sometvnetwork.com*, the animation files grant permission to both domains. To load the animations, the animation player uses the following code:

```
var loader:Loader = new Loader();
loader.load(
    new URLRequest("http://animation.sometvnetwork.com/animationName.swf"));
```

As soon as each animation's main class constructor method runs, the animation player can immediately begin controlling the loaded animation.

To ensure that cross-scripting permissions are applied immediately after a *.swf* file initializes, call *Security.allowDomain()* within that *.swf* file's main class constructor method.

A *.swf* file can determine whether it is currently authorized to cross-script a loaded *.swf* file by checking the childAllowsParent variable of the loaded *.swf* file's *LoaderInfo* object.

For more information on loading *.swf* files, see Chapter 28. For information on invoking movie clip methods on loaded *.swf* files, see the section "Compile-time Type Checking for Runtime-Loaded Assets" in Chapter 28.

Allowing .swf Files Served Over HTTP to Cross-Script .swf Files Served Over HTTPS

When a *.swf* file is served over HTTPS, Flash Player prevents *allowDomain()* call from granting authorization to non-HTTPS origins. However, developers wishing to authorize non-HTTPS origins from a *.swf* file served over HTTPS can, with due caution, use *Security.allowInsecureDomain()*.

Authorizing a non-HTTPS origin from a *.swf* file loaded over HTTPS is considered dangerously insecure and is strongly discouraged.

The syntax and usage of *allowInsecureDomain()* is identical to that of *allowDomain()*, as discussed in the previous section. The *allowInsecureDomain()* method is different only in its ability to authorize non-HTTPS origins from a *.swf* file served over HTTPS. In the vast majority of situations, you should use *allowDomain()* rather than *allowInsecureDomain()* when issuing creator permissions. For a description of the special situations that call for the use of *allowInsecureDomain()*, see *Security.allowInsecureDomain()* in Adobe's ActionScript Language Reference.

Import Loading

In Chapter 28, we'll see how a parent *.swf* file can load a child *.swf* file in a special way that lets the parent use the child's classes directly, as though they were defined by the parent. The technique requires that the parent *.swf* file import the child *.swf* file's classes into its *application domain*. Here's the basic code required in the parent *.swf* file (notice the use of the *LoaderContext* class's instance variable applicationDomain):

```
var loaderContext:LoaderContext = new LoaderContext( );
loaderContext.applicationDomain = ApplicationDomain.currentDomain;
var loader:Loader = new Loader( );
```

```
loader.load(new URLRequest("child.swf"), loaderContext);
```

When the preceding code runs, the attempt to import the child's classes into the parent's application domain will be blocked by Flash Player's security system in the following situations:

- If the parent *.swf* file and the child *.swf* file are loaded from different remote regions in the remote realm
- If the parent *.swf* file is loaded from the local realm and has a different security-sandbox-type than the child *.swf* file

In the first of the preceding cases, the distributor of the child *.swf* file can use a policy file to give the parent *.swf* file permission to import the child *.swf* file's classes. The steps required by the child *.swf* file's distributor and the parent *.swf* file's creator are as follows:

1. The child *.swf* file's distributor must post a policy file authorizing the parent *.swf* file's origin, as shown in the earlier section, "Distributor Permissions (Policy Files)."
2. If the policy file is not in the default location, the parent must load it manually with *Security.loadPolicyFile()*, again, per the earlier section, "Distributor Permissions (Policy Files)."
3. When loading the child *.swf* file, the parent *.swf* file must pass *load()* a *LoaderContext* object whose securityDomain variable is set to flash.system. SecurityDomain.currentDomain.

For example, suppose *site-a.com* has the following default policy file, which authorizes *site-b.com* and *www.site-b.com*:

```
<?xml version="1.0"?>
<!DOCTYPE cross-domain-policy
  SYSTEM "http://www.adobe.com/xml/dtds/cross-domain-policy.dtd">
<cross-domain-policy>
  <allow-access-from domain="www.site-b.com"/>
  <allow-access-from domain="site-b.com"/>
</cross-domain-policy>
```

Now suppose *site-b.com/parent.swf* wants to import *site-a.com/child.swf*'s classes into its application domain. To do so, *site-b.com/parent.swf* uses the following code (notice that *Security.loadPolicyFile()* is not used because the policy file is in the default policy file location):

```
var loaderContext:LoaderContext = new LoaderContext();
loaderContext.applicationDomain = ApplicationDomain.currentDomain;
loaderContext.securityDomain    = SecurityDomain.currentDomain;
loader.load(new URLRequest("http://site-a.com/child.swf"), loaderContext);
```

Using the securityDomain variable to gain distributor permission to import a *.swf* file's classes into an application domain (as shown in the preceding code) is known as *import loading*.

Note that when a given *.swf* file, *a.swf*, uses import loading to load another *.swf* file, *b.swf*, Flash Player treats *b.swf* as though it were first copied to, and then loaded directly from *a.swf*'s server. Hence, *b.swf* adopts *a.swf*'s security privileges, and *b.swf*'s original security relationship with its actual origin is annulled. For example, *b.swf* file loses the ability to access resources from its actual origin via relative URLs. Hence, when using import loading, always test whether the loaded *.swf* file continues to function as desired once loaded.

Import loading is not required in the following situations because the parent *.swf* file is inherently permitted to import the child *.swf* file's classes into its application domain:

- A local *.swf* imports classes from another local *.swf* with the same security-sandbox-type.

- A remote *.swf* imports classes from another remote *.swf* from the same remote region.

For a full discussion of accessing classes in loaded *.swf* files, see the section "Compile-time Type Checking for Runtime-Loaded Assets" in Chapter 28 and see Chapter 31.

Handling Security Violations

Throughout this chapter we've seen a variety of security rules that govern a *.swf* file's ability to perform various ActionScript operations. When an operation fails because it violates a security rule, ActionScript 3.0 either throws a *SecurityError* exception or dispatches a SecurityErrorEvent.SECURITY_ERROR.

A *SecurityError* exception is thrown when an operation can immediately be judged to be in violation of a security rule. For example, if a *local-with-filesystem .swf* file attempts to open a socket connection, ActionScript immediately detects a security violation and throws a *SecurityError* exception.

By contrast, a SecurityErrorEvent.SECURITY_ERROR event is dispatched when, after waiting for some asynchronous task to complete, ActionScript deems an operation in violation of a security rule. For example, when a *local-with-networking .swf* file uses the *URLLoader* class's instance method *load()* to load a file from the remote realm, ActionScript must asynchronously check for a valid policy file authorizing the load operation. If the policy-file check fails, ActionScript dispatches a SecurityErrorEvent.SECURITY_ERROR event (note, not a *SecurityError* exception).

In the debug version of Flash Player, uncaught *SecurityError* exceptions and unhandled SecurityErrorEvent.SECURITY_ERROR events are easy to spot; every time one occurs, Flash Player launches a dialog box explaining the problem. By stark contrast, in the release version of Flash Player, uncaught *SecurityError* exceptions and unhandled SecurityErrorEvent.SECURITY_ERROR events cause a silent failure that can be extremely difficult to diagnose.

To ensure that no security violation goes unnoticed, always test code in the debug version of Flash Player.

To handle security errors, we use the *try/catch/finally* statement. To handle SecurityErrorEvent.SECURITY_ERROR events, we use event listeners. For example, the following code generates a *SecurityError* by attempting to open a socket connection to a port above 65535. When the error occurs, the code adds a failure message to an onscreen *TextField*, output.

```
var socket:Socket = new Socket( );
try {
  socket.connect("example.com", 70000);
} catch (e:SecurityError) {
  output.appendText("Connection problem!\n");
  output.appendText(e.message);
}
```

Similarly, by attempting to load a datafile from a web site that does not have a policy file, a *local-with-networking .swf* file containing the following code would cause a SecurityErrorEvent.SECURITY_ERROR event. Before attempting the load operation, the code registers an event listener that executes when the SecurityErrorEvent.SECURITY_ERROR is dispatched.

```
var urlloader:URLLoader = new URLLoader( );
// Register event listener
urlloader.addEventListener(SecurityErrorEvent.SECURITY_ERROR,
                           securityErrorListener);
// Perform security violation
urlloader.load(new URLRequest("http://www.example.com/index.xml"));
```

 As of the printing of this book, *example.com* does not have a policy file posted in the default location, and the preceding code, therefore, causes a SecurityErrorEvent.SECURITY_ERROR event.

The event listener for the preceding SecurityErrorEvent.SECURITY_ERROR event, shown next, adds a failure message to an onscreen *TextField*, output:

```
private function securityErrorListener (e:SecurityErrorEvent):void {
  output.appendText("Loading problem!\n");
  output.appendText(e.text);
}
```

To determine whether a given operation can potentially generate a *SecurityError* exception or cause a SecurityErrorEvent.SECURITY_ERROR event, consult that operation's entry in Adobe's ActionScript Language Reference. Each operation's entry lists potential *SecurityError* exceptions under the heading "Throws" and potential SecurityErrorEvent.SECURITY_ERROR events under the heading "Events."

In most cases, the class that defines the operation that generates a `SecurityErrorEvent.SECURITY_ERROR` event is also the class with which event listeners should be registered. For example, the *URLLoader* class defines the *load()* operation, which has the potential to cause `SecurityErrorEvent.SECURITY_ERROR` events. Event listeners that handle `SecurityErrorEvent.SECURITY_ERROR` events caused by the *URLLoader* class's instance method *load()*, are registered with the *URLLoader* instance on which *load()* is invoked. The following code demonstrates:

```
// When using URLLoader, register for events with the URLLoader instance.
var urlloader:URLLoader = new URLLoader();
urlloader.addEventListener(SecurityErrorEvent.SECURITY_ERROR,
                           securityErrorListener);
```

However, in some cases, the class that defines the operation that generates a `SecurityErrorEvent.SECURITY_ERROR` event is not also the class with which event listeners should be registered. For example, the *Loader* class defines the *load()* operation, which has the potential to cause `SecurityErrorEvent.SECURITY_ERROR` events. But event listeners that handle those events must be registered with the *LoaderInfo* instance associated with the *load()* operation—not with the *Loader* instance on which *load()* was invoked. Again, the following code demonstrates:

```
// When using Loader, register for events with the LoaderInfo instance.
var loader:Loader = new Loader();
loader.contentLoaderInfo.addEventListener(SecurityErrorEvent.SECURITY_ERROR,
                                          securityErrorListener);
```

To determine the class with which `SecurityErrorEvent.SECURITY_ERROR` event listeners should be registered for any given operation, see Adobe's ActionScript Language Reference. Specifically, look under the class description for the class that defines the operation causing the `SecurityErrorEvent.SECURITY_ERROR` event.

Security Domains

This section is intended to equip you with a basic understanding of the term *security domain* and its casual equivalent *security sandbox*, which is commonly used in Adobe's documentation and other third-party resources. For reasons described in the next section this book avoids the use of both terms.

Taken in combination, a given *.swf* file and the logical set of resources which that *.swf* file can freely access via accessing-content-as-data, loading-data, and cross-scripting operations (per Table 19-3 through Table 19-6) conceptually form a group known as a *security domain*. From the perspective of a *.swf* file from each of the four security-sandbox-types, Table 19-9 lists the constituents of that *.swf* file's security domain.

 Don't confuse *security-sandbox-type* with *security domain*. A *security-sandbox-type* is a *.swf* file's general security status, while a *security domain* is a logical set of resources. A *.swf* file's security-sandbox-type actually *determines* its security domain, much as an employee's corporate rank might determine the accessible areas of a company building.

Table 19-9. Security domains by security-sandbox-type

.swf file's security-sandbox-type	Security domain constituents
Remote	• Non-*.swf* resources from the *.swf*'s region of origin • *.swf* files from the *.swf*'s region of origin
Local-with-filesystem	• Non-*.swf* resources in the local realm • *local-with-filesystem .swf* files in the local realm
Local-with-networking	• *local-with-networking .swf* files in the local realm
Local-trusted	• All non-*.swf* resources in the local and remote realms • *local-trusted .swf* files in the local realm

For the purposes of discussion, security domains are often described in regional terms, as a metaphorical safe zone. Therefore, a *.swf* file might be said to belong to, reside in, or be placed in its security domain. Likewise, a resource might be described as accessible to a *.swf* file because it belongs to that *.swf* file's security domain.

There are only four security-sandbox-types, but for each security-sandbox-type there are many security domains. For example, every *.swf* file in the remote realm has the same security-sandbox-type: *remote*. But a *remote .swf* file from *site-a.com* and a *remote .swf* file from *site-b.com* are part of two different security domains (one for *site-a.com* and one for *site-b.com*). Likewise, every *.swf* file in a trusted location of the local realm has the same security-sandbox-type: *local-trusted*. But two *local-trusted .swf* files from different corporate LANs are part of two different security domains (one for each LAN).

Adobe's documentation often uses the term security domain (and its casual equivalent *security sandbox*) when describing the resources that a *.swf* file can and cannot access.

Ambiguous Use of the Term "Sandbox"

As we learned in the previous section, both third-party literature on Flash Player security and Adobe's documentation often use the term security sandbox or even simply sandbox as a casual equivalent of the formal term security domain. Furthermore, in some rare cases, third-party literature and Adobe's documentation also use the term security sandbox as a casual equivalent of the term security-sandbox-type.

 When reading security-related documentation outside this book, be aware that the term "sandbox" is normally used to mean *security domain*, and might, in some cases, be used to mean *security-sandbox-type*.

To avoid similar confusion, this book forgoes the use of the casual terms security sandbox and sandbox entirely, and uses the official term security domain only when absolutely necessary (for example, when discussing the built-in *SecurityDomain*

class). Rather than use those terms, this book always describes a *.swf* file's security status relative to its *security-sandbox-type*. This book also lists the resources a *.swf* file can access explicitly, rather than using the general term *security domain* to describe a logical group of accessible resources.

For example, consider the following sentence from Adobe's Programming Action-Script 3.0 → Flash Player APIs → Flash Player Security → Security sandboxes → Local sandboxes:

> Local files that are registered as trusted are placed in the local-trusted sandbox.

In the vocabulary preferred by this book, the preceding excerpt would read:

> Local files that are registered as trusted are assigned a security-sandbox-type of local-trusted.

Next, consider this sentence, this time from Adobe's Programming ActionScript 3.0 → Flash Player APIs → Flash Player Security → Accessing loaded media as data:

> By default, a SWF file from one *security sandbox* cannot obtain pixel data or audio data from graphic or audio objects rendered or played by loaded media in another *sandbox*.

In the vocabulary preferred by this book, the preceding excerpt would read:

> By default, a SWF file from one *security domain* cannot obtain pixel data or audio data from graphic or audio objects rendered or played by loaded media *outside that security domain*.

In Adobe's documentation and third-party sources, if the meaning of the term "sandbox" seems ambiguous, focus on the security-sandbox-type being discussed and the operation being allowed or prohibited. If all else fails, simply attempt to perform the operation you wish to perform, and rely on compiler and runtime security error messages to determine if the operation is allowed. However, to be sure you encounter all possible security error messages, follow the guidance provided earlier in the section "Developers Automatically Trusted" and test in the debug version of Flash Player. Also remember that you can check a *.swf* file's security-sandbox-type at runtime via the flash.system.Security.sandboxType variable. Knowing a *.swf* file's security-sandbox-type will help you identify the security restrictions placed on that *.swf* file by Flash Player.

Two Common Security-Related Development Issues

Over the course of this chapter we've studied a variety of security restrictions and permissions systems. Let's finish our study of Flash Player security by looking at two security scenarios that commonly occur in the typical ActionScript development process: accessing Internet subdomains and accessing the Loader class's instance variable content. Each scenario presents a limitation and the corresponding workaround for that limitation.

Accessing Internet Subdomains

Earlier in Table 19-3, we learned that a *remote .swf* can load data from its remote region of origin only. In the section "The Local Realm, the Remote Realm, and Remote Regions," we also learned that two different Internet subdomains, such as *www.example.com* and *games.example.com* are considered different remote regions. Hence, a *.swf* loaded from *http://example.com* can load any datafile posted at *http://example.com*, but cannot load datafiles posted on any other domain, including subdomains such as *games.example.com*. Perhaps surprisingly, this means that a *.swf* file loaded from *http://example.com* cannot use an absolute URL to access a file posted on *www.example.com*. To grant a *.swf* file loaded from *example.com* permission to load assets from *www.example.com*, use a policy file, as described in the earlier section "Distributor Permissions (Policy Files)."

The following steps describe how the owner of *example.com* would supply a policy file allowing *.swf* files accessed via *example.com* to load datafiles from *www.example.com*, and vice versa.

1. Create a new text file named *crossdomain.xml*.

2. Open *crossdomain.xml* in a text editor.

3. Add the following XML code to the file:

```
<?xml version="1.0"?>
<!DOCTYPE cross-domain-policy
  SYSTEM "http://www.adobe.com/xml/dtds/cross-domain-policy.dtd">
<cross-domain-policy>
  <allow-access-from domain="www.example.com" />
  <allow-access-from domain="example.com" />
</cross-domain-policy>
```

4. Save *crossdomain.xml*.

5. Upload *crossdomain.xml* to the root directory of *example.com* (i.e., so that the file can be accessed at *http://example.com/crossdomain.xml*).

Accessing the Loader Class's Instance Variable Content

When an external display asset is loaded using a *Loader* object, an instance of the loaded asset is placed in the *Loader* object's content variable. As we learned in the earlier section "Accessing Content as Data," accessing the content variable is considered either an accessing-content-as-data operation (if the object contained by content is an image) or a cross-scripting operation (if the object contained by content is a *.swf* file's main-class instance). Therefore, according to the security-sandbox-type restrictions covered in Table 19-3, Table 19-4, and Table 19-5, accessing a loaded asset using content without appropriate permission will cause a security error in the following situations:

- When a *remote* .swf file uses content to access a resource that originates from a different remote region
- When a *local-with-networking* .swf file uses content to access a resource that originates from the remote realm
- When a *local-with-networking* .swf file uses content to access a *local-trusted* .swf file
- When a *local-with-filesystem* .swf file uses content to access a *local-trusted* .swf file

If you face any of the preceding situations in your code, you should consider whether you can avoid using content entirely. If your application needs only to display the loaded asset on screen, then access to content is not required. To display a loaded asset onscreen without accessing content, simply add its *Loader* object—rather than the value of content—directly to the display list. For details and example code, see the section "Displaying the Loaded Asset On Screen" in Chapter 28.

Note however, that in the following situations, content is required, and the appropriate creator or distributor permissions must be in place to avoid security violations:

- When the .swf file that loaded the asset needs access to the asset's data—for example, to read the pixels of a bitmap image
- When the .swf file that loaded the asset needs to cross-script the loaded asset
- When the loaded asset must be accessed directly as an object—for example, when the object representing the loaded asset must be passed to a method that expects an *Bitmap* object as an argument

For more information on the *Loader* class, see Chapter 28. For more information on the display list, see Chapter 20.

On to Part II!

Over the past 19 chapters, we've examined most of ActionScript's core concepts. In Part II, we'll turn our attention to a specific part of the Flash runtime API known as the *display API*. There are lots of code examples and real-world programming scenarios to come, so get ready to apply your hard-earned knowledge of the core Action-Script language!

Display and Interactivity

Part II explores techniques for displaying content on screen and responding to input events. Topics covered include the Flash runtime display API, hierarchical event handling, mouse and keyboard interactivity, animation, vector graphics, bitmap graphics, text, and content loading operations.

When you complete Part II, you will be ready to add graphical content and interactivity to your own applications.

The Display API and the Display List

One of the primary activities of ActionScript programming is displaying things on the screen. Accordingly, the Flash platform provides a wide range of tools for creating and manipulating graphical content. These tools can be broken into two general categories:

- The Flash runtime *display API*, a set of classes for working with interactive visual objects, bitmaps, and vector content
- Ready-made user interface components:
  - The *Flex framework's UI component set*, a sophisticated collection of customizable user-interface widgets built on top of the display API
  - The *Flash authoring tool's UI component set*, a collection of user-interface widgets with a smaller file size, lower memory usage, and fewer features than Flex framework's UI component set

The display API is built directly into all Flash runtimes and is, therefore, available to all *.swf* files. The display API is designed for producing highly customized user interfaces or visual effects, such as those often found in motion graphics and games. This chapter focuses entirely on the display API.

The Flex framework's UI component set is part of the Flex framework, an external class library included with Adobe Flex Builder and also available in standalone form for free at: *http://www.adobe.com/go/flex2_sdk*. The Flex framework's UI component set is designed for building applications with relatively standard user interface controls (scrollbars, pull-down menus, data grids, etc.). The Flex framework's interface widgets are typically used in MXML applications, but can also be included in primarily ActionScript-based applications. For details on using the Flex framework in ActionScript, see Chapter 30.

The Flash authoring tool's UI component set is designed for use with *.swf* files created in the Flash authoring tool, and for situations where file size and low memory usage are more important than advanced component features such as data binding and advanced styling options. The Flash authoring tool's UI component set and the

Flex framework's UI component set share a very similar API, allowing developers to reuse knowledge when moving between the two component sets.

In Flash Player 8 and older, ActionScript provided the following four basic building blocks for creating and managing visual content:

Movie clip
    A container for graphical content, providing interactivity, primitive drawing, hierarchical layout, and animation feature

Text field
    A rectangular region containing a formatted text

Button
    An input control representing a very simple interactive "push button"

Bitmap (introduced in Flash Player 8)
    A graphic in bitmap-format

The preceding items continue to be available in the display API, but the classes representing them in ActionScript 3.0 (*MovieClip*, *TextField*, *SimpleButton*, and *Bitmap*) have been enhanced and revised, and situated logically within a larger context.

Display API Overview

In ActionScript, all graphical content is created and manipulated using the classes in the display API. Even the interface widgets in the Flex framework and Flash authoring tool component sets use the display API as a graphical foundation. Many display API classes directly represent a specific type of on-screen graphical content. For example, the *Bitmap* class represents bitmap graphics, the *Sprite* class represents interactive graphics, and the *TextField* class represents formatted text. For the purposes of discussion, we'll refer to classes that directly represent on-screen content (and superclasses of such classes) as *core display classes*. The remaining classes in the display API define supplementary graphical information and functionality but do not, themselves, represent on-screen content. For example, the *CapStyle* and *JointStyle* classes define constants representing line-drawing preferences, while the *Graphics* and *BitmapData* classes define a variety of primitive drawing operations. We'll refer to these nondisplay classes as *supporting display classes*. Whether core or supporting, most of the display API classes reside in the package *flash.display*.

The core display classes, shown in Figure 20-1, are arranged in a class hierarchy that reflects three general tiers of functionality: display, user interactivity, and containment. Accordingly, the three central classes in the display API are: *DisplayObject*, *InteractiveObject*, and *DisplayObjectContainer*. Those three classes cannot be instantiated directly but rather provide abstract functionality that is applied by various concrete subclasses.

As discussed in Chapter 6, ActionScript 3.0 does not support true abstract classes. Hence, in Figure 20-1, *DisplayObject*, *InteractiveObject*, and *DisplayObjectContainer* are listed not as abstract classes, but as abstract-style classes. However, despite this technicality, for the sake of brevity in the remainder of this chapter, we'll use the shorter term "abstract" when referring to the architectural role played by *DisplayObject*, *InteractiveObject*, and *DisplayObjectContainer*.

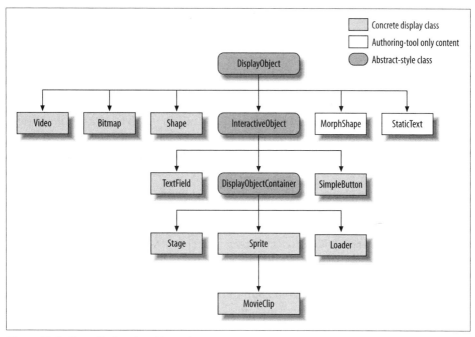

Figure 20-1. Core-display class hierarchy

DisplayObject, the root of the core-display class hierarchy, defines the display API's first tier of graphical functionality: on-screen display. All classes that inherit from *DisplayObject* gain a common set of fundamental graphical characteristics and capabilities. For example, every descendant of *DisplayObject* can be positioned, sized, and rotated with the variables x, y, width, height, and rotation. More than just a simple base class, *DisplayObject* is the source of many sophisticated capabilities in the display API, including (but not limited to):

- Converting coordinates (see the *DisplayObject* class's instance methods *localToGlobal()* and *globalToLocal()* in Adobe's ActionScript Language Reference)

- Checking intersections between objects and points (see the *DisplayObject* class's instance methods *hitTestObject()* and *hitTestPoint()* in Adobe's ActionScript Language Reference)

- Applying filters, transforms, and masks (see the *DisplayObject* class's instance variables `filters`, `transform`, and `mask` in Adobe's ActionScript Language Reference)

- Scaling disproportionately for "stretchy" graphical layouts (see the *DisplayObject* class's instance variable `scale9grid` in Adobe's ActionScript Language Reference)

Note that this book occasionally uses the informal term "display object" to mean any instance of a class descending from the *DisplayObject* class.

DisplayObject's direct concrete subclasses—*Video*, *Bitmap*, *Shape*, *MorphShape*, and *StaticText*—represent the simplest type of displayable content: basic on-screen graphics that cannot receive input or contain nested visual content. The *Video* class represents streaming video. The *Bitmap* class renders bitmap graphics created and manipulated with the supporting *BitmapData* class. The *Shape* class provides a simple, lightweight canvas for vector drawing. And the special *MorphShape* and *StaticText* classes represent, respectively, shape tweens and static text created in the Flash authoring tool. Neither *MorphShape* nor *StaticText* can be instantiated with ActionScript.

DisplayObject's only abstract subclass, *InteractiveObject*, establishes the second tier of functionality in the display API: interactivity. All classes that inherit from *InteractiveObject* gain the ability to respond to input events from the user's mouse and keyboard. *InteractiveObject*'s direct concrete subclasses—*TextField* and *SimpleButton*—represent two distinct kinds of interactive graphical content. The *TextField* class represents a rectangular area for displaying formatted text and receiving text-based user input. The *SimpleButton* class represents Button symbols created in the Flash authoring tool and can also quickly create interactive buttons via Action-Script code. By responding to the input events broadcast by the *TextField* or *SimpleButton,* the programmer can add interactivity to an application. For example, a *TextField* instance can be programmed to change background color in response to a `FocusEvent.FOCUS_IN` event, and a *SimpleButton* instance can be programmed to submit a form in response to a `MouseEvent.CLICK` event.

InteractiveObject's only abstract subclass, *DisplayObjectContainer*, is the base of the third and final functional tier in the display API: containment. All classes that inherit from *DisplayObjectContainer* gain the ability to physically contain any other *DisplayObject* instance. Containers are used to group multiple visual objects so they can be manipulated as one. Any time a container is moved, rotated, or transformed, the objects it contains inherit that movement, rotation, or transformation. Likewise, any time a container is removed from the screen, the objects it contains are removed with it. Furthermore, containers can be nested within other containers to create hierarchical groups of display objects. When referring to the objects in a display hierarchy, this book use standard tree-structure terminology; for example, an object that contains another object in a display hierarchy is referred to as that object's *parent*, while the contained object is referred to as the parent's *child*. In a multilevel display hierarchy, the objects above a given object in the hierarchy are referred to as the object's *ancestors*. Conversely, the objects below a given object in the hierarchy are referred to as the object's *descendants*. Finally, the top-level object in the hierarchy (the object from which all other objects descend) is referred to as the *root* object.

 Don't confuse the ancestor objects and descendant objects in a display hierarchy with the ancestor classes and descendant classes in an inheritance hierarchy. For clarity, this book occasionally uses the terms "display ancestors" and "display descendants" when referring to ancestor objects and descendant objects in a display hierarchy.

DisplayObjectContainer's subclasses—*Sprite*, *MovieClip*, *Stage*, and *Loader*—each provide a unique type of empty containment structure, waiting to be filled with content. *Sprite* is the centerpiece of the container classes. As a descendant of both the *InteractiveObject* the *DisplayObjectContainer* classes, *Sprite* provides the perfect foundation for building custom user interface elements from scratch. The *MovieClip* class is an enhanced type of *Sprite* that represents animated content created in the Flash authoring tool. The *Stage* class represents the Flash runtime's main *display area* (the viewable region within the borders of the application window). Finally, the *Loader* class is used to load external graphical content locally or over the Internet.

 Prior to ActionScript 3.0, the *MovieClip* class was used as an all-purpose graphics container (much like ActionScript 3.0's *Sprite* class is used). As of ActionScript 3.0, *MovieClip* is used only to control instances of movie clip symbols created in the Flash authoring tool. Because ActionScript 3.0 does not provide a way to create timeline elements such as frames and tweens, there is no need to create new empty movie clips at runtime in ActionScript 3.0. Instead, all programmatically created graphics should be instances of the appropriate core display class (*Bitmap*, *Shape*, *Sprite*, *TextField*, etc.).

The display API provides a vast amount of functionality, dispersed over hundreds of methods and variables. While this book covers many of them, our focus in the coming chapters is on fundamental concepts rather than methodical coverage of each method and variable. For a dictionary-style reference to the display API, see Adobe's ActionScript Language Reference.

Extending the Core-Display Class Hierarchy

While in many cases. the core display classes can productively be used without any modification, most nontrivial programs extend the functionality of the core display classes by creating subclasses suited to a custom purpose. For example, a geometric drawing program might define *Ellipse*, *Rectangle*, and *Triangle* classes that extend the *Shape* class. Similarly, a news viewer might define a *Heading* class that extends

TextField, and a racing game might define a *Car* class that extends *Sprite*. In fact, the user interface widgets in the Flex framework are all descendants of the *Sprite* class. In the chapters ahead, we'll encounter many examples of custom display classes. As you learn more about the core display classes, start thinking about how you could add to their functionality; ActionScript programmers are expected and encouraged to expand and enhance the core display classes with custom code. For more information, see the section "Custom Graphical Classes," later in this chapter.

The Display List

As we've just discussed, the core display classes represent the types of graphical content available in ActionScript. To create actual graphics from those theoretical types, we create instances of the core display classes and then add those instances to the *display list*. The display list is the hierarchy of all graphical objects currently displayed by the Flash runtime. When a display object is added to the display list and is positioned in a visible area, the Flash runtime renders that display object's content to the screen.

The root of the display list is an instance of the *Stage* class, which is automatically created when the Flash runtime starts. This special, automatically created *Stage* instance serves two purposes. First, it acts as the outermost container for all graphical content displayed in the Flash runtime (i.e., it is the root of the display list). Second, it provides information about, and control over, the global characteristics of the display area. For example, the *Stage* class's instance variable `quality` indicates the rendering quality of all displayed graphics; `scaleMode` indicates how graphics scale when the display area is resized; and `frameRate` indicates the current preferred frames per second for all animations. As we'll see throughout this chapter, the *Stage* instance is always accessed relative to some object on the display list via the `DisplayObject` class's instance variable `stage`. For example, if `output_txt` is a *TextField* instance currently on the display list, then the *Stage* instance can be accessed using `output_txt.stage`.

Prior to ActionScript 3.0, the *Stage* class did not contain objects on the display list. Furthermore, all *Stage* methods and variables were accessed via the *Stage* class directly, as in:

```
trace(Stage.align);
```

In ActionScript 3.0, *Stage* methods and variables are not accessed through the *Stage* class, and there is no global point of reference to the *Stage* instance. In ActionScript 3.0, the preceding line of code causes the following error:

```
Access of possibly undefined property 'align' through a
reference with static type 'Class'
```

To avoid that error, access the *Stage* instance using the following approach:

```
trace(someDisplayObj.stage.align);
```

where *someDisplayObj* is an object currently on the display list. ActionScript 3.0's *Stage* architecture allows for the future possibility of multiple *Stage* instances and also contributes to Flash Player's security (because unauthorized externally-loaded objects have no global point of access to the *Stage* instance).

Figure 20-2 depicts the state of the display list for an empty Flash runtime before any *.swf* file has been opened. The left side of the figure shows a symbolic representation of the Flash runtime, while the right side shows the corresponding display list hierarchy. When the Flash runtime is empty, the display list hierarchy contains one item only (the lone *Stage* instance). But we'll soon add more!

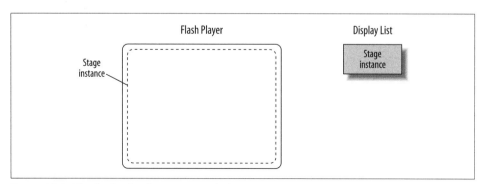

Figure 20-2. The display list for an empty Flash runtime

When an empty Flash runtime opens a new *.swf* file, it locates that *.swf* file's main class, creates an instance of it, and adds that instance to the display list as the *Stage* instance's first child.

 Recall that a *.swf* file's main class must inherit from either *Sprite* or *MovieClip*, both of which are descendants of *DisplayObject*. Techniques for specifying a *.swf* file's main class are covered in Chapter 7.

The .swf file's main class instance is both the program entry point and the first visual object displayed on screen. Even if the main class instance does not create any graphics itself, it is still added to the display list, ready to contain any graphics created by the program in the future. The main class instance of the first .swf file opened by the Flash runtime plays a special role in ActionScript; it determines certain global environment settings, such as relative-URL resolution and the type of security restrictions applied to external operations.

 In honor of its special role, the main-class instance of the first .swf file opened by the Flash runtime is sometimes referred to as the "stage owner."

Let's consider an example that shows how the stage owner is created. Suppose we start the standalone version of Flash Player and open a .swf file named *GreetingApp. swf*, whose main class is *GreetingApp*. If *GreetingApp.swf* contains the class *GreetingApp* only, and *GreetingApp* creates no graphics, then Flash Player's display list will contain just two items: the *Stage* instance and a *GreetingApp* instance (contained by the *Stage* instance). Figure 20-3 demonstrates.

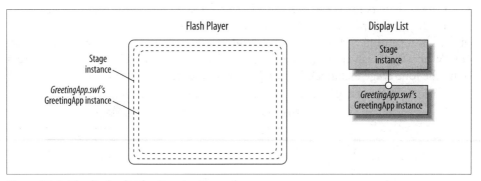

Figure 20-3. The display list for GreetingApp.swf

Once an instance of a .swf file's main class has been added to the *Stage* instance, a program can add new content to the screen by following these general steps:

1. Create a displayable object (i.e., an instance of any core display class or any class that extends a core display class).

2. Invoke the *DisplayObjectContainer* class's instance method *addChild()* on either the *Stage* instance or the main-class instance, and pass *addChild()* the displayable object created in Step 1.

Let's try out the preceding general steps by creating the *GreetingApp* class, then adding a rectangle, a circle, and a text field to the display list using *addChild()*. First, here's the skeleton of the *GreetingApp* class:

```
package {
  import flash.display.*;
  import flash.text.TextField;
```

```
public class GreetingApp extends Sprite {
  public function GreetingApp () {
  }
 }
}
```

Our *GreetingApp* class will use the *Shape* and *Sprite* classes, so it imports the entire *flash.display* package in which those classes reside. Likewise, *GreetingApp* will use the *TextField* class, so it imports *flash.text.TextField*.

Notice that, by necessity, *GreetingApp* extends *Sprite*. *GreetingApp* must extend either *Sprite* or *MovieClip* because it is the program's main class.

 In ActionScript 3.0, a *.swf* file's main class must extend either *Sprite* or *MovieClip*, or a subclass of one of those classes.

In cases where the main class represents the root timeline of a *.fla* file, it should extend *MovieClip*; in all other cases, it should extend *Sprite*. In our example, *GreetingApp* extends *Sprite* because it is not associated with a *.fla* file. It is intended to be compiled as a standalone ActionScript application.

Now let's create our rectangle and circle in *GreetingApp*'s constructor method. We'll draw both the rectangle and the circle inside a single *Shape* object. *Shape* objects (and all graphical objects) are created with the *new* operator, just like any other kind of object. Here's the code we use to create a new *Shape* object:

```
new Shape( )
```

Of course, we'll need to access that object later in order to draw things in it, so let's assign it to a variable, rectAndCircle:

```
var rectAndCircle:Shape = new Shape( );
```

To draw vectors in ActionScript, we use the supporting display class, *Graphics*. Each *Shape* object maintains its own *Graphics* instance in the instance variable graphics. Hence, to draw a rectangle and circle inside our *Shape* object, we invoke the appropriate methods on rectAndCircle.graphics. Here's the code:

```
// Set line thickness to one pixel
rectAndCircle.graphics.lineStyle(1);

// Draw a blue rectangle
rectAndCircle.graphics.beginFill(0x0000FF, 1);
rectAndCircle.graphics.drawRect(125, 0, 150, 75);

// Draw a red circle
rectAndCircle.graphics.beginFill(0xFF0000, 1);
rectAndCircle.graphics.drawCircle(50, 100, 50);
```

For more information on vector drawing in ActionScript 3.0, see Chapter 25.

Vector drawing operations are not limited to the *Shape* class. The *Sprite* class also provides a *Graphics* reference via its instance variable graphics, so we could have created a *Sprite* object to hold the rectangle and circle rather than a *Shape* object. However, because each *Sprite* object requires more memory than each *Shape* object, we're better off using a *Shape* object when creating vector graphics that do not contain children or require interactivity.

Strictly speaking, if we wanted to incur the lowest possible memory overhead in the *GreetingApp* example, we would draw our shapes directly inside the *GreetingApp* instance (remember *GreetingApp* extends *Sprite*, so it supports vector drawing). The code would look like this:

```
package {
  import flash.display.*;
  public class GreetingApp extends Sprite {
    public function GreetingApp () {
      graphics.lineStyle(1);

      // Rectangle
      graphics.beginFill(0x0000FF, 1);
      graphics.drawRect(125, 0, 150, 75);

      // Circle
      graphics.beginFill(0xFF0000, 1);
      graphics.drawCircle(50, 100, 50);
    }
  }
}
```

That code successfully draws the rectangle and circle on screen but is less flexible than placing them in a separate *Shape* object. Placing drawings in a *Shape* object allows them to be moved, layered, modified, and removed independent of other graphical content in the application. For example, returning to our earlier approach of drawing in a *Shape* instance (rectAndCircle), here's how we'd move the shapes to a new position:

```
// Move rectAndCircle to the right 125 pixels and down 100 pixels
rectAndCircle.x = 125;
rectAndCircle.y = 100;
```

Notice that at this point in our code, we have a display object, rectAndCircle, that has not yet been added to the display list. It's both legal and common to refer to and manipulate display objects that are not on the display list. Display objects can be added to and removed from the display list arbitrarily throughout the lifespan of a program and can be programmatically manipulated whether they are on or off the display list. For example, notice that the preceding positioning code occurs *before* rectAndCircle has even been placed on the display list! Each display object maintains its own state regardless of the parent it is attached to—indeed, regardless of whether it is attached to the display list at all. When and if rectAndCircle is eventually added to a display container, it is automatically placed at position (125, 100) in that container's coordinate space. If rectAndCircle is then removed from that container and added to a different one, it is positioned at (125, 100) of the new container's coordinate space.

 Each display object carries its characteristics with it when moved from container to container, or even when removed from the display list entirely.

Now the moment we've been waiting for. To actually display our rectangle and circle on screen, we invoke *addChild()* on the *GreetingApp* instance within the *GreetingApp* constructor and pass along a reference to the *Shape* instance in rectAndCircle.

```
// Display rectAndCircle on screen by adding it to the display list
addChild(rectAndCircle);
```

Flash Player consequently adds rectAndCircle to the display list, as a child of the *GreetingApp* instance.

 As a *Sprite* subclass, *GreetingApp* is a descendant of *DisplayObjectContainer*, and, thus, inherits the *addChild()* method and the ability to contain children. For a refresher on the display API class hierarchy, refer back to Figure 20-1.

Wow, displaying things on screen is fun! Let's do it again. Adding the following code to the *GreetingApp* constructor causes the text "Hello world" to appear on screen:

```
// Create a TextField object to contain some text
var greeting_txt:TextField = new TextField( );

// Specify the text to display
greeting_txt.text = "Hello world";

// Position the TextField object
greeting_txt.x = 200;
greeting_txt.y = 300;

// Display the text on screen by adding greeting_txt to the display list
addChild(greeting_txt);
```

Once an object has been added to a display container, that container can be accessed via the *DisplayObject* class's instance variable parent. For example, from within the

GreetingApp constructor, the following code is a valid reference to the *GreetingApp* instance:

```
greeting_txt.parent
```

If a display object is not currently on the display list, its parent variable has the value null.

Example 20-1 shows the code for *GreetingApp* in its entirety.

Example 20-1. Graphical "Hello world"

```
package {
  import flash.display.*;
  import flash.text.TextField;

  public class GreetingApp extends Sprite {
    public function GreetingApp( ) {
      // Create the Shape object
      var rectAndCircle:Shape = new Shape( );

      // Set line thickness to one pixel
      rectAndCircle.graphics.lineStyle(1);

      // Draw a blue rectangle
      rectAndCircle.graphics.beginFill(0x0000FF, 1);
      rectAndCircle.graphics.drawRect(125, 0, 150, 75);

      // Draw a red circle
      rectAndCircle.graphics.beginFill(0xFF0000, 1);
      rectAndCircle.graphics.drawCircle(50, 100, 50);

      // Move the shape to the right 125 pixels and down 100 pixels
      rectAndCircle.x = 125;
      rectAndCircle.y = 100;

      // Show rectAndCircle on screen by adding it to the display list
      addChild(rectAndCircle);

      // Create a TextField object to contain some text
      var greeting_txt:TextField = new TextField( );

      // Specify the text to display
      greeting_txt.text = "Hello world";

      // Position the text
      greeting_txt.x = 200;
      greeting_txt.y = 300;

      // Show the text on screen by adding greeting_txt to the display list
      addChild(greeting_txt);
    }
  }
}
```

Figure 20-4 shows the graphical results of the code in Example 20-1. As in the previous two figures, on-screen graphics are depicted on the left, with the corresponding Flash Player display list hierarchy shown on the right.

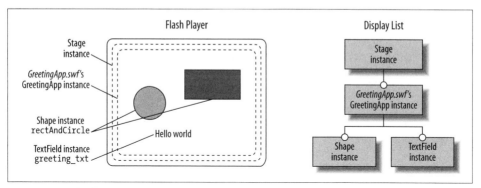

Figure 20-4. The display list for GreetingApp

Containers and Depths

In the previous section, we gave *GreetingApp* two display children (rectAndCircle and greeting_txt). On screen, those two children were placed in such a way that they did not visually overlap. If they had overlapped, one would have obscured the other, based on the *depths* of the two objects. A display object's *depth* is an integer value that determines how that object overlaps other objects in the same display object container. When two display objects overlap, the one with the greater depth position (the "higher" of the two) obscures the other (the "lower" of the two). All display objects in a container, hence, can be thought of as residing in a visual stacking order akin to a deck of playing cards, counted into a pile starting at zero. The lowest object in the stacking order has a depth position of 0, and the highest object has a depth position equal to the number of child objects in the display object container, minus one (metaphorically, the lowest card in the deck has a depth position of 0, and the highest card has a depth position equal to the number of cards in the deck, minus one).

 ActionScript 2.0's depth-management API allowed "unoccupied" depths. For example, in a container with only two objects, one object might have a depth of 0 and the other a depth of 40, leaving depths 1 through 39 unoccupied. In ActionScript 3.0's depth-management API, unoccupied depths are no longer allowed or necessary.

Display objects added to a container using *addChild()* are assigned depth positions automatically. Given an empty container, the first child added via *addChild()* is placed at depth 0, the second is placed at depth 1, the third is placed at depth 2, and so on. Hence, the object most recently added via *addChild( )* always appears visually on top of all other children.

As an example, let's continue with the *GreetingApp* program from the previous section. This time we'll draw the circle and rectangle in their own separate *Shape* instances so they can be stacked independently. We'll also adjust the positions of the circle, rectangle, and text so that they overlap. Here's the revised code (this code and other samples in this section are excerpted from *GreetingApp*'s constructor method):

```
// The rectangle
var rect:Shape = new Shape( );
rect.graphics.lineStyle(1);
rect.graphics.beginFill(0x0000FF, 1);
rect.graphics.drawRect(0, 0, 75, 50);

// The circle
var circle:Shape = new Shape( );
circle.graphics.lineStyle(1);
circle.graphics.beginFill(0xFF0000, 1);
circle.graphics.drawCircle(0, 0, 25);
circle.x = 75;
circle.y = 35;

// The text message
var greeting_txt:TextField = new TextField( );
greeting_txt.text = "Hello world";
greeting_txt.x = 60;
greeting_txt.y = 25;
```

Now let's try adding the rectangle, circle, and text as *GreetingApp* children, in different sequences. This code adds the rectangle, then the circle, then the text:

```
addChild(rect);          // Depth 0
addChild(circle);        // Depth 1
addChild(greeting_txt);  // Depth 2
```

As shown in Figure 20-5, the rectangle was added first, so it appears underneath the circle and the text; the circle was added next, so it appears on top of the rectangle but underneath the text; the text was added last, so it appears on top of both the circle and the rectangle.

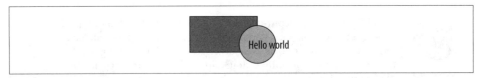

Figure 20-5. Rectangle, circle, text

The following code changes the sequence, adding the circle first, then the rectangle, then the text. Figure 20-6 shows the result. Notice that simply changing the sequence in which the objects are added changes the resulting display.

```
addChild(circle);       // Depth 0
addChild(rect);         // Depth 1
addChild(greeting_txt); // Depth 2
```

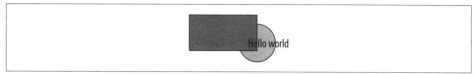

Figure 20-6. Circle, rectangle, text

Here's one more example. The following code adds the text first, then the circle, then the rectangle. Figure 20-7 shows the result.

```
addChild(greeting_txt); // Depth 0
addChild(circle);       // Depth 1
addChild(rect);         // Depth 2
```

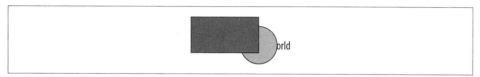

Figure 20-7. Text, circle, rectangle

To retrieve the depth position of any object in a display object container, we use the *DisplayObjectContainer* class's instance method *getChildIndex()*:

```
trace(getChildIndex(rect));  // Displays: 2
```

To add a new object at a specific depth position, we use the *DisplayObjectContainer* class's instance method *addChildAt()* (notice: *addChildAt()* not *addChild()*). The *addChildAt()* method takes the following form:

```
theContainer.addChildAt(theDisplayObject, depthPosition)
```

The `depthPosition` must be an integer between 0 and `theContainer`.numChildren, inclusive.

If the specified `depthPosition` is already occupied by an existing child, then `theDisplayObject` is placed behind that existing child (i.e., the depth positions of all display objects on or above that depth increases by one to make room for the new child).

 Repeat this *addChildAt()* mnemonic to yourself: "If the depth is *occupied*, the new child goes *behind*."

To add a new object above all existing children, we use:

```
theContainer.addChildAt(theDisplayObject, theContainer.numChildren)
```

which is synonymous with the following:

```
theContainer.addChild(theDisplayObject)
```

Typically, *addChildAt()* is used in combination with the *DisplayObjectContainer* class's instance method *getChildIndex()* to add an object below an existing child in a given container. Here's the general format:

```
theContainer.addChildAt(newChild, theContainer.getChildIndex(existingChild))
```

Let's try it out by adding a new triangle behind the circle in *GreetingApp* as it existed in its most recent incarnation, shown in Figure 20-7.

Here's the code that creates the triangle:

```
var triangle:Shape = new Shape();
triangle.graphics.lineStyle(1);
triangle.graphics.beginFill(0x00FF00, 1);
triangle.graphics.moveTo(25, 0);
triangle.graphics.lineTo(50, 25);
triangle.graphics.lineTo(0, 25);
triangle.graphics.lineTo(25, 0);
triangle.graphics.endFill();
triangle.x = 25;
triangle.y = 10;
```

And here's the code that makes `triangle` a new child of *GreetingApp*, beneath the existing object, `circle` (notice that both *addChildAt()* and *getChildIndex()* are implicitly invoked on the current *GreetingApp* object). Figure 20-8 shows the results.

```
addChildAt(triangle, getChildIndex(circle));
```

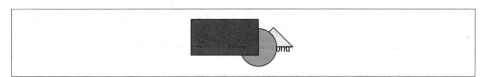

Figure 20-8. New triangle child

As we learned recently, when a new object is added at a depth position occupied by an existing child, the depth positions of the existing child and of all children above it are incremented by 1. The new object then adopts the depth position that was vacated by the existing child. For example, prior to the addition of `triangle`, the depths of *GreetingApp*'s children were:

```
greeting_txt        0
circle              1
rect                2
```

Upon adding `triangle`, circle's depth position changes from 1 to 2, rect's depth position changes from 2 to 3, and `triangle` takes depth 1 (circle's former depth). Meanwhile, greeting_txt's depth position is unaffected because it was below circle's depth from the beginning. Here are the revised depths after the addition of triangle:

```
greeting_txt      0
triangle          1
circle            2
rect              3
```

To change the depth of an existing child, we can swap that child's depth position with another existing child via the *DisplayObjectContainer* class's instance methods *swapChildren()* or *swapChildrenAt()*. Or, we can simply set that child's depth directly using the *DisplayObjectContainer* class's instance method *setChildIndex()*.

The *swapChildren()* method takes the following form:

```
theContainer.swapChildren(existingChild1, existingChild2);
```

where *existingChild1* and *existingChild2* are both children of *theContainer*. The *swapChildren()* method exchanges the depths of *existingChild1* and *existingChild2*. In natural English, the preceding code means, "put *existingChild1* at the depth currently occupied by *existingChild2*, and put *existingChild2* at the depth currently occupied by *existingChild1*."

The *swapChildrenAt()* method takes the following form:

```
theContainer.swapChildrenAt(existingDepth1, existingDepth2);
```

where *existingDepth1* and *existingDepth2* are both depths occupied by children of *theContainer*. The *swapChildrenAt()* method exchanges the depths of the children at *existingDepth1* and *existingDepth2*. In natural English, the preceding code means, "put the child currently at *existingDepth1* at *existingDepth2*, and put the child currently at *existingDepth2* at *existingDepth1*."

The *setChildIndex()* method takes the following form:

```
theContainer.setChildIndex(existingChild, newDepthPosition);
```

where *existingChild* is a child of *theContainer*. The *newDepthPosition* must be a depth position presently occupied by a child object of *theContainer*. That is, *setChildIndex()* can only rearrange the positions of existing child objects; it cannot introduce new depth positions. The *newDepthPosition* parameter of *setChildIndex()* is typically deduced by invoking *getChildIndex()* on an existing child, as in:

```
theContainer.setChildIndex(existingChild1,
                    theContainer.getChildIndex(existingChild2));
```

which means, "put *existingChild1* at the depth currently occupied by *existingChild2*."

Note that when an object's depth is increased to a new position via *setChildIndex()* (i.e., the object is moved higher), the depth of all objects between the old position and the new position is decreased by 1, thus filling the vacant position left by the moved object. Consequently, the moved object appears in front of the object formerly at the new position. For example, continuing with the latest version of

GreetingApp (as shown previously in Figure 20-8), let's change greeting_txt's depth position from 0 to 2. Prior to executing the following code, depth position 2 is held by circle.

```
setChildIndex(greeting_txt, getChildIndex(circle));
```

When greeting_txt moves to depth position 2, the depth positions of circle and triangle are reduced to 1 and 0, respectively, so greeting_txt appears in front of them both. See Figure 20-9.

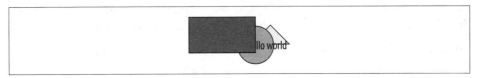

Figure 20-9. Moving the text higher

By contrast, when an object's depth is decreased to a new position via *setChildIndex()* (i.e., the object is moved lower), the depth position of all objects at or above the new position is increased by 1, thus making room for the new object. Consequently, the moved object appears behind the object formerly at the new position (exactly as if the object had been added with *addChildAt()*). Notice the important difference between moving an object to a higher depth versus moving it to a lower depth.

An object moved to a higher depth appears in front of the object at the target position, but an object moved lower appears behind the object at the target position.

For example, continuing from Figure 20-9, let's change rect's depth position from 3 to 1 (where 1 is the depth currently held by circle):

```
setChildIndex(rect, getChildIndex(circle));
```

When rect moves to depth position 1, the depth positions of circle and greeting_txt are increased to 2 and 3, respectively, so rect appears behind them both (see Figure 20-10).

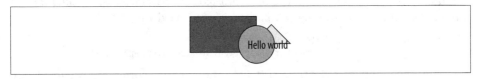

Figure 20-10. Moving the rectangle lower

To move on object to the top of all objects in a given container, use:

```
theContainer.setChildIndex(existingChild, theContainer.numChildren-1)
```

For example, the following code moves the triangle to the top of *GreetingApp*'s children (the following code occurs within the *GreetingApp* class, so *theContainer* is omitted and implicitly resolves to this, the current object):

```
setChildIndex(triangle, numChildren-1);
```

Figure 20-11 shows the results.

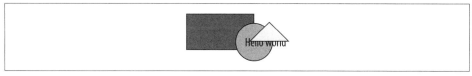

Figure 20-11. Triangle moved to front

The *setChildIndex()* method is easy to understand if you think of a *DisplayObjectContainer*'s children as being modeled after a deck of cards, as discussed earlier. If you move a card from the bottom of the deck to the top, the other cards all move down (i.e., the card that used to be just above the bottom card is now, itself, the new bottom card). If you move a card from the top of the deck to the bottom, the other cards all move up (i.e., the card that used to be the bottom card is now one above the new bottom card).

Removing Assets from Containers

To remove an object from a display object container, we use the *DisplayObjectContainer* class's instance method *removeChild()*, which takes the following form:

```
theContainer.removeChild(existingChild)
```

where *theContainer* is a container that currently contains *existingChild*. For example, to remove the triangle from *GreetingApp* we'd use:

```
removeChild(triangle);
```

Alternatively, we can remove a child based on its depth using *removeChildAt()*, which takes the following form:

```
theContainer.removeChildAt(depth)
```

After *removeChild()* or *removeChildAt()* runs, the removed child's parent variable is set to null because the removed child has no container. If the removed child was on the display list before the call to *removeChild()* or *removeChildAt()*, it is removed from the display list. If the removed child was visible on screen before the call to *removeChild()* or *removeChildAt()*, it is also removed from the screen. If the removed child is, itself, a *DisplayObjectContainer* with its own children, those children are also removed from the screen.

Removing Assets from Memory

It's important to note that the *removeChild()* and *removeChildAt()* methods discussed in the previous section do not necessarily cause the removed object to be purged from memory; they only remove the object from the parent *DisplayObjectContainer* object's display hierarchy. If the removed object is referenced by a variable or array element, it continues to exist and can be re-added to another container at a later time. For example, consider the following code, which creates a *Shape* object, assigns it to the variable rect, and then adds it to parent's display hierarchy:

```
var rect:Shape = new Shape( );
rect.graphics.lineStyle(1);
rect.graphics.beginFill(0x0000FF, 1);
rect.graphics.drawRect(0, 0, 75, 50);
parent.addChild(rect);
```

If we now use *removeChild()* to remove the *Shape* object from parent, rect continues to refer to the *Shape* object:

```
parent.removeChild(rect);
trace(rect);  // Displays: [object Shape]
```

As long as the rect variable exists, we can use it to re-add the *Shape* object to parent's display hierarchy, as follows:

```
parent.addChild(rect);
```

To completely remove a display object from a program, we must both remove it from the screen using *removeChild()* and also remove all references to it. To remove all references to the object, we must manually remove it from every array that contains it and assign null (or some other value) to every variable that references it. Once all references to the object have been removed, the object becomes eligible for garbage collection and will eventually be removed from memory by ActionScript's garbage collector.

However, as discussed in Chapter 14, even *after* all references to an object have been removed, that object continues to be active until the garbage collector deletes it from memory. For example, if the object has registered listeners for the Event.ENTER_FRAME event, that event will still trigger code execution. Likewise, if the object has started timers using *setInterval()* or the *Timer* class, those timers will still trigger code execution. Similarly, if the object is a *MovieClip* instance that is playing, its playhead will continue to advance, causing any frame scripts to execute.

 While an object is waiting to be garbage collected, event listeners, timers, and frame scripts can cause unnecessary code execution, resulting in memory waste or undesired side effects.

To avoid unnecessary code execution when removing a display object from a program, be sure that, before releasing all references to the object, you completely disable it. For more important details on disabling objects, see Chapter 14.

 Always disable display objects before discarding them.

Removing All Children

ActionScript does not provide a direct method for removing all of an object's children. Hence, to remove every display child from a given object, we must use a *while* loop or a *for* loop. For example, the following code uses a *while* loop to remove all children of *theParent* from the bottom up. First, the child at depth 0 is removed, then the depth of all children is reduced by 1, then the new child at depth 0 is removed, and the process repeats until there are no children left.

```
// Remove all children of theParent
while (theParent.numChildren > 0) {
  theParent.removeChildAt(0);
}
```

The following code also removes all children of *theParent*, but from the top down. It should be avoided because it is slower than the preceding approach of removing children from the bottom up.

```
while (theParent.numChildren > 0) {
  theParent.removeChildAt(theParent.numChildren-1);
}
```

The following code removes all children, from the bottom up, using a *for* loop instead of a *while* loop:

```
for (;numChildren > 0;) {
  theParent.removeChildAt(0);
}
```

If you must remove children from the top down (perhaps because you need to process them in that order before removal), be careful never to use a loop that increments its counter instead of decrementing it. For example, never use code like this:

```
// WARNING: PROBLEM CODE! DO NOT USE!
for (var i:int = 0; i < theParent.numChildren; i++) {
  theParent.removeChildAt(i);
}
```

What's wrong with the preceding *for* loop? Imagine *theParent* has three children: A, B, and C, positioned at depths 0, 1, and 2, respectively:

```
Children    Depths
   A          0
   B          1
   C          2
```

When the loop runs the first time, i is 0, so A is removed. When A is removed, B and C's depth is automatically reduced by 1, so B's depth is now 0 and C's depth is now 1:

```
Children    Depths
   B          0
   C          1
```

When the loop runs for the second time, i is 1, so C is removed. With C removed, *theParent*.numChildren becomes 1, so the loop ends because i is no longer less than *theParent*.numChildren. But B was never removed (sneaky devil)!

Reparenting Assets

In ActionScript 3.0, it's perfectly legal and common to remove a child from one *DisplayObjectContainer* instance and move it to another. In fact, the mere act of adding an object to a container automatically removes that object from any container it is already in.

To demonstrate, Example 20-2 presents a simple application, *WordHighlighter*, in which a *Shape* object (assigned to the variable bgRect) is moved between two *Sprite* instances (assigned to the variables word1 and word2). The *Sprite* instances contain *TextField* instances (assigned to the variables text1 and text2) that display the words Products and Services. The *Shape* is a rounded rectangle that serves to highlight the word currently under the mouse pointer, as shown in Figure 20-12. When the mouse hovers over one of the *TextField* instances, the *Shape* object is moved to the *Sprite* containing that *TextField*.

Figure 20-12. Moving an object between containers

We haven't yet covered the mouse-event handling techniques used in Example 20-2. For information on handling input events, see Chapter 22.

Example 20-2. Moving an object between containers

```
package {
  import flash.display.*;
  import flash.text.*;
  import flash.events.*;

  public class WordHighlighter extends Sprite {
    // The first word
    private var word1:Sprite;
    private var text1:TextField;

    // The second word
    private var word2:Sprite;
    private var text2:TextField;
```

Example 20-2. Moving an object between containers (continued)

```
  // The highlight shape
  private var bgRect:Shape;

  public function WordHighlighter () {
    // Create the first TextField and Sprite
    word1 = new Sprite();
    text1 = new TextField();
    text1.text = "Products";
    text1.selectable = false;
    text1.autoSize = TextFieldAutoSize.LEFT;
    word1.addChild(text1)
    text1.addEventListener(MouseEvent.MOUSE_OVER, mouseOverListener);

    // Create the second TextField and Sprite
    word2 = new Sprite();
    text2 = new TextField();
    text2.text = "Services";
    text2.selectable = false;
    text2.autoSize = TextFieldAutoSize.LEFT;
    word2.x = 75;
    word2.addChild(text2)
    text2.addEventListener(MouseEvent.MOUSE_OVER, mouseOverListener);

    // Add the Sprite instances to WordHighlighter's display hierarchy
    addChild(word1);
    addChild(word2);

    // Create the Shape (a rounded rectangle)
    bgRect = new Shape();
    bgRect.graphics.lineStyle(1);
    bgRect.graphics.beginFill(0xCCCCCC, 1);
    bgRect.graphics.drawRoundRect(0, 0, 60, 15, 8);
  }

  // Invoked when the mouse pointer moves over a text field.
  private function mouseOverListener (e:MouseEvent):void {
    // If the TextField's parent Sprite does not already contain
    // the shape, then move it there. DisplayObjectContainer.contains()
    // returns true if the specified object is a descendant
    // of the container.
    if (!e.target.parent.contains(bgRect)) {
      e.target.parent.addChildAt(bgRect, 0);
    }
  }
}
}
```

As it stands, the code in Example 20-2 always leaves one of the text fields highlighted. To remove the highlight when the mouse moves away from both text fields, we would first register both text fields to receive the MouseEvent.MOUSE_OUT event:

```
text1.addEventListener(MouseEvent.MOUSE_OUT, mouseOutListener);
text2.addEventListener(MouseEvent.MOUSE_OUT, mouseOutListener);
```

Then, we would implement code to remove the rectangle in response to `MouseEvent.MOUSE_OUT`:

```
private function mouseOutListener (e:MouseEvent):void {
  // If the highlight is present...
  if (e.target.parent.contains(bgRect)) {
    // ...remove it
    e.target.parent.removeChild(bgRect);
  }
}
```

Traversing Objects in a Display Hierarchy

To traverse objects in a display hierarchy means to systematically access some or all of a container's child objects, typically to manipulate them in some way.

To access the *direct* children of a container (but not grandchildren or any other descendant children), we use a loop statement. The loop iterates over each depth position in the container. Within the loop body, we access each child according to its depth using the *DisplayObjectContainer* class's instance method *getChildAt()*. The following code shows the general technique; it displays the string value of all objects contained by *theContainer*:

```
for (var i:int=0; i < theContainer.numChildren; i++) {
  trace(theContainer.getChildAt(i).toString( ));
}
```

Example 20-3 shows a more concrete, if whimsical, application of display object children traversal. It creates 20 *Shape* instances containing rectangles and then uses the preceding traversal technique to rotate those instances when the mouse is clicked. The traversal code is shown in bold. (In upcoming chapters, we'll study both the vector-drawing techniques and mouse-event-handling techniques used in the example.)

Example 20-3. Rotating rectangles

```
package {
  import flash.display.*;
  import flash.events.*;

  public class RotatingRectangles extends Sprite {
    public function RotatingRectangles () {
      // Create 20 rectangles
      var rects:Array = new Array();
      for (var i:int = 0; i < 20; i++) {
        rects[i] = new Shape();
        rects[i].graphics.lineStyle(1);
        rects[i].graphics.beginFill(Math.floor(Math.random( )*0xFFFFFF), 1);
        rects[i].graphics.drawRect(0, 0, 100, 50);
        rects[i].x = Math.floor(Math.random( )*500);
        rects[i].y = Math.floor(Math.random( )*400);
        addChild(rects[i]);
      }
```

Example 20-3. Rotating rectangles (continued)

```
      // Register for mouse clicks
      stage.addEventListener(MouseEvent.MOUSE_DOWN, mouseDownListener);
    }

    // Rotates rectangles when the mouse is clicked
    private function mouseDownListener (e:Event):void {
      // Rotate each of this object's display children randomly.
      for (var i:int=0; i < numChildren; i++) {
        getChildAt(i).rotation = Math.floor(Math.random( )*360);
      }
    }
  }
}
```

To access not just the direct children of a container, but all of its descendants, we combine the preceding *for* loop with a recursive function. Example 20-4 shows the general approach.

Example 20-4. Recursive display list tree traversal

```
public function processChildren (container:DisplayObjectContainer):void {
  for (var i:int = 0; i < container.numChildren; i++) {
    // Process the child here. For example, the following line
    // prints this child's string value as debugging output.
    var thisChild:DisplayObject = container.getChildAt(i);
    trace(thisChild.toString( ));

    // If this child is, itself, a container, then process its children.
    if (thisChild is DisplayObjectContainer) {
      processChildren(DisplayObjectContainer(thisChild));
    }
  }
}
```

The following function, *rotateChildren()*, applies the generalized code from Example 20-4. It randomly rotates all the descendants of a specified container (not just the children). However, notice the minor change in the approach from Example 20-4: *rotateChildren()* only rotates noncontainer children.

```
public function rotateChildren (container:DisplayObjectContainer):void {
  for (var i:int = 0; i < container.numChildren; i++) {
    var thisChild:DisplayObject = container.getChildAt(i);
    if (thisChild is DisplayObjectContainer) {
      rotateChildren(DisplayObjectContainer(thisChild));
    } else {
      thisChild.rotation =  Math.floor(Math.random( )*360);
    }
  }
}
```

Manipulating Objects in Containers Collectively

In the earlier section "Display API Overview," we learned that child objects automatically move, rotate, and transform when their ancestors are moved, rotated, and transformed. We can use this feature to perform collective visual modifications to groups of objects. To learn how, let's create two rectangular *Shape* instances in a *Sprite* instance:

```
// Create two rectangles
var rect1:Shape = new Shape();
rect1.graphics.lineStyle(1);
rect1.graphics.beginFill(0x0000FF, 1);
rect1.graphics.drawRect(0, 0, 75, 50);

var rect2:Shape = new Shape();
rect2.graphics.lineStyle(1);
rect2.graphics.beginFill(0xFF0000, 1);
rect2.graphics.drawRect(0, 0, 75, 50);
rect2.x = 50;
rect2.y = 75;

// Create the container
var group:Sprite = new Sprite();

// Add the rectangles to the container
group.addChild(rect1);
group.addChild(rect2);

// Add the container to the main application
someMainApp.addChild(group);
```

Figure 20-13 shows the result.

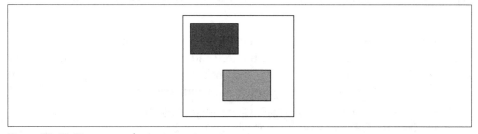

Figure 20-13. Two rectangles in a container

Now let's move, scale, and rotate the container, as follows:

```
group.x = 40;
group.scaleY = .15;
group.rotation = 15;
```

The modifications affect the child *Shape* instances, as shown in Figure 20-14.

Figure 20-14. Move, scale, and rotate

A container's transformations also affect children added *after* the transformations are applied. For example, if we now add a third rectangular *Shape* to group, that *Shape* is moved, scaled, and rotated according to group's existing transformations:

```
// Create a third rectangle
var rect3:Shape = new Shape( );
rect3.graphics.lineStyle(1);
rect3.graphics.beginFill(0x00FF00, 1);
rect3.graphics.drawRect(0, 0, 75, 50);
rect3.x = 25;
rect3.y = 35;
group.addChild(rect3);
```

Figure 20-15 shows the result.

Figure 20-15. A third rectangle

At any time, we can remove or change the container's transformation, and all children will be affected. For example, the following code restores the container to its original state:

```
group.scaleY = 1;
group.x = 0;
group.rotation = 0;
```

Figure 20-16 shows the result. Notice that the third rectangle now appears in its true dimensions and position.

Color and coordinate transformations made to a container via the *DisplayObject* class's instance variable transform are also inherited by its descendants. For example, the following code applies a black color transformation to group, causing all three rectangles to be colored solid black.

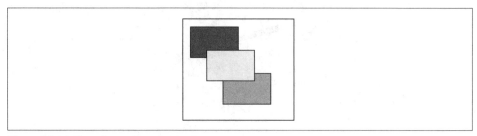

Figure 20-16. Transformations removed

```
import flash.geom.ColorTransform;
var blackTransform:ColorTransform = new ColorTransform( );
blackTransform.color = 0x000000;
group.transform.colorTransform = blackTransform;
```

 For complete details on the types of color and coordinate transformations available in ActionScript, see *flash.geom.Transform* in Adobe's ActionScript Language Reference.

Transformations made to nested containers are compounded. For example, the following code places a rectangle in a *Sprite* that is nested within another *Sprite*. Both *Sprite* instances are rotated 45 degrees. As a result, the rectangle appears rotated on screen by 90 degrees (45 + 45).

```
// Create a rectangle
var rect1:Shape = new Shape( );
rect1.graphics.lineStyle(1);
rect1.graphics.beginFill(0x0000FF, 1);
rect1.graphics.drawRect(0, 0, 75, 50);

var outerGroup:Sprite = new Sprite( );
var innerGroup:Sprite = new Sprite( );

innerGroup.addChild(rect1);
outerGroup.addChild(innerGroup);
innerGroup.rotation = 45;
outerGroup.rotation = 45;
```

Descendant Access to a .swf File's Main Class Instance

In ActionScript 3.0, the display descendants of a *.swf* file's main class instance can retrieve a reference to that instance via the *DisplayObject* class's instance variable root. For example, consider Example 20-5, which shows a *.swf* file's main class, *App*. When the code runs, ActionScript automatically creates an *App* instance and runs its constructor. Within the constructor, two *App* instance descendants (a *Sprite* object and a *Shape* object) use root to access the *App* instance.

Example 20-5. Descendant access to a .swf file's main class instance

```
package {
  import flash.display.*;
  import flash.geom.*;

  public class App extends Sprite {
    public function App () {
      // Make the descendants...
      var rect:Shape = new Shape();
      rect.graphics.lineStyle(1);
      rect.graphics.beginFill(0x0000FF, 1);
      rect.graphics.drawRect(0, 0, 75, 50);
      var sprite:Sprite = new Sprite();
      sprite.addChild(rect);
      addChild(sprite);

      // Use DisplayObject.root to access this App instance
      trace(rect.root);    // Displays: [object App]
      trace(sprite.root);  // Displays: [object App]
    }
  }
}
```

When an object is on the display list but is *not* a descendant of a *.swf* file's main class instance, its root variable returns a reference to the *Stage* instance. For example, the following code modifies the *App* class from Example 20-5 so that the *Sprite* object and its child *Shape* object are added directly to the *Stage* instance. Because the *Sprite* and *Shape* objects are not descendants of a *.swf* file's main class instance, their root variables refer to the *Stage* instance.

```
package {
  import flash.display.*;
  import flash.geom.*;

  public class App extends Sprite {
    public function App () {
      var rect:Shape = new Shape();
      rect.graphics.lineStyle(1);
      rect.graphics.beginFill(0x0000FF, 1);
      rect.graphics.drawRect(0, 0, 75, 50);
      var sprite:Sprite = new Sprite();
      sprite.addChild(rect);
      // Add child to Stage instance, not this App instance
      stage.addChild(sprite);

      trace(rect.root);    // Displays: [object Stage]
      trace(sprite.root);  // Displays: [object Stage]
    }
  }
}
```

For objects that are on the display list but are not descendants of a *.swf* file's main-class instance, the *DisplayObject* class's instance variable root is synonymous with its instance variable stage.

In the first *.swf* file opened by a Flash runtime, the root variable of display objects that are not on the display list has the value null.

In *.swf* files loaded by other *.swf* files, the root variable is set as follows:

- For display objects that are display descendants of the main class instance, the root variable refers to that instance, even if the main class instance is not on the display list.

- For display objects that are not display descendants of the main class instance *and* are not on the display list, the root variable has the value null.

The rebirth of _root

In ActionScript 2.0 and older versions of the language, the global _root variable referred to the top-level movie clip of the current _level. Prior to ActionScript 3.0, conventional wisdom held that _root should be avoided because its meaning was volatile (the object to which it referred changed when loading a *.swf* file into a movie clip).

In ActionScript 3.0, the *DisplayObject* class's instance variable root replaces the global _root variable. *DisplayObject*'s root variable does not suffer from its predecessor's volatility and is considered a clean, safe member of the display API.

 Longtime ActionScript programmers who are used to avoiding the legacy _root variable should feel neither fear nor guilt when using the *DisplayObject* class's instance variable root in ActionScript 3.0.

Whither _level0?

In ActionScript 1.0 and 2.0, the *loadMovieNum()* function was used to stack external .*swf* files on independent Flash Player *levels*. Each level was referred to using the format: _level*n*, where *n* indicated the level's numeric order in the level stack. As of ActionScript 3.0, the concept of levels has been completely removed from the Flash runtime API.

The closest analogue to levels in ActionScript 3.0 is the *Stage* instance's children. However, whereas in ActionScript 1.0 and 2.0, external .*swf* files could be loaded directly onto a _level, in ActionScript 3.0, external .*swf* files cannot be loaded directly into the *Stage* instance's child list. Instead, to add an external .*swf* file to the *Stage* instance's child list, we must first load that .*swf* file via a *Loader* object and then move it to the *Stage* instance via stage.addChild( ), as follows:

```
var loader:Loader = new Loader( );
loader.load(new URLRequest("newContent.swf"));
stage.addChild(loader);
```

Furthermore, it is no longer possible to remove all content in Flash Player by unloading _level0. Code such as the following is no longer valid:

```
// Clear all content in Flash Player. Deprecated in ActionScript 3.0.
unloadMovieNum(0);
```

The closest ActionScript 3.0 replacement for unloadMovieNum(0) is:

```
stage.removeChildAt(0);
```

Using stage.removeChildAt(0) removes the *Stage* instance's first child from the display list but does not necessarily remove it from the program. If the program maintains other references to the child, the child will continue to exist, ready to be re-added to some other container. As shown in the earlier section "Removing Assets from Memory," to completely remove a display object from a program, we must both remove it from its container and remove all references to it. Furthermore, invoking stage.removeChildAt(0) affects the *Stage* instance's first child only; other children are not removed from the display list (contrast this with ActionScript 1.0 and 2.0, where invoking unloadMovieNum(0) removed all content from all _levels). To remove all children of the *Stage* instance, we use the following code within the object that currently resides at depth 0 of the *Stage* instance:

```
while (stage.numChildren > 0) {
  stage.removeChildAt(stage.numChildren-1);
  // When the last child is removed, stage is set to null, so quit
  if (stage == null) {
    break;
  }
}
```

Likewise, the following legacy code—which clears Flash Player of all content and then places *newConent.swf* on _level0—is no longer valid:

```
loadMovieNum("newContent.swf", 0);
```

And there is no ActionScript 3.0 equivalent. However, future versions of Action-Script might re-introduce the ability to clear a Flash runtime of all content, replacing it with a new external *.swf* file.

Containment Events

Earlier we learned how to use the *addChild()* and *addChildAt()* methods to add a new display child to a *DisplayObjectContainer* object. Recall the general code:

```
// The addChild( ) method
someContainer.addChild(newChild)

// The addChildAt( ) method
someContainer.addChild(newChild, depth)
```

We also learned that existing child display objects can be removed from a *DisplayObjectContainer* object via the *removeChild()* and *removeChildAt()* methods. Again, recall the following general code:

```
// The removeChild( ) method
someContainer.removeChild(childToRemove)
// The removeChildAt( ) method
someContainer.removeChildAt(depthOfChildToRemove)
```

Finally, we learned that an existing child display object can be removed from a container by moving that child to another container via either *addChild()* and *addChildAt()*. Here's the code:

```
// Add child to someContainer
someContainer.addChild(child)

// Remove child from someContainer by moving it to someOtherContainer
someOtherContainer.addChild(child)
```

Each of these child additions and removals is accompanied by a built-in Flash runtime event—either `Event.ADDED` or `Event.REMOVED`. The following three sections explore how these two events are used in display programming.

 The following sections require a good understanding of ActionScript's hierarchical event dispatch system, as discussed in Chapter 21. If you are not yet thoroughly familiar with hierarchical event dispatch, read Chapter 21 before continuing with the following sections.

The Event.ADDED and Event.REMOVED Events

When a new child display object is added to a *DisplayObjectContainer* object, ActionScript dispatches an `Event.ADDED` event targeted at the new child. Likewise, when an existing child display object is removed from a *DisplayObjectContainer* object, ActionScript dispatches an `Event.REMOVED` event targeted at the removed child.

As discussed in Chapter 21, when an event dispatch targets an object in a display hierarchy, that object and all of its ancestors are notified of the event. Hence, when the `Event.ADDED` event occurs, the added child, its new parent container, and all ancestors of that container are notified that the child was added. Likewise, when the `Event.REMOVED` event occurs, the removed child and its old parent container and all ancestors of that container are notified that the child is about to be removed. Therefore the `Event.ADDED` and `Event.REMOVED` events can be used in two different ways:

- A *DisplayObjectContainer* instance can use the `Event.ADDED` and `Event.REMOVED` events to detect when it has gained or lost a display descendant.

- A *DisplayObject* instance can use the `Event.ADDED` and `Event.REMOVED` events to detect when it has been added to or removed from a parent container.

Let's take a look at some generalized code that demonstrates the preceding scenarios, starting with a container detecting a new descendant.

We'll start by creating two *Sprite* objects: one to act as a container and the other as a child:

```
var container:Sprite = new Sprite( );
var child:Sprite = new Sprite( );
```

Next we create a listener method, *addedListener()*, to register with container for Event.ADDED events:

```
private function addedListener (e:Event):void {
  trace("Added was triggered");
}
```

Then we register *addedListener()* with container:

```
container.addEventListener(Event.ADDED, addedListener);
```

Finally, we add child to container:

```
container.addChild(child);
```

When the preceding code runs, the Flash runtime dispatches an Event.ADDED event targeted at child. As a result, because container is a display ancestor of child, the *addedListener()* function that we registered with container is triggered during the event's bubbling phase (for more on bubbling, see Chapter 21) .

 When the Event.ADDED event triggers an event listener during the capture phase or the bubbling phase, we know that the object with which the listener registered has a new display descendant.

Now let's add a new child to child, making container a proud grandparent:

```
var grandchild:Sprite = new Sprite( );
child.addChild(grandchild);
```

When the preceding code runs, the Flash runtime again dispatches an Event.ADDED event, this time targeted at grandchild, and *addedListener()* is again triggered during the bubbling phase. Because the listener is triggered during the bubbling phase, we know that container has a new descendant, but we're not sure whether that descendant is a direct child of container. To determine whether the new descendant is a direct child of container, we check if the child's parent variable is equal to the container object, as follows:

```
private function addedListener (e:Event):void {
  // Remember that Event.currentTarget refers to the object
  // that registered the currently executing listener--in
  // this case, container. Remember also that Event.target
  // refers to the event target, in this case grandchild.
  if (DisplayObject(e.target.parent) == e.currentTarget) {
    trace("A direct child was added");
```

```
    } else {
      trace("A descendant was added");
    }
}
```

Continuing with our example, let's make container feel like a kid again by adding it (and, by extension, its two descendants) to the *Stage* instance:

```
stage.addChild(container);
```

When the preceding code runs, the Flash runtime dispatches an Event.ADDED event targeted at container. Once again, *addedListener( )* is triggered—this time during the target phase, not the bubbling phase. Because the listener is triggered during the target phase, we know that container, itself, has been added to a parent container.

 When the Event.ADDED event triggers an event listener during the target phase, we know that the object with which the listener registered was added to a parent container.

To distinguish between container gaining a new descendant and container, itself, being added to a parent container, we examine the current event phase, as follows:

```
private function addedListener (e:Event):void {
  // If this listener was triggered during the capture or bubbling phases...
  if (e.eventPhase != EventPhase.AT_TARGET) {
    // ...then container has a new descendant
    trace("new descendant: " + e.target);
  } else {
    // ...otherwise, container was added to a new parent
    trace("new parent: " + DisplayObject(e.target).parent);
  }
}
```

Now let's turn to the Event.REMOVED event. It works just like the Event.ADDED event, but is triggered by object removals rather than additions:

The following code registers an Event.REMOVED listener, named *removedListener()*, with container for the Event.REMOVED event:

```
container.addEventListener(Event.REMOVED, removedListener);
```

Now let's remove a descendant from the container object:

```
child.removeChild(grandchild)
```

When the preceding code runs, the Flash runtime dispatches an Event.REMOVED event targeted at grandchild, and *removedListener()* is triggered during the bubbling phase.

Next, the following code removes container, itself, from the *Stage* instance:

```
stage.removeChild(container)
```

When the preceding code runs, the Flash runtime dispatches an Event.REMOVED event targeted at container, and *removedListener()* is triggered during the target phase.

Just as with *addedListener()*, within *removedListener()* we can distinguish between container losing a descendant and container, itself, being removed from its parent container by examining the current event phase, as follows:

```
private function removedListener (e:Event):void {
  // If this listener was triggered during the capture or bubbling phases...
  if (e.eventPhase != EventPhase.AT_TARGET) {
    // ...then a descendant is about to be removed from container
    trace("a descendant was removed from container: " + e.target);
  } else {
    // ...otherwise, container is about to be removed from its parent
    trace("container is about to be removed from its parent: "
        + DisplayObject(e.target).parent);
  }
}
```

For reference, Example 20-6 presents the preceding Event.ADDED and Event.REMOVED example code within the context of a test class, *ContainmentEventDemo*. We'll study real-world containment-event examples over the next two sections.

Example 20-6. Containment events demonstrated

```
package {
  import flash.display.*;
  import flash.events.*;

  public class ContainmentEventDemo extends Sprite {
    public function ContainmentEventDemo ( ) {
      // Create Sprite objects
      var container:Sprite = new Sprite( );
      var child:Sprite = new Sprite( );
      var grandchild:Sprite = new Sprite( );

      // Start listening for Event.ADDED and Event.REMOVED events
      container.addEventListener(Event.ADDED, addedListener);
      container.addEventListener(Event.REMOVED, removedListener);

      // Add child to container
      container.addChild(child);  // Triggers addedListener( ) during
                                  // the bubbling phase

      // Add grandchild to child
      child.addChild(grandchild);  // Triggers addedListener( ) during
                                   // the bubbling phase

      // Add container to Stage
      stage.addChild(container);  // Triggers addedListener( ) during
                                  // the target phase

      // Remove grandchild from child
```

Example 20-6. Containment events demonstrated (continued)

```
        child.removeChild(grandchild)  // Triggers removedListener( ) during
                                       // the bubbling phase

      // Remove container from Stage
      stage.removeChild(container)  // Triggers removedListener( ) during
                                    // the target phase
    }

    // Handles Event.ADDED events
    private function addedListener (e:Event):void {
      if (e.eventPhase != EventPhase.AT_TARGET) {
        trace("container has a new descendant: " + e.target);
      } else {
        trace("container was added to a new parent: "
            + DisplayObject(e.target).parent);
      }
    }

    // Handles Event.REMOVED events
    private function removedListener (e:Event):void {
      if (e.eventPhase != EventPhase.AT_TARGET) {
        trace("a descendant was removed from container: " + e.target);
      } else {
        trace("container was removed from its parent: "
            + DisplayObject(e.target).parent);
      }
    }
  }
}

// Running ContainmentEventDemo produces the following output:
container has a new descendant: [object Sprite]
container has a new descendant: [object Sprite]
container was added to a new parent: [object Stage]
a descendant was removed from container: [object Sprite]
container was removed from its parent: [object Stage]
```

A Real-World Containment-Event Example

Now that we've seen how the Event.ADDED and Event.REMOVED events work in theory, let's consider how they can be used in a real application. Suppose we're writing a class, *IconPanel*, that manages the visual layout of graphical icons. The *IconPanel* class is used as one of the parts of a larger window component in a windowing interface. Any time a new icon is added to, or removed from, an *IconPanel* object, that object executes an icon-layout algorithm. To detect the addition and removal of child icons, the *IconPanel* object registers listeners for the Event.ADDED and Event.REMOVED events.

Example 20-7 shows the code for the *IconPanel* class, simplified to illustrate the use of Event.ADDED and Event.REMOVED. Notice that the Event.ADDED and Event.REMOVED event listeners execute icon-layout code when the *IconPanel* gains or loses a new direct child only. No layout code is executed in the following situations:

- When an *IconPanel* object gains or loses a descendant that is not a direct child
- When an *IconPanel* object, itself, is added to a parent container

Example 20-7. Arranging icons in the IconPanel class

```
package {
  import flash.display.*;
  import flash.events.*;

  public class IconPanel extends Sprite {
    public function IconPanel ( ) {
      addEventListener(Event.ADDED, addedListener);
      addEventListener(Event.REMOVED, removedListener);
    }

    public function updateLayout ( ):void {
      // Execute layout algorithm (code not shown)
    }

    // Handles Event.ADDED events
    private function addedListener (e:Event):void {
      if (DisplayObject(e.target.parent) == e.currentTarget) {
        updateLayout( );
      }
    }

    // Handles Event.REMOVED events
    private function removedListener (e:Event):void {
      if (DisplayObject(e.target.parent) == e.currentTarget) {
        updateLayout( );
      }
    }
  }
}
```

The ADDED_TO_STAGE and REMOVED_FROM_STAGE Events

As discussed in the previous two sections, the Event.ADDED and Event.REMOVED events occur when a *DisplayObject* instance is added to, or removed from, a *DisplayObjectContainer* instance. The Event.ADDED and Event.REMOVED events do not, however, indicate whether a given object is currently on the display list. To detect when a *DisplayObject* instance is added to, or removed from, the display list, we use the Event.ADDED_TO_STAGE and Event.REMOVED_FROM_STAGE events, both of which were added to the display API with the release of Flash Player 9.0.28.0.

When a display object (or one of its ancestors) is added to the display list, the Flash runtime dispatches an Event.ADDED_TO_STAGE event targeted at that object. Conversely, when a display object (or one of its ancestors) is about to be removed from the display list, the Flash runtime dispatches an Event.REMOVED_FROM_STAGE event targeted at that object.

 Unlike the Event.ADDED and Event.REMOVED events, Event.ADDED_TO_STAGE and Event.REMOVED_FROM_STAGE events do not bubble. To receive an Event.ADDED_TO_STAGE or Event.REMOVED_FROM_STAGE event through an object's ancestor, register with that ancestor for the event's capture phase.

The generalized code required to register a listener with a *DisplayObject* instance for the Event.ADDED_TO_STAGE event is as follows:

```
theDisplayObject.addEventListener(Event.ADDED_TO_STAGE,
                                  addedToStageListener);
```

The generalized event-listener code required for an Event.ADDED_TO_STAGE listener is:

```
private function addedToStageListener (e:Event):void {
}
```

The generalized code required to register a listener with a *DisplayObject* instance for the Event.REMOVED_FROM_STAGE event is as follows:

```
theDisplayObject.addEventListener(Event.REMOVED_FROM_STAGE,
                                  removedFromStageListener);
```

The generalized event-listener code required for an Event.REMOVED_FROM_STAGE listener is:

```
private function removedFromStageListener (e:Event):void {
}
```

Display objects typically use the Event.ADDED_TO_STAGE event to ensure that the *Stage* object is accessible before using its methods, variables, or events. For example, suppose we're creating a class, *CustomMousePointer*, that represents a custom mouse pointer. Our *CustomMousePointer* class extends the *Sprite* class so that its instances can be added to the display list. In the class, we want to register with the *Stage* instance for the MouseEvent.MOUSE_MOVE event so that we can keep the custom mouse pointer's position synchronized with the system mouse pointer's position. However, when a new *CustomMousePointer* object is created, it is initially not on the display list, so it has no access to the *Stage* instance and cannot register for the MouseEvent.MOUSE_MOVE event. Instead, the *CustomMousePointer* object must wait to be notified that it has been added to the display list (via the Event.ADDED_TO_STAGE event). Once the *CustomMousePointer* object is on the display list, its stage variable refers to the *Stage* instance, and it can safely register for the MouseEvent.MOUSE_MOVE event. The following code shows the relevant Event.ADDED_TO_STAGE excerpt from the *CustomMousePointer* class. For the full *CustomMousePointer* class code listing, see the section "Finding the Mouse Pointer's Position" in Chapter 22.

```
package {
  public class CustomMousePointer extends Sprite {
    public function CustomMousePointer () {
      // Ask to be notified when this object is added to the display list
      addEventListener(Event.ADDED_TO_STAGE, addedToStageListener);
    }

    // Triggered when this object is added to the display list
    private function addedToStageListener (e:Event):void {
      // Now its safe to register with the Stage instance for
      // MouseEvent.MOUSE_MOVE events
      stage.addEventListener(MouseEvent.MOUSE_MOVE, mouseMoveListener);
    }
  }
}
```

Custom Event.ADDED_TO_STAGE and Event.REMOVED_FROM_STAGE events

The initial release of Flash Player 9 did not offer either the Event.ADDED_TO_STAGE event or the Event.REMOVED_FROM_STAGE events. However, using the original display API and a little ingenuity, we can manually detect when a given object has been added to or removed from the display list. To do so, we must monitor the state of that object's ancestors using the Event.ADDED and Event.REMOVED events.

Example 20-8, which follows shortly, shows the approach. In the example, the custom *StageDetector* class monitors a display object to see when it is added to, or removed from, the display list. When the object is added to the display list, *StageDetector* broadcasts the custom StageDetector.ADDED_TO_STAGE event. When the object is removed from the display list, *StageDetector* broadcasts the custom StageDetector.REMOVED_FROM_STAGE event.

The *StageDetector* class's custom ADDED_TO_STAGE and REMOVED_FROM_STAGE events can be used without any knowledge or understanding of the code in the *StageDetector* class. However, the *StageDetector* class serves as an interesting summary of the display list programming techniques we've seen in this chapter, so let's take a closer look at how it works.

In the *StageDetector* class, the object being monitored for ADDED_TO_STAGE and REMOVED_FROM_STAGE events is assigned to the watchedObject variable. The root of watchedObject's display hierarchy is assigned to the watchedRoot variable. The general approach taken by *StageDetector* to detect whether watchedObject is on the display list is as follows:

- Monitor the watchedRoot for Event.ADDED and Event.REMOVED events.

- Any time watchedRoot is added to a *DisplayObjectContainer* object, check if watchedObject is now on the display list (watchedObject is on the display list if its stage variable is non-null.) If watchedObject is now on the display list, dispatch the StageDetector.ADDED_TO_STAGE event. If it's not, start monitoring the new watchedRoot for Event.ADDED and Event.REMOVED events.

- While watchedObject is on the display list, if the watchedRoot or any of the watchedRoot's descendants are removed from a *DisplayObjectContainer* object, then check if the removed object is an ancestor of watchedObject. If the removed object is a watchedObject ancestor, dispatch the StageDetector.REMOVED_FROM_ STAGE event, and start monitoring the watchedObject's new display hierarchy root for Event.ADDED and Event.REMOVED events.

The code for the *StageDetector* class follows.

Example 20-8. Custom ADDED_TO_STAGE and REMOVED_FROM_STAGE events

```
package {
  import flash.display.*;
  import flash.events.*;

  // Monitors a specified display object to see when it is added to or
  // removed from the Stage, and broadcasts the correspoding custom events
  // StageDetector.ADDED_TO_STAGE and StageDetector.REMOVED_FROM_STAGE.

  // USAGE:
  // var stageDetector:StageDetector = new StageDetector(someDisplayObject);
  // stageDetector.addEventListener(StageDetector.ADDED_TO_STAGE,
  //                                addedToStageListenerFunction);
  // stageDetector.addEventListener(StageDetector.REMOVED_FROM_STAGE,
  //                                removedFromStageListenerFunction);
  public class StageDetector extends EventDispatcher {
    // Event constants
    public static const ADDED_TO_STAGE:String = "ADDED_TO_STAGE";
    public static const REMOVED_FROM_STAGE:String = "REMOVED_FROM_STAGE";

    // The object for which ADDED_TO_STAGE and REMOVED_FROM_STAGE events
    // will be generated
    private var watchedObject:DisplayObject = null;

    // The root of the display hierarchy that contains watchedObject
    private var watchedRoot:DisplayObject = null;

    // Flag indicating whether watchedObject is currently on the
    // display list
    private var onStage:Boolean = false;

    // Constructor
    public function StageDetector (objectToWatch:DisplayObject) {
      // Begin monitoring the specified object
      setWatchedObject(objectToWatch);
    }

    // Begins monitoring the specified object to see when it is added to or
    // removed from the display list
    public function setWatchedObject (objectToWatch:DisplayObject):void {
      // Track the object being monitored
      watchedObject = objectToWatch;
```

```
    // Note whether watchedObject is currently on the display list
    if (watchedObject.stage != null) {
      onStage = true;
    }

    // Find the root of the display hierarchy containing the
    // watchedObject, and register with it for ADDED/REMOVED events.
    // By observing where watchedObject's root is added and removed,
    // we'll determine whether watchedObject is on or off the
    // display list.
    setWatchedRoot(findWatchedObjectRoot( ));
  }

  // Returns a reference to the object being monitored
  public function getWatchedObject ( ):DisplayObject {
    return watchedObject;
  }

  // Frees this StageDetector object's resources. Call this method before
  // discarding a StageDetector object.
  public function dispose ( ):void {
    clearWatchedRoot( );
    watchedObject = null;
  }

  // Handles Event.ADDED events targeted at the root of
  // watchedObject's display hierarchy
  private function addedListener (e:Event):void {
    // If the current watchedRoot was added...
    if (e.eventPhase == EventPhase.AT_TARGET) {
      // ...check if watchedObject is now on the display list
      if (watchedObject.stage != null) {
        // Note that watchedObject is now on the display list
        onStage = true;
        // Notify listeners that watchedObject is now
        // on the display list
        dispatchEvent(new Event(StageDetector.ADDED_TO_STAGE));
      }
      // watchedRoot was added to another container, so there's
      // now a new root of the display hierarchy containing
      // watchedObject. Find that new root, and register with it
      // for ADDED and REMOVED events.
      setWatchedRoot(findWatchedObjectRoot());
    }
  }

  // Handles Event.REMOVED events for the root of
  // watchedObject's display hierarchy
  private function removedListener (e:Event):void {
    // If watchedObject is on the display list...
    if (onStage) {
      // ...check if watchedObject or one of its ancestors was removed
```

```
      var wasRemoved:Boolean = false;
      var ancestor:DisplayObject = watchedObject;
      var target:DisplayObject = DisplayObject(e.target);
      while (ancestor != null) {
        if (target == ancestor) {
          wasRemoved = true;
          break;
        }
        ancestor = ancestor.parent;
      }

      // If watchedObject or one of its ancestors was removed...
      if (wasRemoved) {
        // ...register for ADDED and REMOVED events from the removed
        // object (which is the new root of watchedObject's display
        // hierarchy).
        setWatchedRoot(target);

        // Note that watchedObject is not on the display list anymore
        onStage = false;

        // Notify listeners that watchedObject was removed from the Stage
        dispatchEvent(new Event(StageDetector.REMOVED_FROM_STAGE));
      }
    }
  }

  // Returns the root of the display hierarchy that currently contains
  // watchedObject
  private function findWatchedObjectRoot ( ):DisplayObject {
    var watchedObjectRoot:DisplayObject = watchedObject;
    while (watchedObjectRoot.parent != null) {
      watchedObjectRoot = watchedObjectRoot.parent;
    }
    return watchedObjectRoot;
  }

  // Begins listening for ADDED and REMOVED events targeted at the root of
  // watchedObject's display hierarchy
  private function setWatchedRoot (newWatchedRoot:DisplayObject):void {
    clearWatchedRoot( );
    watchedRoot = newWatchedRoot;
    registerListeners(watchedRoot);
  }

  // Removes event listeners from watchedRoot, and removes
  // this StageDetector object's reference to watchedRoot
  private function clearWatchedRoot ( ):void {
    if (watchedRoot != null) {
      unregisterListeners(watchedRoot);
      watchedRoot = null;
    }
  }
```

Example 20-8. Custom ADDED_TO_STAGE and REMOVED_FROM_STAGE events (continued)

```
    // Registers ADDED and REMOVED event listeners with watchedRoot
    private function registerListeners (target:DisplayObject):void {
      target.addEventListener(Event.ADDED, addedListener);
      target.addEventListener(Event.REMOVED, removedListener);
    }

    // Unregisters ADDED and REMOVED event listeners from watchedRoot
    private function unregisterListeners (target:DisplayObject):void {
      target.removeEventListener(Event.ADDED, addedListener);
      target.removeEventListener(Event.REMOVED, removedListener);
    }
  }
}
```

In Chapter 22, we'll see the custom `StageDetector.ADDED_TO_STAGE` and `StageDetector.REMOVED_FROM_STAGE` events used in the *CustomMousePointer* class.

We've now finished our look at the container API. Now let's consider one last short, but fundamental display programming topic: custom graphical classes.

Custom Graphical Classes

We've drawn lots of rectangles, circles, and triangles in this chapter. So many, that some of the examples we've studied have had a distinct "code smell": their code was repetitive, and therefore error-prone.

Learn more about code smell (common signs of potential problems in code) at *http://xp.c2.com/CodeSmell.html*.

To promote reuse and modularity when working with primitive shapes, we can move repetitive drawing routines into custom classes that extend the *Shape* class. Let's start with a custom *Rectangle* class, using an extremely simple approach that provides a very limited set of stroke and fill options, and does not allow the rectangle to be changed once drawn. Example 20-9 shows the code. (We'll expand on the *Rectangle* class's features in Chapter 25.)

Example 20-9. Rectangle, a simple shape subclass

```
package {
  import flash.display.Shape;

  public class Rectangle extends Shape {
    public function Rectangle (w:Number,
                               h:Number,
                               lineThickness:Number,
                               lineColor:uint,
                               fillColor:uint) {
```

Example 20-9. Rectangle, a simple shape subclass (continued)

```
    graphics.lineStyle(lineThickness, lineColor);
    graphics.beginFill(fillColor, 1);
    graphics.drawRect(0, 0, w, h);
  }
 }
}
```

Because *Rectangle* extends *Shape*, it inherits the *Shape* class's graphics variable, and can use it to draw the rectangular shape.

To create a new *Rectangle*, we use the following familiar code:

```
var rect:Rectangle = new Rectangle(100, 50, 3, 0xFF0000, 0x0000FF);
```

Because *Shape* is a *DisplayObject* descendant, *Rectangle* inherits the ability to be added to the display list (as does any descendant of *DisplayObject*), like this:

```
someContainer.addChild(rect);
```

As a descendant of *DisplayObject*, the *Rectangle* object can also be positioned, rotated, and otherwise manipulate like any other displayable object. For example, here we set the *Rectangle* object's horizontal position to 15 and vertical position to 30:

```
rect.x = 15;
rect.y = 30;
```

And the fun doesn't stop at rectangles. Every class in the display API can be extended. For example, an application could extend the *TextField* class when displaying a customized form of text. Example 20-10 demonstrates, showing a *TextField* subclass that creates a hyperlinked text header.

Example 20-10. ClickableHeading, a TextField subclass

```
package {
  import flash.display.*;

  public class ClickableHeading extends TextField {
    public function ClickableHeading (headText:String, URL:String) {
      html = true;
      autoSize = TextFieldAutoSize.LEFT;
      htmlText = "<a href='" + URL + "'>" + headText + "</a>";
      border = true;
      background = true;
    }
  }
}
```

Here's how we might use the *ClickableHeading* class in an application:

```
var head:ClickableHeading = new ClickableHeading(
                              "Essential ActionScript 3.0",
                              "http://www.moock.org/eas3");
addChild(head);
```

Figure 20-17 shows the resulting on-screen content. When the example runs in a Flash runtime, the text is linked to the companion web site for this book.

Figure 20-17. A ClickableHeading instance

We'll see lots more examples of display subclasses in the upcoming chapters. As you conceive of the visual assets required by your applications, consider the possibility of extending an existing display class rather than writing classes from scratch.

Go with the Event Flow

By now, you should feel relatively comfortable creating displayable content and adding it to the screen. Many of the examples in this book rely heavily on the fundamentals that were covered in this chapter, so you'll have plenty of opportunities to review and expand on what you've learned. In the next chapter, we'll learn how Action-Script 3.0's event architecture caters to objects on the display list.

CHAPTER 21

Events and Display Hierarchies

In Chapter 12, we studied ActionScript's built-in event architecture in general terms. In this chapter, we'll take a closer look at how that event architecture specifically caters to objects in display hierarchies.

 ActionScript's system of dispatching events through an object hierarchy, as described in this chapter, is based on the W3C Document Object Model (DOM) Level 3 Events Specification, available at *http:// www.w3.org/TR/DOM-Level-3-Events*.

Hierarchical Event Dispatch

As we saw in Chapter 12, when ActionScript dispatches an event targeted at an object that is not part of a display hierarchy, that target is the sole object notified of the event. For example, when a *Sound* object's sound finishes playing, ActionScript dispatches an Event.COMPLETE event targeted at the associated *SoundChannel* object. The *SoundChannel* object is not part of a display hierarchy, so it is the sole object notified that the event occurred.

By contrast, when ActionScript dispatches an event targeted at an object that *is* part of a display hierarchy, that target and all of its display hierarchy ancestors are notified that the event occurred. For example, if a *Sprite* object contains a *TextField* object, and the user clicks the *TextField* object, both the *TextField* object (the event target) and the *Sprite* object (the event target's ancestor) are notified that the mouse click occurred.

ActionScript's hierarchical event dispatch system enables every display object container to register event listeners that handle events targeted at its descendant display objects. For example, a *Sprite* representing a dialog box might register a listener that handles mouse click events targeted at a nested "OK button" control. Or a *Sprite* representing a login form might register a listener that handles focus events targeted at nested input fields. This centralized architecture helps reduce code repetition, particularly for code that responds to user input events. In the later section "Using the Event Flow to Centralize Code," we'll study a code example that demonstrates the benefits of centralized event handling. But first, let's cover the basics of hierarchical event dispatch and registration.

In this chapter, the terms "ancestor" and "descendant" refer primarily to objects in a display hierarchy, not to superclasses and subclasses in an inheritance hierarchy. To avoid confusion, this chapter sometimes uses the informal terms "display ancestor" and "display descendant" when referring to ancestor objects and descendant objects in a display hierarchy.

Event Dispatch Phases

As we just learned, when ActionScript dispatches an event targeted at an object in a display hierarchy, it notifies not just that target but also its display ancestors. The process by which the target and its ancestors are notified of the event is broken into three distinct phases. In the first phase of the event dispatch, known as the *capture phase*, each of the target's ancestors is notified that the event has occurred. Once the target object's ancestors have all been notified of the event, then the second phase of the event dispatch, known as the *target phase*, begins. During the target phase, ActionScript notifies the target object that the event occurred.

For some event types, the event dispatch ends once the target phase is complete. For other event types, the event dispatch continues into a third phase, known as the *bubbling phase*. During the bubbling phase, the ancestors of the target object are notified that the target successfully received the event notification. Events with a bubbling phase are known as *bubbling events*; events without a bubbling phase are known as *nonbubbling events*.

The four event types Event.ACTIVATE, Event.DEACTIVATE, Event.ENTER_FRAME, and Event.RENDER, have a target phase only. All other event dispatches targeted at an object in a display hierarchy have a capture phase and a target phase. Some event types also have a bubbling phase.

The order in which objects are notified of an event during an event dispatch is governed by the event phase. During the capture phase, ancestors are notified in an order that starts from the root of the target's display hierarchy and proceeds down through each descendant to the target's direct parent. During the target phase, the target, itself is notified. During the bubbling phase, ancestors are notified in the opposite order of the capture phase, from the target's direct parent up to the root of the hierarchy. The process by which event notification passes down through a target's ancestors (capture phase), to the target (target phase), and then back up through the target's ancestors (bubbling phase) is known as the *event flow*. As event notification passes through event flow, the event is said to *propagate* from object to object.

Let's consider a simple event-flow example. Suppose the *Stage* instance contains a *Sprite* object that contains a *TextField* object, as depicted in Figure 21-1. As Figure 21-1 shows, the root of the *TextField* object's display hierarchy is the *Stage* instance, and the *TextField*'s direct parent is the *Sprite* object.

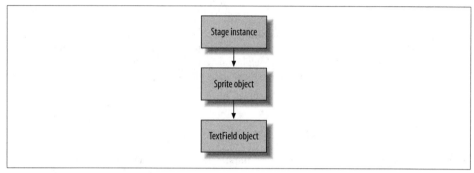

Figure 21-1. A sample display hierarchy

Now further suppose that the user enters some text into the *TextField*, causing the Flash runtime to dispatch a TextEvent.TEXT_INPUT event targeted at the *TextField* object. Because the *TextField* object is part of a display hierarchy, the event passes through the event flow. During the first phase of the event dispatch (the capture phase), the *Stage* instance, then the *Sprite* instance are notified of the event. During the second phase of the dispatch (the target phase), the *TextField* itself is notified of the event. Finally, during the third phase of the dispatch (the bubbling phase), the *Sprite* instance, then the *Stage* instance are notified that the target received event notification. In all, five event notifications are carried out during the TextEvent.TEXT_INPUT event-dispatch, as depicted in Figure 21-2.

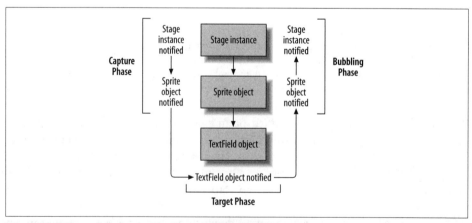

Figure 21-2. Event flow for the TextEvent.TEXT_INPUT event

Event Listeners and the Event Flow

As we've just seen, during an event dispatch targeted at a given display object, that object's display ancestors receive event notification during the capture phase and potentially also during the bubbling phase (if the event is a bubbling event). Accordingly, when we register a listener with an event target's ancestor we must indicate whether that listener should be triggered during the capture phase or the bubbling phase.

To register a listener with an event target's ancestor for the capture phase of an event dispatch, we set *addEventListener()*'s third parameter, useCapture, to true, as in:

```
theAncestor.addEventListener(theEvent, theListener, true)
```

The preceding line of code causes *theListener()* to be executed whenever Action-Script dispatches *theEvent* targeted at one of *theAncestor*'s descendants, *before* that descendant receives notification of the event.

To register a listener with an event target's ancestor for the bubbling phase of an event dispatch, we set *addEventListener()*'s third parameter to false, as in:

```
theAncestor.addEventListener(theEvent, theListener, false)
```

Alternatively, because useCapture's default value is false, we can simply omit the useCapture argument, as in:

```
theAncestor.addEventListener(theEvent, theListener)
```

The preceding line of code causes *theListener()* to be executed whenever Action-Script dispatches *theEvent* targeted at one of *theAncestor*'s descendants, *after* that descendant receives notification of the event.

 For brevity over the remainder of this chapter, we'll use the unofficial term *ancestor listener* to mean "an event listener registered with an event target's display ancestor." Likewise, we'll use the term *target listener* to mean "an event listener registered directly with an event target."

When registering an ancestor listener for a *nonbubbling* event, we always register for the capture phase (i.e., set useCapture to true); otherwise, the listener will not be triggered. When registering an ancestor listener for a *bubbling* event, we choose either capture-phase notification (useCapture set to true) or bubbling-phase notification (useCapture set to false), or both, according to the needs of the application.

The capture phase gives ancestor listeners a chance to process an event before the event target's listeners have responded to it. Typically, capture phase listeners are used to conditionally stop an event from ever reaching its target. For example, a panel widget with an "enabled" state and a "disabled" state might use a capture-phase listener to prevent the panel's descendants from receiving mouse events when the panel is disabled. (We'll learn how to stop events in the later section "Stopping an Event Dispatch.")

By contrast, the bubbling phase gives ancestor listeners a chance to process an event after the event target's listeners have responded to it. Typically, the bubbling phase is used to respond to changes in the state of the target object before the program continues, and before the screen is updated. For example, a panel widget containing draggable icons might use a bubbling-phase listener to trigger automatic icon-alignment after a specific icon has been dragged.

Unlike ancestor listeners, listeners registered with an event target can be triggered during a single phase only—the target phase. To register a listener with an event target for the target phase of an event dispatch, we register that listener using *addEventListener()* with useCapture set to false—exactly as if we were registering an ancestor listener for notification during the bubbling phase. The following generalized code shows the approach:

```
theEventTarget.addEventListener(theEvent, theListener, false)
```

Or, simply:

```
theEventTarget.addEventListener(theEvent, theListener)
```

The preceding line of code causes *theListener()* to be executed whenever Action-Script dispatches *theEvent* targeted at *theEventTarget*, after *theEventTarget*'s ancestors receive capture-phase notification of the event.

 When registering an event listener directly with an event target for target-phase notification, the useCapture parameter should always be either set to false or omitted. Otherwise, the listener will never be triggered.

The following sections present a variety of useCapture examples and discuss several phase-specific event-registration topics.

Registering an Ancestor Listener for the Capture Phase

As we've just learned, to register a given ancestor listener for capture-phase event notification, we set *addEventListener()*'s useCapture parameter to true, as in:

```
theAncestor.addEventListener(theEvent, theListener, true)
```

Now let's apply that code to a working example. For a sample display hierarchy, we'll use the scenario depicted earlier in Figure 21-1, where the *Stage* instance contains a *Sprite* object that contains a *TextField* object. Example 21-1 shows the code we use to create the hierarchy.

Example 21-1. A sample display hierarchy

```
// Create the Sprite
var theSprite:Sprite = new Sprite();

// Create the TextField
var theTextField:TextField = new TextField();
```

Example 21-1. A sample display hierarchy (continued)

```
theTextField.text      = "enter input here";
theTextField.autoSize  = TextFieldAutoSize.LEFT;
theTextField.type      = TextFieldType.INPUT;

// Add the TextField to the Sprite
theSprite.addChild(theTextField);

// Add the Sprite to the Stage instance. Note that someDisplayObject must
// be on the display list in order to access the Stage instance.
someDisplayObject.stage.addChild(theSprite);
```

Now suppose we want to register a function, *textInputListener()*, with theSprite for TextEvent.TEXT_INPUT events. Here's the *textInputListener()* function:

```
private function textInputListener (e:TextEvent):void {
  trace("The user entered some text");
}
```

We want *textInputListener()* to be triggered during the capture phase (i.e., before the *TextField* is notified), so we use the following code to register it:

```
theSprite.addEventListener(TextEvent.TEXT_INPUT, textInputListener, true)
```

The preceding line of code causes *textInputListener()* to be executed whenever ActionScript dispatches a TextEvent.TEXT_INPUT event targeted at theTextField, before theTextField receives notification of the event.

Registering an Ancestor Listener for the Bubbling Phase

Recall that to register a given ancestor listener for bubbling-phase event notification, we set *addEventListener()*'s useCapture parameter to false, as in:

```
theAncestor.addEventListener(theEvent, theListener, false)
```

Continuing again with our *TextField* from Example 21-1, suppose we want to register *textInputListener()* with theSprite for TextEvent.TEXT_INPUT events, and we want *textInputListener()* to be triggered during the bubbling phase (i.e., after the *TextField* is notified). We use the following code:

```
theSprite.addEventListener(TextEvent.TEXT_INPUT, textInputListener, false)
```

Or, we could do the same thing by omitting the useCapture parameter value entirely:

```
theSprite.addEventListener(TextEvent.TEXT_INPUT, textInputListener)
```

The preceding line of code causes *textInputListener()* to be executed whenever ActionScript dispatches a TextEvent.TEXT_INPUT event targeted at theTextField, but after theTextField receives notification of the event.

Note that if the TextEvent.TEXT_INPUT event were a nonbubbling event, then *textInputListener()* would never be triggered. It's worth repeating what we learned earlier: if an ancestor listener registers for a nonbubbling event with useCapture either omitted or set to false, then that listener will never be triggered. In order for an ancestor listener to be triggered when a nonbubbling event is dispatched, it must register for the capture phase by setting useCapture to true.

To determine whether an event is a bubbling or nonbubbling event, we can either:

- Consult the event's entry in Adobe's ActionScript Language Reference.
- Handle the event with an event listener during either the capture or target phases, and check the bubbles variable of the *Event* object passed to the listener. If bubbles is true, then the event bubbles; otherwise, the event does not bubble.

The following code shows the latter technique:

```
// Register a function, clickListener( ), with the Stage instance for
// MouseEvent.CLICK events. Note that someDisplayObject must be on the
// display list in order to access the Stage instance.
someDisplayObject.stage.addEventListener(MouseEvent.CLICK, clickListener);

// ...later in the code, define clickListener( )
private function clickListener (e:MouseEvent):void {
  // When the event occurs, check if it is a bubbling event
  if (e.bubbles) {
    trace("The MouseEvent.CLICK event is a bubbling event.");
  } else {
    trace("The MouseEvent.CLICK event is a non-bubbling event.");
  }
}
```

For convenient reference, Adobe's ActionScript Language Reference lists the value of the *Event* class's instance variable bubbles under all built-in event entries. As a general rule, most built-in events targeted at display objects bubble.

Registering an Ancestor Listener for Both the Capture Phase and the Bubbling Phase

To specify that an ancestor listener should be triggered both during the capture phase and the bubbling phase (i.e., before and after the target receives the event notification), we must register that listener twice—once with useCapture set to true and once with useCapture set to false. For example, returning to our *TextField* scenario, suppose we want to register our *textInputListener()* listener with theSprite for TextEvent.TEXT_INPUT events, and we want *textInputListener()* to be triggered during both the capture phase and the bubbling phase. We use the following code:

```
theSprite.addEventListener(TextEvent.TEXT_INPUT, textInputListener, true)
theSprite.addEventListener(TextEvent.TEXT_INPUT, textInputListener, false)
```

 If an ancestor listener wishes to be triggered during both the capture phase and the bubbling phase of an event dispatch, it must register for the event twice.

Registering a Listener with the Event Target

Recall that to register a target listener for target-phase notification, we set *addEventListener()*'s useCapture parameter to false, as in:

```
theEventTarget.addEventListener(theEvent, theListener, false)
```

Hence, in our ongoing *TextField* scenario, to register *textInputListener()* with *theTextField* for TextEvent.TEXT_INPUT events, we use the following code:

```
theTextField.addEventListener(TextEvent.TEXT_INPUT,
                              textInputListener,
                              false)
```

or, simply:

```
theTextField.addEventListener(TextEvent.TEXT_INPUT, textInputListener)
```

The preceding code causes *textInputListener()* to be executed whenever ActionScript dispatches a TextEvent.TEXT_INPUT event targeted at theTextField. The *textInputListener()* method executes after the *Stage* instance and theSprite have received capture-phase notification, but before the *Stage* instance and theSprite receive bubbling-phase notification.

The Dual Purpose of the useCapture Parameter

As shown in the preceding two sections, *addEventListener()*'s useCapture parameter is set to false in two different circumstances:

- When registering an ancestor listener to be triggered during the bubbling phase
- When registering a target listener to be triggered during the target phase

Therefore, when a listener registers for an event with useCapture set to false, that listener will be triggered when the event is dispatched, and either of the following is true:

- The event target is the object with which the listener registered (in this case, the listener is triggered during the target phase).
- The event target is a descendant of the object with which the listener registered (In this case, the listener is triggered during the bubbling phase, after that descendant has processed the event).

For example, the following code registers *clickListener()* with the *Stage* instance for MouseEvent.CLICK events:

```
someDisplayObject.stage.addEventListener(MouseEvent.CLICK,
                                         clickListener,
                                         false);
```

Because useCapture is false, *clickListener()* will be triggered in both of the following situations:

- When the user clicks the display area (in which case the Flash runtime dispatches an event targeted at the *Stage* instance).
- When the user clicks any on-screen display object (in which case the Flash runtime dispatches an event targeted at the clicked object, which is always a descendant of the *Stage* instance).

Notice that although *clickListener()* registered with a single object (the *Stage* instance), at runtime *clickListener()* might be triggered by event dispatches targeted at that object or at that object's descendants! Therefore, in some cases, a listener function must include code to ignore event dispatches in which it has no interest. We'll study the code required to ignore event dispatches in the later section "Distinguishing Events Targeted at an Object from Events Targeted at That Object's Descendants."

Removing Event Listeners

When unregistering an event listener from an object in a display hierarchy, we must indicate whether that listener originally registered to be triggered during the capture phase or during the target or bubbling phases. To do so, we use *removeEventListener()*'s third parameter, useCapture, which mirrors *addEventListener()*'s useCapture parameter.

If the listener being unregistered was originally registered for the capture phase (i.e., with *addEventListener()*'s useCapture parameter set to true), we must unregister it with *removeEventListener()*'s useCapture parameter set to true. If the listener was originally registered to be triggered during the target or bubbling phases (i.e., with *addEventListener()*'s useCapture parameter set to false), we must unregister it with *removeEventListener()*'s useCapture parameter set to false.

 When unregistering a listener, always set *removeEventListener()*'s useCapture parameter to match the value used for useCapture when *addEventListener()* was originally invoked.

For example, in the following code, we register *clickListener()* with *someDisplayObject* for the capture phase by specifying true as the value of *addEventListener()*'s useCapture parameter:

```
someDisplayObject.addEventListener(MouseEvent.CLICK,
                                   clickListener,
                                   true);
```

Accordingly, when unregistering *clickListener()* from *someDisplayObject*, we must specify true as the value of *removeEventListener()*'s useCapture parameter:

```
someDisplayObject.removeEventListener(MouseEvent.CLICK,
                                      clickListener,
                                      true);
```

When unregistering an event listener that has registered twice with the same object (to be triggered during both the capture phase and the target or bubbling phases), then we must, likewise, invoke *removeEventListener()* twice. For example, the following code registers a MouseEvent.CLICK listener twice with the *Stage* instance, to be triggered during both the capture phase and the target or bubbling phases:

```
someDisplayObject.stage. addEventListener(MouseEvent.CLICK,
                                          clickListener,
                                          true);
someDisplayObject.stage.addEventListener(MouseEvent.CLICK,
                                         clickListener,
                                         false);
```

The following code removes both preceding MouseEvent.CLICK event listeners. Because *clickListener()* was registered separately for both the capture phase and the target or bubbling phases, it must also unregister separately for those phases.

```
someDisplayObject.stage.removeEventListener(MouseEvent.CLICK,
                                            clickListener,
                                            true);
someDisplayObject.stage.removeEventListener(MouseEvent.CLICK,
                                            clickListener,
                                            false);
```

Each listener registration performed with *addEventListener()* is treated separately, requiring its own *removeEventListener()* invocation for unregistration.

Now that were familiar with the basics of the event flow, let's look at an example showing how it can help centralize code in a real-world application.

Using the Event Flow to Centralize Code

If you're waiting for room in a fully booked hotel, it's easier to ask the hotel manager to tell you when a vacancy opens up than it is to ask every guest in the hotel to tell you when they leave. Likewise, when handling event dispatches, it's often more efficient to register event listeners with a display object container than it is to register with each of its descendants.

For example, suppose we're building a simple checkbox control, comprised of the following two classes:

- *CheckBox*, a *Sprite* subclass that acts as a container for the entire control
- *CheckBoxIcon*, a *Sprite* subclass that represents the checkbox's graphical icon

At runtime, each *CheckBox* instance creates two child objects: a *CheckBoxIcon* instance for the checkbox's icon and a *TextField* instance for the checkbox's text label. For reference, let's call the main *CheckBox* instance container and its two children icon and label. Figure 21-3 shows our checkbox control.

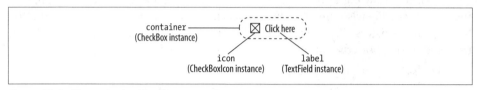

Figure 21-3. Objects in the Checkbox control

We want our checkbox to be easy to use, so we design it to toggle on or off when the user clicks either the checkbox icon or the checkbox label. Accordingly, in our implementation, we must detect mouse-click events targeted at both icon and label. To do so, we could register a separate mouse-click listener with each of those objects. However, registering two event listeners would increase development time and, due to the repetition of near-identical event registration code, increase the potential for bugs in our checkbox. To avoid repetitive code, we can instead handle all mouse-click events through a single listener registered with container. Because container is a display ancestor of both icon and label, it is informed any time the Flash runtime dispatches a mouse-click event targeted at either of those objects. Whenever container's mouse-click listener runs, we know that either the icon or the label was clicked, and we can toggle the checkbox on or off in response.

Example 21-2 shows the code for our example checkbox, with event-handling sections in bold.

Example 21-2. Handling a Checkbox's events hierarchically

```
// File CheckBox.as
package {
  import flash.display.*;
  import flash.events.*;
  import flash.text.*;

  // A very simple checkbox widget
  public class CheckBox extends Sprite {
    private var label:TextField;     // The checkbox's text label
    private var icon:CheckBoxIcon;   // The checkbox's graphical icon
    private var checked:Boolean;     // Flag indicating whether the
                                     // checkbox is currently checked
    // Constructor
    public function CheckBox (msg:String) {
      // When first created, the checkbox is not checked
      checked = false;

      // Create the graphical icon
      icon = new CheckBoxIcon( );
```

Example 21-2. Handling a Checkbox's events hierarchically (continued)

```
      // Create the text label
      label = new TextField( );
      label.text = msg;
      label.autoSize = TextFieldAutoSize.LEFT;
      label.selectable = false;

      // Position the text label next to the graphical icon
      label.x = icon.x + icon.width + 5;

      // Add the label and icon to this object as display children
      addChild(icon);
      addChild(label);

      // Start listening for mouse click event dispatches targeted at this
      // object or any of its children (i.e., the label or the icon)
      addEventListener(MouseEvent.CLICK, clickListener);
    }

    // Handles mouse click events. This method runs whenever either the
    // label or the icon is clicked.
    private function clickListener (e:MouseEvent):void {
      if (checked) {
        icon.uncheck( );
        checked = false;
      } else {
        icon.check( );
        checked = true;
      }
    }
  }
}

// File CheckBoxIcon.as
package {
  import flash.display.*;

  // The graphical icon for a checkbox widget
  public class CheckBoxIcon extends Sprite {

    // Constructor
    public function CheckBoxIcon () {
      uncheck( );
    }

    // Draws a checkbox icon in the "checked" state
    public function check ():void {
      graphics.clear( );
      graphics.lineStyle(1);
      graphics.beginFill(0xFFFFFF);
      graphics.drawRect(0, 0, 15, 15);
      graphics.endFill( );
```

Example 21-2. Handling a Checkbox's events hierarchically (continued)

```
      graphics.lineTo(15, 15);
      graphics.moveTo(0, 15);
      graphics.lineTo(15, 0);
    }

    // Draws a checkbox icon in the "unchecked" state
    public function uncheck ():void {
      graphics.clear();
      graphics.lineStyle(1);
      graphics.beginFill(0xFFFFFF);
      graphics.drawRect(0, 0, 15, 15);
    }
  }
}

// File CheckBoxDemo.as (a main class that uses the CheckBox class)
package {
  import flash.display.Sprite;

  // Demonstrates the use of the CheckBox class
  public class CheckboxDemo extends Sprite {
    public function CheckboxDemo() {
      var c:CheckBox = new CheckBox("Click here");
      addChild(c);
    }
  }
}
```

We've now covered the basics of ActionScript's hierarchical-event-dispatch system, but there are several more topics left to explore. Let's soldier on.

Determining the Current Event Phase

As we learned in the earlier section "Registering an Ancestor Listener for Both the Capture Phase and the Bubbling Phase," by invoking *addEventListener()* twice, we can register a single event-listener function to be executed during both the capture phase and bubbling phases of an event dispatch. Similarly, in the section "The Dual Purpose of the useCapture Parameter," we learned that when an event listener is registered with useCapture set to false, that listener might be triggered during the target phase or during the bubbling phase of an event dispatch. Hence, when an event-listener function is executed in response to an event, the current event phase is not always known. Accordingly, ActionScript provides the *Event* class's instance variable eventPhase, which can be used within an event listener function to deduce the current event phase.

The eventPhase variable indicates whether the current event dispatch is in the capture phase, the target phase, or the bubbling phase. When the event dispatch is in the capture phase, eventPhase is set to EventPhase.CAPTURING_PHASE, indicating that the target object has not yet received event notification. When the event dispatch is in the target phase, eventPhase is set to EventPhase.AT_TARGET, indicating that the target object is currently processing the event. When the event dispatch is in the bubbling phase, eventPhase is set to EventPhase.BUBBLING_PHASE, indicating that the target object has finished processing the event.

Typically, the EventPhase.CAPTURING_PHASE, EventPhase.AT_TARGET, and EventPhase.BUBBLING_PHASE constants have the integer values 1, 2, and 3, respectively, but those values are considered subject to change, and should never be used directly. Instead, to determine the current event phase within an event listener function, always compare the eventPhase variable to the *EventPhase* class constants. For example, always use code like this:

```
private function someListener (e:Event):void {
  if (e.eventPhase == EventPhase.AT_TARGET) {
    // This listener was triggered during the target phase...
  }
}
```

And never use code like this:

```
private function someListener (e:Event):void {
  // Bad code! Never use the EventPhase constant values directly!
  if (e.eventPhase == 2) {
    // This listener was triggered during the target phase...
  }
}
```

The following code demonstrates the general use of the eventPhase variable. First, the code adds a *TextField* object to the *Stage* instance. Then the code registers *clickListener()* with the *Stage* instance for capture-phase MouseEvent.CLICK event notification. Finally, the code registers *clickListener()* with the *Stage* instance for target-phase and bubbling-phase MouseEvent.CLICK event notification.

When *clickListener()* executes, it outputs the current phase. Notice that the current phase is determined by comparing eventPhase to the three *EventPhase* class constants.

```
var t:TextField = new TextField();
t.text = "click here";
t.autoSize = TextFieldAutoSize.LEFT;
stage.addChild(t);

// Register for capture phase
stage.addEventListener(MouseEvent.CLICK, clickListener, true);

// Register for target or bubbling phase
stage.addEventListener(MouseEvent.CLICK, clickListener, false);

// ...elsewhere in the class
private function clickListener (e:MouseEvent):void {
  var phase:String;
```

```
switch (e.eventPhase) {
  case EventPhase.CAPTURING_PHASE:
  phase = "Capture";
  break;

  case EventPhase.AT_TARGET:
  phase = "Target";
  break;

  case EventPhase.BUBBLING_PHASE:
  phase = "Bubbling";
  break;
}
trace("Current event phase: " + phase);
}
```

When the preceding code runs, if the user clicks the *TextField* object, the Flash runtime dispatches a MouseEvent.CLICK event targeted at the *TextField* object, and the output of the preceding code is:

```
Current event phase: Capture
Current event phase: Bubbling
```

(Remember, *clickListener()* registered with the *Stage* instance for both the capture phase and the bubbling phase, so it is triggered twice during event dispatches that target the *Stage* instance's descendants.)

On the other hand, if the user clicks the display area, the Flash runtime dispatches a MouseEvent.CLICK event targeted at the *Stage* object, and the output of the preceding code is:

```
Current event phase: Target
```

As discussed in the next section, the eventPhase variable is typically used to differentiate between events targeted at an object and events targeted at that object's descendants. Less commonly, the eventPhase variable is used to distinguish the capture phase from the bubbling phase within ancestor listeners that are registered for both of those phases.

Distinguishing Events Targeted at an Object from Events Targeted at That Object's Descendants

When the eventPhase variable of the *Event* object passed to a listener function is set to EventPhase.AT_TARGET, we know that the event dispatch is targeted at the object with which the listener registered. On the other hand, when eventPhase is set to either EventPhase.CAPTURING_PHASE or EventPhase.BUBBLING_PHASE, we know that the event dispatch is targeted at a *descendant* of the object with which the listener registered.

Therefore, a listener can use the following code to ignore events targeted at descendants of the object with which it registered:

```
private function someListener (e:SomeEvent):void {
  if (e.eventPhase == EventPhase.AT_TARGET) {
    // Code here is executed only when the object that registered this
    // listener is the event target.
  }
}
```

We can use the preceding technique to write code that responds to input received by a given object but not by any of its descendants. For example, imagine an application in which the *Stage* instance contains many buttons, text fields, and other input-receiving objects. To respond to mouse clicks when they occur over vacant areas of the *Stage* instance only, we use the following code:

```
// Register with the Stage instance for MouseEvent.CLICK events.
// As a result, clickListener() will be invoked when *any* object
// on the display list is clicked.
stage.addEventListener(MouseEvent.CLICK, clickListener);

// ...elsewhere, define the MouseEvent.CLICK event listener
private function clickListener (e:MouseEvent):void {
  // If this listener was triggered during the target phase...
  if (e.eventPhase == EventPhase.AT_TARGET) {
    // ...then the Stage instance was clicked. Proceed with
    // "Stage instance was clicked" response code.
  }
}
```

To create an event listener that ignores events targeted at the object with which it registered, we use the following code:

```
private function someListener (e:SomeEvent):void {
  if (e.eventPhase != EventPhase.AT_TARGET) {
    // Code here is executed only when the object that registered this
    // listener is a descendant of the event target.
  }
}
```

For example, the following listener responds to mouse clicks that occur over any object on the display list, but not over a vacant area of the *Stage* instance:

```
// Register with the Stage instance for MouseEvent.CLICK events
stage.addEventListener(MouseEvent.CLICK, clickListener);

// ...elsewhere, define the MouseEvent.CLICK event listener
private function clickListener (e:SomeInputEvent):void {
  // If this listener was not triggered during the target phase...
  if (e.eventPhase != EventPhase.AT_TARGET) {
    // ...then the target must be a descendant of the Stage instance.
    // Hence, the mouse must have clicked some object on the display list
    // other than the Stage instance.
  }
}
```

Now let's move on to the next hierarchical-event-dispatch topic: stopping an event dispatch.

Stopping an Event Dispatch

At any point during the event flow, every event listener—including those registered with the target object and those registered with its ancestors—can put a stop to the entire event dispatch. Stopping an event's dispatch is referred to as *consuming the event*.

To stop an event dispatch, we invoke the *Event* class's instance method *stopImmediatePropagation()* or *stopPropagation()* on the *Event* object passed to a listener function. The *stopImmediatePropagation()* method stops the event dispatch immediately, without allowing any remaining listeners to be triggered; the *stopPropagation()* method stops the event dispatch after ActionScript triggers the remaining listeners registered with object currently being notified of the event.

For example, suppose we have a *Sprite*, container, that contains a *TextField*, child:

```
var container:Sprite = new Sprite( );
var child:TextField = new TextField( );
child.text = "click here";
child.autoSize = TextFieldAutoSize.LEFT;
container.addChild(child);
```

Further suppose we have three event listener functions: *containerClickListenerOne()*, *containerClickListenerTwo()*, and *childClickListener()*. Register *containerClickListenerOne()* and *containerClickListenerTwo()* with container for MouseEvent.CLICK event notification during the capture phase:

```
container.addEventListener(MouseEvent.CLICK,
                           containerClickListenerOne,
                           true);
container.addEventListener(MouseEvent.CLICK,
                           containerClickListenerTwo,
                           true);
```

Then we register *childClickListener()* with child for MouseEvent.CLICK event notification during the target phase:

```
child.addEventListener(MouseEvent.CLICK, childClickListener, false);
```

Under normal circumstances, when the user clicks child, all three event listeners are triggered—two during the capture phase, and one during the target phase. If, however, *containerClickListenerOne()* consumes the event using *stopImmediatePropagation()*, then neither *containerClickListenerTwo()* nor *childClickListener()* is triggered.

```
public function containerClickListenerOne (e:MouseEvent):void {
  // Prevent containerClickListenerTwo() and childClickListener( ) from
  // receiving the event
  e.stopImmediatePropagation( );
}
```

On the other hand, if *containerClickListenerOne()* consumes the event using *stopPropagation()* rather than *stopImmediatePropagation()*, then container's remaining `MouseEvent.CLICK` event listeners are triggered before the event dispatch stops. Hence, *containerClickListenerTwo()* receives the event, but *childClickListener()* does not.

```
public function containerClickListenerOne (e:MouseEvent):void {
  // Prevent just childClickListener( ) from receiving the event
  e.stopPropagation( );
}
```

Note that the preceding example relies on *containerClickListenerOne()* being registered before *containerClickListenerTwo()*. For information on the order in which event listeners are triggered, see Chapter 12.

Events are typically consumed in order to stop or override a program's normal response to an event. For example, suppose a *Sprite* subclass, *ToolPanel*, contains a group of interface controls, each of which accepts user input. The *ToolPanel* class has two operational states: enabled and disabled. When a *ToolPanel* object is disabled, the user should not be able to interact with any of its nested interface controls.

To implement the "disabled" state, each *ToolPanel* object registers a method, *clickListener()*, for capture-phase `MouseEvent.CLICK` event notification. When a *ToolPanel* object is disabled, the *clickListener()* method stops all click events from reaching child *Tool* objects. Example 21-3 shows the *ToolPanel* class, greatly simplified to emphasize its event consumption code (shown in bold). In the example, the *ToolPanel* class's child interface controls are instances of a generic *Tool* class that is not shown. In a real application, however, the controls might be buttons or menus or any other form of interactive tool.

Example 21-3. Consuming an event

```
package {
  import flash.display.Sprite;
  import flash.events.*;

  public class ToolPanel extends Sprite {
    private var enabled:Boolean;

    public function ToolPanel ( ) {
      enabled = false;

      var tool1:Tool = new Tool( );
      var tool2:Tool = new Tool( );
      var tool3:Tool = new Tool( );

      tool2.x = tool1.width + 10;
      tool3.x = tool2.x + tool2.width + 10;

      addChild(tool1);
      addChild(tool2);
```

Example 21-3. Consuming an event (continued)

```
    addChild(tool3);

    // Register with this object for MouseEvent.CLICK event notification
    // during the capture phase
    addEventListener(MouseEvent.CLICK, clickListener, true);
  }

  private function clickListener (e:MouseEvent):void {
    // If this ToolPanel object is disabled...
    if (!enabled) {
      // ...then stop this click event from reaching this ToolPanel
      // object's descendants
      e.stopPropagation( );
      trace("Panel disabled. Click event dispatch halted.");
    }
  }
 }
}
```

In typical application development, the *stopPropagation()* method is used much more frequently than the *stopImmediatePropagation()* method. Nevertheless, the *stopImmediatePropagation()* method is used in the following situations:

- When a target object wishes to prevent its own listeners from being triggered by an event

- When a program wishes to prevent all listeners from responding to a given event

Let's consider an example for each of the preceding situations, starting with a target object that prevents its own listeners from being triggered by an event. Imagine a space-shooter game that includes the following classes:

- *GameManager*, a class that manages gameplay
- *PlayerShip*, a class that represents the player's spacecraft

The *GameManager* defines a custom event, GameManager.SHIP_HIT, which is dispatched when an enemy's missile hits the player's ship. Each GameManager.SHIP_HIT event dispatch is targeted at the *PlayerShip* object. The *PlayerShip* object registers two listeners to respond to GameManager.SHIP_HIT events. One listener plays an explosion animation, and the other plays an explosion sound.

When the player dies, a new player ship is created, and that ship is invincible for five seconds. While the ship is invincible, the *PlayerShip* object's GameManager.SHIP_HIT listeners should not play the "damaged-ship" animation or sound.

To prevent the GameManager.SHIP_HIT listeners from executing when the ship is invincible, the *PlayerShip* class registers a third listener, *hitListener()*, designed to consume GameManager.SHIP_HIT events based on the current ship status (invincible or not invincible). The *hitListener()* method is registered in *PlayerShip*'s constructor, with a priority of int.MAX_VALUE, as follows:

```
public class PlayerShip {
  public function PlayerShip () {
    addEventListener(GameManager.HIT, hitListener, false, int.MAX_VALUE);
  }
}
```

In Chapter 12 we learned that, by default, an object's event listeners are triggered according to the order in which they were registered. We also learned that this default "trigger order" can be superceded by *addEventListener()*'s priority parameter.

Because *hitListener()* is registered in the *PlayerShip* constructor with the highest possible priority, it is always the first of *PlayerShip*'s GameManager.SHIP_HIT listeners executed. When the *PlayerShip* object is not invincible, and a GameManager.SHIP_HIT event occurs, *hitListener()* does nothing. But when the *PlayerShip* object is invincible, and a GameManager.SHIP_HIT event occurs, *hitListener()* first consumes the event, and then dispatches a new event, PlayerShip.HIT_DEFLECTED. Listeners registered for PlayerShip.HIT_DEFLECTED then play a special animation and sound indicating that the ship was not damaged.

The code for *hitListener()* follows; notice the use of the *stopImmediatePropagation()* method:

```
private function hitListener (e:Event):void {
  if (invincible) {
    // Prevent other PlayerShip listeners from receiving event notification
    e.stopImmediatePropagation();
    // Broadcast a new event
    dispatchEvent(new Event(PlayerShip.HIT_DEFLECTED, true));
  }
}
```

In the preceding *PlayerShip* scenario, note that although the *PlayerShip* object can prevent its own GameManager.SHIP_HIT listeners from being triggered, it cannot prevent GameManager.SHIP_HIT listeners registered with its display ancestors from being triggered. Specifically, any listeners registered for the capture phase with the *PlayerShip* object's display ancestors will always be notified of the GameManager.SHIP_HIT event even if the *PlayerShip* object consumes it. However, after the *PlayerShip* object consumes the GameManager.SHIP_HIT event, its ancestors do not receive notification during the bubbling phase.

Now let's turn to the second *stopImmediatePropagation()* scenario, in which a program wishes to prevent all listeners from responding to a given event. Suppose we're writing a set of user-interface components that automatically change to an inactive state when the Flash runtime loses operating-system focus, and change to an active state when the Flash runtime gains operating-system focus. In order to detect the gaining or losing of operating system focus, our components register listeners for the built-in events Event.ACTIVATE and Event.DEACTIVATE (for details on Event.ACTIVATE and Event.DEACTIVATE, see Chapter 22).

Now further suppose we're writing a testing application to stress test our components. Our stress-test application programmatically triggers the components' interactive behavior. In our test, we must ensure that the built-in Event.DEACTIVATE event does not make the test components inactive; otherwise, our test application will not be able to trigger them programmatically. Hence, in our test application's main class constructor, we register an Event.DEACTIVATE listener with the *Stage* instance. That listener uses *stopImmediatePropagation()* to consume all built-in Event.DEACTIVATE events, as follows.

```
private function deactivateListener (e: Event):void {
  e.stopImmediatePropagation( );
}
```

Because our test application consumes all Event.DEACTIVATE events, the components never receive Event.DEACTIVATE notifications, and, hence, never become inactive in response to the Flash runtime losing system focus. The administrator of the test application can then focus and defocus the Flash runtime while the test runs without interfering with the test application's ability to control the components programmatically.

Event Priority and the Event Flow

When an event listener registers with an object in a display hierarchy, the priority parameter affects the trigger order of listeners registered with that object only. The priority parameter does not, and cannot, alter the order in which objects in the event flow are notified.

 There is no way to force a listener of one object in the event flow to be triggered before or after a listener of another object in the same event flow.

For example, suppose a *Sprite* object contains a *TextField* object. The *Sprite* object registers a MouseEvent.CLICK listener, *spriteClickListener()*, with useCapture set to false and priority set to 2:

```
theSprite.addEventListener(MouseEvent.CLICK, spriteClickListener, false, 2)
```

Likewise, the *TextField* object registers a MouseEvent.CLICK listener, *textClickListener()*, with useCapture set to false and priority set to 1:

```
theTextField.addEventListener(MouseEvent.CLICK, textClickListener, false, 1)
```

When the user clicks the *TextField* object, the Flash runtime dispatches a MouseEvent.CLICK event targeted at the *TextField* object. In response, *textClickListener()* is triggered during the target phase, before *spriteClickListener()*, which is triggered during the bubbling phase. The two event listeners are triggered according to the order of the event flow, even though *spriteClickListener()* registered with a higher priority than *textClickListener()*.

For more information on event priority, see Chapter 12.

Display-Hierarchy Mutation and the Event Flow

Immediately before ActionScript dispatches a given event, it predetermines the entire event flow for that dispatch based on the current state of the event target's display hierarchy. That is, the list of objects that will be notified of the event, and the order in which those objects will be notified, is predetermined before the event dispatch begins. Once the event dispatch begins, objects are notified of the event according to that predetermined order—even if the structure of the target object's display hierarchy is modified by event listeners during the event dispatch.

For example, suppose we have a *TextField* instance contained by a *Sprite* instance that is, itself, contained by the *Stage* instance. Further suppose we register a listener, *stageClickListener()*, with the *Stage* instance for capture-phase MouseEvent.CLICK event notification, as shown in the following code:

```
stage.addEventListener(MouseEvent.CLICK, stageClickListener, true);
```

Finally, suppose that the registered *stageClickListener()* function contains code that removes the *TextField* object from its *Sprite* object parent, as follows:

```
private function stageClickListener (e:MouseEvent):void {
  // If the TextField object was clicked...
  if (e.target == textField) {
    // ...remove it
    removeChild(textField);
    textField = null;
  }
}
```

When the user clicks the text field, ActionScript dispatches a MouseEvent.CLICK event targeted at the *TextField* object. Before the dispatch begins, ActionScript predetermines the entire event flow, as follows:

```
CAPTURE PHASE:   (1) Stage object
                 (2) Sprite object
TARGET PHASE:    (3) TextField object
BUBBLING PHASE:  (4) Sprite object
                 (5) Stage object
```

When the event dispatch begins, ActionScript first notifies the *Stage* object of the event (1). That notification triggers the *Stage* object's listener, *stageClickListener()*, which removes the *TextField* object from the display list. Next, even though the *Sprite* object is now no longer an ancestor of the *TextField* object, ActionScript notifies the *Sprite* object of the event (2). Then, even though the *TextField* object is no longer on the display list, ActionScript notifies the *TextField* object of the event (3).

Finally, during the bubbling phase, ActionScript again notifies the *Sprite* object (4) and the *Stage* object (5) of the event. Even though the display hierarchy containing the event target was modified during the event dispatch, the event still propagates through the entire predetermined event flow.

 Once the event flow is established for a given event dispatch, it is fixed for the duration of that dispatch.

Example 21-4 shows the code for the preceding scenario in the context of an example class, *DisappearingTextField*. In the example, an instance of the custom class *DisappearingTextField* (a *Sprite* subclass) plays the role of the preceding scenario's *Sprite* object.

Example 21-4. The immutable event flow

```
package {
  import flash.display.*;
  import flash.events.*;
  import flash.text.*;

  public class DisappearingTextField extends Sprite {
    private var textField:TextField;
    public function DisappearingTextField () {
      // Create the TextField object
      textField = new TextField();
      textField.text = "Click here";
      textField.autoSize = TextFieldAutoSize.LEFT;

      // Add the TextField object to the DisappearingTextField object
      addChild(textField);

      // Register with the Stage instance for MouseEvent.CLICK events
      stage.addEventListener(MouseEvent.CLICK, stageClickListener, true);

      // To prove that the TextField object receives MouseEvent.CLICK event
      // notification even after it is removed from this
      // DisappearingTextField instance, we register a listener with the
      // TextField object for MouseEvent.CLICK events
      textField.addEventListener(MouseEvent.CLICK, textFieldClickListener);
    }

    // This function runs when the user clicks any object on the
    // display list
    private function stageClickListener (e:MouseEvent):void {
      // If the TextField object was clicked...
      if (e.target == textField) {
        // ...remove it
        removeChild(textField);
        textField = null;
      }
    }
  }
```

Example 21-4. The immutable event flow (continued)

```
    // This function runs when the user clicks the TextField object
    private function textFieldClickListener (e:MouseEvent):void {
      // By now, stageClickListener() has removed the TextField object,
      // but this listener is still triggered.
      trace("textFieldClickListener triggered");
    }
  }
}
```

Event Listener List Mutation

As we've just learned, when a given event occurs, ActionScript notifies the appropriate objects according to the predetermined order of the event flow. In turn, when each object receives notification of the event, its event listeners are triggered. The specific list of listeners that are triggered by a given event notification is determined immediately before that notification occurs. Once the notification has begun, that listener list cannot be altered.

For example, consider a MouseEvent.CLICK event dispatch targeted at a *Sprite* object that is contained by the *Stage* instance. The event flow comprises three event notifications, as follows:

```
CAPTURE PHASE:   (1) Stage object notified
TARGET PHASE:    (2) Sprite object notified
BUBBLING PHASE:  (3) Stage object notified
```

Suppose that, during the first notification (1), code in a *Stage* listener registers a new MouseEvent.CLICK listener with the *Sprite* object. Because the event has not yet propagated to the *Sprite* object, the new listener will be triggered during the second notification (2).

Now further suppose that, during the first notification (1), code in a *Stage* listener registers a new MouseEvent.CLICK listener with the *Stage* instance, for bubbling-phase notification. Because the first notification (1) has already begun, the *Stage* instance's list of listeners has already been frozen, so the new listener is not triggered during the first notification (1). However, the new listener is triggered later in the event flow, during the third notification (3).

Finally, suppose that, during the second notification (2), code in a *Sprite* listener unregisters an existing MouseEvent.CLICK listener from the *Sprite* object. Because the second notification (2) has already begun, its list of listeners has already been frozen, so the removed listener is still triggered during the second notification. Of course, if another MouseEvent.CLICK event were dispatched, the removed listener would not be triggered.

 At any point during a given event dispatch, the list of listeners being triggered during the current notification cannot be modified, but the list of listeners to be triggered by notifications that occur later in the event flow can be modified.

Custom Events and the Event Flow

ActionScript's hierarchical event system applies to all event-dispatches targeted display objects—even those event dispatches instigated manually by the programmer. When a custom event dispatch targets an object in a display hierarchy, the ancestors of that target object are notified of the event.

The generalized code shown in Example 21-5 demonstrates how, just like built-in events, custom events propagate through the event flow. In the example, a test class, *CustomEventDemo* instructs ActionScript to dispatch a custom event targeted at a *Sprite* object on the display list.

Example 21-5. A custom event dispatched through the event flow

```
package {
  import flash.display.*;
  import flash.events.*;
  import flash.text.*;

  public class CustomEventDemo extends Sprite {
    public static const SOME_EVENT:String = "SOME_EVENT";

    public function CustomEventDemo () {
      var sprite:Sprite = new Sprite();
      addChild(sprite);

      // Register someEventListener() with the Stage instance for
      // CustomEventDemo.SOME_EVENT notification.
      stage.addEventListener(CustomEventDemo.SOME_EVENT, someEventListener);

      // Dispatch a CustomEventDemo.SOME_EVENT event to an object on
      // the display list. Set the Event constructor's second parameter
      // to true so the event bubbles.
      sprite.dispatchEvent(new Event(CustomEventDemo.SOME_EVENT, true));
    }

    private function someEventListener (e:Event):void {
      trace("SOME_EVENT occurred.");
    }
  }
}
```

In response to the *dispatchEvent()* invocation in Example 21-5, ActionScript dispatches a CustomEventDemo.SOME_EVENT event into the event flow, targeted at sprite. The event flow is as follows:

```
Stage instance
  |
  |-> CustomEventDemo object
        |
        |-> Sprite object
```

During the capture phase, the `CustomEventDemo.SOME_EVENT` event dispatch propagates from the *Stage* instance to the *CustomEventDemo* object. During the target phase, the event propagates to the *Sprite* object. Finally, during the bubbling phase, the event propagates back to the *CustomEventDemo* object and then back to the *Stage* instance. When the *Stage* instance receives event notification during the bubbling phase, *someEventListener()* is triggered. Even though `CustomEventDemo.SOME_EVENT` is a custom event, it still propagates through the event flow.

As with the built-in events, ActionScript's hierarchical event architecture can help centralize code that responds to custom events. For example, suppose we're building an online ordering system with a shopping-basket widget that contains selectable product icons. The shopping-basket widget is represented by an instance of the custom class, *ShoppingBasket*. Likewise, each product icon is represented by an instance of the custom class, *Product*. The *Product* instances are display children of the *ShoppingBasket* instance. The *ShoppingBasket* instance has a title bar that displays the name of the currently selected product.

When the user selects a product icon in the shopping-basket widget, our application dispatches a custom `Product.PRODUCT_SELECTED` event targeted at the corresponding *Product* instance. Because the *ShoppingBasket* instance is an ancestor of all *Product* instances, it is notified every time the `Product.PRODUCT_SELECTED` event is dispatched. Hence, to keep the *ShoppingBasket* instance's title bar synchronized with the currently selected product, we simply register a single `Product.PRODUCT_SELECTED` listener—*productSelectedListener()*—with the *ShoppingBasket* instance. When *productSelectedListener()* is triggered, we know a product has been selected, so we update the shopping-basket's title bar with the name of the newly selected product.

Examples 21-6 and 21-7 show the *ShoppingBasket* and *Product* classes. The comments will guide you through the code. Event-related sections are shown in bold.

Example 21-6. The ShoppingBasket class

```
package {
  import flash.display.*;
  import flash.text.*;
  import flash.events.*;

  // An online shopping basket that can visually contain Product objects.
  public class ShoppingBasket extends Sprite {
    // The on-screen title bar for the shopping basket panel
    private var title:TextField;
    // An array of the products in this basket
    private var products:Array;
    // The currently selected product
    private var selectedProduct:Product;

    // Constructor
    public function ShoppingBasket () {
      // Create a new empty array to hold Product objects
      products = new Array();
```

Example 21-6. The ShoppingBasket class (continued)

```
    // Create the on-screen title bar
    title = new TextField( );
    title.text = "No product selected";
    title.autoSize = TextFieldAutoSize.LEFT;
    title.border     = true;
    title.background = true;
    title.selectable = false;
    addChild(title);

    // Start listening for Product.PRODUCT_SELECTED event dispatches
    // targeted at child Product objects.
    addEventListener(Product.PRODUCT_SELECTED, productSelectedListener);
  }

  // Adds a new Product object to the shopping basket
  public function addProduct (product:Product):void {
    // Create a new product and add it to the products array
    products.push(product);
    // Add the new product to this object's display hierarchy
    addChild(products[products.length-1]);

    // Now that there's a new product, reposition all products
    updateLayout( );
  }

  // A very simple product-layout algorithm that sorts all products
  // into a single horizontal line in the order they were added, from left
  // to right
  public function updateLayout ( ):void {
    var totalX:Number = 0;
    for (var i:int = 0; i < products.length; i++) {
      products[i].x = totalX;
      totalX += products[i].width + 20;   // 20 is the gutter width
      products[i].y = title.height + 20;  // 20 is the gutter height
    }
  }

  // Responds to Product.PRODUCT_SELECTED event dispatches targeted at
  // child Product objects. When a product is selected, this method
  // updates the shopping basket's title bar to match the selected
  // product's name.
  private function productSelectedListener (e:Event):void {
    // Remember the selected product in case we need to reference it
    // in future
    selectedProduct = Product(e.target);

    // Update the shopping basket's title
    title.text = selectedProduct.getName( );
  }
 }
}
```

Example 21-7 shows the code for the *Product* class.

Example 21-7. The Product class

```
package {
  import flash.display.*;
  import flash.events.*;
  import flash.text.*;

  // A product icon that can be placed in a ShoppingBasket object using
  // ShoppingBasket.addProduct(). In this simplified version, the icon is
  // simply a text field with no corresponding graphical icon.
  public class Product extends Sprite {
    // An event constant for the custom PRODUCT_SELECTED event
    public static const PRODUCT_SELECTED:String = "PRODUCT_SELECTED";
    // The on-screen label showing the product's name
    private var label:TextField;
    // The product's name
    private var productName:String;

    // Constructor
    public function Product (productName:String) {
      // Record the product's name
      this.productName = productName;

      // Create the on-screen label
      label = new TextField();
      label.text = productName;
      label.autoSize = TextFieldAutoSize.LEFT;
      label.border     = true;
      label.background = true;
      label.selectable = false;
      addChild(label);

      // Start listening for mouse clicks. By registering for
      // MouseEvent.CLICK events with this object, we'll receive
      // notification any time its children (e.g., the label) are clicked.
      addEventListener(MouseEvent.CLICK, clickListener);
    }

    // Returns the product's name
    public function getName ():String {
      return productName;
    }

    // Handles MouseEvent.CLICK events. In this example, simply clicking a
    // product selects it, and causes the Product.PRODUCT_SELECTED event to
    // be dispatched. In a more complete implementation, other factors
    // might be involved. For example, products might be selectable
    // via the keyboard, and selection might be disabled during a
    // transaction with the server.
    private function clickListener (e:MouseEvent):void {
      // Notify all registered listeners that this product was selected.
      // Thanks to ActionScript's hierarchical event dispatch system,
      // by dispatching a custom event targeted at this object, we trigger
```

Example 21-7. The Product class (continued)

```
    // not only this object's Product.PRODUCT_SELECTED listeners, but also
    // Product.PRODUCT_SELECTED listeners registered with the
    // ShoppingBasket instance.
    dispatchEvent(new Event(Product.PRODUCT_SELECTED, true));
  }
 }
}
```

Example 21-8 presents a very simple application demonstrating the basic usage of the *ShoppingBasket* and *Product* classes from Example 21-6 and Example 21-7.

Example 21-8. A ShoppingBasket demo

```
package {
  import flash.display.Sprite;

  public class ShoppingBasketDemo extends Sprite {
    public function ShoppingBasketDemo () {
      var basket:ShoppingBasket = new ShoppingBasket();
      basket.addProduct(new Product("Nintendo Wii"));
      basket.addProduct(new Product("Xbox 360"));
      basket.addProduct(new Product("PlayStation 3"));
      addChild(basket);
    }
  }
}
```

On to Input Events

We've now studied pretty much everything there is to know about the core workings of ActionScript's hierarchical event system. In the next chapter, we'll put our new theoretical knowledge into practice as we explore Flash Player's built-in user-input events.

Interactivity

In this chapter, we'll see how to add interactivity to an application by responding to Flash Player's input events. Specifically, we'll explore five different categories of input events:

- Mouse events
- Focus events
- Keyboard events
- Text events
- Flash Player-level events

For each of the preceding event categories, we'll consider the specific events offered by Flash Player's API and the code required to handle those events.

The descriptions of the events covered in this chapter apply specifically to Flash Player (both the browser add-on and standalone versions) but are also generally applicable to any Flash runtime that supports mouse and keyboard input (such as Adobe AIR). When working with other Flash runtimes, be sure to consult the appropriate documentation for information on input events. For official reference material covering Flash Player's input events, see Adobe's ActionScript Language Reference under the Constants heading of the *Event* class and its subclasses. Also see the Events heading under the *TextField*, *DisplayObject*, *InteractiveObject*, and *Stage* classes.

Before we start our examination of specific input events, let's take a quick look at some general rules that govern all input events:

InteractiveObject instances only

> Input-event notifications are sent to instances of classes that inherit from *InteractiveObject* only (*Sprite*, *TextField*, *Stage*, *Loader*, *MovieClip*, *SimpleButton* and subclasses of those classes.) Other types of objects are not notified of input events, even if those objects are on the display list. For example, instances of the *Shape* class can be placed on the display list, but the *Shape* class does not inherit

from *InteractiveObject*, so *Shape* instances do not receive input-event notifications. If a *Shape* object visually overlaps a *TextField* object, and the user clicks the *Shape* object, then the *TextField* object—not the *Shape* object—will be the target of the resulting mouse-click event. To handle interaction with a *Shape* or *Bitmap* object, place that object in a container (*Sprite* or *MovieClip*) and register with that container for input events.

Display list objects only

Objects that are not on the display list when Flash Player dispatches a given input event cannot receive notification of that event.

Default behavior

Some input events trigger a native response by Flash Player, known as a *default behavior*. For example, moving the mouse pointer over a *SimpleButton* instance causes that instance to display its "overstate" graphic. In some cases, Flash Player's default behavior can be prevented using the *Event* class's instance method *preventDefault( )*. For details see the section "Preventing Default Event Behavior" in Chapter 12.

Now on to the events!

Mouse-Input Events

Flash Player dispatches mouse-input events when the user manipulates the system pointing device. Examples of pointing devices that can trigger mouse-input events include: a mouse, a trackball, a laptop touchpad, a laptop pointing stick, and a stylus. For convenience, however, this book uses the catch-all term "mouse" when referring to the system pointing device. The following types of mouse manipulations can trigger mouse-input events:

- Pressing or releasing the primary mouse button
- Moving the mouse pointer
- Using mouse's scrolling device (e.g., spinning the mouse wheel)

Notice that "right-clicking" (i.e., pressing the secondary mouse button) is not included in the preceding list. Flash Player generates mouse input events for the primary mouse button only. However, Flash Player's standard context menu, which is accessed via a secondary mouse-button click, is customizable; for details, see the *ContextMenu* class in Adobe's ActionScript Language Reference.

Flash Player's Built-in Mouse Events

Table 22-1 lists Flash Player's built-in mouse-event types. For each type of event, the "Event type" column lists the *MouseEvent*-class constant that indicates the event type's official string name. The "Description" column describes the specific user action that triggers the event. The "Target" column lists the object that serves as the event target when the event is dispatched. The "Default behavior" column lists Flash Player's native response to the event. The "Bubbles" column indicates whether the event has a bubbling phase. The "Datatype of object passed to listener function" column specifies the datatype of the object passed to the listener function that handles the event. Finally, the "Notes" column lists important information regarding the event's use.

Spend a little time getting to know Flash Player's mouse events by perusing Table 22-1. Here are a few general issues to bear in mind as you review the table:

System focus
The following events are triggered even when Flash Player does not have system focus: `MouseEvent.MOUSE_MOVE`, `MouseEvent.MOUSE_OVER`, `MouseEvent.MOUSE_OUT`, `MouseEvent.ROLL_OVER`, and `MouseEvent.ROLL_OUT`. All other mouse events are triggered when Flash Player has system focus only.

Location matters
With one exception, mouse events are not dispatched when the user manipulates the mouse outside Flash Player's display area. The exception: if the user presses the primary mouse button within Flash Player's display area and then releases it outside Flash Player's display area, `MouseEvent.MOUSE_UP` is dispatched. To be notified when the mouse pointer leaves Flash Player's display area, register for the `Event.MOUSE_LEAVE` event, as discussed in the later section "Flash Player-Level Input Events."

Vector graphics ignored in main-class instance
Mouse interactions with vector content drawn via the instance variable `graphics` of a *.swf* file's main class do not trigger mouse events. However, mouse interactions with vector content drawn via the instance variable `graphics` of any other instance of *InteractiveObject* or its subclasses do trigger mouse events.

Default behavior not cancelable
Flash Player's default behavior cannot be prevented for any type of mouse event.

Immediate screen updates
To refresh the screen immediately after handling any mouse event, use the *MouseEvent* class's instance method *updateAfterEvent()*. For complete details, see the section "Post-event Screen Updates" in Chapter 23.

Table 22-1. Flash Player mouse events

Event type	Description	Target	Default behavior	Bubbles	Data type of bject passed to listener function	Notes
MouseEvent.MOUSE_DOWN	Primary mouse button depressed while mouse pointer is over Flash Player's display area.	The *InteractiveObject* under the mouse pointer when the mouse button was depressed	If target is a *SimpleButton*, downState is displayed. If target is *TextField* with selection enabled, selection begins. Not cancelable.	Yes	*MouseEvent*	
MouseEvent.MOUSE_UP	Primary mouse button released while mouse pointer is over Flash Player's display area.	The *InteractiveObject* under the mouse pointer when the mouse button is released	If target is a *SimpleButton*, its overState is displayed. If target is a *TextField* with selection enabled, selection ends. Not cancelable.	Yes	*MouseEvent*	
MouseEvent.CLICK	Primary mouse button depressed and then released over the same *InteractiveObject*. Or, the user activates a *SimpleButton*, *Sprite*, or *MovieClip* instance via the space or Enter key. See the section "Focus Events" later in this chapter.	The *InteractiveObject* that was clicked or activated	None	Yes	*MouseEvent*	

Table 22-1. Flash Player mouse events (continued)

Event type	Description	Target	Default behavior	Bubbles	Data type of object passed to listener function	Notes
MouseEvent.DOUBLE_CLICK	Two MouseEvent. CLICK events occur in rapid succession over the same *InteractiveObject*.	The *InteractiveObject* that was double-clicked	If target is a *TextField* with selection enabled, the word under the pointer is selected.	Yes	*MouseEvent*	• Triggered only if the programmer first sets the target's doubleClickEnabled variable to true. • In a double-click sequence, the first click triggers MouseEvent. CLICK; the second triggers M.ouseEvent. DOUBLE_CLICK. • Double-click speed is operating-system determined.
MouseEvent.MOUSE_MOVE	Mouse pointer moved while over Flash Player's display area.	The *InteractiveObject* under the mouse pointer when the mouse pointer moved	If target is a *TextField* being selected, selection is updated. Not cancelable.	Yes	*MouseEvent*	
MouseEvent.MOUSE_OVER	Mouse pointer moved onto a display object.	The *InteractiveObject* onto which the mouse pointer moved	When target is a *SimpleButton*, if primary mouse button is down, upState is displayed; if primary mouse button is up, overState is displayed. Not cancelable.	Yes	*MouseEvent*	• Not triggered for *Stage* instance. • Use MouseEvent. relatedObject to access the *InteractiveObject* previously under the mouse pointer.

Table 22-1. Flash Player mouse events (continued)

Event type	Description	Target	Default behavior	Bubbles	Data type of bject passed to listener function	Notes
MouseEvent.MOUSE_OUT	Mouse pointer moved off of a display object.	The *InteractiveObject* off of which the mouse pointer moved	If target is a *SimpleButton*, upState is displayed. Not cancelable.	Yes	*MouseEvent*	• Not triggered for *Stage* instance. • Use MouseEvent. relatedObject to access the *InteractiveObject* now under the mouse pointer.
MouseEvent.ROLL_OVER	Mouse pointer moved onto a given *InteractiveObject* or one of its descendants.	The *InteractiveObject* that registered the event listener being executed	None	No	*MouseEvent*	• Not triggered for *Stage* instance. • Use MouseEvent. relatedObject to access the *InteractiveObject* previously under the mouse pointer.
MouseEvent.ROLL_OUT	Mouse pointer had previously moved onto a given *InteractiveObject* or one of its descendants, but is no longer over that display object or any of its descendants.	The *InteractiveObject* that registered the event listener being executed	None	No	*MouseEvent*	• Not triggered for *Stage* instance. • Use MouseEvent. relatedObject to access the *InteractiveObject* now under the mouse pointer.
MouseEvent.MOUSE_WHEEL	Mouse's scrolling device used while Flash Player has system focus.	The *InteractiveObject* under the mouse pointer when the scrolling device was used	If target is a *TextField*, it scrolls. Not cancelable via the *Event* class's instance method *preventDefault( )*, but see Notes column.	Yes	*MouseEvent*	• To prevent scrolling for text fields, set target's mouseWheelEnabled to false.

Registering for Mouse Events

Here's the general procedure for registering an event listener for a mouse event:

1. Based on the "Description" column in Table 22-1, find the constant for the desired event type in "Event type" column.

2. Create a listener function with a single parameter whose datatype is *MouseEvent*.

3. Consult the "Target" column in Table 22-1 to determine the event's target object.

4. Finally, register the function from Step 3 with either the event target (for target phase notification) or with one of the event target's ancestors (for capture or bubbling phase notification). Most mouse events are handled by listeners registered with the event target (i.e., the object that conceptually received the input).

Let's apply the preceding steps to an example. Suppose we want to register a listener function to be notified when the following *TextField* object is clicked:

```
var theTextField:TextField = new TextField( );
theTextField.text       = "Click here";
theTextField.autoSize   = TextFieldAutoSize.LEFT;
theTextField.border     = true;
theTextField.background = true;
theTextField.selectable = false;
```

Here are the steps to follow:

1. Based on the "Description" column in Table 22-1, we determine that the event constant for mouse clicking is MouseEvent.CLICK.

2. Next, we create a function, *clickListener()*, that will be notified of MouseEvent.CLICK events. We're careful to set *clickListener()*'s parameters datatype to *MouseEvent*.

   ```
   private function clickListener (e:MouseEvent):void {
      trace("Mouse was clicked");
   }
   ```

3. Next, according to the "Target" column in Table 22-1, we find that the target of a MouseEvent.CLICK event dispatch is the *InteractiveObject* that was clicked. We want to know when the theTextField is clicked, so we'll need to register our event listener with either theTextField or one of its display ancestors.

4. For this example, we'll register *clickListener()* directly with the target *TextField* object, theTextField, as follows:

   ```
   theTextField.addEventListener(MouseEvent.CLICK, clickListener);
   ```

As a result of following the preceding steps, our *clickListener()* method executes whenever the user clicks theTextField. Example 22-1 shows the code from the preceding steps in the context of a simple class, *ClickableText*.

Example 22-1. Handling the MouseEvent.CLICK event

```
package {
  import flash.display.*;
  import flash.text.*;
  import flash.events.*;

  public class ClickableText extends Sprite {
    public function ClickableText () {
      var theTextField:TextField = new TextField();
      theTextField.text       = "Click here";
      theTextField.autoSize    = TextFieldAutoSize.LEFT;
      theTextField.border      = true;
      theTextField.background = true;
      theTextField.selectable = false;
      addChild(theTextField);

      theTextField.addEventListener(MouseEvent.CLICK, clickListener);
    }

    private function clickListener (e:MouseEvent):void {
      trace("Mouse was clicked");
    }
  }
}
```

That was pretty painless. Let's try another example. The following code registers *mouseMoveListener()* to be executed whenever the mouse moves while the mouse pointer is over the *Sprite* object referenced by the variable triangle.

```
// Create the triangle
var triangle:Sprite = new Sprite();
triangle.graphics.lineStyle(1);
triangle.graphics.beginFill(0x00FF00, 1);
triangle.graphics.moveTo(25, 0);
triangle.graphics.lineTo(50, 25);
triangle.graphics.lineTo(0, 25);
triangle.graphics.lineTo(25, 0);
triangle.graphics.endFill();
triangle.x = 200;
triangle.y = 100;

// Register with triangle for MouseEvent.MOUSE_MOVE events
triangle.addEventListener(MouseEvent.MOUSE_MOVE, mouseMoveListener);

// ...elsewhere in the class, define the listener
private function mouseMoveListener (e:MouseEvent):void {
  trace("mouse move");
}
```

As the preceding code shows, listeners can register for mouse events with an object that is not on the display list. However, such listeners will not be triggered unless or until the object is subsequently added to the display list.

An object cannot receive input-event notification unless it is on the display list.

Example 22-2 puts the preceding triangle code in the context of a *.swf* file's main class, *MouseMotionSensor*. In the example, triangle is added to the display list so it can receive mouse-event notifications.

Example 22-2. Handling MouseEvent.MOUSE_MOVE over a triangle

```
package {
  import flash.display.*;
  import flash.events.*;

  public class MouseMotionSensor extends Sprite {
    public function MouseMotionSensor () {
      // Create the triangle
      var triangle:Sprite = new Sprite();
      triangle.graphics.lineStyle(1);
      triangle.graphics.beginFill(0x00FF00, 1);
      triangle.graphics.moveTo(25, 0);
      triangle.graphics.lineTo(50, 25);
      triangle.graphics.lineTo(0, 25);
      triangle.graphics.lineTo(25, 0);
      triangle.graphics.endFill();
      triangle.x = 200;
      triangle.y = 100;

      // Add the triangle to the display list
      addChild(triangle);

      // Register with triangle for MouseEvent.MOUSE_MOVE events
      triangle.addEventListener(MouseEvent.MOUSE_MOVE, mouseMoveListener);
    }

    private function mouseMoveListener (e:MouseEvent):void {
      trace("mouse move");
    }
  }
}
```

The basic listener-definition and event-registration code shown in Example 22-2 can be applied to any event in Table 22-1.

Reader exercise: Try adding new code to Example 22-2 that registers event listeners for each of the events listed in Table 22-1. Use the listener-definition and event-registration code for the MouseEvent.MOUSE_MOVE event as a template. To help get you started, here's the code required to register an event listener for the MouseEvent.MOUSE_DOWN event (the first event listed in Table 22-1):

```
// Add this event-registration code to the class constructor
triangle.addEventListener(MouseEvent.MOUSE_DOWN, mouseDownListener);
```

```
// Add this listener-definition code to the class body
private function mouseDownListener (e:MouseEvent):void {
  trace("mouse down");
}
```

Mouse Events and Overlapping Display Objects

By default, when a mouse event occurs over two or more overlapping *InteractiveObject* instances, Flash Player targets the event at the visually front-most instance only. Objects behind the front-most object are not notified of the event.

For example, if a *TextField* object visually overlaps a *Sprite* object, and the user clicks the *TextField* object, then Flash Player dispatches a MouseEvent.CLICK event targeted at the *TextField* object only. The *Sprite* object is not notified that the mouse click occurred.

Example 22-3 shows a simple application that demonstrates the preceding "*TextField* over *Sprite*" scenario. The application's main class, *ClickSensor*, registers a MouseEvent.CLICK listener, *clickListener()*, with a *Sprite* object, circle. The *Sprite* object is partially obscured by a *TextField* object, textfield. When *clickListener()* is triggered, it moves circle 10 pixels to the right.

Example 22-3. A mouse event listener registered with a partially obscured object

```
package {
  import flash.display.*;
  import flash.events.*;
  import flash.text.*;

  public class ClickSensor extends Sprite {
    public function ClickSensor () {
      // Create the circle
      var circle:Sprite = new Sprite();
      circle.graphics.beginFill(0x999999, 1);
      circle.graphics.lineStyle(1);
      circle.graphics.drawEllipse(0, 0, 100, 100);

      // Create the TextField object
      var textfield:TextField = new TextField();
      textfield.text = "Click here";
      textfield.autoSize = TextFieldAutoSize.LEFT;
      textfield.x = 30;
      textfield.y = 30;
      textfield.border = true;
      textfield.background = true;

      // Add circle to the display list
      addChild(circle);
      // Add textfield to the display list, in front of circle
      addChild(textfield);
```

```
      // Register to be notified when the user clicks circle
      circle.addEventListener(MouseEvent.CLICK, clickListener);
    }

    // Handles MouseEvent.CLICK events targeted at circle.
    private function clickListener (e:MouseEvent):void {
      trace("User clicked: " + e.target);
      DisplayObject(e.target).x += 10;
    }
  }
}
```

Figure 22-1 shows the output of the code in Example 22-3.

Figure 22-1. ClickSensor output

When the *ClickSensor* application runs, if the user clicks the visible portion of circle, then circle moves to the right. But if the user clicks a portion of circle that is obscured by textfield, then circle does not receive the MouseEvent.CLICK notification and, hence, does not move to the right.

It is, however, possible to force textfield to ignore all mouse events, thus allowing circle to detect mouse clicks even where it is obscured by textfield. To force textfield to ignore all mouse events, we set its mouseEnabled variable to false, as follows:

```
      textfield.mouseEnabled = false;
```

If the preceding line of code were added to *ClickSensor*'s constructor method, then all mouse clicks over any portion of circle, whether visible or not, would cause circle to move to the right.

When an *InteractiveObject* instance's mouseEnabled variable is set to false, it receives no mouse-input event notifications. Instead, mouse event dispatches are targeted at the next highest mouse-enabled *InteractiveObject* instance on the display list.

Finding the Mouse Pointer's Position

As we learned earlier, when Flash Player triggers a mouse-event listener-function, it passes that function a *MouseEvent* object. That *MouseEvent* object indicates the mouse pointer's current position with the following instance variables:

- localX and localY
- stageX and stageY

The localX and localY variables give the mouse pointer's position in the event target's coordinate space (i.e., relative to the event target's top left corner). Meanwhile, the stageX and stageY variables give mouse pointer's position in the *Stage* instance's coordinate space (i.e., relative to the *Stage* instance's top left corner).

Example 22-4 demonstrates the use of localX, localY, stageX, and stageY. In the example, we create a *TextField* object, add it directly to the *Stage* instance, and then position it at coordinate (100, 100). When the user clicks the *TextField* object, we output the location of the mouse pointer relative to both the *TextField* object (i.e., the event target) and the *Stage* instance. For example, if the user clicks 10 pixels to the right and 20 pixels down from the *TextField* object's top left corner, then the output is:

```
Position in TextField's coordinate space: (10, 20)
Position in Stage instance's coordinate space: (110, 120)
```

Here's the code:

Example 22-4. Finding the mouse pointer's position

```
package {
  import flash.display.*;
  import flash.events.*;
  import flash.text.*;

  public class MousePositionChecker extends Sprite {
    public function MousePositionChecker () {
      // Create the TextField
      var textfield:TextField = new TextField();
      textfield.text = "Click here";
      textfield.autoSize = TextFieldAutoSize.LEFT;
      textfield.x = 100;
      textfield.y = 100;

      // Add textfield to the display list, as a direct child of
      // the Stage instance
      stage.addChild(textfield);

      // Register with textfield for click events
      textfield.addEventListener(MouseEvent.CLICK, clickListener);
    }

    // When textfield is clicked, display the mouse pointer position
    private function clickListener (e:MouseEvent):void {
      // Mouse pointer position relative to the TextField object
      trace("Position in TextField's coordinate space: ("
            + e.localX + ", " + e.localY + ")");
      // Mouse pointer position relative to the Stage instance
      trace("Position in Stage instance's coordinate space: ("
            + e.stageX + ", " + e.stageY + ")");
    }
  }
}
```

By updating the position of an object in response to changes in the mouse position, we can make that object appear to follow the mouse. Example 22-5 shows the ActionScript 3.0 code for a custom mouse pointer. The example combines many of the techniques we learned so far in this book. In particular, the example relies on the *StageDetector* class covered in the section "Custom Event.ADDED_TO_STAGE and Event.REMOVED_FROM_STAGE events" in Chapter 20. The example also includes two techniques we haven't yet learned about: coordinate conversion and post-event screen updates. Crossreferences to supporting information are supplied in the code comments.

Example 22-5. A custom mouse pointer

```
package {
  import flash.display.*;
  import flash.ui.*;
  import flash.events.*;
  import flash.geom.*;

  // A display class that replaces the mouse pointer with a new graphic.
  // When a CustomMousePointer object is added to the display list,
  // it automatically hides the system pointer and begins following
  // its location. When a CustomMousePointer object is removed from the
  // display list, it automatically restores the system mouse pointer.
  public class CustomMousePointer extends Sprite {
    // Constructor
    public function CustomMousePointer () {
      // Create a blue triangle to use as the custom mouse pointer
      graphics.lineStyle(1);
      graphics.beginFill(0x0000FF, 1);
      graphics.lineTo(15, 5);
      graphics.lineTo(5, 15);
      graphics.lineTo(0, 0);
      graphics.endFill();

      // Register to be notified when this object is added to or removed
      // from the display list (requires the custom helper class,
      // StageDetector)
      var stageDetector:StageDetector = new StageDetector(this);
      stageDetector.addEventListener(StageDetector.ADDED_TO_STAGE,
                          addedToStageListener);
      stageDetector.addEventListener(StageDetector.REMOVED_FROM_STAGE,
                          removedFromStageListener);
    }

    // Handles StageDetector.ADDED_TO_STAGE events
    private function addedToStageListener (e:Event):void {
      // Hide the system mouse pointer
      Mouse.hide();

      // Register to be notified when the system mouse pointer moves
      // over, or leaves Flash Player's display area
      stage.addEventListener(MouseEvent.MOUSE_MOVE, mouseMoveListener);
```

Example 22-5. A custom mouse pointer (continued)

```
    stage.addEventListener(Event.MOUSE_LEAVE, mouseLeaveListener);
  }

  // Handles StageDetector.REMOVED_FROM_STAGE events
  private function removedFromStageListener (e:Event):void {
    // Show the system mouse pointer
    Mouse.show( );

    // Unregister for mouse events with the Stage instance
    stage.removeEventListener(MouseEvent.MOUSE_MOVE, mouseMoveListener);
    stage.removeEventListener(Event.MOUSE_LEAVE, mouseLeaveListener);
  }

  // Handles Event.MOUSE_LEAVE events
  private function mouseLeaveListener (e:Event):void {
    // When the mouse leaves Flash Player's display area, hide the
    // custom pointer. Otherwise, the custom mouse pointer and the system
    // mouse pointer will be shown on the screen at the same time. Spooky.
    visible = false;
  }

  // Handles MouseEvent.MOUSE_MOVE events
  private function mouseMoveListener (e:MouseEvent):void {
    // When the mouse moves, update the position of the custom mouse
    // pointer to match the position of the system mouse pointer.
    // (For information on converting points between coordinate spaces,
    // see DisplayObject.globalToLocal( ) in Adobe's ActionScript
    // Language Reference).
    var pointInParent:Point = parent.globalToLocal(new Point(e.stageX,
                                                             e.stageY));
    x = pointInParent.x;
    y = pointInParent.y;

    // Request post-event screen update so that the animation of the
    // pointer is as smooth as possible. For details on
    // MouseEvent.updateAfterEvent( ), see Chapter 23, Screen Updates.
    e.updateAfterEvent( );

    // The MouseEvent.MOUSE_MOVE has fired, so the system pointer
    // must be within Flash Player's display area. Therefore, make sure
    // the custom mouse pointer is visible (it might have been hidden
    // because the system pointer left Flash Player's display area).
    // This code is unfortunate here--it rightfully belongs in an
    // Event.MOUSE_ENTER event, but no such event exists in
    // Flash Player 9.
    if (!visible) {
      visible = true;
    }
  }
 }
}
```

Example 22-6 shows a simple example class that demonstrates the use of the *CustomMousePointer* class shown in Example 22-5.

Example 22-6. A demonstration class showing the use of CustomMousePointer

```
package {
  import flash.display.*;

  // Demonstrates the use of the CustomMousePointer class
  public class CustomMousePointerDemo extends Sprite {
    private var pointer:CustomMousePointer;

    // Constructor
    public function CustomMousePointerDemo () {
      // Create a new CustomMousePointer object and add it to the display
      // list. The act of adding the CustomMousePointer object to the
      // display list automatically replaces the system mouse pointer with
      // the CustomMousePointer object.
      pointer = new CustomMousePointer();
      addChild(pointer);
    }
  }
}
```

Reader exercise: Try following the thread of execution that starts in the *CustomMousePointerDemo* constructor from Example 22-6 and ends with the invocation of the *CustomMousePointer* class's instance method *addedToStageListener()* method. You should eventually find yourself mentally executing the code in the *StageDetector* class from Chapter 20, which will help you become more intimate with the display API and the display list. To help you get started, here are the first seven steps in the execution thread:

1. Create a new *CustomMousePointer* object.
2. Run constructor method for the *CustomMousePointer* object created in Step 1.
3. Draw a blue triangle in the *CustomMousePointer* object.
4. Create a new *StageDetector* object, passing the *CustomMousePointer* object to its constructor.
5. Invoke *StageDetector* object's *setWatchedObject()* method, passing the *CustomMousePointer* object as its only argument.
6. Assign the *CustomMousePointer* object to the *StageDetector* object's watchedObject instance variable.
7. The watchedObject.stage variable is null (because the *CustomMousePointer* object is not currently on the display list), so set the *StageDetector* object's onStage variable to false.

You can take over from here…have fun!

Mentally executing code is a good way to understand how a program works and a nutritious part of a healthy programming diet.

Handling Mouse Events "Globally"

Flash Player defines no truly global mouse events. However, by registering for mouse events with the *Stage* instance, we can handle mouse interaction no matter where it occurs within Flash Player's display area. For example, the following code registers *mouseMoveListener()* with the *Stage* instance for MouseEvent.MOUSE_MOVE events:

```
package {
  import flash.display.*;
  import flash.events.*;

  public class GlobalMouseMotionSensor extends Sprite {
    public function GlobalMouseMotionSensor () {
      stage.addEventListener(MouseEvent.MOUSE_MOVE, mouseMoveListener);
    }

    private function mouseMoveListener (e:MouseEvent):void {
      trace("The mouse moved.");
    }
  }
}
```

When the preceding code runs, any time the mouse moves anywhere over Flash Player's display area, Flash Player dispatches a MouseEvent.MOUSE_MOVE event, triggering *mouseMoveListener()*.

Let's look at another "global" mouse-event handling example. To detect every mouse press in an application, we use the following code:

```
package {
  import flash.display.*;
  import flash.events.*;

  public class GlobalMouseDownSensor extends Sprite {
    public function GlobalMouseDownSensor () {
      stage.addEventListener(MouseEvent.MOUSE_DOWN, mouseDownListener);
    }

    private function mouseDownListener (e:MouseEvent):void {
      trace("The primary mouse button was pressed.");
    }
  }
}
```

When the preceding code runs, any time the primary mouse button is pressed while the mouse pointer is over Flash Player's display area, Flash Player dispatches a MouseEvent.MOUSE_DOWN event, triggering *mouseDownListener()*.

When a mouse-button press occurs over an "empty" region of Flash Player's display area (i.e., where no program-created display object resides), the event is targeted at the *Stage* instance. When a mouse-button press occurs over any other display object, the event is targeted at that object. Hence, by checking the event target within *mouseDownListener()*, we can write code that responds specifically to mouse-button presses over empty regions of Flash Player's display area. The following application, *CircleClicker*, demonstrates the technique. When the user clicks an empty region of Flash Player's display area, *CircleClicker* draws a randomly sized and colored circle. But when the user clicks a circle, *CircleClicker* removes that circle from the screen.

```
package {
  import flash.display.*;
  import flash.events.*;

  public class CircleClicker extends Sprite {
    public function CircleClicker () {
      stage.addEventListener(MouseEvent.CLICK, clickListener);
    }

    private function clickListener (e:MouseEvent):void {
      // If the event target is the Stage instance
      if (e.target == stage) {
        // ...draw a circle
        drawCircle(e.stageX, e.stageY);
      } else {
        // ... otherwise, the event target must be a Sprite object
        // containing a circle, so remove it
        removeChild(DisplayObject(e.target));
      }
    }

    public function drawCircle (x:int, y:int):void {
      var randomColor:int = Math.floor(Math.random( )*0xFFFFFF);
      var randomSize:int = 10 + Math.floor(Math.random( )*150);
      var circle:Sprite = new Sprite( )
      circle.graphics.beginFill(randomColor, 1);
      circle.graphics.lineStyle( );
      circle.graphics.drawEllipse(0, 0, randomSize, randomSize);
      circle.x = x-randomSize/2;
      circle.y = y-randomSize/2;
      addChild(circle);
    }
  }
}
```

Note that, for security reasons, a loaded *.swf* file might be prevented from accessing Flash Player's *Stage* instance. In such situations, to handle mouse events "globally," use the techniques covered in Chapter 12, in the section "Handling Events Across Security Boundaries."

Now let's turn our attention to another type of input events—those triggered by focus changes.

Focus Events

When an object has *keyboard focus*, it acts as the logical recipient of all keyboard input and becomes the target of all keyboard-input event dispatches. An object can gain keyboard focus either programmatically (via the Stage class's instance variable focus) or through user interaction, via the mouse, the Tab key, or the arrow keys. However, in order to gain keyboard focus, an object must be an instance of a class that inherits from *InteractiveObject*. Furthermore, in Flash Player, only one object can have keyboard focus at a time.

 For brevity, the term "keyboard focus" is normally shortened to "focus."

Focusing Objects Programmatically

To focus an object programmatically, we assign that object to the *Stage* instance's focus variable.

For example, the following code creates a *Sprite* object and then immediately focuses it (it assumes that someDisplayContainer is on the display list):

```
var rect:Sprite = new Sprite();
rect.graphics.lineStyle(1);
rect.graphics.beginFill(0x0000FF);
rect.graphics.drawRect(0, 0, 150, 75);
someDisplayContainer.addChild(rect);
someDisplayContainer.stage.focus = rect;
```

When the preceding code runs, rect gains focus, and, hence, becomes the target of all keyboard input event dispatches.

Focusing Objects with the Keyboard

To focus an object via the keyboard, the user presses the Tab key or arrow keys. However, in order for an object to receive focus via those keys, it must be part of Flash Player's tab order. The *tab order* is the set of all objects on the display list that can potentially receive focus via the keyboard. The tab order also determines the sequence in which objects receive focus when the user presses the Tab key.

There are two distinct tab orders in Flash Player: the automatic tab order and the custom tab order. The *automatic tab order* is Flash Player's default tab order, used when no custom tab order is defined. The automatic tab order includes the following objects:

- Instances of *TextField* that are on the display list and have their type variable set to TextFieldType.INPUT
- Instances of *Sprite* or *MovieClip* that are on the display list and have their buttonMode variable set to true or their tabEnabled variable set to true
- Instances of *SimpleButton* that are on the display list

When the automatic tab order is in use, and the user presses the Tab key, focus moves away from the currently focused object to the next object in the automatic tab order. The sequence of Flash Player's automatic tab order is determined by the locations of the objects it contains, proceeding visually from left to right, then top to bottom (regardless of the position of those objects in the display hierarchy).

In contrast to the automatic tab order, the *custom tab order* is a program-defined tab-order including an arbitrary sequence of objects whose tabIndex variable is set to a nonnegative integer. The following types of objects can be included in the custom tab order:

- Instances of *TextField* whose type variable is set to TextFieldType.INPUT
- Instances of *Sprite*, *MovieClip*, or *SimpleButton*

When at least one object currently on the display list has a tabIndex variable set to 0 or greater, the custom tab order is used, and pressing the Tab key causes objects to be focused according to their tabIndex value, from lowest to highest. For example, if the currently focused object has a tabIndex value of 2, and the Tab key is pressed, then the object with tabIndex 3 is focused. If the Tab key is pressed again, the object with tabIndex 4 is focused, and so on. If two objects have the same tabIndex value, the object with the lower depth comes first in the tab order. Objects without an explicitly assigned tabIndex value are excluded from the tab order.

Regardless of whether the automatic tab order or the custom tab order is currently in use, when an instance of the *Sprite*, *MovieClip*, or *SimpleButton* class is focused with the Tab key, then the user can subsequently use the four arrow keys to change focus to an object located in a specific direction (up, down, left, or right).

To exclude an object from the automatic or custom tab order, we set its tabEnabled variable to false. Objects with _visible set to false are automatically excluded from the tab order. To exclude all of a given display-object container's descendants from the automatic or custom tab order, we set its tabChildren variable to false.

By default, Flash Player displays a yellow rectangle around *Sprite*, *MovieClip*, or *SimpleButton* instances when they are focused via the keyboard. To disable the yellow rectangle for an individual object, we set its focusRect variable to false. To disable the yellow rectangle for all objects, we set the *Stage* instance's stageFocusRect variable to false. Note that the value of the stageFocusRect variable is not reflected by the focusRect variable of individual objects. However, setting an individual object's focusRect variable overrides the stageFocusRect variable's setting.

Focusing Objects with the Mouse

Just as the user can assign keyboard focus using the Tab key or the arrow keys, the user can also assign focus by clicking an object with the primary mouse button. However, by default, only *SimpleButton* and *TextField* instances can be focused with the mouse. To allow the user to focus a *Sprite* or *MovieClip* instance with the mouse, we use one of the following approaches:

- Set the instance's buttonMode variable to true (while ensuring that its tabEnabled variable is not explicitly set to false)
- Set the instance's tabEnabled variable to true
- Assign a nonnegative integer to the instance's tabIndex variable (while ensuring that its tabEnabled variable is not explicitly set to false)

For example, the following code creates a *Sprite* object that receives keyboard focus when clicked:

```
var rect:Sprite = new Sprite( );
rect.graphics.lineStyle(1);
rect.graphics.beginFill(0x0000FF);
rect.graphics.drawRect(0, 0, 150, 75);
rect.tabEnabled = true;
```

To prevent an object from being focused with the mouse, we set its mouseEnabled variable to false. To prevent a display object container's descendants from being focused with the mouse, we set that container's mouseChildren variable to false.

An object cannot be focused with the mouse if its mouseEnabled variable is set to false, or the object is a display descendant of a container with the mouseChildren variable set to false.

Furthermore, when the tabEnabled variable of a *Sprite*, *MovieClip*, or *SimpleButton* instance is explicitly set to false, then that instance cannot be focused with the mouse. Likewise, when a *Sprite*, *MovieClip*, or *SimpleButton* instance is a descendant of a container whose tabChildren variable is set to false, then that instance cannot be focused with the mouse. However, due to a Flash Player bug, a *TextField* object whose tabEnabled variable is explicitly set to false can still be focused with the mouse. Likewise, due to the same bug, a *TextField* object that is a descendant of a container whose tabChildren variable is set to false can still be focused with the mouse.

Handling descendant focus through a single ancestor

To instruct ActionScript to treat a display object container and all of its descendants as a group that can receive focus via a single mouse click, follow these steps:

1. Enable mouse-based focusing for the container by setting the container's `buttonMode` or `tabEnabled` variable to `true` or by setting its `tabIndex` variable to a nonnegative integer.

2. Disable mouse interaction for the container's children by setting the container's `mouseChildren` variable to `false`.

Flash Player's Focus Events

When an application's keyboard focus changes to a new object (as described in the previous three sections), Flash Player dispatches one or more focus events describing the change. Table 22-2 lists Flash Player's built-in focus-event types. For each type of event, the "Event type" column lists the *FocusEvent*-class constant that indicates the event type's official string name. The "Description" column describes the specific user action that triggers the event. The "Target" column lists the object that serves as the event target when the event is dispatched. The "Default behavior" column lists Flash Player's native response to the event. The "Bubbles" column indicates whether the event has a bubbling phase. Finally, the "Datatype of object passed to listener function" column specifies the datatype of the object passed to the listener function that handles the event.

Table 22-2. Flash Player focus events

Event type	Description	Target	Default behavior	Bubbles	Datatype of object passed to listener function
FocusEvent.FOCUS_IN	Focus has been gained by a given object.	The object that gained focus. (Use the *FocusEvent* class's instance variable relatedObject to access the object that lost focus, if any).	None	Yes	*FocusEvent*
FocusEvent.FOCUS_OUT	Focus has been lost by a given object.	The object that lost focus. (Use the *FocusEvent* class's instance variable relatedObject to access the object that gained focus, if any).	None	Yes	*FocusEvent*
FocusEvent.KEY_FOCUS_CHANGE	User has attempted to change focus via the keyboard.	The currently focused object. (Use the FocusEvent class's instance variable relatedObject to access the object the user is attempting to focus).	Flash Player changes the focus. Can be canceled via the *Event* class's instance method *preventDefault( )*.	Yes	*FocusEvent*
FocusEvent.MOUSE_FOCUS_CHANGE	User has attempted to change focus via the mouse.	The currently focused object. (Use the FocusEvent class's instance variable relatedObject to access the object the user is attempting to focus).	Flash Player changes the focus. Can be canceled via the *Event* class's instance method *preventDefault( )*.	Yes	*FocusEvent*

As Table 22-2 indicates, the FocusEvent.FOCUS_IN and FocusEvent.FOCUS_OUT events are used to detect when an object has gained or lost focus. By the time those two events are dispatched, the change in focus has already occurred. By contrast, the FocusEvent.KEY_FOCUS_CHANGE and FocusEvent.MOUSE_FOCUS_CHANGE events are used to detect when an object is about to gain or lose focus, but has not yet gained or lost it. An application typically uses the FocusEvent.KEY_FOCUS_CHANGE and FocusEvent.MOUSE_FOCUS_CHANGE events to prevent the user from changing focus via the keyboard or mouse, perhaps in order to force the user to interact with a specific part of the interface, such as a modal dialog box.

As with mouse events, Flash Player defines no truly global focus events. However, by registering for focus events with the *Stage* instance, we can handle all focus changes that occur within Flash Player. Example 22-7 demonstrates the technique, showing an application that creates two *TextField* objects, and sets their background color to green whenever they are focused.

Example 22-7. Handling focus events globally

```
package {
  import flash.display.*;
  import flash.events.*;
  import flash.text.*;

  public class GlobalFocusSensor extends Sprite {
    public function GlobalFocusSensor ( ) {
      // Create text fields
      var field1:TextField = new TextField( );
      field1.width      = 100;
      field1.height     = 30;
      field1.border     = true;
      field1.background = true;
      field1.type = TextFieldType.INPUT;

      var field2:TextField = new TextField( );
      field2.width      = 100;
      field2.height     = 30;
      field2.y          = 50;
      field2.border     = true;
      field2.background = true;
      field2.type = TextFieldType.INPUT;

      // Add text fields to the display list
      addChild(field1);
      addChild(field2);

      // Register for FocusEvent.FOCUS_IN events
      stage.addEventListener(FocusEvent.FOCUS_IN, focusInListener);
    }

    // Handle all FocusEvent.FOCUS_IN events in this application
    private function focusInListener (e:FocusEvent):void {
```

Example 22-7. Handling focus events globally (continued)

```
      // Set the background color of the focused TextField object to green
      TextField(e.target).backgroundColor = 0xFF00FF00;

      // Set the background color of the TextField object that lost focus
      // to white
      if (e.relatedObject is TextField) {
        TextField(e.relatedObject).backgroundColor = 0xFFFFFFFF;
      }
    }
  }
}
```

Focus events can also be handled by listeners registered with the event target or with any of the event target's display ancestors. Example 22-8 shows an application that creates an input *TextField* that, once focused, cannot be unfocused until at least three characters have been entered. Similar code is often found in applications that validate input entered via fill-in forms, such as a login screen or a product order form.

Example 22-8. Handling focus events for a particular object

```
package {
  import flash.display.*;
  import flash.events.*;
  import flash.text.*;

  // Demonstrates how to handle FocusEvent.FOCUS_IN events for a single
  // object. Creates a TextField that, once focused, cannot be unfocused
  // until at least three characters have been entered.
  public class ObjectFocusSensor extends Sprite {
    private var namefield:TextField;
    private var passfield:TextField;

    public function ObjectFocusSensor () {
      // Create text fields
      namefield = new TextField();
      namefield.width      = 100;
      namefield.height     = 30;
      namefield.border     = true;
      namefield.background = true;
      namefield.type = TextFieldType.INPUT;

      passfield = new TextField();
      passfield.width      = 100;
      passfield.height     = 30;
      passfield.y          = 50;
      passfield.border     = true;
      passfield.background = true;
      passfield.type = TextFieldType.INPUT;
```

Example 22-8. Handling focus events for a particular object (continued)

```
    // Add text fields to the display list
    addChild(namefield);
    addChild(passfield);

    // Register for focus change events
    namefield.addEventListener(FocusEvent.MOUSE_FOCUS_CHANGE,
                               focusChangeListener);
    namefield.addEventListener(FocusEvent.KEY_FOCUS_CHANGE,
                               focusChangeListener);
  }

  // Handles all focus change events targeted at namefield
  private function focusChangeListener (e:FocusEvent):void {
    if (e.target == namefield && namefield.text.length < 3) {
      trace("Name entered is less than three characters long");
      e.preventDefault( );
    }
  }
 }
}
```

Keyboard-Input Events

Flash Player dispatches keyboard-input events when the user presses or releases the keys on a keyboard. Broadly speaking, keyboard input events are typically used to trigger a response from either the application as a whole or from a specific interface element. For example, pressing the "S" key might trigger a global "save user data" command while pressing the Down Arrow key might select an item in a specific menu component.

Keyboard-input events that trigger application-wide commands are typically handled globally, by listeners registered with Flash Player's *Stage* instance. By contrast, keyboard-input events that trigger a specific interface-element response are typically handled by listeners registered with the object that currently has keyboard focus.

 Flash Player's keyboard-input events are intended for use when developing keyboard-controlled applications but are not suitable for responding to textual input in *TextField* objects. To respond to textual input, use the TextEvent.TEXT_INPUT event, described later in the section "Text-Input Events."

Table 22-3 lists Flash Player's built-in keyboard-event types. For each type of event, the "Event type" column lists the *KeyboardEvent*-class constant that indicates the event type's official string name. The "Description" column describes the specific user action that triggers the event. The "Target" column lists the object that serves as the event target when the event is dispatched. The "Default behavior" column lists

Flash Player's native response to the event. Unlike mouse events and focus events, keyboard events have no default behavior. The "Bubbles" column indicates whether the event has a bubbling phase. Finally, the "Datatype of object passed to listener function" column specifies the datatype of the object passed to the listener function that handles the event.

Note that keyboard events are not dispatched unless Flash Player has system focus. To be notified when Flash Player gains or loses system focus, register for the Event.ACTIVATE and Event.DEACTIVATE events (described later in the section "Flash Player-Level Input Events").

Table 22-3. Flash Player Keyboard Events

Event type	Description	Target	Default behavior	Bubbles	Datatype of object passed to listener function
KeyboardEvent.KEY_DOWN	Key depressed	Either the *InteractiveObject* with keyboard focus or, if no object is focused, the *Stage* instance	None	Yes	*KeyboardEvent*
KeyboardEvent.KEY_UP	Key released	Either the *InteractiveObject* with keyboard focus or, if no object is focused, the *Stage* instance	None	Yes	*KeyboardEvent*

Global Keyboard-Event Handling

As with mouse events and focus events, Flash Player defines no truly global keyboard events. However, by registering for keyboard events with the *Stage* instance, we can handle all keyboard interaction whenever it occurs while Flash Player has system focus. Example 22-9 demonstrates the technique, showing a simplified class that displays a debugging message whenever a key is pressed.

Example 22-9. Handling keyboard events globally

```
package {
  import flash.display.*;
  import flash.events.*;

  public class GlobalKeyboardSensor extends Sprite {
    public function GlobalKeyboardSensor () {
      // Register to be notified whenever a key is pressed
```

Example 22-9. Handling keyboard events globally (continued)

```
      stage.addEventListener(KeyboardEvent.KEY_DOWN, keyDownListener);
   }

   // This function is invoked whenever a key is pressed while
   // Flash Player has system focus
   private function keyDownListener (e:KeyboardEvent):void {
     trace("A key was pressed.");
   }
  }
}
```

Object-Specific Keyboard-Event Handling

As described in Table 22-3, when no object has keyboard focus, the *Stage* instance is the target of all keyboard event dispatches. By contrast, when an *InteractiveObject* instance has keyboard focus, that instance is the target of all keyboard events dispatched by Flash Player.

Hence, to respond to keyboard input that is directed at a particular object, we register listeners with that object. Example 22-10 demonstrates, showing an application that creates two *Sprite* objects, rect1 and rect2. When rect1 is focused, and a key is pressed, the application moves rect1 to the right. When rect2 is focused, and a key is pressed, the application rotates rect2.

Example 22-10. Handling keyboard events for a particular object

```
package {
  import flash.display.*;
  import flash.events.*;

  public class ObjectKeyboardSensor extends Sprite {
    public function ObjectKeyboardSensor () {
      // Create the rectangles
      var rect1:Sprite = new Sprite();
      rect1.graphics.lineStyle(1);
      rect1.graphics.beginFill(0x0000FF);
      rect1.graphics.drawRect(0, 0, 75, 75);
      rect1.tabEnabled = true;

      var rect2:Sprite = new Sprite();
      rect2.graphics.lineStyle(1);
      rect2.graphics.beginFill(0x0000FF);
      rect2.graphics.drawRect(0, 0, 75, 75);
      rect2.x = 200;
      rect2.tabEnabled = true;

      // Add the rectangles to the display list
      addChild(rect1);
      addChild(rect2);
```

```
    // Register rectangles for keyboard events
    rect1.addEventListener(KeyboardEvent.KEY_DOWN, rect1KeyDownListener);
    rect2.addEventListener(KeyboardEvent.KEY_DOWN, rect2KeyDownListener);
  }

  // Executed when rect1 has focus and a key is pressed
  private function rect1KeyDownListener (e:KeyboardEvent):void {
    Sprite(e.target).x += 10;
  }

  // Executed when rect2 has focus and a key is pressed
  private function rect2KeyDownListener (e:KeyboardEvent):void {
    Sprite(e.target).rotation += 10;
  }
 }
}
```

Now that we know how to detect when the user presses or releases a key on the keyboard, let's explore how to determine *which* key was pressed or released.

Determining the Most Recently Pressed or Released Key

Flash Player assigns an arbitrary numeric identifier, known as a *key code*, to all detectable keys on the keyboard. To determine the key code for the most recently pressed or released key, we retrieve the value of the *KeyboardEvent* class's instance variable keyCode within a KeyboardEvent.KEY_UP or KeyboardEvent.KEY_DOWN listener function, as shown in Example 22-11.

Example 22-11. Retrieving a pressed key's key code

```
package {
  import flash.display.*;
  import flash.events.*;
  import flash.text.*;

  // Displays the key code for any key pressed.
  public class KeyViewer extends Sprite {
    private var keyoutput:TextField;
    public function KeyViewer () {
      keyoutput = new TextField();
      keyoutput.text = "Press any key...";
      keyoutput.autoSize = TextFieldAutoSize.LEFT;
      keyoutput.border     = true;
      keyoutput.background = true;
      addChild(keyoutput);

      stage.addEventListener(KeyboardEvent.KEY_DOWN, keyDownListener);
    }
```

Example 22-11. Retrieving a pressed key's key code (continued)

```
  private function keyDownListener (e:KeyboardEvent):void {
    // Display the key code for the key that was pressed
    keyoutput.text = "The key code for the key you pressed is: "
                     + e.key code;
  }
 }
}
```

To detect the pressing or releasing of a specific key, we compare that key's key code to the value of the *KeyboardEvent* class's instance variable keyCode within a KeyboardEvent.KEY_UP or KeyboardEvent.KEY_DOWN listener function. For example, the following KeyboardEvent.KEY_DOWN listener function detects the pressing of the Escape key by comparing its key code, 27, to the value of keyCode.

```
  private function keyDownListener (e:KeyboardEvent):void {
    if (e.keyCode == 27) {
      trace("The Escape key was pressed");
    }
  }
```

The key codes for all control keys and numeric keypad keys can be accessed via constants of the *flash.ui.Keyboard* class. Hence, the preceding code would normally be written as follows (notice the use of the Keyboard class's static variable ESCAPE in place of the literal value 27):

```
  import flash.ui.Keyboard;
  private function keyDownListener (e:KeyboardEvent):void {
    if (e.keyCode == Keyboard.ESCAPE) {
      trace("The Escape key was pressed");
    }
  }
```

Key codes are language and operating-system dependent.

> For a list of the key codes for the keys on a U.S. English keyboard, see:
> *http://livedocs.macromedia.com/flash/8/main/00001686.html*.

When writing expressions that detect the pressing or releasing of a key that is not included among the *flash.ui.Keyboard* constants, always follow these steps:

1. Run the *KeyViewer* application from Example 22-11 on a computer with the operating system and keyboard of the target user.
2. Press the desired key.
3. Record the returned key code in a constant.
4. Use the constant from Step 3 when detecting the pressing or releasing of the desired key.

For example, suppose we wish to detect the pressing of the "A" key on a computer running Mac OS with a U.S. English keyboard. We run *KeyViewer* and press the A key. In response, the *KeyViewer* application displays the key code 65. We then record that key code in a constant of a custom class, perhaps named *KeyConstants*, as follows:

```
public static const A_KEY:int = 65;
```

Then, to detect the pressing of the A key, we use the following code:

```
private function keyDownListener (e:KeyboardEvent):void {
  if (e.keyCode == KeyConstants.A_KEY) {
    trace("The A key was pressed");
  }
}
```

The following code shows the technique in the context of an extremely simple test application:

```
package {
  import flash.display.*;
  import flash.events.*;

  public class AKeySensor extends Sprite {
    //
    public static const A_KEY:int = 65;

    public function AKeySensor () {
      stage.addEventListener(KeyboardEvent.KEY_DOWN, keyDownListener);
    }

    private function keyDownListener (e:KeyboardEvent):void {
      if (e.keyCode == AKeySensor.A_KEY) {
        trace("The A key was pressed");
      }
    }
  }
}
```

Note that the KeyboardEvent class's instance variable keyCode is not supported when an input method editor (IME) is in use. For information on IMEs, see the *flash.system.IME* class in Adobe's ActionScript Language Reference and Flash Player APIs → Client System Environment → IME class in Adobe's Programming ActionScript 3.0.

Multilocation keys

On some keyboards, certain individual key codes represent keys that occur in multiple places on the keyboard. For example, on a computer running Microsoft Windows with a U.S. English keyboard, the key code 16 represents both the left Shift key and the right Shift key; the key code 17 represents both the left Control key and the right Control key; and the key code 13 represents both the main Enter key and the numeric keypad's Enter key. To distinguish between these multiposition keys, we use the *KeyboardEvent* class's instance variable keyLocation, whose value indicates a logical position, expressed as one of the four constants defined by the *flash.ui.KeyLocation* class (LEFT, NUM_PAD, RIGHT, and STANDARD). The following code demonstrates the technique, showing a KeyboardEvent.KEY_DOWN listener function that outputs one debugging message for the pressing of the left Shift key and another for the pressing of the right Shift key:

```
private function keyDownListener (e:KeyboardEvent):void {
  if (e.keyCode == Keyboard.SHIFT) {
    if (e.keyLocation == KeyLocation.LEFT) {
      trace("The left Shift key was pressed");
    } else if (e.keyLocation == KeyLocation.RIGHT) {
      trace("The right Shift key was pressed");
    }
  }
}
```

Detecting Multiple Simultaneous Key Presses

To detect the pressing of the Shift key or the Control key (Command key on Macintosh) in combination with any other key, we use the *KeyboardEvent* class's instance variables shiftKey and ctrlKey within a KeyboardEvent.KEY_DOWN listener function. For example, the following simple application detects the pressing of the key combination Control+S (Command+S on Macintosh):

```
package {
  import flash.display.*;
  import flash.events.*;

  public class CtrlSSensor extends Sprite {
    public static const S_KEY:int = 83;

    public function CtrlSSensor () {
      stage.addEventListener(KeyboardEvent.KEY_DOWN, keyDownListener);
    }

    private function keyDownListener (e:KeyboardEvent):void {
      if (e.keyCode == CtrlSSensor.S_KEY
          && e.ctrlKey == true) {
        trace("Ctrl+S was pressed");
      }
    }
  }
}
```

 In the standalone and web browser plug-in versions of Flash Player, ActionScript cannot detect the pressing of the Alt key (or, for that matter, the F10 key).

To detect the simultaneous pressing of two or more arbitrary keys other than the Shift key and the Control key, we must manually track each key's current state. The following code demonstrates the technique, showing an application that displays a debugging message when the Left arrow key and the Up arrow key are both down. Similar code might be used to steer a car or a spaceship diagonally in a video game.

```
package {
  import flash.display.*;
  import flash.events.*;
  import flash.ui.*;

  // Detects the simultaneous pressing of the Up Arrow and Left Arrow keys
  public class UpLeftSensor extends Sprite {
    // Tracks the state of the Up Arrow key
    // (true when pressed; false otherwise)
    private var upPressed:Boolean;
    // Tracks the state of the Left Arrow key
    // (true when pressed; false otherwise)
    private var leftPressed:Boolean;

    public function UpLeftSensor () {
      // Register for keyboard events
      stage.addEventListener(KeyboardEvent.KEY_DOWN, keyDownListener);
      stage.addEventListener(KeyboardEvent.KEY_UP, keyUpListener);
    }

    // Handles KeyboardEvent.KEY_DOWN events
    private function keyDownListener (e:KeyboardEvent):void {
      // Make a note of whether the Up Arrow key or Left Arrow
      // key was pressed
      if (e.keyCode == Keyboard.UP) {
        upPressed = true;
      } else if (e.keyCode == Keyboard.LEFT) {
        leftPressed = true;
      }

      // If the Up Arrow key and the Left Arrow key are both pressed...
      if (upPressed && leftPressed) {
        // ...take some application-specific action, such as steering a
        // spaceship diagonally and up and to the left
        trace("Up Arrow key and Left Arrow key are both pressed");
      }
    }

    // Handles KeyboardEvent.KEY_UP events
    private function keyUpListener (e:KeyboardEvent):void {
      // Make a note of whether the Up Arrow key or Left Arrow
      // key was released
      if (e.keyCode == Keyboard.UP) {
        upPressed = false;
      } else if (e.keyCode == Keyboard.LEFT) {
        leftPressed = false;
      }
    }
  }
}
```

Mouse Events and Modifier Keys

Just as ActionScript offers a convenient way to check whether the Shift or Control keys are down during a keyboard-input event dispatch, ActionScript also enables you to check whether the Shift or Control keys are down during a mouse-input event dispatch. To determine whether the Shift key or the Control key is depressed during a mouse-input event dispatch, we use the *MouseEvent* class's instance variables shiftKey and ctrlKey within a listener function registered for the event. For example, the following code outputs a debugging message when a mouse click occurs while the Shift key is depressed. Similar code might be used in a drawing program to constrain the dragging of an object to the horizontal or vertical axis.

```
package {
  import flash.display.*;
  import flash.events.*;

  public class ControlClickSensor extends Sprite {
    public function ControlClickSensor () {
      stage.addEventListener(MouseEvent.CLICK, clickListener);
    }

    private function clickListener (e:MouseEvent):void {
      if (e.shiftKey) {
        trace("Shift+click detected");
      }
    }
  }
}
```

Determining the Character Associated with a Key

Earlier we learned how to determine the key code for the most recently pressed or released key. To retrieve the actual character associated with the most recently pressed or released key, we check the value of the *KeyboardEvent* class's instance variable charCode within a KeyboardEvent.KEY_UP or KeyboardEvent.KEY_DOWN listener function.

When a U.S. English keyboard is used, charCode indicates the ASCII character code of the character that logically corresponds to the most recently pressed or released key. In some cases, the charCode value for a single key has two potential values, depending on whether or not the Shift key is depressed. For example, the character code for the key marked "S" on a U.S. English keyboard is 115 when the Shift key is not depressed, but 83 when Shift is depressed. For keys that display characters with no ASCII value, KeyboardEvent.charCode has the value 0.

When a non-U.S. English keyboard is used, charCode indicates the ASCII character code for the equivalent key on a U.S. English keyboard. For example, on a Japanese keyboard, the key in the U.S. English "A" position displays the glyph ち, but charCode still returns either 97 or 65 (ASCII's "a" and "A", respectively)—not 12385 (the Unicode code point for さ).

To convert a character code into an actual string, we use the *String* class's instance method *fromCharCode()*. Example 22-12 demonstrates the technique by updating the *KeyViewer* class (presented earlier in Example 22-11) to display the character associated with the most recently pressed key.

Example 22-12. Retrieving a pressed key's key code and character code

```
package {
  import flash.display.*;
  import flash.events.*;
  import flash.text.*;
  import flash.ui.*;

  // Displays the key code and character code for any key pressed.
  public class KeyViewer extends Sprite {
    private var keyoutput:TextField;
    public function KeyViewer () {
      keyoutput = new TextField();
      keyoutput.text = "Press any key...";
      keyoutput.autoSize = TextFieldAutoSize.LEFT;
      keyoutput.border     = true;
      keyoutput.background = true;
      addChild(keyoutput);

      stage.addEventListener(KeyboardEvent.KEY_DOWN, keyDownListener);
    }

    private function keyDownListener (e:KeyboardEvent):void {
      keyoutput.text = "The key code for the key you pressed is: "
                     + e.keyCode + "\n";
      keyoutput.appendText("The character code for the key you pressed is: "
                         + e.charCode + "\n");
      keyoutput.appendText("The character for the key you pressed is: "
                         + String.fromCharCode(e.charCode));
    }
  }
}
```

The result of running the *KeyViewer* application from Example 22-12 and pressing the key marked "S" on a U.S. English keyboard is:

```
The key code for the key you pressed is: 83
The character code for the key you pressed is: 115
The character for the key you pressed is: s
```

The result of running the *KeyViewer* application from Example 22-12 and pressing the Shift key in combination with the key marked "S" on a U.S. English keyboard is:

```
The key code for the key you pressed is: 83
The character code for the key you pressed is: 83
The character for the key you pressed is: S
```

As with the *KeyboardEvent* class's instance variable keyCode, charCode is not supported when an input method editor is in use, and is not intended as a means of receiving textual input. To retrieve textual input, we use the TextEvent.TEXT_INPUT event in conjunction with a *TextField* object, as described in the next section.

Text-Input Events

Flash Player dispatches text-input events in the following situations:

- When the user adds new text to an input text field
- When the user activates an "event:"-protocol hypertext link in a text field (by clicking the link)
- When a text field is scrolled, either programmatically or by the user

Table 22-4 lists Flash Player's built-in text-input fsevent types. For each type of event, the "Event Type" column lists the class constant that indicates the event type's official string name. The "Description" column describes the specific user action that triggers the event. The "Target" column lists the object that serves as the event target when the event is dispatched. The "Default behavior" column lists Flash Player's native response to the event. The "Bubbles" column indicates whether the event has a bubbling phase. Finally, the "Datatype of object passed to listener function" column specifies the datatype of the object passed to the listener function that handles the event.

Table 22-4. Flash Player text-input events

Event Type	Description	Target	Default behavior	Bubbles	Data Type of Object Passed to Listener Function
TextEvent.TEXT_INPUT	User has attempted to add new text to an input text field.	The *TextField* object to which the user is attempting to add new text	The text is added to the text field. This default behavior can be canceled via the *Event* class's instance method *preventDefault( )*.	Yes	*TextEvent*
Event.CHANGE	New text added to an input text field by the user.	The *TextField* object to which the new text was added	None	Yes	*Event*
Event.SCROLL	Text field scrolled programmatically or by the user.	The *TextField* object that was scrolled	None	No	*Event*
TextEvent.LINK	"event:"-protocol hypertext link activated.	The *TextField* object containing the activated link	None	Yes	*TextEvent*

Like mouse events, keyboard events, and focus events, a text-input event can be handled by listeners registered with the event target or with any of that target's display ancestors. In the coming sections, however, we'll focus solely on using listeners registered with the event target.

Let's take a closer look at the four events in Table 22-4.

The TextEvent.TEXT_INPUT and Event.CHANGE Events

The TextEvent.TEXT_INPUT and Event.CHANGE events let us detect new text input from the user. Specifically, the following techniques for entering text can trigger the TextEvent.TEXT_INPUT and Event.CHANGE events:

- Pressing a key on the keyboard
- Pasting text via keyboard shortcuts or Flash Player's built-in context menu (accessed via a secondary mouse click)
- Speaking into speech recognition software
- Composing text content with an input method editor

The TextEvent.TEXT_INPUT event indicates that the user is attempting to add new text to an input text field and provides the application with an opportunity to either thwart or allow that attempt. The TextEvent.TEXT_INPUT event offers a convenient way to accessing the text content being added to a text field before it is actually added to that text field. By contrast, the Event.CHANGE event indicates that a user's attempt to add new text to an input text field has succeeded, and that Flash Player has finished updating the text field's content accordingly.

The generalized code required to register a listener with a *TextField* object for the TextEvent.TEXT_INPUT event is as follows:

```
theTextField.addEventListener(TextEvent.TEXT_INPUT, textInputListener);
```

The generalized event-listener code required for a TextEvent.TEXT_INPUT listener is:

```
private function textInputListener (e:TextEvent):void {
}
```

To prevent user-entered text from appearing in a *TextField*, we use the *Event* class's instance method *preventDefault()*, as follows:

```
private function textInputListener (e:TextEvent):void {
  // Stop user-entered text from appearing
  e.preventDefault();
}
```

To access the text entered by the user, we use the *TextEvent* class's instance variable text, as follows:

```
private function textInputListener (e:TextEvent):void {
  // Output a debugging message showing the user-entered text
  trace(e.text);
}
```

The TextEvent.TEXT_INPUT event might be used to auto-format user input in a fill-in form application, as shown in Example 22-13. In the example, all text entered into an input text field is converted to uppercase. Similar code might be used in the "shipping address" section of an online product-order form.

Example 22-13. Converting user input to uppercase

```
package {
  import flash.display.*;
  import flash.events.*;
  import flash.text.*;

  public class UppercaseConverter extends Sprite {
    private var inputfield:TextField;

    public function UppercaseConverter () {
      inputfield = new TextField();
      inputfield.text = "";
      inputfield.width  = 150;
      inputfield.height = 30;
      inputfield.border      = true;
      inputfield.background = true;
      inputfield.type = TextFieldType.INPUT;
      addChild(inputfield);

      // Register with inputfield for TextEvent.TEXT_INPUT events
      inputfield.addEventListener(TextEvent.TEXT_INPUT, textInputListener);
    }

    // Triggered whenever the user attempts to add new text to inputfield
    private function textInputListener (e:TextEvent):void {
      // Prevent the user-supplied text from being added to the text field
      e.preventDefault();
      // Add the equivalent uppercase character to the text field
      inputfield.replaceText(inputfield.caretIndex,
                             inputfield.caretIndex,
                             e.text.toUpperCase());
      // Set the insertion point (caret) to the end of the new text, so
      // the user thinks they entered the text
      var newCaretIndex:int = inputfield.caretIndex + e.text.length;
      inputfield.setSelection(newCaretIndex, newCaretIndex);
    }
  }
}
```

Now let's turn to the Event.CHANGE event. The generalized code required to register a listener with a *TextField* object for the Event.CHANGE event is as follows:

```
theTextField.addEventListener(Event.CHANGE, changeListener);
```

The generalized event listener code required for an Event.CHANGE listener is:

```
private function changeListener (e:Event):void {
}
```

The Event.CHANGE event might be used to synchronize the content of two text fields, as shown in Example 22-14. The example shows an excerpt from a hypothetical panel widget containing labeled photos. For simplicity, the example includes one photo label only, without its corresponding image. The code uses Event.CHANGE to keep the panel's title bar updated to match the name of the currently selected photo. For review, the code also uses the FocusEvent.FOCUS_IN and FocusEvent.FOCUS_OUT events to update the panel title when the user changes focus in the application.

Example 22-14. Synchronizing two TextField objects

```
package {
  import flash.display.*;
  import flash.events.*;
  import flash.text.*;

  public class PhotoPanel extends Sprite {
    private static const defaultTitle:String =
                                    "Photo Viewer [No photo selected]";
    private static const defaultPhotoName:String =
                                    "Enter Photo Name Here";

    private var title:TextField;
    private var photoname:TextField;

    public function PhotoPanel () {
      // Create the TextField object for the panel's title bar
      title = new TextField();
      title.text = PhotoPanel.defaultTitle;
      title.width  = 350;
      title.height = 25;
      title.border     = true;
      title.background = true;
      title.selectable = false;
      addChild(title);

      // Create a title TextField object for an individual photo
      photoname = new TextField();
      photoname.text = PhotoPanel.defaultPhotoName;
      photoname.width  = 150;
      photoname.height = 30;
      photoname.x = 100;
      photoname.y = 150;
      photoname.border     = true;
      photoname.background = true;
      photoname.type = TextFieldType.INPUT
      addChild(photoname);


      // Register with photoname for Event.CHANGE events
      photoname.addEventListener(Event.CHANGE, changeListener);

      // Register with photoname for focus in and out events
```

Example 22-14. Synchronizing two TextField objects (continued)

```
    photoname.addEventListener(FocusEvent.FOCUS_IN, photoFocusInListener);
    photoname.addEventListener(FocusEvent.FOCUS_OUT,
                                photoFocusOutListener);

    // Register with the stage for focus out events
    stage.addEventListener(FocusEvent.FOCUS_OUT, panelFocusOutListener);
  }

  // Triggered whenever new text is added to photoname
  private function changeListener (e:Event):void {
    // The photo's name changed, so update title to match photoname's text
    if (photoname.text.length == 0) {
      title.text = "Photo Viewer [Unnamed Photo]";
    } else {
      title.text = "Photo Viewer [" + photoname.text + "]";
    }
  }

  // Triggered whenever photoname gains focus
  private function photoFocusInListener (e:FocusEvent):void {
    // If the photo hasn't been named yet...
    if (photoname.text == PhotoPanel.defaultPhotoName) {
      // ...clear the photoname text field so the user can enter a name
      photoname.text = "";
      // Update the panel title to indicate that an unnamed photo is
      // selected
      title.text = "Photo Viewer [Unnamed Photo]";
    } else {
      // ...the selected photo already has a name, so update the panel
      // title to display that name
      title.text = "Photo Viewer [" + photoname.text + "]";
    }
  }

  // Triggered whenever photoname loses focus
  private function photoFocusOutListener (e:FocusEvent):void {
    // If the user didn't enter a name for the photo...
    if (photoname.text.length == 0) {
      // ...set the photo's name to the default value
      photoname.text = PhotoPanel.defaultPhotoName;
    }
  }

  // Triggered whenever any object loses focus
  private function panelFocusOutListener (e:FocusEvent):void {
    // If no object is currently focused...
    if (e.relatedObject == null) {
      // ...set the panel title to the default value
      title.text = PhotoPanel.defaultTitle;
    }
  }
 }
}
```

The Event.SCROLL Event

The Event.SCROLL event is triggered when any of the following variables changes on a *TextField* object: scrollH, scrollV, maxscrollH, or maxscrollV. In other words, the Event.SCROLL event indicates that one of the following changes has occurred to the text field:

- The text field has been scrolled vertically or horizontally (either by the user or programmatically via the scrollH or scrollV variables).
- The text field has new content that changes its maximum vertical or horizontal scrolling range.
- A change in the dimensions of the text field has changed the text field's maximum vertical or horizontal scrolling range.

The generalized code required to register a listener with a *TextField* object for the Event.SCROLL event is as follows:

```
theTextField.addEventListener(Event.SCROLL, scrollListener);
```

The generalized event listener code required for a Event.SCROLL listener is:

```
private function scrollListener (e: Event):void {
}
```

Typically, the Event.SCROLL event is used to synchronize a scrollbar interface with the content of a text field, as shown in Example 22-15. The scrollbar in the example has the following features:

- Can be applied to any *TextField* object
- Can be dragged by the mouse to scroll a text field vertically
- Automatically updates in response to changes in the text field's size, content, or scroll position

For the sake of simplicity, however, the scrollbar does not include up and down scrolling buttons. Example 22-15 uses many of the techniques we've learned in this chapter and also contains some techniques that we have not yet studied; where appropriate, crossreferences to supplemental topics are provided.

Example 22-15. Using Event.SCROLL in a scrollbar implementation

```
package {
  import flash.display.*;
  import flash.text.*;
  import flash.events.*;
  import flash.utils.*;
  import flash.geom.*;

  // A simple draggable scrollbar that automatically updates its size
  // in response to changes in the size of a specified text field.
  // Usage:
  //   var theTextField:TextField = new TextField( );
  //   someContainer.addChild(theTextField);
```

Example 22-15. Using Event.SCROLL in a scrollbar implementation (continued)

```
//   var scrollbar:ScrollBar = new ScrollBar(theTextField);
//   someContainer.addChild(scrollbar);
public class ScrollBar extends Sprite {
  // The text field to which this scrollbar is applied
  private var t:TextField;
  // The current height of the text field. If the text field's height
  // changes, we update the height of this scrollbar.
  private var tHeight:Number;
  // The background graphic for the scrollbar
  private var scrollTrack:Sprite;
  // The scrollbar's draggable "scroll thumb"
  private var scrollThumb:Sprite;
  // The scrollbar's width
  private var scrollbarWidth:int = 15;
  // The minimum height of the scrollbar's scroll thumb
  private var minimumThumbHeight:int = 10;
  // A flag indicating whether the user is currently dragging the
  // scroll thumb
  private var dragging:Boolean = false;
  // A flag indicating whether the scrollbar should be redrawn at the next
  // scheduled screen update
  private var changed:Boolean = false;

  // Constructor.
  // @param textfield The TextField object to which to apply
  //                  this scrollbar.
  public function ScrollBar (textfield:TextField) {
    // Retain a reference to the TextField to which this
    // scrollbar is applied
    t = textfield;
    // Remember the text field's height so that we can track it for
    // changes that require a scrollbar redraw.
    tHeight = t.height;

    // Create the scrollbar background
    scrollTrack = new Sprite();
    scrollTrack.graphics.lineStyle();
    scrollTrack.graphics.beginFill(0x333333);
    scrollTrack.graphics.drawRect(0, 0, 1, 1);
    addChild(scrollTrack);

    // Create the draggable scroll thumb on the scrollbar
    scrollThumb = new Sprite();
    scrollThumb.graphics.lineStyle();
    scrollThumb.graphics.beginFill(0xAAAAAA);
    scrollThumb.graphics.drawRect(0, 0, 1, 1);
    addChild(scrollThumb);

    // Register an Event.SCROLL listener that will update the scrollbar
    // to match the current scroll position of the text field
    t.addEventListener(Event.SCROLL, scrollListener);
```

```
    // Register with scrollThumb for mouse down events, which will trigger
    // the dragging of the scroll thumb
    scrollThumb.addEventListener(MouseEvent.MOUSE_DOWN,mouseDownListener);

    // Register to be notified when this object is added to or removed
    // from the display list (requires the custom helper class,
    // StageDetector). When this object is added to the display list,
    // register for stage-level mouse move and mouse up events that
    // will control the scroll thumb's dragging operation.
    var stageDetector:StageDetector = new StageDetector(this);
    stageDetector.addEventListener(StageDetector.ADDED_TO_STAGE,
                                   addedToStageListener);
    stageDetector.addEventListener(StageDetector.REMOVED_FROM_STAGE,
                                   removedFromStageListener);

    // Register to be notified each time the screen is about to be
    // updated. Before each screen update, we check to see whether the
    // scrollbar needs to be redrawn. For information on the
    // Event.ENTER_FRAME event, see Chapter 24.
    addEventListener(Event.ENTER_FRAME, enterFrameListener);

    // Force an initial scrollbar draw.
    changed = true;
  }

  // Executed whenever this object is added to the display list
  private function addedToStageListener (e:Event):void {
    // Register for "global" mouse move and mouse up events
    stage.addEventListener(MouseEvent.MOUSE_UP, mouseUpListener);
    stage.addEventListener(MouseEvent.MOUSE_MOVE, mouseMoveListener);
  }

  // Executed whenever this object is removed from the display list
  private function removedFromStageListener (e:Event):void {
    // Unregister for "global" mouse move and mouse up events
    stage.removeEventListener(MouseEvent.MOUSE_UP, mouseUpListener);
    stage.removeEventListener(MouseEvent.MOUSE_MOVE, mouseMoveListener);
  }

  // Executed once for each screen update. This method checks
  // whether any changes in the text field's scroll position, content,
  // or size have occurred since the last time the scrollbar was drawn.
  // If so, we redraw the scrollbar. By performing this "draw or not"
  // check once per screen-update only, we eliminate redundant calls to
  // updateScrollbar(), and we also avoid some Flash Player timing issues
  // with TextField.maxScrollV.
  private function enterFrameListener (e:Event):void {
    // If the text field has changed height, request a redraw of the
    // scrollbar
    if (t.height != tHeight) {
      changed = true;
      tHeight = t.height;
```

Example 22-15. Using Event.SCROLL in a scrollbar implementation (continued)

```
      // The height has changed, so stop any dragging operation in
      // progress. The user will have to click again to start dragging
      // the scroll thumb once the scroll bar has been redrawn.
      if (dragging) {
        scrollThumb.stopDrag( );
        dragging = false;
      }
    }

    // If the scrollbar needs redrawing...
    if (changed) {
      // ...call the scrollbar drawing routine
      updateScrollbar( );
      changed = false;
    }
  }

  // Handles Event.SCROLL events
  private function scrollListener (e:Event):void {
    // In certain cases, when lines are removed from a text field,
    // Flash Player dispatches two events: one for the reduction in
    // maxScrollV (dispatched immediately) and one for the reduction in
    // scrollV (dispatched several screen updates later). In such cases,
    // the scrollV variable temporarily has an erroneous value that
    // is greater than maxScrollV. As a workaround, we ignore the event
    // dispatch for the change in maxScrollV, and wait for the event
    // dispatch for the change in scrollV (otherwise, the rendered
    // scrollbar would temporarily not match the text field's actual
    // content).
    if (t.scrollV > t.maxScrollV) {
      return;
    }

    // If the user is not currently dragging the scrollbar's scroll
    // thumb, then note that this scrollbar should be redrawn at the next
    // scheduled screen update. (If the user is dragging the scroll thumb,
    // then the scroll change that caused this event was the result of
    // dragging the scroll thumb to a new position, so there's no need to
    // update the scrollbar because the scroll thumb is already in the
    // correct position.)
    if (!dragging) {
      changed = true;
    }
  }

  // Sets the size and position of the scrollbar's background and scroll
  // thumb in accordance with the associated text field's size and
  // content. For information on the TextField variables scrollV,
  // maxScrollV, and bottomScrollV, see Adobe's ActionScript Language
  // Reference.
  public function updateScrollbar ():void {
    // Set the size and position of the scrollbar background.
```

Example 22-15. Using Event.SCROLL in a scrollbar implementation (continued)

```
    // This code always puts the scrollbar on the right of the text field.
    scrollTrack.x = t.x + t.width;
    scrollTrack.y = t.y;
    scrollTrack.height = t.height;
    scrollTrack.width = scrollbarWidth;

    // Check the text field's number of visible lines
    var numVisibleLines:int = t.bottomScrollV - (t.scrollV-1);
    // If some of the lines in the text field are not currently visible...
    if (numVisibleLines < t.numLines) {
      // ... make the scroll thumb visible
      scrollThumb.visible = true;
      // Now set the scroll thumb's size
      //   The scroll thumb's height is the percentage of lines showing,
      //   times the text field's height
      var thumbHeight:int = Math.floor(t.height *
                                        (numVisibleLines/t.numLines));
      //   Don't set the scroll thumb height to anything less
      //   than minimumThumbHeight
      scrollThumb.height = Math.max(minimumThumbHeight, thumbHeight);
      scrollThumb.width  = scrollbarWidth;

      // Now set the scroll thumb's position
      scrollThumb.x = t.x + t.width;
      //   The scroll thumb's vertical position is the number lines the
      //   text field is scrolled, as a percentage, times the height of
      //   the "gutter space" in the scrollbar (the gutter space is the
      //   height of the scroll bar minus the height of the scroll thumb).
      scrollThumb.y = t.y + (scrollTrack.height-scrollThumb.height)
                  * ((t.scrollV-1)/(t.maxScrollV-1));
    } else {
      // If all lines in the text field are currently visible, hide the
      // scrollbar's scroll thumb
      scrollThumb.visible = false;
    }
  }

  // Sets the text field's vertical scroll position to match the relative
  // position of the scroll thumb
  public function synchTextToScrollThumb ( ):void {
      var scrollThumbMaxY:Number = t.height-scrollThumb.height;
      var scrollThumbY:Number = scrollThumb.y-t.y;
      t.scrollV = Math.round(t.maxScrollV
                          * (scrollThumbY/scrollThumbMaxY));
  }


  // Executed when the primary mouse button is depressed over the scroll
  // thumb
  private function mouseDownListener (e:MouseEvent):void {
    // Start dragging the scroll thumb. (The startDrag( ) method is
    // inherited from the Sprite class.)
```

Example 22-15. Using Event.SCROLL in a scrollbar implementation (continued)

```
    var bounds:Rectangle = new Rectangle(t.x + t.width,
                                         t.y,
                                         0,
                                         t.height-scrollThumb.height);
    scrollThumb.startDrag(false, bounds);
    dragging = true;
  }

  // Executes when the primary mouse button is released (anywhere over, or
  // even outside of, Flash Player's display area)
  private function mouseUpListener (e:MouseEvent):void {
    // If the scroll thumb is being dragged, update the text field's
    // vertical scroll position, then stop dragging the scroll thumb
    if (dragging) {
      synchTextToScrollThumb( );
      scrollThumb.stopDrag( );
      dragging = false;
    }
  }

  // Executes when the mouse pointer is moved (anywhere over Flash
  // Player's display area)
  private function mouseMoveListener (e:MouseEvent):void {
    // If the scroll thumb is being dragged, set the text field's vertical
    // scroll position to match the relative position of the scroll thumb
    if (dragging) {
      synchTextToScrollThumb( );
    }
  }
 }
}
```

Example 22-16 shows a simple example class that demonstrates the use of the *ScrollBar* class shown in Example 22-15.

Example 22-16. A demonstration class showing the use of scrollBar

```
package {
  import flash.display.*;
  import flash.text.*;
  import flash.events.*;
  import flash.utils.*;

  // Demonstrates the use of the ScrollBar class
  public class ScrollBarDemo extends Sprite {
    public function ScrollBarDemo ( ) {
      // Create a TextField
      var inputfield:TextField = new TextField( );
      // Seed the text field with some initial content
      inputfield.text = "1\n2\n3\n4\n5\n6\n7\n8\n9";
      inputfield.height = 50;
      inputfield.width  = 100;
```

```
    inputfield.border     = true;
    inputfield.background = true;
    inputfield.type = TextFieldType.INPUT;
    inputfield.multiline = true;
    addChild(inputfield);

    // Create a scrollbar, and associate it with the TextField
    var scrollbar:ScrollBar = new ScrollBar(inputfield);
    addChild(scrollbar);
  }
 }
}
```

The TextEvent.LINK Event

The TextEvent.LINK event is used to trigger ActionScript code in response to the clicking of a hypertext link in a *TextField*. The TextEvent.LINK event occurs when the user clicks a hypertext link whose URL starts with the pseudoprotocol "event."

 For an introduction to using hypertext links in ActionScript text fields, see Chapter 27.

The generalized code required to create a hypertext link that triggers ActionScript code is as follows:

```
    theTextField.htmlText = "<a href='event:linkContent'>linkText</a>";
```

In the preceding code, *theTextField* is the *TextField* object that contains the link, and *linkText* is the text that appears on screen for the user to click. When the user clicks *linkText*, Flash Player executes all listeners registered with *theTextField* or its display ancestors for the TextEvent.LINK event. Each listener is passed a *TextEvent* object whose text variable's value is the supplied *linkContent* string. The *linkContent* string typically identifies an ActionScript operation to be carried out when the link is clicked.

The generalized code required to register a listener with a *TextField* object for the TextEvent.LINK event is as follows:

```
    theTextField.addEventListener(TextEvent.LINK, linkListener);
```

The generalized event listener code required for a TextEvent.LINK listener function is:

```
    private function linkListener (e:TextEvent):void {
    }
```

Using the preceding generalized code as a guide, let's create an example hypertext link that starts a game when clicked. Here's the code for the link: notice that the supplied *linkContent* indicates the name of the operation the link triggers: "startGame."

```
var t:TextField = new TextField();
t.htmlText = "<a href='event:startGame'>Play now!</a>";
t.autoSize = TextFieldAutoSize.LEFT;
addChild(t);
```

Next, the following code registers *linkListener()* with the preceding *TextField* object, t, for TextEvent.LINK events:

```
t.addEventListener(TextEvent.LINK, linkListener);
```

Finally, the following code shows the *linkListener()* method, which is executed when the link is clicked. Within the *linkListener()* method, we perform the operation specified by the supplied *linkContent* string, which we access via the *TextEvent* class's instance variable text.

```
private function linkListener (e:TextEvent):void {
  var operationName:String = e.text;
  if (operationName == "startGame") {
    startGame();
  }
}
```

Now let's try creating a hypertext link that not only triggers an ActionScript operation but also passes an argument to that operation. The code for the hypertext link follows. Notice that this time the supplied *linkContent* indicates the name of the operation (displayMsg) and an argument (hello world), separated by an arbitrary delimiter (a comma).

```
var t:TextField = new TextField();
t.htmlText = "<a href='event:displayMsg,hello world'>click here</a>";
t.autoSize = TextFieldAutoSize.LEFT;
addChild(t);
```

Next, the following code registers *linkListener()* with the preceding *TextField* object, t, for TextEvent.LINK events:

```
t.addEventListener(TextEvent.LINK, linkListener);
```

Finally, the following code shows the *linkListener()* method, where we use the *String* class's instance method *split()* to separate the operation name (displayMsg) from the argument (hello world).

```
private function linkListener (e:TextEvent):void {
  var linkContent:Array    = e.text.split(",");
  var operationName:String = linkContent[0];
  var argument:String      = linkContent[1];

  if (operationName == "displayMsg") {
    displayMsg(argument);
  }
}
```

Unlike in JavaScript, arbitrary ActionScript code cannot be included within an <A> tag's HREF attribute.

Example 22-17 shows the TextEvent.LINK event used in a hypothetical chat application, in which the user can request a private chat by clicking any username in the chat text field. Example 22-17 is highly simplified in order to focus on the use of TextEvent.LINK; it does not show any code relating to actually receiving or sending messages.

Example 22-17. Using the TextEvent.LINK to make usernames clickable

```
package {
  import flash.display.*;
  import flash.text.*;
  import flash.events.*;

  // Demonstrates the use of the TextEvent.LINK event in a simplified
  // chat room example with clickable user names.
  public class ChatRoom extends Sprite {
    // A text field containing chat messages
    private var messages:TextField;

    public function ChatRoom () {
      // Create a text field with 'event:' protocol links
      messages = new TextField();
      messages.multiline = true;
      messages.autoSize = TextFieldAutoSize.LEFT;
      messages.border     = true;
      messages.background = true;
      // Supply sample chat messages with clickable user names
      messages.htmlText =
        "<a href='event:privateChat,user1'>Andy</a> says: What's up?<br>"
      + "<a href='event:privateChat,user2'>Mike</a> says: I'm busy...<br>"
      + "<a href='event:privateChat,user1'>Andy</a> says: Ok see you later";
      addChild(messages);

      // Register with the 'messages' TextField object for
      // TextEvent.LINK events
      messages.addEventListener(TextEvent.LINK, linkListener);
    }

    // Executed any time the user clicks an 'event:' protocol link in
    // the 'messages' TextField object
    private function linkListener (e:TextEvent):void {
      // The content of e.text is the full string that follows "event:" in
      // the href attribute. For example, "privateChat,user1". Here we
      // split that text into an operation ("privateChat") the
      // corresponding argument ("user1").
      var requestedCommand:Array = e.text.split(",");
      var operationName:String = requestedCommand[0];
      var argument:String      = requestedCommand[1];
```

```
      // If the operation requested is a private chat request, invoke
      // the requestPrivateChat( ) method.
      if (operationName == "privateChat") {
        requestPrivateChat(argument);
      }
    }

    // Sends a private chat invitation to the specified user
    private function requestPrivateChat (userID:String):void {
      trace("Now requesting private chat with " + userID);
      // Networking code not shown...
    }
  }
}
```

Flash Player-Level Input Events

As we've seen throughout this chapter, the majority of Flash Player's input events are triggered by user interaction with specific objects on the display list. However, Flash Player also supports a small set of events that are triggered by user interaction with the Flash Player application, itself. We'll refer to these "application events" as Flash Player-level input events. Flash Player-level input events are dispatched in the following situations:

- When the Flash Player's display area is resized
- When the mouse pointer moves out of Flash Player's display area
- When the Flash Player application gains or loses operating-system focus (the standalone version of Flash Player gains system focus when the application window is focused; the web browser plug-in version of Flash Player gains system focus when the user clicks Flash Player's display area or—where supported—the user navigates to the embedded Flash Player object with the keyboard)

Table 22-5 lists the Flash Player-level input-event types. For each type of event, the "Event type" column lists the *Event*-class constant that indicates the event type's official string name. The "Description" column describes the specific user action that triggers the event. The "Target" column lists the object that serves as the event target when the event is dispatched. The "Default behavior" column lists Flash Player's native response to the event (Flash Player-level input-event types have no default behavior). The "Bubbles" column indicates whether the event has a bubbling phase. The "Datatype of object passed to listener function" column specifies the datatype of the object passed to the listener function that handles the event. Finally, the "Notes" column lists important information regarding the event's use.

Table 22-5. Player-level Input Events

Event type	Description	Target	Default behavior	Bubbles	Datatype of object passed to listener function	Notes
Event.ACTIVATE	Flash Player gains system focus.	The display object that registered the event listener	None	Yes	*Event*	Triggered even when target is not on display list.
Event.DEACTIVATE	Flash Player loses system focus.	The display object that registered the event listener	None	Yes	*Event*	Triggered even when target is not on display list
Event.RESIZE	Flash Player's display area resized.	The *Stage* instance	None	Yes	*Event*	
Event.MOUSE_LEAVE	Mouse pointer moves out of Flash Player's display area.	The *Stage* instance	None	Yes	*Event*	There is no companion Event. MOUSE_ENTER event. Use MouseEvent.MOUSE_MOVE to detect re-entry.

Let's take a closer look at the four events in Table 22-5.

The Event.ACTIVATE and Event.DEACTIVATE Events

The Event.ACTIVATE and Event.DEACTIVATE events are typically used to develop applications that enable or disable themselves in response to Flash Player gaining or losing operating-system focus. For example, in response to Flash Player losing application focus, an application might mute all sounds, dismiss an open menu, or pause an in-progress animation.

Unlike the other input events we've studied so far, the Event.ACTIVATE and Event.DEACTIVATE events have no capture phase and no bubbling phase. Instead, Event.ACTIVATE and Event.DEACTIVATE can be handled by listeners registered with any instance of any class that inherits from *EventDispatcher* (note: not just classes that inherit from *DisplayObject*). Furthermore, when a listener function is registered for Event.ACTIVATE or Event.DEACTIVATE events with a display object, it is triggered even when that object is not on the display list.

Example 22-18 demonstrates the basic use of Event.ACTIVATE and Event.DEACTIVATE, showing an application that starts a "rotating rectangle" animation when Flash Player gains system focus, and stops the animation when Flash Player loses system focus. (We'll study animation techniques in Chapter 24).

Example 22-18. Responding to Event.ACTIVATE and Event.DEACTIVATE

```
package {
  import flash.display.*;
  import flash.utils.*;
  import flash.events.*;

  public class Spinner extends Sprite {
    private var timer:Timer;
    private var rect:Sprite;

    public function Spinner () {
      // Create a rectangle graphic
      rect = new Sprite();
      rect.x = 200;
      rect.y = 200;
      rect.graphics.lineStyle(1);
      rect.graphics.beginFill(0x0000FF);
      rect.graphics.drawRect(0, 0, 150, 75);
      addChild(rect);

      // Register to be notified when Flash Player gains or loses
      // system focus
      addEventListener(Event.ACTIVATE, activateListener);
      addEventListener(Event.DEACTIVATE, deactivateListener);

      // Create a timer to use for animation
      timer = new Timer(50, 0);
      timer.addEventListener(TimerEvent.TIMER, timerListener);
    }
```

Example 22-18. Responding to Event.ACTIVATE and Event.DEACTIVATE (continued)

```
// Rotates the rectangle graphic
private function timerListener (e:TimerEvent):void {
  rect.rotation += 10;
}

// Handles Event.ACTIVATE events
private function activateListener (e:Event):void {
  // Start rotating the rectangle graphic
  timer.start( );
}

// Handles Event.DEACTIVATE events
private function deactivateListener (e:Event):void {
  // Stop rotating the rectangle graphic
  timer.stop( );
  }
 }
}
```

The Event.RESIZE Event

The Event.RESIZE event is typically used when developing applications with "stretchy" content, where the size of interface elements is automatically adjusted to fit the available space in Flash Player's display area.

The Event.RESIZE event is triggered when Flash Player's *Stage* instance's scaleMode variable is set to StageScaleMode.NO_SCALE and the dimensions of Flash Player's display area change. The dimensions change when either:

- The Standalone Player is resized by the user or in response to an fscommand("fullscreen", "true") call.

- The user resizes a browser window containing a *.swf* file embedded using percentage values for the <OBJECT> or <EMBED> tags' HEIGHT or WIDTH attributes.

The following HTML code shows how to embed a *.swf* file, *app.swf*, using percentage values for the <OBJECT> and <EMBED> tags' WIDTH attributes. Notice that one dimension is set to a fixed pixel size (HEIGHT="75"), while the other is set to a percentage (WIDTH="100%").

```
<OBJECT classid="clsid:D27CDB6E-AE6D-11cf-96B8-444553540000"
codebase="http://fpdownload.macromedia.com/get/flashplayer/current/swflash.cab"
  WIDTH="100%"
  HEIGHT="75">
  <PARAM NAME="movie" VALUE="app.swf">
  <EMBED src="app.swf"
    WIDTH="100%"
    HEIGHT="75"
    TYPE="application/x-shockwave-flash"
    PLUGINSPAGE="http://www.adobe.com/go/getflashplayer">
  </EMBED>
</OBJECT>
```

Listeners for the Event.RESIZE event must be registered with Flash Player's *Stage* instance, as shown in the following code. Notice the mandatory setting of scaleMode to StageScaleMode.NO_SCALE.

```
package {
  import flash.display.*;
  import flash.events.*;

  public class ResizeSensor extends Sprite {
    public function ResizeSensor () {
      stage.scaleMode = StageScaleMode.NO_SCALE;
      stage.addEventListener(Event.RESIZE, resizeListener);
    }

    private function resizeListener (e:Event):void {
      trace("Flash Player was resized");
    }
  }
}
```

Example 22-19 expands on the preceding code, showing how to position a *Sprite* object, rect, in the top-right corner of Flash Player's display area every time Flash Player is resized. Notice that the example application triggers its initial layout code manually because Event.RESIZE is not triggered when a *.swf* file first loads into Flash Player.

Example 22-19. A stretchy layout

```
package {
  import flash.display.*;
  import flash.events.*;

  // Positions a Sprite object, rect, in the top-right corner of Flash
  // Player's display area every time a Flash Player is resized
  public class StretchyLayout extends Sprite {
    private var rect:Sprite;
    public function StretchyLayout () {
      // Create a rectangle graphic and add it to the display list
      rect = new Sprite();
      rect.graphics.lineStyle();
      rect.graphics.beginFill(0x0000FF);
      rect.graphics.drawRect(0, 0, 150, 75);
      addChild(rect);

      // Prevent content scaling
      stage.scaleMode = StageScaleMode.NO_SCALE;
      // Position the .swf file at the top-left corner of Flash Player's
      // display area
      stage.align     = StageAlign.TOP_LEFT;
      // Register for Event.RESIZE events
      stage.addEventListener(Event.RESIZE, resizeListener);
```

Example 22-19. A stretchy layout (continued)

```
    // Manually trigger initial layout code
    positionRectangle( );
  }

  // Handles Event.RESIZE events
  private function resizeListener (e:Event):void {
    positionRectangle( );
  }

  // Positions rect in top-right corner of Flash Player's display area
  private function positionRectangle ( ):void {
    rect.x = stage.stageWidth - rect.width;
    rect.y = 0;
  }
 }
}
```

The Event.MOUSE_LEAVE Event

The Event.MOUSE_LEAVE event is typically used to disable or remove mouse-reactive content when the mouse pointer leaves Flash Player's display area. For example, in an application that hides the system mouse pointer in order to replace it with a custom mouse-pointer graphic (as shown earlier in Example 22-5), the custom mouse-pointer graphic is hidden when the mouse pointer leaves Flash Player's display area.

As with the Event.RESIZE event, listeners for the Event.MOUSE_LEAVE event must be registered with Flash Player's *Stage* instance. The following code shows the basic code required to handle Event.MOUSE_LEAVE events:

```
package {
  import flash.display.*;
  import flash.events.*;

  public class MouseLeaveSensor extends Sprite {
    public function MouseLeaveSensor ( ) {
      // Register for Event.MOUSE_LEAVE events
      stage.addEventListener(Event.MOUSE_LEAVE, mouseLeaveListener);
    }

    // Handle Event.MOUSE_LEAVE events
    private function mouseLeaveListener (e:Event):void {
      trace("The mouse has left the building.");
    }
  }
}
```

From the Program to the Screen

Over the past few chapters we've seen lots of techniques for creating visual content and modifying it in response to user interaction. In the next chapter, we'll examine how Flash runtimes automatically update the screen to reflect the current display-content in a program. Once we're familiar with the Flash runtime screen-update system, we'll move on to Chapter 24, where we'll use the screen-update cycle to create programmatic animation.

Screen Updates

Conceptually speaking, all screen updates in ActionScript can be separated into two categories: those that occur at regular intervals (*scheduled updates*), and those that occur immediately following the execution of certain event listener functions (*post-event updates*). Regardless of the category, all screen updates are automated. In ActionScript there is no general, arbitrary means of requesting an immediate screen update. Instead, new visual content created programmatically or manually in the Flash authoring tool is rendered automatically by a scheduled or post-event update. This chapter investigates ActionScript's two varieties of screen updates.

While most of this book focuses on pure ActionScript code rather than specific *.swf* authoring tools, the following discussion requires some basic knowledge of the Flash authoring tool's timeline and timeline-scripting techniques. If you are unfamiliar with the Flash authoring tool, you should read Chapter 29 before continuing with this chapter.

Scheduled Screen Updates

In ActionScript, screen updates are inexorably linked to the Flash runtime's animation capabilities. Even pure ActionScript applications created with Flex Builder 2 or the *mxmlc* command-line compiler are governed by the Flash runtime's animation-centric screen-update system.

The Flash runtime's screen-update system is designed to accommodate the Flash authoring tool's model for creating scripted animated content. In the Flash authoring tool, animated content is produced manually as a series of frames on a timeline, exactly like the frames in a physical filmstrip. Each visual frame can be associated with a block of code known as a *frame script*. In very general terms, when the Flash runtime plays an animation that was created in the Flash authoring tool, it adheres to the following screen-update cycle:

1. Execute current frame's code.
2. Update screen.

3. Go to next frame.

4. Repeat.

For example, suppose we have a three-frame-long animation, created in the Flash authoring tool, and each frame has a frame script. The general process by which the Flash runtime plays the animation is as follows:

1. Execute Frame 1's frame script.

2. Display Frame 1's content.

3. Execute Frame 2's frame script.

4. Display Frame 2's content.

5. Execute Frame 3's frame script.

6. Display Frame 3's content

At Steps 1, 3, and 5, each frame script might create new visual content or modify existing visual content. Therefore, a more accurate description of the preceding animation-playback steps would be:

1. Execute Frame 1's frame script.

2. Display Frame 1's content and render visual output of Frame 1's frame script.

3. Execute Frame 2's frame script.

4. Display Frame 2's content and render visual output of Frame 2's frame script.

5. Execute Frame 3's frame script.

6. Display Frame 3's content and render visual output of Frame 3's frame script.

In the preceding list, notice that before rendering the visual output of a given frame script, the Flash runtime always finishes executing that script in its entirety.

 The Flash runtime *never* interrupts a frame script in order to update the screen.

The speed with which the preceding six steps are performed is determined by the Flash runtime's frame rate, which is measured in number of frames per second. For example, suppose the frame rate for the preceding animation is set to a very slow 1 frame per second. Further suppose that each frame script takes exactly 100 millliseconds (ms) to execute and that each frame's content takes exactly 50 milliseconds (ms) to render. Relative to the starting of the animation, the theoretical times at which the preceding six steps would be performed are as follows:

```
0ms:    Begin executing Frame 1's frame script
100ms:  Finish executing Frame 1's frame script
1000ms: Begin rendering Frame 1's content and frame-script output
1050ms: Finish rendering Frame 1's content and frame-script output
```

```
1051ms: Begin executing Frame 2's frame script
1151ms: Finish executing Frame 2's frame script
2000ms: Begin rendering Frame 2's content and frame-script output
2050ms: Finish rendering Frame 2's content and frame-script output

2051ms: Begin executing Frame 3's frame script
2151ms: Finish executing Frame 3's frame script
3000ms: Begin rendering Frame 3's content and frame-script output
3050ms: Finish rendering Frame 3's content and frame-script output
```

Notice that after each frame script has finished executing, the Flash runtime does not immediately update the screen. Instead, it renders the script's output at the next scheduled frame-render time. The Flash runtime's screen updates can, therefore, be thought of as *scheduled screen updates* because they occur according to the preset schedule dictated by the frame rate.

Hence, an even more accurate description of the preceding animation-playback steps would be:

1. Execute Frame 1's frame script.
2. Wait until the next scheduled frame-render time.
3. Display Frame 1's content and render visual output of Frame 1's frame script.
4. Execute Frame 2's frame script.
5. Wait until the next scheduled frame-render time.
6. Display Frame 2's content and render visual output of Frame 2's frame script.
7. Execute Frame 3's frame script.
8. Wait until the next scheduled frame-render time.
9. Display Frame 3's content and render visual output of Frame 3's frame script.

Now let's suppose Frame 1's frame script registers an event-listener function, *clickListener()*, with the *Stage* instance for MouseEvent.CLICK events. Every time *clickListener()* runs, it draws a red line to the current mouse pointer position. Here's the code for Frame 1's frame script:

```
import flash.events.*;
import flash.display.*;

stage.addEventListener(MouseEvent.CLICK, clickListener);

function clickListener (e:MouseEvent):void {
  graphics.lineStyle(2, 0xFF0000);
  graphics.lineTo(e.stageX, e.stageY);
}
```

Immediately after Frame 1's frame script executes, *clickListener()* becomes eligible for MouseEvent.CLICK event notification.

Now suppose the user clicks the Flash runtime's display area 500 ms after the animation starts playing (i.e., during the wait period described in Step 2 of the preceding list). The *clickListener()* method executes immediately, but the visual output of clickListener( ) is not rendered until the next scheduled frame-render time. At the next frame-render time, the visual output of *clickListener( )* is rendered along with Frame 1's content and Frame 1's frame-script output.

Hence, an even more accurate description of the preceding animation-playback steps would be:

1. Execute Frame 1's frame script.
2. Wait until the next scheduled frame-render time. While waiting, if any events are triggered, execute associated event listeners.
3. Display Frame 1's content; render visual output of Frame 1's frame script; render visual output of any event listeners executed during Step 2.
4. Execute Frame 2's frame script.
5. Wait until the next scheduled frame-render time. While waiting, if any events are triggered, execute associated event listeners.
6. Display Frame 2's content; render visual output of Frame 2's frame script; render visual output of any event listeners executed during Step 5.
7. Execute Frame 3's frame script.
8. Wait until the next scheduled frame-render time. While waiting, if any events are triggered, execute associated event listeners.
9. Display Frame 3's content; render visual output of Frame 3's frame script; render visual output of any event listeners executed during Step 8.

 The preceding steps reflect the Flash runtime's default screen-update behavior. However, for certain event types, the Flash runtime can be forced to update the screen more immediately. For details, see the section "Post-Event Screen Updates," later in this chapter.

Now suppose that Frame 2's content is identical to Frame 1's content, that Frame 2's frame script does not generate any visual output, and that no event listeners are triggered between Frame 1 and Frame 2. In such a case, the Flash runtime does not rerender the display area. Instead, when the frame-render time for Frame 2 arrives, the Flash runtime merely checks whether the screen needs updating. Frame 2 has no visual changes, so the screen is not rerendered.

Hence, a still more accurate description of the preceding animation-playback steps would be:

1. Execute Frame 1's frame script.
2. Wait until the next scheduled frame-render time. While waiting, if any events are triggered, execute all registered event listeners.
3. At frame-render time, check if the screen needs updating. The screen needs updating if any of the following is true:

- Frame 1 contains changes to the contents of the *Stage* made manually in the Flash authoring tool.
- Code in Frame 1's frame script created new visual content or modified existing visual content.
- Code in a listener function executed during Step 2 created new visual content or modified existing visual content.

4. If necessary, update the screen to reflect all changes detected in Step 3.

5. Repeat Steps 1-4 for Frames 2 and 3.

For reference in the remainder of this chapter, and in the following chapter, we'll refer to the screen-update check that occurs at Step 3 as a *scheduled screen-update check*. Each time the Flash runtime performs a scheduled screen-update check, it dispatches the Event.ENTER_FRAME event (even when the screen is not actually updated). By responding to the Event.ENTER_FRAME event, objects can perform recurring tasks synchronized with each screen-update opportunity. In Chapter 24, we'll learn how to use the Event.ENTER_FRAME event to create animated content entirely through code.

Ready for one last hypothetical scenario? Suppose we remove Frames 2 and 3 from our animation, leaving Frame 1 only. As before, Frame 1's frame script defines the MouseEvent.CLICK event listener, *clickListener()*. Once Frame 1's content and frame-script output has been rendered (Step 4 in the preceding list), the animation has finished playing. Nevertheless, in order to allow for continued event-processing, the Flash runtime's screen-update cycle must remain active. Therefore, for a *.swf* file that contains a single-frame only, the screen-update cycle is as follows (the following steps apply equally to a multiframe *.swf* file that is simply paused on Frame 1):

1. Execute Frame 1's frame script.

2. Wait until the next scheduled frame-render time. While waiting, if any events are triggered, execute all registered event listeners.

3. At frame-render time, check if the screen needs updating. The screen needs updating if any of the following is true:
   - Frame 1 contains changes to the contents of the *Stage* made manually in the Flash authoring tool.
   - Code in Frame 1's frame script created new visual content or modified existing visual content.
   - Code in a listener function executed during Step 2 created new visual content or modified existing visual content.

4. If necessary, update the screen to reflect all changes detected in Step 3.

5. Wait until the next scheduled frame-render time. While waiting, if any events are triggered, execute all registered event listeners.

6. At frame-render time, check if the screen needs updating. The screen needs updating if code in a listener function executed during Step 5 created new visual content or modified existing visual content.

7. If necessary, update the screen to reflect all changes detected in Step 6.

8. Repeat Steps 5 through 7.

Steps 5 through 8 in the preceding list repeat indefinitely as long as the *.swf* file is running in the Flash runtime, thus binding all subsequent code execution to the frame-rate-based screen-update cycle.

In Chapter 20, we learned that when an empty Flash runtime opens a new *.swf* file, it locates that *.swf* file's main class, creates an instance of it, and adds that instance to the display list as the *Stage* instance's first child. For pure ActionScript programs, immediately after the main class instance's constructor method completes, the screen is updated. All subsequent screen updates occur in accordance with the frame-rate-based screen-update cycle presented in Steps 5 through 8 of the preceding list. For example, consider the following extremely simple drawing program, which emphasizes screen updates by setting the frame rate to one frame per second:

```
package {
  import flash.display.*;
  import flash.events.*;

  public class SimpleScribble extends Sprite {
    public function SimpleScribble () {
      stage.frameRate = 1;
      graphics.moveTo(stage.mouseX, stage.mouseY);
      stage.addEventListener(MouseEvent.MOUSE_MOVE, mouseMoveListener);
    }

    private function mouseMoveListener (e:MouseEvent):void {
      graphics.lineStyle(2, 0xFF0000);
      graphics.lineTo(e.stageX, e.stageY);
    }
  }
}
```

The *SimpleSribble* constructor method creates no graphical content but does register a listener, *mouseMoveListener()*, for the MouseEvent.MOUSE_MOVE event. Whenever the mouse moves, *mouseMoveListener()* draws a line to the current mouse position. However, that line is not actually displayed on screen until the next scheduled screen update, which occurs once per second. Hence, once every second, the Flash runtime updates the screen with a series of lines showing the mouse pointer's path through the display area since the last screen update. For a smoother drawing effect, we could increase the frame rate to 30 frames per second, or we could force immediate screen updates using the techniques described in the later section "Post-Event Screen Updates."

Let's review some key points covered so far:

- ActionScript's screen-update system is fully automated.

- For pure ActionScript applications, the frame rate can be thought of as the number of times per second the Flash runtime automatically checks to see if the screen needs updating. For example, if the Flash runtime's frame rate is 1, then all visual changes made by a program will automatically be rendered once per second; if the frame rate is 10, then visual changes will automatically be rendered 10 times per second (every 100 ms).

- If the frame rate is very low (say, in the range of 1–10 frames per second), then there may be noticeable delays between the execution of code that generates visual output and the rendering of that output to the screen.

- Each time the Flash runtime performs a scheduled screen-update check, it dispatches the Event.ENTER_FRAME event.

- Flash Player will never interrupt the execution of a block of code in order to update the screen.

The last of the preceding points is critically important, so let's examine it more closely.

No Screen Updates Within Code Blocks

As we learned in the preceding section, the Flash runtime will never interrupt the execution of a block of code in order to update the screen. Before a scheduled screen update can occur, all functions in the call stack and all code on the current frame must finish executing. Likewise, before a post-event screen update can occur, the event listener within which *updateAfterEvent()* is invoked must finish executing.

In fact, even when a screen update is scheduled to occur at a given time, that update will be delayed if code is still executing. Screen updates and code execution are mutually exclusive tasks for the Flash runtime; they always occur in succession, never simultaneously.

As a rule of thumb, always remember that in ActionScript, the screen can never be updated between two lines of code. For example, the following function, *displayMsg()*, creates a *TextField* and sets its horizontal position twice; first to 50, then to 100:

```
public function displayMsg ():void {
  var t:TextField = new TextField();
  t.text = "Are we having fun yet?";
  t.autoSize = TextFieldAutoSize.LEFT;
  addChild(t);
  t.x = 50;
  t.x = 100;
}
```

When *displayMsg()* executes, the screen will not and cannot be updated between the last two lines in the function. As a result, the *TextField* never appears on screen at horizontal position 50. Instead, the function is completed in its entirety before the screen is rendered, and the *TextField* appears at horizontal position 100. Even though the value of x actually does change briefly to 50, the visual result of that change is never rendered to the screen.

In some cases, code execution can delay screen updates for many seconds, up to a maximum determined by the max-execution-time compiler option, which is set to 15 seconds by default. Any script that does not complete within the amount of time specified by max-execution-time generates a *ScriptTimeoutError* exception. For information on handling *ScriptTimeoutError* exceptions, see *flash.errors.ScriptTimeoutError* in Adobe's ActionScript Language Reference.

To avoid *ScriptTimeoutError* exceptions, all code must be designed to complete execution within the limit set by the max-execution-time compiler option. To perform a task that requires more than the allowed time limit, break it into segments that can complete within the amount of time specified by max-execution-time, and then use a *Timer* to orchestrate the execution of those segments.

Setting the Frame Rate

Flash Player's frame rate can be set in one of three ways:

- Using the *mxmlc* compiler argument default-frame-rate
- Using the Document Properties dialog in the Flash authoring tool
- Using the Stage class's instance variable frameRate within a running *.swf* file

The first *.swf* file loaded into the Flash runtime establishes the initial frame rate for all *.swf* files subsequently loaded.

Regardless of how the frame rate is set, it is observed by all subsequently loaded *.swf* files (overriding their own specified frame rate). However, once the first *.swf* file has been loaded, the Flash runtime's designated frame rate can be reassigned via the Stage class's instance variable frameRate, which accepts values in the range of .01 (one frame every 100 seconds) to 1,000 (1,000 frames per second). For example, the following class sets the frame rate to 150 frames per second:

```
package {
  import flash.display.*;
  public class SetFrameRate extends Sprite {
    public function SetFrameRate () {
      stage.frameRate = 150;
    }
  }
}
```

While the frame rate can be set through any object with access to the *Stage* instance, display objects cannot run at independent frame rates. All objects on the display list are rendered at the same time, according to the Flash runtime's single frame rate.

 Prior to ActionScript 3.0, the Flash runtime's frame rate could not be changed programmatically.

Designated Frame Rate Versus Actual Frame Rate

Even though the Flash runtime performs scheduled screen updates according to the frame rate, the number of screen updates that can actually be achieved per second (the *actual frame rate*) is often less than the frame rate specified by the programmer (the *designated frame rate*). The actual frame rate varies greatly depending on factors such as the speed of the computer, available system resources, the physical refresh rate of the display device, and the complexity of the content running in the Flash runtime. Therefore, the designated frame rate should be thought of as a speed limit. The actual frame rate will never exceed the designated frame rate but will fall short of it under some conditions.

 Flash Player cannot always achieve the designated frame rate.

To determine the current designated frame rate, we examine the Stage class's instance variable frameRate. For example, the following class displays the designated frame rate in a *TextFiel:*.

```
package {
  import flash.display.*;
  import flash.text.*;

  public class ShowFrameRate extends Sprite {
    public function ShowFrameRate () {
      var t:TextField = new TextField();
      t.autoSize = TextFieldAutoSize.LEFT;
      t.text = stage.frameRate.toString();
      addChild(t);
    }
  }
}
```

To determine the *actual* frame rate, we use the Event.ENTER_FRAME event to measure the elapsed time between the Flash runtime's scheduled screen-update checks. Example 23-1 demonstrates the technique. We'll take a closer look at the Event.ENTER_FRAME event in Chapter 24.

Example 23-1. Measuring the actual frame rate

```
package {
  import flash.display.*;
  import flash.events.*;
  import flash.utils.*;
  import flash.text.*;

  public class FrameRateMeter extends Sprite {
    private var lastFrameTime:Number;
    private var output:TextField;

    public function FrameRateMeter( ) {
      output = new TextField( );
      output.autoSize = TextFieldAutoSize.LEFT;
      output.border     = true;
      output.background = true;
      output.selectable = false;
      addChild(output);

      addEventListener(Event.ENTER_FRAME, enterFrameListener);
    }

    private function enterFrameListener (e:Event):void {
      var now:Number = getTimer( );
      var elapsed:Number = now - lastFrameTime;
      var framesPerSecond:Number = Math.round(1000/elapsed);
      output.text = "Time since last frame: " + elapsed
             + "\nExtrapolated actual frame rate: " + framesPerSecond
             + "\nDesignated frame rate: " + stage.frameRate;
      lastFrameTime = now;
    }
  }
}
```

 The actual frame rate is often much slower in the debugging version of the Flash runtime than it is in the release version.

Post-Event Screen Updates

In the previous section, we learned that scheduled screen updates automatically occur at intervals governed by the frame rate. We also learned that visual changes made by event listeners are not rendered until the next scheduled screen-update time. At a typical frame rate of 24 frames per second, the delay between the execution of an event listener and the rendering of its visual output is typically imperceptible. However, for visual changes that are triggered by mouse and keyboard input, even slight delays can make an application feel jittery or sluggish. Accordingly, ActionScript gives every mouse and keyboard event listener function the special ability to trigger a post-event screen update. A *post-event screen update* is an update that occurs immediately following the dispatch of an event, ahead of the next scheduled update.

To request a post-event screen update in response to a mouse event, we invoke *MouseEvent.updateAfterEvent()* on the *MouseEvent* object passed to any mouse event listener function. For example, the following code triggers a post-event screen update in response to a MouseEvent.MOUSE_MOVE event:

```
private function mouseMoveListener (e:MouseEvent):void {
  e.updateAfterEvent();  // Trigger update
}
```

To request a post-event screen update in response to a keyboard event, we invoke *KeyboardEvent.updateAfterEvent()* on the *KeyboardEvent* object passed to any keyboard event listener function. For example, the following code triggers a post-event screen update in response to a KeyboardEvent.KEY_DOWN event:

```
private function keyDownListener (e:KeyboardEvent):void {
  e.updateAfterEvent();  // Trigger update
}
```

In both cases, invoking *updateAfterEvent()* causes the Flash runtime to update the screen immediately following the dispatch of the event, ahead of the next scheduled screen update. However, even though the post-event screen update occurs ahead of the next scheduled screen update, it does not occur until after all event listeners triggered during the event dispatch have completed executing.

 As with scheduled screen updates, the Flash runtime never interrupts the execution of a block of code to perform a post-event screen update.

For an example of *updateAfterEvent()* used in a real-world scenario, see the custom mouse pointer class, *CustomMousePointer*, in Chapter 22, in the section "Finding the Mouse Pointer's Position." The *CustomMousePointer* class draws a blue triangle in a *Sprite* representing the mouse pointer and uses a MouseEvent.MOUSE_MOVE event listener to make that *Sprite* follow the mouse. Within the *mouseMoveListener()* method, *updateAfterEvent()* is used to trigger a post-event screen update that ensures smooth pointer animation, no matter what the frame rate.

Here is the *mouseMoveListener()* method from the *CustomMousePointer* class; notice the *updateAfterEvent()* invocation, shown in bold:

```
private function mouseMoveListener (e:MouseEvent):void {
  // When the mouse moves, update the position of the custom mouse
  // pointer to match the position of the system mouse pointer
  var pointInParent:Point = parent.globalToLocal(new Point(e.stageX,
```

```
                                                                        e.stageY));
    x = pointInParent.x;
    y = pointInParent.y;

    // Request post-event screen update so that the animation of the
    // pointer is as smooth as possible
    e.updateAfterEvent( );

    // Make sure the custom mouse pointer is visible (it might have been
    // hidden because the system pointer left Flash Player's display area).
    if (!visible) {
      !visible = true;
    }
  }
}
```

Note that when the Flash runtime updates the screen in response to *updateAfterEvent()*, it renders not just the changes made by the event listener function that requested the update but all visual changes since the last screen update.

Post-Event Updates for Timer Events

To allow the screen to be updated immediately following the passage of some arbitrary amount of time, ActionScript provides the *TimerEvent.updateAfterEvent()* method, which forces a post-event screen update after a TimerEvent.TIMER event.

The *TimerEvent.updateAfterEvent()* method is used within TimerEvent.TIMER event listener functions, in exactly the same way that *MouseEvent.updateAfterEvent()* and *KeyboardEvent.updateAfterEvent()* are used within mouse and keyboard event listener functions.

To demonstrate the use of *TimerEvent.updateAfterEvent()*, let's create an exaggerated example that triggers a TimerEvent.TIMER event 10 times more frequently than the Flash runtime's frame rate. We start by setting the frame rate to one frame per second:

```
    stage.frameRate = 1;
```

Next, we create a *Timer* object that dispatches a TimerEvent.TIMER event every 100 ms (10 times a second):

```
    var timer:Timer = new Timer(100, 0);
```

Next, we register a listener function, *timerListener()*, with timer for TimerEvent.TIMER events, as follows:

```
    timer.addEventListener(TimerEvent.TIMER, timerListener);
```

Then we start the timer:

```
    timer.start( );
```

Within the *timerListener()* function, we draw a rectangle and place it in a random position on the screen. To ensure that the rectangle appears immediately after the

`TimerEvent.TIMER` event dispatch completes (rather than at the next scheduled screen update), we use *TimerEvent.updateAfterEvent()* to request a post-event screen update. Here's the code for *timerListener()*:

```
private function timerListener (e:TimerEvent):void {
  // Create the rectangle
  var rect:Sprite = new Sprite();
  rect.graphics.lineStyle(1);
  rect.graphics.beginFill(0x0000FF);
  rect.graphics.drawRect(0, 0, 150, 75);
  rect.x = Math.floor(Math.random( )*stage.stageWidth);
  rect.y = Math.floor(Math.random( )*stage.stageHeight);

  // Add the rectangle to the screen
  addChild(rect);

  // Request a post-event screen update
  e.updateAfterEvent( );
}
```

As a result of the preceding call to *TimerEvent.updateAfterEvent()*, visual changes made within *timerListener()* are rendered approximately every 100 ms, rather than once per second.

For reference, the following code shows our preceding timer scenario in the context of a class, *RandomRectangles*:

```
package {
  import flash.display.*;
  import flash.events.*;
  import flash.utils.*;

  public class RandomRectangles extends Sprite {
    public function RandomRectangles () {
      stage.frameRate = 1;
      var timer:Timer = new Timer(100, 0);
      timer.start();
      timer.addEventListener(TimerEvent.TIMER, timerListener);
    }

    private function timerListener (e:TimerEvent):void {
      var rect:Sprite = new Sprite();
      rect.graphics.lineStyle(1);
      rect.graphics.beginFill(0x0000FF);
      rect.graphics.drawRect(0, 0, 150, 75);
      rect.x = Math.floor(Math.random( )*stage.stageWidth);
      rect.y = Math.floor(Math.random( )*stage.stageHeight);

      addChild(rect);

      e.updateAfterEvent()
    }
  }
}
```

In Chapter 24, we'll continue our study of the *Timer* class, using it to create motion and other forms of animation.

 ActionScript 2.0's *setInterval( )* can also use *updateAfterEvent( )* to trigger a post-event screen update, but *flash.utils.Timer* is preferred over *setInterval( )* because it offers the ability to start and stop timed events, and to notify multiple listeners of timed events. Consider avoiding *setInterval( )* in ActionScript 3.0.

Automatic Post-Event Screen Updates

In Flash Player 9, certain button-style interactions with objects of any class that inherits from *Sprite* will trigger an automatic post-event screen update (exactly as though the programmer had invoked *updateAfterEvent( )*). Specifically, the following interactions will trigger an automatic post-event screen update:

- Moving the mouse over or off of an instance of a class that inherits from *Sprite*
- Pressing or releasing the primary mouse button while the mouse pointer is over an instance of a class that inherits from *Sprite*
- Using the spacebar or Enter key to activate an instance of a class that inherits from *Sprite*

 In future versions of Flash Player, there is a small potential that this special automated screen-update behavior will apply to *SimpleButton* objects only. Accordingly, you might want to avoid relying on it in your code.

Redraw Region

As we learned earlier in the section "Scheduled Screen Updates," the Flash runtime updates the screen only when necessary (that is, when visual content has been changed or added). More specifically, when the Flash runtime updates the screen, it renders only those areas that have changed since the last update. For example, consider an animation with two frames, in which the first frame contains a circle, and the second contains the same circle but also adds a triangle. When the Flash runtime renders the second frame, it redraws the rectangular area containing the triangle but doesn't redraw the circle. The rectangular area encompassing all content that has changed is known as the *redraw region* (sometimes referred to in graphics programming as the *dirty rectangle*).

 In debugging versions of the Flash runtime, the redraw region can be shown by right-clicking the Player window and choosing Show Redraw Regions.

Optimization with the Event.RENDER Event

The Event.RENDER event is a specialized type of screen-update event used in advanced situations where graphics performance is critical. Its primary purpose is to let the programmer defer the execution of all custom drawing routines until the precise moment before the screen is rendered, thus eliminating duplicate drawing-routine execution. Unlike all other built-in Flash runtime events, the Event.RENDER event must be requested manually by the programmer. The Flash runtime dispatches the Event.RENDER event when the following two conditions are both true:

- The Flash runtime is about to check if the screen needs updating (whether due to a frame passing or an *updateAfterEvent()* call).
- The programmer has invoked *stage.invalidate()*. (*stage.invalidate()* is the programmer's way of asking the Flash runtime to dispatch the Event.RENDER event the next time a screen-update check occurs).

Let's consider an example showing how the Event.RENDER event can be used to improve performance. Suppose we're creating an *Ellipse* class that represents an on-screen ellipse shape. For the sake of simplicity, assume that the ellipse is always filled white, with a black, 1 pixel-thick outline. Our *Ellipse* class has two responsibilities:

- It must manage the conceptual data for an ellipse (i.e., store the ellipse width and height).
- It must draw an onscreen ellipse based on the conceptual ellipse and redraw the onscreen ellipse if the conceptual ellipse changes.

Given the preceding responsibilities, Example 23-2 shows how we might create the *Ellipse* class if performance were no concern:

Example 23-2. A simple Ellipse class

```
package {
  import flash.display.Shape;

  public class Ellipse extends Shape {
    private var w:Number;
    private var h:Number;

    public function Ellipse (width:Number, height:Number) {
      w = width;
      h = height;
      draw( );
    }

    public function setWidth (newWidth:Number):void {
      w = newWidth;
      draw( );
    }
```

Example 23-2. A simple Ellipse class (continued)

```
    public function getWidth ( ):Number {
      return w;
    }

    public function setHeight (newHeight:Number):void {
      h = newHeight;
      draw( );
    }

    public function getHeight ( ):Number {
      return h;
    }

    private function draw ( ):void {
      graphics.lineStyle(1);
      graphics.beginFill(0xFFFFFF, 1);
      graphics.drawEllipse(0, 0, w, h);
    }
  }
}
```

Notice that there are three places in the *Ellipse* class where the conceptual ellipse changes: the *setWidth() method,* the *setHeight()* method, and the *Ellipse* constructor method. In order to maintain parity between the conceptual ellipse and the on-screen ellipse, we must ensure that the onscreen ellipse is redrawn in each of those three places. The code in Example 23-2 takes a brute force approach to meeting that parity requirement; it simply invokes *draw()* every time *getWidth(), getHeight(),* or the *Ellipse* constructor method is executed. Of course, if those functions are invoked multiple times within the same screen-update cycle, *draw()* is invoked redundantly. The following code demonstrates:

```
    var e:Ellipse = new Ellipse (100, 200);  // draw( ) invoked here
    e.setWidth(25);    // draw( ) invoked again here
    e.setHeight(50);   // draw( ) invoked again here
```

When the preceding three lines of code run, the *draw()* method is invoked three times, but the screen displays the results of the final invocation only. The first two invocations are redundant and wasteful. In a simple application, the redundancy is imperceptible, and therefore, can arguably be tolerated. However, in complex applications, a similar redundancy might cause drawing routines to execute wastefully hundreds or thousands of times, potentially resulting in serious performance problems.

To remove the redundancy in *Ellipse,* we must change its drawing strategy. Instead of invoking *draw()* every time the conceptual ellipse changes, we'll defer invoking *draw()* until the screen updates. This new strategy will make the *Ellipse* class more complicated but will improve its performance.

The first step in implementing the new "single-*draw()*" strategy is removing the calls to *draw()* from *setWidth()*, *setHeight()*, and the constructor method. Instead of executing *draw()* directly, those functions will instead invoke *stage.invalidate()*, which forces the Flash runtime to dispatch the Event.RENDER event the next time it checks if the screen needs updating. Then, from within an Event.RENDER listener function, we'll invoke *draw()*. Example 23-3 presents the revised *Ellipse* class, with the changes from Example 23-2 shown in bold. Note that *draw()* need not be invoked when the *Ellipse* object is not on the display list, so *stage.invalidate()* is invoked when the *Ellipse* object is on the display list only. To determine whether the *Ellipse* object is on the display list, we check the value of that object's inherited instance variable stage. When stage is null, the *Ellipse* object is not on the display list.

> An object that requests an Event.RENDER event notification will receive that notification even when it is not on the display list.

Note that at this interim stage in our development, the *Ellipse* class is not currently functional because it does not yet register for Event.RENDER events; we'll handle that task soon.

Example 23-3. The revised Ellipse class, part 1

```
package {
  import flash.display.Shape;

  public class EllipseInterim extends Shape {
    private var w:Number;
    private var h:Number;

    public function EllipseInterim (width:Number, height:Number) {
      w = width;
      h = height;

      // If this object is on the display list...
      if (stage != null) {
        // ...request an Event.RENDER dispatch
        stage.invalidate();
      }
    }

    public function setWidth (newWidth:Number):void {
      w = newWidth;

      if (stage != null) {
        stage.invalidate();
      }
    }
```

Example 23-3. The revised Ellipse class, part 1 (continued)

```
public function getWidth ( ):Number {
  return w;
}

public function setHeight (newHeight:Number):void {
  h = newHeight;

  if (stage != null) {
    stage.invalidate( );
  }
}

public function getHeight ( ):Number {
  return h;
}

// Event listener triggered when the screen is about to be updated and
// stage.invalidate( ) has been called
private function renderListener (e:Event):void {
  draw( );
}

private function draw ( ):void {
  graphics.clear( );
  graphics.lineStyle(1);
  graphics.beginFill(0xFFFFFF, 1);
  graphics.drawEllipse(0, 0, w, h);
  }
 }
}
```

To make *renderListener()* execute when the Flash runtime dispatches Event.RENDER, we must register *renderListener()* with the *Stage* instance for Event.RENDER events. However, when an *Ellipse* object is not on the display list, its instance variable stage is set to null, and, therefore, cannot be used for event registration. To circumvent this issue, the *Ellipse* class will define event listener functions— *addedToStageListener()* and *removedFromStageListener()*—that listen for the custom events StageDetector.ADDED_TO_STAGE and StageDetector.REMOVED_FROM_STAGE. The StageDetector.ADDED_TO_STAGE event is dispatched when an object is added to the display list, at which point the *Ellipse* class will register *renderListener()* for the Event.RENDER event. The StageDetector.REMOVED_FROM_STAGE event is dispatched when an object is removed from the display list, at which point the *Ellipse* class will unregister *renderListener()* for Event.RENDER events.

Example 23-4 presents the revised *Ellipse* class, again with changes shown in bold. Notice that the *addedToStageListener()* method invokes *stage.invalidate()*, guaranteeing that any changes made to an *Ellipse* object while it is not on the display list are rendered when it is added to the display list.

Example 23-4 relies on the custom events StageDetector.ADDED_TO_STAGE and StageDetector.REMOVED_FROM_STAGE, dispatched by the custom class, *StageDetector*. For a full discussion of *StageDetector*, see the section "The ADDED_TO_STAGE and REMOVED_FROM_STAGE Events" in Chapter 20.

Example 23-4. The revised Ellipse class, part 2

```
package {
  import flash.display.Shape;
  import flash.events.*;

  public class EllipseInterim extends Shape {
    private var w:Number;
    private var h:Number;

    public function EllipseInterim (width:Number, height:Number) {
      // Register for notification when this
      // object is added to, or removed from, the display list
      var stageDetector:StageDetector = new StageDetector(this);
      stageDetector.addEventListener(StageDetector.ADDED_TO_STAGE,
                                     addedToStageListener);
      stageDetector.addEventListener(StageDetector.REMOVED_FROM_STAGE,
                                     removedFromStageListener);

      w = width;
      h = height;

      if (stage != null) {
        stage.invalidate( );
      }
    }

    public function setWidth (newWidth:Number):void {
      w = newWidth;

      if (stage != null) {
        stage.invalidate( );
      }
    }

    public function getWidth ( ):Number {
      return w;
    }

    public function setHeight (newHeight:Number):void {
      h = newHeight;

      if (stage != null) {
        stage.invalidate( );
      }
    }
```

Example 23-4. The revised Ellipse class, part 2 (continued)

```
    public function getHeight ():Number {
      return h;
    }

    // Event listener triggered when this shape is added to the display list
    private function addedToStageListener (e:Event):void {
      // Register to be notified of screen updates
      stage.addEventListener(Event.RENDER, renderListener);

      // Make sure changes made to this object while it was off-screen
      // are rendered when it is added to the display list.
      stage.invalidate();
    }

    // Event listener triggered when this shape
    // is removed from the display list
    private function removedFromStageListener (e:Event):void {
      // No need to receive screen-update events when the object isn't
      // on the display list
      stage.addEventListener(Event.RENDER, renderListener);
    }

    private function renderListener (e:Event):void {
      draw();
    }

    private function draw ():void {
      graphics.clear();
      graphics.lineStyle(1);
      graphics.beginFill(0xFFFFFF, 1);
      graphics.drawEllipse(0, 0, w, h);
    }
  }
}
```

The *Ellipse* class shown in Example 23-4 is now fully functional, but it still suffers from two significant redundancies.

First, the *addedToStageListener()* method always calls *stage.invalidate()* whenever an *Ellipse* object is added to the display list. This triggers a redraw even in cases where one is not necessary because the conceptual ellipse was not changed while offscreen.

Second, remember that the Event.RENDER event occurs whenever *any* object, not just the current object, calls *stage.invalidate()*. Hence, in its current state, *renderListener()* would invoke *draw()* any time any object in the application calls *stage.invalidate()*. In an application with many objects, this redundancy could cause serious performance problems.

To address these two final issues, we'll make one last set of changes to the *Ellipse* class, adding new logic that tracks whether or not the ellipse needs redrawing when *addedToStageListener()* and *renderListener()* are triggered. First, we'll add a new instance variable, changed, that indicates whether the *Ellipse* needs to be redrawn the next time the screen is updated. Then, to set and unset changed, and to check its status, we'll add three new methods: *setChanged()*, *clearChanged()*, and *hasChanged()*. Finally, we'll set changed to true any time the ellipse changes (i.e., any time *setWidth()*, *setHeight()*, or the constructor method is invoked). Example 23-5 shows the final *Ellipse* class, with modifications shown in bold and comments inserted to guide you through the code. As mentioned earlier, the class shown in Example 23-5 is definitely more complex than the original, unoptimized version from Example 23-2. But in applications that demand maximum graphical performance, the deferred-rendering approach used in Example 23-5 is indispensable. For a more extensive library of shape classes that use deferred rendering, see Chapter 25.

Example 23-5. The final, optimized ellipse class

```
package {
  import flash.display.Shape;
  import flash.events.*;

  public class Ellipse extends Shape {
    private var w:Number;
    private var h:Number;
    private var changed:Boolean;

    public function Ellipse (width:Number, height:Number) {
      // Register for notification when this
      // object is added to the display list
      var stageDetector:StageDetector = new StageDetector(this);
      stageDetector.addEventListener(StageDetector.ADDED_TO_STAGE,
                                     addedToStageListener);
      stageDetector.addEventListener(StageDetector.REMOVED_FROM_STAGE,
                                     removedFromStageListener);

      // Set the width and height
      w = width;
      h = height;

      // Note that the object has changed
      setChanged();
    }

    public function setWidth (newWidth:Number):void {
      w = newWidth;
      setChanged();
    }

    public function getWidth ():Number {
      return w;
    }

    public function setHeight (newHeight:Number):void {
      h = newHeight;
      setChanged();
    }
```

Example 23-5. The final, optimized ellipse class (continued)

```
  public function getHeight ():Number {
    return h;
  }

  // Notes that something about this shape has changed
  private function setChanged ():void {
    changed = true;
    if (stage != null) {
      stage.invalidate();
    }
  }

  // Notes that the most recent changes have been rendered
  private function clearChanged ():void {
    changed = false;
  }

  // Indicates whether or not there are changes to this shape
  // that have not yet been rendered
  protected function hasChanged ():Boolean {
    return changed;
  }

  // Event listener triggered when this shape is added to the display list
  private function addedToStageListener (e:Event):void {
    // Register to be notified of screen updates
    stage.addEventListener(Event.RENDER, renderListener);

    // If the object was changed while off the display list,
    // draw those changes at the next render opportunity. But if the
    // object hasn't changed since the last time it was on the display
    // list, then there's no need to draw it.
    if (hasChanged()) {
      stage.invalidate();
    }
  }

  // Event listener triggered when this shape
  // is removed from the display list
  private function removedFromStageListener (e:Event):void {
    // No need to receive screen-update events when the object isn't
    // on the display list
    stage.addEventListener(Event.RENDER, renderListener);
  }

  // Event listener triggered when the screen is about to be updated and
  // stage.invalidate() has been called
  private function renderListener (e:Event):void {
    // Call draw if there are unrendered changes to this shape.
    // If another object triggers a render event, but this object hasn't
    // changed, then this object won't be redrawn.
    if (hasChanged()) {
```

Example 23-5. The final, optimized ellipse class (continued)

```
      draw( );
    }
  }

  private function draw ( ):void {
    graphics.clear( );
    graphics.lineStyle(1);
    graphics.beginFill(0xFFFFFF, 1);
    graphics.drawEllipse(0, 0, w, h);
  }
 }
}
```

Let's Make It Move!

Now that we're familiar with the Flash runtime's screen-update system, we're ready to learn how to write code that relies on it to create animation and motion. Sound fun? See you at the next chapter.

 For some additional reading on the Flash runtime's screen-update system, see Flash Player engineer Tinic Uro's blog post, at: *http://www. kaourantin.net/2006/05/frame-rates-in-flash-player.html.*

CHAPTER 24

Programmatic Animation

This chapter discusses the basic techniques for creating animation with Action-Script. It focuses on integrating animation code with the Flash runtime's automatic screen updates. It does not, however, cover advanced animation topics, such as programming physics-based motion, motion on a path, collision detection, bitmap animation effects, or color transformations.

No Loops

To create animation with ActionScript, we change visual content repeatedly over time, producing the illusion of movement. For example, to animate a *TextField* object horizontally across the screen, we would repeatedly increase, or decrease, its instance variable x. In some programming languages, the natural mechanism for repeatedly altering an instance variable is a loop statement. Consequently, programmers who are new to ActionScript might expect to create animation using a *while* loop, such as the one shown in the following code:

```
public class TextAnimation extends Sprite {
  public function TextAnimation () {
    // Create a TextField
    var t:TextField = new TextField();
    t.text         = "Hello";
    t.autoSize     = TextFieldAutoSize.LEFT;
    addChild(t);

    // Update the TextField's horizontal position repeatedly, and stop
    // when it reaches x-coordinate 300
    while (t.x <= 300) {
      t.x += 10;
    }
  }
}
```

The preceding *while* loop increments a *TextField* object's instance variable x repeatedly, but as an attempt to produce animation it has a fatal flaw: each time the body of the loop executes, the screen is not updated. With each iteration of the loop, the *TextField*'s horizontal location is updated, but the visual effect of that change is not rendered to the screen. The screen is rendered only after the last iteration of the loop has completed, and the *TextAnimation* constructor function exits. Hence, by the time the screen is rendered, the *TextField* is already situated at x-coordinate 300.

 In ActionScript, loop statements *cannot* be used to produce animation. Remember, the screen can never be updated within a block of code. See the section "No Screen Updates Within Code Blocks" in Chapter 23.

In ActionScript, animation is produced not with loops, but by repeatedly calling functions that make visual changes and then exit, allowing the screen to update. There are two mechanisms for repeatedly calling such functions: the Event.ENTER_FRAME event and the TimerEvent.TIMER event.

Animating with the ENTER_FRAME Event

The Flash runtime dispatches the Event.ENTER_FRAME event every time it performs a scheduled screen-update check (as described in Chapter 23). Any function that registers to receive Event.ENTER_FRAME notifications is executed repeatedly, at a frequency determined by the current Flash runtime frame rate. Visual changes made by any Event.ENTER_FRAME listener function are rendered after it exits.

A function can register to receive Event.ENTER_FRAME notifications from any *DisplayObject* instance, whether or not that instance is currently on the display list. As an example, let's use the Event.ENTER_FRAME event to implement the animation discussed in the previous section, in which a *TextField* moves across the screen horizontally to x-coordinate 300. We start by creating a class, *TextAnimation*, which creates a *TextField* object and then adds it to the display list.

```
public class TextAnimation extends Sprite {
  private var t:TextField;

  public function TextAnimation () {
    // Create a TextField
    t = new TextField();
    t.text        = "Hello";
    t.autoSize    = TextFieldAutoSize.LEFT;
    addChild(t);
  }
}
```

Next, we create an Event.ENTER_FRAME listener function, *moveTextRight()*, which moves the *TextField* t to the right by 10 pixels. Invoking *moveTextRight()* repeatedly will produce the animation effect. Notice that because *moveTextRight()* is an

Event.ENTER_FRAME listener function, it defines a single, required, parameter whose datatype is *Event*.

```
public function moveTextRight (e:Event):void {
  t.x += 10;
}
```

Finally, within *TextAnimation*'s constructor function, we register *moveTextRight()* for Event.ENTER_FRAME events. Once *moveTextRight()* is registered as an Event.ENTER_FRAME listener function, it will be invoked repeatedly in time with the Flash runtime's frame rate. The new code is shown in bold:

```
public function TextAnimation () {
  // Create a TextField
  t = new TextField();
  t.text       = "Hello";
  t.autoSize   = TextFieldAutoSize.LEFT;
  addChild(t);

  // Register moveTextRight() for Event.ENTER_FRAME event notifications
  addEventListener(Event.ENTER_FRAME, moveTextRight);
}
```

Example 24-1 shows the *TextAnimation* class, complete with its *moveTextRight()* method.

Example 24-1. Animating a TextField horizontally

```
public class TextAnimation extends Sprite {
  private var t:TextField;

  public function TextAnimation () {
    // Create a TextField
    t = new TextField();
    t.text       = "Hello";
    t.autoSize   = TextFieldAutoSize.LEFT;
    addChild(t);

    // Register moveTextRight() for Event.ENTER_FRAME event notifications
    addEventListener(Event.ENTER_FRAME, moveTextRight);
  }

  public function moveTextRight (e:Event):void {
    t.x += 10;
  }
}
```

When Example 24-1 runs, each time the Flash runtime performs a scheduled screen-update check, it dispatches an Event.ENTER_FRAME event. In response, *moveTextRight()* executes, and the Flash runtime updates the screen. Over time, the repeated execution of *moveTextRight()* makes the *TextField* object animate across the screen. However, so far, *moveTextRight()* moves the *TextField* t to the right infinitely. To prevent the *TextField* from moving beyond x-coordinate 300, we must modify the *moveTextRight()* method so that it adds 10 to t.x only when t.x is less than or equal to 300, as follows.

```
public function moveTextRight (e:Event):void {
  // Add 10 to t.x only when t.x is less than or equal to 300
  if (t.x <= 300) {
    t.x += 10;
    // Prevent t.x from overshooting 300
    if (t.x > 300) {
      t.x = 300;
    }
  }
}
```

The preceding code accomplishes the goal of halting the *TextField* at x-coordinate 300 but also wastefully allows *moveTextRight()* to continue executing after the *TextField* has reached its destination. To eliminate unnecessary function calls, we unregister *moveTextRight()* for Event.ENTER_FRAME events when the *TextField* reaches x-coordinate 300. Here's the code:

```
public function moveTextRight (e:Event):void {
  if (t.x <= 300) {
    t.x += 10;
    if (t.x > 300) {
      t.x = 300;
    }
  } else {
    // Stop listening for the Event.ENTER_FRAME event
    removeEventListener(Event.ENTER_FRAME, moveTextRight);
  }
}
```

Now that *moveTextRight()* has been modified to listen for Event.ENTER_FRAME events only when necessary, our simple *TextAnimation* class is complete. Example 24-2 shows the final code.

Example 24-2. Animating a TextField horizontally to x-coordinate 300

```
package {
  import flash.display.*;
  import flash.events.*;
  import flash.text.*;

  public class TextAnimation extends Sprite {
    private var t:TextField;

    public function TextAnimation () {
      // Create a TextField
      t = new TextField();
      t.text        = "Hello";
      t.autoSize    = TextFieldAutoSize.LEFT;
      addChild(t);
```

```
    // Register moveTextRight( ) for Event.ENTER_FRAME event notifications
    addEventListener(Event.ENTER_FRAME, moveTextRight);
  }

  public function moveTextRight (e:Event):void {
    if (t.x <= 300) {
      t.x += 10;
      if (t.x > 300) {
        t.x = 300;
      }
    } else {
      // Stop listening for Event.ENTER_FRAME notifications
      // when the TextField reaches its destination
      removeEventListener(Event.ENTER_FRAME, moveTextRight);
    }
  }
 }
}
```

Notice that in Example 24-2, the animation of one object (the *TextField*) is managed by another object (the *TextAnimation* class). The structure of "one object animating another" is typical in applications with centralized animation management. In such applications, a single class acts as the director of all animations in the application, registering a single method for Event.ENTER_FRAME notifications and invoking animation routines on all subordinate objects. By contrast, in an application with decentralized animation management, individual classes control their own animation independently by defining their own Event.ENTER_FRAME event listener methods. For comparison, Example 24-3 shows a *TextField* subclass, *TextTo300*, which—as in our previous example—animates to x-coordinate 300 but does so of its own accord. Notice that *TextTo300* defines *start()* and *stop()* methods that can be used to play and pause the animation.

Example 24-3. Decentralized animation management

```
package {
  import flash.display.*;
  import flash.events.*;
  import flash.text.*;

  public class TextTo300 extends TextField {
    public function TextTo300 () {
    }

    public function moveTextRight (e:Event):void {
      if (x <= 300) {
        x += 10;
        if (t.x > 300) {
          t.x = 300;
        }
      } else {
        stop( );
```

Example 24-3. Decentralized animation management (continued)

```
      }
    }

    public function start ():void {
      // Start playing the animation
      addEventListener(Event.ENTER_FRAME, moveTextRight);
    }

    public function stop ():void {
      // Pause the animation
      removeEventListener(Event.ENTER_FRAME, moveTextRight);
    }
  }
}
```

The following code shows a *.swf* file's main class that uses the *TextTo300* class from Example 24-3:

```
package {
  import flash.display.*;
  import flash.text.*;

  public class TextAnimation extends Sprite {
    private var t:TextTo300;

    public function TextAnimation () {
      // Create a TextTo300 instance
      t = new TextTo300();
      t.text        = "Hello";
      t.autoSize    = TextFieldAutoSize.LEFT;
      addChild(t);

      // Start the animation
      t.start();
    }
  }
}
```

Frame Rate's Effect on Event.ENTER_FRAME Animations

Because the Event.ENTER_FRAME event is synchronized to the frame rate, a higher frame rate will cause Event.ENTER_FRAME listener functions to be triggered more frequently than a lower frame rate. Hence, if we're moving an object around the screen with an Event.ENTER_FRAME listener function, an increase in frame rate can mean an increase in the speed of the animation.

For example, when we programmed the movement of the *TextField* t in the previous section, we implicitly specified its velocity in relation to the frame rate. Our code says, "With each frame that passes, move t 10 pixels to the right":

```
ball_mc._x += 10;
```

Consequently, t's velocity is dependent on the frame rate. If the frame rate is 12 frames per second, then t moves 120 pixels per second. If the frame rate is 30 frames per second, t moves 300 pixels per second!

When developing scripted animations, it's tempting to calculate the distance to move an item in relation to the designated frame rate. For example, if the designated frame rate is 20 frames per second, and we want an item to move 100 pixels per second, we might naturally expect to set the speed of the object to 5 pixels per frame (5 pixels × 20 frames per second = 100 pixels per second).

There are two serious flaws to this approach:

- Any time we wish to change the designated frame rate, we must update all code that calculates speed based on that frame rate.

- As discussed in Chapter 23, the Flash runtime does not always achieve the designated frame rate. If the computer is too slow to render frames fast enough to keep up with the designated frame rate, the animation slows down. This slowdown can even vary depending on the system load; if other programs are running or if Flash is performing some processor-intensive task, the frame rate may drop for only a short period and then resume its normal pace.

In some cases, an animation that plays back at slightly different speeds can be deemed acceptable. But when visual accuracy matters or when we're concerned with the responsiveness of, say, an action game, it's much more appropriate to calculate the distance to move an object based on elapsed time rather than relative to the designated frame rate. For more information, see the section "Velocity-Based Animation," later in this chapter.

Animating with the TimerEvent.TIMER Event

In the previous section, we learned how to use `Event.ENTER_FRAME` to create animations synchronized with the Flash runtime's frame rate. In this section, we'll see how to synchronize animations with an arbitrary time interval, specified using the *flash.utils.Timer* class.

The *Timer* class is a general utility class for executing code after a specified time interval. Each *Timer* object dispatches `TimerEvent.TIMER` events at a programmer-specified frequency. Functions wishing to be executed at that frequency register with the *Timer* object for `TimerEvent.TIMER` events.

 The *Timer* class does not guarantee the frequency with which its listener functions are executed. If the system or the Flash runtime is busy at the time a *Timer* is scheduled to execute its listener functions, the execution will be delayed. For information on accounting for these delays in an animation, see the section "Velocity-Based Animation."

The general steps required to use the *Timer* class are as follows:

1. Create a new *Timer* object:

   ```
   var timer:Timer = new Timer();
   ```

2. Set the frequency with which `TimerEvent.TIMER` events should be triggered, in milliseconds. For example, the following code sets the frequency to 100 milliseconds (10 `TimerEvent.TIMER` event dispatches per second):

   ```
   timer.delay = 100;
   ```

3. Set the total number of `TimerEvent.TIMER` events to be triggered. For example, the following code tells timer to dispatch a total of five `TimerEvent.TIMER` events.

   ```
   timer.repeatCount = 5;
   ```

   The special value 0 indicates no limit (trigger `TimerEvent.TIMER` events forever or until told to stop):

   ```
   timer.repeatCount = 0;   // Unlimited TimerEvent.TIMER events
   ```

4. Create one or more functions to be invoked periodically in response to the *Timer* object's `TimerEvent.TIMER` events. Functions registered for `TimerEvent.TIMER` events must define a single parameter whose datatype is *TimerEvent*.

   ```
   function timerListener (e:TimerEvent):void {
     // Code here will execute when triggered by a TimerEvent.TIMER event
   }
   ```

5. Register the function(s) created in Step 4 with the *Timer* object for `TimerEvent.TIMER` events:

   ```
   timer.addEventListener(TimerEvent.TIMER, timerListener);
   ```

6. Use the *Timer* class's instance method *start()* to start the timer. Once the timer is started, it begins dispatching `TimerEvent.TIMER` events according to the specified `delay` and `repeatCount`.

   ```
   timer.start();
   ```

As an alternative to Steps 2 and 3 in the preceding list, `delay` and `repeatCount` can be set through *Timer*'s constructor parameters, as in:

```
var timer:Timer = new Timer(100, 5);  // Sets delay to 100, repeatCount to 5
```

The following code applies the preceding steps to a simple practical situation: displaying the word "GO!" after a three-second delay. Notice that the *Timer* constructor function's second argument is 1, indicating that only one `TimerEvent.TIMER` event will be dispatched. Similar code might be used at the beginning of a timed quiz or racing game.

```
package {
  import flash.display.*;
  import flash.events.*;
  import flash.utils.*;
  import flash.text.*;

  public class Race extends Sprite {
    private var startMsg:TextField;
```

```
public function Race () {
  // Execute TimerEvent.TIMER listeners once after 3 seconds
  var timer:Timer = new Timer(3000, 1);
  timer.addEventListener(TimerEvent.TIMER, timerListener);
  timer.start( );

  startMsg = new TextField( );
  startMsg.autoSize = TextFieldAutoSize.LEFT;
  startMsg.text = "Get Ready!";
  addChild(startMsg);
}

private function timerListener (e:TimerEvent):void {
  startMsg.text = "GO!";
}
}
}
```

Now that we're comfortable with the *Timer* class in general, let's use it to recreate the *TextAnimation* class from Example 24-2, this time using a *Timer* object for animation instead of Event.ENTER_FRAME. As before, we start by creating the class constructor and properties. This time we add a new instance variable, timer, that will refer to our *Timer* object.

```
public class TextAnimation extends Sprite {
  private var t:TextField;
  private var timer:Timer;

  public function TextAnimation ( ) {
    // Create a TextField
    t = new TextField( );
    t.text        = "Hello";
    t.autoSize    = TextFieldAutoSize.LEFT;
    addChild(t);
  }
}
```

Next, within the *TextAnimation* constructor, we create a *Timer* object, set to generate TimerEvent.TIMER events every 50 milliseconds (i.e., 20 times a second). After creating the *Timer* object, we invoke its *start()* method so that it begins generating TimerEvent.TIMER events.

```
public function TextAnimation ( ) {
  // Create a TextField
  t = new TextField( );
  t.text        = "Hello";
  t.autoSize    = TextFieldAutoSize.LEFT;
  addChild(t);

  timer = new Timer(50, 0);
  timer.start( );
}
```

Next, we create our listener function, *moveTextRight()*, which moves the *TextField* t to the right by 10 pixels until t reaches x-coordinate 300. This time, *moveTextRight()* listens for TimerEvent.TIMER events rather than Event.ENTER_FRAME events, so it defines a single, required, parameter whose datatype is *TimerEvent*.

```
public function moveTextRight (e:TimerEvent):void {
}
```

As before, we want to stop the animation when t reaches x-coordinate 300. To do so, we invoke the *Timer* object's *stop()* method, which stops the generation of TimerEvent.TIMER events:

```
public function moveTextRight (e:TimerEvent):void {
  if (t.x <= 300) {
    t.x += 10;
    if (t.x > 300) {
      t.x = 300;
    }
  } else {
    // Stop the timer when the TextField reaches its destination
    timer.stop( );
  }
}
```

To force a screen update immediately after *moveTextRight()* exits, we use the *TimerEvent* class's instance method *updateAfterEvent()*. (For complete coverage of *updateAfterEvent()*, see Chapter 23.)

```
public function moveTextRight (e:TimerEvent):void {
  if (t.x <= 300) {
    t.x += 10;
    if (t.x > 300) {
      t.x = 300;
    }
    e.updateAfterEvent( );  // Update the screen after this function exits
  } else {
    // Stop the timer when the TextField reaches its destination
    timer.stop( );
  }
}
```

Finally, we register *moveTextRight()* with the *Timer* object for TimerEvent.TIMER events. We perform the registration immediately before starting the timer, in the *TextAnimation* constructor, as follows:

```
public function TextAnimation ( ) {
  // Create a TextField
  t = new TextField( );
  t.text       = "Hello";
  t.autoSize   = TextFieldAutoSize.LEFT;
  addChild(t);
```

```
      timer = new Timer(50, 0);
      timer.addEventListener(TimerEvent.TIMER, moveTextRight);
      timer.start( );
   }
```

Example 24-4 shows the complete code for the *Timer*-based version of *TextAnimation*.

Example 24-4. Animating a TextField horizontally to x-coordinate 300, timer version

```
package {
  import flash.display.*;
  import flash.events.*;
  import flash.utils.*;
  import flash.text.*;

  public class TextAnimation extends Sprite {
    private var t:TextField;
    private var timer:Timer;

    public function TextAnimation ( ) {
      // Create a TextField
      t = new TextField( );
      t.text          = "Hello";
      t.autoSize      = TextFieldAutoSize.LEFT;
      addChild(t);

      timer = new Timer(50, 0);
      timer.addEventListener(TimerEvent.TIMER, moveTextRight);
      timer.start( );
    }

    public function moveTextRight (e:TimerEvent):void {
      if (t.x <= 300) {
        t.x += 10;
        if (t.x > 300) {
          t.x = 300;
        }
        e.updateAfterEvent( );  // Update the screen following this function
      } else {
        // Stop the timer when the TextField reaches its destination
        timer.stop( );
      }
    }
  }
}
```

For another comparison between *Timer*-based animation and Event.ENTER_FRAME-based animation, Example 24-5 shows the analogous *Timer* version of the *TextTo300* class shown earlier Example 24-3.

Example 24-5. TextTo300, timer version

```
package {
  import flash.display.*;
  import flash.events.*;
  import flash.utils.*;
  import flash.text.*;

  public class TextTo300 extends TextField {
    private var timer:Timer;

    public function TextTo300 () {
      timer = new Timer(50, 0);
      timer.addEventListener(TimerEvent.TIMER, moveTextRight);
    }

    public function moveTextRight (e:Event):void {
      if (x <= 300) {
        x += 10;
        if (t.x > 300) {
          t.x = 300;
        }
      } else {
        stop();
      }
    }

    public function start ():void {
      // Start playing the animation
      timer.start();
    }

    public function stop ():void {
      // Pause the animation
      timer.stop();
    }
  }
}
```

Example 24-6 shows another *Timer*-based animation example; it's ActionScript 3.0's version of an old friend: blinking text.

Example 24-6. It lives!

```
package {
  import flash.display.TextField;
  import flash.util.Timer;
  import flash.events.*;

  public class BlinkText extends TextField {
    private var timer:Timer;

    public function BlinkText (delay:Number = 1000) {
      timer = new Timer(delay, 0);
```

Example 24-6. It lives! (continued)

```
      timer.addEventListener(TimerEvent.TIMER, timerListener);
      timer.start();
   }

   private function timerListener (e:TimerEvent):void {
      // If this object is currently visible, make it invisible; or, if this
      // object is currently invisible, make it visible.
      visible = !visible;
      e.updateAfterEvent();
   }

   public function setDelay (newDelay:Number):void {
      timer.delay = newDelay;
   }

   public function startBlink ():void {
      timer.start();
   }

   public function stopBlink ():void {
      visible = true;
      timer.stop();
   }
  }
}
```

Frame Rate's Effect on Timer

Although the *Timer* class may seem to provide a completely arbitrary way to execute a function after a given time period, it is, perhaps surprisingly, still dependent on the Flash runtime's frame rate. A TimerEvent.TIMER event can occur at most 10 times for every scheduled screen-update check (i.e., 10 times the frame rate). For example, given a frame rate of 1 frame per second, a TimerEvent.TIMER event can occur only every 100 ms at most, even when a smaller delay value is specified for a *Timer* object. At 10 frames per second, a TimerEvent.TIMER event can occur 100 times per second (every 10 ms). At 100 frames per second, a TimerEvent.TIMER event can occur 1,000 times per second (every 1 ms).

When a TimerEvent.TIMER event is set to run less often than the frame rate, it will execute after the interval time has expired, at the next scheduled screen update. To request an update before the next scheduled update, use the *TimerEvent* class's instance method *updateAfterEvent()*, as discussed in Chapter 23.

Choosing Between Timer and Event.ENTER_FRAME

As we've just seen, the *Timer* class and the Event.ENTER_FRAME event can both be used to produce animation. So which one is right for your family? Here are the major factors to consider:

Frame rate is subject to change
> When a *.swf* file is loaded by another application, the frame rate of that application might be vastly different than the *.swf* file's designated frame rate, potentially causing the *.swf* 's animations to play too quickly or too slowly. The loaded *.swf* file can, of course, set the frame rate, but that change in frame rate might cause undesirable playback behavior in the parent application. The *Timer* class offers some frame-rate independence (subject to the limitations discussed in the earlier section "Frame Rate's Effect on Timer").

Using many Timer objects requires more memory
> In decentralized animation management architectures, using a separate *Timer* to control the animation of each object requires more memory than would be required by the analogous Event.ENTER_FRAME implementation.

Using many Timer objects can cause excessive screen update requests
> In decentralized animation management architectures, using a separate *Timer* in conjunction with *updateAfterEvent()* to control the animation of each object leads to multiple independent requests for screen updates, possibly leading to performance problems.

Based on those factors, here are the recommended best practices:

- In applications that must synchronize the display of programmatic content with the display of frame-based content created manually in the Flash authoring tool, use Event.ENTER_FRAME.

- In applications where variations in the Flash runtime's frame rate must be mitigated, use a single *Timer* object to orchestrate all animations, and use velocity based animation (see the section "Velocity-Based Animation").

- When variations in the Flash runtime's frame rate are considered acceptable, use Event.ENTER_FRAME (because the code for Event.ENTER_FRAME-based animation is generally simpler than its *Timer*-based equivalent).

- Avoid using individual *Timer* objects to animate individual display objects. Where possible, use a single *Timer* object to orchestrate all animations. That said, if you want to update different objects different times, individual *Timer* objects can be appropriate.

A Generalized Animator

In many examples presented so far in this chapter, the code for creating a visual object and the code for animating that object has been combined in the same class. In real-world applications, it's wiser and more typical to externalize animation code and reuse it across multiple classes.

The simple *Animator* class shown in Example 24-7 demonstrates one possible way to abstract animation features away from objects being animated. Each *Animator* instance can move a specified *DisplayObject* to a given position within a given amount of time. Note that Example 24-7 focuses on the class structure used to externalize animation code. The *Animator* class does not, therefore, provide sophisticated animation capabilities. For more advanced animation features, consider using the Flex framework's *mx.effects.Tween* class or Flash CS3's *fl.transitions.Tween* and *fl.motion.Animator* classes.

The *Animator* class listing follows. Comments will guide you through the code.

Example 24-7. A generalized animation utility class

```
package {
  import flash.display.*;
  import flash.events.*;
  import flash.utils.*;

  // A very simple animation class that demonstrates how to separate
  // animation duties from an object being animated
  public class Animator extends EventDispatcher {
    // Refers to the object being animated
    private var target:DisplayObject;
    // Each time an animation starts we record its start time in startTime
    private var startTime:Number;
    // The duration of an animation, in milliseconds
    private var duration:Number;
    // Each time an animation starts we record the target's start
    // position in startX and startY
    private var startX:Number;
    private var startY:Number;
    // Each time an animation starts we record the difference between the
    // starting position and the end position in deltaX and deltaY
    private var deltaX:Number;
    private var deltaY:Number;

    // The constructor function accepts a reference to the object that
    // will be animated
    public function Animator (target:DisplayObject) {
      this.target = target;
    }

    // Starts an animation that moves the target object from its current
    // position to the specified new position (toX, toY), over
```

Example 24-7. A generalized animation utility class (continued)

```
    // 'duration' milliseconds
    public function animateTo (toX:Number, toY:Number,
                                duration:Number):void {
      // Remember where the target was when this animation started
      startX = target.x;
      startY = target.y;

      // Calculate the difference between the target's starting position
      // and final destination
      deltaX = toX - target.x;
      deltaY = toY - target.y;
      startTime = getTimer( );

      // Remember how long this animation should take
      this.duration = duration;

      // Begin listening for Event.ENTER_FRAME events. Each time a
      // scheduled screen-update occurs, we'll update the position of
      // the target object
      target.addEventListener(Event.ENTER_FRAME, enterFrameListener);
    }

    // Handles Event.ENTER_FRAME events.
    private function enterFrameListener (e:Event):void {
      // Calculate the time elapsed since the animation started
      var elapsed:Number = getTimer( )-startTime;
      // Calculate how much time has passed in the animation, as a
      // percentage of its total duration
      var percentDone:Number = elapsed/duration;
      // If the animation is not yet complete...
      if (percentDone < 1) {
        // ...update the position of the target object
        updatePosition(percentDone);
      } else {
        // ...otherwise place the target object at its final destination,
        // and stop listening for Event.ENTER_FRAME events
        updatePosition(1);
        target.removeEventListener(Event.ENTER_FRAME, enterFrameListener);
      }
    }

    // Sets the position of the target object to a percentage of the
    // distance between the animation start point and end point
    private function updatePosition (percentDone:Number):void {
      target.x = startX + deltaX*percentDone;
      target.y = startY + deltaY*percentDone;
    }
  }
}
```

The *SlidingText* class shown next, in Example 24-8, demonstrates the use of the *Animator* class. Each *SlidingText* object is a text field that can be animated to a position.

 The Flex framework includes text components that can be animated and styled with many customizable effects. For more information, see *mx.controls.Text* and *mx.controls.TextArea* in Adobe's Flex 2 Language Reference.

Example 24-8. A sliding text class

```
package {
  import flash.text.*;

  public class SlidingText extends TextField {
    private var animator:Animator;

    public function SlidingText (toX:Number, toY:Number, duration:Number) {
      animator = new Animator(this);
      slideTo(toX, toY, duration);
    }

    public function slideTo (toX:Number, toY:Number, duration:Number):void {
      animator.animateTo(toX, toY, duration);
    }
  }
}
```

The *AnimationLibDemo* class shown, in Example 24-9 demonstrates how to use both the *Animator* class and the *SlidingText* class. It creates a circle that moves to the mouse pointer position when the Flash runtime's display area is clicked. It also animates the text "Hello" to position (300, 0), one last riveting time.

Example 24-9. An Animator demo

```
package {
  import flash.display.*;
  import flash.events.*;
  import flash.text.*;

  // Demonstrates the use of the Animator class
  public class AnimationLibDemo extends Sprite {
    private var circleAnimator:Animator;

    public function AnimationLibDemo () {
      // Create a message that animates to position (300, 0) over
      // the course of one second (1000 ms)
      var welcome:SlidingText = new SlidingText(300, 0, 1000);
      welcome.text      = "Welcome!";
      welcome.autoSize  = TextFieldAutoSize.LEFT;
      addChild(welcome);
```

Example 24-9. An Animator demo (continued)

```
        // Create a circle to animate
        var circle:Shape = new Shape( );
        circle.graphics.lineStyle(10, 0x666666);
        circle.graphics.beginFill(0x999999);
        circle.graphics.drawCircle(0, 0, 25);
        addChild(circle);

        // Create an Animator to animate the circle
        circleAnimator = new Animator(circle);

        // Register for mouse clicks
        stage.addEventListener(MouseEvent.MOUSE_DOWN, mouseDownListener);
      }

    // When the user clicks the stage, animate the
    // circle to the point that was clicked.
    private function mouseDownListener (e:MouseEvent):void {
      // Convert the point from the Stage instance's coordinate system
      // to this AnimationLibDemo instance's coordinate system
      var mousePt:Point = globalToLocal(new Point(e.stageX, e.stageY));
      circleAnimator.animateTo(mousePt.x, mousePt.y, 500);
    }
  }
}
```

 When creating user interface controls with animated effects, consider extending the Flex framework's *mx.core.UIComponent* class rather than creating a custom animation library. The *UIComponent* class comes equipped with an extensive toolset for adding effects to custom user interface controls.

Velocity-Based Animation

In the Flash runtime, the specific timing of both scheduled screen-update checks and TimerEvent.TIMER events is not guaranteed. The Event.ENTER_FRAME event often executes later than the time scheduled by the designated frame rate, and TimerEvent.TIMER events often occur later than the time specified by a *Timer* object's delay variable.

These delays can result in unpredictable animation. To guarantee that a given object will travel a specified distance in a specified amount of time, we must set its position according to its velocity (i.e., its rate of speed in a particular direction). Example 24-10 shows the basic technique.

Example 24-10. Calculating position based on velocity

```
package {
  import flash.display.*;
  import flash.events.*;
  import flash.utils.*;
```

Example 24-10. Calculating position based on velocity (continued)

```
// Moves an object a specified number of pixels per second, no matter what
// the frame rate
public class Animation extends Sprite {
  private var distancePerSecond:int = 50;  // Pixels to move per second
  private var now:int;                      // The current time
  private var then:int;                     // The last screen-update time
  private var circle:Shape;                 // The object to animate

  public function Animation () {
    // Create the object to animate
    circle = new Shape();
    circle.graphics.beginFill(0x0000FF, 1);
    circle.graphics.lineStyle(1);
    circle.graphics.drawEllipse(0, 0, 25, 25);
    addChild(circle);

    // Initialize timestamps
    then = getTimer();
    now  = then;

    // Register for notification of scheduled screen-update checks
    addEventListener(Event.ENTER_FRAME, enterFrameListener);
  }

  //  Handles Event.ENTER_FRAME events
  private function enterFrameListener (e:Event):void {
    // Calculate how much time has passed since the last move
    then = now;
    now = getTimer();
    var elapsed:int = now - then;
    var numSeconds:Number = elapsed / 1000;

    // Calculate the amount move based on the amount of time that
    // has passed since the last move
    var moveAmount:Number = distancePerSecond * numSeconds;

    // Move the object. In this case, the object's direction is 0 degrees.
    circle.x += moveAmount;
  }
 }
}
```

The *Animator* class shown earlier in Example 24-7 likewise uses velocity to guarantee that the object it animates will travel a specified distance in a specified amount of time.

Moving On to Strokes 'n' Fills

Over the past few chapters, we've spent most of our time working with interactivity and animation. Over the next several chapters, we'll change our focus to the creation of three specific kinds of visual content: vectors, bitmaps, and text fields.

Drawing with Vectors

In ActionsScript, primitive vectors, lines, and shapes are drawn via the *Graphics* class. However, the *Graphics* class is never instantiated directly; instead, each Action-Script class that supports programmatic vector drawing creates a *Graphics* instance automatically and provides access to it via the instance variable graphics. The display classes that support vector drawing are *Sprite*, *MovieClip*, and *Shape*.

 Shape objects consume less memory than *Sprite* and *MovieClip* objects. Hence, to conserve memory, vector content should be drawn in *Shape* objects whenever the containment and interactive capabilities of the *Sprite* and *MovieClip* classes are not required.

Graphics Class Overview

As shown in Table 25-1, the *Graphics* class's drawing tools can be broken down into five general categories: drawing lines, drawing shapes (also known as *fills*), defining line styles, moving the drawing pen, and removing graphics.

Table 25-1. Graphics class overview

Purpose	Graphics method
Drawing lines	*curveTo( ), lineTo( )*
Drawing shapes	*beginBitmapFill( ), beginFill( ), beginGradientFill( ), drawCircle( ), drawEllipse( ), drawRect( ), drawRoundRect( ), drawRoundRectComplex( ), endFill( )*
Defining line styles	*lineGradientStyle( ), lineStyle( )*
Moving the drawing pen	*moveTo( )*
Removing graphics	*clear( )*

Conceptually, lines and curves are drawn in ActionScript by a theoretical "drawing pen." For all new *Sprite*, *MovieClip*, and *Shape* objects, the pen starts out at position (0,0). As lines and curves are drawn (via *lineTo( )* and *curveTo( )*), the pen moves around the object's coordinate space, resting at the end point of the last line or curve drawn. The pen's current position always indicates the starting point of the next line or curve to be drawn. To arbitrarily set the starting point of a line or curve, we use the *moveTo()* method, which "picks up" the drawing pen and moves it to a new position without drawing a line to the specified point.

Drawing Lines

To draw straight lines we use the *lineTo()* method, which draws a line from the current drawing pen position to a specified point (x, y). For example, the following code creates a new Sprite object and draws a line in it from (0, 0) to (25, 35):

```
var canvas:Shape = new Shape();
canvas.graphics.lineTo(25, 35);
addChild(canvas);
```

However, if you try that code as is, you may be surprised to find that no line appears on screen! By default, all lines and shapes drawn have no stroke. To cause a stroke to appear, we must use the *lineStyle()* method, which sets the visual stroke characteristics (thickness, color, etc.) for all lines and shapes subsequently drawn. For reference, here is the method signature for *lineStyle()*, showing the visual options available and their default values. Consult Adobe's ActionScript Language Reference for details on each parameter.

```
lineStyle(thickness:Number = 1.0,
          color:uint = 0,
          alpha:Number = 1.0,
          pixelHinting:Boolean = false,
          scaleMode:String = "normal",
          caps:String = null,
          joints:String = null,
          miterLimit:Number = 3)
```

The *lineStyle()* method must be invoked explicitly for each new *Sprite*, *MovieClip*, and *Shape* object, or no stroke will appear (although filled regions can still be drawn without a stroke).

Let's look at a few examples showing various ways to modify the line style of canvas. The following code clears the line style (subsequent lines, curves, and fills are not stroked):

```
canvas.graphics.lineStyle()
```

The following code sets the line style to 1 pixel-thick, solid black:

```
canvas.graphics.lineStyle(1)
```

The following code sets the line style to 1 pixel-thick, solid green:

```
canvas.graphics.lineStyle(1, 0x00FF00)
```

The following code sets the line style to 2 pixels thick, 50% transparent green:

```
canvas.graphics.lineStyle(1, 0x00FF00, 50)
```

Now let's draw a line from (0, 0) to (25, 35), as before, but this time we'll apply a 3 pixel-thick blue stroke, causing the line to appear on screen:

```
var canvas:Shape = new Shape( );
canvas.graphics.lineStyle(3, 0x0000FF);  // Apply blue stroke
canvas.graphics.lineTo(25, 35);
addChild(canvas);
```

Note that if the preceding line were drawn in a *Sprite* or *MovieClip* containing child display objects, it would appear behind those objects.

 Child display objects are always displayed in front of their parent and, hence, always obscure vector content drawn with ActionScript in that parent.

For example, the following code adds a *TextField* object to a new *Sprite* object and then draws a line in that *Sprite* object. The *TextField* object obscures the line because the *TextField* object is the *Sprite* object's child.

```
// Create the Sprite and put it on screen
var container:Sprite = new Sprite( );
addChild(container);

// Create the TextField
var msg:TextField = new TextField( );
msg.text = "Hello";
msg.border = true;
msg.background = true;
msg.autoSize = TextFieldAutoSize.LEFT;
container.addChild(msg);

// Draw the line
container.graphics.lineStyle(3, 0x0000FF);
container.graphics.lineTo(25, 35);
```

Figure 25-1 shows the result of the preceding code.

Figure 25-1. Vector content behind a TextField

 Content drawn via graphics in a *Sprite* or *MovieClip* always appears behind (i.e., is obscured by) any child objects of that *Sprite* or *MovieClip*.

When drawing multiple lines, each line's stroke style can be set individually by calling *lineStyle()* before drawing each line. For example, the following code draws a square with progressively thicker lines, colored black, red, green, and blue:

```
var canvas:Shape = new Shape( );
canvas.graphics.lineStyle(1, 0x000000);
canvas.graphics.lineTo(100, 0);
canvas.graphics.lineStyle(5, 0xFF0000);
canvas.graphics.lineTo(100, 100);
canvas.graphics.lineStyle(10, 0x00FF00);
canvas.graphics.lineTo(0, 100);
canvas.graphics.lineStyle(15, 0x0000FF);
canvas.graphics.lineTo(0, 0);
addChild(canvas);
```

Figure 25-2 shows the results.

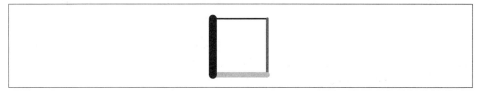

Figure 25-2. Lines of varying thicknesses

Notice the end of the lines (known as the line *caps*) in Figure 25-2 are rounded by default. To select square caps instead of round ones, use the *lineStyle()* method's caps parameter. For example, the following code creates a 10 pixel-thick green line with square caps:

```
canvas.graphics.lineStyle(10, 0x00FF00, 1, false,
                        LineScaleMode.NORMAL, CapsStyle.SQUARE);
```

A thickness of 0 sets the stroke to hairline (a one-pixel line that does not increase in thickness when the object is scaled up or the Flash runtime's display area is zoomed in). Other line-scaling options can be set via the *lineStyle()* method's scaleMode parameter.

To turn the stroke off completely, set thickness to undefined or call *lineStyle()* with no parameters. For example:

```
canvas.graphics.lineStyle(undefined);   // Turn off lines in canvas
canvas.graphics.lineStyle( );           // Same thing
```

To move the drawing pen without drawing any line at all, use *moveTo()*. For example, suppose we want to draw a single straight line from (100,100) to (200, 200) in a new *Shape* object. We first move the pen from (0,0) to (100,100) using *moveTo()* and then draw a line from there to (200,200) using *lineTo()*, as follows:

```
var canvas:Shape = new Shape( );    // Create the Shape to draw in
canvas.graphics.lineStyle(1);       // Set the stroke to 1 point, black
canvas.graphics.moveTo(100, 100);   // Move the pen without drawing a line
canvas.graphics.lineTo(200, 200);   // Draw the line (this also moves the pen)
```

Drawing Curves

To draw curved lines we use the *curveTo()* method, which has this signature:

```
curveTo(controlX:Number, controlY:Number, anchorX:Number, anchorY:Number)
```

The *curveTo()* method draws a quadratic Bézier curve from the current drawing pen position to the point (*anchorX*, *anchorY*) using an off-curve control point of (*controlX*, *controlY*). The curve tangents at each endpoint run in the direction of the line from the endpoint to the control point. The Bézier curve is contained in the convex hull of its three control points.

Conceptually speaking, the straight line that would run from the pen position to the end point (*anchorX*, *anchorY*) is pulled by the control point (*controlX*, *controlY*) to make a curve. If any of *curveTo()*'s arguments are missing, the operation fails silently, and the position of the drawing pen remains unchanged. As with *lineTo()*, the stroke characteristics of the curve (thickness, color, alpha, etc.) are determined by the most recent call to *lineStyle()*.

The following code draws a four-point black curve from the drawing pen's default position (0, 0) to the anchor point (100, 0) using the control point (50, 100). The resulting curve is shown in Figure 25-3.

```
var canvas:Shape = new Shape( );
addChild(canvas);

canvas.graphics.lineStyle(4);  // Set the stroke to 4-point, black
canvas.graphics.curveTo(50, 100, 100, 0);  // Draw the curve
```

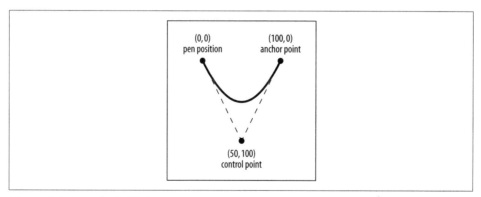

Figure 25-3. A quadratic Bézier curve

After a curve is drawn, the drawing pen remains at the end point of the curve. Hence, multiple calls to *curveTo()* and/or *lineTo()* can be used to draw complex curves or closed shapes, such as circles and polygons, as discussed in the next section.

Curves drawn on fractional pixels often appear blurry. To sharpen blurry, antialiased lines, set *lineStyle()*'s pixelHinting parameter to true.

Sometimes it is more convenient to specify three points on a curve rather than two anchor points and a control point. The following code defines a custom *curveThrough3Pts()* method that accepts three points as arguments and draws a quadratic curve that passes through them. The second point is assumed to be halfway along the curve in time (t = .5):

```
// Adapted from Robert Penner's drawCurve3Pts() method
public function curveThrough3Pts (g:Graphics,startX:Number, startY:Number,
                                  throughX:Number, throughY:Number,
                                  endX:Number, endY:Number) {
  var controlX:Number = (2 * throughX) - .5 * (startX + endX);
  var controlY:Number = (2 * throughY) - .5 * (startY + endY);
  g.moveTo(startX, startY);
  g.curveTo(controlX, controlY, endX, endY);
}

// Usage
var canvas:Shape = new Shape();
addChild(canvas);
canvas.graphics.lineStyle(2, 0x0000FF);
curveThrough3Pts(canvas.graphics, 100, 100, 150, 50, 200, 100);
```

For more information on curve mathematics in ActionScript, see Jim Armstrong's "TechNotes," at *http://www.algorithmist.net/technotes.html*.

Drawing Shapes

To draw an arbitrary shape (i.e., to paint a color into the geometric area between three or more points), follow these steps:

1. Choose the starting point of the shape (either the default (0,0) or a point specified via *moveTo()*).

2. Start the shape with the *beginBitmapFill()*, *beginFill()*, or *beginGradientFill()* method.

3. Draw the shape's outline with a series of *lineTo()* and/or *curveTo()* calls, the last of which should end at the starting point specified in Step 1.

4. Close the shape with *endFill()*.

The *beginFill()* method fills the shape with a solid color; the *beginGradientFill()* method fills the shape with a gradient (a blend between two or more colors); and the *beginBitmapFill()* method fills a shape with the specified bitmap (tiled if desired).

For example, the following code draws a red triangle with a five pixel-thick black outline. Notice that the default start point (0, 0) matches the endpoint:

```
var triangle:Shape = new Shape( );
triangle.graphics.beginFill(0xFF0000, 1);
triangle.graphics.lineStyle(20);
triangle.graphics.lineTo(125, 125); // Draw a line down and right
triangle.graphics.lineTo(250, 0);   // Draw a line up and right
triangle.graphics.lineTo(0, 0);     // Draw a line left
triangle.graphics.endFill( );
addChild(triangle);
```

Figure 25-4 shows the result of the preceding code.

Figure 25-4. A triangle

Notice that the corners of the triangle in Figure 25-4 are rounded. To set the rendering style for corners, we use *lineStyle()*'s joints parameter. For example, the following code changes the corner-rendering style to "mitered" by assigning the constant JointStyle.MITER to the joints parameter:

```
triangle.graphics.lineStyle(20, 0, 1, false, LineScaleMode.NORMAL,
                            CapsStyle.ROUND, JointStyle.MITER);
```

Figure 25-5 shows the result; pay special attention to the new corners of the triangle.

Figure 25-5. Triangle with mitered joints

To draw various kinds of rectangles and ellipses, the *Graphics* class provides the following convenience methods: *drawCircle()*, *drawEllipse()*, *drawRect()*, *drawRoundRect()*, and *drawRoundRectComplex()*. The "round rect" methods draw rectangles with rounded corners. All of the shape-drawing convenience methods are used with the familiar *lineStyle()* and *beginFill()* methods. However, it is not necessary to call *endFill()* after drawing the shape because each convenience method does so automatically.

The following code shows the general use of the shape drawing methods. It uses *drawRect()* to draw a blue rectangle with a black one-pixel outline:

```
var canvas:Shape = new Shape( );
addChild(canvas);

// Set line thickness to one pixel
canvas.graphics.lineStyle(1);
// Set the fill color to blue
canvas.graphics.beginFill(0x0000FF);
// Draw the shape
canvas.graphics.drawRect(0, 0, 150, 75);
// Notice no call to endFill( ) here
```

Removing Vector Content

To remove all vector drawings in an object, we use the *Graphics* class's instance method *clear()*. For example:

```
var canvas:Shape = new Shape( );
// Draw a line
canvas.graphics.lineStyle(3, 0x0000FF);  // Apply blue stroke
canvas.graphics.lineTo(25, 35);
addChild(canvas);

// Erase the line
canvas.graphics.clear( );
```

When the *clear()* method is invoked, the object's line style reverts to undefined (no stroke). After calling *clear()*, *lineStyle()* must be called again, or no stroke will appear on lines and shapes. Calling *clear()* also resets the drawing pen position to (0, 0). Note that *clear()* affects vector content in a single object only; if that object is a *Sprite* or *MovieClip* instance, *clear()* does not erase any vector content in its children, nor does it remove them.

The following code draws a single line with a random stroke style every 250 milliseconds. It uses *clear()* to erase the previously drawn line.

```
package {
  import flash.display.*;
  import flash.utils.*;
  import flash.events.*;

  public class RandomLines extends Sprite {

    private var s:Shape;

    public function RandomLines ( ) {
      s = new Shape( );
      addChild(s);
```

```
    var t:Timer = new Timer(250);
    t.addEventListener(TimerEvent.TIMER, timerListener);
    t.start( );
}

private function timerListener (e:TimerEvent):void {
  s.graphics.clear( );
  s.graphics.lineStyle(random(1, 10), random(0, 0xFFFFFF));
  s.graphics.moveTo(random(0, 550), random(0, 400));
  s.graphics.lineTo(random(0, 550), random(0, 400));
}

// Returns a number in the range of minVal to maxVal, inclusive
public function random (minVal:int, maxVal:int):int {
  return minVal + Math.floor(Math.random( ) * (maxVal + 1 - minVal));
}
  }
}
```

Reader exercise: For comparison, try removing the call to *clear()* on line 1 of the *timerListener()* method.

Example: An Object-Oriented Shape Library

The graphical content created by the built-in shape drawing methods (*drawEllipse()*, *drawRect()*, etc.) does not correspond to any object, and cannot be changed or removed independently once drawn. In ActionScript, there are no classes that give object-oriented access to corresponding onscreen shapes. This section shows one way to address that shortcoming, showing an example implementation of a small class library for creating and manipulating shapes as objects.

The classes in our example shape library are as follows: *BasicShape*, *Rectangle*, *Ellipse*, *Star*, and *Polygon*. *BasicShape* is the base class of the library. It extends the built-in *Shape* class, which provides a lightweight, basic surface on which to draw shapes. The *BasicShape* class manages stroke and fill styles for all shapes and determines when a shape needs to be drawn. Instances of the remaining classes represent geometric shapes that can be added to, and removed from, the display list. Each shape class implements its own specific drawing routine. Once a shape object is created, its stroke, fill, and outline can be updated freely.

The following six examples put many of the techniques we've studied in this book into practice—especially those covered in this chapter. Pay close attention to the numerous comments; they will guide you through the code.

Example 25-1 shows the *BasicShape* class, an abstract-style class that defines the basic functionality of all shapes in the class library. Its main features are implemented in the following methods:

- *setStrokeStyle()* and *setFillStyle()*: Store the visual characteristics of the shape
- *draw()*: Renders the shape but delegates specific line plotting to *drawShape()*, an abstract method implemented by subclasses
- *setChanged()*, *clearChanged()*, and *hasChanged()*: Track whether the shape has changed since the last time it was rendered
- *requestDraw()*, *addedListener()*, *removedListener()*, and *renderListener()*: In combination, these methods determine when a shape needs to be drawn

Example 25-1. The BasicShape class

```
package org.moock.drawing {
  import flash.display.*;
  import flash.events.*;
  import flash.errors.IllegalOperationError;

  // Base class for displayable geometric shapes
  public class BasicShape extends Shape {
    // Fill style
    protected var fillColor:Number = 0xFFFFFF;
    protected var fillAlpha:Number = 1;

    // Line style. Use mitered joints instead of round (the ActionScript
    // default). All other defaults match ActionScript's defaults.
    protected var lineThickness:Number = 1;
    protected var lineColor:uint = 0;
    protected var lineAlpha:Number = 1;
    protected var linePixelHinting:Boolean = false;
    protected var lineScaleMode:String = LineScaleMode.NORMAL;
    protected var lineJoints:String = JointStyle.MITER;
    protected var lineMiterLimit:Number = 3;

    // Flag indicating that the object needs redrawing. Prevents this
    // object from being redrawn in cases where some other object
    // triggers a RENDER event.
    protected var changed:Boolean = false;


    // Constructor
    public function BasicShape () {
      // Register to be notified when this object is added to or removed
      // from the display list (requires the custom helper class,
      // StageDetector)
      var stageDetector:StageDetector = new StageDetector(this);
      stageDetector.addEventListener(StageDetector.ADDED_TO_STAGE,
                              addedToStageListener);
      stageDetector.addEventListener(StageDetector.REMOVED_FROM_STAGE,
                              removedFromStageListener);
    }
```

Example 25-1. The BasicShape class (continued)

```
// Sets the visual characteristics of the line around the shape
public function setStrokeStyle (thickness:Number = 1,
                                color:uint = 0,
                                alpha:Number = 1,
                                pixelHinting:Boolean = false,
                                scaleMode:String = "normal",
                                joints:String = "miter",
                                miterLimit:Number = 10):void {
  lineThickness = thickness;
  lineColor = color;
  lineAlpha = alpha;
  linePixelHinting = pixelHinting;
  lineScaleMode = scaleMode;
  lineJoints = joints;
  lineMiterLimit = miterLimit;

  // The line style has changed, so ask to be notified of the
  // next screen update. At that time, redraw the shape.
  setChanged();
}

// Sets the visual characteristics of the shape's fill
public function setFillStyle (color:uint = 0xFFFFFF,
                              alpha:Number = 1):void {
  fillColor = color;
  fillAlpha = alpha;

  // The fill style has changed, so ask to be notified of the
  // next screen update. At that time, redraw the shape.
  setChanged();
}

// Creates the shape's graphics, delegating specific line-drawing
// operations to individual BasicShape subclasses. For the sake of
// performance, draw() is called only when the stage broadcasts
// an Event.RENDER event.
private function draw ():void {
  // Delete all graphics in this object.
  graphics.clear();
  // Line cap style doesn't matter for a
  // closed shape, so pass null for that argument.
  graphics.lineStyle(lineThickness, lineColor, lineAlpha,
                     linePixelHinting, lineScaleMode, null,
                     lineJoints, lineMiterLimit);
  graphics.beginFill(fillColor, fillAlpha);
  drawShape();  // Call drawing routine, implemented by subclass
  graphics.endFill();

  // Make a note that the most recent changes have been rendered.
  clearChanged();
}
```

Example 25-1. The BasicShape class (continued)

```
// Draws the actual lines for each type of shape. Must be implemented
// by all BasicShape subclasses.
protected function drawShape ():void {
  // Prevent this abstract-style method from being invoked directly
  throw new IllegalOperationError("The drawShape() method can be "
                        + "invoked on BasicShape subclasses only.")
}

// Notes that something about this shape has changed, if the shape
// is currently on stage, causes it to be drawn at the next render
// opportunity
protected function setChanged ():void {
  changed = true;
  requestDraw();
}

// Notes that the most recent changes have been rendered
protected function clearChanged ():void {
  changed = false;
}

// Indicates whether or not there are changes to this shape
// that have not yet been rendered
protected function hasChanged ():Boolean {
  return changed;
}

// If this shape is on screen, requestDraw() causes it to be drawn
// the next time the screen is updated
protected  function requestDraw ():void {
  if (stage != null) {
    stage.invalidate();
  }
}

// Event listener triggered when this shape is added to the display list
private function addedToStageListener (e:Event):void {
  // Register to be notified of screen updates
  stage.addEventListener(Event.RENDER, renderListener);

  // If the object was changed while off the display list,
  // draw those changes at the next render opportunity. But if the
  // object hasn't changed since the last time it was on the display
  // list, then there's no need to draw it.
  if (hasChanged()) {
    requestDraw();
  }
}

// Event listener triggered when this shape
// is removed from the display list
private function removedFromStageListener (e:Event):void {
```

Example 25-1. The BasicShape class (continued)

```
      // No need to listen for Event.RENDER events when the object isn't
      // on the display list
      stage.removeEventListener(Event.RENDER, renderListener);
    }

    // Event listener triggered when the screen is about to be updated and
    // stage.invalidate( ) has been called.
    private function renderListener (e:Event):void {
      // Call draw if there are unrendered changes to this shape.
      // If another object triggers a render event, but this object hasn't
      // changed, then this object won't be redrawn.
      if (hasChanged( )) {
        draw( );
      }
    }
  }
}
```

Example 25-2 shows the *Ellipse* class, a *BasicShape* subclass. Notice that the specific code for drawing an ellipse is contained by the *drawShape()* method. Furthermore, setting the size of an *Ellipse* object does not immediately cause the ellipse to be drawn. Instead, when *setSize()* is invoked, the object calls *setChanged()*, indicating that it needs to be redrawn the next time the Flash runtime renders the screen.

Example 25-2. The Ellipse class

```
package org.moock.drawing {
  // Represents an ellipse that can be drawn to the screen
  public class Ellipse extends BasicShape {
    // The width and height of the ellipse
    protected var w:Number;
    protected var h:Number;

    // Constructor
    public function Ellipse (width:Number = 100, height:Number = 100) {
      super( );
      setSize(width, height);
    }

    // The ellipse drawing routine
    override protected function drawShape ():void {
      graphics.drawEllipse(0, 0, w, h);
    }

    // Sets the width and height of the ellipse
    public function setSize (newWidth:Number, newHeight:Number):void {
      w = newWidth;
      h = newHeight;
```

Example 25-2. The Ellipse class (continued)

```
    // Setting the width and height of the ellipse changes its shape,
    // so it must be redrawn at the next render opportunity.
    setChanged();
  }
 }
}
```

Example 25-3 shows the *Polygon* class, another *BasicShape* subclass. *Polygon* can draw any multisided shape. As such, it acts as the superclass for specific types of polygons, such as *Rectangle* and *Star*. Like *Ellipse*, *Polygon* supplies its own specific drawing routine in the *drawShape()* method. Any time a *Polygon* object's points are set (via *setPoints()*), it calls *setChanged()*, indicating that it needs to be redrawn the next time the Flash runtime renders the screen.

Example 25-3. The Polygon class

```
package org.moock.drawing {
  // Represents a polygon that can be drawn to the screen
  public class Polygon extends BasicShape {
    // The polygon's points.
    //  To reduce memory consumption, the points are stored in two integer
    //  arrays rather than one array of flash.geom.Point objects.
    private var xpoints:Array;
    private var ypoints:Array;

    // Constructor
    public function Polygon (xpoints:Array = null, ypoints:Array = null) {
      super();
      setPoints(xpoints, ypoints);
    }

    // The polygon drawing routine
    override protected function drawShape ():void {
      // Draw lines to each point in the polygon
      graphics.moveTo(xpoints[0], ypoints[0]);
      for (var i:int = 1; i < xpoints.length; i++) {
        graphics.lineTo(xpoints[i], ypoints[i]);
      }
      // Close the shape by returning to the first point
      graphics.lineTo(xpoints[0], ypoints[0]);
    }

    // Assigns the polygon's points
    public function setPoints (newXPoints:Array, newYPoints:Array):void {
      if (newXPoints == null || newYPoints == null) {
        return;
      }

      if (newXPoints.length != newYPoints.length) {
        throw new Error("setPoints() requires a matching "
                        + "number of x and y points");
      }
```

Example 25-3. The Polygon class (continued)

```
      xpoints = newXPoints;
      ypoints = newYPoints;

      // Assigning new points to the polygon changes its shape,
      // so it must be redrawn at the next render opportunity.
      setChanged();
    }
  }
}
```

Example 25-4 shows the *Rectangle* class, a *Polygon* subclass. The *Rectangle* class is similar in structure to the *Ellipse* class but relies on drawing routine in the *Polygon* class's instance method *drawShape()* rather than providing its own.

Example 25-4. The Rectangle class

```
package org.moock.drawing {
  // Represents a rectangle that can be drawn to the screen
  public class Rectangle extends Polygon {
    // The width and height of the rectangle
    protected var w:Number;
    protected var h:Number;

    // Constructor
    public function Rectangle (width:Number = 100, height:Number = 100) {
      super();
      setSize(width, height);
    }

    // Sets the width and height of the rectangle
    public function setSize (newWidth:Number, newHeight:Number):void {
      w = newWidth;
      h = newHeight;

      // Translate the width and height into points on the polygon
      setPoints([0,w,w,0],[0,0,h,h]);
    }
  }
}
```

Example 25-5 shows the last class in the library: *Star* class, another *Polygon* subclass. Like *Rectangle*, the *Star* class relies on *Polygon*'s *drawShape()* to plot its outline. The visual characteristics of each *Star* object are assigned via the *setStar()* method.

Example 25-5. The Star class

```
package org.moock.drawing {
  // Represents a star shape that can be drawn to the screen
  public class Star extends Polygon {
    // Constructor
```

Example 25-5. The Star class (continued)

```
    public function Star (numTips:int,
                          innerRadius:Number,
                          outerRadius:Number,
                          angle:Number = 0) {
      super( );
      setStar(numTips, innerRadius, outerRadius, angle);
    }

    // Sets the physical characteristics of the star.
    // Based on Ric Ewing's ActionScript 1.0 drawing methods, available at:
    // http://www.adobe.com/devnet/flash/articles/adv_draw_methods.html
    //    numTips       Number of tips (must be 3 or more)
    //    innerRadius   Radius of the base of the tips
    //    outerRadius   Radius of the summit of the tips
    //    angle         Starting angle in degrees (defaults to 0)
    public function setStar (numTips:int,
                             innerRadius:Number,
                             outerRadius:Number,
                             angle:Number = 0):void {
      // Calculate the polygon points of the star
      if (numTips > 2) {
        // Initialize variables
        var pointsX:Array = [];
        var pointsY:Array = [];
        var centerX:Number = outerRadius;
        var centerY:Number = outerRadius;
        var step:Number, halfStep:Number,
            startAngle:Number, dx:Number, dy:Number;
        // Calculate distance between tips
        step = (Math.PI*2)/numTips;
        halfStep = step/2;
        // Calculate starting angle in radians
        startAngle = (angle/180)*Math.PI;
        // Set starting point
        pointsX[0] = centerX+(Math.cos(startAngle)*outerRadius);
        pointsY[0] = centerY-(Math.sin(startAngle)*outerRadius);
        // Add remaining points
        for (var i:int=1; i <= numTips; i++) {
          dx = centerX+Math.cos(startAngle+(step*i)-halfStep)*innerRadius;
          dy = centerY-Math.sin(startAngle+(step*i)-halfStep)*innerRadius;
          pointsX.push(dx);
          pointsY.push(dy);
          dx = centerX+Math.cos(startAngle+(step*i))*outerRadius;
          dy = centerY-Math.sin(startAngle+(step*i))*outerRadius;
          pointsX.push(dx);
          pointsY.push(dy);
        }
        // Store the star's calculated points
        setPoints(pointsX,pointsY);
      }
    }
  }
}
```

Finally, Example 25-6 shows the *ShapeRandomizer* class, which demonstrates the use of the shape library classes shown in the previous five examples. *ShapeRandomizer*'s constructor method creates four shapes. Clicking the stage randomly modifies the stroke, fill, and outline of those shapes.

Example 25-6. The ShapeRandomizer class

```
package {
  import flash.display.Sprite;
  import flash.events.MouseEvent;

  import org.moock.drawing.*;

  // An org.moock.drawing library demo. Creates random shapes when the
  // mouse clicks the stage.
  public class ShapeRandomizer extends Sprite {

    // The shapes
    private var rect:Rectangle;
    private var ell:Ellipse;
    private var poly:Polygon;
    private var star:Star;

    // Constructor
    public function ShapeRandomizer () {
      // Create a rectangle
      rect = new Rectangle(50, 100);
      rect.setStrokeStyle(1, 0xFF0000);
      rect.setFillStyle(0x0000FF);

      // Create an ellipse
      ell = new Ellipse(250, 50);
      ell.setStrokeStyle(2, 0xFFFF00);
      ell.setFillStyle(0xED994F);

      // Create a triangle (i.e., a 3-sided Polygon)
      poly = new Polygon([0, 50, 100], [50, 0, 50]);
      poly.setStrokeStyle(4, 0x333333);
      poly.setFillStyle(0x00FF00);

      // Create a star
      star = new Star(5, 30, 80);
      star.setStrokeStyle(4, 0x666666);
      star.setFillStyle(0xFF0000);

      // Add the shapes to the display list
      addChild(rect);
      addChild(ell);
      addChild(poly);
      addChild(star);

      // Register for mouse clicks
      stage.addEventListener(MouseEvent.MOUSE_DOWN, mouseDownListener);
    }
```

Example 25-6. The ShapeRandomizer class (continued)

```
  // Event listener triggered when the mouse clicks Flash Player's
  // display area
  private function mouseDownListener (e:MouseEvent):void {
    // Randomly change the shapes
    rect.width  = random(1, 300);
    rect.height = random(1, 300);
    rect.setStrokeStyle(random(1, 10), random(0, 0xFFFFFF));
    rect.setFillStyle(random(0, 0xFFFFFF), Math.random( ));

    ell.width  = random(1, 300);
    ell.height = random(1, 300);
    ell.setStrokeStyle(random(1, 10), random(0, 0xFFFFFF));
    ell.setFillStyle(random(0, 0xFFFFFF), Math.random( ));

    poly.setPoints([random(1, 300), random(1, 300), random(1, 300)],
              [random(1, 300), random(1, 300), random(1, 300)]);
    poly.setStrokeStyle(random(1, 10), random(0, 0xFFFFFF));
    poly.setFillStyle(random(0, 0xFFFFFF), Math.random( ));

    star.setStar(random(3, 15), random(10, 20), random(30, 80));
    star.setStrokeStyle(random(1, 10), random(0, 0xFFFFFF));
    star.setFillStyle(random(0, 0xFFFFFF), Math.random( ));
  }

  // Returns a number in the range of minVal to maxVal, inclusive
  public function random (minVal:int, maxVal:int):int {
    return minVal + Math.floor(Math.random( ) * (maxVal + 1 - minVal));
  }
 }
}
```

Figure 25-6 shows one set of random shapes produced by the *ShapeRandomizer* class.

Figure 25-6. Shapes produced by ShapeRandomizer

From Lines to Pixels

In this chapter, we learned how to create and manipulate vector-based graphical content. In the next chapter, we'll see how to create and manipulate *bitmap-based* graphical content.

 For further vector graphics study, see the *Graphics* class documentation in Adobe's ActionScript Language Reference.

CHAPTER 26
Bitmap Programming

In programming terms, a *bitmap image* is an image stored in bitmap data format. The bitmap data format treats an image as a rectangular grid of pixels, where each pixel in the grid is assigned a number that indicates its color. For example, in bitmap data format, an image with a width and height of 16 pixels would be stored as a list of 256 numbers, each indicating a specific color. Figure 26-1 demonstrates, showing a 16×16-pixel image magnified to reveal its individual pixels. The right side of the figure shows the grid position and color values of three sample pixels in the image. Notice that positions on the grid are zero-based, so the top-left pixel's coordinate is (0, 0), while the bottom-right pixel's coordinate is (15, 15).

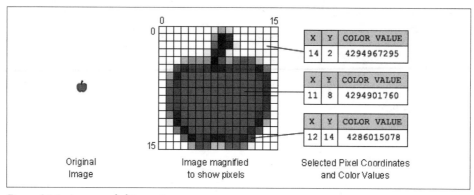

Figure 26-1. An example bitmap image

In this chapter, we'll explore a sampling of common bitmap programming techniques. Bear in mind, however, that exhaustive coverage of bitmap programming in ActionScript could well fill a book of its own. For further study, consult Adobe's ActionScript Language Reference.

The BitmapData and Bitmap Classes

In ActionScript, the *BitmapData* class represents bitmap-formatted image data such as that in Figure 26-1. Each *BitmapData* instance contains a list of pixel color values, and instance variables width and height that governs how those pixels are arranged on screen. Using the *BitmapData* class, we can create the data for a completely new bitmap image, or examine and modify the data of any existing bitmap image, including externally loaded bitmap images.

The *BitmapData* class provides a wide range of tools for setting and retrieving the color value of a given pixel or group of pixels, and for producing common graphic effects such as blur or drop shadow. As we'll see later, the *BitmapData* class can even be used to create animated effects and to perform bitmap-based collision detection. To use most of *BitmapData*'s tools, we must understand the format ActionScript uses to describe a pixel's color value, discussed in the next section.

As the name suggests, a *BitmapData* object is not, itself, an image; it is only the bitmap-formatted data representing an image. To create an actual on-screen image based on the information in a *BitmapData* object, we must pair that object with an instance of the *Bitmap* class, as described in the later section "Creating a New Bitmap Image." The *Bitmap* class is a *DisplayObject* descendant that wraps a *BitmapData* object for on-screen display.

 When working with a bitmap image, we use the *Bitmap* class to manipulate the image as a display object, and the *BitmapData* class to manipulate the image's underlying pixel data.

By separating image display (*Bitmap*) from data storage (*BitmapData*), Action-Script's bitmap architecture lets many different *Bitmap* objects simultaneously display the *same BitmapData* object, each with its own display characteristics (i.e., different scale, rotation, cropping, filters, transforms, and transparency).

Before we learn how to create a new bitmap image, let's take a quick look at how colors are represented in ActionScript.

Pixel Color Values

In ActionScript, the color values of pixels in bitmaps are stored in 32-bit unsigned integers, providing a vast range of 4,294,967,296 possible color values. Each individual color value in a *BitmapData* object is conceptually made up of four separate numbers, representing four different color components—Alpha (i.e., transparency), Red, Green, and Blue. These four components are known as color *channels*. The amount of each channel in a given color ranges from 0 to 255. Accordingly, in binary, each channel occupies 8 of the 32 bits in the color value, as follows: Alpha, bits 24–31 (the most significant byte); Red, bits 16–23; Green, bits 8–15; and Blue, bits 0–7. The higher the value of Red, Green, or Blue, the more each color contributes to the final color. If all three RGB channels are equal, the result is a shade of gray; if they are all 0, the result is black; if they are all 255, the result is white. This 32-bit color format allows for a possible 16,777,216 colors, each with a separate Alpha level between 0 (transparent) and 255 (opaque).

For example, pure red is described by the following channel values:

```
Alpha: 255, Red: 255, Green: 0, Blue: 0
```

Those values correspond to the following bit settings in a 32-bit unsigned integer color value (shown with spaces separating the four bytes):

```
11111111 11111111 00000000 00000000
```

In decimal, the preceding integer value reads:

```
4294901760
```

Of course, when presented as a single decimal number, the different channels in a color value are not obvious. Hence, for the sake of legibility, pixel color values are typically written in the hexadecimal form 0xAARRGGBB, where AA, RR, GG, and BB are each two-digit hex numbers representing Alpha, Red, Green and Blue. For example, the preceding pure red color value (A:255, R:255, G:0, B:0) is written in hexadecimal as:

```
0xFFFF0000   // Much easier to read!
```

For comparison, Figure 26-2 shows the image in Figure 26-1, but this time with the color values of the three sample pixels broken down into their respective color channels, written in hexadecimal.

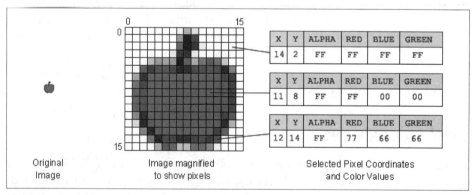

Figure 26-2. A bitmap image with hexadecimal color values

For a primer on hexadecimal numbers, see *http://www. moock.org/ asdg/technotes/basePrimer.*

To retrieve the value of a single channel from a 32-bit color value, we can use the right shift and bitwise AND operators together, as follows:

```
var colorValue:uint  = 0xFFFFCC99; // A sample color
var alpha:uint = (colorValue >> 24) & 0xFF; // Isolate the Alpha channel
var red:uint   = (colorValue >> 16) & 0xFF; // Isolate the Red channel
var green:uint = (colorValue >> 8) & 0xFF;  // Isolate the Green channel
var blue:uint  = colorValue & 0xFF;         // Isolate the Blue channel

trace(alpha, red, green, blue);  // Displays: 255 255 204 153
```

 For a primer on bitwise operations, see the online tech note at *http:// www.moock.org/asdg/technotes/bitwise.*

While numbers cannot be modified directly, we can achieve the effect of setting the value of a single channel in an existing 32-bit color value through binary combinations. First, we clear the desired channel's byte in the existing color value; then we combine the resulting number with a new color channel value. The following code shows the technique; it produces a number that is the effective result of inserting the hex value AA into an existing color value:

```
var colorValue:uint   = 0xFFFFCC99; // A sample color
// Clear the red byte in the original color value, and assign
// the result back to colorValue
colorValue &= 0xFF00FFFF;
// Combine colorValue with the new red value
colorValue |= (0xAA<<16);
trace(colorValue.toString(16));  // Displays: ffaacc99
```

Take a closer look at the last line of the code:

```
trace(colorValue.toString(16));  // Displays: ffaacc99
```

That code generates a hexadecimal string for a numeric color value by invoking the *toString()* method on the value with the radix parameter set to 16. The hexadecimal string is easier to read than its numeric decimal equivalent. However, as a means of making a color value human-readable, *toString()* is imperfect because it omits all leading zeros. For example, given the number:

```
var n:uint = 0x0000CC99;
```

the expression, n.toString(16) returns cc99, omitting the four leading zeros. To improve the legibility of color values during debugging, we can write custom code such as that shown in Example 26-1. Example 26-1 shows a class for working with color values, *Pixel*. The *Pixel* class wraps binary operations into convenient methods such as *setRed()* and *setAlpha()*. Its methods can retrieve and set the individual color channels in a color value, and generate strings describing color values in various human-readable formats. The *Pixel* class is available online at *http://www.moock.org/ eas3/examples.*

Example 26-1. The Pixel class

```
package {
  public class Pixel {
    private var value:uint;  // The pixel's color value

    public function Pixel (n1:uint, n2:int=0, n3:int=0, n4:int=0) {
      if (arguments.length == 1) {
        value = n1;
      } else {
        value = n1<<24 | n2<<16 | n3<<8 | n4;
      }
    }

    public function setAlpha (n:int):void {
      if (n < 0 || n > 255) {
        throw new RangeError("Supplied value must be in the range 0-255.");
      }
      value &= (0x00FFFFFF);
      value |= (n<<24);
    }

    public function setRed (n:int):void {
      if (n < 0 || n > 255) {
        throw new RangeError("Supplied value must be in the range 0-255.");
      }
      value &= (0xFF00FFFF);
      value |= (n<<16);
    }

    public function setGreen (n:int):void {
      if (n < 0 || n > 255) {
        throw new RangeError("Supplied value must be in the range 0-255.");
      }
      value &= (0xFFFF00FF);
      value |= (n<<8);
    }

    public function setBlue (n:int):void {
      if (n < 0 || n > 255) {
        throw new RangeError("Supplied value must be in the range 0-255.");
      }
      value &= (0xFFFFFF00);
      value |= (n);
    }

    public function getAlpha ():int {
      return (value >> 24) & 0xFF;
    }
```

Example 26-1. The Pixel class (continued)

```
    public function getRed ():int {
      return (value >> 16) & 0xFF;
    }

    public function getGreen ():int {
      return (value >> 8) & 0xFF;
    }

    public function getBlue ():int {
      return value & 0xFF;
    }

    public function toString ():String {
      return toStringARGB();
    }

    public function toStringARGB (radix:int = 16):String {
      var s:String =
          "A:" + ((value >> 24)&0xFF).toString(radix).toUpperCase()
        + " R:" + ((value >> 16)&0xFF).toString(radix).toUpperCase()
        + " G:" + ((value >> 8)&0xFF).toString(radix).toUpperCase()
        + " B:" + (value&0xFF).toString(radix).toUpperCase();

      return s;
    }

    public function toStringAlpha (radix:int = 16):String {
      return ((value >> 24)&0xFF).toString(radix).toUpperCase();
    }

    public function toStringRed (radix:int = 16):String {
      return ((value >> 16)&0xFF).toString(radix).toUpperCase();
    }

    public function toStringGreen (radix:int = 16):String {
      return ((value >> 8)&0xFF).toString(radix).toUpperCase();
    }

    public function toStringBlue (radix:int = 16):String {
      return (value&0xFF).toString(radix).toUpperCase();
    }
  }
}

// Usage examples:
var p:Pixel = new Pixel(0xFFFFCC99);  // A sample color
p.setRed(0xAA);
trace(p);                   // Displays: A:FF R:AA G:CC B:99
trace(p.getRed());          // Displays: 170
trace(p.toStringRed());    // Displays: AA

var p2:Pixel = new Pixel(0x33,0x66,0x99,0xCC);
trace(p2.toStringARGB(10)); // Displays: A:51 R:102 G:153 B:204
```

Creating a New Bitmap Image

To create and display a brand new bitmap image, follow these steps:

1. Create a *BitmapData* object.
2. Set the *BitmapData* object's pixel colors as desired.
3. Associate the *BitmapData* object with a *Bitmap* object.
4. Add the *Bitmap* object to the display list.

Let's try it out!

Our goal is to display a 10×10 blue square centered on a 20×20 green background. First, we'll create the *BitmapData* object using the following general code:

```
new BitmapData(width, height, transparent, fillColor)
```

The *width* and *height* parameters indicate the pixel dimensions of the image, which have a maximum value of 2880. The image dimensions cannot be changed after the *BitmapData* object is created. The *transparent* parameter indicates whether the image should support per-pixel transparency (i.e., whether the Alpha channel of each pixel's color value can be set to anything less than 255). If the image does not need to be transparent, then *transparent* should be set to false because the Flash runtime renders opaque bitmaps faster than transparent ones. Finally, the *fillColor* parameter indicates the color value that is initially assigned to all pixels in the image.

The image we want to create is 20×20 pixels square, does not require transparency, and has a green background. Hence, to create our *BitmapData* object, we use the following code:

```
// 0xFF00FF00 means Alpha: 255, Red: 0, Green: 255, Blue: 0
var imgData:BitmapData = new BitmapData(20, 20, false, 0xFF00FF00);
```

Next, we need to set the color of a 10×10 square region of pixels to blue. The *BitmapData* class offers a variety of tools for setting pixel colors: *setPixel()*, *setPixel32()*, *setPixels()*, *fillRect()*, and *floodFill()*. The *fillRect()* method suits our purpose perfectly; it sets a specified rectangular region of pixels to a specified color. Our specified *Rectangle* is 10 pixels wide and high, with a top-left corner coordinate of (5, 5). As a result, all the pixels in the bitmap from (5, 5) to (14, 14), inclusive, will be colored blue.

```
imgData.fillRect(new Rectangle(5, 5, 10, 10), 0xFF0000FF);
```

We've now finished setting the color of pixels in our *BitmapData* object and are ready to associate it with a *Bitmap* object for on-screen display. We can associate a *BitmapData* object with a *Bitmap* object in two ways: by passing it to the *Bitmap* constructor or by assigning it to the instance variable bitmapData of an existing *Bitmap* object. The following code shows both approaches:

```
// Pass the BitmapData object to the Bitmap constructor
var bmp:Bitmap = new Bitmap(imgData);
```

```
// Assign the BitmapData object to bitmapData
var bmp:Bitmap = new Bitmap( );
bmp.bitmapData = imgData;
```

Once the *BitmapData* object is associated with a *Bitmap* object, adding that *Bitmap* object to the display list displays the image described by the *BitmapData* object.:// Display the image on screen

```
addChild(bmp);
```

In summary, here is the code required to create and display a new bitmap image containing a 10×10 blue square centered on a 20×20 green background:

```
var imgData:BitmapData = new BitmapData(20, 20, false, 0xFF00FF00);
imgData.fillRect(new Rectangle(5, 5, 10, 10), 0xFF0000FF);
var bmp:Bitmap = new Bitmap(imgData);
addChild(bmp);
```

Figure 26-3 shows the result of the preceding code.

Figure 26-3. A bitmap image from scratch

As mentioned earlier, many different *Bitmap* objects can simultaneously display representations of the same *BitmapData* object. For example, the following code uses our imgData object as the source for two different *Bitmap* objects. The first *Bitmap* object presents the imgData without alteration, while the second *Bitmap* object is rotated and scaled.

```
var imgData:BitmapData = new BitmapData(20, 20, false, 0xFF00FF00);
imgData.fillRect(new Rectangle(5, 5, 10, 10), 0xFF0000FF);

var bmp1:Bitmap = new Bitmap(imgData);
addChild(bmp1);

var bmp2:Bitmap = new Bitmap(imgData);
bmp2.rotation = 45;
bmp2.x = 50;
bmp2.scaleX = 2;   // 200%
bmp2.scaleY = 2;   // 200%
addChild(bmp2);
```

Figure 26-4 shows the result.

Figure 26-4. Two bitmaps with the same BitmapData source

Note that transformations applied to a *Bitmap* object do not affect its associated *BitmapData* object. The actual pixel data stored in a *BitmapData* object cannot directly be transformed (i.e., rotated, scaled, or moved). It is, however, possible to transform pixel data in the process of copying it to a new *BitmapData* object. For details, see the section "Copying Graphics to a BitmapData Object," later in this chapter.

Loading an External Bitmap Image

In the previous section, we learned how to create a brand new bitmap. Now let's try loading an existing bitmap image from disk. The types of bitmap images that can be loaded and displayed are: JPEG, GIF, and PNG.

 Externally loaded JPEG images can be in progressive or nonprogressive format. Animated GIF images do not animate; only their first frame is displayed.

External bitmaps can be loaded in two ways: at runtime, using the *Loader* class, or at compile time, using the [Embed] metadata tag. For reference, Examples 26-2 and 26-3 present sample code showing both techniques; for much deeper coverage, see Chapter 28.

Example 26-2 shows how to load a bitmap named *photo.jpg* at runtime. The code assumes that both the bitmap file and the *.swf* file loading the bitmap file are in the same directory.

Example 26-2. Loading a bitmap at runtime

```
package {
  import flash.display.*;
  import flash.events.*;
  import flash.net.*;

  // A simple example showing how to load an image
  public class BitmapLoader extends Sprite {
    private var loader:Loader;  // The bitmap loader

    public function BitmapLoader() {
      // Create the loader
      loader = new Loader();

      // Register to be notified when the bitmap has been loaded
      // and initialized
      loader.contentLoaderInfo.addEventListener(Event.INIT,
                                                initListener);

      // Load the bitmap
      loader.load(new URLRequest("photo.jpg"));
    }
```

Example 26-2. Loading a bitmap at runtime (continued)

```
    // Triggered when the bitmap has been loaded and initialized
    private function initListener (e:Event):void {
      // Add the loaded bitmap to display list
      addChild(loader.content);

      // Retrieve the color value for
      // the top-left pixel in the loaded bitmap
      trace(Bitmap(loader.content).bitmapData.getPixel(0, 0));
    }
  }
}
```

Notice that once a bitmap has loaded, its pixel data can be accessed via the *Bitmap* class's instance variable bitmapData, as follows (note the cast to *Bitmap*, which is required when compiling in strict mode; see Chapter 8):

```
    Bitmap(loader.content).bitmapData
```

Example 26-3 shows how to embed a bitmap named *photo.jpg* at compile time. The code assumes that both the class file embedding the bitmap and the bitmap file are in the same directory.

> The [Embed] metadata tag shown in Example 26-3 is supported by Flex Builder 2 and the standalone compiler *mxmlc*, but not Flash CS3. It requires the use of the Flex compiler-support library, *flex.swc*. For full details, see the section "Embedding Display Assets at CompileTime" in Chapter 28.

Example 26-3. Embedding a bitmap at compile time

```
package {
  import flash.display.*;
  import flash.events.*;
  import mx.core.BitmapAsset;

  public class BitmapEmbedder extends Sprite {
    // Embed the bitmap
    [Embed(source="photo.jpg")]
    private var Photo:Class;

    public function BitmapEmbedder () {
      // Create an instance of the embedded bitmap
      var photo:BitmapAsset = new Photo( );
      addChild(photo);
      trace(photo.bitmapData.getPixel(0, 0));
    }
  }
}
```

As in Example 26-2, the pixel data for the embedded bitmap can be accessed via `bitmapData`, as follows (this time, no cast is required because photo's datatype is a descendent of *Bitmap*):

```
photo.bitmapData
```

Examining a Bitmap

Having learned how to create and load a new bitmap, we can now explore the tools for examining the pixels of an existing bitmap.

To retrieve the complete 32-bit integer color value of any pixel in a bitmap, we use the *BitmapData* class's instance method *getPixel32()*, which takes the following form:

```
theBitmapDataObject.getPixel32(x, y)
```

where *theBitmapDataObject* is the *BitmapData* instance from which the pixel color value will be retrieved, and *x* and *y* are the horizontal and vertical location of the pixel whose color value will be retrieved. For example, the following code creates a blue square bitmap, then displays the color value of its top-left pixel (i.e., the pixel at coordinates (0, 0)):

```
var imgData:BitmapData = new BitmapData(20, 20, false, 0xFF0000FF);
trace(imgData.getPixel32(0, 0));  // Displays: 4278190335
```

The pixel's color value is a large number (4278190335) because the alpha channel's value is 255, so the bits in the color value's most significant byte are all 1's:

```
11111111 00000000 00000000 11111111
```

In decimal format, the individual channels in a color value returned by *getPixel32()* are indecipherable. Hence, for debugging purposes, code such as that shown in the earlier *Pixel* class must be used to extract human-readable channel values from the number returned by *getPixel32()*:

```
// Displays: A:FF R:0 G:0 B:FF
trace(new Pixel(imgData.getPixel32(0, 0)));
```

Note that the Alpha channel value for pixels in nontransparent bitmaps is always 255, even when a different Alpha value is assigned. For example, the following code creates a blue square, nontransparent bitmap, and sets the Alpha channel of all of its pixels to 0x33. Because the bitmap is nontransparent, the Alpha channel assignment is ignored:

```
var imgData:BitmapData = new BitmapData(20, 20, false, 0x330000FF);
trace(imgData.getPixel32(0, 0));  // Displays: 4278190335
                                  // (Alpha is 0xFF, not 0x33)
```

The alpha value of pixels can be set in transparent bitmaps only (i.e., bitmaps created with the value true passed to the transparent parameter of the *BitmapData* constructor). For example, the following code again creates a blue square bitmap but this time enables transparency. Because the bitmap is transparent, the assignment of 0x33 to the Alpha channel succeeds.

```
var imgData:BitmapData = new BitmapData(20, 20, true, 0x330000FF);
trace(imgData.getPixel32(0, 0));  // Displays: 855638271
                                  // (Alpha is 0x33)
```

getPixel32() Versus getPixel( )

To provide a convenient way to retrieve a pixel's color value without its Alpha channel information, ActionScript offers the *BitmapData* class's instance method *getPixel()*. The *getPixel()* method takes the exact same form as *getPixel32()* and also returns 32-bit integer color value. However, unlike *getPixel32()*, *getPixel()* sets the Alpha channel bits in the returned integer to 0. That is, a call to *getPixel()* produces the exact same result as the expression:

```
theBitmapDataObject.getPixel32( ) & 0x00FFFFFF
```

The actual Alpha channel of the pixel in the bitmap is unaffected; only the number returned is altered. For example, recall the blue square bitmap from the preceding section:

```
var imgData:BitmapData = new BitmapData(20, 20, false, 0xFF0000FF);
```

When we retrieve the color value of the top-left pixel in that bitmap using *getPixel()*, we receive the value 255 because the bits in the Alpha channel have been set to 0 (contrast 255 with 4278190335, the earlier value returned by *getPixel32()*):

```
trace(imgData.getPixel(0, 0));  // Displays: 255
```

The *getPixel()* method should be used only to retrieve the combined value of the Red, Green, and Blue channels as a single number. When retrieving a color value in order to process one or more channels individually, use *getPixel32()*. The *getPixel32()* method is the appropriate method to use in the majority of color-processing situations.

 The *getPixel32()* method returns a 32-bit integer containing the entire 4-channel color value for a given pixel. The *getPixel()* method returns a 32-bit integer containing the Red, Green, and Blue channel values for a given pixel, and an Alpha channel of 0.

Transparency's Effect on Color-Value Retrieval

Due to the Flash runtime's internal rendering architecture, pixel color values in transparent images cannot be retrieved reliably using *getPixel32()*, *getPixel()*, or any other means. For the sake of rendering performance, when the Flash runtime stores a pixel color value in a *BitmapData* object, it converts that value to an internal format known as a *premultiplied color value*. A premultiplied color value combines a color's Alpha channel value with its Red, Green, and Blue channels. For example, if the original color's Alpha channel is 50% of 255, then the premultiplied color value stores

50% of 255 for the Alpha channel, and 50% of the original Red value, 50% of the original Green value, and 50% of the original Blue value. As a result, the original values assigned to the Red, Green, and Blue channels are lost. When pixel color values are retrieved from a transparent image, ActionScript automatically converts them from premultiplied format to the standard (*unmultiplied*) ARGB format we've used throughout this chapter, resulting in a loss of precision. In many cases, the converted, unmultiplied value does not exactly match the original color value assigned to the pixel. For example, the following code creates a new *BitmapData* object in which every pixel is pure white, and fully transparent (i.e., the alpha channel is 0):

```
var imgData:BitmapData = new BitmapData(20, 20, true, 0x00FFFFFF);
```

When we retrieve the color value of any pixel from the preceding bitmap, the result is 0 (i.e., all four channels have the value 0):

```
trace(imgData.getPixel32(0, 0)); // Displays: 0
```

The original values of 255 for the Red, Green, and Blue channels, have been lost.

Hence, programs wishing to store, and then later retrieve, transparent pixel color values without data loss should do so by storing those values in a *ByteArray*. As a general rule, transparent pixel color values should be considered irretrievable once written to a bitmap:

By contrast, nontransparent pixel color values are safely retrievable, without risk of data loss:

```
// Retrieve a pixel from a nontransparent image
var imgData:BitmapData = new BitmapData(20, 20, false, 0xFFFFFFFF);
trace(imgData.getPixel32(0, 0)); // Displays: 4294967295
                                 // (original data was preserved)
```

As the following code shows, the color value of any pixel whose Alpha channel is set to 255 is preserved across assignment and retrieval operations, even if the pixel is stored in a transparent bitmap:

```
// Retrieve a pixel with Alpha set to 255, from a transparent image
var imgData:BitmapData = new BitmapData(20, 20, true, 0xFFFFFFFF);
trace(imgData.getPixel32(0, 0)); // Displays: 4294967295
                                 // (original data was preserved)
```

ColorPicker: A getPixel32( ) Example

Now that we understand how to retrieve a pixel's color value, let's apply our knowledge to a real-world situation. Suppose we're building an online application for creating party invitations. Users of the application select a photo to place on the front of the invitation and choose a matching color for the text on the invitation. To allow the user to experiment with different colors, the application provides a special form of color picker; when the user moves the mouse over the chosen image, the color of the text on the invitation automatically changes to match the color of the pixel currently under the mouse pointer. Example 26-4 shows the code for the color picker, with an example image, *sunset.jpg*. Study the comments to see how the color value under the mouse pointer is retrieved.

Example 26-4. An image-based color picker

```
package {
  import flash.display.*;
  import flash.events.*;
  import flash.text.*;
  import flash.net.*;

  // Sets the color of a TextField to match the color of a selected
  // pixel in an image.
  public class ColorPicker extends Sprite {
    private var img:Bitmap;          // The Bitmap object
    private var imgContainer:Sprite; // Container for the Bitmap object
    private var t:TextField;         // The TextField that will be colored

    // Constructor method
    public function ColorPicker( ) {
      // Create the TextField and add it to
      // the ColorPicker's display hierarchy
      t =  new TextField( );
      t.text = "Please come to my party...";
      t.autoSize = TextFieldAutoSize.LEFT;
      addChild(t);

      // Load the image
      var loader:Loader = new Loader( );
      loader.contentLoaderInfo.addEventListener(Event.INIT,
                                                initListener);
      loader.load(new URLRequest("sunset.jpg"));
    }

    // Invoked when the image has initialized
    private function initListener (e:Event):void {
      // Obtain a reference to the loaded Bitmap object
      img = e.target.content;
      // Put the loaded bitmap in a Sprite so we can detect mouse
      // interaction with it
      imgContainer = new Sprite( );
      imgContainer.addChild(img);
      // Add the Sprite to the ColorPicker's display hierarchy
      addChild(imgContainer);
      imgContainer.y = 30;
      // Start listening for mouse movement
      imgContainer.addEventListener(MouseEvent.MOUSE_MOVE,
                                    mouseMoveListener);
    }
```

Example 26-4. An image-based color picker (continued)

```
    // Invoked when the mouse moves over the Sprite containing the image
    private function mouseMoveListener (e:MouseEvent):void {
      // Set the text color to the pixel currently under the mouse
      t.textColor = img.bitmapData.getPixel32(e.localX, e.localY);
    }
  }
}
```

Retrieving the Color of a Region of Pixels

The *BitmapData* class's instance methods *getPixel32()* and *getPixel()* are used to retrieve the color value of an individual pixel. By contrast, the *BitmapData* class's instance method *getPixels()* method is used to retrieve the color values of an entire rectangular region of pixels. The *getPixels()* method might be used in any of the following scenarios:

- When passing a region of a bitmap between sections of a program
- When using a custom algorithm to process a section of a bitmap
- When sending part or all of a bitmap to a server in raw binary format

The *getPixels()* method takes the following general form:

```
theBitmapDataObject.getPixels(rect)
```

where *theBitmapDataObject* is the *BitmapData* object whose pixel color values will be returned, and *rect* is a *flash.geom.Rectangle* object describing the region of pixels to retrieve. The *getPixels()* method returns a *ByteArray* of 32-bit integer color values. The *ByteArray* is a flat list of color values for the pixels in the specified rectangular region, assembled from left to right, and top to bottom. For example, consider the following diagram of a 4×4 bitmap, whose pixels, for the sake of discussion, are labeled A through P:

```
A B C D
E F G H
I J K L
M N O P
```

Recalling that the upper-left corner pixel in a bitmap resides at coordinate (0,0), if we use *getPixels()* to retrieve the rectangular region of pixels from (2, 1) through (3, 3), then the returned *ByteArray* will contain the following pixels in the following order:

```
G, H, K, L, O, P
```

Notice that the *ByteArray* is a flat, one-dimensional list, and does not include any information about the dimensions or position of the rectangular region from which the pixels originated. Therefore, to reconstitute a bitmap from pixels in a *ByteArray* in the same rectangular order as they originated, we must have independent access to the width, height, and position of the original rectangle. Information about the original rectangle might be assigned to a variable or even added to the *ByteArray* itself.

To practice using *getPixels()*, let's copy a rectangular region from one bitmap to another. First, we make the two *BitmapData* objects. The first is a 20×20 blue square, and the second is a 30×30 green square:

```
var blueSquare:BitmapData = new BitmapData(20, 20, false, 0xFF0000FF);
var greenSquare:BitmapData = new BitmapData(30, 30, false, 0xFF00FF00);
```

Next, we define the rectangular region of pixels we want to retrieve from the green square. The rectangle is positioned at coordinate (5,5) and is 10 pixels wide and high.

```
var rectRegion:Rectangle = new Rectangle(5, 5, 10, 10);
```

Now we retrieve the green pixels:

```
var greenPixels:ByteArray = greenSquare.getPixels(rectRegion);
```

To write the green pixels into the blue square, we'll use the *BitmapData* class's instance method *setPixels()* method. However, before we call *setPixels()*, we must set the *ByteArray*'s file pointer to 0, so that *setPixels()* starts reading pixel color values from the beginning of the list:

```
greenPixels.position = 0;
```

Now we can read the pixels from the greenPixels *ByteArray* into the blueSquare *BitmapData* object:

```
blueSquare.setPixels(rectRegion, greenPixels);
```

To verify that everything worked out as expected, we display the two bitmaps on screen:

```
var blueBmp:Bitmap = new Bitmap(blueSquare);
var greenBmp:Bitmap = new Bitmap(greenSquare);
addChild(blueBmp);
addChild(greenBmp);
greenBmp.x = 40;
```

Figure 26-5 shows the results.

Figure 26-5. Pixels copied from a ByteArray

When copying pixels between two bitmaps, if the rectangle being copied is the same size in the source and the destination (as it was in the previous example), we can use the *BitmapData* class's convenient instance method *copyPixels()* rather than the combination of *getPixels()* and *setPixels()*. Other built-in *BitmapData* instance methods that offer convenient access to typical copy operations include *copyChannel()*, *clone()*, *merge()*, and *draw()*. For details, see the section "Copying Graphics to a BitmapData Object" later in this chapter.

Other Examination Tools

In this section we learned how to examine the pixels of a *BitmapData* object using *getPixel32()*, *getPixel()*, and *getPixels()*. The *BitmapData* class also offers several other, more specialized, tools for examining pixels:

compare()
  Checks the difference between pixels in two bitmap images

getColorBoundsRect()
  Determines which area of a bitmap image contains a given color

hitTest()
  Detects whether the pixels in a bitmap overlap a given point, rectangle, or other bitmap image

For complete details on the preceding methods, see the *BitmapData* class in Adobe's ActionScript Language Reference.

Modifying a Bitmap

The basic tools for assigning new colors to the pixels of an existing bitmap exactly mirror those for examining a bitmap. They are: *setPixel32()*, *setPixel()*, and *setPixels()*. The *setPixel32()* method assigns a new 4-channel color value to a pixel as a 32-bit unsigned integer. It takes the following form:

```
thatBitmapDataObject.setPixel32(x, y, color)
```

where *theBitmapDataObject* is the *BitmapData* instance containing the pixel whose color value will be changed, *x* and *y* are the horizontal and vertical location of that pixel, and *color* is the new color value to assign to the pixel. For example, the following code creates a blue, square bitmap, and then sets the color value of its top-left pixel to white:

```
var imgData:BitmapData = new BitmapData(20, 20, false, 0xFF0000FF);
imgData.setPixel32(0, 0, 0xFFFFFFFF);
```

By contrast, the *setPixel()* method, which takes the same general form as *setPixel32()*, sets only the Red, Green, and Blue channels of a pixel's color value, leaving the pixel's original Alpha channel unaltered. For example, the following code creates a partially transparent blue, square bitmap, and then sets the color value of its top-left pixel to white. Because *setPixel()* is used instead of *setPixel32()*, the top left pixel retains its original Alpha channel value (0x66):

```
var imgData:BitmapData = new BitmapData(20, 20, true, 0x660000FF);
imgData.setPixel(0, 0, 0xFFFFFF);
```

After the *setPixel()* operation completes, the top-left pixel's color value is 0x66FFFFFF.

Any Alpha channel value specified in the number passed to *setPixel()* is ignored. For example, in the following code, we assign a pixel value using a number that specifies an Alpha channel of CC; nevertheless, after the operation, the top-left pixel's color value is still 0x66FFFFFF:

```
imgData.setPixel(0, 0, 0xCCFFFFFF);
```

Improve Performance with BitmapData.lock( )

By default, *Bitmap* instances that reference a given *BitmapData* object are notified every time *setPixel32()* or *setPixel()* is called on that object. When *setPixel32()* or *setPixel()* are used in rapid succession within the same frame cycle—such as when setting the color of every pixel in a bitmap—these notifications can reduce performance. To improve performance, we can use the *BitmapData* class's instance method *lock()*.

Calling *lock()* on a *BitmapData* object forces ActionScript to *not* notify dependent *Bitmap* objects when executing *setPixel32()* or *setPixel()*. Hence, before using *setPixel32()* or *setPixel()* in rapid succession, always call *lock()*. After calling *lock()*, assign all desired pixel color values; then call the *BitmapData()* class's instance method *unlock()*. Calling *unlock()* instructs ActionScript to notify all dependent *Bitmap* objects as necessary. Example 26-5 demonstrates the approach. The example uses a loop to assign a random color to every pixel in a 500 × 500 *BitmapData* object. Notice the call to *lock()* before the loop and *unlock()* after the loop, shown in bold.

Example 26-5. Using BitmapData.lock() to improve performance

```
// Create the bitmap
var imgData:BitmapData = new BitmapData(500, 500, true, 0x00000000);
var bmp:Bitmap = new Bitmap(imgData);

// Invoke lock()
imgData.lock();

// Set pixel color-values
var color:uint;
for (var i:int = 0; i < imgData.height ; i++) {
  for (var j:int = 0; j < imgData.width; j++) {
    color = Math.floor(Math.random()*0xFFFFFFFF);
    imgData.setPixel32(j, i, color);
  }
}

// Invoke unlock()
imgData.unlock();
```

In tests, when running Example 26-5 in the release version of Flash Player on a computer with a Pentium 4 2.6-GHz processor, a single iteration of the loop takes approximately 100 ms. Without *lock()*, a single iteration takes approximately 125 ms. That is, code runs approximately 20% faster when *lock()* is used.

When measuring Flash runtime performance, always be sure to test in the release version, not in the debug version. The release version is often more than two times faster than the debug version.

ScribbleAS3: A setPixel32( ) Example

Setting the color of a pixel in a bitmap has many practical applications—from custom effects, to photo correction, to dynamic interface generation. Let's take a look at just one practical application for *setPixel32()*: a simple drawing program. Example 26-6 presents an ActionScript 3.0 adaptation of the venerable classic, Scribble. The code creates an empty bitmap onto which the user draws with the mouse. Whenever the mouse moves with the primary mouse button depressed, the code draws a black pixel on the empty bitmap.

Example 26-6. A very simple drawing program, ScribbleAS3

```
package {
  import flash.display.*;
  import flash.events.*;
  import flash.ui.*;
  import flash.geom.*;

  // A basic drawing application. Draws a single dot on a
  // BitmapData object every time the MouseEvent.MOUSE_MOVE event
  // occurs while the primary mouse button is depressed.
  public class ScribbleAS3 extends Sprite {
    // The on-screen bitmap
    private var canvas:Bitmap;
    // Contains the bitmap, providing interactivity
    private var canvasContainer:Sprite;
    // Line around the bitmap
    private var border:Shape;
    // Indicates whether the mouse is currently depressed
    private var isDrawing:Boolean = false;

    // Constructor
    public function ScribbleAS3 () {
      createCanvas();
      registerForInputEvents();

      // Prevent the app from resizing
      stage.scaleMode = StageScaleMode.NO_SCALE;
    }

    // Creates the empty bitmap object where drawing will occur
    private function createCanvas (width:int = 200, height:int = 200):void {
      // Define the BitmapData object that will store the pixel
      // data for the user's drawing
      var canvasData:BitmapData = new BitmapData(width, height,
                                            false, 0xFFFFFFFF);
```

Example 26-6. A very simple drawing program, ScribbleAS3 (continued)

```
    // Create a new displayable Bitmap, used to render the
    // canvasData object
    canvas = new Bitmap(canvasData);

    // Create a Sprite to contain the Bitmap. The Bitmap class doesn't
    // support input events; hence, put it in a Sprite so the user
    // interact with it.
    canvasContainer = new Sprite( );
    // Add the canvas bitmap to the canvasContainer Sprite
    canvasContainer.addChild(canvas);

    // Add the canvasContainer Sprite (and the Bitmap it contains) to
    // the this object's display hierarchy
    addChild(canvasContainer);

    // Make a border around the drawing surface.
    border = new Shape( );
    border.graphics.lineStyle(1, 0xFF000000);
    border.graphics.drawRect(0, 0, width, height);
    addChild(border);
  }

  // Registers for the required mouse and keyboard events
  private function registerForInputEvents ( ):void {
    // Register for mouse down and movement events from canvasContainer
    canvasContainer.addEventListener(MouseEvent.MOUSE_DOWN,
                                     mouseDownListener);
    canvasContainer.addEventListener(MouseEvent.MOUSE_MOVE,
                                     mouseMoveListener);

    // Register for mouse up and key events from the Stage (i.e.,
    // globally). Use the Stage because a mouse up event should always
    // exit drawing mode, even if it occurs while the mouse pointer is
    // not over the drawing. Likewise, the spacebar should always clear
    // the drawing, even when canvasContainer isn't focused.
    stage.addEventListener(MouseEvent.MOUSE_UP, mouseUpListener);
    stage.addEventListener(KeyboardEvent.KEY_DOWN, keyDownListener);
  }

  // Sets the color of a specified pixel
  public function drawPoint (x:int, y:int, color:uint = 0xFF000000):void {
    canvas.bitmapData.setPixel32(x, y, color);
  }

  // Responds to MouseEvent.MOUSE_DOWN events
  private function mouseDownListener (e:MouseEvent):void {
    // Set a flag indicating that the primary
    // mouse button is currently down
    isDrawing = true;
    // Draw a dot where the mouse was clicked.
    drawPoint(e.localX, e.localY);
  }
```

Example 26-6. A very simple drawing program, ScribbleAS3 (continued)

```
    // Responds to MouseEvent.MOUSE_MOVE events
    private function mouseMoveListener (e:MouseEvent):void {
      // Draw a dot when the mouse moves over the drawing
      // while the primary mouse button is depressed
      if (isDrawing) {
        // Use localX and localY to obtain pointer position relative to
        // the canvasContainer.
        drawPoint(e.localX, e.localY);

        // Update the screen immediately following the execution of
        // this event listener function
        e.updateAfterEvent();
      }
    }

    // Responds to MouseEvent.MOUSE_UP events
    private function mouseUpListener (e:MouseEvent):void {
      // Set a flag indicating that the primary mouse button is currently up
      isDrawing = false;
    }

    // Responds to KeyboardEvent.KEY_DOWN events
    private function keyDownListener (e:KeyboardEvent):void {
      // Clear the drawing when the spacebar is pressed. To clear the
      // drawing, we set all pixels to the color white.
      if (e.charCode == Keyboard.SPACE) {
        canvas.bitmapData.fillRect(new Rectangle(0, 0,
                                   canvas.width,
                                   canvas.height),
                                   0xFFFFFFFF);
      }
    }
  }
}
```

Assigning the Color of a Region of Pixels

The *setPixel32()* and *setPixel()* methods are used to set the color value of an individual pixel. By contrast, the *BitmapData* class's instance method *setPixels()* method is used to set the color values of an entire rectangular region of pixels.

The *setPixels()* method takes the following general form:

```
    theBitmapDataObject.setPixels(rect, pixelByteArray)
```

where *theBitmapDataObject* is the *BitmapData* object whose pixel color values will be assigned, *rect* is a *flash.geom.Rectangle* object describing the region of pixels to assign, and *pixelByteArray* is a *ByteArray* of unsigned 32-bit integers specifying the color values to be assigned. The *setPixels()* method fills the specified rectangular region from left to right and top to bottom, starting with the color value *pixelByteArray* located at the current file pointer position (i.e., at *pixelByteArray*.position).

For example, consider the following diagram of a 4×4 bitmap, whose pixels, for the sake of discussion, are labeled A through P:

```
A B C D
E F G H
I J K L
M N O P
```

And consider the following diagram of a byte array containing six 32-bit unsigned integer color values, labeled C1 through C6:

```
C1 C2 C3 C4 C5 C6
```

Recalling that the upper-left corner pixel in a bitmap resides at coordinate (0,0), if we use *setPixels()* to fill the rectangular region of pixels from (1, 0) through (3, 1) with the preceding byte array, then the bitmap will subsequently look like this:

```
A C1 C2 C3
E C4 C5 C6
I  J  K  L
M  N  O  P
```

Let's try the same thing in code. First, we'll create a 4×4-pixel red square:

```
var imgData:BitmapData = new BitmapData(4, 4, false, 0xFFFF0000);
```

Now, we'll create a byte array containing six color values, all green. For demonstration purposes, we create the byte array manually, but normally, the byte array would be created programmatically, perhaps by calling *getPixels()* or by running a custom algorithm that outputs color values.

```
var byteArray:ByteArray = new ByteArray();
byteArray.writeUnsignedInt(0xFF00FF00);
byteArray.writeUnsignedInt(0xFF00FF00);
byteArray.writeUnsignedInt(0xFF00FF00);
byteArray.writeUnsignedInt(0xFF00FF00);
byteArray.writeUnsignedInt(0xFF00FF00);
byteArray.writeUnsignedInt(0xFF00FF00);
```

Next, we set the position at which *setPixels()* should start reading color values from the byte array. We want *setPixels()* to begin reading at the beginning of the byte array, so we set the *ByteArray* class's instance variable position to 0:

```
byteArray.position = 0;
```

Finally, we fill the rectangular region in the bitmap with the colors from the byte array:

```
imgData.setPixels(new Rectangle(1,0,3,2), byteArray);
```

 Notice that the position and size of the *Rectangle* passed to *setPixels()* is specified using top-left coordinate and width/height, not top-left coordinate and bottom-right coordinate.

Note that if the *pixelByteArray* ends before the specified rectangular region is filled, ActionScript throws an *EOFError*. For example, if we increase the size of the preceding rectangular region from 3×2 (6 pixels) to 3×3 (9 pixels):

```
imgData.setPixels(new Rectangle(1,0,3,3), byteArray);
```

then the following error occurs:

```
Error: Error #2030: End of file was encountered.
```

The preceding error would also occur if we had forgotten to set the position of the *ByteArray* to zero after creating it (which is a much more common programming mistake than specifying the wrong size of rectangle or providing an insufficient number of color values).

 Before calling *setPixels()*, always remember to set the position of the specified input byte array.

The *setPixels()* method is typically used to generate a bitmap image based on serialized binary data retrieved from an external source such as a server or a local shared object.

Other Manipulation Tools

In this section we learned how to change the pixels of a *BitmapData* object using *setPixel32()*, *setPixel()*, and *setPixels()*. The *BitmapData* class also offers several other, more specialized, tools for manipulating pixels:

fillRect()
> Sets a rectangular region of pixels to a specified color

floodFill()
> For a given pixel, *p*, assigns a specified color to all surrounding pixels that match *p*'s color (similar to the paint bucket tool found in many graphics programs)

scroll()
> Repositions all pixels in a bitmap by a given horizontal and vertical amount

For complete details on the preceding methods, see the *BitmapData* class in Adobe's ActionScript Language Reference.

The *BitmapData* class also supports various filters, effects, and copy operations that can be used to manipulate a bitmap's pixels. For details, see the sections "Copying Graphics to a BitmapData Object" and "Applying Filters and Effects," later in this chapter.

Resizing a Bitmap

When a *Bitmap* object that references a *BitmapData* object is resized using either scaleX and scaleY, or width and height, the bitmap will appear to have changed size on screen, but the underlying *BitmapData* object will not have changed. To truly change the size of the underlying *BitmapData* object, we must resample it using the *BitmapData* class's instance method *draw()* (to *resample* means to change the number of pixels in an image). The general technique is as follows:

1. Retrieve a reference to the original *BitmapData* object.
2. Draw a scaled version of the original *BitmapData* object into a new *BitmapData* object.
3. Associate the original *Bitmap* object with the new, scaled *BitmapData* object.

Example 26-7 demonstrates the preceding steps.

Example 26-7. Resampling a bitmap

```
// Retrieve a temporary reference to the original BitmapData object
var originalBitmapData:BitmapData = originalBitmap.bitmapData;

// Set the amount by which to scale the bitmap
var scaleFactor:Number = .5;

// Calculate the new dimensions of the scaled bitmap
var newWidth:int = originalBitmapData.width * scaleFactor;
var newHeight:int = originalBitmapData.height * scaleFactor;

// Create a new BitmapData object, sized to hold the scaled bitmap
var scaledBitmapData:BitmapData = new BitmapData(newWidth, newHeight,
                                    originalBitmapData.transparent);

// Create a transformation matrix that will scale the bitmap
var scaleMatrix:Matrix = new Matrix();
matrix.scale(scaleFactor, scaleFactor);

// Draw the scaled bitmap into the new BitmapData object
scaledBitmapData.draw(originalBitmapData, matrix);

// Replace the original BitmapData object with the
// new, scaled BitmapData object
originalBitmap.bitmapData = scaledBitmapData;
```

In the next section, we'll learn more about the *draw()* method.

Copying Graphics to a BitmapData Object

Pixel color values can be copied to a *BitmapData* object from one of two sources: another *BitmapData* object, or any *DisplayObject* instance.

To copy any *DisplayObject* instance to a *BitmapData* object, we use the *draw()* method, which copies the color values from a source object to a destination *BitmapData* object. As part of the copying process, pixels written to the *BitmapData* object can be transformed, blended, and smoothed.

To copy color values from another *BitmapData* object, we can use either *draw()* or any of the following *BitmapData*-specific methods:

copyPixels()
> Copies the color values from a rectangular region of pixels in a source *BitmapData* object to a destination *BitmapData* object. The source and destination can be the same, allowing pixels to be copied from one area to another within the same image.

copyChannel()
> Copies a single color channel from a rectangular region of pixels in a source *BitmapData* object to a destination *BitmapData* object. The source and destination can be the same, allowing one channel to be copied into another channel within the same image.

clone()
> Creates a new *BitmapData* object by duplicating an existing *BitmapData* object.

merge()
> Blends the channels of two *BitmapData* objects together, producing a new image in which one image appears superimposed over the other. The source and destination *BitmapData* object can be the same, allowing two channels of the same image to be blended.

In this section, we'll focus on *draw()* and *copyPixels()*. For details on the other copying methods, see the *BitmapData* class in Adobe's ActionScript Language Reference.

The BitmapData Class's Instance Method draw( )

The *draw()* method has the following general form:

```
destinationBitmapData.draw(source, transformMatrix, colorTransform, blendMode,
    clipRect, smoothing)
```

where *destinationBitmapData* is the *BitmapData* object into which the pixels will be drawn, and the parameters to *draw()* are as follows:

source

The *DisplayObject* or *BitmapData* instance that will be drawn into *destinationBitmapData*. This is *draw()*'s only required parameter. Note that if *source* is a *DisplayObject*, its transformations are not included when it is drawn into *destinationBitmapData*. However, *source*'s transformations can be manually included by passing *source*.transform.matrix as *draw()*'s *transformMatrix* parameter and *source*.transform.colorTransform as *draw()*'s *colorTransform* parameter. Alternatively, *destinationBitmapData* can be associated with a *Bitmap* object whose instance variable transform refers to *source*.transform.

transformMatrix

An optional *Matrix* object describing any translation (i.e., change in position), scaling, rotation, and skew that should be applied to the pixels being drawn into *destinationBitmapData*. For information on using a *Matrix* object to perform graphical transformations, see Adobe's ActionScript Language Reference, under the *Matrix* class, and Adobe's Programming ActionScript 3.0, under Flash Player APIs → Working with Geometry → Using Matrix objects. For a general primer on matrix transforms, see *http://windowssdk.msdn.microsoft.com/en-us/library/ms536397.aspx* and *http://www.senocular.com/flash/tutorials/transformmatrix*. Note that it is the developer's responsibility to ensure that *destinationBitmapData* is large enough to accommodate the transformed *source*. The Flash Player 9 API does not provide any way to predict the size of the transformed *source*. Future Flash runtimes may include such a feature, perhaps in the form of a "*generateTransformRect()*" method (designed after the existing *generateFilterRect()* method). To voice your support for such a method, visit *http://www.adobe.com/cfusion/mmform/index.cfm?name=wishform*.

colorTransform

An optional *ColorTransform* object describing any color adjustments that should be applied to the pixels being drawn into *destinationBitmapData*. Color transformations are specified independently for each color channel using either a multiplier (a number by which the existing channel value will be multiplied) or an offset (a number that will be added to the existing channel value), or both. For information on using a *ColorTransform* object to perform graphical transformations, see Adobe's ActionScript Language Reference, under the *ColorTransform* class.

blendMode

An optional constant of the *BlendMode* class, indicating the type of blending that should be applied to the pixels being drawn into *destinationBitmapData*. *Blending* means using equations to combine the color values of the *source* object with the display objects behind it, typically producing a superimposing effect. Supported blend modes include BlendMode.MULTIPLY, BlendMode.SCREEN, BlendMode.HARDLIGHT, and many others that will be familiar to Adobe Photoshop users. ActionScript's blend mode implementation is based on the W3C SVG standard (see *http://www. w3.org/TR/2003/WD-SVG12-20030715/#compositing*), and Jens Gruschel's research, published at *http://www.pegtop.net/delphi/articles/blendmodes*. For a description and image illustrating each available blend mode, see Adobe's ActionScript Language Reference, under the *DisplayObject* class's instance variable `blendMode`.

`clipRect`

An optional *Rectangle* object indicating the rectangular region of `destinationBitmapData` into which *source* will be drawn.

`smoothing`

An optional Boolean indicating whether bitmap smoothing should be applied during the drawing operation. This parameter has an effect only when *source* is a *BitmapData* object *and* the specified `transformMatrix` causes scaling or rotation. In such a case, when `smoothing` is `true`, *source* is rendered into `destinationBitmapData` using ActionScript's bitmap-smoothing algorithm. When `smoothing` is `false`, *source* is rendered into `destinationBitmapData` without any smoothing. An image rendered with smoothing looks less "jagged" or "pixelated" than an image rendered without smoothing. Figure 26-6 demonstrates, showing a small source image (top), scaled up by a factor of 3 using a *Matrix* object, with smoothing applied (left) and smoothing not applied (right).

Rendering a bitmap with smoothing takes longer than rendering it without smoothing. For the fastest possible performance, set `smoothing` to `false`; for the best possible image quality, set `smoothing` to `true`. The `smoothing` parameter affects the single *draw()* operation in progress only; it does not govern whether smoothing is applied to the `destinationBitmapData` in the future.

Figure 26-6. Bitmap smoothing

The *draw()* method is typically used for the following purposes:

- To combine multiple display objects into a single bitmap
- To *rasterize* vector content (i.e., convert vectors to a bitmap) for the sake of performing some effect

Let's look at an example of each case. First, we'll create two vector shapes—a rectangle and an ellipse—and draw them both into a single *BitmapData* object. Example 26-8 shows the code.

Vector shapes need not be on the display list in order to be drawn into a *BitmapData* object. It is perfectly normal to create vector objects off screen simply for the sole purpose of being copied to a bitmap (as shown in Examples 26-8 and 26-9).

Example 26-8. Display objects composited into a bitmap

```
// Make the rectangle
var rect:Shape = new Shape( );
rect.graphics.beginFill(0xFF0000);
rect.graphics.drawRect(0,0,25,50);

// Make the ellipse
var ellipse:Shape = new Shape( );
ellipse.graphics.beginFill(0x0000FF);
ellipse.graphics.drawEllipse(0,0,35,25);

// Make the BitmapData object. It will play the role of
// a drawing canvas, so we assign it to a variable named canvas.
var canvas:BitmapData = new BitmapData(100, 100, false, 0xFFFFFFFF);

// Draw the vector rectangle on to the bitmap
canvas.draw(rect);

// Draw the vector ellipse on to the bitmap. Use a transformation
// matrix to place the ellipse at coordinate (10, 10) within the
// BitmapData object.
var matrix:Matrix = new Matrix( );
matrix.translate(10, 10);
canvas.draw(ellipse, matrix);

// Associate the BitmapData object with a Bitmap object so it can
// be displayed on screen
var bmp:Bitmap = new Bitmap(canvas);
addChild(bmp);
```

Figure 26-7 shows the bitmap image resulting from the preceding code, zoomed for the sake of close examination. Notice that ActionScript antialiases the ellipse, so it blends into the existing rectangle.

Content drawn into a *BitmapData* object is antialiased against the existing background in the bitmap.

Next, we'll use *draw()* to rasterize a *TextField* so that we can apply a pixel-level dissolve effect to it. Example 26-9 shows the code.

Figure 26-7. Display objects composited into a bitmap

Example 26-9. Rasterizing, then dissolving a TextField

```
package {
  import flash.display.*;
  import flash.utils.*;
  import flash.events.*;
  import flash.geom.*;
  import flash.text.*;

  public class DissolveText extends Sprite {
    // Variables used for the dissolve effect
    private var randomSeed:int = Math.floor(Math.random( ) * int.MAX_VALUE);
    private var destPoint:Point = new Point(0, 0);
    private var numberOfPixels:int = 10;
    private var destColor:uint = 0xFF000000;

    // The BitmapData object into which the text will be drawn
    private var bitmapData:BitmapData;
    // A timer used to repeatedly invoke pixelDissolve( )
    private var t:Timer;

    // Constructor
    public function DissolveText ( ) {
      // Create the text
      var txt:TextField = new TextField( );
      txt.text = "Essential ActionScript 3.0";
      txt.autoSize = TextFieldAutoSize.LEFT;
      txt.textColor = 0xFFFFFF;

      // Make the BitmapData object, sized to accommodate the text
      bitmapData - new BitmapData(txt.width, txt.height, false, destColor);
      // Draw the text into the BitmapData object
      bitmapData.draw(txt);

      // Associate the BitmapData object with a Bitmap object so it can
      // be displayed on screen
      var bitmap:Bitmap = new Bitmap(bitmapData);
      addChild(bitmap);

      // Start repeatedly invoking pixelDissolve( )
      t = new Timer(10);
      t.addEventListener(TimerEvent.TIMER, timerListener);
      t.start( );
    }
```

Example 26-9. Rasterizing, then dissolving a TextField (continued)

```
    // Handles TimerEvent.TIMER events
    private function timerListener (e:TimerEvent):void {
      dissolve();
    }

    // Performs the dissolve
    public function dissolve():void {
      // Call pixelDissolve() to dissolve the specified number of pixels,
      // and remember the returned random seed for next time. Using the
      // returned random seed ensures a smooth dissolve.
      randomSeed = bitmapData.pixelDissolve(bitmapData,
                                            bitmapData.rect,
                                            destPoint,
                                            randomSeed,
                                            numberOfPixels,
                                            destColor);
      // Stop the dissolve when all pixels are the target color (i.e.,
      // when the width and height of the region in which the target color
      // does not exist are both 0)
      var coloredRegion:Rectangle =
              bitmapData.getColorBoundsRect(0xFFFFFFFF, destColor, false);
      if (coloredRegion.width == 0 && coloredRegion.height == 0 ) {
        t.stop();
      }
    }
  }
}
```

The *draw()* method is also used to rasterize vector content for the sake of improved performance. For example, recall the simple ScribbleAS3 drawing program presented earlier in Example 26-6. That program draws dots wherever the mouse moves but does not connect those dots with lines. One way to connect the dots with lines would be to use the *Graphics* class's instance method *lineTo()*, which draws a vector line between two points. However, using vectors to draw lines introduces a performance limitation: the user could potentially draw enough lines to make the application unresponsive (due to limits in the Flash runtime's vector renderer). To solve this problem, we can draw lines using *lineTo()* into an off-screen *Shape* instance. After each line is drawn, we copy it from the *Shape* object to a *BitmapData* object and then clear the drawing in the *Shape* instance. Because only one vector line exists at a time, the application never becomes unresponsive. Example 26-10 shows the code, some of which will be familiar from Example 26-6. Pay special attention to the *drawLine()* method, shown in bold.

Example 26-10. ScribbleAS3, off-screen vector version

```
package {
  import flash.display.*;
  import flash.events.*;
  import flash.ui.*;
  import flash.geom.*;
```

Example 26-10. ScribbleAS3, off-screen vector version (continued)

```
// A basic drawing application. This version draws a vector off screen
// and then copies that vector to a bitmap surface, thus avoiding
// the performance degradation associated with drawing too many vectors.
public class ScribbleAS3_VectorV2 extends Sprite {
  private var canvas:Bitmap;;            // The on-screen bitmap canvas
  private var virtualCanvas:Shape;       // The off-screen vector canvas
  private var canvasContainer:Sprite;    // Contains the bitmap,
                                         // providing interactivity
  private var isDrawing:Boolean = false; // Indicates whether the mouse
                                         // is currently depressed
  private var border:Shape; // Line around the bitmap
  private var lastX:int;     // Most recently clicked x-position
  private var lastY:int;     // Most recently clicked y-position

  // Constructor
  public function ScribbleAS3_VectorV2 () {
    createCanvas();
    registerForInputEvents();

    // Prevent the app from resizing.
    stage.scaleMode = StageScaleMode.NO_SCALE;
  }

  // Creates the on-screen bitmap canvas and off-screen vector canvas
  private function createCanvas (width:int = 200, height:int = 200):void {
    // Create a new off-screen object into which individual
    // vector lines are drawn before being copied to canvasData
    virtualCanvas = new Shape();

    // Define the data object that will store the actual pixel
    // data for the user's drawing. Lines are copied from virtualCanvas
    // to this object.
    var canvasData:BitmapData = new BitmapData(width,
                                               height, false, 0xFFFFFFFF);

    // Create a new displayable Bitmap, used to render the
    // canvasData object
    canvas = new Bitmap(canvasData);

    // Create a Sprite to contain the Bitmap. The Bitmap class
    // doesn't broadcast input events, so put it in a Sprite so the
    // user can interact with it.
    canvasContainer = new Sprite();
    canvasContainer.addChild(canvas);

    // Add the canvasContainer Sprite (and the Bitmap it contains) to
    // this object's display hierarchy
    addChild(canvasContainer);
```

Example 26-10. ScribbleAS3, off-screen vector version (continued)

```
    // Put a border around the drawing surface.
    border = new Shape();
    border.graphics.lineStyle(1);
    border.graphics.drawRect(0, 0, width, height);
    addChild(border);
  }

  // Registers for the required mouse and keyboard events
  private function registerForInputEvents ():void {
    // Register for mouse down and movement events from canvasContainer
    canvasContainer.addEventListener(MouseEvent.MOUSE_DOWN,
                             mouseDownListener);
    canvasContainer.addEventListener(MouseEvent.MOUSE_MOVE,
                             mouseMoveListener);

    // Register for mouse up and key events from the Stage (i.e.,
    // globally). Use the Stage because a mouse up event should always
    // exit drawing mode, even if it occurs while the mouse pointer is
    // not over the drawing. Likewise, the spacebar should always clear
    // the drawing, even when canvasContainer isn't focused.
    stage.addEventListener(MouseEvent.MOUSE_UP, mouseUpListener);
    stage.addEventListener(KeyboardEvent.KEY_DOWN, keyDownListener);
  }

  // Sets the color of a specified pixel. Use this for drawing a single
  // pixel because Graphics.lineTo() won't draw a single pixel
  public function drawPoint (x:int, y:int, color:uint = 0xFF000000):void {
    // Set the color of the specified pixel
    canvas.bitmapData.setPixel(x, y, color);
  }

  // Draws a vector line in virtualCanvas, then copies that line's bitmap
  // representation to canvasData (which is accessed via
  // canvas.bitmapData)
  public function drawLine (x1:int, y1:int, x2:int, y2:int,
                        color:uint = 0xFF000000):void {
    // Draw line in virtualCanvas
    virtualCanvas.graphics.clear();
    virtualCanvas.graphics.lineStyle(1, 0x000000, 1, true,
                                LineScaleMode.NORMAL, CapsStyle.NONE);
    virtualCanvas.graphics.moveTo(x1, y1);
    virtualCanvas.graphics.lineTo(x2, y2);
    // Copy line to canvasData
    canvas.bitmapData.draw(virtualCanvas);
  }

  // Responds to MouseEvent.MOUSE_DOWN events
  private function mouseDownListener (e:MouseEvent):void {
    // Set a flag indicating that the primary
    // mouse button is currently down
    isDrawing = true;
    // Remember the point clicked so we can draw a line to it if
```

Example 26-10. ScribbleAS3, off-screen vector version (continued)

```
        // the mouse moves
        lastX = e.localX;
        lastY = e.localY;
        // Draw a dot where the mouse was clicked
        drawPoint(e.localX, e.localY);
      }

      // Responds to MouseEvent.MOUSE_MOVE events
      private function mouseMoveListener (e:MouseEvent):void {
        // Draw a line when the mouse moves over the drawing
        // while the primary mouse button is depressed
        if (isDrawing) {
          // Use localX and localY to obtain pointer position relative to
          // the canvasContainer.
          var thisX:int = e.localX;
          var thisY:int = e.localY;

          // Draw a line to the new mouse location
          drawLine(lastX, lastY, thisX, thisY);

          // Remember the last mouse position for next time
          lastX = thisX;
          lastY = thisY;

          // Update the screen immediately following the execution of
          // this event listener function
          e.updateAfterEvent();
        }
      }

      // Responds to MouseEvent.MOUSE_UP events
      private function mouseUpListener (e:MouseEvent):void {
        // Set a flag indicating that the primary mouse button is currently up
        isDrawing = false;
      }

      // Responds to KeyboardEvent.KEY_DOWN events
      private function keyDownListener (e:KeyboardEvent):void {
        // Clear the drawing when the spacebar is pressed. To clear the
        // drawing, we set all pixels to the color white.
        if (e.charCode == Keyboard.SPACE) {
          canvas.bitmapData.fillRect(new Rectangle(0, 0,
                                           canvas.width, canvas.height),
                             0xFFFFFFFF);
        }
      }
    }
  }
}
```

How draw( ) handles Alpha channel values

When a transparent source *BitmapData* object is copied to a transparent destination bitmap data object using *draw()*, the Alpha channels of the two *BitmapData* objects are merged together on a per-pixel level, using the `BlendMode.SCREEN` algorithm, which is:

```
(sourceAlpha * (256-destinationAlpha) / 256) + destinationAlpha
```

When two Alpha values being combined are both between 1 and 254, the result is a more opaque Alpha value than either of the original Alpha values. Wherever the source being drawn is transparent, the destination *BitmapData* retains its original Alpha channel value. Wherever the destination is transparent, the new destination Alpha channel value is entirely replaced with the source Alpha channel value.

To completely replace the Alpha channel values in the destination *BitmapData* object with those from the source *BitmapData* object (instead of merging the two), use *copyPixels()* rather than *draw()*. See the upcoming section, "The BitmapData Class's Instance Method copyPixels( )."

No arbitrary screen captures

Note that it is not possible to take a screen capture of an arbitrary rectangular region of the screen via ActionScript. ActionScript can only copy display objects to bitmap format. ActionScript's closest analog to screen capturing the display area is to use the *Stage* instance as *draw()*'s source parameter, as in:

```
var canvas:BitmapData = new BitmapData(100, 100, false, 0xFFFFFFFF);
canvas.draw(someDisplayObject.stage);
```

where *someDisplayObject* is a *DisplayObject* instance on the display list. The preceding code will produce a bitmap containing every object currently on the display list, with the following caveats:

- The *.swf* file's background color is not copied to the bitmap.
- If any objects on the display list are inaccessible due to security restrictions, they are not copied to the bitmap, and a *SecurityError* exception is thrown.

The BitmapData Class's Instance Method copyPixels( )

Like *draw()*, *copyPixels()* is used to copy pixel color values from a source object to a destination *BitmapData* object. However, unlike *draw()*—which can copy pixel data from any *DisplayObject* instance or *BitmapData* object—*copyPixels()* can copy pixel data from *BitmapData* objects only. The *copyPixels()* method is used for its speed and convenience. In casual testing, *copyPixels()* operations proved to be 25% to 300% faster than equivalent *draw()* operations.

For best possible performance when copying pixel color values between two *BitmapData* objects, use *copyPixels()*, not *draw()*.

In addition to being faster than *draw()*, the *copyPixels()* method provides the developer with easy access to the following operations:

- Placing pixels from the source at a specific point in the destination
- Combining one bitmap with another bitmap's Alpha channel
- Overwriting the Alpha channel of a destination bitmap when copying pixels to it

Even though all three of the preceding operations can also be accomplished using *draw()* in combination with other *BitmapData* methods, *copyPixels()* is normally preferred due to its convenience.

The *copyPixels()* method has the following form:

```
destinationBitmapData.copyPixels(sourceBitmapData, sourceRect, destPoint,
alphaBitmapData, alphaPoint, mergeAlpha)
```

where *destinationBitmapData* is the *BitmapData* object into which the pixels will be drawn, and the parameters to *draw()* are as follows:

sourceBitmapData

The *BitmapData* instance that will be copied to *destinationBitmapData*. The *sourceBitmapData* and *destinationBitmapData* object can be the same, allowing pixels to be copied from one area to another within the same image.

sourceRect

A *Rectangle* object specifying the region of *sourceBitmapData* that will be copied into *destinationBitmapData*. To copy the entire *sourceBitmapData* object, use *sourceBitmapData*.rect. When *alphaBitmapData* is supplied, this parameter also specifies the width and height of the rectangular region within *alphaBitmapData* whose Alpha channel will be copied into *destinationBitmapData*.

destPoint

A *Point* object specifying the top-left corner of the rectangular region within *destinationBitmapData* where the copied pixels will be placed.

alphaBitmapData

An optional *BitmapData* object, separate from *sourceBitmapData*, whose Alpha channel values will become the new Alpha channel values of the pixels written to *destinationBitmapData*. The height and width of the specific rectangular region whose Alpha channel will be copied into *destinationBitmapData* are specified by *sourceRect*.

Using this parameter, we can combine the RGB channels from one bitmap (*sourceBitmapData*) with the Alpha channel of another bitmap (*alphaBitmapData*). Such a technique could be used, for example, to produce an irregular, aged effect on photographs in an electronic scrapbook application. Each photograph would be stored in its own *BitmapData* object, while the feathered edge would be stored as an Alpha channel in a single, reusable *BitmapData* object. Using *copyPixel()*'s `alphaBitmapData` parameter, the Alpha channel of the feathered edge bitmap would be combined with the photographs at runtime.

alphaPoint

A *Point* object specifying the top-left corner of the rectangular region within `alphaBitmapData` from which Alpha channel values will be retrieved. The width and height of the rectangular region are specified by `sourceRect`.

mergeAlpha

A Boolean indicating whether, during the copy operation, the Alpha channels of `destinationBitmapData` and `sourceBitmapData` should be combined (`true`) or the Alpha channel of `sourceBitmapData` should completely replace the existing `destinationBitmapData` Alpha channel (`false`). This parameter has an effect only when both `destinationBitmapData` and `sourceBitmapData` are transparent bitmaps. The default value is `false`, meaning that `sourceBitmapData`'s Alpha channel completely replaces the existing `destinationBitmapData`'s Alpha channel. The algorithm used to combine the Alpha channels matches that discussed in the earlier section "How draw( ) handles Alpha channel values."

The *copyPixels()* method is the method of choice for moving pixels between two *BitmapData* objects. Moving pixels between bitmaps is a common operation in graphics applications and video games. Let's look at a couple of examples.

First, let's practice the basic syntax of *copyPixels()* by creating a blue square and a red square, and copying a portion of the blue square to the red square.

```
// Create the squares (20x20 pixels each)
var redSquare:BitmapData = new BitmapData(20, 20, true, 0xFFFF0000);
var blueSquare:BitmapData = new BitmapData(20, 20, true, 0xFF0000FF);

// Define the rectangular region that will be copied from
// blueSquare to redSquare
var sourceRect:Rectangle = new Rectangle(5, 5, 10, 5);

// Define the point at which the rectangular region from
// blueSquare will be placed into redSquare
var destPoint:Point = new Point(0,0);

// Copy the pixels
redSquare.copyPixels(blueSquare, sourceRect, destPoint);

// Associate the redSquare BitmapData object with a Bitmap
// object for on-screen display
var b:Bitmap = new Bitmap(redSquare);
addChild(b);
```

Example 26-11 presents another example—aging a photograph, as discussed earlier under the *alphaBitmapData* parameter description. The comments will guide you through the code. Pay special attention to the *makeScrapbookImage()* method.

Example 26-11. An aged photograph effect

```
package {
  import flash.display.*;
  import flash.events.*;
  import flash.geom.*;
  import flash.net.*;

  public class ScrapbookImage extends Sprite {
    private var numLoaded:int = 0;
    private var photoLoader:Loader;   // The photo loader
    private var borderLoader:Loader;  // The borter loader

    // Constructor
    public function ScrapbookImage () {
      // Load the photograph
      photoLoader = new Loader();
      photoLoader.contentLoaderInfo.addEventListener(Event.INIT,
                                                     initListener);
      photoLoader.load(new URLRequest("photo.jpg"));

      // Load the border
      borderLoader = new Loader();
      borderLoader.contentLoaderInfo.addEventListener(Event.INIT,
                                                      initListener);
      borderLoader.load(new URLRequest("border.png"));
    }

    // Handles Event.INIT events for the loaded images
    private function initListener (e:Event):void {
      numLoaded++;
      if (numLoaded == 2) {
        makeScrapbookImage();
      }
    }

    // Combines the border image with the photo image to produce
    // the aged photograph effect
    public function makeScrapbookImage ():void {
      // Retrieve the BitmapData object for the photograph
      var photoData:BitmapData = Bitmap(photoLoader.content).bitmapData;
      // Retrieve the BitmapData object for the border
      var borderData:BitmapData = Bitmap(borderLoader.content).bitmapData;
      // Create a BitmapData object that will hold the final
      // photograph image
      var scrapbookImage:BitmapData = new BitmapData(borderData.width,
                                                     borderData.height,
                                                     true,
                                                     0xFFFFFFFF);
```

Example 26-11. An aged photograph effect (continued)

```
        // Copy the pixels  from the photograph, while applying the
        // border's Alpha channel
        scrapbookImage.copyPixels(photoData,
                                  borderData.rect,
                                  new Point(0,0),
                                  borderData,
                                  new Point(0,0),
                                  true);

        // Associate the scrapbookImage BitmapData object with a Bitmap
        // object for on-screen display
        var b:Bitmap = new Bitmap(scrapbookImage);
        addChild(b);
        b.x = 100;
        b.y = 75;
    }
  }
}
```

Figure 26-8 shows the result of the code from Example 26-11. The original image appears on the left and the "aged" image appears on the right.

Figure 26-8. An aged photograph effect

The images and code for Example 26-11 are available online at *http://www.moock. org/eas3/examples*.

The *copyPixels()* method also offers an efficient way to reuse a collection of pixel values. For example, in 2D video games, backgrounds are often dynamically generated from a small group of ready-made bitmap graphics known as *tiles*. As the player moves around the world, the program displays the appropriate set of background tiles. Using *copyPixels()*, each tile is copied from a reusable *BitmapData* object to the on-screen background image. While full discussion of a tiled-background system is beyond the scope of this book, a fully functional ActionScript tile example can be downloaded from this book's companion web site, at *http://www.moock.org/eas3/examples*.

Applying Filters and Effects

To produce graphical effects, we can choose from the following wide range of tools provided by the *BitmapData* class:

colorTransform()

> Adjusts colors using a *ColorTransform* object, which provides a basic interface for simple color transformations. (For more complex control over color transformations, use the *ColorMatrixFilter* class.)

applyFilter()

> Modifies a bitmap using a preset filter effect such as drop shadow or blur. See the section "Applying Filters."

noise()

> Fills a bitmap with random color values in configurable ranges. Figure 26-9 shows an image generated by the *noise()* method.

Figure 26-9. A noise-filled bitmap

perlinNoise()

> Fills a bitmap with a random organic-style pattern of color values. Figure 26-10 shows an image generated by the *perlinNoise()* method. The result of *perlinNoise()* is not normally used directly; it is typically combined with other filters to produce simulated waves, flames, clouds, water, wood grain, and landscapes. For a general discussion of Perlin noise, see Ken Perlin's introductory lecture at *http://www.noisemachine.com/talk1*. For an ActionScript example showing how to use *perlinNoise()* to create a wood texture, see *http://www.connectedpixel.com/blog/texture/wood*. For a marble texture, see *http://www.connectedpixel.com/blog/texture/marble*.

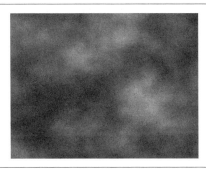

Figure 26-10. A Perlin-noise-filled bitmap

paletteMap( )

Replaces colors in an image with colors from a lookup table or another image.

pixelDissolve( )

When used repeatedly in an animation, produces fade effect between two images, or fades an image to a specific color, pixel by pixel (for example of an image-to-color fade, see Example 26-9).

threshold( )

Convert pixels in a given color-range to a specific new color value.

While each of the preceding methods offers a wealth of graphical possibilities, in this section, we'll focus on the tool with perhaps the most general usefulness, *applyFilter( )*. For details on the other effects methods, see the *BitmapData* class in Adobe's Action-Script Language Reference.

Applying Filters

To provide programmers with a convenient way to apply common graphics effects to a bitmap image, ActionScript's provides a selection of built-in graphics filters.

> The filters discussed in this section can be applied permanently to a *BitmapData* object on the pixel level but can also dynamically be applied to, and removed from, any display object. For details, see the *DisplayObject* class's instance variable `filters` in Adobe's Action-Script Language Reference.

Each built-in filter is represented by its own class in the `flash.filters` package. For example, the blur filter, which makes a bitmap look blurry, is represented by the *flash.filters.BlurFilter* class.

Some filters are easy to use even for developers without any graphics programming experience. These include: bevel, blur, drop shadow, and glow, represented by the classes *BevelFilter* (and its gradient variety, *GradientBevelFilter*), *BlurFilter*, *DropShadowFilter*, and *GlowFilter* (and its gradient variety, *GradientGlowFilter*).

Other filters require an existing understanding of fundamental graphics programming techniques, such as convolution, displacement, and color matrices. These include: matrix convolution, displacement mapping, and color matrix transformations, represented by the classes *ConvolutionFilter*, *DisplacementMapFilter*, and *ColorMatrixFilter*.

Whatever the type of filter, the technique for applying a filter to a bitmap in Action-Script is the same:

1. Create an instance of the desired filter class.

2. Pass the filter instance to the *applyFilter()* method.

For example, to apply a blur filter to a bitmap, we create an instance of the *BlurFilter* class, using the following general format:

```
new BlurFilter(blurX, blurY, quality)
```

where *blurX* and *blurY* indicate the distance to blur each pixel, horizontally and vertically, and *quality* indicates the rendering quality of the effect, expressed using one of the three constants of the *BitmapFilterQuality* class.

The following code creates a medium quality blur effect that spans 15 pixels both vertically and horizontally:

```
var blurFilter:BlurFilter =
                    new BlurFilter(15, 15, BitmapFilterQuality.MEDIUM);
```

Once the filter has been created, we apply it to a *BitmapData* object using the following code:

```
destinationBitmapData.applyFilter(sourceBitmapData, sourceRect, destPoint, filter);
```

where *destinationBitmapData* is the *BitmapData* object into which the filtered pixels will be drawn, and the parameters to *draw()* are as follows:

sourceBitmapData
> The *BitmapData* object to which the filter will be applied. The *sourceBitmapData* and *destinationBitmapData* object can be the same, allowing a filter to be applied directly to a single *BitmapData* object.

sourceRect
> A *Rectangle* object specifying the region of *sourceBitmapData* to which the filter will be applied. To apply the filter to an entire bitmap, use *sourceBitmapData*.rect.

destPoint
> A *Point* object specifying the position within *destinationBitmapData* where the filtered pixels will be placed. Note that the *destPoint* corresponds to the top-left corner of the specified *sourceRect*, *not* to the top-left corner of the region of pixels affected by the filter operation. See the discussion of *generateFilterRect()* that follows.

filter

> The filter object to apply; for example, an instance of one of the following classes: *BevelFilter*, *GradientBevelFilter*, *BlurFilter*, *DropShadowFilter*, *GlowFilter*, *GradientGlowFilter*, *ConvolutionFilter*, *DisplacementMapFilter*, or *ColorMatrixFilter*.

For example, the following code applies the *BlurFilter* object we made earlier to an entire *BitmapData* object:

```
bitmapData.applyFilter(bitmapData, bitmapData.rect, new Point(0,0), blurFilter);
```

Figure 26-11 shows the result of applying a 15×15 *BlurFilter* to an image.

Figure 26-11. A blur filter applied

When a filter is applied to a bitmap, the resulting bitmap is often larger than the original. For example, applying a drop-shadow filter may produce a shadow that falls outside the bounds of the original bitmap. In order to accommodate the full effect of a filter, we must be sure to draw the filtered pixels into a bitmap large enough to hold them. To determine the size of a bitmap that will be large enough to accommodate a filter effect, we use the *BitmapData* class's instance method *generateFilterRect()*. The *generateFilterRect()* method returns a *Rectangle* object indicating the area of pixels that will be affected by a given filter operation. The general form of *generateFilterRect()* is:

```
sourceBitmapData.generateFilterRect(sourceRect, filter)
```

The *generateFilterRect()* method returns a *Rectangle* object indicating the area of pixels that would be affected if the specified filter object (*filter*) were applied to the specified rectangular region (*sourceRect*) of the specified *BitmapData* object (*sourceBitmapData*).

 The *generateFilterRect()* method does not actually apply the filter it simply indicates the area of pixels that would be affected by the filter if it were applied.

Let's try using *generateFilterRect()* in practice. Our goal is to produce a bitmap that has a drop-shadow effect applied. First, we create the original bitmap, with no drop-shadow effect applied. The original bitmap is a 20×20 gray square.

```
var origBitmap:BitmapData = new BitmapData(20, 20, false, 0xFFDDDDDD);
```

Next, we create the *DropShadowFilter* object. The *DropShadowFilter* constructor has the following form:

```
DropShadowFilter(distance:Number=4.0, angle:Number=45, color:uint=0,
                 alpha:Number=1.0, blurX:Number=4.0, blurY:Number=4.0,
                 strength:Number=1.0, quality:int=1, inner:Boolean=false,
                 knockout:Boolean = false, hideObject:Boolean = false)
```

For details on the various *DropShadowFilter* constructor parameters, see Adobe's ActionScript Language Reference, under *DropShadowFilter*. Here's our *DropShadowFilter* object:

```
var dsFilter:DropShadowFilter = new DropShadowFilter(4, 45, 0,
                                        1, 10, 10,
                                        2, BitmapFilterQuality.MEDIUM);
```

Next, we use *generateFilterRect()* to determine how big our original bitmap will be after the *DropShadowFilter* is applied:

```
var filterRect:Rectangle = origBitmap.generateFilterRect(origBitmap.rect,
                                                         dsFilter);
```

Now we can create an appropriately sized new bitmap into which to draw the original bitmap with the drop-shadow filter applied. Notice that we specify the height and width of the new bitmap using the results supplied by *generateFilterRect()* (shown in bold):

```
var finalBitmap:BitmapData = new BitmapData(filterRect.width,
                                            filterRect.height, true);
```

 The destination *BitmapData* object for a drop-shadow filter effect must be transparent.

Now that we have a source bitmap, a *DropShadowFilter* object, and an appropriately sized destination bitmap, we can apply our drop-shadow filter, as follows:

```
finalBitmap.applyFilter(origBitmap, origBitmap.rect,
                        new Point(-filterRect.x, -filterRect.y),
                        dsFilter);
```

In the preceding code, notice that the supplied *destPoint* offsets the filtered pixels by an amount equal to the distance that the filter effect extends above and to the left of the supplied *sourceRect*. In our example, the filter effect is applied to the entire bitmap, so the top-left corner of the *sourceRect* is at coordinate (0, 0). The blur of the drop shadow extends above the original bitmap by 9 pixels and to the left of the original bitmap by 9 pixels. Hence, the x-coordinate of the generated filter rectangle is –9, and the y-coordinate of the generated filter rectangle is –9. To move the top-left corner of the filtered pixels down and to the right (to the top-left corner of the filtered bitmap), we specify a *destPoint* that negates the values of the filter rectangle's x and y coordinates:

```
new Point(-filterRect.x, -filterRect.y)
```

For review, here is the drop-shadow code in its entirety:

```
var origBitmap:BitmapData = new BitmapData(20, 20, false, 0xFFDDDDDD);
var dsFilter:DropShadowFilter = new DropShadowFilter(4, 45, 0,
                                     1, 10, 10,
                                     2, BitmapFilterQuality.MEDIUM);
var filterRect:Rectangle = origBitmap.generateFilterRect(origBitmap.rect,
                                                dsFilter);
var finalBitmap:BitmapData = new BitmapData(filterRect.width,
                                     filterRect.height, true);
finalBitmap.applyFilter(origBitmap, origBitmap.rect,
                     new Point(-filterRect.x, -filterRect.y),
                     dsFilter);
```

Figure 26-12 shows the results of the preceding code.

Figure 26-12. A drop-shadow filter applied

Now that we understand the basics of using filters, let's revisit Example 26-11 to improve the aged photograph effect. Example 26-12 shows the new code. The general creation and application of filters in the example should now be familiar. However, the example introduces the use of a specific filter we haven't explored: *ColorMatrixFilter*. A *ColorMatrixFilter* alters the colors in a bitmap using a matrix transformation, producing effects such as brightness, contrast, saturation adjustments, and hue rotation. The example shows how to use *ColorMatrixFilter* in its raw state, but at least two developers offer freely available code for performing common matrix transformations:

Mario Klingemann's ColorMatrix Class
> *http://www.quasimondo.com/archives/000565.php*

Grant Skinner's ColorMatrix Class
> *http://www.gskinner.com/blog/archives/2005/09/flash_8_source.html*

For background information on color matrix transformations, see *Using Matrices for Transformations, Color Adjustments, and Convolution Effects in Flash*, by Phil Chung, at *http://www.adobe.com/devnet/flash/articles/matrix_transformations_04.html*.

Example 26-12. An aged photograph effect, now with filters

```
package {
  import flash.display.*;
  import flash.events.*;
  import flash.geom.*;
  import flash.net.*;
  import flash.filters.*;

  public class ScrapbookImage extends Sprite {
    private var numLoaded:int = 0;
    private var photoLoader:Loader;    // The photo loader
    private var borderLoader:Loader;   // The borter loader

    public function ScrapbookImage () {
      // Load the photograph
      photoLoader = new Loader();
      photoLoader.contentLoaderInfo.addEventListener(Event.INIT,
                                               initListener);
      photoLoader.load(new URLRequest("photo.jpg"));

      // Load the border
      borderLoader = new Loader();
      borderLoader.contentLoaderInfo.addEventListener(Event.INIT,
                                               initListener);
      borderLoader.load(new URLRequest("border.png"));
    }


    // Handles Event.INIT events for the loaded images
    private function initListener (e:Event):void {
      numLoaded++;
      // When those images have loaded, apply the effect
      if (numLoaded == 2) {
        makeScrapbookImage();
      }
    }

    // Combines the border image with the photo image to produce
    // the aged photograph effect
    public function makeScrapbookImage ():void {
      // Retrieve the BitmapData object for the photograph
      var photoData:BitmapData = Bitmap(photoLoader.content).bitmapData;
      // Retrieve the BitmapData object for the border
      var borderData:BitmapData = Bitmap(borderLoader.content).bitmapData;
      // Create a BitmapData object that will hold the final
      // photograph image
      var tempBitmapData:BitmapData = new BitmapData(borderData.width,
                                               borderData.height,
                                               true,
                                               0x00000000);

      // Copy the pixels  from the photograph, while applying the
      // border's Alpha channel
```

Example 26-12. An aged photograph effect, now with filters (continued)

```
tempBitmapData.copyPixels(photoData,
                          borderData.rect,
                          new Point(0,0),
                          borderData,
                          new Point(0,0),
                          false);

// A ColorMatrixFilter that will increase brightness
var brightnessOffset:int = 70;
var brightnessFilter:ColorMatrixFilter = new ColorMatrixFilter(
    new Array(1,0,0,0,brightnessOffset,
              0,1,0,0,brightnessOffset,
              0,0,1,0,brightnessOffset,
              0,0,0,1,0));

// A blur filter to make the image look fuzzy
var blurFilter:BlurFilter = new BlurFilter(1, 1);

// A drop shadow filter to make the image look like it's on paper
var dropShadowFilter:DropShadowFilter = new DropShadowFilter(4, 35,
                  0x2E2305, .6, 5, 12, 4, BitmapFilterQuality.MEDIUM);

// Calculate the area required to display the image
// and its drop shadow
var filteredImageRect:Rectangle = tempBitmapData.generateFilterRect(
                       tempBitmapData.rect, dropShadowFilter);

// Create a BitmapData object that will hold the final image
var scrapbookImage:BitmapData =
                       new BitmapData(filteredImageRect.width,
                           filteredImageRect.height,
                           true,
                           0xFFFFFFFF);

// Apply the ColorMatrixFilter, which increases the brightness
tempBitmapData.applyFilter(tempBitmapData,
                       tempBitmapData.rect,
                       new Point(0,0),
                       brightnessFilter);

// Apply the BlurFilter
tempBitmapData.applyFilter(tempBitmapData,
                       tempBitmapData.rect,
                       new Point(0,0),
                       blurFilter);

// Apply the DropShadowFilter
scrapbookImage.applyFilter(tempBitmapData,
                       tempBitmapData.rect,
                       new Point(-filteredImageRect.x,
                                 -filteredImageRect.y),
                       dropShadowFilter);
```

Example 26-12. An aged photograph effect, now with filters (continued)

```
    // Associate the scrapbookImage BitmapData object with a Bitmap
    // object for on-screen display
    var b:Bitmap = new Bitmap(scrapbookImage);
    addChild(b);
    b.x = 100;
    b.y = 75;
  }
 }
}
```

Figure 26-13 shows the result of the code from Example 26-12.

Figure 26-13. An aged photograph effect, now with filters

Freeing Memory Used by Bitmaps

Every pixel in every *BitmapData* object occupies a little bit of system memory—four bytes to be precise (one byte for each color channel). Though the memory used by each pixel is insignificant on its own, pixels can collectively add up to form a significant memory demand. Hence, to reduce the amount of memory required by the Flash runtime when working with bitmaps, every ActionScript program should ensure that all *BitmapData* objects become eligible for garbage collection when they are no longer required.

To make a given *BitmapData* object eligible for garbage collection, either remove all references to it or remove all references to objects that reference it. Either way, the memory used by the *BitmapData* object will automatically be freed by the garbage collector in a future mark-and-sweep cycle.

To *immediately* free the memory occupied by the pixels of the *BitmapData* object (rather than waiting for the garbage collector to free it), use the *BitmapData* class's instance method *dispose()*. For example, the following code creates a *BitmapData* object that consumes 1600 bytes (20 pixels wide × 20 pixels high × 4 bytes per pixel):

```
var imgData:BitmapData = new BitmapData(20, 20, false, 0xFF00FF00);
```

To immediately free the 1600 bytes of memory, we use *dispose()*, as follows:

```
imgData.dispose();  // Free memory used by imgData
```

The *dispose()* method frees the memory consumed by imgData's pixel information, but does not immediately free the memory consumed by the imgData object, itself. The imgData object's memory is freed according to the normal garbage collection cycle.

Once *dispose()* has been invoked on a *BitmapData* object, that object can no longer be used. Accessing its methods and variables generates an *ArgumentError* exception.

The *dispose()* method can be useful for controlling memory consumed by functions or loops that use a bitmap only temporarily, as might be the case when generating a filtered image by combining multiple temporary images.

Words, Words, Words

We've spent the preceding two chapters creating images to display on screen. In the next chapter, we'll learn how to create text to display on screen.

CHAPTER 27
Text Display and Input

Flash Player offers an extensive, sophisticated API for working with text. In this chapter we'll look at some of its key features: creating and displaying text, formatting text, and handling text input.

The information presented in this chapter applies specifically to Flash Player (both the browser add-on and standalone versions) but is also generally applicable to any Flash runtime that supports full-featured text display and input, such as Adobe AIR. Note, however, that unlike Flash Player, Adobe AIR provides full-featured HTML and CSS support, analogous to that found in web browsers such as Microsoft Internet Explorer and Mozilla Firefox. When working with other Flash runtimes, be sure to consult the appropriate documentation for information on text support.

The centerpiece of Flash Player's text API is the *TextField* class, which provides control over text displayed on screen.

 In this book (and in most ActionScript documentation), the term "text field," refers, in a general sense, to a given text field on screen and its corresponding ActionScript *TextField* instance. Meanwhile, the phrase "a *TextField* object" refers more specifically to the ActionScript object that controls a text field.

Before we start creating and working with text, let's take a quick look at the core classes in Flash Player's text API, listed in Table 27-1. The text API's feature set can be broken into the following general categories:

- Controlling on-screen text
- Formatting text
- Setting FlashType text-rendering options
- Managing fonts (e.g, determining available fonts)
- Retrieving text metrics (measurements)
- Supplying constant values

Table 27-1 presents a brief overview of each class in the text API, categorized according to the preceding general categories. All classes in the text API reside in the package *flash.text*. Note that this chapter offers a good introduction to ActionScript's text API but does not cover all its features exhaustively. The text API is vast. For further study, be sure to explore the *flash.text* package in Adobe's ActionScript Language Reference. Furthermore, for additional and more specialized control over text, consider using the *Label*, *Text*, *TextArea*, and *TextInput* components provided by the Flex framework or the *Label*, *TextArea*, and *TextInput* components provided by the Flash authoring tool.

Table 27-1. Text API overview

Purpose	Class	Description
Controlling on-screen text	*TextField*	Represents the following types of text fields: • Text fields created with ActionScript code • Text fields of type "dynamic" or "input," created in the Flash authoring tool
	StaticText	Represents text fields of type "static", created in the Flash authoring tool.
	TextSnapshot	A string containing the text of all static text fields in a given *DisplayObjectContainer* instance.
Formatting text	*TextFormat*	A simple data class representing character-formatting information.
	StyleSheet	Represents a style sheet that specifies character-formatting information. Based on the W3C's Cascading style sheet Level 1 (CSS1) specification.
Setting FlashType rendering options	*CSMSettings*	A simple data class used to provide Flash Player's FlashType text renderer with custom antialiasing settings for rendering a particular font at a particular size. Used with the *TextRenderer* class's static method *setAdvancedAntiAliasingTable( )*.
	TextRenderer	Controls rendering settings for Flash Player's FlashType text renderer.
Managing fonts	*Font*	Provides access to the list of fonts available on the system or embedded in .swf files, and registers runtime-loaded fonts.
Retrieving text measurements	*TextLineMetrics*	Describes measurements for a single line of text in a text field.

Table 27-1. Text API overview (continued)

Purpose	Class	Description
Supplying constant values	*AntiAliasType, FontStyle, FontType, GridFitType, TextColorType, TextDisplayMode, TextFieldAutoSize, TextFieldType, TextFormatAlign*	These classes define constants used to specify various variable and parameter values in the text API. For details, see Table 27-2.

Table 27-2 presents a brief overview of text-API classes whose purpose is simply to provide access to special values via class constants.

Table 27-2. Text API constant-value classes

Purpose	Class	Description
Constants used when choosing a text renderer	*AntiAliasType*	Defines constants that describe types of antialiasing. Used with the *TextField* class's instance variable `antiAliasType`.
Constants used when setting FlashType rendering options	*FontStyle*	Defines constants that describe font variations (e.g., bold, italic). Used with the *TextRenderer* class's static method *setAdvancedAntiAliasingTable( )* and the *Font* class's instance variable `fontStyle`.
	GridFitType	Defines constants that describe types of pixel-grid fitting. Used with the *TextField* class's instance variable `gridFitType`.
	TextColorType	Defines constants that describe types of text color ("dark" or "light"). Used with the *TextRenderer* class's static method *setAdvancedAntiAliasingTable( )*.
	TextDisplayMode	Defines constants that describe types of subpixel anti-aliasing. Used with the *TextRenderer* class's static variable `displayMode`.
Constants used when setting text field options	*TextFieldAutoSize*	Defines constants that describe automatic sizing options. Used with the *TextField* class's instance variable `autoSize`.
	TextFieldType	Defines constants that describe types of text fields ("dynamic" or "input"). Used with the *TextField* class's instance variable `type`.
Constants used when retrieving font lists	*FontType*	Defines constants that describe types of font locations ("device" or "embedded"). Used with the *Font* class's static method *enumerateFonts( )*.
Constants used when setting text alignment	*TextFormatAlign*	Defines constants that describe types of text alignment (i.e., "center", "left", "right", or "justify"). Used with the *TextFormat* class's instance variable `align`.

Now that we have a general familiarity of the tools available in the text API, let's make some text!

Creating and Displaying Text

To display text with ActionScript, we first create a *TextField* object. The *TextField* object represents a rectangular text container that can be displayed on screen and filled with formatted text via code or user input. For example, the following code creates a *TextField* object and assigns it to the variable t:

```
var t:TextField = new TextField();
```

After creating a *TextField* object, we use the *TextField* class's instance variable text to specify the text to display. For example, the following code specifies "Hello world" as the text to display in t:

```
t.text = "Hello world";
```

Finally, to display the text field on screen, we pass the *TextField* object to the *addChild()* or *addChildAt()* method of any *DisplayObjectContainer* that is currently on the display list. For example, assuming *someContainer* is on the display list, the following code causes the text field t to appear on screen:

```
someContainer.addChild(t);
```

Example 27-1 shows the preceding code in the context of a demonstration class, *HelloWorld*. In the example, notice that we import the *TextField* class (along with all classes in the *flash.text* package) before using it.

Example 27-1. Displaying text

```
package {
  import flash.display.*;
  import flash.text.*;  // Import TextField and other classes
                        // in the flash.text package

  public class HelloWorld extends Sprite {
    public function HelloWorld () {
      // Create a TextField object
      var t:TextField = new TextField();

      // Specify the text to display
      t.text = "Hello world";

      // Add the TextField object to the display list
      addChild(t);
    }
  }
}
```

The result of the code from Example 27-1 is shown in Figure 27-1. The figure shows the text as it would appear by default on Windows XP; we'll cover fonts and formatting later in this chapter.

Figure 27-1. A text field

While the preceding figure shows the text in the text field, it does not show the text field's rectangular display region. By default, a text field's rectangular display region is set to 100 pixels wide by 100 pixels high. Figure 27-2 revises Figure 27-1 to show a dashed line representing the text field's rectangular display region.

Figure 27-2. A text field and its rectangular display region

The width and height of a text field's rectangular display region can be set explicitly using the *TextField* class's instance variables width and height. For example, the following code sets t's rectangular display region's width to 200 and height to 50:

```
t.width = 200;
t.height = 50;
```

Figure 27-3 shows the result of the changes made by the preceding code, again using a dashed line to represent the text field's rectangular display region.

Figure 27-3. Custom size for a text field's rectangular display region

By default, a text field's rectangular display region is not visible on screen. However, we can make it visible by setting one or both of the *TextField* class's instance variables background and border to true. The background variable specifies whether to fill the text field's rectangular display region with a solid color, while the border variable specifies whether to draw a 1-pixel-thick line around the text field's rectangular display region. The color of the background and border is specified by assigning 24-bit RGB color values to backgroundColor and borderColor.

Example 27-2 updates our *HelloWorld* class to display t's rectangular display region with a dark gray border and a light gray background. The new code is shown in bold.

Example 27-2. Displaying text with a border and background

```
package {
  import flash.display.*;
  import flash.text.*;  // Import TextField and other classes
                        // in the flash.text package

  public class HelloWorld extends Sprite {
    public function HelloWorld () {
      var t:TextField = new TextField();  // Create TextField object
      t.text = "Hello world";             // Set text to display
      t.background = true;                // Turn on background
      t.backgroundColor = 0xCCCCCC;       // Set background color to light gray
      t.border = true;                    // Turn on border
      t.borderColor = 0x333333;           // Set order color to dark gray

      addChild(t);                        // Add text field to the display list
    }
  }
}
```

The result of the code from Example 27-2 is shown in Figure 27-4.

Figure 27-4. A text field with a border and background

Word Wrapping

By default, when the width of the text in a text field exceeds the width of the text field's rectangular display area, the excess text is hidden from view. For example, the following code sets t's text to a string that is wider than 100 pixels in the default font on Windows XP:

```
t.text = "Hello world, how are you?";
```

The result is shown in Figure 27-5.

Figure 27-5. Excess text hidden from view

To prevent text that exceeds the width of a text field's rectangular display area from being hidden, we can enable automatic line-breaking in a text field by setting the *TextField* class's instance variable `wordWrap` to `true`. When automatic line-breaking is enabled, long lines of text *soft wrap*—that is, any line that is wider than the text field's rectangular display region will automatically flow onto the following line. For example, this code enables automatic line-breaking for the *TextField* object t:

```
t.wordWrap = true;
```

The result is shown in Figure 27-6.

Figure 27-6. Automatic line-breaking

Word wrapping is a display feature only; no carriage return or newline character appears in the source text where wrapping occurs. If `wordWrap` is `true`, changing the text field's `width` causes long lines to soft wrap at a different point (i.e., the text reflows). Hard returns can be added to a text field using the "\n" escape sequence or, in HTML text, the <BR> tag. (We'll study the use of HTML in text fields later in this chapter, in the section "Formatting Text with HTML.")

 Don't confuse `wordWrap` with `multiline` (covered later in the section "Formatting Text with HTML" and "Text Field Input"). The `multiline` variable affects the ability of HTML and user input to cause line breaks, while `wordWrap` dictates whether ActionScript performs automatic line-breaking.

Automatic Resizing

To force a text field's rectangular display region to automatically resize to match the size of the text field's text, we use the *TextField* class's instance variable `autoSize`. Setting `autoSize` to anything other than `TextFieldAutoSize.NONE` (the default) ensures that a text field will always be large enough to display its assigned text.

 The `autoSize` variable overrides any absolute sizes specified by a *TextField* object's `height` or `width`.

The `autoSize` variable has four possible values: `TextFieldAutoSize.NONE`, `TextFieldAutoSize.LEFT`, `TextFieldAutoSize.RIGHT`, and `TextFieldAutoSize.CENTER`. These values dictate the direction in which the text field should expand or contract to fit its text, where NONE means don't resize, LEFT means keep the left side anchored and resize right, RIGHT means keep the right side anchored and resize left, and CENTER means resize evenly on both sides. In the latter three cases, where word wrapping or hard line breaks occur, the text field's bottom border will also resize to accommodate multiple lines in the text.

Example 27-3 creates a text field whose rectangular display region resizes on the right and, where line breaks occur, on the bottom.

Example 27-3. Resizable right and bottom borders

```
package {
  import flash.display.*;
  import flash.text.*;

  public class HelloWorld extends Sprite {
    public function HelloWorld () {
      var t:TextField = new TextField();
      t.text = "Hello world, how are you?";
      t.background = true;
      t.backgroundColor = 0xCCCCCC;
      t.border = true;
      t.borderColor = 0x333333;

      // Make t's rectangular display region automatically resize to
      // accommodate t.text.
      t.autoSize = TextFieldAutoSize.LEFT;

      addChild(t);
    }
  }
}
```

The result of the code from Example 27-3 is shown in Figure 27-7. Compare Figure 27-7 with the earlier Figure 27-5, which showed a text field that uses neither automatic resizing nor word wrap.

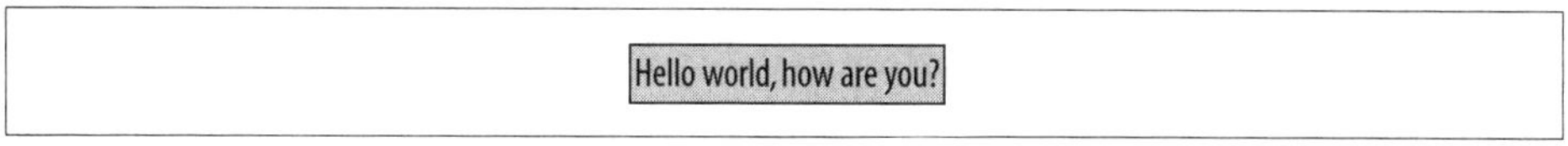

Figure 27-7. Resizable right and bottom borders

Now suppose we add a line break to t's text, as follows (the line break is inserted using the character sequence "\n"):

```
t.text = "Hello world." + "\n" + "How are you?";
```

Figure 27-8 shows the resulting text field. Notice that ActionScript automatically resizes the text field's rectangular display region to perfectly accommodate the text by expanding both the right and bottom borders.

Figure 27-8. Resizable right and bottom borders, with line break

Setting wordWrap to true and autoSize to anything but TextFieldAutoSize.NONE results in a text field whose bottom border automatically expands or contracts, but whose left, right, and top borders remained fixed. Example 27-4 demonstrates, showing a text field with a resizable bottom border.

Example 27-4. Resizable bottom border only

```
package {
  import flash.display.*;
  import flash.text.*;

  public class HelloWorld extends Sprite {
    public function HelloWorld ( ) {
      var t:TextField = new TextField( );
      t.text = "Hello world, how are you?";
      t.background = true;
      t.backgroundColor = 0xCCCCCC;
      t.border = true;
      t.borderColor = 0x333333;

      // In combination, the following two lines make t's bottom border
      // automatically resize to accommodate t.text.
      t.autoSize = TextFieldAutoSize.LEFT;
      t.wordWrap = true;

      addChild(t);
    }
  }
}
```

The result of the code in Example 27-4 is shown in Figure 27-9. Notice that the rectangular display container's width is fixed at 100 pixels (the default), but the bottom border expands to accommodate wrapped text.

Figure 27-9. Resizable bottom border only

To create a text field with an expandable bottom border and a fixed width, set autoSize to anything but TextFieldAutoSize.NONE, and set wordWrap to true.

Rotated, Skewed, and Transparent Text Requires Embedded Fonts

By default, Flash Player does not render rotated or skewed text fields to the screen. For example, if we were to add the following text field to the display list, the text "Hello world" would not appear on screen because the text field is rotated:

```
var t:TextField = new TextField( );
t.text = "Hello world";
t.rotation = 30;  // Rotate text
```

Likewise, if we were to add the following text field to the display list, the text "Hello world" would not appear on screen because the text field is skewed:

```
var t:TextField = new TextField( );
t.text = "Hello world";
t.transform.matrix = new Matrix(1, 1, 0, 1);  // Skew text
```

Also by default, Flash Player renders all text fields at full opacity, even when they are set to transparent via the *TextField* class's instance variable alpha. For example, if we were to add the following text field to the display list, the text "Hello world" would appear fully opaque, even though the text field's alpha percentage is set to 20%:

```
var t:TextField = new TextField( );
t.text = "Hello world";
t.alpha = .2;
```

Flash Player renders accurate rotation, skew, and transparency for text fields that use embedded fonts only. For information on rendering text using embedded fonts, see the section "Fonts and Text Rendering," later in this chapter.

Modifying a Text Field's Content

Once a text field's text content has been set, it can be reassigned via the text variable. For example, the following code creates a *TextField* object and sets it text content to "Hello":

```
var t:TextField = new TextField( );
t.text = "Hello";
```

The following code completely reassigns t's text to the string "Goodbye":

```
t.text = "Goodbye";
```

To add new text following a text field's existing text (rather than completely reassigning the text field's text), we use either the *TextField* class's instance method *appendText()* or the += operator. For example, the following code adds the string "...hope to see you again!" to the text "Goodbye":

```
t.appendText("...hope to see you again!");
```

After the preceding line of code executes, t.text has the value:

```
"Goodbye...hope to see you again!"
```

The appended text adopts the formatting of the last character in the text field, and any existing text retains its original formatting. If the text field contains no text when *appendText()* is called, the appended text is formatted with the text field's default text format.

For information on text formatting and the default text format, see the next section, "Formatting Text Fields."

Like the preceding code, the following code adds new text at the end of a text field's existing text, but does so with the += operator rather than *appendText()*:

```
t.text += " Come again soon.";
```

Unlike *appendText()*, the += operator resets the formatting of *all* text in the text field to the default text format. The += operator is also much slower than *appendText()*, and should, therefore, be avoided.

To replace an arbitrary sequence of characters in a text field with a new sequence of characters, we use the *TextField* class's instance method *replaceText()*, which has the following general form:

```
theTextField.replaceText(beginIndex, endIndex, newText)
```

The *replaceText()* method deletes the characters in *theTextField* from *beginIndex* to *endIndex*-1, and replaces them with *newText*. The new amalgamated value is reflected by *theTextField*.text.

For example, the following code replaces the characters "bcd" in the text "abcde" with the new text "x":

```
var t:TextField = new TextField();
t.text = "abcde";
t.replaceText(1, 4, "x");
trace(t.text);  // Displays: axe
```

If *beginIndex* and *endIndex* are equal, the *newText* is inserted immediately before the specified *beginIndex*. For example, the following code inserts the character "s" immediately before the character "t":

```
var t:TextField = new TextField();
t.text = "mat";
t.replaceText(2, 2, "s");
trace(t.text);  // Displays: mast
```

The remainder of this section describes formatting issues related to *replaceText()* and requires an understanding of the text formatting techniques discussed in the next section.

The formatting of text inserted via *replaceText()* varies according to the supplied values for *beginIndex* and *endIndex*. When *beginIndex* and *endIndex* are different, the inserted text adopts the formatting of the character after the inserted text (i.e., the character at *endIndex*). Any existing text retains its original formatting. For example, consider the following code, which creates a text field that displays the word "lunchtime," with the characters "time" formatted in bold:

```
var boldFormat:TextFormat = new TextFormat();
boldFormat.bold = true;

var t:TextField = new TextField();
t.text = "lunchtime";
t.setTextFormat(boldFormat, 5, 9);  // Bold the word "time"
```

The resulting output is:

lunch**time**

If we now use *replaceText()* to replace the word "lunch" with the word "dinner," as follows:

```
t.replaceText(0, 5, "dinner");      // Replace "lunch" with "dinner"
```

then the word "dinner" is formatted in bold, matching the formatting of the character at endIndex ("t"). The resulting output is:

dinnertime

To insert text in a new format, rather than adopt the existing format of the text field, we use *replaceText()* to assign the new text, then immediately assign the desired format to the new text. For example, the following code again replaces the word "lunch" with the word "dinner," but this time also formats the newly added text:

```
t.replaceText(0, 5, "dinner");      // Replace "lunch" with "dinner"
var regularFormat:TextFormat = new TextFormat();
regularFormat.bold = false;
t.setTextFormat(regularFormat, 0, 6);  // Un-bold the word dinner
```

The output of the preceding code is:

dinner**time**

When *replaceText()*'s *beginIndex* and *endIndex* arguments are both 0, text is inserted at the beginning of the text field, and the inserted text adopts the text field's default text format. Any existing text retains its original formatting.

When *beginIndex* and *endIndex* are equal, and are both greater than 0, the inserted text adopts the formatting of the character immediately preceding the inserted text (i.e., the character at *endIndex*-1). Any existing text retains its original formatting. For example, the following code once again creates a text field that displays the word "lunchtime," with "time" in bold:

```
var boldFormat:TextFormat = new TextFormat();
boldFormat.bold = true;
```

```
var t:TextField = new TextField( );
t.text = "lunchtime";
t.setTextFormat(boldFormat, 5, 9);  // Bold the word "time"
```

This time, we insert the text "break" immediately before the character "t":

```
t.replaceText(5, 5, "break");      // Insert "break" before "t"
```

Because the character at endIndex-1 ("h") is not formatted in bold, the word "break" is also not formatted in bold, and the resulting output is:

lunchbreak**time**

Now let's take a closer look at text formatting techniques.

Formatting Text Fields

ActionScript provides three different tools for applying text formatting: the *flash.text. TextFormat* class, HTML, and the *flash.text.StyleSheet* class. All three tools offer control over the following paragraph and character formatting options, but use different syntax:

Paragraph-level formatting
    Alignment, indentation, bullets, leading (line spacing, pronounced "led-ing"), tab stops

Character-level formatting
    Font face, font size, font weight (bold or normal), font color, font style (italic or normal), kerning, letter spacing (tracking), text underline, hypertext links

Paragraph-level formatting applies to entire paragraphs, where a paragraph is defined as a span of text delimited by line breaks (\n, <BR>, or <P>). By contrast, character-level formatting applies to arbitrary spans of individual characters, delimited using text indices or HTML or XML tags.

The *TextFormat* class offers detailed programmatic control over text formatting and is typically used when generating textual output dynamically. The *StyleSheet* class helps separate formatting instructions from formatted content and is typically used when formatting large bodies of HTML or XML content. HTML formatting instructions offer a simple, intuitive way to format text, but pollute text content with formatting markup. HTML is typically used when convenience is more important than flexibility, as might be the case when formatting text in an application prototype or when formatting short runs of text that are guaranteed not to change over the course of a project.

 The *TextFormat* class is fully compatible and interchangeable with HTML-based formatting instructions. However, the *StyleSheet* class is compatible with neither the *TextFormat* class nor HTML-based formatting instructions. Text fields that use style sheets can be formatted with instances of the *StyleSheet* class only.

The following sections discuss the general usage of *TextFormat* objects, HTML, and *StyleSheet* objects. Each section shows examples of common formatting operations. For coverage of each individual formatting option, see the following entries in Adobe's ActionScript Language Reference:

- *TextFormat* class
- TextField class's instance variable htmlText
- *StyleSheet* class

> Assigning a value to a *TextField* object's text variable removes any custom formatting associated with the field. Use the *TextField* class's instance method *replaceText( )* to add text to a field while retaining its formatting.

Formatting Text with the TextFormat Class

The general process for applying text formatting using the *TextFormat* class is as follows:

1. Create a *TextFormat* object.
2. Set the *TextFormat* object's variables to reflect the desired formatting.
3. Apply the format to one or more characters using the *TextField* class's instance method *setTextFormat( )*.

Let's apply the preceding steps to an example. Our goal is to format all the text in a text field using the font Arial, size 20 pt, in bold.

> In ActionScript, all font sizes are specified in pixels. A font size measurement of 20 pt is interpreted by Flash Player to mean 20 pixels.

We'll start our formatting code by creating a text field that will automatically resize to fit our formatted text:

```
var t:TextField = new TextField( );
t.text = "ActionScript is fun!";
t.autoSize = TextFieldAutoSize.LEFT;
```

Next, we'll create the *TextFormat* object:

```
var format:TextFormat = new TextFormat( );
```

Then, we'll set the font, size, and bold variables of our text field object to our desired values: "Arial", 20, and true, as follows:

```
format.font = "Arial";
format.size = 20;
format.bold = true;
```

Taken in combination, the *TextFormat* object's variables describe a formatting style that can be applied to a given character or span of characters. The available variables are listed in the next section, "Available TextFormat variables."

Once we've created a *TextFormat* object and set its variables, we can then apply the format to a character or span of characters using *setTextFormat()*, which takes the following form:

```
theTextField.setTextFormat(textFormat, beginIndex, endIndex)
```

In the preceding generalized code, `theTextField` is the text field whose text will be formatted, and `textFormat` is the *TextFormat* object containing formatting instructions. The `beginIndex` parameter is an optional integer indicating the index of the first character whose formatting will be set by `textFormat`. The `endIndex` parameter is an optional integer indicating the index of the character after the last character whose formatting will be set by `textFormat`.

When `beginIndex` and `endIndex` are both supplied, *setTextFormat()* formats the span of characters from `beginIndex` to `endIndex`-1 according to the variables of `textFormat`. When `beginIndex` is supplied but `endIndex` is not supplied, *setTextFormat()* formats the single character at `beginIndex` according to the variables of `textFormat`. When neither `beginIndex` nor `endIndex` are supplied, *setTextFormat()* formats all characters in `theTextField` according to the variables of `textFormat`. Any `textFormat` variable whose value is set to `null` has no affect on the formatting of the target span of characters (the existing formatting for the variable in question is retained).

Let's try using *setTextFormat()* to format the characters in our example text field, t. Here's the code:

```
t.setTextFormat(format);
```

For review, Example 27-5 shows the complete code required to format all the text in a text field using the font Arial, 20 pt, bold.

Example 27-5. Formatting a text field

```
// Create the text field
var t:TextField = new TextField();
t.text = "ActionScript is fun!";
t.autoSize = TextFieldAutoSize.LEFT;

// Create the TextFormat object and set its variables
var format:TextFormat = new TextFormat();
format.font = "Arial";
format.size = 20;
format.bold = true;

// Apply the format
t.setTextFormat(format);
```

The result of the code in Example 27-5 is shown in Figure 27-10.

```
┌─────────────────────────────────────────────────────────────────┐
│                                                                   │
│                      ActionScript is fun!                         │
│                                                                   │
└─────────────────────────────────────────────────────────────────┘
```

Figure 27-10. Text formatted with a TextFormat object

Now suppose we want to format all the text in our text field using Arial, 20 pt, but we want the word "fun" only in bold. We need two *TextFormat* objects, one for the general font settings and one for the specific bold setting. Example 27-6 shows the code (note the use of the *beginIndex* and *endIndex* parameters in the second call to *setTextFormat()*):

Example 27-6. Two formats

```
// Create the text field
var t:TextField = new TextField( );
t.text = "ActionScript is fun!";
t.autoSize = TextFieldAutoSize.LEFT;

// Create the TextFormat object for the general font settings
var fontFormat:TextFormat = new TextFormat( );
fontFormat.font = "Arial";
fontFormat.size = 20;

// Create the TextFormat object for the specific bold setting
var boldFormat:TextFormat = new TextFormat( );
boldFormat.bold = true;

// Apply the general font settings to the entire text field
t.setTextFormat(fontFormat);

// Apply the specific bold settings to the word fun only
t.setTextFormat(boldFormat, 16, 19);
```

Notice that sequential formatting is not destructive; formatting changes are applied only for variables that are set, so in the second call to *setTextFormat()* the word "fun" retains its font face (Arial) and size (20), and gains the formatting option bold.

Now that we've seen how to apply a format, let's briefly consider the complete list of formatting options available through the *TextFormat* class.

Available TextFormat variables

Tables 27-3 and 27-4 list the character and paragraph-level formatting variables of the *TextFormat* class. Skim over the tables for general familiarity. For detailed descriptions of each variable, see the *TextFormat* class entry in Adobe's ActionScript Language Reference.

Table 27-3 lists the *TextFormat* variables used to set character-level formatting options.

Table 27-3. Character-level TextFormat variables

Variable	Description
bold	Boolean; specifies bold character display
color	Specifies character color as a 24-bit integer (e.g., 0xFF0000)
font	Specifies the font
italic	Boolean; specifies italicized character display
kerning	Boolean; specifies whether to automatically kern character pairs
letterSpacing	Specifies the distance between letters (tracking), in pixels
size	Specifies character font size, in points (1/72 inch)
target	Specifies the window or frame for a hypertext link
underline	Boolean; specifies underlined character display
url	Specifies a hypertext link

Table 27-4 lists the *TextFormat* variables used to set paragraph-level formatting options.

Table 27-4. Paragraph-level TextFormat variables

Variable	Description
align	Specifies horizontal paragraph alignment (left, right, center, or justify), using one of the *TextFormatAlign* class constants
blockIndent	Specifies the distance, in pixels, a paragraph is indented from the text field's left border
bullet	Specifies whether to add bullets to paragraphs
indent	Specifies the distance, in pixels, a paragraph's first line is indented from the text field's left border
leading	Specifies the amount of vertical space, in pixels, between lines of text
leftMargin	Specifies the horizontal distance, in pixels, between the left border of the text field and the left edge of a paragraph
rightMargin	Specifies the horizontal distance, in pixels, between the right border of the text field and the right edge of a paragraph
tabStops	Specifies horizontal tab stops, in pixels

Of all of the variables listed in the preceding two tables, the TextFormat class's instance variable font bears special attention. Its value specifies the name of a font, as a string. As we'll learn later in the section "Fonts and Text Rendering," developers can instruct Flash Player to display text using fonts installed on the end user's local system (known as *device fonts*) or fonts included with a *.swf* file (known as *embedded fonts*). Accordingly, the font variable must specify either the name of a font on the local system or the name of a font embedded in a *.swf* file. For device fonts only, ActionScript also offers three special font names—"_sans," "_serif," and "_typewriter"—which can be used to indicate that text should be rendered in the default sans-serif, serif, or monospace font for the local system. For example, specifying "_sans" as a font name when using device fonts results in the font Arial on Microsoft Windows XP and Helvetica on MacOS X in the United States.

We'll learn more about specifying font names later in this chapter. For the purposes of the current discussion, we'll assume text is displayed using fonts installed on the end user's local system (device fonts), and we'll use names of fonts installed on Microsoft's Windows XP operating system.

Embedded font warning: Bold and italic require separate fonts

Note that when text formatted in bold or italic is rendered using embedded fonts, the bold and italic variations of the appropriate font(s) must be made available to Flash Player as embedded fonts. For example, consider the following code, which creates a text field containing the words "hello" and "world," with "hello" formatted in Courier New and "world" formatted in Courier New, bold:

```
// Create the text field
var t:TextField = new TextField( );
t.text = "hello world";

// Create TextFormat objects
var fontFormat:TextFormat = new TextFormat( );
fontFormat.font = "Courier New";
var boldFormat:TextFormat = new TextFormat( );
boldFormat.bold = true;

// Apply formatting
t.setTextFormat(fontFormat, 0, 11);
t.setTextFormat(boldFormat, 6, 11);
```

In order to render the preceding text field using embedded fonts, Flash Player must be given access to embedded versions of both Courier New and Courier New Bold. For complete details, see the section "Using bold and italic with embedded fonts," later in this chapter.

setTextFormat( ) does not apply to future text assignments

The *setTextFormat()* method can be used to format a text field's text only *after* that text has been added to the text field. For example, in the following code, we mistakenly invoke *setTextFormat()* before assigning the text we intend to format:

```
// Create the text field
var t:TextField = new TextField( );
t.autoSize = TextFieldAutoSize.LEFT;

// Create the TextFormat object and set its variables
var format:TextFormat = new TextFormat( );
format.font = "Arial";
format.size = 20;
format.bold = true;
```

```
// Apply the format
t.setTextFormat(format);

// Assign the text
t.text = "ActionScript is fun!";
```

When the *setTextFormat()* method is invoked in the preceding code, t does not yet contain any text, so the attempt to apply formatting has no effect. The correct code is:

```
// Create the text field
var t:TextField = new TextField();
t.autoSize = TextFieldAutoSize.LEFT;

// Create the TextFormat object and set its variables
var format:TextFormat = new TextFormat();
format.font = "Arial";
format.size = 20;
format.bold = true;

// Assign the text
t.text = "ActionScript is fun!";

// Apply the format
t.setTextFormat(format);
```

 When formatting text with *setTextFormat()*, always assign the text before formatting it.

For information on applying formatting to a text field before assigning its text, see the upcoming section, "Default formatting for text fields."

Applying paragraph-level formatting

To apply any of the paragraph-level formatting shown earlier in Table 27-4, we must apply the format to the first character in a paragraph (recall that in ActionScript, a paragraph is defined as a span of text delimited by line breaks).

For example, consider the following code, which first creates a text field with two paragraphs, and then creates a *TextFormat* object that specifies a paragraph-level formatting option, center alignment:

```
// Create the text field
var t:TextField = new TextField();
t.width = 300;
t.border = true;
// The paragraphs are separated by a single line break (represented by
// the escape sequence "\n")
t.text = "This is paragraph one.\nThis is paragraph two.";

// Create the TextFormat object
var alignFormat:TextFormat = new TextFormat();
alignFormat.align = TextFormatAlign.CENTER;
```

To set the alignment for the first paragraph in the text field only, we apply the format to the first character in the first paragraph, which resides at index 0:

```
t.setTextFormat(alignFormat, 0);
```

To set the alignment for the second paragraph only, we apply the format to the first character in the second paragraph, which resides at index 23:

```
t.setTextFormat(alignFormat, 23);
```

To set the alignment for a range of paragraphs, we apply the format using *beginIndex* and *endIndex* arguments that include the desired paragraphs:

```
t.setTextFormat(alignFormat, 0, 24);
```

When word wrapping is enabled, if any paragraph wraps to the next line, the specified format range must include the subsequent line's first character; otherwise, the format will not apply to the wrapped line. Hence, for best results when applying paragraph-level formatting to a paragraph in a text field that has wrapping enabled, always apply the format to the entire span of characters in the paragraph. To dynamically determine the beginning and end indices of the characters in a paragraph, use the *TextField* class's instance methods *getFirstCharInParagraph()* and *getParagraphLength()*. For example, the following code uses *getParagraphLength()* to dynamically determine the beginning and end indices of the two paragraphs in the text field from the preceding example code. The code then uses those indices to apply alignment formatting to the entire span of characters in the second paragraph.

```
// Create the text field
var t:TextField = new TextField();
t.width = 100;
t.border = true;
t.wordWrap = true;
t.text = "This is paragraph one.\nThis is paragraph two.";

// Create TextFormat object
var alignFormat:TextFormat = new TextFormat();
alignFormat.align = TextFormatAlign.CENTER;

// Determine paragraph start and end indices
var firstParagraphStart:int = 0;
var firstParagraphEnd:int = t.getParagraphLength(firstParagraphStart)-1;
var secondParagraphStart:int = firstParagraphEnd+1;
var secondParagraphEnd:int = secondParagraphStart
                          + t.getParagraphLength(secondParagraphStart)-1;

// Apply formatting
t.setTextFormat(alignFormat, secondParagraphStart, secondParagraphEnd);
```

Retrieving formatting information for a span of characters

To examine the existing formatting of one or more characters already in a field, we use the *TextField* class's instance method *getTextFormat()*. The *getTextFormat()* method returns a *TextFormat* object whose variables describe the formatting of the specified characters. The general form of *getTextFormat()* is as follows:

```
theTextField.getTextFormat(beginIndex, endIndex)
```

When *getTextFormat()* is invoked with one integer argument, or if *endIndex* is equal to *beginIndex*+1, the returned *TextFormat* object reflects the formatting for the single character at *beginIndex*. For example, here we apply a format to the first four characters of a text field, and then we check the font of the first character:

```
// Create the text field
var t:TextField = new TextField();
t.width = 100;
t.border = true;
t.wordWrap = true;
t.text = "What time is it?";

// Create a TextFormat object with a font variable of "Arial"
var arialFormat:TextFormat = new TextFormat();
arialFormat.font = "Arial";

// Apply the format to the word 'What', characters 0 to 3 (inclusive)
t.setTextFormat(arialFormat, 0, 4);

// Retrieve a TextFormat object for the first character
var firstCharFormat:TextFormat = t.getTextFormat(0);

// Check the font variable
trace(firstCharFormat.font); // Displays: Arial
```

When *getTextFormat()* is invoked with two integer arguments, the returned *TextFormat* object represents the formatting for the span of characters from beginIndex to endIndex-1. And when *getTextFormat()* is invoked with no arguments, the returned *TextFormat* object represents the formatting for all the characters in the field.

If a specific format (e.g., font, bold, or italic) is not the same for all characters in a specified span, the corresponding variable of the *TextFormat* object for that span will be null. Continuing with our example, if we retrieve a *TextFormat* object for the entire text of t, we find that variables shared by all characters return nonnull values:

```
// Retrieve a TextFormat object for all characters in theField_txt
var allCharsFormat:TextFormat = t.getTextFormat();

// Now check whether all the characters are bold
trace(allCharsFormat.bold); // Displays: false
```

But variables that vary between characters return null:

```
// Check the font for all characters
trace(allCharsFormat.font); // Displays: null (the font is not uniform)
```

The first four characters in t have a different font than the remaining characters, so no single font variable value can accurately describe the entire span; hence, font is set to null.

Note that changes to a *TextFormat* object returned by *getTextFormat()* do not have any effect on the text of *theTextField* unless the *TextFormat* object is subsequently reapplied with *setTextFormat()*. For example, on its own, the following assignment of the font variable has no effect on t:

```
allCharsFormat.font = "Courier New";
```

But when we add a call to *setTextFormat()*, the change is applied:

```
// Applies the "Courier New" font to the whole text field
t.setTextFormat(allCharsFormat);
```

Default formatting for text fields

Whenever new text is added to a text field, whether programmatically or through user input, ActionScript formats it with the *default text format* for the text field. The text field's default text format is an internal *TextFormat* object that specifies how new text should be formatted when no explicit formatting is specified.

However, a text field's default text format is not static; it dynamically adjusts itself to match the formatting of text at the insertion point (also known as the *caret position*). Accordingly, when the user inputs new text after a given character in a text field, that character's format determines the format of the new text. Likewise, as we learned earlier, when *replaceText()* is used to add new text to a text field, the new text takes on the formatting of either the character following the new text (if any existing text was deleted) or the character preceding the new text (if no existing text was deleted).

In general, the default text format should not be thought of as a developer tool for formatting new text added to a text field but rather as ActionScript's internal means of determining the formatting for new text added to a text field. To format new text in a given format, use *setTextFormat()* after the text is added. For example, consider the following code, which creates a text field whose text is all bold:

```
var t:TextField = new TextField();
t.width = 400;
t.text = "This is bold text.";
var boldFormat:TextFormat = new TextFormat();
boldFormat.bold = true;
t.setTextFormat(boldFormat);
```

Normally, any new text added to t would automatically also be formatted in bold. For example, the following new text is formatted in bold:

```
t.appendText(" This is bold too.");
```

To add new nonbold text to t, we must apply a nonbold format after appending the text, as follows:

```
// Add the text
t.appendText(" This isn't bold.");

// Immediately format the new text in non-bold. Notice that the
// indices of the first and last characters of the new text are
// retrieved dynamically via String.indexOf( ) and TextField.length.
var regularFormat:TextFormat = new TextFormat( );
regularFormat.bold = false;
t.setTextFormat(regularFormat,
                t.text.indexOf("This isn't bold."),
                t.length);
```

A similar approach for formatting new text added by the user is shown in the later section "Text Field Input."

Even though the default text format is primarily an internal ActionScript tool, developers can use it in one important way: to set the formatting of an *empty* text field. The format for an empty *TextField* object is specified by assigning a *TextFormat* object to the *TextField* object's defaultTextFormat variable, as follows:

```
// Create the text field
var t:TextField = new TextField( );
t.width = 300;

// Create the TextFormat object
var defaultFormat:TextFormat = new TextFormat( );
defaultFormat.size  = 20;
defaultFormat.color = 0xFF0000;
defaultFormat.font  = "Verdana";

// Assign the TextFormat object to t's defaultTextFormat variable
t.defaultTextFormat = defaultFormat;
```

Once an empty *TextField* object's defaultTextFormat is assigned, all future text added to the text field, whether programmatically or through user input, will be formatted according to that defaultTextFormat—unless new custom formatting is applied to the characters in the text field. For example, the following code adds new text to t; the new text is automatically formatted in 20 pt red Verdana (per t.defaultTextFormat):

```
t.text = "This is 20 pt red Verdana";
```

Once custom formatting has been applied to the characters in the text field, future text added to the text field will be formatted to match the formatting of text at the insertion point.

Now that we're familiar with the basics of formatting text using the *TextFormat* class, let's move on to formatting text with HTML.

Formatting Text with HTML

To apply formatting to a text field using HTML, we follow these general steps:

1. Create a *TextField* object.

2. Create a string of text containing HTML-based formatting instructions using ActionScript's limited set of HTML formatting tags.

3. Assign the HTML-formatted text to the *TextField* object's htmlText variable. Any HTML-formatted text assigned to the htmlText variable is displayed as formatted text on screen.

Let's apply the preceding steps to an example. Our goal is to format all the text in a text field using the font Arial, size 20 pt, in bold (as we did earlier with a *TextFormat* object).

We'll start by creating a text field that will automatically resize to fit our formatted text:

```
var t:TextField = new TextField( );
t.autoSize = TextFieldAutoSize.LEFT;
```

Next, we'll create our formatted text string using the <B> tag and <FONT> tag:

```
var message:String = "<FONT FACE='Arial' SIZE='20'>"
                   + "<B>ActionScript is fun!</B></FONT>";
```

Finally, we assign the HTML string to t's htmlText variable:

```
t.htmlText = message;
```

The result is shown in Figure 27-11.

ActionScript is fun!

Figure 27-11. Text formatted with HTML

Often, HTML text is assigned directly to the htmlText variable, as shown in the following code:

```
t.htmlText = "<FONT FACE='Arial' SIZE='20'>"
           + "<B>ActionScript is fun!</B></FONT>";
```

Using HTML we can apply any of the formatting options available through the *TextFormat* class. Table 27-5 lists ActionScript's supported set of HTML tags and attributes, complete with cross references to equivalent *TextFormat* class variables. For additional information on ActionScript HTML support, see the entry for *TextField* class's instance variable htmlText in Adobe's ActionScript Language Reference.

Unlike the Flash Player plug-in and standalone Flash Player, Adobe AIR includes a full-featured HTML parser and renderer, capable of handling the full range of HTML, CSS, and JavaScript normally used with web browsers.

Note that when style sheets are not in use, Flash Player automatically adds HTML markup to htmlText if the HTML source assigned to htmlText does not fully describe the text field's formatting. For example, the following code sets htmlText without using any <P> or <FONT> tags:

```
var t:TextField = new TextField( );
t.htmlText = "This field contains <B>HTML!</B>";
```

When we examine the value of t.htmlText, we find that <P> and <FONT> tags have been added:

```
trace(t.htmlText);
// Displays:
<P ALIGN="LEFT"><FONT FACE="Times New Roman" SIZE="12" COLOR="#000000"
LETTERSPACING="0" KERNING="0">This field contains <B>HTML!</B></FONT></P>
```

Now let's look at ActionScript's supported set of HTML tags and attributes in Table 27.5.

Table 27-5. ActionScript's supported HTML tags

Tag	Description	Attributes	Description	Equivalent *TextFormat* instance variable
<A>	Specifies a hypertext link	HREF	Specifies the destination of a hypertext link	url
		TARGET	Specifies the window or frame for a hypertext link	target
<B>	Specifies bold character display	None		bold
 	Causes a line break in a body of text; functionally equivalent to the \n escape sequence	None		None
<FONT>	Specifies font information	FACE	Specifies the font name	font
		SIZE	Specifies the font size, in points	size

Table 27-5. ActionScript's supported HTML tags (continued)

Tag	Description	Attributes	Description	Equivalent *TextFormat* instance variable
		COLOR	Specifies the font color, as a 24-bit integer hexadecimal number preceded by the pound sign (#). For example, red is #FF0000	`color`
		KERNING	Specifies whether to kern character pairs (1 means kern, 0 means don't kern)	`kerning`
		LETTERSPACING	Specifies the distance between letters (i.e., the tracking), in pixels	`lettterSpacing`
`<I>`	Specifies italic character display	None		`italic`
`<IMAGE>`	Specifies a display asset to embed in the text field	SRC	The location of the asset (image, *.swf* file, or movie clip symbol) to embed in the text field	None
		WIDTH	The optional width of the embedded asset	None
		HEIGHT	The optional height of the embedded asset	None
		ALIGN	The optional horizontal alignment of the embedded asset	None
		HSPACE	The optional horizontal space surrounding the embedded asset	None
		VSPACE	The optional vertical space surrounding the embedded asset	None
		ID	Specifies an optional identifier by which the embedded asset can be referenced via the *TextField* class's instance method *getImageReference( )*	None

Table 27-5. ActionScript's supported HTML tags (continued)

Tag	Description	Attributes	Description	Equivalent *TextFormat* instance variable
		CHECKPOLICYFILE	Specifies whether a policy file should be checked before the asset is accessed as data (see Chapter 19)	None
`<LI>`	Specifies a paragraph displayed with a preceding bullet; note that the bullet cannot be modified, and that no `<UL>` or `<OL>` is required	None		bullet
`<P>`	Specifies a paragraph	ALIGN	Specifies horizontal paragraph alignment (left, right, center, or justify)	align
		CLASS	Specifies the CSS class, for use with style sheets	None
`<SPAN>`	Marks an arbitrary span of text so it can be formatted with a style sheet	CLASS	Specifies the CSS class, for use with style sheets	None
`<TEXTFORMAT>`	Specifies formatting information for a span of text	LEFTMARGIN	Specifies the horizontal distance, in pixels, between the left border of the text field and the left edge of a paragraph	leftMargin
		RIGHTMARGIN	Specifies the horizontal distance, in pixels, between the right border of the text field and the right edge of a paragraph	rightMargin
		BLOCKINDENT	Specifies the distance, in pixels, a paragraph is indented from the text field's left border	blockIndent
		INDENT	Specifies the distance, in pixels, a paragraph's first line is indented from the text field's left border	indent

Table 27-5. ActionScript's supported HTML tags (continued)

Tag	Description	Attributes	Description	Equivalent *TextFormat* instance variable
		LEADING	Specifies the amount of vertical space, in pixels, between lines of text	`leading`
		TABSTOPS	Specifies horizontal tab stops, in pixels	`tabStops`
`<U>`	Specifies underlined character display	None		`underline`

Generally speaking, the usage of the HTML tags in ActionScript listed in Table 27-5 matches that found in common web browsers. That said, there are some significant differences between the use of HTML in ActionScript and the use of HTML in web browsers, as follows:

- The `<TABLE>` tag is not supported; use tab stops to simulate HTML tables.
- In ActionScript, HTML is used primarily for formatting, and HTML content is not organized using the web-browser document metaphor. Therefore, the `<HTML>` and `<BODY>` tags are not required (but the `<BODY>` tag can optionally be used when formatting HTML with style sheets).
- Unsupported tags are ignored, although their text content is preserved.
- Flash requires quotes around the values assigned to tag attributes. See the section "Quoting attribute values."
- Hypertext links are not underlined automatically in Flash and must be underlined manually using the `<U>` tag or the CSS `text-decoration` variable.
- The `<LI>` tag does not support multilevel bullets or the `<OL>` (numbered list) tag.
- Unterminated `<P>` tags do not cause line breaks in Flash Player as they do in regular HTML. Closing `</P>` tags are required by Flash Player in order for line breaks to be added.
- In Flash Player, `<P>` causes a single line break, exactly like `<BR>`, whereas in web browsers, `<P>` traditionally causes a double line break.
- The `<P>` and `<BR>` tags do not cause a line break in text fields whose `multiline` variable is set to `false`. Furthermore, `multiline` is set to `false` by default. Hence, set `multiline` to `true` when using `<P>` and `<BR>`.
- Hypertext links can be used to execute ActionScript code. For details, see the section "Hypertext Links," later in this chapter.
- The `NAME` attribute of the `<A>` tag is not supported by Flash Player, so internal links within a body of text are not possible.
- In Flash, anchor tags are not added to the tab order and are therefore not accessible via the keyboard.

Entity support

ActionScript's supported special character entities are listed in Table 27-6. Wherever an entity appears in a text field's htmlText variable, Flash Player displays the corresponding character on screen. Numeric entities such as ™ (trademark symbol) are also supported.

Table 27-6. Supported entities

Entity	Character represented
&lt;	<
&gt;	>
&amp;	&
&quot;	"
&apos;	'
	nonbreaking space

Quoting attribute values

Outside Flash Player, HTML attribute values may be quoted with single quotes, double quotes, or not at all. The following tags are all valid in most web browsers:

```
<P ALIGN=RIGHT>
<P ALIGN='RIGHT'>
<P ALIGN="RIGHT">
```

But in Flash Player, unquoted attribute values are not allowed. For example, the syntax <P ALIGN=RIGHT> is illegal in ActionScript. However, both single and double quotes may be used to delimit attribute values. When composing text field values that include HTML attributes, use one type of quote to demarcate the string itself and another to demarcate attribute values. For example, these examples are both valid:

```
t.htmlText = "<P ALIGN='RIGHT'>hi there</P>";
t.htmlText = '<P ALIGN="RIGHT">hi there</P>';
```

However, this example would cause an error because double quotation marks are used to demarcate both the string and the attribute:

```
// ILLEGAL! Do not use!
t.htmlText = "<P ALIGN="RIGHT">hi there</P>";
```

Interactions between the text and htmlText variables

Because the *TextField* variables text and htmlText can both assign the textual content of a text field, care must be taken when using those variables in combination.

When HTML tags are assigned to htmlText, the value of text will be that of htmlText, but with all HTML tags stripped out. For example, here we assign some HTML to a text field's htmlText variable:

```
var t:TextField = new TextField();
t.htmlText = '<P ALIGN="LEFT">' +
    + '<FONT FACE="Times New Roman" SIZE="12" COLOR="#000000" '
    + 'LETTERSPACING="0" KERNING="0">This field contains <B>HTML!</B>'
    + '</FONT></P>';
```

After the assignment, htmlText has the value:

```
<P ALIGN="LEFT"><FONT FACE="Times New Roman" SIZE="12" COLOR="#000000"
LETTERSPACING="0" KERNING="0">This field contains <B>HTML!</B></FONT></P>
```

But text has the value:

```
This field contains HTML!
```

Take heed that successive assignments to htmlText and text overwrite each other. That is, assigning a new value to text overwrites the value of htmlText and vice versa. By contrast, successive concatenations (not reassignments) do not overwrite each other. For example, the following code assigns some HTML content to htmlText, then concatenates a string to that content via the text variable:

```
var t:TextField = new TextField();
t.htmlText = "<B>hello</B>";
t.text += " world";
```

After the concatenation, the value of htmlText is:

```
<P ALIGN="LEFT"><FONT FACE="Times New Roman" SIZE="12" COLOR="#000000"
LETTERSPACING="0" KERNING="0">hello world</FONT></P>
```

As the preceding code shows, concatenating text to htmlText resets the text field's formatting. When we assigned the value "world" to text, Flash removed the <B> tag we originally assigned to htmlText! Hence, mixing text and htmlText assignments is generally not recommended.

HTML tags assigned directly to the *TextField* class's instance variable text are never interpreted as HTML; they are always displayed verbatim. For example, the following code assigns a string including HTML tags to text and then concatenates a plain string to that content via the htmlText variable:

```
var t:TextField = new TextField();
t.text = "<B>world</B>";
t.htmlText += "hello";
```

After the concatenation, the value of htmlText is as follows:

```
<P ALIGN="LEFT"><FONT FACE="Times New Roman" SIZE="12" COLOR="#000000"
LETTERSPACING="0" KERNING="0">&lt;B&gt;world&lt;/B&gt;hello</FONT></P>
```

Notice that the < and > characters in the <B> tag were converted to the HTML entities < and >.

Unrecognized tags and attributes

Like web browsers, Flash Player ignore tags and attributes it does not recognize. For example, if we were to assign the following value to htmlText:

```
<P>Please fill in and print this form</P>
<FORM><INPUT TYPE="TEXT"></FORM>
<P>Thank you!</P>
```

The output would be:

> Please fill in and print this form
>
> Thank you!

The <FORM> and <INPUT> elements are not supported by Flash Player so both are ignored (in fact, the unknown tags are stripped from htmlText!)

Similarly, if we use container elements such as <TD>, the content is preserved but the markup is ignored. For example, in the following code:

```
theTextField.htmlText = "<TABLE><TR><TD>table cell text</TD></TR></TABLE>";
```

outputs the following line without table formatting:

> table cell text

However, if a tag is not terminated, the entire text that follows is considered part of the tag and will not display on screen. For example, given the following assignment:

```
theTextField.htmlText = "We all know that 5 < 20. That's obvious.";
```

Flash Player displays:

> We all know that 5

To include a < character in an HTML text field, use the entity < as follows:

```
theTextField.htmlText = "We all know that 5 &lt; 20. That's obvious.";
```

Flash Player displays:

> We all know that 5 < 20. That's obvious.

For more information on including HTML source code in an HTML text field, see http://moock.org/asdg/technotes/sourceInHtmlField/

We've now seen how to format a text field using the *TextFormat* class and HTML. Now let's look at the last tool for formatting text, the *StyleSheet* class.

Formatting Text with the StyleSheet Class

ActionScript's *StyleSheet* class is used to format text fields using style sheets. Its functionality is based on a very limited subset of the W3C's Cascading style sheets, Level 1 Recommendation (CSS1).

This section assumes a prior understanding of basic CSS concepts. If you are new to CSS, you should read the following introductions to CSS before continuing:

- *http://www.w3.org/TR/CSS21/intro.html*
- *http://www.w3.org/MarkUp/Guide/Style*

But bear in mind that ActionScript does not support the full range of features in the W3C recommendation.

As described in the W3C's CSS recommendation, a *stylesheet* is a collection of rules that specify the presentation of a document. Each rule describes the style for a particular element in an HTML or XML document. The following code shows an example rule that specifies the font color red for ‹H1› elements:

```
h1 { color: #FF0000 }
```

Within that rule, the selector (h1) indicates the element to which the style should be applied. The declaration block ({ color: #FF0000 }) contains one or more declarations describing the style that should be applied to the selected element. Each declaration (color: #FF0000) contains a style property (color) and a value (#FF0000).

Selectors are not case-sensitive, but style property names are.

Here's a simple style sheet that contains two rules, one for ‹p› elements and one for ‹li› elements:

```
p {
  font-family: sans-serif
  font-size: 12px;
}

li {
  font-family: serif
  font-size: 10px;
  margin-left: 10px;
}
```

In ActionScript 3.0, a style sheet such as that shown in the preceding code is represented by an instance of the *StyleSheet* class. Using the methods of the *StyleSheet* class, we can create a new style sheet programmatically or parse an existing external style sheet. To associate a *StyleSheet* object with a particular *TextField* object, we assign it to that *TextField* object's styleSheet variable (covered later). Each text field can be associated with a single *StyleSheet* object only, in stark contrast to CSS1, where multiple style sheets can be associated with a single HTML or XML document.

The specific properties available for use in an ActionScript style sheet are listed in Table 27-7. ActionScript supports only those W3C style properties that map to the formatting options of the *TextFormat* class. Compared to the full range of properties defined by the W3C, ActionScript's set of supported properties is extremely limited.

Table 27-7. Supported CSS style properties

Style property name	Description
color	Specifies the font color, as a 24-bit integer hexadecimal number preceded by the pound sign (#). For example, red is #FF0000.
display	Specifies whether the element should be hidden (none), followed by an automatic line break (block) or not followed by an automatic line break (inline).
font-family	Specifies the device or embedded font name.
font-size	Specifies the font size, in pixels.
font-style	Specifies italicized character display (italic) or normal character display (normal, default).
font-weight	Specifies bold character display (bold) or normal character display (normal, default).
kerning	Specifies whether character pairs should be automatically kerned (true) or not (false, default). This property is an unofficial extension to the W3C set of supported style properties.
leading	Specifies the amount, in pixels, of vertical space between lines of text. This property is an unofficial extension to the W3C set of supported style properties. Compare with the W3C property line-height.
letter-spacing	Specifies the distance, in pixels, between letters (i.e., the tracking).
margin-left	Specifies the horizontal distance, in pixels, between the left border of the text field and the left edge of a paragraph.
margin-right	Specifies the horizontal distance, in pixels, between the right border of the text field and the right edge of a paragraph.
text-align	Specifies horizontal paragraph alignment (left—the default—right, center, or justify).
text-decoration	Specifies graphical embellishments added to the text. Supported values in ActionScript are underline and none (the default).
text-indent	Specifies the distance, in pixels, a paragraph's first line is indented from the text field's left border (exactly like the *TextFormat* class's instance variable indent).

Style sheets can be used to add formatting to both XML elements and HTML elements. However, among the HTML elements that Flash Player uses for formatting (see Table 27-5), only <P>, <LI>, and <A> tags can be formatted with style sheets. Other built-in tags (e.g., <B> and <I>) always perform their intended HTML-formatting duty, and cannot be formatted with style sheets. Furthermore, <P> and <LI> always display as block elements, even when instructed to display as inline elements by a style sheet.

To add formatting to the various interactive states of a hypertext link, use the following pseudo class selectors: a:link, a:hover, and a:active. For example, the following rule specifies that hypertext links should be underlined when under the mouse pointer:

```
a:hover {
  text-decoration: underline;
}
```

Style sheets give developers the critically important ability to separate style information from content, and to apply a single style definition to multiple bodies of content. However, in ActionScript, style sheets have many limitations that diminish their potential usefulness. Before we learn how to format text using style sheets, let's peruse those limitations.

Notable style sheet limitations in ActionScript

By design, Flash Player provides a minimal style sheet implementation only, intended as a style sheet–inspired interface for setting text field formatting options. As a result, Flash Player's style sheet support lacks several important features found in the W3C's CSS recommendation. Readers accustomed to working with CSS and HTML should stay mindful of the following Flash Player limitations:

- All lengths are expressed in pixels. The relative unit em is not supported, and points are treated as pixels.

- Each text field can be associated with one style sheet at a time only. Flash Player style sheets do not "cascade."

- Reassigning a text field's style sheet does not cause the text field to be rendered in the newly assigned style sheet (for a workaround, see the example following this list).

- The `margin-top` and `margin-bottom` properties are not supported.

- Elements cannot be arbitrarily displayed as list items. The `display` property value `list-item` is not supported. Furthermore, list-item markers (i.e., bullets) cannot be customized, even for the built-in `<LI>` HTML element.

- Flash Player supports basic type selectors and class selectors only. All other varieties of selectors are not supported. Furthermore, type selectors and class selectors cannot be combined (e.g., the following selector is illegal in Flash Player: `p.someCustomClass`). If a style sheet contains a descendant selector, the entire style sheet is ignored and no formatting is applied.

- When a style sheet is assigned to a text field, that text field's text content cannot be modified via *replaceText( )*, *appendText( )*, *replaceSelText( )* or user input.

To change a text field's style sheet, first assign the desired *StyleSheet* object to styleSheet, then assign htmlText to itself, as follows:

```
t.styleSheet = someNewStyleSheet;
t.htmlText = t.htmlText;
```

Note, however, that the new style sheet must set all style properties set by the old style sheet; otherwise, any unset old style property values will be retained.

Now that we're familiar with the general features and limitations of Flash Player's style sheets, let's see them in action. The following two sections describe how to apply a style sheet to a text field, first using a programmatically created style sheet, then using a style sheet loaded from an external *.css* file.

Formatting text with a programmatically created style sheet

To format text with a programmatically created style sheet, follow these general steps:

1. Create one or more generic objects representing rule declaration blocks.

2. Create a *StyleSheet* object.

3. Use the *StyleSheet* class's instance method *setStyle()* to create one or more rules based on the declaration blocks created in Step 1.

4. Use the *TextField* class's instance variable styleSheet to register the *StyleSheet* object with the desired *TextField* object.

5. Assign the desired HTML or XML content to the *TextField* object's htmlText variable.

 Always register the *StyleSheet* object (Step 4) before assigning the HTML or XML content (Step 5). Otherwise, the style sheet will not be applied to the content.

Let's apply the preceding steps to an example. Our goal is to format all the text in a text field using the font Arial, size 20 pt, in bold (as we did earlier with the *TextFormat* class and with HTML). Once again, the text we'll be formatting is the following simple HTML fragment:

```
<p>ActionScript is fun!</p>
```

In our style sheet, we'll define a rule that tells Flash Player to display the content of all <P> tags in Arial, size 20 pt, bold. The declaration block for our rule is a simple generic object with dynamic instance variable names matching CSS-style properties and variable values specifying corresponding CSS-style values. Here's the code:

```
// Create the object that will serve as the declaration block
var pDeclarationBlock:Object = new Object();

// Assign style properties
pDeclarationBlock.fontFamily = "Arial"
pDeclarationBlock.fontSize   = "20";
pDeclarationBlock.fontWeight = "bold";
```

In the preceding code, notice that when style sheets are created programmatically, the format for CSS property names changes slightly: hyphens are removed and characters following hyphens are capitalized. For example, `font-family` becomes `fontFamily`.

Now that we have our declaration block ready, we'll create the *StyleSheet* object. Here's the code:

```
var styleSheet:StyleSheet = new StyleSheet();
```

To create the <P> tag rule, we use the *StyleSheet* class's instance method *setStyle()*. The *setStyle()* method creates a new style rule, based on two parameters: a selector name (as a *String*), and a declaration block (as an *Object*), as shown in the following generic code:

```
theStyleSheet.setStyle("selector", declarationBlock);
```

Accordingly, here's the code for our <P> tag rule:

```
styleSheet.setStyle("p", pDeclarationBlock);
```

Our style sheet is now complete. Next we'll create the text field to format. The following code creates the text field and assigns our *StyleSheet* object to its `styleSheet` variable:

```
var t:TextField = new TextField();
t.width  = 200
t.styleSheet = styleSheet;
```

Finally, we assign the `htmlText` to be formatted:

```
t.htmlText = "<p>ActionScript is fun!</p>";
```

Example 27-7 shows the code for our formatted text field in its entirety.

Example 27-7. Text Formatted with a programmatically created style sheet

```
// Create the declaration block
var pDeclarationBlock:Object = new Object();
pDeclarationBlock.fontFamily = "Arial"
pDeclarationBlock.fontSize   = "20";
pDeclarationBlock.fontWeight = "bold";

// Create the stylesheet
var styleSheet:StyleSheet = new StyleSheet();

// Create the rule
styleSheet.setStyle("p", pDeclarationBlock);

// Create the text field
var t:TextField = new TextField();
t.width  = 200

// Assign the stylesheet
t.styleSheet = styleSheet;

// Assign the HTML code to be styled
t.htmlText = "<p>ActionScript is fun!</p>";
```

The result of the code in Example 27-7 is identical to the result shown earlier in Figures 27-10 and 27-11.

Class selectors

To apply a style to one specific variety of paragraph rather than all paragraphs, we use a CSS class selector. For example, suppose we want to draw special attention to important notes in a document. We place the notes in <p> tags with the class attribute set to the custom value specialnote, as follows:

```
<p class='specialnote'>Set styleSheet before htmlText!</p>
```

Then, we create a rule for that specialnote class using a class selector, as follows:

```
styleSheet.setStyle(".specialnote", specialnoteDeclarationBlock);
```

As in CSS, an ActionScript class selector is made up of a period followed by the desired class attribute value (in our case, specialnote).

Example 27-8 revises our earlier style sheet example to demonstrate the use of CSS class selectors in ActionScript.

Example 27-8. Formatting applied to a specific class of paragraph

```
var specialnoteDeclarationBlock:Object = new Object( );
specialnoteDeclarationBlock.fontFamily = "Arial"
specialnoteDeclarationBlock.fontSize   = "20";
specialnoteDeclarationBlock.fontWeight = "bold";

var styleSheet:StyleSheet = new StyleSheet( );
styleSheet.setStyle(".specialnote", specialnoteDeclarationBlock);

// Create the text field
var t:TextField = new TextField( );
t.width     = 300;
t.wordWrap  = true;
t.multiline = true;
t.styleSheet = styleSheet;
t.htmlText = "<p>Always remember...</p>"
  + "<p class='specialnote'>Set styleSheet before htmlText!</p>"
  + "<p>Otherwise, the stylesheet will not be applied.</p>";
```

The result of the code in Example 27-8 is shown in Figure 27-12.

> Always remember...
> ### Set styleSheet before
> ### html Text!
> Otherwise, the stylesheet will not be applied.

Figure 27-12. Formatting applied to a specific class of paragraph

Formatting XML tags with CSS

To apply a style to a specific variety of content, we can create a custom XML tag for that content. For example, rather than describing a special note as a class of paragraph (as we did in the preceding section), we could instead create a completely new XML tag, as follows:

```
<specialnote>Set styleSheet before htmlText!</specialnote>
```

To apply a style rule to the <specialnote> tag, we use a normal type selector (with no leading period), as follows:

```
styleSheet.setStyle("specialnote", specialnoteDeclarationBlock);
```

And to specify that our <specialnote> tag should behave like a paragraph, we set the display variable to block in the <specialnote> rule. Example 27-9 shows the complete code for styling a custom XML tag, with noteworthy differences from our preceding class-selector code shown in bold.

Example 27-9. Formatting XML content with a style sheet

```
var specialnoteDeclarationBlock:Object = new Object( );
specialnoteDeclarationBlock.fontFamily = "Arial"
specialnoteDeclarationBlock.fontSize   = "20";
specialnoteDeclarationBlock.fontWeight = "bold";
specialnoteDeclarationBlock.display    = "block";

var styleSheet:StyleSheet = new StyleSheet( );
styleSheet.setStyle("specialnote", specialnoteDeclarationBlock);

var t:TextField = new TextField( );
t.width     = 300;
t.wordWrap  = true;
t.multiline = true;
t.styleSheet = styleSheet;
t.htmlText = "<p>Always remember...</p>"
  + "<specialnote>Set styleSheet before htmlText!</specialnote>"
  + "<p>Otherwise, the stylesheet will not be applied.</p>";
```

The result of the code shown in Example 27-9 is identical to that shown in Figure 27-12.

Formatting text with an externally loaded style sheet

To format text with an externally loaded style sheet, follow these general steps:

1. Create a style sheet in an external *.css* file.
2. Use the *URLLoader* class to load the *.css* file.
3. Once the *.css* file has loaded, create a *StyleSheet* object.
4. Use the *StyleSheet* class's instance method *parseCSS( )* to import the rules from the *.css* file into the *StyleSheet* object.

5. Use the *TextField* class's instance variable styleSheet to register the *StyleSheet* object with the desired *TextField* object.

6. Assign the desired HTML or XML content to the *TextField* object's htmlText variable.

Let's apply the preceding steps to an example. Our goal is, once again, to create an application that formats all the text in a text field using the font Arial, size 20 pt, in bold. As before, the text we'll be formatting is the following simple HTML fragment:

```
<p>ActionScript is fun!</p>
```

We start by adding the following CSS rule to a text file named *styles.css*:

```
p {
  font-family: Arial;
  font-size: 20px;
  font-weight: bold;
}
```

Next we create our application's main class, *StyleSheetLoadingDemo*. *StyleSheetLoadingDemo* uses a *URLLoader* object to load *styles.css*, as follows:

```
package {
  import flash.display.*;
  import flash.text.*;
  import flash.events.*;
  import flash.net.*;

  public class StyleSheetLoadingDemo extends Sprite {
    public function StyleSheetLoadingDemo () {
      // Load styles.css
      var urlLoader:URLLoader = new URLLoader();
      urlLoader.addEventListener(Event.COMPLETE, completeListener);
      urlLoader.load(new URLRequest("styles.css"));
    }

    private function completeListener (e:Event):void {
      // Code here is executed when styles.css finishes loading
    }
  }
}
```

When *styles.css* has finished loading, *completeListener()* executes. Within *completeListener()*, we create a new *StyleSheet* object and import the rules from *styles.css* into it, as follows:

```
private function completeListener (e:Event):void {
  var styleSheet:StyleSheet = new StyleSheet();
  styleSheet.parseCSS(e.target.data);
}
```

Once the rules have been imported into the *StyleSheet* object, we create our *TextField* object, register our style sheet, then assign the text to be styled, as follows:

```
var t:TextField = new TextField( );
t.width = 200;
t.styleSheet = styleSheet;
t.htmlText = "<p>ActionScript is fun!</p>";
```

Example 27-10 shows the code for the *StyleSheetLoadingDemo* class in its entirety.

Example 27-10. Text formatted with an external style sheet

```
package {
  import flash.display.*;
  import flash.text.*;
  import flash.events.*;
  import flash.net.*;

  public class StyleSheetLoadingDemo extends Sprite {
    public function StyleSheetLoadingDemo ( ) {
      var urlLoader:URLLoader = new URLLoader( );
      urlLoader.addEventListener(Event.COMPLETE, completeListener);
      urlLoader.load(new URLRequest("styles.css"));
    }

    private function completeListener (e:Event):void {
      var styleSheet:StyleSheet = new StyleSheet( );
      styleSheet.parseCSS(e.target.data);

      var t:TextField = new TextField( );
      t.width = 200;
      t.styleSheet = styleSheet;
      t.htmlText = "<p>ActionScript is fun!</p>";

      addChild(t);
    }
  }
}
```

The result of the code in Example 27-10 is identical to the result shown earlier in Figures 27-10 and 27-11.

We've now finished our study of ActionScript's text formatting techniques. In the next section, we'll study several issues relating to font rendering and the use of fonts in a *.swf* file.

Fonts and Text Rendering

By default, Flash Player displays text using *device fonts*. Device fonts are fonts that are installed on the end user's system. When Flash Player displays text with a device font, it completely delegates the text-rendering process to the local environment (i.e., operating system). For example, consider the following simple *HelloWorld* application, which creates a text field formatted with the font Arial:

```
package {
  import flash.display.*;
  import flash.text.*;

  public class HelloWorld extends Sprite {
    public function HelloWorld () {
      var fontFormat:TextFormat = new TextFormat();
      fontFormat.font = "Arial";

      var t:TextField = new TextField();
      t.text = "Hello world";
      t.setTextFormat(fontFormat);

      addChild(t);
    }
  }
}
```

When that code runs, Flash Player adds t to the display list, and prepares to update the screen. To display the characters "Hello world," Flash Player passes the string "Hello world" to the operating system's text renderer, and asks it to render those characters using the system font "Arial." The operating system then renders the characters directly to Flash Player's frame buffer. For example, on Microsoft Windows XP, the string "Hello world" is rendered using Microsoft's ClearType renderer.

If the preceding *HelloWorld* application runs on two different computers with two different operating systems, those computers may have two different native text renderers, and perhaps even two different versions of the font Arial. Hence, even when the required font is available, the character that appears on screen may look quite different from computer to computer. Additionally, using cacheAsBitmap or filters can subtly change text-rendering behavior. For example, if a *TextField* object is placed in a *Sprite* object whose cacheAsBitmap variable is true, Windows XP will use normal antialiasing instead of ClearType.

If a font specified for a given character is not installed on the end user's operating system, Flash Player will automatically ask the operating system to render the character in an appropriate substitute font. For example, if the font for a given character is set to Verdana, and that character is displayed on the default installation of MacOS X (which does not include Verdana), then the character will be rendered in the default sans-serif font, Helvetica. Hence, depending on the availability of fonts on the end-user's operating system, text rendered in device fonts on two different computers with two different operating systems might have a drastically different appearance.

When device fonts are used, text display varies by operating system and, for the plug-in version of Flash Player, by web browser.

If no font is specified at all for a given character, the local renderer renders the character in an arbitrary default font of Flash Player's choosing. For example, on Microsoft Windows XP, the default font is Times New Roman.

To eliminate differences in text rendering across computers and devices, Flash Player enables developers to embed font outlines in a *.swf* file. Text that is rendered using embedded font outlines is guaranteed to have a very similar appearance across varied computers, operating systems, and devices. However, this consistency comes at a price; embedding outlines for a complete Roman font typically adds 20 to 30 KB to a *.swf* file (Asian fonts can be much larger). Device fonts, by contrast, do not increase a *.swf* file's size at all. Hence, device fonts are typically used when small file size is more important than visual integrity, and embedded font outlines are typically used when visual integrity is more important than small file size.

To use an embedded font we must first embed that font's outlines and then enable embedded fonts for the desired text field(s) at runtime. When embedded fonts are enabled for a text field, that text field is rendered by either Flash Player's standard vector renderer or the specialized FlashType renderer, not the local environment's text renderer. Note that every variation of a font style must be embedded individually. If a text field uses embedded versions of Courier New in bold, italic, and bold italic, then we must embed all three font variations, or the text will not display correctly. Underline is not considered a font variation, nor is font size or color.

The technique for embedding font outlines at compile time varies for different development tools. The following two sections explain how to embed fonts in the Flash authoring tool and Flex Builder 2.0 or the *mxmlc* command line compiler. Each section describes how to embed an example font, Verdana. Once a font's outlines are embedded in a *.swf* file, they can be used to format text, as described in the section "Formatting Text with an Embedded Font."

Embedding Font Outlines in the Flash Authoring Tool

To embed Verdana outlines in the Flash authoring tool, follow these steps:

1. Select Window → Library.
2. From the pop-up Options menu in the upper-right corner of the panel, select New Font. The Font Symbol Properties dialog box appears.
3. Under Font, select Verdana.
4. Under Name, enter "Verdana" (this is a cosmetic name, used in the Library only).
5. Click OK.
6. In the Library, select the Verdana font symbol.
7. From the pop-up Options menu, select Linkage.

8. In the Linkage Properties dialog box, under Linkage, select Export For ActionScript.

9. The Class box should automatically be set to Verdana. If not, enter Verdana in the Class box. This class name is used when loading fonts at runtime, as discussed in the later section "Loading Fonts at Runtime."

10. Click OK.

 The Flash authoring tool can embed the outlines for any font it displays in the Font Symbol Properties dialog's Font menu.

To export a font without antialiasing, add the following step to the preceding procedure, between Steps 2 and 3:

- In the Font Symbol Properties dialog box, (Step 2) select "Bitmap text," and then choose a font size.

When "Bitmap text" is selected, the compiler snaps shapes to whole pixels when calculating glyph outlines. The result is a crisp vector shape for each glyph at the designated size, with no antialiasing applied. For best results when using "Bitmap text," always set the font size of text formatted with the embedded font to match the font size selected in the Font Symbols Properties dialog box. Also avoid scaling text formatted with the embedded font.

 The "Bitmap text" option is not available in Flex Builder 2 or *mxmlc*.

Embedding Font Outlines in Flex Builder 2 and mxmlc

To embed font outlines in a Flex Builder 2 ActionScript project or with the standalone compiler, *mxmlc*, we use the [Embed] metadata tag. To use [Embed], we must give the compiler access to the Flex compiler-support library, *flex.swc*. By default, all Flex Builder 2 projects automatically include *flex.swc* in the ActionScript library path, so in Flex Builder 2, the techniques covered in this section work without any special compiler configuration.

Assets embedded using the [Embed] metadata tag, including fonts, can be embedded at the variable level or the class level. However, variable-level font embedding is more convenient than class-level font embedding, so fonts are rarely embedded at the class level.

 For more information on the [Embed] metadata tag, see Chapter 28.

The generalized code required to embed a font at the variable level in a Flex Builder 2 ActionScript Project or with *mxmlc* is as follows:

```
[Embed(source="pathToFont",
       fontFamily="fontName")]
private var className:Class;
```

In the preceding code, which must occur within a class body, *pathToFont* specifies the path to a font file on the local filesystem, *fontName* is an arbitrary name by which the font will be referenced in the application, and *className* is the name of the variable that will refer to the class that represents the embedded font. (The class that represents the font is used only when loading fonts at runtime, as discussed in the later section "Loading Fonts at Runtime.")

For example, the following code shows how to embed font outlines for the font Verdana on Windows XP. Notice that the *pathToFont* must use forward slashes, but is not case-sensitive.

```
[Embed(source="c:/windows/fonts/verdana.ttf",
       fontFamily="Verdana")]
private var verdana:Class;
```

When the preceding code runs, ActionScript automatically generates a class representing the embedded font asset and assigns that class to the variable verdana.

 The [Embed] metadata tag can be used to embed TrueType fonts only.

In simple cases, the code that embeds a font resides in the same class that uses that font to format text. Example 27-11 demonstrates, showing a simple class, *HelloWorldVerdana*, that displays the text "Hello world" formatted using an embedded font. (We'll learn more about formatting text with embedded fonts in the next section.)

Example 27-11. Hello World, in Verdana

```
package {
  import flash.display.*;
  import flash.text.*;

  public class HelloWorldVerdana extends Sprite {
    // Embed the font Verdana
    [Embed(source="c:/windows/fonts/verdana.ttf",
           fontFamily="Verdana")]
    private var verdana:Class;

    public function HelloWorldVerdana () {
      var t:TextField = new TextField();
      t.embedFonts = true;
      // Format text using the font Verdana
```

Example 27-11. Hello World, in Verdana (continued)

```
    t.htmlText = "<FONT FACE='Verdana'>Hello world</FONT>";
    addChild(t);
    }
  }
}
```

In more complex applications with multiple embedded fonts, a single central class is typically responsible for all font embedding—thus keeping font-embedding code separate from text-formatting code. Example 27-12 demonstrates, showing two classes: *FontEmbedder*, which embeds a font, and *HelloWorld*, a main class that formats text with the font embedded by *FontEmbedder*. Notice that *HelloWorld*, by necessity, makes reference to *FontEmbedder*, forcing *FontEmbedder* and its fonts to be compiled into the *.swf* file.

Example 27-12. Embedding fonts centrally

```
// The FontEmbedder class
package {
  // Embeds the fonts for this application
  public class FontEmbedder {
    [Embed(source="c:/windows/fonts/verdana.ttf",
           fontFamily="Verdana")]
    private var verdana:Class;
  }
}

// The HelloWorld class
package {
  import flash.display.*;
  import flash.text.*;

  public class HelloWorld extends Sprite {
    // Make a reference to the class that embeds the fonts for this
    // application. This reference causes the class and, by extension, its
    // fonts to be compiled into the .swf file.
    FontEmbedder;

    public function HelloWorld () {
      var t:TextField = new TextField();
      t.embedFonts = true;
      t.htmlText = "<FONT FACE='Verdana'>Hello world</FONT>";
      addChild(t);
    }
  }
}
```

For comparison, Example 27-13 demonstrates how to embed a font at the class level. Notice that the class that uses the embedded font must reference the class that embeds the font.

Example 27-13. Class-level font embedding

```
// The font-embedding class
package {
  import flash.display.*;
  import mx.core.FontAsset;

  [Embed(source="c:/windows/fonts/verdana.ttf", fontFamily="Verdana")]
  public class Verdana extends FontAsset {
  }
}

// The class that uses the embedded fonts
package {
  import flash.display.*;
  import flash.text.*;

  public class HelloWorld extends Sprite {
    // Make a reference to the class that embeds the font. This reference
    // causes the class and, by extension, its font to be compiled into
    // the .swf file.
    Verdana;

    // Constructor
    public function HelloWorld () {
      var t:TextField = new TextField();
      t.embedFonts = true;
      t.htmlText = "<FONT FACE='Verdana'>Hello world</FONT>";
      addChild(t);
    }
  }
}
```

 Note that due to a bug in Flex Builder 2 and *mxmlc*, fonts embedded with the [Embed] syntax discussed in this section cannot be kerned. However, fonts embedded using the Flash authoring tool can be kerned. When kerning is required in an application compiled with Flex Builder 2 or mxmlc, embed the desired font in a *.swf* file using the Flash authoring tool, then load that font dynamically (see the section "Loading Fonts at Runtime").

Now that we've seen how to embed fonts using both the Flash authoring tool and the [Embed] metadata tag, let's examine how to format text with embedded fonts.

Formatting Text with an Embedded Font

To format a given *TextField* object with embedded fonts, we must first set that object's embedFonts variable to true. Setting embedFonts to true tells Flash Player to use embedded fonts when rendering the text field's content. The following code demonstrates:

```
// Create a TextField object
var t:TextField = new TextField();

// Tell Flash Player to use embedded fonts when rendering t's content
t.embedFonts = true;
```

 Setting embedFonts to true does not cause any fonts to be added to a *.swf* file; it merely indicates that the text field should be rendered with embedded fonts if they are available.

The embedFonts variable must be set separately for each text field that uses a particular font, even if multiple text fields use the same font. However, file size is not affected when multiple text fields use the same embedded font: only one copy of the font is downloaded with the *.swf* file.

Once we have set the *TextField* object's embedFonts variable to true, we then set the font for the text field using the *TextFormat* class's instance variable font, the <font> tag's face attribute, or the CSS fontFamily property, as discussed in the earlier section "Formatting Text Fields." For example:

```
// Set the font with a TextFormat object
var format:TextFormat = new TextFormat();
format.font = "fontName";
var t:TextField = new TextField();
t.embedFonts = true;
t.defaultTextFormat = format;
t.text = "hello world";

// Or set the font with HTML
var t:TextField = new TextField();
t.embedFonts = true;
t.htmlText = "<FONT FACE='fontName'>Hello world</FONT>";

// Or set the font with CSS
var styleSheet:StyleSheet = new StyleSheet();
var pStyle:Object = new Object();
pStyle.fontFamily = "fontName";
styleSheet.setStyle("p", pStyle);
var t:TextField = new TextField();
t.embedFonts = true;
t.styleSheet = styleSheet; // Assign styleSheet before assigning htmlText!
t.htmlText = "<p>hello world</p>";
```

In the preceding code, *fontName* specifies the name of an embedded font, as defined by the tool used to compiled the *.swf* file in which the font is embedded.

For fonts embedded using the [Embed] metadata tag, *fontName* must match the string value specified for the fontFamily parameter of the [Embed] tag used to embed the font.

For fonts embedded via the Flash authoring tool, *fontName* must match the name that appears in the Font menu of the Font Symbol Properties dialog box used to embed the font (see Step 3 in the earlier section, "Embedding Font Outlines in the Flash Authoring Tool"). For fonts embedded with the Bitmap text option selected, *fontName* must match the following pattern:

```
nameInFontMenu_sizeInFontMenupt_variationCode
```

In the preceding pattern, *nameInFontMenu* is the name that appears in the Font menu of the Font Symbol Properties dialog box, *sizeInFontMenu* is the font size selected in the Font Symbol Properties dialog box, and *variationCode* is one of st (standard), b (bold), i (italic), or bi (bold italic), matching the selected variation in the Font Symbol Properties dialog box.

 The preceding pattern applies to Flash CS3 and Flash Player 9 but may change in the future. That said, for backwards compatibility, hypothetical future versions of Flash Player will continue to support the preceding pattern.

Table 27-8 presents several examples of the preceding *fontName* pattern required when the Bitmap text option is selected.

Table 27-8.

Name in font menu	Font variation	Font size	Example fontName value
Verdana	Standard	12	Verdana_12pt_st
Verdana	Bold	12	Verdana_12pt_b
Verdana	Italic	12	Verdana_12pt_i
Verdana	Bold Italic	12	Verdana_12pt_bi

Notice that the general technique for specifying a character's font is the same whether the text rendered is rendered with a device font or an embedded font. In the case of device fonts, the supplied font name must match the name of a font installed on the end user's system. In the case of embedded fonts, the supplied font name must match the name of an embedded font.

Using bold and italic with embedded fonts

To use the bold, italic, or bold-italic variations of a font in a *TextField* object whose embedFonts variable is set to true, we must embed those variations separately. For example, if we use Arial bold, Arial italic, and Arial bold italic in a *TextField* object whose embedFonts variable is set to true, then we must embed all three Arial font variations.

Each variation of a font embedded via the Flash authoring tool must be assigned a unique class name in the Font Symbol Properties dialog box. Likewise, each variation of a font embedded via the [Embed] metadata tag must correspond to its own variable (for variable-level embeds) or class (for class-level embeds). Furthermore, each variation of a given font must specify the same value for the [Embed] tag's fontFamily parameter, and must use the appropriate font-variation parameter (either fontWeight or fontStyle) to specify the variation being embedded.

For example, the following code embeds the bold and italic variations of Verdana. The bold variation of the font specifies a fontFamily of "Verdana" and a fontWeight of "bold." The italic variation of the font specifies a fontFamily of "Verdana" and a fontStyle of "italic." Notice that the source parameter for each embed statement specifies the location of the font file containing the appropriate font variation (*verdanab.ttf* and *verdanai.ttf*, respectively).

```
[Embed(source="c:/windows/fonts/verdanab.ttf",
       fontFamily="Verdana",
       fontWeight="bold")]
private var verdanaBold:Class;

[Embed(source="c:/windows/fonts/verdanai.ttf",
       fontFamily="Verdana",
       fontStyle="italic")]
private var verdanaItalic:Class;
```

For reference, Example 27-14 shows the code required to embed and use the regular and bold variations of the font Verdana.

Example 27-14. Embedding multiple font variations

```
// The font-embedding class
package {
  public class FontEmbedder {
    // Embed regular variation
    [Embed(source="c:/windows/fonts/verdana.ttf",
           fontFamily="Verdana")]
    private var verdana:Class;

    // Embed bold variation
    [Embed(source="c:/windows/fonts/verdanab.ttf",
           fontFamily="Verdana",
           fontWeight="bold")]
    private var verdanabold:Class;
  }
}

// The class that uses the embedded fonts
package {
  import flash.display.*;
  import flash.text.*;
```

Example 27-14. Embedding multiple font variations (continued)

```
public class HelloWorld extends Sprite {
  // Force FontEmbedder and, by extension, its fonts to be compiled into
  // the .swf file.
  FontEmbedder;

  public function HelloWorld () {
    var t:TextField = new TextField();
    t.embedFonts = true;
    // Use two variations of Verdana (normal, and bold)
    t.htmlText = "<FONT FACE='Verdana'>Hello <b>world</b></FONT>";

    addChild(t);
  }
 }
}
```

Loading Fonts at Runtime

Imagine we're building a travel booking application in which the user can book air transportation, accommodation, and ground transportation. Each booking section has its own design that uses its own fonts. In some cases, users book air transportation only, and completely skip the accommodation-booking and ground-transportation-booking sections of the application.

To speed up the initial loading of our travel application, we can defer loading fonts until they are actually required by the application. Immediately before the user accesses each booking section, we load the fonts required by that section. Thus, users that access only one section load the fonts required for that section only, and do not have to wait for other sections' fonts to load before using the application.

To load fonts at runtime, follow these general steps:

1. Embed the font(s) in a *.swf* file (using the techniques covered in the earlier sections "Embedding Font Outlines in the Flash Authoring Tool" and "Embedding Font Outlines in Flex Builder 2 and mxmlc").

2. In the *.swf* file that embeds the font, use the *Font* class's static method *registerFont()* to add the font to the global font list.

3. Load the *.swf* file with the embedded font.

Let's apply the preceding steps to an example. We'll start by creating a *.swf* file, *Fonts.swf*, that embeds Verdana (regular) and Verdana (bold) using the [Embed] metadata tag. Here's the code for *Fonts.swf* file's main class:

```
package {
  import flash.display.*;
  import flash.text.*;

  // Embed fonts for use by any .swf file that loads this file
  public class Fonts extends Sprite {
```

```
      [Embed(source="c:/windows/fonts/verdana.ttf",
            fontFamily="Verdana")]
      private var verdana:Class;

      [Embed(source="c:/windows/fonts/verdanab.ttf",
            fontFamily="Verdana",
            fontWeight="bold")]
      private var verdanaBold:Class;
    }
  }
```

Next, we must add our embedded fonts to the global font list. To do so we use the *Font* class's static method *registerFont()*, which takes a single parameter, font. The font parameter expects a reference to the *Font* class that represents the font to be added to the global font list. Once a font is added to the global font list, it can be used by any *.swf* file running in Flash Player.

In the preceding code, the classes representing our two Verdana font variations are assigned to the variables verdana and verdanaBold. Hence, to add those fonts to the global font list, we pass the value of those variables to the *registerFont()* method, as follows:

```
Font.registerFont(verdana);
Font.registerFont(verdanaBold);
```

To ensure that our fonts are added to the global font list as soon as they load, we invoke *registerFont()* within the *Fonts* class constructor, as follows:

```
package {
  import flash.display.*;
  import flash.text.*;

  // Embed fonts for use by any .swf file that loads this file
  public class Fonts extends Sprite {
    [Embed(source="c:/windows/fonts/verdana.ttf",
          fontFamily="Verdana")]
    private var verdana:Class;

    [Embed(source="c:/windows/fonts/verdanab.ttf",
          fontFamily="Verdana",
          fontWeight="bold")]
    private var verdanaBold:Class;

    // Constructor
    public function Fonts () {
      // Register this class's embedded fonts in the global font list
      Font.registerFont(verdana);
      Font.registerFont(verdanaBold);
    }
  }
}
```

If we had embedded our fonts using Font symbols in the Flash authoring tool, we would have added the preceding *registerFont()* calls to the first frame of the main timeline, and we would have passed *registerFont()* the font classes listed in the Class box of the Linkage Properties dialog box for each embedded Font symbol (see Step 8 in the section "Embedding Font Outlines in the Flash Authoring Tool").

Next, we compile *Fonts.swf* and load it at runtime using the *Loader* class. As soon as *Fonts.swf* finishes loading, its fonts immediately become available for use by any other *.swf* file running in Flash Player. Example 27-15 shows an example class that loads and then uses the fonts embedded in *Fonts.swf*.

 For complete information on loading *.swf* files, see Chapter 28.

Example 27-15. Using loaded fonts

```
package {
  import flash.display.*;
  import flash.text.*;
  import flash.events.*;
  import flash.net.*;

  // This class demonstrates how to format text using loaded fonts.
  // The fonts, themselves, are embedded in the file Fonts.swf,
  // shown earlier.
  public class HelloWorld extends Sprite {
    public function HelloWorld () {
      // Load the .swf file that contains the embedded fonts
      var loader:Loader = new Loader();
      loader.contentLoaderInfo.addEventListener(Event.INIT, initListener);
      loader.load(new URLRequest("Fonts.swf"));
    }

    // Executed when Fonts.swf has initialized, and its fonts are available
    private function initListener (e:Event):void {
      // For debugging, show the available embedded fonts
      showEmbeddedFonts();

      // The font has loaded, so now display the formatted text
      outputMsg();
    }

    // Displays text formatted with the embedded fonts
    private function outputMsg ():void {
      // Create the text field
      var t:TextField = new TextField();
      t.embedFonts = true;  // Tell ActionScript to render this
                            // text field using embedded fonts
      // Use two variations of Verdana (normal, and bold)
      t.htmlText = "<FONT FACE='Verdana'>Hello <b>world</b></FONT>";
```

Example 27-15. Using loaded fonts (continued)

```
    // Add the text field to the display list
    addChild(t);
  }

  // Outputs a list of the currently available embedded fonts
  public function showEmbeddedFonts ():void {
    trace("========Embedded Fonts========");

    var fonts:Array = Font.enumerateFonts();
    fonts.sortOn("fontName", Array.CASEINSENSITIVE);
    for (var i:int = 0; i < fonts.length; i++) {
      trace(fonts[i].fontName + ", " + fonts[i].fontStyle);
    }
  }
}
```

 Most browsers cache *.swf* files, so applications comprised of multiple *.swf* files can achieve an overall reduction in load time by loading fonts from a single *.swf* file at runtime.

Missing Fonts and Glyphs

Earlier we learned that when a text field is rendered using device fonts, if a given character's font is not installed on the end user's operating system, Flash Player will automatically ask the operating system to render the character in an appropriate substitute font.

By contrast, when a text field is rendered using embedded fonts and a given character's font is not available in the list of embedded fonts, Flash Player first attempts to render the character using any available variation of the specified font. For example, consider the following code, which uses two variations of the font Verdana:

```
    var t:TextField = new TextField();
    t.embedFonts = true;
    t.htmlText = "<FONT FACE='Verdana'>Hello <b>world</b></FONT>";
```

Notice that the font for the word "Hello" is set to Verdana, normal variation, while the font for the word "world" is set to Verdana, bold variation. At runtime, if the embedded font Verdana, bold-variation is not available, but the embedded font Verdana, normal-variation *is* available, then the text "Hello world" will be rendered entirely in Verdana, normal-variation. If, however, *neither* the normal variation nor the bold variation of Verdana is available, then the character is not rendered at all, and no text appears on screen!

When using embedded fonts, if the text in your application mysteriously goes missing or appears in the wrong font variation, chances are the required fonts are not available. To determine which fonts are available at runtime, use the *Font* class's static method *enumerateFonts()*, as discussed in the section "Determining Font Availability."

When embedded fonts are in use, and a text field contains a character whose glyph is not available in the specified font, that character is not rendered. By contrast, when device fonts are in use, and a text field contains a character whose glyph is not available in the specified font, Flash Player will automatically search the system for a substitute font containing the missing glyph. If such a font is found, the character will be rendered in the substitute font. If no font is found, then the character is not rendered.

When a program supplies no formatting information for a *TextField* object whose embedFonts variable is set to true, Flash Player attempts to render that object's content using an embedded font whose name matches the name of the default font for the current environment ("Times New Roman" on Microsoft Windows). If no such embedded font exists, then the text is not rendered.

Determining Font Availability

To determine the list of device fonts and embedded fonts available at runtime, use the *Font* class's static method *enumerateFonts()*. The *enumerateFonts()* method returns an array of *Font* objects, each of which represents an available device font or embedded font. The *enumerateFonts()* method defines a single Boolean parameter, enumerateDeviceFonts, which dictates whether the returned array includes device fonts. By default, enumerateDeviceFonts is false, so the array returned by *enumerateFonts()* does not include device fonts. Each *Font* object in the returned array defines the following variables describing the font it represents:

fontName

Indicates the name of the font. For device fonts, fontName is the name that appears in the system font list. For fonts embedded in the Flash authoring tool, fontName is the name that appears in the Font menu of the Font Symbol Properties dialog box used to embed the font. For fonts embedded using the [Embed] metadata tag, fontName is the string value specified for the fontFamily parameter of the [Embed] tag used to embed the font.

fontStyle

Indicates the font variation (regular, bold, italic, or bold-italic) as one of the following four ActionScript constants: FontStyle.REGULAR, FontStyle.BOLD, FontStyle.ITALIC, FontStyle.BOLD_ITALIC.

fontType

> Indicates whether the font is an embedded font or a device font. This variable refers to one of the following two ActionScript constants: FontType.EMBEDDED, or FontType.DEVICE.

Example 27-16 demonstrates how to generate an alphabetical list of all available embedded fonts.

Example 27-16. Listing all embedded fonts

```
var fonts:Array = Font.enumerateFonts();
fonts.sortOn("fontName", Array.CASEINSENSITIVE);
for (var i:int = 0; i < fonts.length; i++) {
  trace(fonts[i].fontName + ", " + fonts[i].fontStyle);
}
```

Example 27-17 demonstrates how to generate an alphabetical list of all available device fonts.

Example 27-17. Listing all device fonts

```
var fonts:Array = Font.enumerateFonts(true);
fonts.sortOn("fontName", Array.CASEINSENSITIVE);
for (var i:int = 0; i < fonts.length; i++) {
  if (fonts[i].fontType == FontType.DEVICE) {
    trace(fonts[i].fontName + ", " + fonts[i].fontStyle);
  }
}
```

Example 27-18 demonstrates how to generate an alphabetical list of all available embedded and device fonts.

Example 27-18. Listing all embedded and device fonts

```
var fonts:Array = Font.enumerateFonts(true);
fonts.sortOn("fontName", Array.CASEINSENSITIVE);
for (var i:int = 0; i < fonts.length; i++) {
    trace(fonts[i].fontType + ": "
          + fonts[i].fontName + ", " + fonts[i].fontStyle);
}
```

The *enumerateFonts()* function can be used to allow the user to choose an application's fonts, or to select a fallback font automatically, as shown in Example 27-19.

Example 27-19. Automatically selecting a fallback font

```
package {
  import flash.display.*;
  import flash.text.*;

  public class FontFallbackDemo extends Sprite {
    public function FontFallbackDemo () {
      var format:TextFormat = new TextFormat();
```

Example 27-19. Automatically selecting a fallback font (continued)

```
      // Assigns the first font available
      format.font = getFont(["ZapfChancery", "Verdana", "Arial", "_sans"]);

      var t:TextField = new TextField( );
      t.text = "ActionScript is fun!";
      t.autoSize = TextFieldAutoSize.LEFT;
      t.setTextFormat(format)

      addChild(t);
    }

    // Given a list of fonts, returns the name of the first font in the list
    // that is available either as an embedded font or a device font
    public function getFont (fontList: Array):String {
      var availableFonts:Array = Font.enumerateFonts(true);
      for (var i:int = 0; i < fontList.length; i++) {
        for (var j:int = 0; j < availableFonts.length; j++) {
          if (fontList[i] == Font(availableFonts[j]).fontName) {
            return fontList[i];
          }
        }
      }
      return null;
    }
  }
}
```

Determining Glyph Availability

To determine whether a specific embedded font has a glyph for a specific character or set of characters, we use the *Font* class's instance method *hasGlyphs( )*. When provided with a string argument, the *hasGlyphs( )* method returns a Boolean value indicating whether the font has all the glyphs required to display that string.

> The *Font* class's instance method *hasGlyphs( )* works with embedded fonts only. There is no way to determine whether a given device font has a glyph for a specific character.

To use the *hasGlyphs( )* method, we must first obtain a reference to the *Font* object for the font in question. To do so, we use a *for* loop to search the array returned by *enumerateFonts( )*. For example, the following code retrieves a reference to the *Font* object for the font Verdana, and assigns it to the variable font:

```
var fontName:String = "Verdana";
var font:Font;
var fonts:Array = Font.enumerateFonts(true);
for (var i:int = 0; i < fonts.length; i++) {
  if (fonts[i].fontName == fontName) {
```

```
        font = fonts[i];
        break;
    }
}
```

Once a reference to the desired *Font* object has been obtained, we can then use *hasGlyphs()* to check if the corresponding font has the glyphs required to display a given string. For example, the following code checks if the font Verdana can display the English string "Hello world":

```
trace(font.hasGlyphs("Hello world"));  // Displays: true
```

The following code checks if the font Verdana can display the Japanese string "みんなさん、こんにちは":

```
trace(font.hasGlyphs(みんなさん、こんにちは));  // Displays: false
```

Embedded-Text Rendering

Perhaps surprisingly, for *TextField* objects with embedFonts set to true, Flash Player offers two different text-rendering modes. These modes are known somewhat generically as *normal* mode and *advanced* mode.

In normal mode, Flash Player renders text with the standard vector-renderer that is used to render all vector shapes in a *.swf* file. The standard vector-renderer draws text with an antialiasing algorithm that executes quickly and produces smooth-looking lines. Text rendered with the standard vector-renderer is typically considered clear and legible at medium to large font sizes (approximately 16 point and greater), but fuzzy and illegible at small font sizes (12 point and smaller).

In advanced mode, Flash Player renders text with a specialized text-renderer known as FlashType. FlashType is a licensed implementation of the Saffron Type System, created by Mitsubishi Electric Research Laboratories (MERL). The FlashType renderer is specifically designed to clearly render the types of shapes commonly found in fonts at small sizes. Currently, FlashType generates better results for Western fonts than Asian fonts. However, Asian text rendered with FlashType is still generally clearer than text rendered with Flash Player's standard vector renderer. Text rendered with the FlashType renderer is typically considered more legible than text rendered with Flash Player's standard vector-renderer. At small font sizes, FlashType also renders text faster than Flash Player's standard vector-renderer. However, at large font sizes, FlashType takes significantly longer to render text than Flash Player's standard vector-renderer.

 For background information on the Saffron Type System, see Mitsubishi's official Saffron project overview at *http://www.merl.com/projects/ADF-Saffron*, and Ronald Perry's technical presentation notes for Saffron at *http://www.merl.com/people/perry/SaffronOverview.ppt*.

Developers can choose between Flash Player's two text-rendering modes dynamically at runtime, on a per-text field basis. To tell Flash Player to render a given *TextField* object using the standard vector-renderer, set that object's `antiAliasType` to `AntiAliasType.NORMAL`. For example, the following code creates a *TextField* object, and then tells Flash Player to render it with embedded fonts using the standard vector-renderer. Notice that in addition to setting the value of `antiAliasType`, the code sets the *TextField* object's `embedFonts` variable to true; Flash Player's text-rendering modes apply to text rendered with embedded fonts only.

```
// Create the TextField object
var t:TextField = new TextField( );

// Tell Flash Player to render this text field with embedded fonts
t.embedFonts = true;

// Tell Flash Player to use the standard vector-renderer when rendering
// this text field
t.antiAliasType = AntiAliasType.NORMAL;
```

By contrast, the following code creates a *TextField* object and then tells Flash Player to render it with embedded fonts using the FlashType renderer:

```
// Create the TextField object
var t:TextField = new TextField( );

// Tell Flash Player to render this text field with embedded fonts
t.embedFonts = true;

// Tell Flash Player to use the FlashType renderer when rendering
// this text field
t.antiAliasType = AntiAliasType.ADVANCED;
```

The default value of `antiAliasType` is `AntiAliasType.NORMAL` (standard vector-renderer).

> By default, Flash Player renders *TextField* objects whose `embedFonts` variable is true using the standard vector-renderer.

Figure 27-13 shows the English alphabet rendered in 10-point Verdana using both FlashType (left) and the standard vector-renderer (right). On screen, the alphabet rendered using FlashType is considerably more legible than the alphabet rendered using Flash Player's standard vector-renderer.

For reference, Example 27-20 shows the code used to produce the demonstration alphabets shown in Figure 27-13.

FlashType	Standard Vecto-Renderer
abcdefghijklmnopqrstuvwxyz	abcdefghijklmnopqrstuvwxyz

Figure 27-13. FlashType versus Flash Player's standard vector-renderer

Example 27-20. FlashType versus Flash Player's standard vector-renderer

```
package {
  import flash.display.*;
  import flash.text.*;

  public class FlashTypeDemo extends Sprite {
    // Forward slashes are required, but case doesn't matter.
    [Embed(source="c:/windows/fonts/verdana.ttf",
           fontFamily="Verdana")]
    private var verdana:Class;

    public function FlashTypeDemo () {
      // FlashType
      var t:TextField = new TextField();
      t.width = 200;
      t.embedFonts = true;
      t.htmlText = "<FONT FACE='Verdana' SIZE='10'>"
                   + "abcdefghijklmnopqrstuvwxyz</FONT>";
      t.antiAliasType = AntiAliasType.ADVANCED;
      addChild(t);

      // Standard vector-renderer
      var t2:TextField = new TextField();
      t2.width = 200;
      t2.embedFonts = true;
      t2.htmlText = "<FONT FACE='Verdana' SIZE='10'>"
                    + "abcdefghijklmnopqrstuvwxyz</FONT>";
      t2.antiAliasType = AntiAliasType.NORMAL;
      addChild(t2);
      t2.x = 180;
    }
  }
}
```

 For best text-animation quality use the standard vector-renderer (set antiAliasType to AntiAliasType.NORMAL). For best legibility, use the FlashType renderer (set antiAliasType to AntiAliasType.ADVANCED).

Note that *FlashType* rendering is automatically disabled when text is skewed or flipped.

Tweaking the FlashType Renderer

The attractiveness and legibility of text is highly subjective. ActionScript offers a variety of advanced tools for fine-tuning the specific behavior of the FlashType renderer.

While a complete discussion of the FlashType renderer's optional settings is beyond the scope of this book, for the sake of familiarity, Table 27-9 lists the available tools and their basic purpose. For further study, see each item's entry in Adobe's ActionScript Language Reference.

Table 27-9. Variables and methods used to set FlashType options

Variable or method	Description
TextField's instance variable `sharpness`	Sets the sharpness of the text field's text to an integer value between −400 (blurry) and 400 (sharp).
TextField's instance variable `thickness`	Sets the thickness of the lines in a text field's text to an integer value between −200 (thin) and 200 (thick). Setting a text field's `thickness` to a high value gives a bold appearance to its text.
TextField's instance variable `gridFitType`	Sets pixel-level grid-fitting options that affect the legibility of text at different alignments (left, center, and right). *Grid fitting* is a technique that positions the stems of a displayed glyph on whole pixels to improve its readability.
TextRenderer's static variable `displayMode`	Instructs FlashType's antialiasing algorithm to favor either LCD or CRT screens. This setting applies globally to all text rendered by the FlashType renderer.
TextRenderer's static variable `maxLevel`	Sets the quality level of adaptively sampled distance fields (part of FlashType's internal structure for describing glyph outlines). This setting applies globally to all text rendered by the FlashType renderer (but Flash Player automatically increases this setting for any individual glyph rendered at a font size over 64 pixels). Higher values reduce performance.
TextRenderer's static method *setAdvancedAntiAliasingTable( )*	Assigns values that precisely determine the weight and sharpness of a specific font at a specific size, style, and color type ("light" or "dark").

Now let's change our focus from formatting and fonts to receiving input through text fields.

Text Field Input

Text fields can receive a variety of forms of user input, including text entry, text selection, hypertext-link activation, keyboard focus, scrolling, and mouse interaction. In this section, we'll study text entry, text selection, and hypertext links. For information on keyboard focus, scrolling, and mouse interaction, see Chapter 22.

Text Entry

Each text field's ability to receive user input is governed by the value of its type variable. By default, for text fields created with ActionScript, the instance variable type is set to `TextFieldType.DYNAMIC`, meaning that text can be modified through Action-Script but not by the user. To allow a text field to receive user input, we must set type to `TextFieldType.INPUT`, as shown in the following code:

```
var t:TextField = new TextField();
t.type = TextFieldType.INPUT;
```

When a *TextField* object's type variable is set to `TextFieldType.INPUT`, the user can add text to or delete text from the text field. The user's modifications are automatically reflected by the text and htmlText variables.

To be notified when a text field's text is modified by the user, we can register with that text field for `TextEvent.TEXT_INPUT` and `Event.CHANGE` events. The `TextEvent.TEXT_INPUT` event is dispatched when the user attempts to change the text of the text field, before the text and htmlText variables are updated. The `Event.CHANGE` event is dispatched after the text and htmlText variables have been updated in response to user input. For complete details on `TextEvent.TEXT_INPUT` and `Event.CHANGE`, see Chapter 22.

By default, users are not allowed to enter line breaks into text fields. To allow the user to enter line breaks (for example by pressing the Enter key or Return key), set multiline to true, as shown in the following code:

```
var t:TextField = new TextField();
t.type = TextFieldType.INPUT;
t.multiline = true;
```

To restrict the set of characters that the user can enter into a text field, use the *TextField* class's instance variable restrict. For example, the following text field allows numeric text entry only, as might be required for a credit-card input field:

```
var t:TextField = new TextField();
t.width = 200;
t.height = 20;
t.border     = true;
t.background = true;
t.type = TextFieldType.INPUT;
t.restrict = "0-9";
```

To limit the number of characters the user can enter into a text field, use the *TextField* class's instance variable maxChars. For example, the following text field allows eight characters only, as might be required for the name field of a login form:

```
var t:TextField = new TextField();
t.width = 100;
t.height = 20;
t.border     = true;
t.background = true;
t.type = TextFieldType.INPUT;
t.maxChars = 8;
```

To specify that characters should be obscured for screen privacy, use the *TextField* class's instance variable `displayAsPassword`. When `displayAsPassword` is true, all characters are displayed as asterisks (*). For example, the words "hi there" are displayed as "********". This allows users to enter text without casual onlookers seeing it. The following code demonstrates a text field that obscures characters, as might be required for the password field of a login form:

```
var t:TextField = new TextField( );
t.width = 100;
t.height = 20;
t.border    = true;
t.background = true;
t.type = TextFieldType.INPUT;
t.displayAsPassword = true;
```

Formatting user input

By default, new text entered by the user automatically adopts the formatting of the character before the insertion point or the character at index 0 if the new text is inserted before index 0. If the text field was previously empty, the new text is formatted according to the text field's default text format (which is set via `defaultTextFormat`, as discussed in the earlier section "Default formatting for text fields").

To override the automatic formatting applied to new text input, follow these steps:

1. Intercept the input with the `TextEvent.TEXT_INPUT` event.

2. Manually insert equivalent text.

3. Add formatting to the manually inserted text.

Example 27-21 demonstrates the technique in an example class, *FormattedInputDemo*. Comments will guide you through the code.

Example 27-21. Formatting user input

```
package {
  import flash.display.*;
  import flash.text.*;
  import flash.events.*;

  public class FormattedInputDemo extends Sprite {
    public function FormattedInputDemo ( ) {
      // Create the TextFormat objects
      var boldFormat:TextFormat = new TextFormat( );
      boldFormat.bold = true;
      var italicFormat:TextFormat = new TextFormat( );
      italicFormat.italic = true;

      // Create the text field
      var t:TextField = new TextField( );
      t.text = "lunchtime";
```

Example 27-21. Formatting user input (continued)

```
      // Format the word "lunch" with italics
      t.setTextFormat(italicFormat, 0, 5);
      // Format the word "time" with bold
      t.setTextFormat(boldFormat, 5, 9);
      t.type = TextFieldType.INPUT;

      // Register with t for TextEvent.TEXT_INPUT events
      t.addEventListener(TextEvent.TEXT_INPUT, textInputListener);

      // Add the text field to the display list
      addChild(t);
    }

    // Triggered whenever the user attempts to add new text to t
    private function textInputListener (e:TextEvent):void {
      // Retrieve a reference to the text field that received text input
      var t:TextField = TextField(e.target);

      // Prevent the user-supplied text from being added to the text field
      e.preventDefault();

      // Add the user-supplied text manually. This way, the TextField
      // object's text variable is forced to update immediately, allowing
      // us to format the new text within this function.
      t.replaceText(t.caretIndex, t.caretIndex, e.text);

      // Set the format for the new text
      var regularFormat:TextFormat = new TextFormat();
      regularFormat.bold   = false;
      regularFormat.italic = false;
      t.setTextFormat(regularFormat,
                      t.caretIndex,
                      t.caretIndex+e.text.length)

      // Set the insertion point to the end of the new text, so
      // the user thinks they entered the text
      var newCaretIndex:int = t.caretIndex + e.text.length;
      t.setSelection(newCaretIndex, newCaretIndex);
    }
  }
}
```

Text Selection

By default, the text in all programmatically created text fields can be selected by the
user. To disable user-selection for a text field, set selectable to false. Normally, a
text field's selection is shown only when the text field is focused; to force a text
field's selection to be shown even when that text field does not have focus, set
alwaysShowSelection to true. In Flash Player 9, the color of the selection highlight
cannot be set; future versions of Flash Player might support configurable selection-
highlight color.

To determine the index of the first selected character in a text field, use the *TextField* class's instance variable `selectionBeginIndex`. To determine the index of the last selected character in a text field, use the *TextField* class's instance variable `selectionEndIndex`. To determine the position of the insertion point (caret), use the *TextField* class's instance variable `caretIndex`. To programmatically select characters in a text field or set the insertion point, use the *TextField* class's instance method *setSelection( )*.

Note that Flash Player does not include any events to indicate when a text field's selection changes. To detect changes in a text field's selection, poll the value of `selectionBeginIndex` and `selectionEndIndex`.

To replace the current selection with new text, as might be required in an application with word processor-style text editing, use the *TextField* class's instance method *replaceSelectedText( )*. Note, however, that *replaceSelectedText( )* works only when a text field has focus or has `alwaysShowSelection` set to true. The *replaceSelectedText( )* method is a convenience version of the *replaceText( )* method we studied in the earlier section "Modifying a Text Field's Content." *replaceSelectedText( )* behaves exactly like *replaceText( )* except that it automatically sets the *beginIndex* and *endIndex* parameters to match the current selection.

Hypertext Links

To add a hypertext link to a text field, we use the `TextFormat` class's instance variable `url` or the HTML anchor tag, `<A>`. Typically, hypertext links are used to open specified resources at specified URLs. For example, the following code creates a text field containing a hypertext link that, when activated, causes Flash Player to open O'Reilly's web site in the system's default browser.

```
var t:TextField = new TextField( );
t.htmlText = "To visit O'Reilly's web site, "
             + "<a href='http://www.oreilly.com'>click here</a>";
t.autoSize = TextFieldAutoSize.LEFT;
```

However, hypertext links can also be used to trigger ActionScript code execution. For complete details, see the section "The TextEvent.LINK Event" in Chapter 22.

We're almost done with our study of text fields. But before we move on to the next chapter, let's briefly consider how text fields created manually in the Flash authoring tool are represented in ActionScript.

Text Fields and the Flash Authoring Tool

In the Flash authoring tool, text fields can be created manually using the Text tool. Each manually created text field is set to one of three author-time text field types: static text, dynamic text, or input text. At runtime, each manually created text field is represented in ActionScript by an object that matches its author-time text field type.

Text fields of type "static text" are represented by *StaticText* instances. Text fields of type "dynamic text" are represented by *TextField* instances with type set to TextFieldType.DYNAMIC. Text fields of type "input text" are represented by *TextField* instances with type set to TextFieldType.INPUT.

The text content of text fields of type "static text" can be read at runtime through ActionScript code but cannot be modified. By contrast, the text content of text fields of type "dynamic text" or "input text" can be both read and modified. Hence, Flash authors should choose the static text type when a text field's content does not need to be modified at runtime. To create text fields whose content can be modified at runtime Flash authors should choose the dynamic text or input text types.

To access all the text in all the static text fields in a given *DisplayObjectContainer* instance, use the *TextSnapshot* class (whose primary purpose is enabling character selection across multiple individual *StaticText* objects).

 Text fields that are static text type cannot be created with Action-Script code; the *StaticText* and *TextSnapshot* classes exist solely to provide programmatic access to these text fields created in the Flash authoring tool.

Just as ActionScript programmers can choose text-rendering options at runtime, Flash authors can use the Properties panel to select the rendering mode for text fields at compile-time. The Flash authoring tool rendering options (and their ActionScript equivalents) are listed in Table 27-10.

Table 27-10. Flash authoring tool text rendering options

Properties panel setting	Description	ActionScript equivalent
Use device fonts	Rely on the local playback environment to render text using fonts installed on the end user's system.	Set embedFonts to false.
Bitmap text (no antialias)	When "Bitmap text" is selected, the compiler snaps shapes to whole pixels when calculating glyph outlines (so the font does not appear antialiased). At runtime, those glyph outlines are rendered by Flash Player's built-in vector renderer, not FlashType.	Embed font using Flash authoring tool's "Bitmap text" option, then set embedFonts to false. Not available when compiling with Flex Builder 2 or *mxmlc*.
Antialias for animation	Render text using Flash Player's standard vector-renderer.	Set antiAliasType to AntiAliasType.NORMAL.
Antialias for readability	Render text using the FlashType renderer, with default settings.	Set antiAliasType to AntiAliasType.ADVANCED.
Custom antialias	Render text with the FlashType renderer, with custom settings.	Set antiAliasType to AntiAliasType.ADVANCED, and apply custom settings using the techniques described in the earlier section "Tweaking the FlashType Renderer."

Loading...Please Wait...

Over the past eight chapters, we've learned a great deal about creating and manipulating visual content using the display API. In the next chapter, we'll finish our study of display programming with a deep look at ActionScript's tools for loading external display assets.

Loading External Display Assets

In ActionScript, there are three ways to programmatically add an external display asset to an application:

- Use the *flash.display.Loader* class to load the asset at runtime
- Use the *flash.net.Socket* class in combination with the *Loader* class's instance method *loadBytes()* to load the asset at runtime over a direct TCP/IP socket
- Use the [Embed] metadata tag to include the asset from the local filesystem at compile-time

The *Loader* and *Socket* classes are built-in to the Flash runtime API, while the [Embed] metadata tag requires the Flex framework. All three approaches support the following display asset formats:

- SWF (compiled Flash applications)
- JPEG, GIF, or PNG (bitmap images)

Additionally, the [Embed] metadata tag supports SVG-formatted display assets.

The *Loader* class replaces the following ActionScript 2.0 loading tools:

- *MovieClipLoader* class
- *loadMovie()* and *loadMovieNum()*
- global functions*MovieClip* class's instance methods *loadMovie()* and *loadMovieNum()*

In this chapter, we'll learn how to use *Loader*, *Socket*, and [Embed] to load external display assets. For information on loading fonts, see Chapter 27. For information on loading XML, see Chapter 18. For information on loading other nondisplay assets, such as variables, binary data, or sound, see the *URLLoader*, *URLStream*, and *Sound* class entries in Adobe's ActionScript Language Reference.

Using Loader to Load Display Assets at Runtime

The *Loader* class loads an external display asset at runtime. The asset can be retrieved over HTTP or from the local filesystem. There are three basic steps to using the *Loader* class:

1. Create the *flash.display.Loader* instance.
2. Create a *flash.net.URLRequest* instance that specifies the asset's location.
3. Pass the *URLRequest* instance to the *Loader* instance's *load()* method.

Over the next few sections we'll create an example class, *SunsetViewer*, that demonstrates the preceding steps in detail. Our example class will load a single bitmap image, *sunset.jpg*. Once we're comfortable with the basics of loading an asset, we'll then examine how to monitor the progress of a load operation using the *flash.display.LoaderInfo* class. Finally, we'll consider the code required to access the loaded asset and add it to the display list.

 Load operations are subject to Flash Player security limitations. For complete coverage, see Chapter 19.

In our *SunsetViewer* example, we'll presume that the application *.swf* file, *SunsetViewer.swf*, will be posted to a web site in the same directory as the image we're loading, *sunset.jpg*.

Creating the Loader Instance

As we just learned, the first step in loading any display asset at runtime using *Loader* is creating a *Loader* instance. The *Loader* instance manages the load operation and provides access to the loaded asset. We'll create our *Loader* instance in *SunsetViewer*'s constructor method and assign it to an instance variable named loader, as shown in Example 28-1.

Example 28-1. Creating the Loader instance

```
package {
  import flash.display.*;

  public class SunsetViewer extends Sprite {
    private var loader:Loader;

    public function SunsetViewer () {
      loader = new Loader();  // Create the Loader instance
    }
  }
}
```

Specifying the Asset's Location

To load an external display asset using a *Loader* instance, we must specify the asset's location with a *flash.net.URLRequest* object. Each individual *URLRequest* object describes the location of a single external resource, either on the network or the local filesystem. To create a *URLRequest* object that specifies an asset's location, use the following general code, which assigns the asset's location to the instance variable url:

```
var urlRequest:URLRequest = new URLRequest( );
urlRequest.url = "theAssetURL";
```

Alternatively, the asset's location can be passed to the *URLRequest* constructor, as:

```
var url:URLRequest = new URLRequest("theAssetURL");
```

In both cases, *theAssetURL* is a string containing a standard URL. For example:

```
new URLRequest("http://www.example.com/image.jpg");
```

The set of network protocols allowed in the *theAssetURL* is dependent on the operating system. For example, http://, https://, and ftp:// are all supported by Windows, Macintosh, and UNIX, but a request for Windows help content (ms-its:) might be supported on Windows only. For security reasons, Flash Player might also block some protocols. However, Adobe does not currently publish a list of blocked protocols. Furthermore, ActionScript does not generate any security error messages relating specifically to protocol blocking. Hence, when working with unusual protocols, be aware that load operations involving some unusual protocols may fail silently.

In addition to specifying a URL, each *URLRequest* object can also provide supplementary information for requesting a resource over HTTP. To specify an HTTP request's header, method, POST data, query string, and MIME content type, simply set the appropriate *URLRequest* variables, as documented in Adobe's ActionScript Language Reference. For example, to specify an HTTP request's headers, set the *URLRequest* class's instance variable, requestHeaders.

An asset's location can be specified as an absolute or relative URL. However, note that Flash Player's system for resolving relative URLs varies depending on how Flash Player is launched:

- If Flash Player is launched in order to display a *.swf* file embedded in a web page via the <OBJECT> or <EMBED> tag, then all relative URLs are resolved in relation to that web page—not in relation to any *.swf* file. Further, if the web page was opened locally, relative URLs are resolved locally; if the web page was opened over the Internet, relative URLs are resolved over the Internet.

- If Flash Player is launched as a standalone application or by browsing directly to a *.swf* file in a Flash-enabled web browser, then all relative URLs are resolved in relation to the *first .swf* file opened by Flash Player—known as the *stage owner*. Further, if the stage owner was opened locally, relative URLs are resolved locally; if the stage owner was opened over the Internet, relative URLs are resolved over the Internet.

Even if the first *.swf* file opened by Flash Player is removed from the stage, it is still considered the stage owner and still governs relative-URL resolution.

Let's consider a relative-URL example that demonstrates the preceding two relative-URL-resolution systems. Suppose we embed an application, *SunsetViewer.swf*, on a web page, *SunsetViewer.html*, and we store those two files in the following separate directories:

```
/viewer/SunsetViewer.html
/viewer/assets/SunsetViewer.swf
```

Suppose also that from *SunsetViewer.swf* we want to load an image, *sunset.jpg*, which also resides in the */assets/* directory:

```
/viewer/assets/sunset.jpg
```

If we expect the user to view *SunsetViewer.swf* by browsing to the web page *SunsetViewer.html*, then we must compose our relative URL in relation to the web page, as follows:

```
new URLRequest("assets/sunset.jpg");
```

However, if we expect the user to browse directly to *SunsetViewer.swf*, then we would compose our relative URL in relation to the *.swf* file, not the web page, as follows:

```
new URLRequest("sunset.jpg");
```

When distributing content for playback in Flash Player, compose all relative URLs according to how you expect your users to launch Flash Player.

Even when a *.swf* file loads another *.swf* file that, itself, loads external assets, relative URLs are still resolved in relation to either the stage owner (in the case of a direct launch) or the web page containing the embedded Flash Player (in the case of a web page launch).

For example, suppose we open a hypothetical application, *SlideShow.swf*, directly in Flash Player. Next suppose *SlideShow.swf* loads the preceding *SunsetViewer.swf* example. In such a case, all relative URLs in *SunsetViewer.swf* would have to be composed relative to *SlideShow.swf* (notice: *not* relative to *SunsetViewer.swf*!). Similarly, if *SlideShow.swf* were viewed via a web page, then all relative URLs in *SunsetViewer.swf* would have to be composed relative to that web page.

You can completely avoid the issue of varying relative URL-resolution by storing all *.html* files, *.swf* files, and external-display-asset files in the same directory.

Now let's return to our example *SunsetViewer* class. Earlier, in Example 28-1 we created a *Loader* instance. Example 28-2 updates the *SunsetViewer* class, adding code that creates a request for the relative URL *"sunset.jpg"*. As mentioned earlier, for the sake of our example, we'll assume that *sunset.jpg* is stored in the same directory as *SunsetViewer.swf*, thus avoiding any relative-URL complexity.

Example 28-2. Specifying the asset's location

```
package {
  import flash.display.*;
  import flash.net.URLRequest;  // Import the URLRequest class

  public class SunsetViewer extends Sprite {
    private var loader:Loader;

    public function SunsetViewer () {
      loader = new Loader();
      // Specify asset location as "sunset.jpg"
      var urlRequest:URLRequest = new URLRequest("sunset.jpg");
    }
  }
}
```

Now that we've specified the location of *sunset.jpg*, let's actually load it.

Starting the Load Operation

So far, we've created a *Loader* object and a *URLRequest* object. Now we'll put them together to load an asset. To start a load operation, we pass our *URLRequest* instance to the *Loader* instance's *load()* method, as shown in Example 28-3.

Example 28-3. Starting the load operation

```
package {
  import flash.display.*;
  import flash.net.URLRequest;

  public class SunsetViewer extends Sprite {
    private var loader:Loader;

    public function SunsetViewer () {
      loader = new Loader();
      var url:URLRequest = new URLRequest("sunset.jpg");
      // Start the load operation
      loader.load(url);
    }
  }
}
```

So in summary, here's the basic code required to load an external display asset at runtime:

```
var loader:Loader = new Loader( );
var url:URLRequest = new URLRequest("assetURL");
loader.load(url);
```

where *assetURL* is the location of the asset to load. It's also legitimate and common to combine the preceding second and third lines into one, as in:

```
var loader:Loader = new Loader( );
loader.load(new URLRequest("assetURL"));
```

 To cancel an in-progress load operation, use the *Loader* class's instance method *close( )*.

Once an asset has started loading, we'll eventually want to access it and then display it on screen. The next two sections cover those tasks.

Accessing the Loaded Asset

Before a loaded asset can safely be accessed, ActionScript must first initialize it. During the initialization phase, ActionScript instantiates the asset, adds it to the *Loader* object that loaded it, and performs any tasks required to ready the asset for use.

The instantiation stage of the initialization process varies for different types of assets:

- For bitmaps, instantiation occurs when the external file has completely loaded. At that time, the loaded pixel data is automatically placed in a *BitmapData* object, which is then associated with a new *Bitmap* object. The *Bitmap* object represents the loaded image.

- For *.swf* files, instantiation occurs when all assets and classes on frame 1 (including the *.swf*'s main class) have been received. At that time, ActionScript creates an instance of the *.swf*'s main class and executes its constructor. The main class instance represents the loaded *.swf* file.

 For the sake of the following discussion, we'll refer to the instantiated object (either the *Bitmap* object or the instance of the *.swf*'s main class) as the *asset object*.

Once the loaded asset has been instantiated, the asset object is automatically added to the *Loader* object. The asset object is the *Loader* object's first, and only allowed, child. If the asset is a *.swf* file, any code on its first frame executes immediately after its main class instance is added to the *Loader* object.

After the asset object has been added to the *Loader* object, and all initialization is complete, the Flash runtime dispatches an `Event.INIT` event. When `Event.INIT` occurs, the asset is considered ready for use. Any code that needs to access a loaded asset should, therefore, be executed only after `Event.INIT` occurs.

 Do not attempt to access a loading asset before `Event.INIT` occurs.

Listeners wishing to be notified when the `Event.INIT` event occurs must register with the asset object's *LoaderInfo* object—not the *Loader* object that originally invoked *load( )*. The *LoaderInfo* object is a separate object that provides information about a loaded asset. Each *Loader* instance provides a reference to its loading asset's *LoaderInfo* object via the instance variable `contentLoaderInfo`. Hence, to register an event listener for a given asset's `Event.INIT` event, we use the following general code:

```
theLoader.contentLoaderInfo.addEventListener(Event.INIT, initListener);
```

where *theLoader* is the *Loader* object loading the asset, and *initListener* is a reference to the function that will handle the `Event.INIT` event. Once `Event.INIT` occurs, the loaded asset can safely be accessed via the *Loader* object's content variable or *getChildAt( )* method, as in:

```
theLoader.content
theLoader.getChildAt(0)
```

Notice the 0 in `getChildAt(0)`. The asset is the *Loader* object's only child, so it resides at depth index 0.

The following code shows an `Event.INIT` event listener that sets the position of an asset that has been loaded and initialized. In order to demonstrate the two different ways of accessing the loaded asset, the code sets the horizontal position using the content variable and the vertical position using `getChildAt(0)`.

```
private function initListener (e:Event):void {
  theLoader.content.x = 50;
  theLoader.getChildAt(0).y = 75;
}
```

Alternatively, a loaded asset can be accessed through the *Event* object passed to the `Event.INIT` listener function. An *Event* object passed to an `Event.INIT` listener defines a target variable that refers to the asset's *LoaderInfo* object. And each *LoaderInfo* object references its corresponding asset via the instance variable content. Hence, within an `Event.INIT` listener function, a reference to the loaded asset can be retrieved using the expression *theEvent*.`target.content`. For example, the following code sets the horizontal position of a loaded asset to 100:

```
private function initListener (e:Event):void {
  e.target.content.x = 100;
}
```

When accessing loaded assets, beware that, because an asset is not added to its *Loader* until it has sufficiently loaded, invoking *theLoader*.getChildAt(0) before a load operation commences causes an error. (Recall that a bitmap asset is not added to its *Loader* until after the external file has completely loaded. A *.swf* asset is not added to its *Loader* until after all assets and classes on the first frame, including the *.swf*'s main class, have been received.)

Likewise, before a load operation commences, the content variable contains the value null. The following code demonstrates:

```
// Start a load operation
var loader:Loader = new Loader( );
loader.load(new URLRequest("sunset.jpg"));

// Immediately attempt to access the loading asset
// before the load operation completes
trace(loader.getChildAt(0));   // RangeError: Error #2006:
                               // The supplied index is out of bounds.
trace(loader.content);         // Displays: null
```

Even once a load operation has started, if an asset has not sufficiently loaded, accessing either content or getChildAt(0) causes the following error:

```
Error: Error #2099: The loading object is not sufficiently loaded
                    to provide this information.
```

The lesson, once again, is: do not attempt to access a loading asset before Event.INIT occurs. In fact, the reverse is also true: before accessing its parent *Loader* object, code in a loaded *.swf* file's main class should wait for Event.INIT to occur. In particular, code in the constructor of a loaded *.swf* file's main class does not have access to the parent *Loader* object. That said, code placed in the first frame of a loaded *.swf* file's timeline (in the Flash authoring tool) can access the parent *Loader* object (before Event.INIT occurs).

Let's apply our new asset-access knowledge to the *SunsetViewer* class. Example 28-4 shows how to access the loaded *sunset.jpg* from an Event.INIT listener function. It displays the height, width, and rotation of the loaded image using the asset-access techniques covered in this section.

Example 28-4. Accessing the loaded asset

```
package {
  import flash.display.*;
  import flash.net.URLRequest;
  import flash.events.*;

  public class SunsetViewer extends Sprite {
    private var loader:Loader;

    public function SunsetViewer ( ) {
      loader = new Loader( );
```

Example 28-4. Accessing the loaded asset (continued)

```
    // Register for Event.INIT
    loader.contentLoaderInfo.addEventListener(Event.INIT, initListener);
    var urlRequest:URLRequest = new URLRequest("sunset.jpg");
    loader.load(urlRequest);
  }

  // Listener invoked when Event.INIT occurs
  private function initListener (e:Event):void {
    // Access asset in three different ways
    trace(loader.content.width);
    trace(loader.getChildAt(0).height);
    trace(e.target.content.rotation);
  }
 }
}
```

 To use the methods and variables of the *Bitmap* class, the *MovieClip* class, or a *.swf* file's main class with a loaded asset, follow the techniques covered in the later section "Compile-Time Type-Checking for Runtime-Loaded Assets."

Displaying the Loaded Asset On Screen

Once an asset is ready to be accessed, it is also ready to be added to the display list for on-screen display. To add a loaded asset to the display list, we use the *DisplayObjectContainer* class's instance method *addChild( )*, just as we would when adding any other display object to the display list. Example 28-5 adds the *Bitmap* object representing *sunset.jpg* to the main application class, *SunsetViewer*.

Example 28-5. Adding an asset to the display list

```
package {
  import flash.display.*;
  import flash.net.URLRequest;
  import flash.events.*;

  public class SunsetViewer extends Sprite {
    private var loader:Loader;

    public function SunsetViewer ( ) {
      loader = new Loader( );
      loader.contentLoaderInfo.addEventListener(Event.INIT, initListener);
      var urlRequest:URLRequest = new URLRequest("sunset.jpg");
      loader.load(urlRequest);
    }

    private function initListener (e:Event):void {
      addChild(loader.content);  // Add Bitmap object to SunsetViewer
    }
  }
}
```

Adding a loaded asset object to a new *DisplayObjectContainer* as shown in Example 28-5 automatically removes that asset from its original parent *Loader* object. To demonstrate, let's add some code to Example 28-5's *initListener()* method. The added code checks how many children loader has, both before and after the loaded asset (*sunset.jpg*) is added to *SunsetViewer*. Notice that after the asset is moved, loader has no child display objects.

```
private function initListener (e:Event):void {
  trace(loader.numChildren);  // Displays: 1 (the lone child is the asset)
  addChild(loader.content);
  trace(loader.numChildren);  // Displays: 0 (because the asset was moved)
}
```

An alternative technique for displaying a loaded asset on screen is to add the asset's *Loader* object, rather than the asset object, to the display list. The *Loader* class, itself, is a descendent of *DisplayObject*, so it can be added to any *DisplayObjectContainer* directly. Once again, let's revise the *initListener()* method from Example 28-5. This time we'll add loader to *SunsetViewer* directly. In so doing, we implicitly make the *Bitmap* object representing *sunset.jpg* a grandchild of *SunsetViewer*.

```
private function initListener (e:Event):void {
  addChild(loader);  // Add loader and its child asset to the display list
}
```

In fact, a *Loader* object can be added to the display list before any load operation starts. When a display asset is subsequently loaded, it is automatically added to the *Loader* object and, by extension, to the display list. Example 28-6 demonstrates. It adds loader to the display list before loading *sunset.jpg*. After *sunset.jpg* is instantiated and initialized, it is added to loader and—because loader is already on the display list—appears on screen. Therefore, no Event.INIT event listener is required.

Example 28-6. Adding a Loader to the display list

```
package {
  import flash.display.*;
  import flash.net.URLRequest;

  public class SunsetViewer extends Sprite {
    private var loader:Loader;

    public function SunsetViewer () {
      loader = new Loader();
      addChild(loader);
      var urlRequest:URLRequest = new URLRequest("sunset.jpg");
      loader.load(urlRequest);
    }
  }
}
```

Hence, the simplest possible way to load a display asset and display it on screen is:

```
var loader:Loader = new Loader( );
addChild(loader);
loader.load(new URLRequest(theAssetURL));
```

The preceding three lines of code work for many simple situations, but in cases where the loaded asset must be managed separately from its *Loader* object, or where the timing for displaying the loaded asset must be managed manually, the code shown earlier in Example 28-5 is more appropriate.

We've now learned how to load and display an external asset, but there's often a noticeable delay between those two operations while the asset downloads. Next we'll learn how to use the *LoaderInfo* class to display the progress of a download operation.

Displaying Load Progress

To display the progress of an asset-load operation we follow four general steps:

1. Before loading the asset, create a visual load-progress indicator (e.g., a text field or "loading bar").

2. When the load operation starts, add the progress indicator to the display list.

3. As the asset loads, update the state of the progress indicator (much to the user's delight).

4. When the load operation completes, remove the progress indicator from the screen.

Let's see how the preceding steps work in practice by adding a simple text-based load-progress indicator to our *SunsetViewer* class.

We'll start by giving *SunsetViewer* a new instance variable, progressOutput, which refers to a standard *TextField* object. The progressOutput text field will display load-progress information.

```
private var progressOutput:TextField;
```

Next, we'll give *SunsetViewer* two new methods: *createProgressIndicator( )* and *load( )*. The first new method, *createProgressIndicator( )*, creates the progressOutput *TextField*. We'll invoke *createProgressIndicator( )* from *SunsetViewer*'s constructor. Here's the code:

```
private function createProgressIndicator ( ):void {
  progressOutput  = new TextField( );
  progressOutput.autoSize   = TextFieldAutoSize.LEFT;
  progressOutput.border     = true;
  progressOutput.background = true;
  progressOutput.selectable = false;
  progressOutput.text       = "LOADING...";
}
```

The second new method, *load( )*, will add progressOutput to the display list and start the asset-load operation. Any time a load operation is requested via *load( )*, progressOutput will be placed on screen; any time a load operation completes, progressOutput will be removed from the screen. This architecture lets *SunsetViewer* reuse the same *TextField* object when displaying load-progress information. Here's the code for *load( )*:

```
private function load (urlRequest:URLRequest):void {
  // Start the load operation
  loader.load(urlRequest);
  // If progressOutput isn't already a descendant of this object...
  if (!contains(progressOutput)) {
    // ...add it
    addChild(progressOutput);
  }
}
```

During loading, we'll listen for the ProgressEvent.PROGRESS event, which indicates that a new portion of *sunset.jpg* has arrived and provides the latest load-progress information. Each time the ProgressEvent.PROGRESS event occurs, we'll update progressOutput. The ProgressEvent.PROGRESS event is targeted at our loading asset's *LoaderInfo* object. As we learned earlier, an asset's *LoaderInfo* object can be accessed via the *Loader* class's instance variable contentLoaderInfo. Hence, to register to receive ProgressEvent.PROGRESS notifications, we use the following code:

```
loader.contentLoaderInfo.addEventListener(ProgressEvent.PROGRESS,
                                          progressListener);
```

In the preceding code, progressListener is a reference to the function we want to run when the ProgressEvent.PROGRESS event occurs. The progressListener function is passed a ProgressEvent object whose variables indicate:

- The file size of the loading asset (bytesTotal)
- The number of bytes that have been received so far (bytesLoaded)

The following code shows the progressListener function for our *SunsetViewer* class; notice how it retrieves load progress information from the *ProgressEvent* object, e:

```
private function progressListener (e:ProgressEvent):void {
  // Update progress indicator. 1 Kb is 1024 bytes, so divide by
  // 1024 to convert output to Kb.
  progressOutput.text = "LOADING: "
                    + Math.floor(e.bytesLoaded / 1024)
                    + "/" + Math.floor(e.bytesTotal / 1024) + " KB";
}
```

When an asset has been received in its entirety, the Flash runtime dispatches an Event.COMPLETE event targeted at the asset's *LoaderInfo* object. When Event.COMPLETE occurs, we can remove the progress indicator (progressOutput) from the display list.

To register with our loading asset's *LoaderInfo* object for Event.COMPLETE events, we use the following code:

```
loader.contentLoaderInfo.addEventListener(Event.COMPLETE,
                                          completeListener);
```

where completeListener is a reference to the function we want to run when Event.COMPLETE occurs. The following code shows the completeListener function. Its job is simply to remove progressOutput from the display list.

```
private function completeListener (e:Event):void {
  // Remove progress indicator.
  removeChild(progressOutput);
}
```

Finally, for the sake of reusability and easier reading, we'll move our *Loader*-creation code and event-registration code into a new method, *createLoader()*, shown next. Notice that the code in *createLoader()* registers not only for ProgressEvent.PROGRESS and Event.COMPLETE but also for the Event.INIT event discussed in the earlier section "Accessing the Loaded Asset." As before, we'll place our loaded asset on the display list when Event.INIT occurs. Here's the code for *createLoader()*:

```
private function createLoader ():void {
  // Create the Loader
  loader = new Loader();

  // Register for events
  loader.contentLoaderInfo.addEventListener(ProgressEvent.PROGRESS, progressListener);
  loader.contentLoaderInfo.addEventListener(Event.COMPLETE, completeListener);
  loader.contentLoaderInfo.addEventListener(Event.INIT, initListener);
}
```

Code that removes a progress indicator from the display list (as our *completeListener()* does) should always use the Event.COMPLETE event rather than the Event.INIT event. Be careful not to confuse these two events. Event.INIT expresses a qualitative state of "asset readiness" while Event.COMPLETE expresses a quantitative state of download completion. Event.INIT indicates that an asset is ready for use, even though—in the case of a *.swf* file—it might still be downloading. By contrast, Event.COMPLETE indicates that all the bytes in the file containing an asset have been received.

 Use the Event.INIT event to determine when an asset can be safely accessed. Use the Event.COMPLETE event to determine when a load operation has finished.

Because some types of assets can be initialized before they are fully loaded, Event.INIT always occurs before Event.COMPLETE. For example, suppose we're loading a *.swf* file containing a 2,000-frame animation. When the first frame has loaded and been initialized, Event.INIT occurs. At that time, we add the animation to the display list and let it

---

play while the *.swf* continues to load. As the *.swf* loads, a load-bar indicates download progress. When the *.swf* finishes loading, Event.COMPLETE occurs, and we remove the load-bar from the screen.

Example 28-7 shows our *SunsetViewer* class once again, this time revised to include the load-progress-display code covered in this section.

Example 28-7. Displaying load progress

```
package {
  import flash.display.*;
  import flash.net.URLRequest;
  import flash.events.*
  import flash.text.*;

  public class SunsetViewer extends Sprite {
    private var loader:Loader;              // The asset loader
    private var progressOutput:TextField;  // The text field in which
                                           // to display load progress
    // Constructor
    public function SunsetViewer () {
      // Create Loader object and register for events
      createLoader();

      // Create the progress indicator
      createProgressIndicator();

      // Start the load operation
      load(new URLRequest("sunset.jpg"));
    }

    private function createLoader ():void {
      // Create the Loader
      loader = new Loader();

      // Register for events
      loader.contentLoaderInfo.addEventListener(ProgressEvent.PROGRESS,
                                          progressListener);
      loader.contentLoaderInfo.addEventListener(Event.COMPLETE,
                                          completeListener);
      loader.contentLoaderInfo.addEventListener(Event.INIT,
                                          initListener);
    }

    private function createProgressIndicator ():void {
      progressOutput  = new TextField();
      progressOutput.autoSize   = TextFieldAutoSize.LEFT;
      progressOutput.border     = true;
      progressOutput.background = true;
      progressOutput.selectable = false;
      progressOutput.text       = "LOADING...";
    }
```

Example 28-7. Displaying load progress (continued)

```
    private function load (urlRequest:URLRequest):void {
      loader.load(urlRequest);
      if (!contains(progressOutput)) {
        addChild(progressOutput);
      }
    }

    // Listener invoked whenever data arrives
    private function progressListener (e:ProgressEvent):void {
      // Update progress indicator.
      progressOutput.text = "LOADING: "
                          + Math.floor(e.bytesLoaded / 1024)
                          + "/" + Math.floor(e.bytesTotal / 1024) + " KB";
    }

    private function initListener (e:Event):void {
      addChild(loader.content);  // Add loaded asset to display list
    }

    // Listener invoked when the asset has been fully loaded
    private function completeListener (e:Event):void {
      // Remove progress indicator.
      removeChild(progressOutput);
    }
  }
}
```

Why not use Event.OPEN?

If you've browsed through the Flash runtime API documentation you might have noticed a convenient-looking event called Event.OPEN, which occurs when a loading operation commences. In theory, Event.OPEN offers a nice clean place from which to add a progress indicator to the display list. As we learned earlier, progress-display code breaks down into four general tasks:

1. Create the progress indicator.
2. Add the progress indicator to the display list.
3. Update the progress indicator.
4. Remove the progress indicator from the display list.

The first operation typically occurs during a setup phase. The remaining three operations correspond to the three loading events: Event.OPEN, Event.PROGRESS, and Event.COMPLETE. You might wonder, then, why the *SunsetViewer* class in Example 28-7 added progressOutput to the display list in the *load( )* method rather than in an Event.OPEN listener.

```
    private function load (urlRequest:URLRequest):void {
      loader.load(urlRequest);
```

```
    if (!contains(progressOutput)) {
      // Why do this here...
      addChild(progressOutput);
    }
  }

  private function openListener (e:Event):void {
    if (!contains(progressOutput)) {
      // ...rather than here?
      addChild(progressOutput);
    }
  }
```

In fact, an Event.OPEN listener would theoretically be a good place to add progressOutput to the display list. Unfortunately, in practice, idiosyncratic browser behavior complicates the use of Event.OPEN, so this book avoids its use. For complete details, see the later section "Environment-specific behavior for load failures."

So far we've learned how to load an external asset, display it on screen, and show its load progress to the user. Now let's study the code required to recover from load errors.

Handling Load Errors

As we learned in Chapter 19, any time an attempt to load an asset fails due to security restrictions, Flash Player either throws a *SecurityError* exception or dispatches a SecurityErrorEvent.SECURITY_ERROR. Any time an attempt to load an asset fails for any other reason, ActionScript dispatches an IOErrorEvent.IO_ERROR event targeted at the asset's *LoaderInfo* object. By handling that event, we can attempt to recover from any nonsecurity-related load failure. For example, we might write code in an IOErrorEvent.IO_ERROR listener that asks the user to check for a faulty Internet connection.

Let's add load-error handling code to our *SunsetViewer* class. To register to be notified when IOErrorEvent.IO_ERROR occurs, we use the now-familiar code:

```
loader.contentLoaderInfo.addEventListener(IOErrorEvent.IO_ERROR,
                                          ioErrorListener);
```

where *ioErrorListener* is a reference to the function that will handle the event. The following code shows the *ioErrorListener* function. In our *SunsetViewer* application, *ioErrorListener()* simply displays an error message to the user in the progressOutput text field.

```
// Listener invoked when a load error occurs
private function ioErrorListener (e:IOErrorEvent):void {
  progressOutput.text = "LOAD ERROR";
}
```

Unlike other loading events, when Flash Player dispatches an IOErrorEvent.IO_ERROR event targeted at a *LoaderInfo* object, but no listener function is registered to handle it, ActionScript generates a runtime error. For example:

```
Error #2044: Unhandled IOErrorEvent:. text=Error #2035: URL Not Found.
```

Of course, like all runtime error events, the "Unhandled IOErrorEvent" error is displayed in the debug version of Flash Player only. In the release version of Flash Player, ActionScript does not display load errors to the user; instead, ActionScript expects application code to respond to the error as it sees fit.

Example 28-8 updates *SunsetViewer* one last time, showing the class in its final state, complete with load-error handling code. The new code is shown in bold.

Example 28-8. The final SunsetViewer, with load-error handling

```
package {
  import flash.display.*;
  import flash.net.URLRequest;
  import flash.events.*
  import flash.text.*;

  public class SunsetViewer extends Sprite {
    private var loader:Loader;
    private var progressOutput:TextField;

    public function SunsetViewer () {
      createLoader();
      createProgressIndicator();
      load(new URLRequest("sunset.jpg"));
    }

    private function createLoader ():void {
      loader = new Loader();
      loader.contentLoaderInfo.addEventListener(ProgressEvent.PROGRESS,
                                      progressListener);
      loader.contentLoaderInfo.addEventListener(Event.COMPLETE,
                                      completeListener);
      loader.contentLoaderInfo.addEventListener(Event.INIT,
                                      initListener);
      loader.contentLoaderInfo.addEventListener(IOErrorEvent.IO_ERROR,
                                      ioErrorListener);
    }

    private function createProgressIndicator ():void {
      progressOutput    = new TextField();
      progressOutput.autoSize    = TextFieldAutoSize.LEFT;
      progressOutput.border      = true;
      progressOutput.background  = true;
      progressOutput.selectable  = false;
      progressOutput.text        = "LOADING...";
    }
```

```
    private function load (urlRequest:URLRequest):void {
      loader.load(urlRequest);
      if (!contains(progressOutput)) {
        addChild(progressOutput);
      }
    }

    private function progressListener (e:ProgressEvent):void {
      progressOutput.text = "LOADING: "
                          + Math.floor(e.bytesLoaded / 1024)
                          + "/" + Math.floor(e.bytesTotal / 1024) + " KB";
    }

    private function initListener (e:Event):void {
      addChild(loader.content);
    }

    private function completeListener (e:Event):void {
      removeChild(progressOutput);
    }

    // Listener invoked when a load error occurs
    private function ioErrorListener (e:IOErrorEvent):void {
      progressOutput.text = "LOAD ERROR";
    }
  }
}
```

Environment-specific behavior for load failures

To perform load operations, the Flash runtime depends on its local environment (i.e., the operating system and host application, which is often a web browser). As a result, some ActionScript loading behaviors are environment-specific. As much as possible, ActionScript attempts to reduce the programmer's exposure to environment-specific behaviors. Nevertheless, in Flash Player 9, there are two load-failure behaviors—presented in Table 28-1—that are unique to Internet Explorer on Windows, and require special programmer attention.

Table 28-1. Internet Explorer-specific load behaviors

Feature	Internet Explorer behavior	Standalone player, firefox, and Adobe AIR behavior
Event.OPEN	All load operations trigger the Event. OPEN event, even those that eventually fail due to a "file not found" condition.	The Event.OPEN event is *not* triggered for load operations that fail due to a "file not found."
IOErrorEvent's instance variable text	When a load operation fails due to a "file not found" condition, text is set to "Error #2036: Load Never Completed."	When a load operation fails due to a "file not found" condition, text is set to "Error #2035: URL Not Found."

None of the differing behaviors described in Table 28-1 is the "correct" behavior. Each behavior is simply determined by the Flash runtime's environment. However, because the behaviors are not consistent across all environments, care must be taken when writing code that uses Event.OPEN or the *IOErrorEvent* class's instance variable text. To achieve platform neutrality, follow these two guidelines:

- Never make logical branching decisions based on the value of the *IOErrorEvent* class's instance variable text. Use that variable for debugging purposes only.
- Avoid using Event.OPEN for anything other than debugging.

Let's consider one example showing why the use of Event.OPEN could cause problems in an application. Suppose an application uses a custom class, *LoadBar*, to display progress for a load operation. The application adds the *LoadBar* instance to the display list whenever a load operation starts, from within an Event.OPEN event listener:

```
private function openListener (e:Event):void {
  addChild(loadBar);
}
```

Now suppose the application attempts to load a file that cannot be found. If the application is viewed in Internet Explorer, *openListener()* is executed, and the *LoadBar* instance appears on screen. But if the application is viewed in any other browser, *openListener()* is *not* executed, and the *LoadBar* instance does not appear on screen. In the best case, the developer notices the discrepancy and writes Internet Explorer-specific code to remove the *LoadBar* instance from the screen in the event of a load failure. Such code complicates the application and increases the possibility of code errors. In the worst case, the developer does not notice the discrepancy, and in Internet Explorer, the *LoadBar* is stranded on screen for the lifetime of the application. To avoid the problem completely, it's safest to never use the Event.OPEN event. Instead, simply follow the approach we took in Example 28-7: add any load progress indicators to the screen manually before starting load operations.

In future versions of ActionScript, the environment-specific behaviors described in Table 28-1 might be standardized, eliminating the need to avoid the Event.OPEN event.

Debugging with HTTPStatusEvent

When an HTTP client requests an asset over HTTP, the HTTP server responds with a status code indicating how the request was handled. For example, if an HTTP request succeeds, the HTTP server sends a status code of 200. If an HTTP request fails, the server sends a failure status describing what went wrong. HTTP-status codes for load failures often provide more detailed information than ActionScript's generic IOErrorEvent.IO_ERROR event, so they are useful for debugging. However, HTTP-status codes are not supported in all environments.

Flash Player plug-ins for Netscape, Mozilla (Firefox), Safari, Opera, and Internet Explorer (Macintosh version) do not support HTTP-status codes.

When Flash Player receives an HTTP-status code from the server, it dispatches an HTTPStatusEvent.HTTP_STATUS event targeted at the loading asset's *LoaderInfo* object. To register to be notified when HTTPStatusEvent.HTTP_STATUS occurs, we use the following code:

```
theLoader.contentLoaderInfo.addEventListener(HTTPStatusEvent.HTTP_STATUS,
                                    httpStatusListener);
```

where *theLoader* is the *Loader* object loading the asset and *httpStatusListener* is a reference to the function that will handle the event. The *httpStatusListener* function is passed an *HTTPStatusEvent* object whose status variable contains the HTTP-status code. The following code shows a typical *httpStatusListener* function; notice how it retrieves the HTTP-status code from the *HTTPStatusEvent* object, e:

```
private function httpStatusListener (e:HTTPStatusEvent):void {
  trace("http status: " + e.status);
}
```

Perhaps surprisingly, Flash Player actually dispatches an HTTPStatusEvent.HTTP_STATUS for every single load operation, even when Flash Player does not receive an HTTP-status code from the server. When no HTTP-status code is received, the value of the *HTTPStatusEvent* class's instance variable status is set to 0. For example, in all of the following situations, status is set to 0:

- A file is loaded locally or from a non-HTTP source.
- The HTTP server cannot be reached.
- The request URL is malformed.
- The environment does not support HTTP-status codes (e.g., Flash Player is running in Mozilla Firefox).

We've now covered all general tasks relating to loading display assets, at runtime with a *Loader* object. The upcoming sections cover issues relating specifically to using loaded *.swf* files.

Compile-Time Type-Checking for Runtime-Loaded Assets

In the earlier section "Accessing the Loaded Asset," we learned that the *Loader* class's instance variable content refers to an object representing a loaded asset. We also learned that—depending on which type of asset was loaded—content might refer to an instance of either the *Bitmap* class or a *.swf* file's main class. Instances of those disparate classes can legally be assigned to content because its datatype is

DisplayObject, and both the *Bitmap* class and all *.swf* file main classes inherit from *DisplayObject*. As a result, any object assigned to content can be operated on using the variables and methods of *DisplayObject* but cannot be operated on using the more specific variables and methods of either the *Bitmap* class or a *.swf*'s main class.

For example, the following code legally accesses the *DisplayObject* class's instance variable width on an object referenced via content:

```
// DisplayObject defines width, so no error
loader.content.width
```

The following code similarly attempts to access the Bitmap class's instance variable bitmapData on an object referenced via content. But this time, the code causes a compiler error because the *DisplayObject* class does not define the bitmapData variable.

```
ERROR: "Access of possibly undefined property bitmapData through a
        reference with static type flash.display:DisplayObject."
```

```
loader.content.bitmapData.getPixel(0, 0)
```

To avoid compile-time errors when referencing *Bitmap* methods and variables through content, we cast content to *Bitmap*, as shown in the following code:

```
Bitmap(loader.content).bitmapData.getPixel(1, 1);
```

The cast operation informs the compiler that the loaded asset is an instance of the *Bitmap* class, which defines the bitmapData variable.

Likewise, when using *MovieClip* methods and variables on a loaded *.swf* file, we cast content to *MovieClip*. For example, the following code starts playing a hypothetical animation by invoking the *MovieClip* class's instance method *play()* on a loaded asset. The (required) cast operation informs the compiler that the loaded asset is a descendent of the *MovieClip* class, and, therefore, supports the *play()* method.

```
MovieClip(loader.content).play( );
```

In the same way, when using the custom methods and variables of a loaded *.swf* file's main class, you might naturally expect to cast content to that main class. For example, suppose an application, *Main.swf* loads another application, *Module.swf*, whose main class is *Module*. Further suppose that *Module* defines a custom method, *start()*. When *Main.swf* loads *Module.swf*, ActionScript automatically creates a *Module* instance and assigns it to content. Hence, to invoke *start()* on the loaded *Module* instance, you might expect to use the following cast operation:

```
Module(loader.content).start( );
```

While the preceding code is conceptually correct, it will actually cause a compile-time error unless special measures are taken when compiling *Main.swf*. Let's consider why.

Suppose we've created *Main.swf* and *Module.swf* as separate projects in Flex Builder 2. The two projects are designed as self-contained, independent applications, so they have completely separate code bases, and do not link to each other in any way. *Module.swf*'s project defines the class *Module*, but *Main.swf*'s project has no knowledge of that class. When we build *Main.swf*, the compiler encounters this code:

```
Module(loader.content).start()
```

and cannot resolve the reference to *Module* within *main.swf*'s ActionScript Build Path. Unable to find *Module*, the compiler assumes that the expression `Module(loader.content)` is a method call. However, no method named *Module* exists, so the compiler generates the following datatype error:

```
1180: Call to a possibly undefined method Module.
```

There are two ways to address this issue: we can opt-out of compile-time type-checking or we can give the compiler access to the *Module* class when compiling *Main.swf*. The next two sections cover these two options.

Opting Out of Compile-Time Type-Checking

To opt-out of compile-time type-checking when using the custom methods and variables of a loaded *.swf* file's main class, we can either cast `loader.content` to the *Object* datatype, as in:

```
Object(loader.content).start();  // No compiler error
```

or, we can assign `loader.content` to an untyped variable, as in:

```
var module:* = loader.content;
module.start();  // No compiler error
```

Alternatively, we can access the loaded object via the expression *initEvent*.`target.content` within an `Event.INIT` event listener function. The *Event* class's instance variable `target` is not type-checked at compile-time because target's datatype is *Object*.

```
private function initListener (e:Event):void {
  e.target.content.start();  // No compiler error
}
```

In each of the preceding cases, when *start()* is accessed, the compiler does not generate an error. Instead, our use of `loader.content` is not type-checked until runtime. However, as we learned in Chapter 8, opting out of compile-time type-checking comes at a productivity cost. When type checking is deferred until runtime, errors are not reported until potential problem code is actually executed, so testing time is increased.

To avoid increased testing time, we can choose instead to give the compiler access to the *Module* class when compiling *Main.swf*. The next section describes the process in detail.

Give the Compiler Access to the Loaded Class

To avoid compiler errors when casting loader.content to a loaded *.swf* file's main class, we can give ActionScript compile-time access to that class. There are three different techniques for doing so: the *source-path* technique, the *library-path* technique, and the *external-library-path* technique. Continuing with the *Module* class example from the previous section, each technique is covered in the following three sections. In each case, the compiler is given access to the *Module* class when compiling *Main.swf*.

The three techniques covered in the following sections are appropriate in different situations. Use the *source-path* technique when both of the following are true:

- An increase in the file size of the overall application is acceptable.
- You are willing to make the source code of the loaded *.swf* file (*Module.swf* in our example) directly available to the author of the accessing *.swf* file (*Main.swf* in our example).

Use the the *library-path* technique when an increase in the file size of the overall application is acceptable *and* one of the following is true:

- You do not wish to make the source code of the loaded *.swf* file directly available to the author of the accessing *.swf* file.
- The time required to compile the accessing *.swf* file must be minimized.

Use the tthe *external-library-path* technique when an increase in the overall application's file size is not acceptable.

Note that in all three of the following technique examples, if *Main.swf* already contains a class named *Module*, *Main.swf*'s version is used instead of the *Module.swf*'s. To avoid that possibility, always qualify your class names with a unique package name (as discussed in Chapter 1).

Add the Module Class File to Main.swf's source-path

The first technique for giving the compiler access to the *Module* class when compiling *Main.swf* is to add *Module*'s class file to *Main.swf*'s *source-path*.

The following steps describe the process in Flex Builder 2:

1. In the Navigator panel, select the project folder for the *Main.swf* application.
2. On the Project Menu, choose Properties.
3. On the Properties dialog, choose ActionScript Build Path.
4. On the Source path tab, click the Add Folder button.
5. On the Add Folder dialog, specify the path to the folder containing *Module*'s class file.

---

6. On the Add Folder dialog, click OK.

7. On the Properties dialog, click OK.

The following steps describe the equivalent process for adding *Module*'s class file to *Main.swf*'s *source-path* in Flash CS3:

1. Open *Main.swf*'s corresponding *.fla* file, *Main.fla*. (Note that the steps for creating *Main.fla* are not discussed in this section. The file *Main.fla* is assumed to be *.fla* file with its document class set to *Main*.)

2. Select File → Publish Settings.

3. In the Publish Settings dialog, on the Flash tab, next to "ActionScript version: ActionScript 3.0," click the Settings button.

4. On the ActionScript 3.0 Settings dialog, under Classpath, click the plus button (+), and specify the path to the folder containing *Module*'s class file.

Once *Module*'s class file is in *main.swf*'s *source-path*, the compiler will be able to type-check any reference to *Module* that occurs in *main.swf*. The compiler also adds the bytecode for *Module* (and all dependent definitions) directly into *main.swf*, ensuring that *Module* will be accessible within *Main.swf* at runtime. The *source-path* technique, hence, increases the overall file size of the application because the *Module* class and its dependent definitions are included in both *Main.swf* and *Module.swf*. Furthermore, the *source-path* technique compiles *Module* from scratch every time the *Main.swf* is built, which can be time-consuming.

Add the Module Class File to Main.swf's library-path

The second technique for giving the compiler access to the *Module* class when compiling *Main.swf* is to create a *.swc* file containing *Module* and include that *.swc* file in *Main.swf*'s *library-path*.

To create the *.swc* file containing *Module* in Flex Builder 2, we use the command-line component compiler, *compc* (*compc* resides in the Flex Builder 2 install directory, under *Flex SDK 2\bin*). The general form for compiling a *.swc* file using *compc* is:

```
compc -source-path path_to_definitions -output path_to_swc_file -include-classes
definitionNames
```

where *path_to_definitions* is a list of locations in which the compiler should look for classes and other definitions when creating the *.swc* file, *path_to_swc_file* is the path to the *.swc* file that will be created, and *definitionNames* is a list of definitions to include in the *.swc* file (the compiler automatically includes all dependent definitions). For example, suppose we're using Windows XP, and we want to create a *.swc* file named *module.swc* in the folder *c:\apps\module\bin*. We want *module.swc* to include *Module*, whose class file resides in the folder *c:\apps\module\src*. To create *module.swc*, we use the following command:

```
compc -source-path c:\apps\module\src -output c:\apps\module\bin\module.swc -include-
classes Module
```

Note that, despite its name, the *compc* compiler option -include-classes can be used to include any kind of definition, not just classes. Future versions of the compiler may include a more appropriately named option, -include-definitions.

Now let's consider the equivalent process for creating a *.swc* file containing *Module* in Flash CS3. Here are the steps:

1. Create a new Flash document (*.fla* file) named *Module.fla*.
2. In the Properties panel (Window → Properties), for Document class, enter **Module**.
3. Select File → Publish Settings.
4. On the Formats tab, under Type, uncheck HTML.
5. On the Flash tab, under Options, check Export SWC.
6. Click Publish, then click OK.

Once *module.swc* has been created, we include it in the *library-path* when compiling *main.swf*. To do so in Flex Builder 2, follow these steps:

1. In the Navigator panel, select the project folder for the *Main.swf* application.
2. On the Project Menu, choose Properties.
3. On the Properties dialog, choose ActionScript Build Path.
4. On the Library path tab, click the Add SWC button.
5. On the Add SWC dialog, specify the path to *module.swc*.
6. On the Add SWC dialog, click OK.
7. On the Properties dialog, click OK.

In Flash CS3, to include *module.swc* in the *library-path* when compiling *main.swf*, follow these steps:

1. In the Flash authoring tool installation folder, under *Configuration\Components*, create a new folder named *Module*. (On Windows XP, the default location for *Configuration\Components* is: *C:\Program Files\Adobe\Adobe Flash CS3\en\ Configuration\Components*. On Mac OS X, the default location for *Configuration\ Components* is: *Macintosh HD:Applications:Adobe Flash CS3:Configuration: Components*).
2. Copy the *module.swc* file to the *Module* folder created in Step 1. Copying the *module.swc* file to a subfolder of *Configuration\Components* adds it to the Flash authoring tool's Components panel.
3. In the Flash authoring tool, open Components panel (Window → Components).

4. Select the pop-up Options menu in the top-right corner of the Components panel, and choose the Reload option. The folder *Module* will appear in the Components panel.

5. In the Components panel, open the *Module* folder.

6. Open *Main.fla*'s Library (Window → Library).

7. Drag the Module component from the Components panel to *Main.fla*'s Library.

Once *module.swc* is in *Main.swf*'s *library-path*, the compiler will be able to type-check any reference to *Module* that occurs in *Main.swf*. The compiler also copies the bytecode for *Module* (and all dependent classes) directly from *module.swc* to *main.swf*, ensuring that *Module* will be accessible within *Main.swf* at runtime. Hence, like the *source-path* technique, the *library-path* technique increases the overall file size of the application because the *Module* class and its dependent definitions are included in both *Main.swf* and *Module.swf*. However, because the *library-path* technique does not require *Module* to be compiled from scratch every time the *Main.swf* is built, building *Main.swf* using the *library-path* technique is typically faster than using the *source-path* technique.

Copying precompiled bytecode from a *.swc* file to a *.swf* file is faster than compiling from raw definition files.

Of course, every time the *Module* class changes, *module.swc* must, itself, be recreated. Therefore, if *Module* changes more frequently than *Main.swf*, the time saved by copying bytecode directly from *module.swc* to *Main.swf* will be fully offset by the time spent compiling *module.swc*. In the parlance of our time, your mileage may vary.

Add the Module Class File to Main.swf's external-library-path

The third technique for giving the compiler access to the *Module* class when compiling *Main.swf* is to create a *.swc* file containing *Module*, and include that *.swc* file in the *external-library-path* when compiling *main.swf*.

We start this technique by following the instructions from the previous section for creating the *module.swc* file. Once *module.swc* is created, we add it to *Main.swf*'s *external-library-path*. To do so in Flex Builder 2, follow these steps:

1. In the Navigator panel, select the project folder for the *Main.swf* application.

2. On the Project Menu, choose Properties.

3. On the Properties dialog, choose ActionScript Build Path.

4. On the Library path tab, click the Add SWC button.

5. On the Add SWC dialog, specify the path to *module.swc*.

6. On the Add SWC dialog, click OK.

7. Under "Build path libraries," expand *module.swc* in the tree.

8. Under *module.swc*, select "Link Type: Merged into code."

9. Click the Edit button.

10. On the Library Path Item Options dialog, for Link Type, choose External.

11. On the Library Path Item Options dialog, click OK.

12. On the Properties dialog, click OK.

In Flash CS3, to include *module.swc in* the *external-library-path*, we simply place it in the same folder as *Main.fla* (or in any folder in *Main.fla*'s classpath) and delete the Module component from *Main.fla*'s Library.

Once *module.swc* is in *Main.swf*'s *external-library-path*, the compiler will be able to type-check any reference to *Module* that occurs in *Main.swf*. However, in contrast to both the *library-path* technique and the *source-path* technique, when *Main.swf* is built using the *external-library-path* technique, the compiler does *not* copy *Module*'s bytecode to *Main.swf*. Thus, the overall file size of the application is kept to a minimum. However, excluding *Module*'s bytecode from *Main.swf* raises a new issue: any reference to the *Module* class within *Main.swf* is unknown to ActionScript at runtime. Hence, the following code:

```
Module(loader.content).start( )
```

will cause the following runtime error:

```
ReferenceError: Error #1065: Variable Module is not defined.
```

To avoid that error, we must instruct ActionScript to import *Module.swf*'s classes into *Main.swf*'s *application domain* at runtime.

 A *.swf* file's application domain provides access to its classes. Application domains govern how classes and other definitions are shared among loaded *.swf* files. For more information, see Adobe's Programming ActionScript 3.0, under Flash Player APIs → Client System Environment → ApplicationDomain class. Also see Chapter 31.

To import *Module.swf*'s classes into *Main.swf*'s application domain, we use a *LoaderContext* object when issuing the request to load *Module.swf*. Here's the code as it would appear in *Main.swf*'s main class:

```
// First, import the ApplicationDomain and LoaderContext classes...
import flash.system.*;

// ...later in the class, use a LoaderContext object to
// import Module.swf's classes and other definitions
// into Main.swf's application domain
loader.load(new URLRequest("Module.swf"),
        new LoaderContext(false, ApplicationDomain.currentDomain));
```

The preceding code makes *Module.swf*'s classes (and other definitions) directly accessible to code in *Main.swf*—as though *Main.swf* had, itself, defined them.

Note that if *Main.swf* and *Module.swf* are from different remote regions, or if *Main.swf* originates from the local realm and has a different security-sandbox-type than *Module. swf*, then the attempt to import *Module.swf*'s classes into *Main.swf*'s application domain will fail silently. In such a case, the code:

```
Module(loader.content).start( )
```

will cause the same error that would occur if *Module.swf*'s classes had never been imported into *Main.swf*'s application domain—namely:

```
ReferenceError: Error #1065: Variable Module is not defined.
```

In certain situations, this security limitation can be avoided using *import loading*, wherein *Main.swf* uses a *LoaderContext* object to import *Module.swf* into its security domain. The following code demonstrates:

```
var loaderContext:LoaderContext = new LoaderContext( );
loaderContext.applicationDomain = ApplicationDomain.currentDomain;
var loader:Loader = new Loader( );
loader.load(new URLRequest("Module.swf"), loaderContext);
```

For complete information on import loading, see the section "Import Loading" in Chapter 19.

For review and reference, Example 28-9 shows the code for the *Main* and *Module* classes discussed in this section. The code shown presumes that *module.swc* has already been created and added to *Module.swf*'s *external-library-path*.

Example 28-9. The Main and Module classes

```
// The Main class
package {
  import flash.display.*;
  import flash.net.*;
  import flash.events.*;
  import flash.system.*;

  public class Main extends Sprite {
    private var loader:Loader;

    public function Main( ) {
      loader = new Loader( );
      loader.contentLoaderInfo.addEventListener(Event.INIT,
                                                initListener);
      loader.load(new URLRequest("Module.swf"),
                new LoaderContext(false,
                                  ApplicationDomain.currentDomain));
    }

    private function initListener (e:Event):void {
      trace("init");
```

Example 28-9. The Main and Module classes (continued)

```
      Module(e.target.content).start();
    }
  }
}

// The Module class
package {
  import flash.display.Sprite;

  public class Module extends Sprite {
    public function Module() {
    }

    public function start ():void {
      trace("Module.start() was invoked...");
    }
  }
}
```

We've now learned several techniques for accessing the main class of a loaded asset without causing datatype errors. In the next section, we'll learn how to safely access assets created after the first frame in a loaded *.swf* file.

Accessing Assets in Multiframe .swf Files

In the earlier section "Accessing the Loaded Asset," we learned that when a *.swf* file loads another *.swf* file, all visual assets and programmatic objects on the loaded *.swf* file's first frame are available as soon as the Event.INIT event occurs. Hence, code in an Event.INIT event listener can immediately operate on those assets and objects. However, code within an Event.INIT event listener cannot operate on assets and objects created on subsequent frames in the loaded *.swf* file.

Any code wishing to access assets and objects created on or after the second frame of a loaded *.swf* file must first verify that those assets and objects exist. There are two ways to verify that assets and objects in a loaded *.swf* file exist:

- In the accessing *.swf* file, use a *Timer* object to poll for the existence of the asset or object.
- In the accessing *.swf* file, register for a custom event that is dispatched by the loaded *.swf* file when the asset or object becomes available.

Let's consider an example for each of the preceding techniques. We'll again use the scenario of *Main.swf* loading *Module.swf* from the previous section. Suppose *Module.swf* has a script on the second frame of its main timeline that creates a *TextField* object, t. *Main.swf* loads *Module.swf* and wishes to access t. Here's the timeline script in *Module.swf*:

```
    stop( );
    var t:TextField = new TextField( );
    t.text = "hello";
    addChild(t);
```

Example 28-10 shows how *Main.swf* loads *Module.swf* and then polls for the existence of the *TextField* before using it.

Example 28-10. Polling for the existence of a loaded object

```
package {
  import flash.display.*;
  import flash.events.*;
  import flash.net.*;
  import flash.utils.*;

  public class Main extends Sprite {
    private var loader:Loader;

    public function Main( ) {
      // Load Module.swf
      loader = new Loader( );
      loader.contentLoaderInfo.addEventListener(Event.INIT,
                                                initListener);
      loader.load(new URLRequest("Module.swf"));
    }

    private function initListener (e:Event):void {
      // The loaded .swf file has been initialized, so start polling for
      // the existence of the TextField.
      var timer:Timer = new Timer(100, 0);
      timer.addEventListener(TimerEvent.TIMER, timerListener);
      timer.start( );
    }

    private function timerListener (e:TimerEvent):void {
      // Check whether the loaded .swf file's TextField has been created
      if (loader.content.hasOwnProperty("t")) {
        // The TextField exists now, so we can safely access it
        trace(Object(loader.content).t.text);

        // Stop the timer
        e.target.stop( );
      }
    }
  }
}
```

Now suppose again that *Main.swf* loads *Module.swf* and wishes to access t. This time, however, *Module.swf*'s main class, *Module*, broadcasts a custom event—Module.ASSETS_READY—when t becomes available. *Main.swf* registers for

Module.ASSETS_READY and accesses t after the event occurs. Here's the code for the *Module* class, where the event constant is defined:

```
package {
  import flash.display.MovieClip;

  class Module extends MovieClip {
    // Define the event constant
    public static const ASSETS_READY:String = "ASSETS_READY";
  }
}
```

And here's the script on thte second frame of *Module.swf* 's main timeline, which dispatches the event indicating that t is available:

```
stop( );

var t:TextField = new TextField( );
t.text = "hello";
addChild(t);

dispatchEvent(new Event(Module.ASSETS_READY));
```

Finally, Example 28-11 shows the code for *Main.swf*'s main class. The example assumes that ActionScript has not been given compile-time access to the loaded *.swf* file's class definitions. As a result, the code refers to the Module.ASSETS_READY event by its string name, "ASSETS_READY":

```
loader.content.addEventListener("ASSETS_READY", assetsReadyListener);
```

Likewise, the code casts loader.content to the *Object* type so that type-checking is deferred until runtime:

```
Object(loader.content).t.text
```

For complete information on type-checking loaded assets, see the section "Compile-Time Type-Checking for Runtime-Loaded Assets."

Example 28-11. Handling an event announcing a loaded object's availability

```
package {
  import flash.display.*;
  import flash.events.*;
  import flash.net.*;
  import flash.utils.*;

  public class Main extends Sprite {
    private var loader:Loader;

    public function Main( ) {
      // Load Module.swf
      loader = new Loader( );
      loader.contentLoaderInfo.addEventListener(Event.INIT,
                                                initListener);
      loader.load(new URLRequest("Module.swf"));
    }
```

```
  private function initListener (e:Event):void {
    // The loaded .swf file has been initialized, so register for
    // the Module.ASSETS_READY event.
    loader.content.addEventListener("ASSETS_READY",
                                    assetsReadyListener);
  }

  private function assetsReadyListener (e:Event):void {
    // The TextField exists now, so we can safely access it
    trace(Object(loader.content).t.text);
  }
 }
}
```

So far, this chapter's coverage of loaded assets has been restricted to the automatically created asset object referenced by loader.content. Let's now explore how to manually create additional new instances of a loaded asset.

Instantiating a Runtime-Loaded Asset

The technique for creating a new instance of a runtime-loaded asset varies according to whether that asset is a *.swf* file or a bitmap. The following two sections describe the instantiation process for both types of assets.

Instantiating a Loaded .swf File

To create a new instance of a loaded *.swf* file, we must first obtain a reference to that *.swf* file's main class. Once the class reference is obtained, we use the *new* operator to create the instance. There are two general approaches for obtaining a reference to a loaded *.swf* file's main class:

- Retrieve a direct reference to the class using the *source-path*, *library-path*, or *external-library-path* techniques covered in the earlier section "Compile-Time Type-Checking for Runtime-Loaded Assets."
- Retrieve a reference to the class using the *ApplicationDomain* class's instance method *getDefinition()*.

Let's look at examples for both approaches by returning to the "*Main.swf* loads *Module.swf* " scenario from earlier sections.

Suppose we want to make a new instance of *Module.swf* in *Main.swf*. We first make the *Module* class directly available to *Main.swf* by following the *source-path* technique, the *library-path* technique, or the *external-library-path* technique covered earlier. Reviewing what we've already learned, recall that once the *Module* class is available to *Main.swf*, we can reference it directly, as shown in the cast operation excerpted from the Event.INIT event listener in Example 28-9:

```
private function initListener (e:Event):void {
  trace("init");
  Module(e.target.content).start();  // Direct reference to Module
}
```

In the same way, to make a new instance of *Module*, we simply use the *new* operator:

```
private function initListener (e:Event):void {
  var moduleObj:Module = new Module();
}
```

Now suppose that *Main.swf* does not have compile-time access to *Module*, but we still want to make a new instance of *Module.swf* in *Main.swf*. In such a situation, we must retrieve a reference to *Module* using the *ApplicationDomain* class's instance method *getDefinition()*. When passed a class name, *getDefinition()* method returns a reference to the specified class. The returned reference can be assigned to a variable of type *Class*, for use in subsequent instantiation expressions. The following code shows the general technique:

```
var SomeClass:Class = someApplicationDomain.getDefinition("SomeClassName");
var obj:Object = new SomeClass();
```

where *someApplicationDomain* is a reference to the *.swf* file's *ApplicationDomain* object, and *SomeClassName* is the fully qualified, string name of the class to retrieve. Therefore, in order to retrieve a reference to the *Module* class from within *Main.swf*, we need the following:

- A reference to *Module.swf*'s *ApplicationDomain* object
- The fully qualified name for the *Module* class

A *.swf* file's *ApplicationDomain* object can be accessed via its *LoaderInfo* object, which is accessed via the loaderInfo variable of any *DisplayObject* instance in the *.swf* file. The fully qualified class name for a *.swf* file's main class can be deduced with the help of *flash.utils.getQualifiedClassName()*. Once *Module.swf* has loaded, within *Main.swf*'s Event.INIT listener, we can use the following code to retrieve a reference to *Module.swf*'s main class:

```
var ModuleClassName:String = getQualifiedClassName(e.target.content);
var appDomain:ApplicationDomain =
                      e.target.content.loaderInfo.applicationDomain;
// After the following line of code runs, ModuleClass refers
// to Module.swf's main class
var ModuleClass:Class = appDomain.getDefinition(ModuleClassName);
```

Once we have a reference to the module class, we can use it to create *new* objects:

```
var newModule:Object = new ModuleClass();
```

As usual, be careful to let a loading *.swf* file initialize before attempting to access it; *getDefinition()* should be used only after the Flash runtime dispatches the `Event.INIT` event.

Note that the datatype of `newModule` in the preceding code is *Object*, not *Module*, because, in this example, *Main.swf* does not have direct access to *Module.swf*'s main class. Hence, any subsequent access of *Module*'s methods and variables through `newModule` is not type-checked until runtime. If compile-time type checking is required, use the *source-path*, *library-path*, or *external-library-path* techniques rather than *getDefinition()*.

Note that the techniques covered in this section apply not only to creating a new instance of a *.swf* file but also to creating an instance of any symbol in that *.swf* file. For example, suppose we wanted to create an instance of a symbol named *Ball*, from *Module.swf*. We would export *Ball* for ActionScript, then either of the following:

- Obtain a reference to the exported *Ball* class using the *ApplicationDomain* class's instance method *getDefinition()*

- Make the *Ball* class directly available to *Main.swf* by following either the *source-path* , *library-path* , or *external-library-path* technique.

Instantiating a Loaded Image

Unlike *.swf* file assets, a new copy of a loaded bitmap asset cannot be created with the *new* operator. Instead, to create a new copy of a loaded bitmap asset, we must clone the bitmap's pixel data and associate the cloned data with a new *Bitmap* object.

As we learned earlier, when an image file is loaded, the loaded pixel data is automatically placed in a *BitmapData* object. To clone a loaded bitmap's pixel data, we invoke *BitmapData.clone()* method on that *BitmapData* object. The following code demonstrates. It clones a loaded bitmap's data and passes the cloned data to the constructor of a new *Bitmap* object. That new *Bitmap* object is a copy of the loaded bitmap asset. The loaded asset is, as always, accessed only after the `Event.INIT` event has occurred.

```
private function initListener (e:Event):void {
  // e.target.content is the asset object representing the loaded bitmap
  var newImage:Bitmap = new Bitmap(e.target.content.bitmapData.clone());

  // newImage now has a copy of the loaded bitmap
}
```

Using Socket to Load Display Assets at Runtime

At the beginning of this chapter, we learned that ActionScript provides two different mechanisms for adding an external display asset to an application at runtime:

- The *flash.display.Loader* class
- The *flash.net.Socket* class, used in combination with the *Loader* class's instance method *loadBytes( )*

Now that we're comfortable with the *Loader* class, let's examine how it can be combined with the *Socket* class to retrieve display assets over a raw TCP/IP socket. The technique described in this section might be used when loading assets for a socket-based application such as a multiuser game, or simply to prevent the loaded asset from appearing in the end user's cache.

Here's the general process for retrieving display assets over a raw TCP/IP socket:

1. Connect to a server that can transfer a GIF, PNG, JPEG, or SWF file in binary format to the Flash runtime.

2. Retrieve the bytes for the desired asset.

3. Convert the loaded bytes to an asset object, suitable for on-screen display.

To accomplish the first two of the preceding steps, we use ActionScript's *flash.net.Socket* class. The *Socket* class communicates with a server in binary data format (in raw bytes). To accomplish the final step, we use the *Loader* class's instance method *loadBytes( )* method. The *loadBytes( )* method converts raw bytes to an ActionScript display object.

The following sections describe the preceding process in detail.

Server-Side: Sending the Asset

Using the *Socket* class, we can retrieve the bytes for a display asset from any server that knows how to send a GIF, PNG, JPEG, or SWF file in binary format. For example, the *Socket* class can be used to retrieve images from most mail servers, chat servers, and news servers—all of which typically support image-transfers in binary format.

Rather than studying how to load an asset from an existing type of server (e.g., mail, chat, or news), let's consider the more complete scenario, in which we create not only the Flash client that retrieves the asset but also the server that sends it. We'll call our custom-created server *FileSender*, and we'll write it in Java. FileSender's behavior is extremely simple: when a client connects, it automatically sends that client a single file, followed by the ASCII character 4 (End of Transmission), and then closes the connection. Notice that FileSender's behavior is fully automated: the client does not need to request the asset from the server, nor send any form of acknowledgment once the asset is received. This architecture allows us to concentrate solely on the asset-transfer process.

Example 28-12 shows the Java source code for FileSender, contributed to this book by Derek Clayton.

Example 28-12. The FileSender server

```java
import java.net.ServerSocket;
import java.net.Socket;
import java.io.IOException;
import java.io.InputStream;
import java.io.File;
import java.io.FileInputStream;
import java.io.BufferedOutputStream;

/**
 * FileSender is a simple server that takes a Socket connection
 * and transmits a file after which the connection is closed.
 *
 * Usage: java FileSender [port] [file]
 *
 * [port] = the port on which the server will listen (on all
 *          local ip addresses) for connections
 * [filename] = the path to the file that will be transmitted
 *
 */
public class FileSender implements Runnable {
    private int port;
    private File file;
    private String filename;
    private ServerSocket server;
    private Thread thisThread;
    private byte[] bytes;

    public FileSender(int p, String f) {
        port = p;
        filename = f;
    }

    public void start() {
        InputStream is = null;
        try {
            // --- read the file in to our byte array
            file = new File(filename);
            is = new FileInputStream(file);
            bytes = new byte[(int)file.length( )+1];
            int offset = 0;
            int byteRead = 0;
            while (offset < bytes.length
                    && (byteRead=is.read(bytes, offset, bytes.length-offset))
                        >= 0) {
                offset += byteRead;
            }
            bytes[bytes.length-1] = 4;
```

Example 28-12. The FileSender server (continued)

```
            // --- create the ServerSocket
            server = new ServerSocket(port);
        } catch (Exception e) {
            e.printStackTrace();
            System.exit(1);
        } finally {
            if (is != null) {
                try {
                    is.close();
                } catch (Exception e) {
                    e.printStackTrace();
                    System.exit(1);
                }
            }
        }

        // --- start the Thread which will accept connections
        thisThread = new Thread(this);
        thisThread.start();
    }

    public void run() {
        // --- while the server is active...
        while (thisThread != null) {
            BufferedOutputStream ps = null;
            Socket socket = null;
            try {
                // --- ...accept socket connections
                //     (blocks until a connection is made)
                socket = server.accept();

                // --- create the output stream
                ps = new BufferedOutputStream(socket.getOutputStream());

                // --- write the bytes and close the connection
                ps.write(bytes);
                ps.close();
                ps = null;
                socket.close();
                socket = null;
            } catch(Exception e) {
                thisThread = null;
                e.printStackTrace();
            } finally {
                if (ps != null) {
                    try {
                        ps.close();
                    } catch (IOException e) {
                        e.printStackTrace();
                        System.exit(1);
                    }
                }
            }
```

Example 28-12. The FileSender server (continued)

```
            if (socket != null) {
                try {
                    socket.close( );
                } catch (IOException e) {
                    e.printStackTrace( );
                    System.exit(1);
                }
            }
        }
    }

    // --- cleanup the server
    if (server != null) {
        try {
            server.close( );
        } catch (IOException e) {
            e.printStackTrace( );
            System.exit(1);
        }
    }
}

public final static void main(String [] args) {
    // --- check for the proper number of arguments
    if (args.length != 2) {
        System.out.println("usage: java FileSender [port] [file]");
        System.exit(1);
    }

    try {
        // --- set the arguments to their proper type
        int port = Integer.parseInt(args[0]);
        String filename = args[1];

        // --- create and start the FileSender
        //     (which will run in its own thread)
        FileSender fs = new FileSender(port, filename);
        fs.start( );
    } catch (Exception e) {
        e.printStackTrace( );
        System.exit(1);
    }
}
}
```

The source code for FileSender can be downloaded at: *http://moock.org/eas3/examples*.

To start FileSender, we issue Java the following command:

```
java FileSender port filename
```

where *port* is the port over which the server will accept connections, and *filename* is the name of the file FileSender will send to any connecting client. For example, to start the server on port 3000 and configure it to send a file named *photo.jpg*, we issue Java the following command:

```
java FileSender 3000 photo.jpg
```

For information on security limitations governing socket connections, see Chapter 19.

Client-Side: Receiving the Asset

We've just seen the code for a custom Java server that automatically sends a specified file to any client that connects. Now let's build a corresponding ActionScript client that connects to the server and receives a file.

Unlike many traditional programming languages, ActionScript's socket communication system is entirely event-based.

 In ActionScript, it is not possible to pause program execution while waiting for data to arrive over a socket. That is, ActionScript socket operations are *asynchronous*, not *synchronous*.

In ActionScript, data can be read from a socket only after that socket's ProgressEvent.SOCKET_DATA event has occurred. The ProgressEvent.SOCKET_DATA event indicates that some arbitrary amount of new data is available for the client to read. However, once the client has finished reading the new data, it must again wait for the next ProgressEvent.SOCKET_DATA event to occur before reading additional data from the socket. Here's the general process:

1. Client connects to socket.
2. Socket receives some data.
3. ProgressEvent.SOCKET_DATA event occurs.
4. Client reads all available data.
5. Socket receives more data.
6. ProgressEvent.SOCKET_DATA event occurs.
7. Client reads all available data.
8. Repeat Steps 5 through 7 until socket is closed.

The amount of data that arrives with each ProgressEvent.SOCKET_DATA event is completely arbitrary. Often, the data available to a client when the ProgressEvent.SOCKET_DATA event occurs constitutes only part of some larger whole. Therefore, special care must be taken to manually assemble all required data before processing it. For example, suppose an image is sent to a client over a socket. The client might receive the image data in, say, three segments—each of which triggers a ProgressEvent.SOCKET_DATA event. Client code wishing to process the image must reassemble the three segments before processing the image as a whole.

To reassemble small segments of data into a larger whole, a client must manually add each segment to a temporary byte array (i.e., a "byte buffer") while the larger whole loads. The "larger whole" might be a file, an object, a complete instruction, a mail message, a chat message, or any other logical data structure that must be processed as a single entity. Each time a new segment arrives, the client checks to see if the larger whole has fully loaded. If so, the client processes it. If not, the client waits for more data to arrive. Note, however, that there is no one official way to check whether some logical body of data has been received in its entirety. Each binary socket protocol will provide its own means of indicating the completeness of a given transmission. For example, a server might tell its client how many bytes to expect before it starts a subsequent transmission, or a client might inspect a loaded byte stream manually for beginning-of-file and end-of-file markers. In our example client, we'll process the loaded display asset when the socket connection is closed by the server. Closing the socket connection is the server's (very simple) way of telling our client that it has finished sending the asset's data.

Let's see how all this looks in code. Our simple ActionScript client consists of a single class, *DisplayAssetLoader*. Here are the steps *DisplayAssetLoader* follows to receive and display an asset sent by FileSender:

1. Create a *Socket* object.
2. Register the *DisplayAssetLoader* object for *Socket* object's events.
3. Use the *Socket* object to connect to the server.
4. When new binary data is received over the socket, place that data in a temporary buffer.
5. When the socket disconnects, use the *Loader* class's instance method *loadBytes()* to load the binary data from the temporary buffer into a *Loader* object.
6. Display the loaded asset object on screen.

Example 28-13 shows the complete code for the *DisplayAssetLoader* class. A discussion of *DisplayAssetLoader*'s key features follows the code listing; minor details are covered by inline code comments.

Example 28-13. The DisplayAssetLoader class

```
package {
  import flash.display.*;
  import flash.events.*;
  import flash.net.*;
  import flash.text.*;
  import flash.utils.*;
```

Example 28-13. The DisplayAssetLoader class (continued)

```
public class DisplayAssetLoader extends Sprite  {
  // A constant representing the ASCII character for "end of transmission"
  public static const EOT:int = 4;
  // An on-screen TextField in which to display status messages
  private var statusField:TextField;
  // The socket object over which communication will occur
  private var socket:Socket;
  // A byte buffer in which to place the asset's binary data as it loads
  private var buffer:ByteArray = new ByteArray();
  // The Loader object used to generate the asset from
  // the loaded binary data
  private var loader:Loader;

  // Class constructor
  public function DisplayAssetLoader () {
    // Create the status TextField
    statusField = new TextField();
    statusField.border      = true;
    statusField.background = true;
    statusField.width = statusField.height = 350;
    addChild(statusField);

    // Create the socket object
    socket = new Socket();

    // Register for socket events
    socket.addEventListener(Event.CONNECT, connectListener);
    socket.addEventListener(Event.CLOSE, closeListener);
    socket.addEventListener(ProgressEvent.SOCKET_DATA,
                            socketDataListener);
    socket.addEventListener(IOErrorEvent.IO_ERROR, ioErrorListener);

    // Tell the user we're about to try connecting to the socket
    out("Attempting connection...");

    // Attempt to connect to the socket
    try {
      socket.connect("localhost", 3000);
    } catch (e:Error) {
      out("Connection problem!\n");
      out(e.message);
    }
  }

  // Handles socket connection events
  private function connectListener (e:Event):void {
    out("Connected! Waiting for data...");
  }

  // Handles newly received data
  private function socketDataListener (e:ProgressEvent):void {
    out("New socket data arrived.");
```

Example 28-13. The DisplayAssetLoader class (continued)

```
      // When new bytes arrive, place them in a buffer for later processing
      socket.readBytes(buffer, buffer.length, socket.bytesAvailable);
    }

    // Handles socket disconnection events. When a disconnection occurs,
    // attempt to generate a display asset from the loaded bytes
    private function closeListener (e:Event):void {
      // First, check if we received the whole asset...
      // Retrieve the last byte in the buffer
      buffer.position = buffer.length - 1;
      var lastByte:int = buffer.readUnsignedByte( );
      // If an "end of transmission" byte was never received, the
      // asset's binary data didn't fully arrive, so don't
      // generate the asset
      if (lastByte != DisplayAssetLoader.EOT) {
        return;
      }

      // All clear, we can safely generate an asset from the bytes that
      // were loaded. The last byte in the buffer is not part of the asset,
      // so truncate it.
      buffer.length = buffer.length - 1;

      // Now, create the Loader object that will generate
      // the asset from the loaded bytes
      loader = new Loader( );

      // Generate an asset from the loaded bytes
      loader.loadBytes(buffer);

      // Wait for the asset to initialize
      loader.contentLoaderInfo.addEventListener(Event.INIT,
                                                assetInitListener);
    }

    // Puts the asset on screen when it's done initializing
    private function assetInitListener (e:Event):void {
      addChild(loader.content);
      out("Asset initialized.");
    }

    // Handles I/O errors
    private function ioErrorListener (e:IOErrorEvent):void {
      out("I/O Error: " + e.text);
    }

    // Print status messages to the screen and the debugging console
    private function out (msg:*):void {
      trace(msg);
      statusField.appendText(msg + "\n");
    }
  }
}
```

Let's look at three key sections of the *DisplayAssetLoader* class: the creation and connection of the socket, the placing of bytes in a buffer, and the creation of the display asset from the loaded bytes.

Creating and connecting to the socket

To establish and manage the socket connection, we use a *Socket* instance, which we assign to a private variable, socket:

```
socket = new Socket();
```

To connect to the socket, we use the *Socket* class's instance method *connect()*. However, because socket connections can potentially generate security and I/O errors, we wrap the call to *connect()* in a *try/catch* block:

```
try {
  socket.connect("localhost", 3000);
} catch (e:Error) {
  out("Connection problem!\n");
  out(e.message);
}
```

Placing bytes in a buffer

As we learned earlier, when new data is received over the socket, the Flash runtime dispatches the ProgressEvent.SOCKET_DATA event. The target of that event dispatch is the *Socket* object that received the data. Hence, to be notified when new data arrives, we register with socket for the ProgressEvent.SOCKET_DATA event, as follows:

```
socket.addEventListener(ProgressEvent.SOCKET_DATA, socketDataListener);
```

Whenever the ProgressEvent.SOCKET_DATA event occurs, the *DisplayAssetLoader* class's instance method *socketDataListener()* is invoked. Within *socketDataListener()*, the *Socket* class's instance variable bytesAvailable indicates the number of bytes in the socket currently available for reading. The *socketDataListener()* adds the newly received data to a *ByteArray* referenced by the variable buffer. To read the new data into buffer, we use the *Socket* class's instance method *readBytes()*, which takes the following general form:

```
theSocket.readBytes(bytes, offset, length)
```

where *theSocket* is the *Socket* object from which the bytes will be read, *bytes* is a *ByteArray* object into which the bytes will written, *offset* is the position within *bytes* at which writing will begin, and *length* is the number of bytes to read from the socket. In our case, we want to read all the bytes from the socket and write them into buffer, starting at the end of buffer. Hence, we use the following code:

```
socket.readBytes(buffer, buffer.length, socket.bytesAvailable);
```

Here's the full listing for the *socketDataListener()* method:

```
private function socketDataListener (e:ProgressEvent):void {
  out("New socket data arrived.");
  socket.readBytes(buffer, buffer.length, socket.bytesAvailable);
}
```

Creating a display asset from the loaded bytes

Once all of the bytes for an asset have arrived, we can use the *Loader* class's instance method *loadBytes()* to generate an ActionScript *DisplayObject* instance from those bytes. Recall that FileSender indicates that an asset's data has been sent in full by simply closing the socket connection. So, we place the code for generating our *DisplayObject* instance (the "asset object") in an Event.CLOSE event listener. To register for the Event.CLOSE event with socket, we use the following code:

```
socket.addEventListener(Event.CLOSE, closeListener);
```

In the *closeListener()* function, before generating the *DisplayObject* instance, we first check whether the server's End of Transmission byte (ASCII 4) was received. Recall that the server sends an End of Transmission byte as the last byte in the data stream. To retrieve that byte, we use the following code:

```
buffer.position = buffer.length - 1;
var lastByte:int = buffer.readUnsignedByte();
```

If the End of Transmission byte was never received, the asset's binary data didn't fully arrive, so the listener function exits:

```
if (lastByte != DisplayAssetLoader.EOT) {
  return;
}
```

If the End of Transmission byte *was* received, we generate the asset object using *loadBytes()*. However, before we pass the asset's bytes to the *loadBytes()* method, we must first truncate the End of Transmission byte from the buffer, as follows:

```
buffer.length = buffer.length - 1;
```

With the asset's bytes in hand, we can now generate the asset object:

```
loader = new Loader();
loader.loadBytes(buffer);
```

When the preceding code has finished executing, the process of generating the asset object has been set in motion, but the asset object is not yet accessible. As with the *Loader* class's instance method *load()*, attempting to access the asset object via loader.content immediately after invoking *loadBytes()* yields the value null. Therefore, we must wait for the Event.INIT to occur before accessing the asset object:

```
loader.contentLoaderInfo.addEventListener(Event.INIT,
                                 assetInitListener);
```

When the asset becomes available, we add it to the screen:

```
private function assetInitListener (e:Event):void {
  addChild(loader.content);
  out("Asset initialzed.");
}
```

Remember that when the Event.INIT event occurs, the assets and objects created by the .swf file's main class constructor or by code on the first frame of the .swf file's timeline are accessible, but assets and objects created on or after the second frame are not accessible. For further instructions on accessing visual assets and objects created on or after the second frame, see the earlier section, "Accessing Assets in Multiframe .swf Files."

Removing Runtime Loaded .swf Assets

To remove a runtime-loaded .swf asset from an application, we must first nullify all references the application has to the asset and then either nullify all references the application has to the Loader object that loaded the asset or invoke unload() on the Loader object that loaded the asset.

However, before we remove the asset from the application, we must disable the asset and its display children, if any, so that it does not continue to consume system and network resources once removed.

The typical tasks required to disable a loaded .swf asset are divided between the application that loaded the asset and the asset itself. The application that loaded the asset should perform the following tasks before removing the asset:

- If the asset is still loading, the application must stop the load operation. For example:
  ```
  try {
    theAssetLoader.close();
  } catch (e:*) {}
  ```
- As part of nullifying all references to the asset, the application must remove the asset from all parent DisplayObjectContainer instances. For example:
  ```
  container.removeChild(theAsset);
  ```

The asset, itself, should perform the following tasks before being removed:

- Tell any loaded .swf child assets to disable themselves.
- Stop any sounds from playing.
- Stop the main timeline, if it is currently playing.
- Stop any movie clips that are currently playing.
- Close any connected network objects, such as instances of Loader, URLLoader, Socket, XMLSocket, LocalConnection, NetConnections, and NetStream.

- Nullify all references to *Camera* or *Microphone.*
- Unregister all event listeners (particularly `Event.ENTER_FRAME`, and mouse and keyboard listeners).
- Stop any currently running intervals (via *clearInterval( )*).
- Stop any *Timer* objects (via the *Timer* class's instance method *stop( )*).

The asset should perform the preceding tasks in a custom disposal method invoked by the application before it removes the asset.

For more information on disabling objects before disposing of them, see the section"Deactivating Objects" in Chapter 14. See also Grant Skinner's online series of articles, "ActionScript 3.0: Resource Management," posted at: *http://www.gskinner.com/blog/archives/2006/06/as3_resource_ma.html.*

We've now learned all the techniques for adding an external asset to an application at runtime. Next let's consider how to add an external display asset to an application at compile-time.

Embedding Display Assets at CompileTime

To include an external display asset in an ActionScript application at compile-time, we use the [Embed] metadata tag. This tag adds a specified external asset to a *.swf* file, and makes that asset accessible to a program as a user-specified or autogenerated class. Instances of the embedded asset are created from that class using ActionScript's standard *new* syntax.

 The [Embed] metadata tag is supported by Flex Builder 2 and the command-line compiler, *mxmlc.* However, the [Embed] metadata is not supported by Adobe Flash CS3. Future versions of the Flash authoring tool might add support for [Embed].

To use [Embed], we must give the compiler access to the Flex compiler-support library, *flex.swc.* By default, all Flex Builder 2 projects automatically include *flex.swc* in the ActionScript library path, so in Flex Builder 2, the techniques covered in this section work without any special compiler configuration.

A Note on File Size and Memory Consumption

Unlike the runtime asset-loading techniques we've seen so far in this chapter, embedding a display asset at compile time using the [Embed] metadata tag increases the size of the *.swf* file loading the asset and also increases the Flash runtime's memory usage. Consequesntly, you should embed an asset at compile time only when you are certain that the application will definitely need to use that asset. Otherwise, you should load the asset at runtime if and when it is required. For example, imagine a product catalog application with images of thousands of products and one welcome-screen image. The welcome-screen image is shown every time the application starts, and, therefore, could sensibly be embedded using the [Embed] metadata tag. By contrast, each product's image is required only when the user views the product in question, and should, therefore, be loaded at runtime and discarded when the user is finished viewing the product.

Now that we know when to use [Embed] let's see how to actually use it. The next section examines the general code required to use [Embed]. Subsequent sections cover concrete examples for the general code discussed in the next section.

General [Embed] Syntax

The [Embed] metadata tag can be used either at the instance variable-definition level or at the class-definition level.

The following code shows the basic use of [Embed] at the variable-definition level:

```
[Embed(source="pathToFile")]
private var ClassName:Class;
```

When the preceding code is compiled, the ActionScript compiler automatically generates a new class representing the external asset located at *pathToFile* and assigns that class to the private variable named *ClassName*. The new class's superclass is one of the *mx.core* - classes for embedding assets. As we'll see over the upcoming sections, the specific shim class used varies according to the type of asset being embedded. The *pathToFile* must specify the asset file's location using one of the following:

- An absolute reference available locally to the compiler (e.g., *c:/assets/photo.jpg*)
- A relative reference, composed in relation to the ActionScript source file embedding the asset (e.g., *.../images/photo.jpg*)

Notice that, because the *ClassName* variable refers to a class, its datatype is *Class*. When a variable refers to a *Class* object, consider capitalizing the variable name (following the conventional style for class names).

Once the association between the embedded asset and the *ClassName* variable has been made, we use the following familiar code to make a new instance of the asset.

```
new ClassName();
```

Now let's turn to the general syntax for using the [Embed] metadata tag at the class-definition level. The following code shows the basic approach:

```
[Embed(source="pathToFile")]
public class ClassName extends AssetType {
}
```

When the preceding code runs, the external asset located at *pathToFile* is associated with the class *ClassName*. The *ClassName* class must be *public* and extend *AssetType*, which is one of the Flex *mx.core* shim classes for embedding assets. Later sections indicate which specific shim class should be used for the various types of assets that can be embedded at the class level.

To make a new instance of an asset embedded at the class level, we again use the following standard code:

```
new ClassName();
```

Supported Asset Types

When used at either the variable level or the class level, the [Embed] metadata tag supports the following display-asset types:

- Bitmaps in GIF, JPEG, or PNG format
- SVG files
- Symbols from legacy .swf files (i.e., Flash Player 8 and older)
- Any file as binary data

Additionally, at the variable-definition level only, [Embed] supports the embedding of entire .swf files of any version.

Note that individual symbols and classes in a Flash Player 9 (or higher) .swf file cannot be embedded using the [Embed] metadata tag. Instead, individual symbols and classes must be accessed through one of the following means:

- Embed the symbol or class's .swf file at the variable level (see the section "Embedding Entire .swf Files"), then use the *ApplicationDomain* class's instance method *getDefinition()* to access the symbol or class (see the section "Using getDefinition() to Access a Class in an Embedded .swf File").
- Embed the symbol or class's .swf file as raw binary data (see the section "Embedding Files as Binary Data"), then use the *ApplicationDomain* class's instance method *getDefinition()* to access the symbol or class (see the section "Using getDefinition() to Access a Class in an Embedded .swf File").
- Link to a .swc file containing the class or symbol (see the earlier section, "Give the Compiler Access to the Loaded Class").

 In addition to the display assets covered in this section, the [Embed] metadata tag can be used to embed sounds and fonts.

For information on embedding sounds, see Adobe's Flex 2 Developer's Guide, under Flex Programming Topics → Embedding Assets.

For information on embedding fonts, see the section "Fonts and Text Rendering" in Chapter 27. Also see Adobe's Flex 2 Developer's Guide, under Customizing the User

Interface → Using Fonts → Using embedded fonts → Embedded font syntax → Embedding Fonts in ActionScript.

Now that we've seen the basic code used for embedding an external asset at compile time, let's look at some specific examples.

Embedding Bitmap Images

The following code shows how to embed an image named *photo.jpg* at the variable level. The code assumes that both the class file embedding the image and the image file are in the same directory. When the code runs, ActionScript automatically generates a class representing the *photo.jpg* asset and assigns that class to the variable *Photo*, ready for run-time instantiation. The autogenerated class extends *mx.core.BitmapAsset*. Here's the code:

```
[Embed(source="photo.jpg")]
private var Photo:Class;
```

Next, the following code shows how to embed an image named *photo.jpg* at the class level. Again, the class file and the asset file are assumed to be in the same directory. Notice that, by necessity, the class extends *mx.core.BitmapAsset*.

```
package {
  import mx.core.BitmapAsset;

  [Embed(source="photo.jpg")]
  public class Photo extends BitmapAsset {
  }
}
```

To create a new instance of the embedded image, we use the following code (whether the image was embedded at the variable level or the class level):

```
new Photo()
```

When assigning an instance of the embedded image to a variable, we set that variable's datatype to either *mx.core.BitmapAsset* (for variable-level embeds) or *Photo* (for class-level embeds):

```
var photo:BitmapAsset = new Photo();  // Variable level
var photo:Photo = new Photo();        // Class level
```

Once an instance is created, it can be added to the display list like any other display object:

```
addChild(photo);
```

Note that the [Embed] metadata tag supports scale-9 formatting for embedded bitmap images. When scale-9 formatting is specified for an embedded bitmap image, the autogenerated class extends *mx.core.SpriteAsset*, not *mx.core.BitmapAsset*. For complete details on scale-9 formatting and embedded bitmaps, see Adobe's Flex 2 Developer's Guide, under Flex Programming Topics → Embedding Assets → Embedding asset types → Using scale-9 formatting with embedded images.

Embedding SVG

The following code shows how to embed an SVG graphic named *line.svg* at the variable level. The code assumes that both the class file embedding the SVG graphic and the SVG graphic file are in the same directory. When the code runs, ActionScript automatically generates a class representing the *line.svg* asset, and assigns that class to the variable *SVGLine*, ready for runtime instantiation. The autogenerated class extends *mx.core.SpriteAsset*. Here's the code:

```
[Embed(source="line.svg")]
private var SVGLine:Class;
```

Next, the following code shows how to embed an SVG graphic named *line.svg* at the class level. Again, the class file and the asset file are assumed to be in the same directory. Notice that, by necessity, the class extends *mx.core.SpriteAsset*.

```
package {
  import mx.core.SpriteAsset;

  [Embed(source="line.svg")]
  public class SVGLine extends SpriteAsset {
  }
}
```

To create a new instance of the embedded SVG graphic, we use the following code (whether the SVG graphic was embedded at the variable level or the class level):

```
new SVGLine( )
```

When assigning an instance of the embedded SVG graphic to a variable, we set that variable's datatype to *mx.core.SpriteAsset* (for variable-level embeds) or *SVGLine* (for class-level embeds):

```
var line:SpriteAsset = new SVGLine( );  // Variable level
var line: SVGLine = new SVGLine( );     // Class level
```

Once an instance is created, it can be added to the display list like any other display object:

```
addChild(line);
```

Embedding Entire .swf Files

The following code shows how to embed an entire *.swf* file named *App.swf* at the variable level. The code assumes that both the class file embedding the *.swf* file and the *.swf* file, itself, are in the same directory. When the code runs, ActionScript automatically generates a class representing the *App.swf* asset, and assigns that class to the variable App, ready for runtime instantiation. The autogenerated class extends *mx.core.MovieClipLoaderAsset*. Here's the code:

```
[Embed(source="App.swf")]
private var App:Class;
```

Entire *.swf* files can be embedded at the variable level only.

To create a new instance of the embedded *.swf*, we use the following code:

```
new App( )
```

When assigning an instance of the embedded *.swf* to a variable, we set that variable's datatype to *mx.core.MovieClipLoaderAsset*:

```
var app:MovieClipLoaderAsset = new App( );
```

Once an instance is created, it can be added to the display list like any other display object:

```
addChild(app);
```

Embedding Symbols from Legacy .swf Files

The following code shows how to embed an individual symbol named *Ball*, from a Flash Player 8 or older *.swf* file named *fp8app.swf*, at the variable level. The code assumes that both the class file embedding the symbol and the *.swf* file containing the symbol are in the same directory. When the code is compiled, the ActionScript compiler automatically generates a class representing the *Ball* symbol and assigns that class to the variable FP8Ball, ready for runtime instantiation. The autogenerated class extends the *mx.core* asset class matching the *Ball* symbol's type (i.e., one of *MovieClipAsset*, *TextFieldAsset*, *ButtonAsset*, or, for single-frame movie clips, *SpriteAsset*). Here's the code; note the use of the additional [Embed] parameter, symbol:

```
[Embed(source="fp8app.swf", symbol="Ball")]
private var FP8Ball:Class;
```

Next, the following code shows how to embed an individual symbol named *Ball*, from a Flash Player 8 or older *.swf* file named *fp8app.swf*, at the class level. Again, the class file and the asset file are assumed to be in the same directory. In this example, we'll assume that the *Ball* symbol is a movie clip, so the class, by necessity, extends *mx.core.MovieClipAsset*.

```
package {
  import mx.core.MovieClipAsset;

  [Embed(source="fp8app.swf", symbol="Ball")]
  public class FP8Ball extends MovieClipAsset {
  }
}
```

To create a new instance of the embedded symbol, we use the following code (whether the symbol was embedded at the variable level or the class level):

```
new FP8Ball( )
```

When assigning an instance of the embedded symbol to a variable, if the symbol was embedded at the variable level, we set that variable's datatype to the *mx.core* asset class matching the symbol type (i.e., one of *MovieClipAsset*, *TextFieldAsset*, or *ButtonAsset*). For example, our *Ball* symbol is a movie clip, so *FP8Ball* instances should be assigned to variables of type *MovieClipAsset*.

```
var fp8ball:MovieClipAsset = new FP8Ball();
```

If the symbol was embedded at the class level, we set that variable's datatype to the class embedding the symbol. For example:

```
var fp8ball:FP8Ball = new FP8Ball();
```

Once an instance is created, it can be added to the display list like any other display object:

```
addChild(fp8ball);
```

Embedding Files as Binary Data

The [Embed] metadata tag can be used to embed the binary data (bytes) from any file into an application as a byte array. The application can then operate on those bytes. For example, if the embedded binary data is in GIF, JPEG, PNG, or SWF format, the application can use the *Loader* class to convert the data to a display asset.

In the following code, we embed a Flash Player 9-format *.swf* file named *fp9app.swf* as binary data, at the variable level. The code assumes that both the class file embedding the binary data and the file containing that data are in the same directory. When the code runs, ActionScript automatically generates a class representing the binary data and assigns that class to the variable FP9BinaryData, ready for runtime instantiation. The autogenerated class extends *mx.core.ByteArrayAsset*. Here's the code; note the use of the additional [Embed] parameter, mimeType:

```
[Embed(source="fp9app.swf", mimeType="application/octet-stream")]
private var FP9BinaryData:Class;
```

In the following code, we embed a Flash Player 9-format *.swf* file named *fp9app.swf* as binary data, at the class level. Again, the class file and the asset file are assumed to be in the same directory. Notice that, by necessity, the class extends *mx.core.ByteArrayAsset*.

```
package {
  import mx.core.ByteArrayAsset;

  [Embed(source="fp9app.swf", mimeType="application/octet-stream")]
  public class FP9BinaryData extends ByteArrayAsset {
  }
}
```

To create a new instance of the embedded binary data, we use the following code (whether the data was embedded at the variable level or the class level):

```
new FP9BinaryData()
```

When assigning an instance of the embedded binary data to a variable, we set that variable's datatype to *mx.core.ByteArrayAsset* (for variable-level embeds) or to the class embedding the symbol (for class-level embeds):

```
var fp9binarydata:ByteArrayAsset = new FP9BinaryData( );  // Variable level
var fp9binarydata:FP9BinaryData = new FP9BinaryData( );   // Class level
```

Once an instance is created, if the embedded binary data is in GIF, JPEG, PNG, or SWF format, we can use the *Loader* class to generate a display asset as follows:

```
var loader:Loader = new Loader( );
loader.loadBytes(fp9binarydata);
addChild(loader);
```

After the asset initializes, it can be added to the display list using the technique discussed in the earlier section "Displaying the Loaded Asset On Screen."

We can use the technique of embedding an asset as binary data to embed XML files in an application at compile time. Example 28-14 demonstrates.

Example 28-14. Embedding XML at compile time

```
package {
  import flash.display.*;
  import flash.events.*;
  import flash.utils.ByteArray;

  public class EmbedXML extends Sprite {
    [Embed(source="embeds/data.xml", mimeType="application/octet-stream")]
    private var BinaryData:Class;

    public function EmbedXML ( ) {
      // Create a new instance of the embedded data
      var byteArray:ByteArray = new BinaryData( );

      // Convert the data instance to XML
      var data:XML = new XML(byteArray.readUTFBytes(byteArray.length));

      // Display the source code for the embedded XML
      trace(data.toXMLString( ));
    }
  }
}
```

Using getDefinition( ) to Access a Class in an Embedded .swf File

As we learned earlier, individual symbols and classes in a Flash Player 9 (or later) *.swf* file cannot be embedded using the [Embed] metadata tag. Instead, to access a class or a symbol's class in an embedded *.swf* file, we can link to a *.swc* file containing the desired class or symbol's class, or we can use the *ApplicationDomain* class's instance method *getDefinition()* to access the desired class or symbol's class at runtime.

When using *getDefinition()*, we must be sure the *.swf* file instance has initialized before we attempt to access its symbols or classes. To do so, we register with the embedded asset object's *LoaderInfo* object for Event.INIT events. Depending on how the *.swf* file was embedded, we access *LoaderInfo* in different ways. If the *.swf* file was embedded directly at the variable level, we use the following code to register for Event.INIT events:

```
// Instantiate the asset object
var embeddedInstance:MovieClipLoaderAsset = new ClassName();

// Register for Event.INIT
Loader(embeddedInstance.getChildAt(0)).contentLoaderInfo.addEventListener(
                                              Event.INIT,
                                              initListener);
```

In the preceding code, *ClassName* is the variable that refers to the class representing the embedded *.swf* file, *embeddedInstance* is an instance of *ClassName*, and *initListener* is a reference to the function that will execute when the instance is initialized.

On the other hand, if the *.swf* file was embedded as binary data, we use the following code to register for Event.INIT event notification:

```
// Instantiate the asset object
var binarydata:ByteArrayAsset = new BinaryData();

// Generate a display object representing the .swf file
var loader:Loader = new Loader();
loader.loadBytes(binarydata);
addChild(loader);

// Register for Event.INIT
loader.contentLoaderInfo.addEventListener(Event.INIT,
                                          initListener);
```

where *BinaryData* is the variable that refers to the class representing the embedded *.swf* file's binary data, *binarydata* is an instance of *BinaryData*, and *initListener* is, once again, a reference to the function that will execute when the *.swf* file instance is initialized.

The following code shows an example Event.INIT event listener that retrieves a reference to a movie-clip symbol's class named *Ball*. The code also creates an instance of the *Ball* symbol and adds it to the *initListener()*'s class's display hierarchy.

```
private function initListener (e:Event):void {
  // Obtain a reference to the Ball symbol from the embedded .swf file
  var BallSymbol:Class =
  e.target.content.loaderInfo.applicationDomain.getDefinition("Ball");

  // Make a new instance of the Ball symbol
  var ball:MovieClip = MovieClip(new BallSymbol());
```

```
      // Place the Ball instance on screen
      addChild(ball);
  }
```

An [Embed] Example

For reference, Example 28-15 shows a class that demonstrates the variable-level [Embed] scenarios discussed in the preceding sections.

Example 28-15. Variable-level embed demonstration class

```
package {
  import flash.display.*;
  import flash.events.*;
  import mx.core.MovieClipAsset;
  import mx.core.MovieClipLoaderAsset;
  import mx.core.SpriteAsset;
  import mx.core.BitmapAsset;
  import mx.core.ByteArrayAsset;

  public class VariableLevelEmbedDemo extends Sprite {
    [Embed(source="photo.jpg")]
    private var Photo:Class;

    [Embed(source="line.svg")]
    private var SVGLine:Class;

    [Embed(source="fp9app.swf")]
    private var FP9App:Class;

    [Embed(source="fp8app.swf", symbol="Ball")]
    private var FP8Ball:Class;

    [Embed(source="fp9app.swf", mimeType="application/octet-stream")]
    private var FP9BinaryData:Class;

    public function VariableLevelEmbedDemo () {
      // Variable-level bitmap
      var photo:BitmapAsset = new Photo();
      addChild(photo);

      // Variable-level SVG
      var line:SpriteAsset = new SVGLine();
      addChild(line);

      // Variable-level Flash Player 8-format SWF Symbol
      var fp8ball:MovieClipAsset = new FP8Ball();
      addChild(fp8ball);

      // Variable-level Flash Player 9-format SWF
      var fp9app:MovieClipLoaderAsset = new FP9App();
      addChild(fp9app);
```

Example 28-15. Variable-level embed demonstration class (continued)

```
    // To access a symbol's class or regular class in the embedded .swf,
    // wait for the embedded .swf file to initialize
    Loader(fp9app.getChildAt(0)).contentLoaderInfo.addEventListener(
                                           Event.INIT,
                                           fp9appInitListener);

    // Variable-level binary data (FP9 SWF)
    var fp9binarydata:ByteArrayAsset = new FP9BinaryData();
    var loader:Loader = new Loader();
    loader.loadBytes(fp9binarydata);
    addChild(loader);

    // To access a symbol's class or regular class in the embedded .swf,
    // wait for the embedded .swf file to initialize
    loader.contentLoaderInfo.addEventListener(Event.INIT,
                                       fp9binarydataInitListener);
  }

  private function fp9appInitListener (e:Event):void {
    // Obtain a reference to the Ball symbol from the embedded .swf file
    var BallSymbol:Class =
      e.target.content.loaderInfo.applicationDomain.getDefinition("Ball");
    // Make a new instance of the Ball symbol
    var ball:MovieClip = MovieClip(new BallSymbol());
    // Position the Ball instance and place it on screen
    ball.x = 220;
    ball.y = 240;
    addChild(ball);
  }

  private function fp9binarydataInitListener (e:Event):void {
    // Obtain a reference to the Ball symbol from the embedded .swf file
    var BallSymbol:Class =
      e.target.content.loaderInfo.applicationDomain.getDefinition("Ball");
    // Make a new instance of the Ball symbol
    var ball:MovieClip = MovieClip(new BallSymbol());
    // Position the Ball instance and place it on screen
    ball.y = 200;
    addChild(ball);
  }
 }
}
```

Clean the Project to See Changes

We've just seen a variety of ways to embed an external display asset in an application. Typically, when an embedded asset's file is changed, those changes are automatically reflected the next time the associated application is compiled. However, in Flex Builder 2, changes to assets are occasionally not reflected when recompiling an application. To guarantee that all asset changes are reflected at compile time, clean the application's project, as follows:

1. Select Project → Clean.
2. On the Clean dialogue, select the project you wish to clean.
3. Click OK.

On to Part III

We've covered a huge number of ActionScript essentials over the last 28 chapters, and our journey is almost over! In the last section of this book, we'll examine three applied ActionScript topics: programming in the Flash authoring tool, gaining access to the Flex framework with "just enough" MXML, and distributing a group of classes for use in a parent application.

Applied ActionScript Topics

Part III focuses on ActionScript code-production issues. Topics covered include combining ActionScript with assets created manually in the Flash authoring tool, using the Flex framework in Flex Builder 2, and creating a custom code library.

When you complete Part III, you will have learned the practical skills required to create ActionScript applications using the Flash authoring tool and Flex Builder 2. You will also have learned how to share code with other developers on your team or in the world at large.

ActionScript and the Flash Authoring Tool

In Chapter 1, we learned that the Flash authoring tool can be used to combine ActionScript code with graphics, animation, and multimedia assets. Now that we have a good understanding of the core ActionScript language, let's explore the important links between ActionScript and content created in the Flash authoring tool.

 For the benefit of programmers coming from other languages and environments, some of the concepts discussed in this chapter are presented from the perspective of a newcomer to the Flash authoring tool. Some of the upcoming material will, hence, be review for experienced Flash users.

You can download the example files discussed in this chapter at *http://www.moock. org/eas3/examples*.

The Flash Document

In this book, we've created plenty of *.swf* files using "pure code" (i.e., one or more ActionScript classes). In the Flash authoring tool, by contrast, *.swf* files are created using a visual interface for producing graphics, animation, and interactive multimedia content.

To create a *.swf* file with the Flash authoring tool, we must first create a *Flash document*, or *.fla* file. A *.fla* file describes the arrangement of a body of multimedia content over time. To create a *.fla* file suitable for use with ActionScript 3.0, follow these steps:

1. In the Flash authoring tool, select File → New.
2. On the New Document dialog, on the General tab, for Type, select Flash File (ActionScript 3.0).
3. Click OK.

From a *.fla* file, we can compile (or *export*) a corresponding *.swf* file for playback in a Flash runtime.

To export to a *.swf* file for testing in the Flash authoring tool, we use Control → Test Movie. To export a *.swf* file for distribution over the Web, we use File → Publish. A *.swf* file exported from the Flash authoring tool can also be distributed as a desktop application; for information, see the product documentation for Adobe AIR.

Timelines and Frames

Structurally, a *.fla* file is a hierarchy of one or more animations, each with its own *timeline*. A timeline is a linear sequence of *frames*, akin to a physical filmstrip. Each frame can contain audio, video, text, vector graphics, bitmap graphics, and programmatic content.

When a *.swf* file is exported from a *.fla* file, the Flash compiler converts the *.fla* file's timelines to Flash file format (SWF), suitable for playback in a Flash client runtime. When the *.swf* file plays, the frames from the *.fla* file's timelines are displayed in rapid succession, producing the illusion of animation. The speed at which the Flash runtime displays frames is governed by the *frame rate*, which is measured in number of frames per second. (For more information on the frame rate, see Chapter 23).

While some *.fla* files contain a single timeline, most contain multiple timelines, allowing content to be created in discrete parts and combined to form a larger animation. For example, a scene depicting a car driving down a mountainous road might include three timelines—one for the mountains passing slowly, one for the road passing quickly, and one for the car's wheels spinning.

The first timeline created in a new *.fla* file is known as the *main timeline*. The main timeline forms the foundation of all content subsequently added to the *.fla* file.

To produce each frame of content in a timeline, we can either import external assets or create new graphics using Flash's built-in design tools (e.g., Pencil, Brush, and Text). The graphics of each frame are placed on a visual workspace known as the *Stage*.

 Don't confuse the Flash authoring tool's Stage with ActionScript's *Stage* class: the Flash authoring tool's Stage is a design workspace, while ActionScript's *Stage* class represents the root object in the Flash runtime display list.

Figure 29-1 shows a simple *.fla* file, *hello.fla*, opened in the Flash authoring tool. The top half of the figure shows the *.fla* file's main timeline, which in this case contains two frames. The bottom half of the figure shows the Stage, which displays the content of the selected frame. In this case, the selected frame is the main timeline's first frame, as indicated by the thin vertical line running through the frame in the timeline. That thin line indicates the selected frame and is known as the *playhead*.

Figure 29-1. The hello.fla file, showing Frame 1 of the main timeline

Figure 29-2 shows *hello.fla* again, this time with Frame 2 of the main timeline selected. Notice that the position of the playhead, which indicates the selected frame, has moved to the right. Accordingly, the Stage now shows the content of Frame 2.

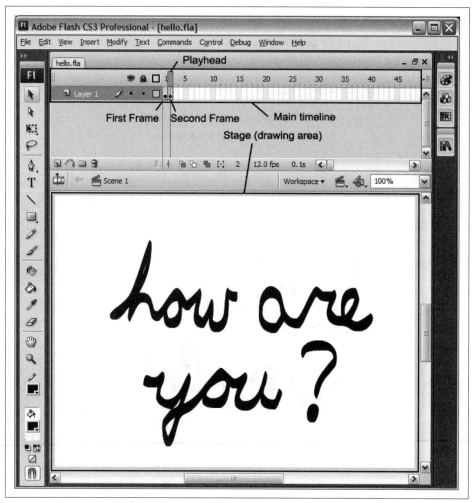

Figure 29-2. The hello.fla file, showing Frame 2 of the main timeline

Keyframes and Regular Frames

The Flash authoring tool defines two types of frames: *keyframes* and *regular frames*. Though Flash animation is not the focus of this book, an understanding of the difference between keyframes and frames is required when creating frame scripts, covered in the next section.

A *keyframe* is a frame whose on-Stage content differs from the preceding frame. To add a new keyframe to a timeline, we select Insert → Timeline → Keyframe.

A *regular frame*, by contrast, is a frame that's on-Stage content is automatically carried over (repeated) from the preceding closest keyframe. To add a new regular frame to a timeline, we select Insert → Timeline → Frame.

By adding regular frames to a timeline, we allow time to pass without changing the image shown on screen. By adding keyframes to a timeline, we can change the content of the screen (typically in order to produce the effect of animation).

For example, suppose we're making an animation of a man running to a house, waiting motionless at the front door for a short time, and then running away. While the man runs to the house, each frame of the animation has different content, so each frame must be a keyframe. While the man waits at the front door, each frame of the animation has the same content (because the man is not moving), so each frame can be a regular frame. While the man runs away from the house, each frame of the animation again has different content, so each frame must be a keyframe.

Figure 29-3 shows the frames of our running-man animation, greatly reduced to fit in this book. Frames 1, 2, 3, 8, and 9 are keyframes, each with their own content. Frames 4 though 7 are regular frames, with content carried forward from Frame 3. In the figure, the content of Frames 4 through 7 is shown in gray, indicating that it is carried forward from Frame 3. The figure indicates keyframes with the letter K and regular frames with the letter R.

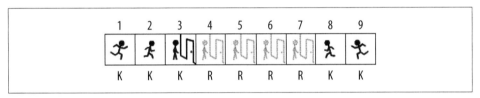

Figure 29-3. Keyframes versus regular frames

Figure 29-4 shows the timeline for our animation as it would appear in the Flash authoring tool, with Frame 1 selected. Notice that keyframes with content are indicated with a filled circle icon. Keyframes without content, known as *blank keyframes*, are indicated with a hollow circle (our animation does not include any blank keyframes). Regular frames have no circle icon at all. The last regular frame before a keyframe has a rectangle icon.

For easy reference in the coming sections, we'll assume that our running-man animation is saved in a file named *runningman.fla*.

Now, let's explore timeline scripting.

Figure 29-4. The running man timeline

Timeline Scripting

In order to execute code at a designated point in a timeline, we use a *frame script*. A frame script is a block of ActionScript code attached to a keyframe in a *.fla* file's timeline.

To add a frame script to a keyframe in a timeline, follow these general steps:

1. Click the desired keyframe in the timeline (select it).
2. Choose Window → Actions to open the Actions panel.
3. Enter the desired code into the Actions panel.

Any code entered into the Actions panel while a keyframe is selected will become part of that keyframe's frame script and will be executed just before that keyframe is rendered in the Flash runtime.

Frame scripts are typically used to control the content present on the frame in which they occur. We'll learn more about controlling content using frame scripts later in this chapter, in the section "Accessing Manually Created Symbol Instances."

Frame scripts cannot contain the *class*, *package*, or *interface* statements, or the *public*, *internal*, *private*, *dynamic*, or *static* attributes, but are free to include any other ActionScript code.

Programming using frame scripts is sometimes referred to as *timeline scripting*. Timeline scripting is the oldest form of ActionScript programming, and indeed was the *only* form of ActionScript programming up to the release of ActionScript 2.0 and Flash Player 7. Arguably, some of the Flash community's most innovative content has been born out of the marriage of timeline content and frame scripts.

As an example frame script, let's add some code to the last frame of the running-man animation. Our example frame script will open the URL *http://moock.org* in a new web browser window. Here's the code:

```
import flash.net.*;
var request:URLRequest = new URLRequest("http://moock.org");
navigateToURL(request, "_blank");
```

Figure 29-5 shows our frame script as it appears in the Actions panel in the Flash authoring tool. Notice that keyframes with frame scripts are indicated with a small "a" icon (for ActionScript) in the timeline.

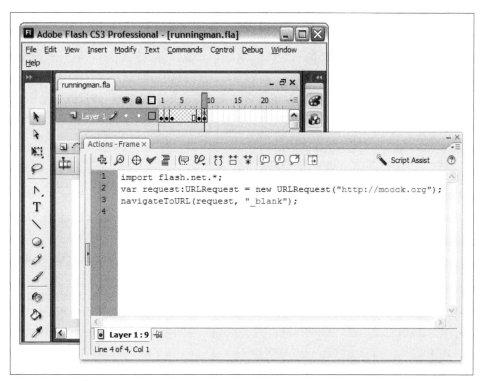

Figure 29-5. A frame script

As it stands, our frame script has a problem. By default, the Flash runtime loops animations (i.e., plays them repeatedly). Hence, our frame script will execute every time the running-man animation loops, causing multiple browser windows to open. To fix our frame script, we must use the *MovieClip* class's instance method *stop()* method to stop the animation from looping, as shown in the following code. We'll take a closer look at the *MovieClip* class's playback-control methods in the later section "Programmatic Timeline Control."

```
import flash.net.*;
var request:URLRequest = new URLRequest("http://moock.org");
navigateToURL(request, "_blank");
stop();
```

In the preceding code, the *stop()* method is invoked on the ActionScript object that represents the main timeline. The next section describes precisely how the main timeline is represented as an object in ActionScript.

Note that frame scripts can refer to any custom class (or other definition) that is accessible via the document classpath (which is set for each *.fla*) or global classpath (which applies to all *.fla* files). To set the document classpath, use File → Publish Settings → Flash → ActionScript Version: Version 3.0 → Settings → Classpath. To set the global classpath, use Edit → Preferences → ActionScript → Language → ActionScript 3.0 Settings → Classpath.

The Document Class

From an ActionScript perspective, a *.fla* file's main timeline is considered an instance of the *document class*, which is specified via File → Publish Settings → Flash → Action-Script Version → Settings → Document class.

The specified document class must inherit from *flash.display.MovieClip* if:

- The main timeline contains any frame scripts.
- The document class wishes to control the main timeline programmatically using *MovieClip* methods.
- The main timeline's Stage contains any components with customized parameters and either of the following is true:
  - The customized parameters are not identical on all frames of the timeline. For example, a Button's label is "OK" on Frame 1 and "Submit" on Frame 2.
  - The component does not appear on all frames of the timeline. For example, a List with a custom data provider appears on Frame 1 but not on Frame 2.
- The main timeline's Stage contains any components with customized accessibility properties or Strings Panel content.

Otherwise, the document class need only inherit from *flash.display.Sprite*.

When specifying the document class for a *.fla* file, include the fully qualified class name only; do not include the file extension (*.as*).

When a document class is specified, but the specified class is not found, the Flash compiler automatically generates a document class by the specified name. The automatically generated class extends *MovieClip*.

If a *.fla* file does not specify a document class, then its document class is assigned automatically. If the following conditions are all met, the automatically assigned document class is *flash.display.MovieClip*:

- The main timeline's Stage contains no named instances (see the section "Accessing Manually Created Symbol Instances").
- The main timeline contains no frame scripts.
- The main timeline's Stage contains no components with customized parameters that vary across frames.
- The main timeline's Stage contains no components with customized accessibility properties or Strings Panel content.

Otherwise, the automatically assigned document class is an automatically generated *MovieClip* subclass.

Each of the main timeline's frame scripts can be thought of as roughly analogous to an instance method of the document class. Code in a frame script of the main timeline executes in its own scope, with the same set of access rules applied to instance methods of the document class. That is, a frame script of the main timeline can access any definition (variable, method, class, interface, or namespace) that would be accessible within any of the document class's instance methods. Likewise, a frame script of the main timeline can use the keyword this to refer to the current object (i.e., the document class instance).

As an example, let's create a document class, *RunningMan*, for the *runningman.fla* file from the preceding section. Because *runningman.fla*'s main timeline includes a frame script, the *RunningMan* class must inherit from *MovieClip*. In *RunningMan*, we'll define a simple method for opening a URL in a web browser. Here's the code:

```
package {
  import flash.display.MovieClip;
  import flash.net.*;

  public class RunningMan extends MovieClip {
    public function goToSite (url:String):void {
      var request:URLRequest = new URLRequest(url);
      navigateToURL(request, "_blank");
    }
  }
}
```

To associate the *RunningMan* class with the running-man animation, we save its source file in the same directory as *runningman.fla*, and then follow these steps:

1. Select File → Publish Settings → Flash → ActionScript Version: Version 3.0 → Settings.
2. For Document class, enter **RunningMan**. (Notice **RunningMan**, not **RunningMan.as**.)
3. On the ActionScript 3.0 Settings dialog, click OK.
4. On the Publish Settings dialog, click OK.

Now that the document class for *runningman.fla* has been set to *RunningMan*, we can update the frame script on Frame 9, from the preceding section. The frame script's previous code was as follows:

```
import flash.net.*;
var request:URLRequest = new URLRequest("http://moock.org");
navigateToURL(request, "_blank");
stop();
```

The following code shows the new frame script for Frame 9. Notice that it refers directly to the *RunningMan* class's instance method *goToSite()*.

```
goToSite("http://moock.org");
stop();
```

In the preceding code, *stop()* refers to the *MovieClip* class's instance method *stop()*, which is inherited by the *RunningMan* class. As a descendant of the *MovieClip* class, the *RunningMan* class also has access to all nonprivate methods and variables defined by *EventDispatcher*, *DisplayObject*, *InteractiveObject*, *DisplayObjectContainer*, and *Sprite*. For example, the following code uses the *DisplayObjectContainer* class's instance method *addChild()* to add a new text field to the main timeline's display hierarchy:

```
// Code in runningman.fla, frame 9 frame script
import flash.text.*;

// Add a new text field to the main timeline's display hierarchy
var msg:TextField = new TextField();
msg.text = "I guess no one was home...";
msg.autoSize = TextFieldAutoSize.LEFT;
msg.border     = true;
msg.background = true;
msg.selectable = false;
addChild(msg);

stop();
```

In response to the preceding code, the *TextField* object referenced by msg is added to the main timeline's display hierarchy. When we export *runningman.swf* from *runningman.fla*, and then load *runningman.swf* into the Flash runtime, the text "I guess no one was home..." appears on screen when the playhead reaches Frame 9. The text appears on screen because the document class instance of the first *.swf* file loaded by the Flash runtime is automatically added to the display list. For plenty of details, see Chapter 20.

Note that the preceding text field-creation code could have alternatively (and more appropriately) been added to a *RunningMan* instance method. Either approach is technically valid, but as a best practice, you should try to store code in external class files rather than on frame scripts.

Variable and Function Definitions in Frame Scripts

A variable definition in a frame script on a *.fla* file's main timeline creates an instance variable in that *.fla* file's document class. Likewise, a function definition in a frame script on a *.fla* file's main timeline creates an instance method in that *.fla* file's document class.

Similarly, a variable definition in a frame script on a Movie Clip symbol's timeline creates an instance variable in the symbol's linked class. And a function definition in a frame script on a Movie Clip symbol's timeline creates an instance method in the symbol's linked class. (We'll learn about Movie Clip symbols and linked classes in the next two sections.)

However, take heed that an instance variable created in a frame script is not initialized until that frame script executes (i.e., the playhead reaches the frame containing the frame script). For example, consider the following code, showing two frame scripts:

```
// Frame script on frame 1
trace(n);  // Displays: 0

// Frame script on frame 2
var n:int = 10;
trace(n);  // Displays: 10
```

When the first of the preceding two frame scripts runs, the instance variable n has been defined, but it has not yet been initialized (the = 10 part of the code hasn't run yet). As a result, the code trace(n) causes 0 (the default value for variables of type *int*) to appear in the Output panel. When the second script runs, the instance variable n *has* been initialized (set to 10), so the code trace(n) causes 10 to appear in the Output panel.

By contrast, after a frame script has been executed, any instance variables it defines can be used for the remainder of the program's execution. For example, suppose we add a third frame script to the hypothetical timeline from the preceding code:

```
// Frame script on frame 3
trace(n);  // Displays: 10
gotoAndStop(1);
```

When the third script runs, the instance variable n still has the value 10, so the code trace(n) causes 10 to appear in the Output panel. Then, the code gotoAndStop(1) causes the playhead to move to Frame 1, so Frame 1's frame script executes for a second time. This time, the instance variable n still has the value 10, so the code trace(n) causes 10 (not 0) to appear in the Output panel.

An instance method created in a frame script can be used even before the playhead reaches the frame containing the instance method definition.

Symbols and Instances

In the earlier section "Timelines and Frames," we learned that a *.fla* file is a hierarchy of one or more animations, each with its own *timeline*. Now that we've seen how to create the main animation in a Flash document, let's explore nested animations. In order to create nested animations, we must understand *symbols*.

In the Flash authoring tool, a *symbol* is a user-defined reusable animation, button, or graphic. Symbols are created off-Stage in a special symbol-editing mode. Each *.fla* file stores its associated symbols in an asset repository known as the *Library*. From a single symbol, an arbitrary number of copies, or *instances*, can be created. For example, to create a sky full of animated twinkling stars, we could create a single star symbol and then add multiple instances of it to the Stage. Figure 29-6 shows what the star symbol and its instances might look like in a *.fla* file. Notice that each star instance is positioned, scaled, and rotated independently.

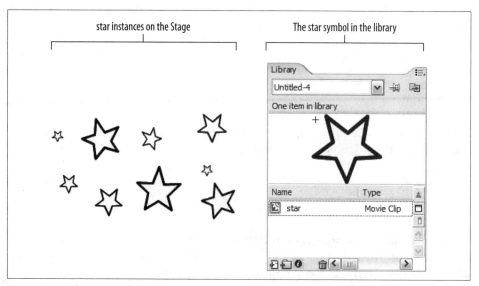

Figure 29-6. The star symbol and star instances

By default, when a *.swf* file is compiled from a *.fla* file, only those symbols whose instances are actually used in the document (i.e., appear on Stage) or are exported for ActionScript (see the section "Instantiating Flash Authoring Symbols via ActionScript") are included in the *.swf* file. Furthermore, each symbol's content is included just once, and then duplicated at runtime as necessary for each instance. Consequently, using symbols and instances (rather than raw graphics) can greatly reduce a *.swf*'s file size.

Types of Symbols

The Flash authoring tool defines three basic types of symbols:

- *Movie Clip* (for animations with programmatic content)
- *Graphic* (for nonprogrammatic animations that can be previewed directly in the Flash authoring tool)
- *Button* (for simple interactivity)

Graphic symbols cannot be accessed with ActionScript, and Button symbols offer primitive interactivity that can also be achieved with the Movie Clip symbol or the *Button* component. Therefore, in this chapter, we'll ignore Graphic and Button symbols, and focus exclusively on Movie Clip symbols.

Movie Clip Symbols

A Movie Clip symbol is a self-contained, reusable animation. Each Movie Clip symbol includes its own timeline and Stage, exactly like the main timeline. Furthermore, instances of Movie Clip symbols can be nested inside each other to produce hierarchically structured graphics or animations. For example, a Movie Clip symbol depicting a cartoon face might contain instances of a separate Movie Clip symbol depicting animated, blinking eyes.

Figure 29-7 shows a Movie Clip symbol being created in the Flash authoring tool. The Stage shows the contents of frame 2 of the Movie Clip's timeline. Note that the timeline in the figure is not the *.fla* file's main timeline, but the separate, independent timeline of the star Movie Clip symbol.

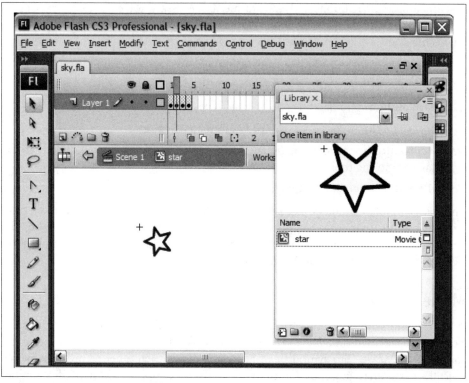

Figure 29-7. Editing a Movie Clip symbol

Linked Classes for Movie Clip Symbols

From an ActionScript perspective, each Movie Clip symbol instance in a *.fla* file is represented at runtime by an instance of the *Sprite* class or one of its subclasses. The class used to represent instances of a specific Movie Clip symbol is known as that symbol's *linked class*. A symbol's linked class can be specified manually or generated automatically.

To set the linked class for a Movie Clip symbol, we use the Linkage Properties dialog. Note that if any of the following are true, the specified linked class must inherit from *flash.display.MovieClip*:

- The symbol's timeline contains any frame scripts.
- The linked class wishes to control instances of the symbol programmatically, using *MovieClip* methods.

- The symbol's Stage contains any components with customized parameters and either of the following is true:
  - The customized parameters are not identical on all frames of the timeline. For example, a Button's label is "OK" on Frame 1 and "Submit" on Frame 2.
  - The component does not appear on all frames of the timeline. For example, a List with a custom data provider appears on Frame 1 but not on Frame 2.
- The symbol's Stage contains any components with customized accessibility properties or Strings Panel content.

Otherwise, the specified linked class need only inherit from *flash.display.Sprite*.

Here are the steps for specifying the linked class for a for a Movie Clip symbol:

1. Select the symbol in the *.fla* file's Library.
2. Select the pop-up Options menu in the top-right corner of the Library panel, and choose the Linkage option.
3. In the Linkage Properties dialog box, for Linkage, select Export for Action-Script. Note that selecting Export for ActionScript forces the symbol to be included in the compiled *.swf* file, even if no instance of that symbol is used in the document.
4. In the Linkage Properties dialog box, for Class, enter the fully qualified class name (i.e., the class name combined with the class's package, if the class resides in a package). The class being linked must be available in either the global classpath or the classpath of the *.fla* file containing the symbol. When specifying a linked class name in the Linkage Properties dialog, always leave the *Base class* field at its default value, except when linking more than one symbol to a single superclass, as discussed in the section "Linking Multiple Symbols to a Single Superclass."
5. Click OK.

In Step 4 of the preceding procedure, if the specified class is not found, the Flash compiler generates a linked class by the specified name automatically. The automatically generated class extends the specified base class.

If no linked class is specified for a given symbol, then the compiler assigns one automatically. If the following conditions are all met, then the automatically assigned linked class is *MovieClip*:

- The symbol's Stage does not contain any named instances.
- The symbol's timeline has no frame scripts.
- The symbol's Stage contains no components with customized parameters that vary across frames.
- The symbol's Stage contains no components with customized accessibility properties or Strings Panel content.

Otherwise, the automatically assigned linked class is an automatically generated *MovieClip* subclass.

Once a symbol is linked to a class, manually created instances of that symbol adopt the programmatic behaviors defined by the linked class. Conversely, programmatically created instances of the class adopt the audiovisual content of the linked symbol. Thus the symbol and the class are coupled together: the symbol defines the graphical content, while the class defines the programmatic behavior.

As an example, let's link our star Movie Clip symbol from the preceding section to a *MovieClip* subclass, *Star*. The *Star* class will randomly change the transparency (alpha value) of each star instance every 100 ms. Here's the code:

```
package {
  import flash.display.MovieClip;
  import flash.utils.Timer;
  import flash.events.TimerEvent;

  public class Star extends MovieClip {
    private var timer:Timer;

    public function Star () {
      timer = new Timer(100, 0);
      timer.addEventListener(TimerEvent.TIMER, timerListener);
      timer.start();
    }

    private function timerListener (e:TimerEvent):void {
      randomFade();
    }

    private function randomFade ():void {
      // Set alpha to a random floating-point value from 0 up to (but
      // not including) 1. The instance variable alpha is inherited from
      // the DisplayObject class (which is ancestor of MovieClip).
      alpha = Math.random();
    }

    // Provide a means of stopping the timer. As discussed in section
    // "Deactivating Objects" in Chapter 14,
    // external code should use this method before removing a star instance
    // from the program.
    public function dispose ():void {
      timer.stop();
    }
  }
}
```

To link the *Star* class to the star Movie Clip symbol, follow these steps:

1. Save the file containing the star symbol as *sky.fla*.

2. Save the *Star* class in a text file named *Star.as*, in the same folder as *sky.fla*.

---

3. Select the star symbol in *sky.fla*'s Library.

4. Select the pop-up Options menu in the top-right corner of the Library panel, and choose the Linkage option.

5. In the Linkage Properties dialog, for Linkage, select Export for ActionScript.

6. In the Linkage Properties dialog, for Class, enter **Star**.

7. Click OK.

Figure 29-8 shows the Linkage Properties dialog as it appears after Step 6 in the preceding procedure.

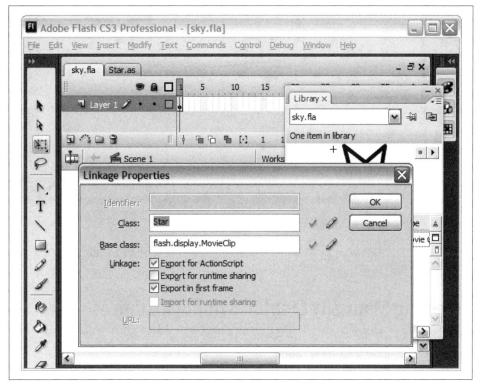

Figure 29-8. Linking the Star symbol to the Star class

To create instances of the star symbol in the Flash authoring tool, we drag the symbol name from the Library to the Stage of the main timeline (or to any other symbol's Stage, but in this case, there are no other symbols in the document). Figure 29-9 ilustrates the procedure; it shows five star-symbol instances being dragged to the Stage of the first frame of *sky.fla*'s main timeline.

Once the star symbol instances are on the main timeline, we can export *sky.swf* from *sky.fla*, and watch the each star's twinkling motion (defined by the star symbol) and fading effect (defined by the *Star* class).

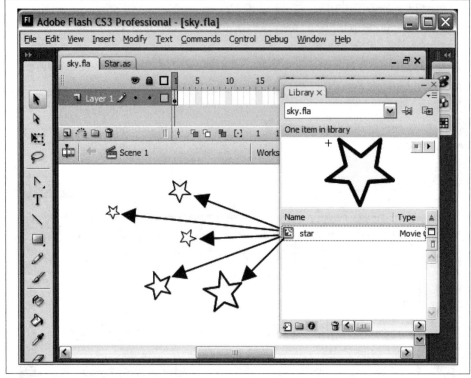

Figure 29-9. Creating instances of the star symbol

Now that we know how to manually create instances of Movie Clip symbols, let's examine how to access and control them.

Accessing Manually Created Symbol Instances

At runtime, every instance of any symbol placed on any timeline in a *.fla* file automatically becomes a display child of the ActionScript object representing that timeline.

For example, in the preceding section, we added five star-symbol instances to the main timeline of *sky.fla*. As a result, at runtime, those five instances become display object children of *sky.fla*'s document-class instance. To prove it, let's create a document class for *sky.fla*, and use *getChildAt()* to list the children of the main timeline. Here's the code:

```
package {
  import flash.display.MovieClip;

  public class Sky extends MovieClip {
    public function Sky () {
      for (var i:int=0; i < numChildren; i++) {
        trace("Found child: " + getChildAt(i));
```

```
      }
    }
  }
}
```

With the preceding document class in place, when *sky.swf* is exported and played in the Flash authoring tool's Test Movie mode, the following output appears in the Output panel:

```
Found child: [object Star]
Found child: [object Star]
Found child: [object Star]
Found child: [object Star]
Found child: [object Star]
```

 Code in a *.swf* file's document class constructor method can access all manually placed child assets on the *.swf* file's first frame but not on the second or subsequent frames (because assets on a subsequent frame are not added as display children until the playhead reaches that frame).

From an ActionScript perspective, the five star-symbol instances on the main time-line are instances of the *Star* class, which inherits from *MovieClip*. As such, we can control the stars using the variables and methods of the *DisplayObject* class (or any other ancestor of *MovieClip*). For example, the following code uses the *DisplayObject* class's instance variable x to align the stars along x-coordinate 100:

```
for (var i:int=0; i < numChildren; i++) {
  getChildAt(i).x = 100;
}
```

The *getChildAt()* method shown in the preceding code, however, has a limitation. Because the depths of individual symbol instances are not readily apparent in the Flash authoring tool, *getChildAt()* cannot easily be used to selectively manipulate a particular symbol instance. To make an individual instance easy to identify and manipulate through code, we assign it an instance name.

Instance Names

An *instance name* is a simple string name assigned to a symbol instance. To give a manually created symbol instance an instance name, we use the Properties panel. For example, to assign instance names to the star symbol instances from in the preceding section, we follow these steps:

1. Open the Properties panel (Window → Properties).

2. Select a star instance on Stage.

3. For <Instance Name>, enter **star1**.

4. Repeat Steps 2-3 to assign the remaining sky the instance names **star2** through **star5**.

Figure 29-10 shows the Properties panel (bottom of figure) as it appears during Step 3 of the preceding procedure.

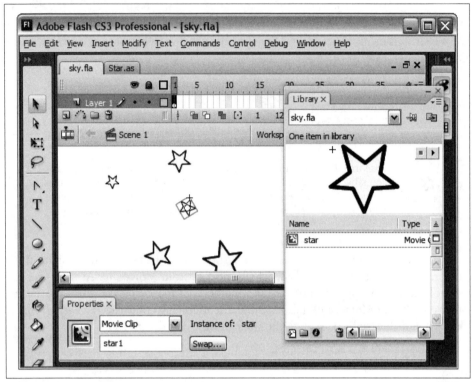

Figure 29-10. Naming a star symbol instance

A manually created symbol instance with an instance name can be accessed in Action-Script via the *DisplayObjectContainer* class's instance method *getChildByName()*. For example, the following code uses *getChildByName()* to move "star3" (the star whose instance name is "star3") to coordinate (0, 0):

```
package {
  import flash.display.MovieClip;

  public class Sky extends MovieClip {
    public function Sky () {
      getChildByName("star3").x = 0;
      getChildByName("star3").y = 0;
    }
  }
}
```

An instance's instance name can be accessed at runtime via the *DisplayObject* class's instance variable name. For example, the following code displays the names of all instances on the first frame of *sky.fla*'s main timeline:

```
for (var i:int=0; i < numChildren; i++) {
  trace(getChildAt(i).name);
}
```

The instance name of an object can also be changed at runtime by assigning a new value to that object's name variable, as in:

```
someDisplayObject.name = "someName";
```

However, changing instance names at runtime typically makes code hard to follow, so you should avoid it in your programs.

Matching Variables for Instance Names

The *getChildByName()* method from the preceding section successfully provides a way to access a particular symbol instance, but it's not particularly convenient. To make manually created symbol instances easier to access through ActionScript, the Flash compiler provides two automated services. First, when the compiler encounters a named instance on a timeline, it automatically assigns that instance to an instance variable of the same name in the timeline's document class or linked class. Second, in certain cases, if the matching instance variable does not already exist in the timeline's document class or linked class, the compiler automatically creates it. Let's consider these two automated services with an example.

Returning to the *sky.fla* example from the preceding section, recall that *sky.fla*'s document class is *Sky*, and that *sky.fla*'s main timeline contains five star-symbol instances, named "star1" through "star5." When the Flash compiler compiles *sky.swf*, it automatically adds code to the *Sky* class that assigns those five star instances to five instance variables, named star1 through star5. The result is the equivalent of adding the following code to the beginning of the *Sky* class constructor:

```
package {
  import flash.display.MovieClip;

  public class Sky extends MovieClip {
    public function Sky () {
      star1 = getChildByName("star1");
      star2 = getChildByName("star2");
      star3 = getChildByName("star3");
      star4 = getChildByName("star4");
      star5 = getChildByName("star5");
    }
  }
}
```

Of course, in this case, the *Sky* class does not actually define the variables `star1` through `star5`. Hence, the preceding automated variable assignment has the potential to cause an error. Whether an error actually occurs depends on a compiler option called "Automatically declare stage instances," which is set on a per-*.fla* basis under File → Publish Settings → Flash → ActionScript Version → Settings → Stage. When "Automatically declare stage instances" is enabled (the default), the compiler not only assigns Stage instances to matching variables, but also automatically declares those variables. For example, if we enable "Automatically declare stage instances" for *sky.fla*, then the compiler automatically declares the instance variables `star1` through `star5` in the *Sky* class. The result is the equivalent of adding the following code to the *Sky* class (notice that the automatically declared variables are *public*):

```
package {
  import flash.display.MovieClip;

  public class Sky extends MovieClip {
    public var star1:Star;
    public var star2:Star;
    public var star3:Star;
    public var star4:Star;
    public var star5:Star;

    public function Sky () {
      star1 = getChildByName("star1");
      star2 = getChildByName("star2");
      star3 = getChildByName("star3");
      star4 = getChildByName("star4");
      star5 = getChildByName("star5");
    }
  }
}
```

As a result of the preceding automatically inserted code, within the *Sky* class, we can refer to the star instances from *sky.fla*'s main timeline directly by instance name. For example, the following code moves "star3" (the star whose instance name is "star3") to coordinate (0, 0):

```
package {
  import flash.display.MovieClip;

  public class Sky extends MovieClip {
    public function Sky () {
      star3.x = 0;
      star3.y = 0;
    }
  }
}
```

Likewise, in any frame script on *sky.fla*'s main timeline, we can also refer to the star instances directly by instance name. For example, when placed in *sky.fla*'s first frame script, the following code rotates "star5" by 30 degrees:

```
star5.rotation = 30;
```

Nifty, eh?

However, in light of the preceding automated behavior, when "Automatically declare stage instances" is enabled, the programmer must take heed not to define instance variables whose names collide with symbol instance names. For example, the following code defines an instance variable, `star1`, whose name collides with a symbol instance from *sky.fla*'s main timeline:

```
package {
  import flash.display.MovieClip;

  public class Sky extends MovieClip {
    public var star1:Star;

    public function Sky () {
    }
  }
}
```

As a result of the instance variable definition in the preceding code, the compiler generates the following error:

```
A conflict exists with definition star1 in namespace internal.
```

By contrast, when "Automatically declare stage instances" is disabled, the compiler does not declare matching variables for Stage instances. For example, if we disable "Automatically declare stage instances" for *sky.fla*, then the compiler does not declare the instance variables `star1` through `star5` in the *Sky* class. However, it still assigns those variables references to the five star-symbol instances on the main timeline. As a result, we must supply the matching variable declarations in the *Star* class, as shown in the following code. Notice that the variables are, by necessity, declared *public*.

```
package {
  import flash.display.MovieClip;

  public class Sky extends MovieClip {
    public var star1:Star;
    public var star2:Star;
    public var star3:Star;
    public var star4:Star;
    public var star5:Star;

    public function Sky () {
    }
  }
}
```

Omitting the variable declarations from the preceding code has two possible results, depending on whether the class is declared with the *dynamic* attribute (see the section "Dynamic Instance Variables" in Chapter 15). If the class is not declared with the *dynamic* attribute (as is the case with the *Sky* class), then the following runtime error occurs because the compiler's automatically added assignment statements refer to nonexistent variables:

```
ReferenceError: Error #1056: Cannot create property star5 on Sky.
```

If, on the other hand, the class *is* declared with the *dynamic* attribute, then the automatically added assignment statements simply add new dynamic instance variables (named star1 through star5) to each instance of the class at runtime.

 Despite the fact that "Automatically declare stage instances" is enabled by default, many programmers prefer to disable it. As we just learned, when "Automatically declare stage instances" is disabled, nondynamic classes linked to timelines must declare variables matching all named Stage instances. Such explicit declarations make the variables more obvious in the class that uses them and prevent compiler errors when editing the class in other development environments (such as Flex Builder 2).

Note that automatically generated document classes and automatically generated linked classes are always compiled with "Automatically declare stage instances" enabled. Consequently, the named Stage instances of any timeline associated with an automatically generated document class or an automatically generated linked class can always be accessed via matching instance variables.

Accessing Manually Created Text

In the preceding sections, we learned three tools for accessing manually created symbol instances through ActionScript:

- The *getChildAt( )* method
- The *getChildByName( )* method
- Automatically assigned instance variables

The same three tools can also be used to access manually created text. In the Flash authoring tool, text fields are created with the Text Tool. Manually created text fields of type Dynamic Text or Input Text are represented at runtime by instances of the *flash.text.TextField* class. Like symbol instances, Dynamic and Input text fields become display children of the object representing the timeline that contains them. Also like symbol instances, Dynamic and Input text fields can be assigned an instance name that corresponds to an automatically assigned instance variable.

For example, the following steps describe how to move a manually created Dynamic text field to coordinate (200, 300) using ActionScript:

1. In the Flash authoring tool, create a new *.fla* file name *message.fla*.
2. In the Tools panel, select the Text Tool.
3. Click the Stage of the first frame of *message.fla*'s main timeline.
4. In the text field that appears, enter the text **hello**.
5. On the Properties panel (Window → Properties), change Static Text to Dynamic Text.
6. Still on the Properties panel, for <Instance Name>, enter **msg**.
7. Click the first frame of *message.fla*'s main timeline (select it).
8. Open the Actions panel (Window → Actions).
9. Enter the following code into the Actions panel:

```
msg.x = 200;
msg.y = 300;
```

Programmatic Timeline Control

Now that we know how to access manually created Movie Clip symbol instances, let's take a quick look at the tools for controlling the playback of those instances. The following list describes the most important timeline-control methods and variables of the *MovieClip* class. For more information on the *MovieClip* class, see Adobe's ActionScript Language Reference.

play( )
> Initiates the sequential display of the frames the movie clip's timeline. Frames are displayed at a speed dictated by the frame rate, which can be assigned via the Flash runtime *Stage* instance's frameRate variable.

stop( )
> Halts the playback of a movie clip. But note that even while a movie clip is stopped, the Flash runtime continues to play sounds, react to user actions, and process events, including Event.ENTER_FRAME events. Similarly, visual changes performed in event handlers or via *setInterval( )* or a *Timer* event are rendered even when the playhead is stopped. The *stop( )* method merely prevents the movie clip's playhead from advancing in the timeline.

gotoAndPlay( )
> Sends the playhead of the movie clip's timeline to the specified frame number or label and then plays the timeline from that point. The state of other movie clips is not affected. To cause other movie clips to play, invoke *play( )* or *gotoAndPlay( )* separately on each movie clip.

gotoAndStop()

Sends the playhead of the movie clip's timeline to the specified frame number or label and then halts the playback of the movie clip.

nextFrame()

Moves the playhead of the movie clip's timeline ahead one frame and stops it there.

prevFrame()

Moves the playhead of the movie clip's timeline back one frame and stops it there.

`currentFrame`

Yields the frame number at which the playhead of the movie clip currently resides. Note that the first frame is 1, not 0; therefore, `currentFrame` ranges from 1 to `totalFrames`.

`currentLabel`

Yields a string representing the label of the current frame, as specified in the Flash authoring tool.

`currentLabels`

Yields an array containing all the labels of the current timeline.

`totalFrames`

Yields the number of frames in the movie clip timeline.

Let's apply some of the preceding methods and variables to our *sky.fla* document. All the following examples could be placed either in a method of the *Sky* class, or on *sky.fla*'s main timeline.

The following code displays frame 4 of "star1:"

```
star1.gotoAndStop(4);
```

The following code stops the playback of the timeline of "star3:"

```
star3.stop();
```

The following code advances the playhead of "star5" by two frames:

```
star5.gotoAndStop(star5.currentFrame + 2);
```

The following code stops the playback of the timeline of all star instances on the main timeline:

```
for (var i:int=0; i < numChildren; i++) {
  getChildAt(i).stop();
}
```

Instantiating Flash Authoring Symbols via ActionScript

In the earlier section "Linked Classes for Movie Clip Symbols," we learned that instances of a symbol can be created manually in the Flash authoring tool by dragging the symbol's name from the Library to the Stage of a timeline. Instances of symbols that are exported for ActionScript can also be created directly through code, using the standard *new* operator.

For example, earlier, we linked the star symbol to the *Star* class. To create an instance of the star symbol through code, we use the following expression:

```
new Star( )
```

To add an instance of the star symbol to the main timeline of *sky.swf* at runtime, we would use the following code in either a frame script on the main timeline, or a method in the *Sky* class:

```
var star:Star = new Star( );
addChild(star);
```

The following code creates 50 star instances, and positions them randomly on screen:

```
var sky:Array = new Array( );
for (var i:int = 0; i < 50; i++) {
  sky.push(new Star( ));
  sky[i].x = Math.floor(Math.random( )*550);
  sky[i].y = Math.floor(Math.random( )*400);
  addChild(sky[i]);
}
```

Note that ActionScript code can be used to create instances of any symbol that is exported for ActionScript, whether or not the symbol has a custom-defined linked class. That is, the class specified on the Linkage Properties dialog need not be a custom class (as *Star* is). As we learned earlier, when the class specified on the Linkage Properties dialog is not found in the classpath, ActionScript automatically generates it. The automatically generated class can be used to create instances of the symbol through code.

For example, suppose we have a Movie Clip symbol named box_symbol, and we want to create instances of it with ActionScript. Here are the steps we follow:

1. Select box_symbol in the Library.
2. Select the pop-up Options menu in the top-right corner of the Library panel, and choose the Linkage option.
3. In the Linkage Properties dialog, for Linkage, select Export for ActionScript.
4. In the Linkage Properties dialog, for Class, enter **Box**.
5. Click OK.
6. By default, the preceding steps will prompt the Flash authoring tool to display a warning dialog stating "A definition for this class could not be found in the classpath, so one will be automatically generated in the SWF file on export." Click OK to dismiss the warning.

Once the preceding steps are complete, to create a box_symbol instance, we use the expression new Box( ) on any timeline or in any class of the *.swf* file that contains box_symbol.

Instance Names for Programmatically Created Display Objects

As it happens, like manually created instances, display objects created programmatically can *also* be assigned an instance name via the name variable. For example, the following code creates a *TextField* instance, gives it the instance name "price," adds it to a container, and then retrieves a reference to it by name.

```
var t:TextField = new TextField( );
t.text = "$99.99";
t.name = "price"
var detailsPage:Sprite = new Sprite( );
detailsPage.addChild(t);
trace(detailsPage.getChildByName("price"));  // Displays: [object TextField]
```

The preceding code may appear convenient because it offers a way to access an object on the display list according to some programmer-determined label, rather than by object reference or depth position. However, using instance names in this way is prone to error because ActionScript does not require instance names to be unique and does not throw an exception for attempts to access nonexistent instance names. Hence, use of instance names with programmatically created display objects should be avoided.

 Instance names should typically be used only when referring to text field instances or instances of Library symbols created manually in the Flash authoring tool.

Programmatically created display objects should always be accessed by reference. For example, the following code shows two versions of *displayPrice( )*, a hypothetical method that displays the price of a product. Both of the following versions of the method display the price in a *TextField*. In the first version (recommended), the *TextField* that will contain the price is passed as an object reference to the method. In the second version (discouraged), the *DisplayObjectContainer* containing the *TextField* is passed to the method, and the method retrieves a reference to the *TextField* by instance name.

```
// Recommended
public function displayPrice (priceField:TextField, price:Number):void {
  priceField.text = "$" + price;
}

// Discouraged
```

```
public function displayPrice (orderForm:Sprite, price:Number):void {
  TextField(orderForm.getChildByName("price")).text = "$" + price;
}
```

Wherever practical, display objects should be made available by reference to dependent parts of a program.

In MXML, a display object's instance name can be set via the id attribute, and named display objects can also be accessed by *getChildByName()*. However, as with pure ActionScript applications, references are preferred over instance names.

Linking Multiple Symbols to a Single Superclass

In the earlier section "Linked Classes for Movie Clip Symbols," we learned how to link a class to a Movie Clip symbol. Now let's consider how to give many different Movie Clip symbols the same programmatic behavior by linking those symbols to a single superclass.

As an example, we'll create a simple login form with two different graphical interface styles. Such a form might be required in an application that offers its users a choice of interface designs, or *skins*. Our forms will look different, but their behavior will be the same.

We'll start by creating a *.fla* file, *LoginApp.fla*, in the Flash authoring tool. In *LoginApp.fla*, we'll create two symbols, one for each graphical style of the login form. We'll name the first symbol LoginForm_Style1, and the second symbol LoginForm_Style2. In each login form symbol, we'll add two manually created input text fields (named username and password) and a submit button (named submitBtn). The submit button is, itself, a hand-drawn instance of a Movie Clip symbol. Figure 29-11 shows the two login form symbols.

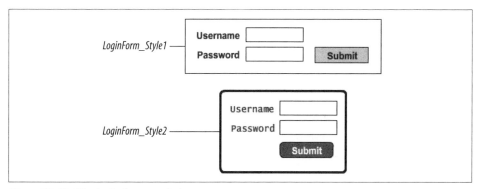

Figure 29-11. The login form symbols

Next, we'll create a *LoginForm* class that controls the behavior of the login form symbols. The *LoginForm* class responds to submit button clicks and transmits login information to a server. In this example, we'll set the compiler option "Automatically declare stage instances" to disabled. Accordingly, within the *LoginForm* class, we'll declare the manually created assets from the login form symbols as instance variables. The instance variable names—username, password, and submitBtn—match the instance names of the instances in the login form symbols.

Here's the code for the *LoginForm* class:

```
package {
  import flash.display.*;
  import flash.text.*;
  import flash.events.*;

  public class LoginForm extends MovieClip {
    public var username:TextField;
    public var password:TextField;
    public var submitBtn:SimpleButton;

    public function LoginForm () {
      submitBtn.addEventListener(MouseEvent.CLICK, submitListener);
    }

    private function submitListener (e:MouseEvent):void {
      submit(username.text, password.text);
    }

    public function submit (name:String, pass:String):void {
      trace("Now submitting user: " + name + " with password: " + pass);

      // Now transmit login information to server (code not shown).
      // Typically, the flash.net.URLLoader class is used to send
      // data to a server.
    }
  }
}
```

Finally, we associate the behavior of the *LoginForm* class with the login form symbols. However, because a single class cannot be linked to more than one symbol, we cannot link the *LoginForm* class directly to the login form symbols. Instead, we must link each login form symbol to a *subclass* of the *LoginForm* class. The following steps describe the process:

1. Select the LoginForm_Style1 symbol in *LoginApp.fla*'s Library.
2. Select the pop-up Options menu in the top-right corner of the Library panel, and choose the Linkage option.
3. In the Linkage Properties dialog box, for Linkage, select Export for ActionScript.
4. In the Linkage Properties dialog box, for Base class, enter **LoginForm**.
5. In the Linkage Properties dialog box, for Class, enter **LoginForm_Style1**.
6. Click OK.

7. By default, the preceding steps will prompt the Flash authoring tool to display a warning dialog stating "A definition for this class could not be found in the classpath, so one will be automatically generated in the SWF file on export." Click OK on this warning dialog.

8. Select the LoginForm_Style2 symbol in *LoginApp.fla*'s Library, then repeat Steps 2–6, substituting **LoginForm_Style2** for **LoginForm_Style1** in Step 6.

In response to the preceding steps, at compile time, the Flash compiler will automatically generate two classes—*LoginForm_Style1* and *LoginForm_Style2*, both of which extend *LoginForm*. The compiler will then link the LoginForm_Style1 symbol to the *LoginForm_Style1* class, and the LoginForm_Style2 symbol to the *LoginForm_Style2* class. Both symbols, thus, inherit the behavior of the *LoginForm* class.

The Composition-Based Alternative to Linked Classes

In this chapter, we've learned to add behavior to Movie Clip symbols by linking them to custom classes. As an alternative practice, to give programmatic behavior to a symbol we can simply create an instance of any custom class on the symbol's timeline and then use that instance to control the symbol.

For example, in the preceding section, we associated the login form symbols with the *LoginForm* class in order to give the symbols the programmatic ability to submit information to a server. But arguably, the *LoginForm* class is not a subtype of *MovieClip*. It is, rather, a simple communication utility that happens to take input from a user interface. As such, it can be (and perhaps should be) defined as a stand-alone class for use by any symbol that agrees to provide the appropriate inputs.

For the sake of comparison, the following code shows a new version of the *LoginForm* class, revised for use as a helper class on a symbol's timeline. The new class has a new name, *LoginManager*, reflecting its new role as a communication utility class. Notice that the new class constructor expects references to user interface objects that will supply user input.

```
package {
  import flash.display.*;
  import flash.text.*;
  import flash.events.*;

  public class LoginManager {
    private var username:TextField;
    private var password:TextField;

    public function LoginManager (username:TextField,
                                  password:TextField,
                                  submitBtn:SimpleButton) {
      this.username = username;
      this.password = password;
      submitBtn.addEventListener(MouseEvent.CLICK, submitListener);
    }
```

```
    private function submitListener (e:MouseEvent):void {
      submit(username.text, password.text);
    }

    public function submit (name:String, pass:String):void {
      trace("Now submitting user: " + name + " with password: " + pass);

      // Now transmit login information to server (code not shown).
      // Typically, the flash.net.URLLoader class is used to send
      // data to a server.
    }
  }
}
```

To use the *LoginManager* class, each of the login form symbols from the preceding section would define a frame script with the following code (presumably on frame 1, but in the case of an animated form, perhaps later in the timeline). In the following code, username, password, and submitBtn are the instance names of the text fields and button in the login form symbol:

```
var loginManager:LoginManager = new LoginManager(username,
                                                 password,
                                                 submitBtn);
```

The difference between the *LoginManager* approach and the *LoginForm* approach from the preceding section is effectively the difference between composition and inheritance, as discussed in the section "Inheritance Versus Composition" in Chapter 6. The potential benefits of the composition-based approach are:

- The *LoginManager* class is free to inherit from any class it chooses, unlike *LoginForm* which must inherit from *MovieClip*.
- The designer of the login form symbol can change the instance names of the form's text fields and submit button without affecting the functionality of the *LoginManager* class.

Let's now move to our final Flash authoring tool topic, preloading classes.

Preloading Classes

By default, when the Flash authoring tool compiles a *.swf* file, it exports all classes in the *.swf* file's first frame. As a result, all classes used in the *.swf* file must finish loading before the *.swf* file's first frame is displayed. Depending on the total size of the classes included in the *.swf* file, this loading process can result in a noticeable delay before the *.swf* file begins to play.

To avoid the class-loading delay, we can export a *.swf* file's classes *after* Frame 1 in the main timeline, and then provide a simple timeline script that displays progress information during the class-loading process.

As an example, let's change our *sky.fla* file so that the classes it uses aren't loaded until Frame 15. Note, however, that a *.swf* file's document class—and every class the document class references, whether directly or indirectly—always loads in Frame 1. Hence, to prevent the *Star* class from loading before Frame 1, we must first remove the instance names from all manually created *Star* instances and we will delete the definitions for the variables star1 through star5 from the *Sky* class code. To remove instance names, we select each *Star* instance on Stage and delete its name from the Properties panel.

The following procedures describe how to load *sky.fla*'s classes at Frame 15 and display a loading message while the classes load.

First, follow these steps to instruct Flash to export *sky.fla*'s classes at Frame 15:

1. Open *sky.fla* in the Flash authoring tool.
2. Choose File → Publish Settings.
3. In the Publish Settings dialog box, on the Flash tab, next to ActionScript Version: Version 3.0, click Settings.
4. In the ActionScript Settings dialog, for Export Classes in Frame, enter **15**.
5. Click OK to confirm the ActionScript Settings.
6. Click OK to confirm the Publish Settings.

Next, we add a very basic timeline preloader to *sky.fla* so that a "Loading" message appears while the classes load.

 The following procedures expect a prior knowledge of timeline layers and frame labels, but even if you are not familiar with those aspects of the Flash authoring tool, you should be able to complete the procedures as described.

First, on the main timeline of *sky.fla*, we double-click Layer 1's name and change it to **sky**. Next, we make the timeline 15 frames long, as follows:

1. On the main timeline, click Frame 1 of the *sky* layer to select it.
2. Click and hold the keyframe at Frame 1, then drag it to Frame 15 of the timeline.

As a result of extending the timeline as described in the preceding steps, the star symbol instances that previously appeared on frame 1 will now appear on Frame 15 (where the *Star* class is loaded).

Next, we'll add a new layer for code, and call it *scripts*:

1. Choose Insert → Timeline → Layer.
2. Double-click the new layer's name, and change it to **scripts**.

Then, we'll add a *labels* layer with two frame labels, loading and main. The labels designate the application's loading state and startup point, respectively.

1. Choose Insert → Timeline → Layer.

2. Double-click the new layer's name and change it to **labels**.

3. At Frames 4 and 15 of the *labels* layer, add a new keyframe (using Insert → Timeline → Keyframe).

4. With Frame 4 of the *labels* layer selected, in the Properties panel, under Frame, change <Frame Label> to **loading**.

5. With Frame 15 of the *labels* layer selected, in the Properties panel, under Frame, change <Frame Label> to **main**.

Now we'll add the preloader script to the *scripts* layer:

1. At Frame 5 of the *scripts* layer, add a new keyframe (using Insert → Timeline → Keyframe).

2. With Frame 5 of the *scripts* layer selected, enter the following code in the Actions panel:

```
if (framesLoaded == totalFrames) {
  gotoAndStop("main");
} else {
  gotoAndPlay("loading");
}
```

Finally, we'll add a loading message that displays while *star.fla*'s classes load:

1. With Frame 1 of the *scripts* layer selected, enter the following code into the Actions panel:

```
import flash.text.*;

var loadMsg:TextField = new TextField();
loadMsg.text = "Loading...Please wait.";
loadMsg.autoSize = TextFieldAutoSize.LEFT;
loadMsg.border     = true;
loadMsg.background = true;
loadMsg.selectable = false;
addChild(loadMsg);
```

2. At Frame 15 of the *scripts* layer, add a new keyframe (using Insert → Timeline → Keyframe).

3. With Frame 15 of the *scripts* layer selected, enter the following code in the Actions panel:

```
removeChild(loadMsg);
```

That's it! You can test *sky.swf* using Control → Test Movie. Once in Test Movie mode, you can watch a simulated download of the *.swf* by enabling the Bandwidth Profiler (View → Bandwidth Profiler) and then choosing View → Simulate Download. Because our *Star* class is so small, you may have to select a very slow download speed (such as 200 bytes per second) to see the preloading message. To change the download speed, choose View → Download Settings.

You can download the preceding *sky.fla* example at *http://www.moock.org/eas3/examples*.

When using the "Export Classes in Frame" compiler option, take note that:

- A *.fla* file's document class is always exported in Frame 1, regardless of the specified value for "Export Classes in Frame."
- All classes referenced by the document class or referenced in a main timeline script are exported in Frame 1, regardless of the specified value for "Export Classes in Frame."
- If "Automatically declare stage instances" is enabled, and the main timeline's Stage contains named instances of a symbol that is linked to a class, then the linked class will be exported in Frame 1 (because the class is referenced in the automatic variable declarations for the instances on Stage).

Up Next: Using the Flex Framework

This chapter covered many applied techniques for working with ActionScript code in the Flash authoring tool. The remaining two chapters of this book are similarly practical. In the next chapter, we'll learn how to use the Flex framework's user interface components in an ActionScript-centric Flex Builder 2 project. Then, in Chapter 31, we'll learn how to share code with other developers.

A Minimal MXML Application

In Chapter 20, we learned that the Flex framework includes a sophisticated collection of customizable components for creating user interfaces. The Flex framework's user interface components are typically used with MXML-based applications, but can also be used in applications written primarily in ActionScript. For the benefit of readers who do not wish to use MXML, this chapter describes the bare minimum steps required to use the Flex framework's UI components in a Flex Builder 2 project, with as little MXML as possible.

For the record, this chapter has nothing against MXML. In general, MXML is an excellent tool for creating standardized interfaces deployed to the Flash platform. This chapter simply caters to situations where either an application's layout is entirely programmatically generated or where the developer does not have the time or interest to learn MXML.

For complete information on MXML and the Flex framework, see Adobe's documentation and O'Reilly's *Programming Flex 2* (Kazoun and Lott, 2007).

 Users of the Flash authoring tool should note that Flash CS3 includes its own set of user interface components in the package *fl*. The Flash CS3 components can also be used (both technically and legally) in ActionScript programs compiled with Flex Builder 2 or *mxmlc*.

The General Approach

Here are the minimal steps for creating an application that uses the Flex framework's UI components via ActionScript:

1. In Flex Builder 2, create a Flex project.
2. In the new project, define a class with a static method that will act as the application's point of entry.

3. In the project's main MXML file, add an MXML event property that listens for the top-level *Application* instance's `FlexEvent.APPLICATION_COMPLETE` event and invokes the static method from Step 2 in response.

4. In the static method from Step 2, create the desired UI components, and add them to the *Application* instance.

The following sections describe the preceding steps in detail.

Create the Flex Project

To create the project for the application, follow these steps:

1. In Flex Builder 2, choose File → New → Flex Project.

2. On the New Flex Project dialog, for "How will your Flex application access data?," select Basic, then click Next.

3. For Project name, enter the desired project name, then click Next.

4. For Main source folder, enter **src**.

5. For Main application file, enter the desired filename, with the extension *.mxml*. For example, **MinimalMXML.mxml**.

6. Click Finish.

In response to the preceding steps, Flex Builder 2 creates a new project whose Library path automatically includes the file *framework.swc*, which contains the UI components.

Once the project has been created, we create the application's point of entry, as described in the next section.

Create the Application Point of Entry

Our application's point of entry is a static method defined by a custom class. In our example, we'll name the static method *main()* and the custom class *EntryClass*. The *main()* method creates the UI component instances and adds them to the top-level *Application* instance's display hierarchy. The top-level *Application* instance is an automatically created object that acts as the basis of all MXML application, and provides access to the display list. Throughout our program, the top-level *Application* instance can be accessed via the *mx.core.Application* class's static variable, `application`.

Example 30-1 shows the code for *EntryClass*.

Example 30-1. The ActionScript class for a minimal MXML application

```
package {
  import mx.controls.*;
  import mx.core.*;
```

Example 30-1. The ActionScript class for a minimal MXML application (continued)

```
public class EntryClass {
  // Application point of entry
  public static function main ():void {
    // Create Flex framework UI components
    // For example:
    var button:Button = new Button();

    // Add UI components to the screen
    // For example:
    var mxmlApp:Application = Application(Application.application);
    mxmlApp.addChild(button);
  }
 }
}
```

Once the *EntryClass.main()* method has been created, we can invoke it in response to the top-level *Application* instance's `FlexEvent.APPLICATION_COMPLETE` event, as described in the next section.

Trigger the Application Point of Entry

In the earlier section "Create the Flex Project," we specified *MinimalMXML.mxml* as our example project's main application file. As a result, Flex Builder 2 automatically inserts the following code into that file:

```
<?xml version="1.0" encoding="utf-8"?>
<mx:Application xmlns:mx="http://www.adobe.com/2006/mxml"
  layout="absolute">
</mx:Application>
```

We need to make only one minor change to the preceding MXML code: we must add an event property that invokes *EntryClass.main()* when the top-level *Application* instance receives `FlexEvent.APPLICATION_COMPLETE` event notification. The following bolded code shows the approach:

```
<?xml version="1.0" encoding="utf-8"?>
<mx:Application xmlns:mx="http://www.adobe.com/2006/mxml"
  layout="absolute" applicationComplete="EntryClass.main()">
</mx:Application>
```

In response to the preceding code, when the application has finished initialization, it will automatically invoke *EntryClass.main()*, which, in turn, creates the desired UI component instances. (Look mom, no MXML!)

Let's apply the general approach covered in the preceding sections to a real example.

A Real UI Component Example

To demonstrate how to use ActionScript to create and control Flex framework UI components, we'll create a simple application that contains only two component instances: a *Button* instance and a *DataGrid* instance. The application simply counts the number of times the *Button* instance has been clicked. The *DataGrid* instance displays the total click count, and the amount of elapsed time between clicks.

We'll name our application's main MXML file *MinimalMXML.mxml*. We'll name the class that defines our program's point of entry *Clickometer*.

Here's the code for *MinimalMXML.mxml*:

```
<?xml version="1.0" encoding="utf-8"?>
<mx:Application xmlns:mx="http://www.adobe.com/2006/mxml"
  layout="vertical" applicationComplete="Clickometer.main( )">
</mx:Application>
```

In the preceding code, notice that the value of the applicationComplete event property indicates the method to invoke (*Clickometer.main()*) when the application has finished initializing. Notice also that the application uses a "vertical" layout scheme. For information on layout options, see the *Application* class's instance variable layout in Adobe's ActionScript Language Reference.

Now here's the code for the *Clickometer* class, where the UI components are created:

```
package {
  import mx.controls.*;
  import mx.core.*;
  import flash.events.*;
  import flash.utils.*;

  public class Clickometer {
    private static var lastClickTime:int = 0;
    private static var numClicks:int = 0;
    private static var grid:DataGrid;
    private static var button:Button;

    // Program entry point
    public static function main ():void {
      // Create a button
      button = new Button( );
      button.label = "Click Quickly!";
      button.addEventListener(MouseEvent.CLICK, clickListener);

      // Create a data grid
      grid = new DataGrid( );
      grid.dataProvider = new Array( );
```

```
// Add visual assets to the screen. Application.application is a
// reference to the top-level Flex application, a general container
// for UI components and visual assets.
var mxmlApp:Application = Application(Application.application);
mxmlApp.addChild(button);
mxmlApp.addChild(grid);
      }

      // This method is invoked every time the button is clicked
      private static function clickListener (e:MouseEvent):void {
        var now:int = getTimer();
        var elapsed:int = now - lastClickTime;
        lastClickTime = now;
        numClicks++;
        grid.dataProvider.addItem({Clicks: numClicks, "Time (ms)": elapsed});
      }
    }
  }
}
```

The preceding example application is available for download at *http://www.moock. org/eas3/examples*.

Sharing with Your Friends

Well, there's only one chapter left in this book. So what's the last ActionScript essential? Sharing your clever code with other programmers. To share ActionScript code, you can simply send that special someone to one or more of your class files. Or, if you're more ambitious, you can create an entire *class library* (i.e., group of classes) for compile time or runtime inclusion in an application. The final chapter of this book describes how to create and distribute code using class libraries.

Distributing a Class Library

This chapter discusses three specific techniques for sharing a group of classes (a *class library*) among multiple projects and multiple developers. By far the easiest way to share classes is to simply distribute the source code. We'll cover this easiest case first, before we discuss how to share classes without distributing source code, as you might want to do when selling a professional class library.

 The term "class library" is programmer jargon for an arbitrary group of classes distributed to a team or to the world at large. Don't confuse it with a *.fla* file's Library or the Flash Library panel. Those terms are unique to the Flash authoring environment and not part of the current discussion.

In ActionScript, a class library can be distributed to other developers simply as a bunch of source *.as* files, in a *.swf* file, or in a *.swc* file. We'll cover all three approaches in this chapter. Note, however, that ActionScript offers a wide range of options for distributing class libraries; this chapter covers three specific canonical situations but is not exhaustive. For more information on distributing class libraries, see the following Adobe documentation:

- Programming ActionScript 3.0 → Flash Player APIs → Client System Environment → Using the ApplicationDomain class (*http://livedocs.macromedia. com/flex/201/html/18_Client_System_Environment_175_4.html*)

- Building and Deploying Flex 2 Applications → Building Flex Applications → Using Runtime Shared Libraries (*http://livedocs.macromedia.com/flex/201/html/ rsl_124_1.html*)

The example files discussed in this chapter are available at *http://www.moock.org/ eas3/examples*.

Sharing Class Source Files

Let's start with the simplest way to distribute a class library: sharing class source files.

Suppose you work in a small web shop called Beaver Code, whose web site is *http:// www.beavercode.com*. You've made a class—*com.beavercode.effects.TextAnimation*— that creates various text effects. You want to use the *TextAnimation* class on two sites you're working on, Barky's Pet Supplies and Mega Bridal Depot. Rather than place a copy of the class file (that is, *TextAnimation.as*) in each project folder, you store the class file centrally and merely refer to it from each project. For example, on Windows, you store *TextAnimation.as* in the following location:

> *c:\data\actionscript\com\beavercode\effects\TextAnimation.as*

To make the *TextAnimation* class accessible to both projects, you add the directory *c:\data\actionscript* to each project's classpath (the classpath is discussed in Chapter 7).

By the same logic, if there were several members on your team, you might think it would be handy to store your classes on a central server so everyone would be able to use them by adding the server folder to their project's classpath. For example, you might want to store all shared classes on a server called *codecentral*, as follows:

> *\\codecentral\com\beavercode\effects\TextAnimation.as*

But working directly off the server is highly perilous and not recommended.

> If you store your classes on a central server and allow developers to modify them directly, the developers are liable to overwrite one another's changes. Furthermore, if the clock of the server and the clock of a programmer's personal computer are not in perfect sync, then the latest version of the class might not be included in the program at compile time. To avoid these problems, you should always use version control software to manage your class files when working on a team. Two popular (and free!) options are CVS (see *http://www. cvshome.org*) and Subversion (*http://subversion.tigris.org*).

On large projects, you might also want to automate the *.swf* export process using a build tool such as Apache Ant (*http://ant.apache.org*).

For information on using Ant with Flex Builder 2, see Using Flex Builder 2 → Programming Flex Applications → Building Projects → Advanced build options → Customizing builds with Apache Ant (*http://livedocs.macromedia.com/flex/201/html/ build_044_12.html*).

To automate *.swf* export in the Flash authoring tool, you'd have to execute a command-line JSFL script to tell Flash to create the *.swf* for each *.fla* file in your project.

Complete coverage of command-line compilation with Flash is outside the scope of this book, but here's a quick sample that gives the general flavor of it on Windows:

```
// Code in exportPetSupplies.jsfl:
// ===============================
// Open the .fla file.
var doc = fl.openDocument("file:///c|/data/projects/pet/petsupplies.fla");
// Export the .swf file.
doc.exportSWF("file:///c|/data/projects/pet/petsupplies.swf", true);
// Quit the Flash authoring tool (optional).
fl.quit(false);

// Command issued on command line from /pet/ directory:
// ====================================================
"[Flash install_folder]\flash.exe" exportPetSupplies.jsfl
```

For the preceding example command to work, Flash must not be running. After the command is issued, the compiled *petsupplies.swf* movie appears in the directory *c:\data\projects\pet*.

Distributing a Class Library as a .swc File

When working with a team of offsite developers or publishing a class library for the world at large, the approach of sharing class files directly can be cumbersome. For the sake of convenience, Adobe's ActionScript tools provide the option to wrap a class library in a single file, known as a *.swc* file.

The following sections describe first, how to create a *.swc* file containing a class library and then how to use classes from that library in an application.

Creating a .swc-Based Class Library in Flex Builder 2

To demonstrate the process of creating a *.swc* file containing a class library in Flex Builder 2, we'll return to the Beaver Code example from the preceding section. Our class library will be called "beavercore," and have a main package of *com.beavercore*. The package name matches a fictional web site, *http://www.beavercore.com*, that the developers at Beaver Code have created to host the beavercore class library.

The following steps describe how to create a *.swc* file, *beavercore.swc*, containing the beavercore class library. For the sake of simplicity, the library contains a single class only, *com.beavercore.effects.TextAnimation*.

1. In Flex Builder, select File → New → Flex Library Project.

2. In the New Flex Library Project dialog, for Project name, enter **beavercore**, then click Next.

3. For Main source folder, enter **src**, then click Finish.

4. With the *src* folder in the *beavercore* project selected, choose File → New → Folder. For Folder name, enter **com**. Repeat this process to create the folder structure *src/com/beavercore/effects*.

5. With the *effects* folder in the *beavercore* project selected, choose File → New → ActionScript Class.

6. On the New ActionScript Class dialog, for name, enter **TextAnimation**, then click Finish.

7. In *TextAnimation.as*, enter the following code:

```
package com.beavercore.effects {
  public class TextAnimation {
    public function TextAnimation () {
      trace("Imagine a text effect with great majesty.");
    }

    public function start ():void {
      trace("Effect now starting.");
    }
  }
}
```

8. In the Navigator panel, select the *beavercore* project folder, then choose Project → Build Project. (Note that the Build Project command is available only if Project → Build Automatically is not selected. When Build Automatically is selected, skip Step 8.)

In response to the preceding steps, Flex Builder 2 generates the file *beavercore.swc* and places it in the folder */bin/*. The file *beavercore.swc* contains the project's classes in compiled form. In our simple example, Flex Builder adds all classes from the *beavercore* project to *beavercore.swc*. In a more complex situation, we could explicitly indicate which classes to include or exclude via Project → Properties → Flex Library Build Path → Classes.

Using a .swc-Based Class Library in Flex Builder 2

Now that we've created a *.swc*-based class library (*beavercore.swc*), let's see how to use it in a project.

Suppose we're creating a Flash-based web site for Barky's Pet Supplies in Flex Builder 2. We want to use the *TextAnimation* class from the *beavercore.swc* class library in the web site. The following steps describe the process:

1. In Flex Builder, select File → New → ActionScript Project.

2. On the New ActionScript Project dialog, for Project name, enter **beaver_barkys**, then click Next.

3. For Main source folder, enter **src**.

4. For Main application file, enter **Barkys**.

---

5. On the Library path tab, click Add SWC.

6. Browse to and select the file *beavercore.swc* from the preceding section, then click Finish.

7. In *Barkys.as* (which opens automatically), enter the following code:

```
package {
  import flash.display.Sprite;
  import com.beavercore.effects.TextAnimation;

  public class Barkys extends Sprite {
    public function Barkys () {
      var textAni:TextAnimation = new TextAnimation();
      textAni.start();
    }
  }
}
```

8. In the Navigator panel, select the *beaver_barkys* project folder, then choose Run → Debug Barkys.

In response to the preceding steps, the compiler generates a *.swf* file (*Barkys.swf*) including the *TextAnimation* class, and runs that *.swf* file. The following messages appear in the Console:

```
Imagine a text effect with great majesty.
Effect now starting.
```

Notice that the *Barkys* class makes direct reference to the *TextAnimation* class as though it were actually part of the *beaver_barkys* project.

Now that we've seen how to create and distribute a class library as a *.swc* file in Flex Builder 2, let's examine how to do the same thing in the Flash authoring tool.

Creating a .swc-Based Class Library in the Flash Authoring Tool

The following steps describe how to use the Flash authoring tool to create a class library named *beavercore.swc*, that contains a single class, *TextAnimation*.

1. Create a new folder named **beavercore** on the filesystem. The *beavercore* folder will contain the source files for the class library.

2. In the *beavercore* folder, create the following subfolder structure: *com/beavercore/effects*.

3. In the *effects* folder, create a new text file named *TextAnimation.as*.

4. In *TextAnimation.as*, enter the following code:

```
package com.beavercore.effects {
  public class TextAnimation {
    public function TextAnimation () {
      trace("Imagine a text effect with great majesty.");
    }
```

```
      public function start ():void {
        trace("Effect now starting.");
      }
    }
  }
```

5. In the *beavercore* folder, create a new text file named *BeaverCore.as*.

6. In *BeaverCore.as*, enter the following code. Notice that the following *BeaverCore* class includes references to the classes (and other definitions) that we want included in the class library.

```
package {
  import com.beavercore.effects.*;
  import flash.display.Sprite;

  public class BeaverCore extends Sprite {
    com.beavercore.effects.TextAnimation;
  }
}
```

7. In the Flash authoring tool, create a new *.fla* file, and save it as *beavercore.fla* in the *beavercore* folder.

8. In the Properties panel (Window → Properties), for Document class, enter **BeaverCore**.

9. Select File → Publish Settings.

10. On the Formats tab, under Type, uncheck HTML.

11. On the Flash tab, under Options, check Export SWC.

12. Click Publish, then click OK.

In response to the preceding steps, Flash generates the file *beavercore.swc* and places it in the folder *beavercore*. The file *beavercore.swc* contains the classes in compiled form.

Using a .swc-Based Class Library in the Flash Authoring Tool

The following steps describe the process we follow to use the *TextAnimation* class from the *beavercore.swc* class library in a web site for Barky's Pet Supplies.

1. Create a new folder named **barkys** on the filesystem. The *barkys* folder will contain the source files for the web site.

2. In the *barkys* folder, create a new text file named *Barkys.as*.

3. In *Barkys.as*, enter the following code:

```
package {
  import flash.display.Sprite;
  import com.beavercore.effects.TextAnimation;

  public class Barkys extends Sprite {
    public function Barkys () {
      var textAni:TextAnimation = new TextAnimation();
      textAni.start();
```

```
        }
      }
    }
```

4. In the Flash authoring tool, create a new *.fla* file, and save it in the *barkys* folder as *barkys.fla*.

5. In the Properties panel (Window → Properties), for Document class, enter **Barkys**.

6. In the Flash authoring tool installation folder, under *Configuration\Components*, create a new folder named *BeaverCode*. (On Windows XP, the default location for *Configuration\Components* is: *C:\Program Files\Adobe\Adobe Flash CS3\en\Configuration\Components*. On Mac OS X, the default location for *Configuration\Components* is: *Macintosh HD:Applications:Adobe Flash CS3: Configuration:Components*).

7. Copy the *beavercore.swc* file from the preceding section to the *BeaverCode* folder created in Step 6. Copying the *beavercore.swc* file to a subfolder of *Configuration\Components* adds it to the Flash authoring tool's Components panel.

8. In the Flash authoring tool, open Components panel (Window → Components).

9. Select the pop-up Options menu in the top-right corner of the Components panel, and choose the Reload option. The folder *BeaverCode* will appear in the Components panel.

10. In the Components panel, open the *BeaverCode* folder.

11. Open *barkys.fla*'s Library (Window → Library).

12. Drag the BeaverCore component from the Components panel to *barkys.fla*'s Library.

13. Select Control → Test Movie.

In response to the preceding steps, the compiler generates a *.swf* file (*Barkys.swf*) including the *TextAnimation* class, and runs that *.swf* file. The following messages appear in the Output panel:

```
Imagine a text effect with great majesty.
Effect now starting.
```

Notice that the *Barkys* class makes direct reference to the *TextAnimation* class, just as it can refer to any class available in the classpath.

Distributing a Class Library as a .swf File

When working with multiple *.swf* files that use the same class, compiling that class into every *.swf* is a waste of space. When file size is a concern, we can prevent such redundancies by producing a class library in the form of a separate *.swf* file and loading that *.swf* file at runtime. Once the library has loaded the first time, it is cached on the end user's machine and can be reused by other *.swf* files without being down-loaded again.

 The process of creating and using a *.swf*-based class library is more complex than using a *.swc*-based class library. Consequently, you should use *.swf*-based class libraries only when you wish to make your application's file size as small as possible.

The following sections describe first, how to create a *.swf* file containing a class library, and then how to use classes from that library in an application.

Creating a .swf-Based Class Library in Flex Builder 2

To demonstrate the process of creating a *.swf* file containing a class library in Flex Builder 2, we'll again return to the beavercore example. The following steps describe how to create a class library, named *beavercore.swf*, that contains a single class, *TextAnimation* (we'll assume we're starting from scratch, even though some of the following steps are repeated from the earlier section "Creating a .swc-Based Class Library in Flex Builder 2").

1. In Flex Builder, select File → New → Flex Library Project.

2. In the New Flex Library Project dialog, for Project name, enter **beavercore**, then click Next.

3. For Main source folder, enter **src**, then click Finish.

4. With the *src* folder in the *beavercore* project selected, choose File → New → Folder. For Folder name, enter **com**. Repeat this process to create the folder structure *src/com/beavercore/effects*.

5. With the *effects* folder in the *beavercore* project selected, choose File → New → ActionScript Class.

6. On the New ActionScript Class dialog, for name, enter **TextAnimation**, then click Finish.

7. In *TextAnimation.as*, enter the following code:

```
package com.beavercore.effects {
  public class TextAnimation {
    public function TextAnimation () {
      trace("Imagine a text effect with great majesty.");
    }

    public function start ():void {
      trace("Effect now starting.");
    }
  }
}
```

Flex Builder 2 does not provide a direct way to compile a *.swf* file from a Flex Library Project. Hence, we must compile *beavercore.swf* using the command-line compiler, *mxmlc*. To be able to compile our classes as a *.swf*, we must create a main class for that *.swf*. In that main class, we include references to the classes (and other definitions) that we want included in the class library. The following steps describe the process on Microsoft Windows.

Compiling a .swf file using mxmlc

1. With the *src* folder in the *beavercore* project selected, choose File → New → ActionScript Class.

2. On the New ActionScript Class dialog, for Name, enter **Main**, then click Finish.

3. In *Main.as*, enter the following code. The *Main* class states the names of all classes (and definitions) to be included in the class library.

```
package {
  import com.beavercore.effects.*;
  import flash.display.Sprite;

  public class Main extends Sprite {
    com.beavercore.effects.TextAnimation;
  }
}
```

4. From the Windows start menu, open a command prompt by choosing Start → All Programs → Accessories → Command Prompt.

5. At the command prompt, change to the *C:\Program Files\Adobe\Flex Builder 2\ Flex SDK 2\bin* directory by entering the following command (note that the location of the compiler varies by version and operating system; consult Adobe's documentation for details):

```
cd C:\Program Files\Adobe\Flex Builder 2\Flex SDK 2\bin
```

6. At the command prompt, enter the following command, then press Enter:

```
mxmlc path_to_project\src\Main.as -output path_to_project\bin\beavercore.swf
```

In response to the preceding steps, Flex Builder 2 generates the file *beavercore.swf* and places it in the folder */bin/*. The *beavercore.swf* file contains our class library, and is now ready to be loaded and used by any application at runtime. However, any application that loads *beavercore.swf* must also be provided with a *.swc* file to use for compile-time type-checking. To create that *.swc* file, we select the *beavercore* project folder in the Navigator panel, then choose Project → Build Project. In response, Flex Builder 2 generates the file *beavercore.swc* and places it in the folder */bin/*.

Using a .swf-Based Class Library in Flex Builder 2

Now that we've created a *.swf*-based class library (*beavercore.swc*), let's see how to use it in a project.

Suppose we're using Flex Builder 2 to create the Mega Bridal Depot web site (mentioned earlier in this chapter), and we want to use the *TextAnimation* class from the *beavercore.swf* class library. We first create the Mega Bridal Depot ActionScript project and add *beavercore.swc* to the external library path. Then we load the *beavercore.swf* class library at runtime.

The following steps describe the process we follow to create the Mega Bridal Depot ActionScript project and add *beavercore.swc*, to the external library path:

1. In Flex Builder, select File → New → ActionScript Project.

2. On the New ActionScript Project dialog, for Project name, enter **beaver_ megabridaldepot**, then click Next.

3. For Main source folder, enter **src**.

4. For Main application file, enter **MegaBridalDepot**.

5. On the Library path tab, click Add SWC.

6. Browse to and select the file *beavercore.swc* from the preceding section, then click Finish.

7. Under Build path libraries, select "Link Type: Merged into code," then click Edit.

8. On the Library Path Item Options dialog, for Link Type, choose External, then click OK.

9. On the New ActionScript Project dialog, click Finish.

The preceding steps add *beavercore.swc* to the Mega Bridal Depot project's external library path. As such, the classes and definitions in *beavercore.swc* are available for compile-time type-checking but will not be included in the compiled *MegaBridalDepot.swf* application. Instead, we must load those classes at runtime.

To load the *beavercore.swf* class library at runtime, we use the *Loader* class's instance method *load()*, as discussed in Chapter 28. When loading *beavercore.swf,* we import it into *MegaBridalDepot.swf*'s application domain so that the classes in *beavercore.swf* can be accessed directly, as though they were part of *MegaBridalDepot.swf*. Note that in *MegaBridalDepot.swf*, we must be sure not to access *beavercore.swf*'s classes before they are fully loaded (i.e., before the Event.INIT event occurs for the load operation that loads *beavercore.swf*).

The following code shows the *MegaBridalDepot* class, which loads the *beavercore. swf* class library at runtime. The code assumes that the *beavercore.swf* file has been moved to the same folder as *MegaBridalDepot.swf*.

```
package {
  import flash.display.*;
  import flash.net.*;
  import flash.system.*;
  import flash.events.*;
  import com.beavercore.effects.TextAnimation;

  public class MegaBridalDepot extends Sprite {
```

```
    public function MegaBridalDepot () {
      var libLoader:Loader = new Loader();
      libLoader.contentLoaderInfo.addEventListener(
                                          Event.INIT, initListener);
      libLoader.load(
          new URLRequest("beavercore.swf"),
          new LoaderContext(false, ApplicationDomain.currentDomain));
    }

    private function initListener (e:Event):void {
      var textAni:TextAnimation = new TextAnimation();
      textAni.start();
    }
  }
}
```

Note that in the preceding libLoader.load() operation, we must be careful not to load *beavercore.swf*'s classes into *beavercore.swf*'s own application domain, as shown in the following code:

```
// WRONG! This code loads beavercore.swf's classes into beavercore.swf's
// own application domain, as a child of the system application
// domain. As a result, beavercore.swf's classes cannot be directly accessed
// from within MegaBridalDepot.swf.
libLoader.load(new URLRequest("beavercore.swf"));
```

The following code, likewise, erroneously loads *beavercore.swf*'s classes into its own application domain, but this time as a child of *MegaBridalDepot.swf*'s application domain:

```
// WRONG! Classes are loaded into beavercore.swf's own application domain.
// This time, even though beavercore.swf's application domain is a child of
// the parent MegaBridalDepot.swf's application domain, code in
// MegaBridalDepot.swf still can't directly access the classes in
// beavercore.swf's application domain. Making MegaBridalDepot.swf's
// application domain the parent of beavercore.swf's application domain
// merely tells beavercore.swf to use MegaBridalDepot.swf's version of any
// classes that are defined by both files.
libLoader.load(new URLRequest("beavercore.swf"),
               new LoaderContext(false,
               new ApplicationDomain(ApplicationDomain.currentDomain)));
```

For more information on application domains, see Adobe's Programming Action-Script 3.0, under Flash Player APIs → Client System Environment → ApplicationDomain class.

Now that we've seen how to create and distribute a class library as a *.swf* file in Flex Builder 2, let's examine how to do the same thing in the Flash authoring tool.

Creating a .swf-Based Class Library in the Flash Authoring Tool

Happily, the process for creating a *.swf*-based class library in the Flash authoring tool is identical to the process for creating a *.swc*-based class library, as described in the earlier section "Creating a .swc-Based Class Library in the Flash Authoring Tool." In fact, publishing a *.swc* file as described in that section creates both a *.swc* file containing the class library *and* a *.swf* file containing the class library. The *.swf* file is placed in the same folder as the *.swc* file.

For example, when we published our earlier beavercore class library as a *.swc* file, the Flash authoring tool also automatically created *beavercore.swf*. Like the *.swc* file, *beavercore.swf* was placed in the *beavercore* folder. The next section describes how to use the *beavercore.swf* class library in an application.

Using a .swf-Based Class Library in Flash CS3

The following steps describe the process we follow to use the *TextAnimation* class from the *beavercore.swf* class library in a web site for Mega Bridal Depot.

1. Create a new folder named **megabridaldepot** on the filesystem. The *megabridaldepot* folder will contain the source files for the web site.

2. In the *megabridaldepot* folder, create a new text file named *MegaBridalDepot.as*.

3. In *MegaBridalDepot.as*, enter the following code (for details on the loading techniques used in the following code, see the section "Using a .swf-Based Class Library in Flex Builder 2"):

```
package {
  import flash.display.*;
  import flash.net.*;
  import flash.system.*;
  import flash.events.*;
  import com.beavercore.effects.TextAnimation;

  public class MegaBridalDepot extends Sprite {
    public function MegaBridalDepot () {
      var libLoader:Loader = new Loader();
      libLoader.contentLoaderInfo.addEventListener(
                                         Event.INIT, initListener);
      libLoader.load(
          new URLRequest("beavercore.swf"),
          new LoaderContext(false, ApplicationDomain.currentDomain));
    }

    private function initListener (e:Event):void {
      var textAni:TextAnimation = new TextAnimation();
      textAni.start();
    }
  }
}
```

4. In the Flash authoring tool, create a new *.fla* file, and save it in the *megabridaldepot* folder as *megabridaldepot.fla*.

5. In the Properties panel (Window → Properties), for Document class, enter **MegaBridalDepot**.

6. Copy *beavercore.swc* to the *megabridaldepot* folder.

7. Copy *beavercore.swf* to the *megabridaldepot* folder.

8. Select Control → Test Movie.

Step 6 in the preceding procedure adds *beavercore.swc* to *megabridaldepot.fla*'s class-path, making the classes and definitions in *beavercore.swc* available for compile-time type-checking. Note, however, that the classes and definitions in the *.swc* file are used for type-checking only and are not included in the exported *megabridaldepot.swf*. To include definitions from a *.swc* file in an exported *.swf* file, add the *.swc* to the Library of the source *.fla* file, as described in the earlier section "Using a .swc-Based Class Library in the Flash Authoring Tool."

 Placing a *.swc* file in a *.fla* file's classpath makes the *.swc* file's definitions available for compile-time type-checking but does not include those definitions in the *.swf* file exported from the *.fla* file. The result is equivalent to adding the *.swc* file to the external library path when compiling with Flex Builder 2 or *mxmlc*. ActionScript 2.0 developers should note that no *_exclude.xml* file is required; the *_exclude.xml* file system is not supported in Flash CS3.

In response to the preceding steps, the compiler generates a *.swf* file, *MegaBridalDepot.swf* and runs that *.swf* file in Test Movie mode. The *MegaBridalDepot.swf* file does not include the *TextAnimation* class; instead, it loads it at runtime. Once the class loads, the following messages appear in the Output panel:

```
Imagine a text effect with great majesty.
Effect now starting.
```

With that, our noble mission to share our code is complete. And, as it happens, so is this book...

But Is It Really Over?

Over the 31 chapters of this book, we've explored many different programming tools and techniques; it's now up to *you* to experiment with them. Take what you've learned and explore your own ideas and projects. If you've previously spent most of your time in ActionScript, don't feel limited to it. Most of the concepts in this book are applicable to many other languages. Your ActionScript training will serve you well in Java, C++, Perl, and Visual Basic, just to name a few. Don't be afraid to venture into that territory.

Programming is an art form. As such, it comes with all the frustrations and elation of sculpture, writing, painting, or music. And it's subject to the primary law of creativity: there is no final destination. Every day that you program, you'll express something new and learn more along the way. The process never stops. So while this book may be over, your journey as a programmer will continue for as long as you write code.

If you see or do something neat along the way, drop me a note at *colin@moock.org*.

Thanks for sharing part of your programmer's journey with me. Happy trails!

The Final Virtual Zoo

This appendix presents the final code for the virtual zoo program, which is covered in Part I. This final version uses the techniques we studied in Part II to add graphics and interactivity to the program.

 You can download the code for the virtual zoo program at *http://www. moock.org/eas3/examples*.

Note that the code in this version of the virtual zoo has been updated structurally to reflect real-world design practices. In particular, two new classes have been added: *FoodButton*, which represents a simple clickable-text button, and *VirtualPetView*, which displays a *VirtualPet* instance graphically.

The *VirtualZoo* class has changed in the following significant ways:

- It now creates an instance of *VirtualPetView*, used to render the pet to the screen.
- It waits for the *VirtualPetView* instance to load the required images before starting the pet simulation.

The *VirtualPet* class has changed in the following significant ways:

- The following constants represent the pet's physical condition: VirtualPet. PETSTATE_FULL, VirtualPet.PETSTATE_HUNGRY, VirtualPet.PETSTATE_STARVING, and VirtualPet.PETSTATE_DEAD.
- The instance variable petState keeps track of the pet's current physical condition.
- Event listeners are notified of changes in the pet's physical condition via the VirtualPet.STATE_CHANGE event.
- Event listeners are notified of changes in the pet's name via the VirtualPet.NAME_ CHANGE event.

- To change the number of calories in a pet's stomach, the *VirtualPet* class uses the *setCalories()* method. When necessary, the *setCalories()* method changes the pet's state via *setPetState()*.

- Changes to the pet's physical condition are performed via the new *setPetState()* method, which triggers a corresponding VirtualPet.STATE_CHANGE event.

- The *VirtualPet* class uses a *Timer* object instead of *setInterval()* to trigger *digest()* calls.

- Each *VirtualPet* object's life cycle (digestion) can be started and stopped via the *start()* and *stop()* methods.

- The *digest()* method no longer determines whether or not digesting food will kill the pet. It delegates that responsibility to *setCalories()*.

- A formal *die()* method deactivates *VirtualPet* objects.

Study the following commented code listings carefully. Then, as an exercise, see if you can add a second pet to the zoo.

Example A-1 shows the code for the *VirtualZoo* class, the program's main class.

Example A-1. The VirtualZoo class

```
package {
  import flash.display.Sprite;
  import zoo.*;
  import flash.events.*;

  // The VirtualZoo class is the main application class. It extends Sprite
  // so that it can be instantiated and added to the display list at
  // program-start time.
  public class VirtualZoo extends Sprite {
    // The VirtualPet instance
    private var pet:VirtualPet;
    // The object that will render the pet to the screen
    private var petView:VirtualPetView;

    // Constructor
    public function VirtualZoo () {
      // Create a new pet, and attempt to give it a name
      try {
        pet = new VirtualPet("Bartholomew McGillicuddy");
      } catch (e:Error) {
        // If attempting to create a VirtualPet object causes an exception,
        // then the object won't be created. Hence, we report the problem
        // and create a new VirtualPet object here with a known-to-be-valid
        // name.
        trace("An error occurred: " + e.message);
        pet = new VirtualPet("Stan");
      }

      // Create the object that will render the pet to the screen
      petView = new VirtualPetView(pet);
```

```
      // Register this VirtualZoo object to be notified when the
      // rendering object (the "petView") has finished initializing
      petView.addEventListener(Event.COMPLETE, petViewCompleteListener);
    }

    // An event listener triggered when the VirtualPetView object (petView)
    // has finished initializing
    public function petViewCompleteListener (e:Event):void {
      // Add the view to the display list
      addChild(petView);
      // Begin the pet's life cycle
      pet.start();
      // Feed the pet
      pet.eat(new Sushi());
    }
  }
}
```

Example A-2 shows the code for the *VirtualPet* class, whose instances represent pets in the zoo.

Example A-2. The VirtualPet class

```
package zoo {
  import flash.utils.*;
  import flash.events.*;

  // The VirtualPet class represents a pet in the zoo. It extends
  // EventDispatcher so that it can be targeted by event dispatches.
  public class VirtualPet extends EventDispatcher {
    // ==STATIC CONSTANTS==
    // VirtualPet-related event types (handled by the VirtualPetView object
    // that displays the pet on screen)
    public static const NAME_CHANGE:String  = "NAME_CHANGE";
    public static const STATE_CHANGE:String = "STATE_CHANGE";

    // States representing the pet's current physical condition
    public static const PETSTATE_FULL:int     = 0;
    public static const PETSTATE_HUNGRY:int    = 1;
    public static const PETSTATE_STARVING:int  = 2;
    public static const PETSTATE_DEAD:int      = 3;

    // ==STATIC VARIABLES==
    // The maximum length of a pet's name
    private static var maxNameLength:int = 20;
    // The maximum number of calories a pet can have
    private static var maxCalories:int = 2000;
    // The rate at which pets digest food
    private static var caloriesPerSecond:int = 100;
    // The default name for pets
    private static var defaultName:String = "Unnamed Pet";
```

Example A-2. The VirtualPet class (continued)

```
// ==INSTANCE VARIABLES==
// The pet's name
private var petName:String;
// The number of calories currently in the pet's "stomach".
private var currentCalories:int;
// The pet's current physical condition
private var petState:int;
// A timer for invoking digest() on a regular basis
private var digestTimer:Timer;

// Constructor
public function VirtualPet (name:String):void {
  // Assign this pet's name
  setName(name);
  // Start this pet out with half the maximum calories (a
  // half-full "stomach").
  setCalories(VirtualPet.maxCalories/2);
}

// Starts the pet's life cycle
public function start ():void {
  // Invoke digestTimerListener() once per second
  digestTimer = new Timer(1000, 0);
  digestTimer.addEventListener(TimerEvent.TIMER, digestTimerListener);
  digestTimer.start();
}

// Pauses the pet's life cycle
public function stop ():void {
  if (digestTimer != null) {
    digestTimer.stop();
  }
}

// Assigns the pet's name, and notifies listeners of the change
public function setName (newName:String):void {
  // Throw an exception if the new name is not valid
  if (newName.indexOf(" ") == 0) {
    throw new VirtualPetNameException();
  } else if (newName == "") {
    throw new VirtualPetInsufficientDataException();
  } else if (newName.length > VirtualPet.maxNameLength) {
    throw new VirtualPetExcessDataException();
  }

  // Assign the new name
  petName = newName;
  // Notify listeners that the name changed
  dispatchEvent(new Event(VirtualPet.NAME_CHANGE));
}

// Returns the pet's name
```

```
  public function getName ():String {
    // If the pet has never been assigned a valid name...
    if (petName == null) {
      // ...return the default name
      return VirtualPet.defaultName;
    } else {
      // ...otherwise, return the pet's name
      return petName;
    }
  }

  // Adds some calories to the pet's stomach, in the form of a Food object
  public function eat (foodItem:Food):void {
    // If the pet is dead, abort
    if (petState == VirtualPet.PETSTATE_DEAD) {
      trace(getName() + " is dead. You can't feed it.");
      return;
    }

    // If the food item is an apple, check it for worms. If it has a worm,
    // don't eat it.
    if (foodItem is Apple) {
      if (Apple(foodItem).hasWorm()) {
        trace("The " + foodItem.getName() + " had a worm. " + getName()
             + " didn't eat it.");
        return;
      }
    }

    // Display a debugging message indicating what the pet ate
    trace(getName() + " ate the " + foodItem.getName()
         + " (" + foodItem.getCalories() + " calories).");
    // Add the calories from the food to the pet's "stomach"
    setCalories(getCalories() + foodItem.getCalories());
  }

  // Assigns the pet a new number of calories, and changes the pet's
  // state if necessary
  private function setCalories (newCurrentCalories:int):void {
    // Bring newCurrentCalories into the legal range, if necessary
    if (newCurrentCalories > VirtualPet.maxCalories) {
      currentCalories = VirtualPet.maxCalories;
    } else if (newCurrentCalories < 0) {
      currentCalories = 0;
    } else {
      currentCalories = newCurrentCalories;
    }

    // Calculate the number of calories in the pet's stomach, as a
    // percentage of the maximum calories allowed
    var caloriePercentage:int = Math.floor(getHunger()*100);
```

Example A-2. The VirtualPet class (continued)

```
        // Display a debugging message indicating how many calories the pet
        // now has
        trace(getName( ) + " has " + currentCalories + " calories"
                + " (" + caloriePercentage + "% of its food) remaining.");

        // If necessary, set the pet's state based on the change in calories
        if (caloriePercentage == 0) {
          // The pet has no food left. So if the pet is not already dead...
          if (getPetState( ) != VirtualPet.PETSTATE_DEAD) {
            // ...deactivate it
            die( );
          }
        } else if (caloriePercentage < 20) {
          // The pet needs food badly. Set its state to starving.
          if (getPetState( ) != VirtualPet.PETSTATE_STARVING) {
            setPetState(VirtualPet.PETSTATE_STARVING);
          }
        } else if (caloriePercentage < 50) {
          // The pet needs food. Set its state to hungry.
          if (getPetState( ) != VirtualPet.PETSTATE_HUNGRY) {
            setPetState(VirtualPet.PETSTATE_HUNGRY);
          }
        } else {
          // The pet doesn't need food. Set its state to full.
          if (getPetState( ) != VirtualPet.PETSTATE_FULL) {
            setPetState(VirtualPet.PETSTATE_FULL);
          }
        }
      }

      // Returns the number of calories in the pet's "stomach"
      public function getCalories ( ):int {
        return currentCalories;
      }

      // Returns a floating-point number describing the amount of food left
      // in the pet's "stomach," as a percentage
      public function getHunger ( ):Number {
        return currentCalories / VirtualPet.maxCalories;
      }

      // Deactivates the pet
      private function die ( ):void {
        // Stop the pet's life cycle
        stop( );
        // Put the pet in the "dead" state
        setPetState(VirtualPet.PETSTATE_DEAD);
        // Display a debugging message indicating that the pet died
        trace(getName( ) + " has died.");
      }

      // Reduces the pet's calories according to the pet's digestion rate.
      // This method is called automatically by digestTimer.
```

```
  private function digest ():void {
    trace(getName() + " is digesting...");
    setCalories(getCalories() - VirtualPet.caloriesPerSecond);
  }

  // Assigns an integer representing the pet's current physical condition
  private function setPetState (newState:int):void {
    // If the pet has not changed state, abort
    if (newState == petState) {
      return;
    }

    // Assign the new state
    petState = newState;
    // Notify listeners that the pet's state changed
    dispatchEvent(new Event(VirtualPet.STATE_CHANGE));
  }

  // Returns an integer representing the pet's current physical condition
  public function getPetState ():int {
    return petState;
  }

  // An event listener for the Timer object that governs digestion
  private function digestTimerListener (e:TimerEvent):void {
    // Digest some food
    digest();
  }
  }
}
```

Example A-3 shows the code for the *Food* class, the superclass of the various types of food that pets eat.

Example A-3. The Food class

```
package zoo {
  // The Food class is the superclass of the various types of food that
  // pets eat.
  public class Food {
    // Tracks the number of calories this piece of food has
    private var calories:int;
    //  This piece of food's human readable name
    private var name:String;

    // Constructor
    public function Food (initialCalories:int) {
      // Record the specified initial number of calories
      setCalories(initialCalories);
    }
```

Example A-3. The Food class (continued)

```
    // Returns the number of calories this piece of food has
    public function getCalories ():int {
      return calories;
    }

    // Assigns the number of calories this piece of food has
    public function setCalories (newCalories:int):void {
      calories = newCalories;
    }

    // Returns this piece of food's human readable name
    public function getName ():String {
      return name;
    }

    // Assigns this piece of food's human readable name
    public function setName (newName:String):void {
      name = newName;
    }
  }
}
```

Example A-4 shows the code for the *Apple* class, which represents a specific type of food that pets eat.

Example A-4. The Apple class

```
package zoo {
  // The Apple class represents one of the types of food a pet can eat
  public class Apple extends Food {
    // The amount of calories in an Apple object, if no specific
    // amount is indicated
    private static var DEFAULT_CALORIES:int = 100;
    // Tracks whether an Apple object has a worm
    private var wormInApple:Boolean;

    // Constructor
    public function Apple (initialCalories:int = 0) {
      // If no valid calorie amount is specified...
      if (initialCalories <= 0) {
        // ...give this Apple object the default amount
        initialCalories = Apple.DEFAULT_CALORIES;
      }
      // Invoke the Food class constructor
      super(initialCalories);

      // Randomly determine whether this Apple object as a worm (50% chance)
      wormInApple = Math.random() >= .5;

      // Give this food item a name
      setName("Apple");
    }
```

Example A-4. The Apple class (continued)

```
    // Returns a Boolean indicating whether the Apple object has a worm
    public function hasWorm ( ):Boolean {
      return wormInApple;
    }
  }
}
```

Finally, Example A-5 shows the code for the *Sushi* class, which represents a specific type of food that pets eat.

Example A-5. The Sushi class

```
package zoo {
  // The Sushi class represents one of the types of food a pet can eat
  public class Sushi extends Food {
    // The amount of calories in a Sushi object, if no specific
    // amount is indicated
    private static var DEFAULT_CALORIES:int = 500;

    // Constructor
    public function Sushi (initialCalories:int = 0) {
      // If no valid calorie amount is specified...
      if (initialCalories <= 0) {
        // ...give this Sushi object the default amount
        initialCalories = Sushi.DEFAULT_CALORIES;
      }
      // Invoke the Food class constructor
      super(initialCalories);

      // Give this food item a name
      setName("Sushi");
    }
  }
}
```

Example A-6 shows the code for the *VirtualPetNameException* class, which represents an exception thrown when an invalid pet name is specified.

Example A-6. The VirtualPetNameException class

```
package zoo {
  // The VirtualPetNameException class represents an exception thrown when
  // a generally invalid pet name is specified for a pet
  public class VirtualPetNameException extends Error {
    // Constructor
    public function VirtualPetNameException (
                           message:String = "Invalid pet name specified.") {
      // Invoke the Error constructor
      super(message);
    }
  }
}
```

Example A-7 shows the code for the *VirtualPetExcessDataException* class, which represents an exception thrown when an excessively long pet name is specified for a pet.

Example A-7. The VirtualPetExcessDataException class

```
package zoo {
  // The VirtualPetExcessDataException class represents an exception
  // thrown when an excessively long pet name is specified for a pet
  public class VirtualPetExcessDataException
                                    extends VirtualPetNameException {
    // Constructor
    public function VirtualPetExcessDataException () {
      // Invoke the VirtualPetNameException constructor
      super("Pet name too long.");
    }
  }
}
```

Example A-8 shows the code for the *VirtualPetInsufficientDataException* class, which represents an exception thrown when an excessively short pet name is specified for a pet.

Example A-8. The VirtualPetInsufficientDataException class

```
package zoo {
  // The VirtualPetInsufficientDataException class represents an exception
  // thrown when an excessively short pet name is specified for a pet
  public class VirtualPetInsufficientDataException
                                    extends VirtualPetNameException {
    // Constructor
    public function VirtualPetInsufficientDataException () {
      // Invoke the VirtualPetNameException constructor
      super("Pet name too short.");
    }
  }
}
```

Example A-9 shows the code for the *VirtualPetView* class, which graphically displays a *VirtualPet* instance.

ExampleA-9. The VirtualPetView class

```
package zoo {
  import flash.display.*;
  import flash.events.*;
  import flash.net.*;
  import flash.text.*;

  // The VirtualPetView class graphically depicts a VirtualPet instance.
  // Images for the pet are loaded at runtime.
  public class VirtualPetView extends Sprite {
    // The pet being displayed
    private var pet:VirtualPet;
```

```
// Container for pet graphics
private var graphicsContainer:Sprite;

// Pet graphics and text
private var petAlive:Loader;        // The pet in its alive state
private var petDead:Loader;         // The pet in its alive state
private var foodHungry:Loader;      // An icon for the hungry state
private var foodStarving:Loader;    // An icon for the starving state
private var petName:TextField;      // Displays the pet's name

// Pet user interface
private var appleBtn:FoodButton;    // Button for feeding the pet an apple
private var sushiBtn:FoodButton;    // Button for feeding the pet sushi

// Load completion detection
static private var numGraphicsToLoad:int = 4; // Total number
                                              // of graphics
private var numGraphicsLoaded:int = 0;   // Number of graphics
                                         // loaded so far

// Constructor
public function VirtualPetView (pet:VirtualPet) {
  // Store a reference to the pet being displayed
  this.pet = pet;

  // Register to be notified when the pet's name changes
  pet.addEventListener(VirtualPet.NAME_CHANGE,
                       petNameChangeListener);
  // Register to be notified when the pet's condition changes
  pet.addEventListener(VirtualPet.STATE_CHANGE,
                       petStateChangeListener);

  // Make and load the pet graphics
  createGraphicsContainer();
  createNameTag();
  createUI();
  loadGraphics();
}

// Creates a container into which to place pet graphics
private function createGraphicsContainer ():void {
  graphicsContainer = new Sprite();
  addChild(graphicsContainer);
}

// Creates a TextField in which to display the pet's name
private function createNameTag ():void {
  petName = new TextField();
  petName.defaultTextFormat = new TextFormat("_sans",14,0x006666,true);
  petName.autoSize = TextFieldAutoSize.CENTER;
  petName.selectable = false;
  petName.x = 250;
  petName.y = 20;
  addChild(petName);
}
```

```
// Creates buttons for the user to feed the pet
private function createUI ():void {
  // The Feed Apple button
  appleBtn = new FoodButton("Feed Apple");
  appleBtn.y = 170;
  appleBtn.addEventListener(MouseEvent.CLICK, appleBtnClick);
  addChild(appleBtn);

  // The Feed Sushi button
  sushiBtn = new FoodButton("Feed Sushi");
  sushiBtn.y = 190;
  sushiBtn.addEventListener(MouseEvent.CLICK, sushiBtnClick);
  addChild(sushiBtn);
}

// Disables the user interface
private function disableUI ():void {
  appleBtn.disable();
  sushiBtn.disable();
}

// Loads and positions the external graphics for the pet
private function loadGraphics ():void {
  // Graphic showing the pet in its alive state
  petAlive = new Loader();
  petAlive.load(new URLRequest("pet-alive.gif"));
  petAlive.contentLoaderInfo.addEventListener(Event.COMPLETE,
                                    completeListener);
  petAlive.contentLoaderInfo.addEventListener(IOErrorEvent.IO_ERROR,
                                    ioErrorListener);

  // Graphic showing the pet in its dead state
  petDead = new Loader();
  petDead.load(new URLRequest("pet-dead.gif"));
  petDead.contentLoaderInfo.addEventListener(Event.COMPLETE,
                                    completeListener);
  petDead.contentLoaderInfo.addEventListener(IOErrorEvent.IO_ERROR,
                                    ioErrorListener);

  // The "needs food" icon
  foodHungry = new Loader();
  foodHungry.load(new URLRequest("food-hungry.gif"));
  foodHungry.contentLoaderInfo.addEventListener(Event.COMPLETE,
                                      completeListener);
  foodHungry.contentLoaderInfo.addEventListener(IOErrorEvent.IO_ERROR,
                                      ioErrorListener);
  foodHungry.x = 15;
  foodHungry.y = 100;

  // The "needs food badly" icon
  foodStarving = new Loader();
  foodStarving.load(new URLRequest("food-starving.gif"));
```

```
    foodStarving.contentLoaderInfo.addEventListener(Event.COMPLETE,
                                   completeListener);
    foodStarving.contentLoaderInfo.addEventListener(IOErrorEvent.IO_ERROR,
                                   ioErrorListener);
    foodStarving.x = 15;
    foodStarving.y = 100;
}

// Triggered when the pet changes state
private function petStateChangeListener (e:Event):void {
  // If the pet is dead...
  if (pet.getPetState() == VirtualPet.PETSTATE_DEAD) {
    // ...disable the feed buttons
    disableUI();
  }
  // Update the graphics to reflect the new state of the pet
  renderCurrentPetState();
}

// Queries the pet for its current state and renders that
// state to the screen
private function renderCurrentPetState ():void {
  // Clear all graphics
  for (var i:int = graphicsContainer.numChildren-1; i >= 0; i--) {
    graphicsContainer.removeChildAt(i);
  }
  // Check the pet's current state
  var state:int = pet.getPetState();

  // Display appropriate graphics
  switch (state) {
    case VirtualPet.PETSTATE_FULL:
      graphicsContainer.addChild(petAlive);
      break;

    case VirtualPet.PETSTATE_HUNGRY:
      graphicsContainer.addChild(petAlive);
      graphicsContainer.addChild(foodHungry);
      break;

    case VirtualPet.PETSTATE_STARVING:
      graphicsContainer.addChild(petAlive);
      graphicsContainer.addChild(foodStarving);
      break;

    case VirtualPet.PETSTATE_DEAD:
      graphicsContainer.addChild(petDead);
      break;
  }
}
```

```
// Triggered when the pet's name changes
private function petNameChangeListener (e:Event):void {
  // Update the pet's name on screen
  renderCurrentPetName();
}

// Queries the pet for its current name, and renders that
// name to the screen
private function renderCurrentPetName ():void {
  petName.text = pet.getName();
}

// Triggered when the "Feed Apple" button is clicked
private function appleBtnClick (e:MouseEvent):void {
  // Feed the pet an apple
  pet.eat(new Apple());
}

// Triggered when the "Feed Sushi" button is clicked
private function sushiBtnClick (e:MouseEvent):void {
  // Feed the pet some sushi
  pet.eat(new Sushi());
}

// Triggered when a graphic finishes loading
private function completeListener (e:Event):void {
  // Increase (by one) the count of the total number of graphics loaded
  numGraphicsLoaded++;
  // If all the graphics have loaded...
  if (numGraphicsLoaded == numGraphicsToLoad) {
    // ...display the appropriate graphics, then broadcast
    // an Event.COMPLETE event, indicating that this VirtualPetView
    // object is ready to use
    renderCurrentPetState();
    renderCurrentPetName();
    dispatchEvent(new Event(Event.COMPLETE));
  }
}

// Triggered if a graphic fails to load properly
private function ioErrorListener (e:IOErrorEvent):void {
  // Display a debugging message describing the loading problem
  trace("Load error: " + e);
}
}
}
```

Example A-10 shows the code for the *FoodButton* class, which represents a simple clickable-text button.

Example A-9. The FoodButton class

```
package zoo {
  import flash.display.*
  import flash.events.*;
  import flash.text.*;

  // The FoodButton class represents a simple clickable-text button
  public class FoodButton extends Sprite {
    // The text to be clicked
    private var text:TextField;
    // The formatting of the text when it is *not* under the mouse pointer
    private var upFormat:TextFormat;
    // The formatting of the text when it *is* under the mouse pointer
    private var overFormat:TextFormat;

    // Constructor
    public function FoodButton (label:String) {
      // Enable the "hand" mouse cursor for interactions with this object
      // (The buttonMode variable is inherited from Sprite.)
      buttonMode = true;
      // Disable mouse events for this object's children
      // (The mouseChildren variable is inherited
      // from DisplayObjectContainer.)
      mouseChildren = false;

      // Define the text formatting used when this object is *not*
      // under the mouse pointer
      upFormat = new TextFormat("_sans",12,0x006666,true);
      // Define the text formatting used when this object *is*
      // under the mouse pointer
      overFormat = new TextFormat("_sans",12,0x009999,true);

      // Create the clickable text field, and add it to this object's
      // display hierarchy
      text = new TextField();
      text.defaultTextFormat = upFormat;
      text.text = label;
      text.autoSize = TextFieldAutoSize.CENTER;
      text.selectable = false;
      addChild(text);

      // Register to be notified when the mouse moves over this object
      addEventListener(MouseEvent.MOUSE_OVER, mouseOverListener);
      // Register to be notified when the mouse moves off of this object
      addEventListener(MouseEvent.MOUSE_OUT, mouseOutListener);
    }

    // Disables mouse event notifications for this object
    public function disable ():void {
```

Example A-9. The FoodButton class (continued)

```
      // (The mouseEnabled variable is inherited from InteractiveObject.)
      mouseEnabled = false;
    }

    // Triggered when the mouse moves over this object
    public function mouseOverListener (e:MouseEvent):void {
      // Apply the "mouse over" text format
      text.setTextFormat(overFormat);
    }

    // Triggered when the mouse moves off of this object
    public function mouseOutListener (e:MouseEvent):void {
      // Apply the "mouse not over" text format
      text.setTextFormat(upFormat);
    }
  }
}
```

Index

We'd like to hear your suggestions for improving our indexes. Send email to *index@oreilly.com*.

C

call expressions, 31
call stack, 255
Caller class, 346
caloriesPerSecond static variable, 96
capture phase, 503
caret position, 717
Cascading Style Sheets (CSS), 727
case expressions, 48
casting, 146
    as operator for casting to Date and Array
        classes, 149
    upcasting and downcasting, 148
catch blocks, 242
character-level formatting, 708
charCode, 563
CheckBox class, 511
    hierarchical handling of events, 512
child nodes, 354
child( ) method (XML), 359, 371
children, 460
children( ) method (XML), 360
Class class, 85
class libraries, 861
    distributing, 861
        as .swc files, 863–867
        as .swf files, 867–873
        source code sharing, 862
    protecting with version control, 862
class scope, 297
classes, 6
    access control modifiers, 12
    ActionScript's native classes, 7
    attributes, 12
    base class, 103
    class APIs, 35
    class blocks, 11
    class definitions, 11
    class extensions, limitations, 161
    class hierarchy, 103
    class initializer, 84, 297
    class interfaces, 35
    class libraries (see class libraries)
    class objects, 85
    derived class, 103
    dynamic classes, 280
        troubleshooting, 281
    inheritance (see inheritance)
    multidatatype classes and interfaces, 161
    naming of classes, 9

Object class, 104
    prototype objects, augmentation
        with, 291
    requirements for program
        compilation, 134
    subclassing built-in classes, 113
classpath and program compilation, 134
clear( ) method, 636
clearChanged( ) method, 638
clickListener( ) method, 515
client runtime environments, 4
clone( ) method, 663, 672
closeListener( ) method, 805
code comments, 13
code sharing (see class libraries, distributing)
coder, 3
coding style and constructor arguments, 25
collision potential, instance variables and
        symbol instance names, 843
color channels, 649
color values, hexadecimal
        representation, 650
color, pixel values for, 649
colorTransform( ) method, 686
comments, 13
comments( ) class instance method
        (XML), 359, 370
compare( ) method, 664
compiler restrictions, 134
compilers, 5
compiling programs, 130–132
    classpath, 134
    Flash authoring tool, 130
    Flex Builder 2, 131
    just-in-time (JIT) compilation, 5
    mxmlc, 133
    reference error detection, 145
    strict mode ignorance of type mismatch
        errors, 143
    strict mode versus standard mode
        compilation, 135
completeListener( ) method, 206, 216
components, xxiv
composition, 117
    delegation, 118
    inheritance, versus, 117–120
compound expressions, 26
concat( ) method, 197
concatenation operator (+), 47
concatenation operator (+=), 183

F

factorials, calculating, 95
FIFO stack, 195
file formats
    .as files, 8
    .swf, xxv, 5
file: protocol, 412
FileSender, 796
fillRect( ) method, 654, 670
filtering predicate operator (E4X), 383
final attribute, 112
finally blocks, 243, 258–260
fixed variables, 280
.fla files, 821
    (see also Flash documents)
Flash, xix
Flash authoring tool, xxiv, 3, 821
    Actions panel, 826
    classes, preloading of, 852–855
    compiling programs with, 130
        standard mode compilation,
            enabling, 136
    document class, 828–831
    document class path and global class
        path, setting, 828
    frame scripts, 826–828
    frame types, 824
    instance names for display objects, 848
    Linkage Properties dialog, 834
    playhead, 822
    Stage, 822
    .swc-based libraries, 865–867
        creating, 865
        using, 866
    .swf files, creating with, 821
    .swf-based libraries, creating in, 871
    symbols
        automatic declaration of stage
            instances, 842
        instance names, 839
        instance names, matching variables
            for, 841–844
        instantiating via ActionScript, 847
        linking multiple symbols to one
            superclass, 849–851
        manually created symbol instances,
            accessing, 838–839
        Movie Clip symbols (see Movie Clip
            symbols)
    text fields, manually creating with, 759

Text Tool, 844
timeline scripting, 826–828
    adding frame scripts to keyframes, 826
timelines
    programmatic control of, 845–846
UI component set, 457
Flash compiler, 5
Flash CS3 and swf-based libraries, 872
Flash documents (.fla files), 821
    document class, automatic assignment
        of, 829
    main timeline, 822
    process of export to .swf files, 822
    .swf files, compiling from, 822
    timelines, 822
Flash file format (SWF), xxv
Flash Lite, xxiii, 4
Flash Player, xxiii, 4
    security restrictions (see security)
Flash runtime APIs, xxiv
Flash runtime clients, xxiii
flash.display.MovieClip document class, 829
flash.filters package, 687
FlashType renderer, tuning, 755
Flex 2 SDK, 5
Flex Builder, 3
Flex Builder 2
    .swf-based libraries, 868–871
    application point of entry, triggering, 858
    cleaning projects, 817
    compiling programs with, 131
        enabling standard mode
            compilation, 136
    projects, creating, 857
    .swc-based class libraries, 863–865
        creating, 863
        using, 864
    .swf-based libraries
        creating in, 868
        using in, 869
    UI component example, 859
Flex compiler, 5
Flex framework, xxiv, 457, 856
    UI component set, 457
floodFill( ) method, 654, 670
focus events, 548–555
    Flash Player built-in focus-event
        types, 551–555
    focusing objects with the mouse, 550
        descendant focus, handling through a
            single ancestor, 550
    tab order and automatic tab order, 548

H

handling events (see events)

hard returns, 702

Has-A relationships, 119

hasChanged( ) method, 638

hitListener( ) method, 520

hitTest( ) method, 664

HTML text formatting, 719–726
- interactions between text and htmlText variables, 724
- quoting attribute values, 724
- special character entities supported by ActionScript, 724
- tags and attributes supported by ActionScript, 720–723
- unrecognized tags and attributes, 726

I

IconPanel class, 492

identity theft using email, 423

IDEs (integrated development environments), 3

IEventDispatcher interfac, 203

if statements, 44–48
- chaining, 47
- else omitted, 47

ImageLoader class, 274

implements keyword, 161

in operator, 181

inequality operator (!=), 182

information theft, 424

inheritance, 101–104
- code reuse, 114
- composition, versus, 117–120
- dynamic binding, 115–117
- extension, 105
- hierarchical modeling, 114
- interface inheritance, 164
- Is-A, Has-A, and Uses-A, 119
- noninheritance of static methods and variables, 104
- overridden instance methods, invoking, 107
- overriding instance methods, 105
- polymorphism, 115–117
- preventing extension of classes and overriding of methods, 112
- redefinition, 105
- reuse, 105
- subclassing built-in classes, 113
- theory, 114–120

inheritance tree, 103

initialization statements, 57

initListener( ) method, 771

input events, 531
- Flash Player-level input events, 580–585
  - Event.ACTIVATE and Event.DEACTIVATE, 582
  - Event.MOUSE_LEAVE, 585
  - Event.RESIZE, 583
  - input-event types, 580
- focus events (see focus events)
- general rules governing, 531
- keyboard-input events (see keyboard-input events)
- mouse-input events (see mouse-input events)
- text-input events (see text-input events)

insignificant whitespace, 354

instance members, 42

instance method scope, 298

instance methods, 31
- access-control modifiers for, 34
- arbitrary number of arguments, 75
- bound methods, 66
- get and set methods, 72–75
  - variable names and, 74
- terminology compared, C++ and Java, 86
- this keyword, omitting from code, 64–66

instance variables, 20–23, 30
- access-control modifiers, 22
- collision potential with symbol instance names, 843
- private accessor modifier, used on, 68
- static variables of the same name, 78
- terminology compared, C++ and Java, 86

instanceof operator, 182

instances, 6

int datatype, conversions of other datatypes to, 151

integrated development environments (IDEs), 3

InteractiveObject class, 458, 460

interfaces (ActionScript), 159
- as datatypes, 139
- curly braces, problems with, 162
- method declarations, 162
- methods, definition before compilation, 163
- methods, listing of, 161
- multidatatype classes and, 161
- multiple datatype example with arrays, 165–170

About the Author

Colin Moock is an independent ActionScript expert whose world-renowned books have educated Flash programmers since 1999. He is the author of the canonical *Essential ActionScript 2.0* (O'Reilly, 2004) and *ActionScript for Flash MX: The Definitive Guide* (O'Reilly, 2003, 2001). Moock runs one of the web's oldest Flash developer sites, *www.moock.org* and is the co-creator of Unity, a client/server framework for creating multiuser applications.

Colophon

The animal on the cover of *Essential ActionScript 3.0* is the coral snake (*Micrurus fulvius tenere*). This highly dangerous snake is found in the southeastern states of North America and can also be found in Mexico. It likes wet, humid, and thick foliage-littered forests, but can be found in any environment.

The coral snake is recognized by its vibrant red, yellow, and black bands. These colors ward off would-be attackers. On the head and tail are bands of black and yellow; on the midsection are black, yellow, and red bands. The red bands are always adjacent to the yellow bands. The average length of a snake is 24 inches, with a maximum length of 47 inches. The coral snake is the only venomous snake in North America to hatch its young from eggs.

Coral snakes have short, grooved, and hollow fangs located at the front of the mouth. They feed on lizards and other snakes. Coral snakes bite their prey to inject neurotoxic venom, which paralyzes the victim; however, unlike snakes of the viper family, which use a stabbing method, when a coral snake bites its victim, it hangs on for a long time to inject as much venom as possible. Coral snakes are seldom seen, due to their habit of living underground, or in cracks and crevices, and their nocturnal tendencies. Coral snakes usually do not bite humans unless handled. If a human or pet is bitten, treatment should take place as soon as possible, since coral snake bites are often fatal.

The cover image is a 19th-century engraving from the Dover Pictorial Archive. The cover font is Adobe ITC Garamond. The text font is Linotype Birka; the heading font is Adobe Myriad Condensed; and the code font is LucasFont's TheSans Mono Condensed.

Better than e-books

Buy *Essential ActionScript 3.0* and access
the digital edition FREE on Safari for 45 days.

Go to www.oreilly.com/go/safarienabled
and type in coupon code USHEDFH

Search
thousands of
top tech books

Download
whole chapters

Cut and Paste
code examples

Find
answers fast

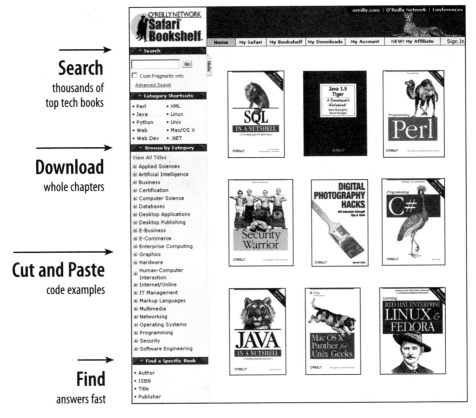

Search Safari! The premier electronic reference
library for programmers and IT professionals.

The Authoritative Resource

Adobe Developer Library

Adobe Developer Library, a co-publishing partnership between O'Reilly Media and Adobe Systems, Inc., is the authoritative resource for developers using Adobe technologies. With top-quality books and innovative online resources, the Adobe Developer Library delivers expert training straight from the source. Topics include ActionScript™, Adobe Flex®, Adobe Flash®, and Adobe Acrobat® software.

Get the latest news about books, online resources, and more at adobedeveloperlibrary.com

Spreading the knowledge of innovators

www.oreilly.com